The
Laurel &
Hardy
Encyclopedia

The Laurel & Hardy Encyclopedia

GLENN MITCHELL

B.T. Batsford Ltd · London

Printed by The Bath Press, Bath

for the publishers
B.T. Batsford Ltd
4 Fitzhardinge Street
London W1H 0AH

ISBN 0 7134 7711 3

To my father, who saw *Hats Off*,
The Rogue Song and Laurel & Hardy
in person; and my mother, tolerant
and encouraging.

Acknowledgements

The illustrations in this book
include many from stills issued to
publicize films made and/or distributed by (primarily) Hal Roach
Studios, Metro-Goldwyn-Mayer,
20th Century-Fox and Franco-
London Films. Others, where
known, are credited within the cap-
tions themselves. Although effort
has been made to trace present
copyright owners, apologies are
made in advance for any unintentional omission or neglect; we will
be happy to insert appropriate
acknowledgement to companies or
individuals in subsequent editions
of the book.

Foreword

I have two very good reasons to cherish Glenn Mitchell's marvellous book.

The first reason has to do with the correspondence attendant on my work as Laurel & Hardy's authorized biographer.

Since 1962 (the publication year of my first book on this renowned pair), I have been the recipient of hundreds and hundreds of letters about them. Even now, over thirty years later, these letters still come to me, and in effect ask 'Where can I find out more information on the boys?', usually concluding with a statistical question about them which I'm unable to answer. To such letters I have usually replied that until there is such a thing as a Laurel & Hardy encyclopedia, detailed questions of this kind are just unanswerable. But now such an encyclopedia exists, thank heaven.

My second reason for treasuring Glenn's superb overview of almost everything relative to Laurel & Hardy is the sheer quality of this book. I must say I am utterly fascinated with all the detailed information, so patiently gleaned from a bewildering multiplicity of sources. Glenn not only knows the films in detail, he knows the genesis of most of them, the influences upon them by other films and performers, and all the ancillary facts about them one could ever need. Where else, to take one example, could one learn that Stan's Lord Paddington could well derive from a George Arliss performance, the same George Arliss who learned much from Stan's father? As it should do, the encyclopedia abounds in interesting minutiae of this kind.

But where the book's greatest value lies, surely, is that, throughout, Glenn brings an evaluative eye to everything he discusses. He not only gives the details but the artistic effect of Laurel & Hardy at work, capsuling the basic events in each film in such a way as to show the reader the key nuances of performance. This is something very difficult to do in print, but the book in hand succeeds masterfully.

And now, blessedly, my correspondence will diminish. Moreover, I now know where to go to find out all the many things about Laurel & Hardy that I never learned.

John McCabe

Introduction

The genesis of this book is straightforward if protracted: as a lifelong *aficionado* of comedy and of Laurel & Hardy in particular, it occurred to me that a Laurel & Hardy book dealing entirely in facts and figures would be worthwhile, especially after being asked for the umpteenth time 'Which is the film in which they work in a sawmill?' (you'll find it under **Sawmills**, by the way). This seemed particularly necessary given the number of sometimes damaging untruths circulated about the pair (see **Apocrypha** for a brief round-up of same). The idea was put vaguely in correspondence with Laurel & Hardy's authorized biographer, John McCabe, who convinced me to go ahead and offered all necessary assistance. In addition to writing a foreword, he has advised, contributed and patiently examined the text, in addition to permitting liberal quotation from his work. Anyone documenting the history of Laurel & Hardy in the last three decades owes him an inestimable debt.

Laurel & Hardy are in any case considered one of the great Anglo-American partnerships and I believe they would have approved of what might be termed trans-Atlantic comparisons. Their widespread exposure through television and video suggests a need for some sort of consumer guide to their work; some subjects, notably the solo films and stage appearances, warrant complete studies of their own, but are presented here in a representative and, it is hoped, useful selection.

The individual entries are cross-referenced where appropriate and may be broken down into the following categories: the Laurel & Hardy films, each of which is documented separately; selected solo films, chosen either to illustrate their development or because of academic or comedic value;

biographical notes on the team; thematic discussions, detailing recurrent motifs, props, theories and activities, which may also benefit archivists seeking themed extracts; and biographies of the key personnel. Suitable space has been devoted to those considered of particular importance, though sometimes more is allocated to interesting but largely undocumented people. Star names in their own right are sufficiently chronicled elsewhere and are detailed mostly for their connection to Laurel & Hardy.

A further hope is that many of the biographical and thematic entries extend the book's usefulness as a general reference; despite its specialist brief, there may be much information unavailable to the enthusiast from similar alphabetical volumes. For some people little or nothing could be traced and apologies to those who search in vain for certain of the team's colleagues. A further apology is due for the occasionally tongue-in-cheek nature of the text, born in part from an awareness of the absurdity inherent in taking comedy too seriously. A number of headings are designed to raise an amused eyebrow until their relevance becomes clear; these serve also to convey anecdotal material from various sources. Some readers may discern a tendency to 'plug' Charley Chase, an unduly neglected Roach comedian: this is entirely deliberate and no apology is offered.

Considerable thanks go to Michael Pointon, tireless source of advice, information and guidance; Robert G. Dickson, co-author (with Juan Heinink) of *Cita en Hollywood*, an invaluable work on American-made films in Spanish, for detailing the foreign-language versions and much else; Robert F. Spiller; Ray Andrew; Barry Anthony; David Barker; Tony Barker, editor of *Music Hall* magazine; the

British Film Institute; Sarah Doonican; Trevor Dorman; the late Malcolm Stuart Fellows; Alex Gleason; Roger L. Gordon; Alison Grimmer; Juan Heinink; Jim Hutchinson; Irv Hyatt; Phil Johnson; Del Kempster; Kodak Ltd.; Robert S. Lewis; Rosina Lawrence McCabe; Willie McIntyre; Camillo Moscati; Mark Newell; Jonathan Pertwee; John Pettigrew; Bram Reijnhout; the late Hal Roach; Vicente Romero; the Shell Art Collection; Randy Skretvedt; Martina Stansbie, my editor who patiently imposed order on my chaos; Carolyn Whitaker; and the late Harry Worth. Naturally, any errors in the text are entirely my responsibility. Thanks also to Chester Chaste and Purser Cryder, behind whose identities were two irreplaceable talents.

Glenn Mitchell
London, 1995

*Academy Awards: Stan with his special Oscar, in a photograph
inscribed to fellow-comedian Max Wall
By kind courtesy of Michael Pointon and the estate of Max Wall*

ACADEMY AWARDS

(Laurel & Hardy appearances *qv*)
Initiated for the 1927-8 season, the
Academy of Motion Picture Arts and
Sciences' annual 'Oscars' continue to
be the industry's most coveted series
of awards. So impressed was the com-
mittee by the Laurel & Hardy short
The Music Box, a new category was
created, permitting its recognition as
'Best Live-Action Comedy Short
Subject' for 1931-2. The following
year's award went to an RKO release,
So This Is Harris, starring Phil Harris
with Laurel & Hardy's own James
Finlayson (*qv*) in the supporting cast.
Tit For Tat was nominated in 1935
but did not receive the award. Two
other near-misses were *Way Out West*
and *Block-Heads*, each nominated for
their music scores. One of the films to
which Laurel & Hardy contributed a
guest appearance, *The Hollywood
Revue of 1929*, was nominated as the
season's 'Best Picture'. Another, *The
Rogue Song*, was nominated for its
star, Lawrence Tibbett (*qv*), as 'Best
Actor'. In 1961, Stan Laurel was presented with an honorary Oscar for his
'creative pioneering in the field of
comedy'. It became his most treasured
possession, yet he insisted it be
dubbed 'Mr Clean', owing to its
resemblance to a character in a TV
commercial. In 1984, the Sons of the
Desert club (*qv*) initiated a 'Mr Clean'
award, an Oscar near-lookalike presented to the winner of the trivia quiz
held at each international convention.

(See also: Kaye, Danny; Screen
Actors' Guild)

ADRIAN, IRIS (1913–94)

Wisecracking actress, a former
Ziegfeld girl who played 'Alice', one
of the dockside ladies in *Our Relations*
(*qv*). During shooting, Babe was separated from his wife and asked the
actress for a date; she accepted, but he
later cancelled saying 'I'm an old fat
fellow... you wouldn't like me'. 'I
didn't think he was so bad', she said
later. Miss Adrian's earliest known
film appearance is *Chasing Husbands*, a
1928 short with Charley Chase (*qv*);
many others include *Paramount On
Parade* (1930), *Go West* (1940), *The
G-String Murders* (1941), *The Paleface*
(1948), *The Odd Couple* (1968) and
Paternity (1981).

(See also: Marriages)

ADVERTISING

In common with most celebrities,
Laurel & Hardy were frequently asked
to endorse various products.
Relatively early instances include a
campaign in which the team forsook
their customary bowlers for stetsons.
Magazine advertisements of the 1930s
saw the team extolling the superiority
of Chesterfield and Old Gold cigarettes and Mobil oil, while in Great
Britain, a drawing of the team
appeared in one of the period's imaginative Shell ads, drawn by John
Patrick. In the 1950s, Laurel & Hardy
found that their revived popularity
had brought a spate of unauthorized
product endorsements within 'Laurel
& Hardy Hours' on American TV, but
took no action after the failure of a
similar complaint brought by Roy

Rogers. Even posthumously, their
images are considered potent advertising material: in the 1980s, several
newspaper campaigns employed stills
from the films, promoting glue, elec-
tricity and TV sets. In the early 1980s,
a British TV campaign used Laurel &
Hardy lookalikes to sell oranges, while
American commercials did the same
for a brand of windscreen wiper.
Foreign-speaking countries have used
stills or caricatures to advertise enterprises ranging from biscuits to
insurance. Advertising for the team's
own films varies worldwide. In the
US, comprehensive press books (even
for the shorts) were let down somewhat by the poor likenesses depicted
in many posters. European counterparts - notably those from Belgium -
tend to be superior, although the
implied content can sometimes be
misleading.

(See also: Caricatures; Impersonators;
In-jokes; Nudity; Television)

AERIAL ANTICS
See: *Hog Wild*

AGEE, JAMES (1909-55)

Critic and screenwriter who in 1949
took the bold step of praising the
silent greats in his *Life* magazine essay
'Comedy's Greatest Era'. At this time,
such material was far from in vogue
and it can be said that Agee's remarks
were instrumental in the subsequent
revival of interest. Laurel & Hardy are
represented in the work by descriptions of the pie fight from *The Battle
of the Century* (*qv*) and the bridge

crossing from *Swiss Miss* (*qv*); although neither scene is entirely representative, the fact that the article was written at all speaks volumes for Agee's value as a commentator.

(See also: Animals; Pianos; Reviews)

A–HAUNTING WE WILL GO
(Laurel & Hardy film)
Released by 20th Century-Fox, 7 August 1942. Produced by Sol M. Wurtzel. Directed by Alfred Werker. Camera: Glen MacWilliams. 67 minutes.
With Stan Laurel and Oliver Hardy, Dante the Magician, Sheila Ryan, John Shelton, George Lynn, Don Costello, Elisha Cook Jr., Addison Richards.

Wanted criminal Darby Mason (George Lynn) plans to travel incognito to collect an inheritance, this to be achieved by posing as a corpse; the coffin will be delivered to a sanitarium run by fellow-crook 'Doc' Lake (Don Costello). An escort is needed for the train journey; Stan and Ollie, ordered out of town for vagrancy, see their

advertisement in a newspaper and apply, taking the grisly job only to avoid arrest. They board the train but fall victim to a pair of confidence tricksters selling a fake money-making machine. Ordering a meal with nothing but play money, they are in trouble until bailed out by a kindly onlooker, Dante the Magician. They arrange to repay him on reaching their destination, where Dante is appearing. Mason's accomplices call attorney Malcolm Kilgore (Addison Richards), executor of the will, claiming to have an injured patient who is believed to be the heir. On examining the coffin, they find it has been switched with one of Dante's props. Stan and Ollie arrive at the theatre where Dante introduces them to stage manager Tommy White (John Shelton), who has become friendly with Dante's assistant Margo (Sheila Ryan). The boys test out an illusion using twin telephone booths and are engaged as comic assistants. The gangster's coffin is hauled to the theatre's ceiling, in preparation for a trick. Mason's henchmen arrive, cornering Stan and Ollie at gunpoint with a demand for

the coffin. The show goes on as the boys search for the coffin backstage; they overhear a police detective reminding Tommy of an earlier instruction never to return to that town, but he promises to remain only for the week's engagement. Onstage, Stan and Ollie join Dante for the Indian Rope Trick, Ollie playing the flute as Stan perches precariously. The boys rest backstage until pursued by one of the gang. Stan hides behind a prop door while Ollie takes refuge in a sabre cabinet. Stan watches helplessly as a propman inserts the swords, but Ollie avoids being impaled. When the box is wheeled before the audience he sneezes, opening the cabinet and sending the swords flying. The gangsters discover the coffin's whereabouts and ask Stan and Ollie for an exit other than the stage door; they are unwittingly directed to a lion's cage. The act continues. Stan is placed in a sarcophagus before Dante fires a bullet into the coffin suspended above. On examination it is found to contain Doc Lake, shot through the heart. The policeman suspects Tommy, who it seems was once innocently involved with Lake; Dante shows that the bullet hole in the coffin is in the wrong position to have killed Lake, who must have been dead when placed inside. The arrogant officer, searching the premises, soon joins the crooks in the lion's cage; they are freed and Mason is captured. Kilgore has arrived to explain that he is really a Federal agent, who set up the inheritance in order to find Mason; Lake was killed because Mason, having left the coffin, saw him firing shots into it. Ollie tries to find Stan, who has vanished during the trick, and discovers him miniaturized inside a prop egg.

Considered valuable for preserving Dante the Magician's act (though he is known to have appeared in other

A-Haunting We Will Go: *Dante the magician has three assistants; guess which one is Sheila Ryan*

films), *A-Haunting We Will Go* serves no other purpose and is perhaps the worst of Laurel & Hardy's Fox series. The implied ghostliness of the title, much in vogue at the time, is nowhere to be seen; instead there is a dull, confusing 'mystery' which has no need of the team and might better have been made without them. The few laughs to be had are from a trick effect using multiple Laurel & Hardys, as if they needed gimmicks to be funny; a reworking of the broken statue gag from *Wrong Again* (qv) is sunk by relegating the payoff to an afterthought. The dialogue seems designed to make them an unlikely blend of imbecile and wiseacre: after Dante saves them from being put off the train, Stan tells an official 'that's where *you* get off'. Admirers must wince when another line refers to their having belonged to a lodge, for *Sons of the Desert* this isn't.

(See also: Black humour; Confidence tricks; Cook, Elisha Jr.; Criminals; Female impersonation; *Great Guns*; Home movies; Magicians; Moreland, Mantan; Music; Trains; 20th Century-Fox; Werker, Alfred; Writers)

AIRCRAFT (all films *qv*)

In Laurel & Hardy's time, air travel was not yet the automatic means of travel we know today. Journeys to Europe were made by sea while inland trips tended to be by rail, although they would sometimes board aircraft while touring in wartime. Airborne vehicles crop up in a handful of films: *Forty-Five Minutes From Hollywood* shows a number of contraptions hovering above California's skyline; Mickey Mouse takes to a makeshift dirigible in *Babes in Toyland*; Stan takes pot shots at a French aviator in *Block-Heads*; the boys are trapped in runaway aeroplanes in *The Flying Deuces* and *The Big Noise*; and in *The Bullfighters*, alight from an airliner. One of the hallmarks of the Fox films is the frequent sound of passing aircraft; distracting evidence of the

studio's lack of concern. It should be noted that *Air Raid Wardens* features no raids whatever.

(See also: Stage appearances; 20th Century-Fox; Wartime)

AIR RAID WARDENS

(Laurel & Hardy film)
Released by M-G-M, early April 1943. Produced by B. F. Zeidman. Directed by Edward Sedgwick. 67 minutes.
With Stan Laurel and Oliver Hardy, Edgar Kennedy, Jacqueline White, Horace (Stephen) McNally, Nella Walker, Donald Meek, Henry O'Neill, Howard Freeman, Paul Stanton, Robert Emmett O'Connor, William Tannen, Russell Hicks, Phil Van Zandt, Frederic Worlock, Don Costello.

The small town of Huxton greets the outbreak of war with a calm determination to help Uncle Sam on the home front. Stan and Ollie, a trail of failed businesses behind them, try to enlist but are rejected by each of the services. Dan Madison (Horace McNally), editor of the local paper and head of Huxton's civil defence, persuades them to help as civilians. Returning to their current business, a bicycle shop, they find the premises being emptied by removal man Joe Bledsoe (Edgar Kennedy). As they do battle, the new proprietor, Eustace Middling (Donald Meek) walks in; they compromise by sharing the business. When Stan and Ollie leave to put up posters for that evening's defence meeting, Middling calls an associate; he is evidently a Nazi spy. At the meeting, Madison speaks of the need to protect a nearby magnesium plant and delegates various key tasks; Stan and Ollie, arriving late and carrying a yapping dog, disrupt the proceedings. They volunteer as Air Raid Wardens and are given a harmless task during an exercise. Receiving the wrong orders, they are sent to 'rescue' the local banker, J. P. Norton (Howard Freeman), with whom they have had several altercations. Norton is accidentally knocked cold, given messy, improvised first-aid and eventually trapped under a truck. Recovering from the ordeal, Norton demands the boys' dismissal; Madison persuades him to give them another chance. Late at night Stan and Ollie receive a call for duty, but the all clear is sounded. Unaware that the blackout is over, they call at a house asking for the lights to be put out; the householder is Joe Bledsoe, who proves unco-operative. As the lights are switched on and off, a neighbour reports someone 'signalling to the Japs'. Bledsoe knocks them cold with a bottle of booze and they are accused of being drunk on duty. Madison reluctantly dismisses them. As the boys leave, they hear Madison speak of an exercise for the benefit of a visiting Major; back at the shop, they spot German-speaking intruders and hide in the back of their car. The spies are thus tracked to their hide-out, where they are seen discussing sabotage plans with Middling. Stan and Ollie try to contact Madison using a carrier pigeon, but the message is intercepted and the boys captured. They are forced to participate in a William Tell-style routine but overpower their captor. Finding an old car, they drive off, but crash into a tree. They reach a telephone and call the authorities, who take the message to be part of the exercise. Wardens are sent to the magnesium plant but the boys realize Middling has infiltrated the force; the wardens round up the spies while Stan and Ollie, heroes of the day, arrive just in time to catch Middling.

First of two M-G-M features spaced between the Fox series, *Air Raid Wardens* benefits from an increased budget but is sabotaged by the wartime requirements of excessive patriotism and stereotyped Nazis. The writing team, including as it does former Roach associates Charles Rogers (*qv*) and Jack Jevne, should have produced brighter results (particularly when reuniting the team with Edgar Kennedy), but the whole is stifled by unwieldy direction and, reportedly, a technical advisor reluctant to permit any genuine kidding of civil defence methods. One can only attribute to the film's two other writers (Martin Rackin, Harry Crane) such moments as an attempt at pathos (Stan's speech

on being dismissed from the service), plus a misconceived reversal of Stanley's undue preparation to sign his name. Unlike parallel scenes in *Double Whoopee* and *Any Old Port* (both *qv*), this version starts with his signing an 'X' before dwelling upon his supposed illiteracy. This is symptomatic of the studio's erasure of their dignity, ignoring the customary sympathy for their well-meaning ineptitude. The original trailer for this film panders both to this and contemporary slang by describing them as 'a gruesome twosome', a description that might have been better placed elsewhere.

(See also: Alcohol; Cars; Characters; Kennedy, Edgar; Jigsaw puzzles; M-G-M; Sedgwick, Edward; Trailers; 20th Century-Fox; Video releases; Wartime; Writers)

ALAN, RAY (b. 1930)
British ventriloquist and scriptwriter. Toured with Laurel & Hardy in post-war variety, a period he has recalled in programmes such as BBC Radio's *Funny You Should Ask*. One rather charming story concerns a visit to Alan's dressing room by Oliver Hardy who, despite having developed some difficulty in walking, climbed a considerable number of steps in order to ask the young entertainer for an autograph.

(See also: Stage appearances)

ALCOHOL
(Laurel & Hardy films *qv*)
Many comedians have depicted the use (or abuse) of alcohol. W. C. Fields built much of his image, both public and private, around a reverence for drink, recalling the days of Falstaff. Chaplin tended towards comic drunk routines even in his Karno days; ironic, considering the part alcohol played in his father's early death. In their solo careers, Laurel & Hardy played quite a number of such scenes, one of which caused a young Hardy

some embarrassment when called upon to explain his apparent drunkenness (see **Freemasons**). Laurel was later to recall an impromptu bit of business from his own solo work, when, as the cameras turned, he decided to incorporate a drunken attempt to don an overcoat, which finished buttoned not just around Stan but also a telegraph pole. As a team, they were to explore this area thoroughly, most obviously in the three-reel comedy *Blotto*, although their intoxication is on this occasion the result of auto-suggestion. One of their wartime films, *Air Raid Wardens*, sees them unjustly dismissed from the service for apparent drunkenness. The Prohibition law central to *Blotto*'s premise surfaces regularly in the gag titles of 1920s comedies. It serves also as an excuse to place Stan and Ollie in jail for *Pardon Us*, when they are convicted for trying to sell home brew to a policeman. The liberated post-Prohibition attitude to beer is accurately reflected in *Our Relations*, where it is considered quite proper for ladies and gentlemen to drink. *Them Thar Hills* concludes with Charlie Hall doing battle with Laurel & Hardy after discovering Mrs Hall (Mae Busch) the worse for some 'mountain water' drawn from a well heavily laced with moonshine. Billy Gilbert (*qv*) contributes a splendidly slurred moment to *One Good Turn*, while Arthur Housman (*qv*), perhaps the most accomplished of specialized comic drunks, staggers hilariously through, among others, *Scram!*, *The Live Ghost* and *Our Relations*. In *The Fixer-Uppers*, Laurel & Hardy join one of his binges and are rendered unconscious, a condition they also experience in a scripted but unfilmed segment of *The Bohemian Girl*. Within the Laurel & Hardy team itself, most of the drinking scenes involve Stan. The operettas *Fra Diavolo* and the aforementioned *The Bohemian Girl* share the idea of Stan filling up with wine, while in *Swiss Miss*, Stan persuades a vigilant St. Bernard to relinquish his cask of brandy by creating a snowstorm from feathers. The radio sketch titled *The Wedding Night* has Stan 'bolstered' by Ollie's supply of prune punch. Hardy as on-screen drinker tends to be confined to his villains of solo days, as in the example quoted above and *Fluttering Hearts*, a 1927 comedy starring Charley Chase (*qv*). An exception may be found in one of the silent Laurel & Hardys, *Early to Bed*, which contains a sequence in which a spoiled, newly-rich Ollie returns from a tipsy evening. There is a beer named after Stan Laurel, brewed in his native town of Ulverston. In 1991, *The Laurel & Hardy Magazine* reported that Glaswegian *aficionados* planned to celebrate the forthcoming Hardy centenary with a brew called Hardy Heavy.

(See also: Aubrey, Jimmy; *Big Noise, the*; Births; *Four Clowns*; *Mumming Birds*; Periodicals; Radio; *That's My Wife*)

ALL-STAR SERIES, THE
Seemingly designed to reflect Hal Roach's acquisition of 'fading stars' (*qv*), the 'All-Star' label came to represent instead comedies featuring various contract players rather than specific names. Although the Laurel & Hardy comedies were promoted under their own name from the autumn of 1927, they retained an in-house designation of 'All-Star Comedies' until *Should Married Men Go Home?* (*qv*), from which point the official 'Laurel & Hardy series' begins.

(See also: Hal Roach Studios, the; *Pair of Tights, a*; *Putting Pants On Philip*; *Second Hundred Years, the*; Teaming)

ALONG CAME AUNTIE (1926)
See: Oakland, Vivien; Risqué humour; Sleeper, Martha and *That's My Wife*

ALTERNATIVE TITLES
(all films *qv*)

One of the most common difficulties for the film scholar is the existence of alternative titles for certain subjects. Where title changes exist, they tend to be between the US and UK markets, sometimes to avoid confusion with another production of the same title, at other times to eliminate expressions either indecipherable or in some way unacceptable in that region. In some instances, changes seem to have been made purely at a whim. Several Laurel & Hardy films have circulated under varying identities, often when the British copies retained working titles jettisoned at the last minute for US release. *You're Darn Tootin'*, an American expression, reverted to its

provisional label of *The Music Blasters* for the UK. *We Faw Down*, deriving from the baby-talk slang popular in 1920s America, became *We Slip Up* for the British market, although *They Go Boom* made the trip unamended. Another American expression, *Hog Wild*, became *Aerial Antics* for the UK. *Beau Hunks* became *Beau Chumps* when exported. *Fra Diavolo* was released under that title almost everywhere except the US, where it

Alternative titles: Atoll K *played most UK dates as* Robinson Crusoeland *and in America as* Utopia

was called *The Devil's Brother*; Stan Laurel always referred to the film under its intended title. *Pardon Us* endured the less witty if more descriptive label *Jailbirds* when opening in London, while *Sons of the Desert* retains its working title of *Fraternally Yours* in most British prints. Other titles for this film have been given as *Sons of the Legion* and *Convention City*, but these seem to be erroneous. Despite the tendency of reissues to derive from American originals, current UK prints of these last three subjects often retain the alternative titles. A number of Laurel & Hardy reissues have borne unfamiliar names: *Fra Diavolo* has been known rather prosaically as *Bogus Bandits*, *Bonnie Scotland* once surfaced as *Heroes of the Regiment*, while the

much-travelled *Babes in Toyland* has been known simply as *Toyland*, *Revenge Is Sweet*, *March of the Toys* and, most commonly, *March of the Wooden Soldiers*, a title retained for the restored edition to which colour has been added. One Laurel & Hardy rediscovery came from material bearing a British title. A long-lost 1931 charity short, *The Stolen Jools* reappeared under the name it was given for its 1932 UK release, *The Slippery Pearls*. American television has seen versions of some Laurel & Hardy films mutilated both in length and titling: a truncated *Pack Up Your Troubles* appeared, aptly, as *Smithereens*; *Pardon Us* was commuted to an extract called *Whatta Stir*; while the single-reel fragment *Sailors' Downfall* bore scant likeness to *Our Relations*.

G. M. Anderson produced an early series of Laurel films, including When Knights Were Cold. *Mae Laurel didn't get to be leading lady, but she seems to have ensnared a King*

(See also: Home movies; Reissues; Television; Working titles)

ANDERSON, GILBERT M.
(1882-1971)

Born Max Aronson, G. M. Anderson achieved fame in early westerns as 'Broncho Billy'. In 1907 he co-founded Essanay, a name derived from the initials of Anderson and his partner, George K. Spoor. Hal Roach (*qv*) worked briefly on their premises during 1915, a time when Essanay's biggest attraction was Charlie Chaplin (*qv*). Anderson's later activities as producer included *Lucky Dog* (*qv*), a Laurel film that included Hardy in its supporting cast. Anderson subsequently produced the following Laurel films for Metro release: *The Egg*, *The Weak-End Party*, *Mud and Sand*, *The Pest* (all 1922), *When Knights Were Cold* and *The Handy Man* (both 1923). Stan Laurel recalled a sequence from *When Knights Were Cold* involving 300 medieval knights on papier-mâché horses of the sort where the rider's legs reach the ground. A further idea of the film's spirit may be gained from a still depicting Laurel, in period costume, answering a telephone. As a parody of Valentino's *Blood and Sand*, *Mud and Sand* connects elsewhere to Laurel & Hardy chronology through the presence in the original of Walter Long (*qv*) and British actor Leo White, the former Chaplin foil who worked with Babe after defecting to imitator Billy West (*qv*). In Laurel & Hardy's *This Is Your Life* tribute, one of the series' directors, Frank Fouce, recalled that in *Mud and Sand* Stan (as 'Rhubarb Vaselino') was required to be chased by a bull, a genuinely dangerous stunt from which he barely escaped. The crew had some fun at Stan's expense by claiming that the scene would have to be redone. According to John McCabe (*qv*), the Laurel-Anderson series ended when the producer reneged on a contractual point concerning payment; Laurel went on to fame elsewhere, while Anderson lived to enjoy a lengthy retirement, receiving a special Oscar in 1957.

(See also: Academy Awards; M-G-M; Parodies; Rolin Film Company, the; Solo films; Superstition; Teaming; Turpin, Ben; Working titles)

ANDRE, LONA (d. 1992)
Actress in films from 1932, among them *College Humor*, *Murder at the Vanities* and *Our Relations* (*qv*), in which she plays 'Lily', one of the waterfront ladies befriended by 'Alfie' Laurel and 'Bertie' Hardy. Left acting

in 1943 to follow a business career, though continuing to live in North Hollywood; she reached managerial status during a stint of more than 25 years with Lockheed.

ANGORA LOVE
(Laurel & Hardy film)
Released by M-G-M, 14 December 1929. Produced by Hal Roach. Directed by Lewis R. Foster. Two reels, synchronized music and effects on disc.
With Stan Laurel and Oliver Hardy, Edgar Kennedy, Charlie Hall, Harry Bernard, Charley Young.

Penelope the goat breaks loose from her moorings at the pet shop and is reported stolen. Stan and Ollie emerge from a bakery, where Stan has spent their last dime on 'pastry with a hole in it': they meet Penelope, who starts to follow them after Stan has given her a piece of doughnut. Ollie considers goats 'bad luck', a viewpoint strengthened when a small boy tells them that the goat has been stolen. Casual attempts to shake her off lead to a full-scale flight; the chase escalates, concluding with another dip for Ollie in that ubiquitous muddy hole in the ground. We are informed by title card that two days have elapsed, during which Laurel & Hardy have failed to escape the goat ('it caught up with them in St Paul'). At their lodgings, Stan and Ollie prepare for bed, hoping to keep their companion a secret from the landlord (Edgar Kennedy). Penelope's habits create sufficient fuss for the landlord to be alerted. The boys manage to hide the goat during his first two visits, but become aware of a certain aroma. Penelope needs a bath, but their preparations lead to Ollie being jammed in the tub, and, after a neighbour has mistakenly called at their room, Stan's head being dunked into the suds in lieu of the goat. The water spillage reaches the landlord as he sleeps below. The police are summoned and when the landlord reaches the boys' room he is drenched with a tub of water. He goes to the kitchen, fills a bucket, and returns to pour it over Stan. An exchange of soakings begins, soon involving the neighbour who had called earlier. A policeman arrives to

One of several attempts to elude the goat, shot for but deleted from the final version of **Angora Love**

receive a well-aimed throw from the landlord. Recognizing the goat, he arrests the landlord for the theft. Ollie, who never wants to see another goat, is dismayed when Stan points out a group of Penelope's offspring left under the bed.

Angora Love was the last of their silent films, though like many late silents it was released with music and sound effects. The track, similar to that for *Bacon Grabbers* (*qv*), comprises theatre organ and a few strategic noises. A rich source of gags, much of *Angora Love* was recycled into their later comedies (all *qv*): the business of Ollie attempting to hang up his clothes while Stan continually uses the same hook resurfaces in *Be Big*, while Ollie massaging Stan's foot in mistake for his own may also be seen in *Beau Hunks*. *Laughing Gravy* is a remake of the entire subject, closer by far than the example recalled by Stan Laurel, *The Chimp*. Laurel's memories of *Angora Love* suggest that there were to have been more elaborate attempts to elude the goat than were eventually included, such as hiding and walking backwards. Stills exist of the team in a theatre lobby, with cameraman George Stevens (*qv*) tending the box office. In one shot they look apprehensively from the doorway, while the goat stands behind them; in another, they seem to be explaining their dilemma to Stevens. The last Laurel & Hardy silents were completed early in 1929 but released throughout that year in between talking subjects. Despite appearing at a time when even silent features were practically ignored, this short gained enthusiastic reviews. Shortly before his death, director Lewis Foster (*qv*) sent an example of such a review to Blackhawk Films (*qv*), who believed it to be from *Film Daily*:

Here is a short comedy, just sizzling over with rapid-fire, laughter-stirring situations that click equally well with youths and

adults. Laurel & Hardy are an unctuous pair of funsters that always boom along on a current of rippling merriment. True, they are the very incarnation of acrobatic tumble bugs and ludicrous what-nots that defy the straight line of analysis; but, oh boy, who cares about the proprieties of cinema construction when two big ginks are pulling off stunts that would shake all the sugar out of a chronic diabetic all tied up in knots of laughter.

(See also: Animals; Beds; Deleted scenes; Landlords; Music; Reciprocal destruction; Remakes; Reviews; Risqué humour; Silent films; Sound)

ANIMALS
(Laurel & Hardy films *qv*)
Familiar showbiz maxim: never work with children or animals. Laurel & Hardy were able to acquit themselves in any company, no matter how scene-stealing. Of the animals to enter their world, those seeming to have greatest comic potential are goats, one of whom (named 'Narcissus') is their companion in *Saps at Sea*. *Do Detectives Think?*, an early silent, uses

a goat to provide a horrifying shadow in a graveyard, while the team's last silent, *Angora Love*, centres around the boys' attempts to conceal a goat (called 'Penelope' this time) from their landlord. *Angora Love* was remade as *Laughing Gravy*, in which they harbour not a goat but the dog after whom the film is named. The same dog appears fleetingly in *The Bohemian Girl* and in the extended edition of *Pardon Us*. 'Laughing Gravy' resembles closely Stan's pet-pooch 'Buster' in *Early to Bed*. 'Buddy' is the family dog placed among the doomed picnic party of *Perfect Day*; a larger cousin is intimidated by a miniature toy bulldog in *Bacon Grabbers*. Prison bloodhounds in *Pardon Us* not only fail to recapture escapees Laurel & Hardy, but actually settle with them and provide a litter of pups. Perhaps the oddest canine in Laurel & Hardy history is Stan himself in a dog skin in *The Pest* (1922), but man's best friend lived up to the title when bringing Laurel & Hardy together for the first time in *Lucky Dog*. Cats are seen less often, but burglars Laurel & Hardy imitate them in *Night Owls*. A genuine cat falls foul of a flying roller skate in *Brats*, but no such fate meets the various lions in *The Chimp*, *Hollywood Party*, *Nothing But Trouble* and *Atoll K*. *The Chimp* is actually a circus gorilla called Ethel, played by Phillipines-born make-up man Charles Gemora (1903-61). He appears once more as a gorilla in *Swiss Miss* and is reported as the occupant of the ape costume in *At The Circus* with the Marx Brothers (*qv*). Still among the larger creatures, horses provide transport for *The Music Box* and in all the films with historical settings. A horse named 'Blue Boy' causes confusion with the painting of that name in *Wrong Again*. A full-scale rodeo takes place in *Great Guns*; none of the participants can compare with the horse representing a reincarnated Ollie in *The Flying Deuces*. Mules occasionally provide an alternative, notably 'Dinah' in *Way Out West*. Taurine encounters include of course *The Bullfighters* and the Laurel solo *Mud and Sand*. Even larger are the elephants who appear infrequently but memorably: Hardy's 1939 solo film *Zenobia* (*qv*) takes its name from a trained elephant who, though talented, cannot match its airborne ancestors in *Flying Elephants*. Such mythological creatures are outside the team's usual scope but the unreal milieu of *Babes in Toyland* permits the fabled Cat and his Fiddle, with the addition of Disney's Three Little Pigs and Mickey Mouse. Mickey is another of the varied attractions in M-G-M's *Hollywood Party*.

(See also: Anderson, G. M.; Animation; Fish; Insects)

ANIMATION

Animation was used frequently for trick effects in silent comedies, particularly in the Sennett films. Roach was less fond of such methods, although a notable exception gives us a glimpse of *Flying Elephants* (*qv*). When Stan and Ollie complete the building of a house in *The Finishing Touch* (*qv*), an animated bird begins the process of collapse by landing on the chimney. In *Brats* (*qv*), Stan and Ollie's small sons take a pop-gun to a small cartoon mouse, while the business of Ollie's neck being stretched in *Way Out West* is once again accomplished by animation. One source attributes the elephants to Walter Lantz who, years before producing the Woody Woodpecker series, spent time at Roach; another credits studio special effects head, Roy Seawright (*qv*), whose province these and similar effects tended to be. During animation's great days of the 1930s and 1940s, film star caricatures proved ideal both for spot gags and as a framework for entire cartoons. Laurel & Hardy were often depicted thus, and formed a friendship with Walt Disney (*qv*) which manifested itself in the inclusion of Mickey Mouse and the Three Little Pigs in *Babes in Toyland* (*qv*). In turn Laurel & Hardy appeared in graphic form in three Disney shorts, *Mickey's Gala Première* (1933), *Mickey's Polo Team* (1936) and *Mother Goose Goes Hollywood* (1938). Laurel & Hardy and Disney each contributed separately to M-G-M's *Hollywood Party* (*qv*). Stan Laurel was depicted as a gorilla in *Mickey's Pet Store* (1933). *Mickey's Polo Team* deserves applause for its skill in characterization; this aspect distinguishes even the studio's short films and serves here to lift the Laurel & Hardy facsimilies far beyond mere exploitation of a popular image. Ollie on horseback is fastidious in his attempts to coax the animal into movement, his gentle requests being made primarily

through tiny gestures (delivered in that symmetrical Hardy fashion using both hands in unison). When Stan lends assistance, he and Ollie mutually confirm their next course of action with the exaggerated nods associated with the genuine article. At one point, Ollie emerges from a collision trapped beneath his horse: pause for a disgusted look to camera followed by the clang of a horseshoe on Ollie's head. Top Disney man Ubbe ('Ub') Iwerks (said to have been the true creator of Mickey Mouse) spent ten years away from the Disney studio as an independent producer, during which period he produced at least four cartoons employing Laurel & Hardy caricatures, including *Movie Mad* (1931) and *Soda Squirt* (1933). A 1935 film, *Balloonland*, sees Laurel & Hardy dancing past the camera as balloon men. *The Brave Tin Soldier* (1934), which includes a brief glimpse of the team as round-bottomed toy dolls, typifies many of these representations - momentary affairs conceived only for a quick laugh. The 1937 Columbia cartoon *Merry Mutineers*, (one of four Columbia cartoons to use their likenesses), is another example, with Laurel & Hardy used only fleetingly among the dancing mariners of the title. Disney's main rival, Max Fleischer, used such motifs sparingly but Popeye the Sailor can be found offering his impression of Stan Laurel in *Puttin' On The Act* (1940). When Disney's main energies began to be channelled into more ambitious projects, supremacy in the short category passed mostly to M-G-M's Tom & Jerry series and to the Warner Brothers cartoons. Laurel & Hardy crop up in various Warner entries, from the early *Bosko's Garage* (1933) and *Buddy's Adventures* (1935) to more polished works, notably *Coo-Coo Nut Grove* (1936), *Hollywood Steps Out* (1941), and *Hollywood Canine*

Animation: Ollie and Stan caricatured as toy dolls in the 1934 Ub Iwerks cartoon The Brave Tin Soldier

Canteen (1946). *Hop, Skip and a Chump* (1942) shows Laurel & Hardy transformed into crows, the authentic Laurel & Hardy timing and mannerisms being captured with remarkable skill; a 1940 Warner entry, *You Ought To Be In Pictures*, presents an accomplished blend of live action and animation, with a moment where Porky Pig attempts to enter a film studio disguised as Oliver Hardy as a highlight. More recently, the television market has been swamped with limited-animation product, including the 1960s Hanna-Barbera films based on Laurel & Hardy caricatures drawn by Larry Harmon (*qv*). Somewhat peripherally, Thames TV's 1978 series *The Kenny Everett Video Show* incorporated two very recognizable figures into an episode of its animated space spoof 'Captain Kremmen'.

(See also: Caricatures; Seawright, Roy; Tashlin, Frank)

ANOTHER FINE MESS
(Laurel & Hardy film)
Released by M-G-M, 29 November 1930. Three reels. Produced by Hal Roach. Directed by James Parrott. Camera: Jack Stevens.
With Stan Laurel and Oliver Hardy, James Finlayson, Thelma Todd, Charles Gerrard, Harry Bernard.

Colonel Buckshot (James Finlayson) is leaving for South Africa, entrusting the task of renting his mansion to his servants. Stan and Ollie, pursued by the law, take refuge in the house and overhear the servants' plans to sneak away for the weekend. Once they have left, the boys make several attempts to leave, foiled each time by the ever-present policeman outside. A complication develops with the arrival of prospective tenants, Lord and Lady Plumtree (Charles Gerrard and Thelma Todd). Ollie tells Stan to borrow the butler's uniform and inform the couple of the Colonel's absence. Stan follows orders but cannot ask them to leave, having spotted the policeman. He calls for 'Colonel Buckshot', forcing Ollie to continue the charade. Greeting the couple with considerable grandeur, Ollie summons 'Agnes', the maid, taking Stan aside with instructions to don the maid's outfit. Back with his visitors, the 'Colonel' is asked to play the piano (producing an elaborately topped-and-tailed performance of 'Chopsticks') before Lord Plumtree asks to be escorted to the billiard room. Attempts to locate the room take them upstairs, where they meet 'Agnes', the bashful maid who trips downstairs straight into conversation with Lady Plumtree. After abandoning the search for the billiard room (with the discovery that Lord Plumtree does not even play), the astonished Ollie learns that Lady Plumtree would like to retain Agnes' services. From here Ollie refines the details of renting the house at a low price, claiming 'I picked it up for practically nothing myself'. Negotiations for staff salaries necessitate a few quick changes of costume for Stan, who at one point combines the butler's uniform with the maid's wig. Back in his 'Agnes' role, he answers the door to none other than the real Colonel, who has returned to fetch his bow and arrows. Ollie takes some time recognizing him, until Stan draws his attention to the Colonel's portrait hanging nearby. They make a run for it; the Colonel

Another Fine Mess: *Colonel Buckshot and Agnes*

calls the police and Lord Plumtree has to flee from the irate householder. Stan and Ollie borrow an outsize goat skin, and escape under it on a tandem. The police chase this two-wheeled animal into a tunnel, where a streetcar tears off their uniforms. The bizarre cycling goat emerges as two separate creatures on unicycles.

This bizarre ending is matched by an eccentric beginning, with the opening credits spoken in unison by twin girls (see **Titling**). In other respects the humour in *Another Fine Mess* is conventional but very funny, bearing a proud heritage as a remake of the early *Duck Soup* (*qv*), itself based on a stage sketch written by Laurel's father. A facetious tone marks the soundtrack, which employs spot effects of slide-whistles and musical stings to punctuate the action more than in any other Laurel & Hardy talkie, effects usually quite alien to the team's sophisticated slapstick. Research suggests that no foreign versions were made, Laurel's personal list of his films noting any alternative editions and including none for this film; this applies also to Roach studio records. A reported version called *De bote en bote* was later confirmed as a Spanish title for *Pardon Us* (*qv*).

(See also: Bicycles; Catch-phrases; Continuity errors; Courtliness; Englishmen; Finlayson, James; Foreign versions; Jefferson, Arthur; Pianos; Remakes; Risqué humour; Servants; Todd, Thelma; Vagrancy)

ANY OLD PORT
(Laurel & Hardy film)
Released by M-G-M, 5 March 1932.
Two reels. Produced by Hal Roach.
Directed by James Horne. Camera: Art Lloyd.
With Stan Laurel and Oliver Hardy, Walter Long, Jacqueline Wells, Harry Bernard, Charlie Hall, Bobby Burns, Dick Gilbert.

Stan and Ollie arrive home from a

Walter Long trapped in **Any Old Port**

whaling voyage (for which Stan was 'bait') and check into a hotel, the Mariner's Rest. The proprietor of this seedy establishment, Mugsy Long (Walter Long) is forcing a young girl in his employ (Jacqueline Wells) into marriage, an activity from which he takes time out to register his new guests. As the boys play pool, the reluctant girl manages to tell them of her dilemma before being locked in a cupboard. Stan and Ollie intervene, but are dissuaded somewhat when Long fails to notice the pool balls aimed at his head. The local justice (Bobby Burns) arrives to officiate, and the boys are summoned as witnesses. They refuse to co-operate and a free-for-all breaks out over the key to the cupboard. Stan swaps the key for another, giving the second one to Ollie; as Long chases Ollie around the building, Stan frees the girl, who makes her exit. Eventually the chase leads to a jetty, where Long is dumped into the water. Stan and Ollie escape only to realize that all their money is in the hotel room. Starvation seems imminent until Ollie is hailed by an old friend (Harry Bernard) seated at a nearby lunch wagon. He is making money as a boxing promoter, and

offers Ollie $50 to fight that evening. Ollie happily accepts both the engagement and an advance of the full amount, before settling down to order a huge meal. Stan cannot do likewise, because he has to fight later on; Ollie, of course, is the manager. At the arena, 'Battling Laurel' displays ignorance even of such basics as limbering up, but these become minor concerns when he discovers his opponent to be Mugsy Long. The vengeful hotelier instructs his second (Dick Gilbert) to 'load' his glove; Ollie, meanwhile, places a bet against Stan winning. The advice of Stan's second (Charlie Hall) is to 'hold him in the clinches', an instruction Stan takes literally until they are prised apart. In the confusion, Long's weighted glove goes to Stan, who is soon chasing Long around the ring. When he tries to retrieve the glove, Long is knocked cold and his second reports Stan to an official. By the ringside, Ollie tells Stan about the bet he had against him; Stan draws back his fist to strike Ollie, but the loaded glove knocks out the official, and the boys make a swift exit.

A deleted first reel of *Any Old Port* began with Stan and Ollie aboard ship with James Finlayson, Tiny Sandford (both *qv*) and an ostrich acquired on their travels. William K. Everson (*qv*) has considered *Any Old Port* to be a parody of D. W. Griffith's 1919 classic *Broken Blossoms*, implying perhaps that Griffith veteran Walter Long might well have contributed a few ideas. More specific technical advice is suggested by contemporary publicity for the film, which reveals Dick Gilbert as a former boxer who, like Edgar Kennedy (*qv*), had once fought Jack Dempsey. Gilbert's 15 years in the ring concluded with a thirty-round fight in Mexico. Elsewhere in the press sheet is a story about a young boxer who, having witnessed the filming, asked Stan Laurel for the shorts he had worn in the film. He wore them in his next three fights and won each by a knockout.

(See also: *Air Raid Wardens*; Bernard, Harry; Boxing; Burns, Bobby; Deleted scenes; *Double Whoopee*; Food; Long, Walter; Parodies; Sailors; Stage appearances; Titling; Wells, Jacqueline)

APOCRYPHA (all films *qv*)

There are many stories circulating about Laurel & Hardy that have no basis in reality; several are quite harmless, but others are more damaging to their memory. Two in the first category have been recounted by Hal Roach (*qv*) in various interviews, clearly in the interests of entertaining his audience: one is that Stan Laurel's blue eyes made him unfilmable until a more sensitive stock was introduced. The truth is that although pale, his eyes were emphasized in early appearances by heavy make-up. The second concerns the filming of *Big Business*, to the effect that the house destroyed was not that intended. Stan Laurel was aware of this story and stated quite clearly that the correct house was used - the home of an amply-compensated studio employee. Other

on-set anecdotes are equally unfounded: Rosina Lawrence (*qv*), heroine of *Way Out West*, denies that 'Dinah', the mule, was killed while being raised in a harness; and the bandsaw dissecting a car in *Busy Bodies* was the product of optical printing, which disproves claims that it had gone wrong and nearly killed the two comedians. More serious are tales from less sympathetic sources: one originated with a British newspaper, depicting Laurel in penniless old age, a condition he averted totally through careful investments; another derives from a magazine of the sort noted for celebrity 'revelations', claiming a long-time hatred between Stan and Babe that is refuted by family, friends and, for that matter, evidence; the third, a creative newspaper headline declaring 'Stan Laurel Marries Eighth Time', is a distortion almost beyond comprehension. Perhaps the most amusing (except, possibly, to those involved) is a belief that actor and director Clint Eastwood might be Stan Laurel's son; varying sources attribute the myth either to a foreign magazine or, incredibly, a letter to a children's comic remarking on the resemblance between the two.

(See also: *Babes in Toyland*; Colouring; Hobbies; Insurance; *Lucky Dog*; Marriages; Plays; Salaries; Seawright, Roy)

ARBUCKLE, ROSCOE 'FATTY'
(1889-1933)

Rotund comedian, whose early days with Selig led to stardom at Sennett's Keystone studio, often with Mabel Normand or Charlie Chaplin (both *qv*). Later starred in shorts for Joseph Schenck, during which period he introduced Buster Keaton (*qv*) to pictures. Signed for Paramount features shortly before his career was ruined; a young actress died at a party in Arbuckle's hotel room, and though cleared of all blame he was banned from the screen for several years. He continued as a director (using the

name William Goodrich) before a successful comeback, first on stage, then in a series of two-reel talkies for Vitaphone, but died just as feature roles started to materialize. Arbuckle's name is still tainted by the scandal, a great injustice for someone known to have been gentle and extremely talented; David A. Yallop's book *The Day the Laughter Stopped* (1976) establishes his innocence beyond question, yet much nonsense is still perpetuated by the uninformed. Yallop quotes an article from the September 1931 *Motion Picture* magazine, in which Laurel & Hardy were among the many to support Arbuckle's return to acting. Babe may well have recalled a few of his comedies from the 'teens which used 'Fatty' in the title, a move suggested by Rick de Croix in *Classic Images* to have been a probable emulation of contemporary Arbuckle films. *Fatty's Fatal Fun* (1916) may be seen excerpted in *Laurel & Hardy's Laughing Twenties* (*qv*). The *Classic Images* piece goes on to detail the use of a specific Arbuckle gag in this film, where Babe uses his large midriff to bounce someone across a room.

(See also: Sennett, Mack; Periodicals; Solo films)

ARLISS, GEORGE
(1868-1946)

British actor of aristocratic bearing, with a face seemingly tailor-made for a monocle. A lengthy, distinguished career on the British stage led ultimately to film success on both sides of the Atlantic, notably the title role in *Disraeli* in both the silent original and the talkie remake. An early autobiography, *On the Stage* (John Murray, 1928), records his repertory days with particular praise for Stan Laurel's father, Arthur Jefferson (*qv*), as a character actor and for passing on much useful advice. Arliss, who also describes Jefferson's considerable skills as a maker of wigs and grease-paint, goes on to mention that he took

The Army: Legionnaires in Beau Hunks

over Jefferson's roles after the latter's departure from the company. Despite his patrician air, Arliss was often associated with robust characters, a dichotomy reflected in his portrayal of pirate-cum-clergyman *Dr Syn* (1937). Another example is his dual role in the 1936 British comedy *His Lordship*, a film which provides him with an *alter ego* believed by some to be the prototype for Stan Laurel's 'Lord Paddington' in *A Chump at Oxford* (*qv*).

ARMETTA, HENRY (1888-1945)
The archetypal excitable European, Italian-born Henry Armetta had a long career in American films, including work with Buster Keaton (*qv*) in *What? No Beer?* and the Marx Brothers (*qv*) in their last M-G-M film, *The Big Store*. He fits perfectly into Laurel & Hardy's *Fra Diavolo* (*qv*) as the worried innkeeper, Matteo; his attempts to emulate Stan's 'kneesie-earsie-nosie' routine are among the film's highlights.

Artists: Babe in creative costume, for 1917's Cupid's Rival
Photograph by Phil Johnson

ARMY, THE
(Laurel & Hardy films *qv*)
Military life has long been a comedy staple. In their lengthy careers Laurel & Hardy encompassed several military adventures, an early example being the 1924 Laurel solo film *Smithy*, in which Stan leaves the ranks (owing to 'a bean shortage'!) to enter the building trade. One of the films to feature Laurel & Hardy before their official teaming, *With Love and Hisses*, sees them as Territorials on a weekend camp. The team's second starring feature, *Pack Up Your Troubles*, opens with the team unable to evade the recruiting officer, but allows them a moment of glory - and promotion - after the accidental capture of an entire enemy platoon. *Block-Heads* offers a variation on their Great War exploits when Private Laurel is left to guard a trench - where he remains for 21 years. On joining 20th Century-Fox in 1941 they were placed in *Great Guns*, a film clearly inspired by Abbott & Costello's *Buck Privates*. This established the unhappy precedent for handing Laurel & Hardy what was at best second-hand material. Other military adventures include *Bonnie Scotland*, where Stan and Ollie join a Highland regiment bound for India, and stints with the Foreign Legion in *Beau Hunks* and *The Flying Deuces*. In 1923 Laurel had parodied the Legion epic *Under Two Flags* as *Under Two Jags*, finding time for another desert adventure later that same year, *Scorching Sands*. In *Air Raid Wardens* they are rejected by every branch of the services, thus reflecting their real life experiences: Hardy volunteered on the day America entered the war in April

The boys are baffled by vanishing food in **Atoll K**; *there's a stowaway on board*

1917, but was laughed out of a New York recruiting office because of his size; Laurel was conscripted early in 1918, but failed the medical examination, entering what he later termed 'the 4-F department'.

(See also: Costello, Lou; Insects; Sailors; 20th Century-Fox)

ARTISTS (Laurel & Hardy films *qv*)
The comic stereotype of an easel-and-beret artist may be spotted intermittently through Laurel & Hardy history. Hardy played just such a character in *Hungry Hearts* (*qv*) and Billy West's *Cupid's Rival* (1917). Much later, Charles Middleton (*qv*) portrayed one Pierre Gustave in Laurel & Hardy's *The Fixer-Uppers*, a man with a strong sense of honour backed up by homicidal wrath. The silent prototype of this film, *Slipping Wives*, presents Herbert Rawlinson (*qv*) in an artist's costume that pales alongside that of paint delivery man Stan Laurel. In *The Flying Deuces*, Stan and Ollie receive their portrait (actually drawn by Harry Langdon) from a fully-fledged Parisian painter, a scene missing from most UK prints.

(See also: Animation; Caricatures; Guest appearances; Langdon, Harry; London, Jean 'Babe'; Paintings; West, Billy)

ASTOR, GERTRUDE (1887-1977)
Statuesque blonde recalled by Laurel & Hardy admirers as the Mrs Hardy of *Come Clean* (*qv*). Also in Roach comedies with Charley Chase and Our Gang (both *qv*). Born in Lakeland, Ohio, she had a lengthy career in silents from the mid-teens, often for Universal and frequently as second female lead. She may be seen in *The Strong Man* (1926) with Harry Langdon (*qv*). Many others include *Stagestruck* (1925), *The Boy Friend* (1926), *The Cat and the Canary* (1927) and *The Butter and Egg Man* (1928). Later in character parts, her roles included a more obscure Langdon film (1940's *Misbehaving Husbands*), *Around the World in Eighty Days* (1956) and *The Man Who Shot Liberty Valance* (1962). In 1975 she was honoured with a lunch by Universal; her death two years later was reported to have been on her 90th birthday. Her birthdate is given sometimes as 1889; implausibly, some early 1930s sources quote it as 1906, implying that she was playing society women at the age of 11.

ATOLL K
(Laurel & Hardy film)
Filmed April 1950-April 1951.
Released at intervals during 1951

(Europe), 1952 (UK) and 1954 (US). Complete running time: approx. 98 minutes (available prints vary between 80 and 90 minutes). Produced by Raymond Eger for Franco-London Films S. A., Films E. G. E., Films Sirius and Fortezza Film. Directed by Leo Joannon and (uncredited) John Berry. Supervision (again uncredited) by Alf Goulding. Alternative titles: *Robinson Crusoeland* (GB) and *Utopia* (US). British and French copies exist with the original title.
With Stan Laurel and Oliver Hardy, Suzy Delair, Max Elloy, Adriano Rimoldi, Luigi Tosi.

Stan and Ollie's inheritance is eroded to zero by crippling taxes of every imaginable variety. One compensation: they are left with an island of their own - and the problem of how to reach it. Chartering a boat, they travel to their sunny legacy accompanied by a stateless refugee as chef and one-man crew; the mysterious disappearance of food reveals the presence of a further companion. When the boat stops, Ollie starts to disassemble the engine, entrusting the parts to Stanley. Once the components have slid into the sea, they realize the fuel tank is empty. Attempts to put up sails are unsuccessful, but Ollie's trousers prove a suitable substitute. All seems lost when the boat founders in a storm, but they reach land in the form of an atoll thrown up by the tempest. Soon the castaways are joined by Cherie (Suzy Delair), a young singer on the run from her boyfriend. Their next visitors are officials who, discovering uranium on the atoll, declare that ownership of the new island should be determined by the nationality of the first person to land. As this is the refugee, no country has a claim and the inhabitants establish 'Crusoeland', a lawless, tax-free utopia. Word spreads and the island is jammed by prospective citizens, all of them keen to enjoy a society without laws. Ollie's attempt to deport troublemakers leads only to a death sentence for himself and the other castaways. Cherie appears to side with the rebels, but is only playing along so she can release her friends. Her attempts fail, but they are saved from the gallows by a second storm. Stan and Ollie are eventually restored to their own private island, secure in the knowledge of regular supplies and a leisurely routine of eating and sleeping. Officialdom intervenes once more, confiscating both island and supplies.

The team's last cinema appearance, *Atoll K* began as an ambitious project with, according to the *Star* of 4 April 1950, appearances by French comedian Fernandel and the Italian clown, Toto. Filming quickly degenerated into chaos and no guest stars are in sight. It suffers chiefly from the difficulties imposed by an international co-production (between France and Italy) and the complication of Laurel's illness during shooting. His widow, Ida, told John McCabe (*qv*) of the need for a miniature hospital on-set with Mrs Laurel functioning as nurse, after the comedian had undergone surgery. Laurel, who was in no condition to work, completed the project through sheer professionalism; according to McCabe, he was later to regret having done so. That professionalism was not shared by the crew, director Leo Joannon spending much of his time photographing the water, while the gagmen proved lazy. Further delay resulted from the need to send to Paris for even minor props - the film's location was near Cannes; even a pencil sharpener (for a single gag) had to be obtained in this way. What gags there are tend to be muted by Laurel's emaciated appearance; although restored to health after his return home, in *Atoll K* he resembles a man close to death. This handicap might almost have been overcome with superior material; however,

despite help from Monty Collins and Alf Goulding (*qv*), the script and direction remain inept. There is even a gag playing directly on Hardy's weight, something seldom emphasized. At this time Hardy, while admittedly at his heaviest, is at least fit for work. The better moments are those making few physical demands, notably with Stan's 'white magic' (*qv*) and Ollie's gallantry toward Suzy Delair (*qv*). Rather more alarming is Stan's desperation when enveloped by a rubber dinghy, his panic being taken beyond comedy by his poor physical condition. *Atoll K* benefits somewhat from its satirical edge, commenting not just on the dangers of humanity's herd instinct but on the sometimes rapacious tax system (Hardy had recently made his own hefty settlement with the US Internal Revenue). It was, as William K. Everson (*qv*) has observed, an attempt at something different, and one can only regret the absence of favourable conditions. In America at least, *Atoll K* is in the public domain, resulting in the distribution of copies from several 8mm, 16mm and video sources. The American version, titled *Utopia*, is also that supplied to UK video. Although it is the shortest in circulation, little of the Laurel & Hardy footage is missing, though two songs by Suzy Delair are deleted. European and American copies vary in that each contains minor scenes missing from the other; for example, the European material omits part of the scene immediately prior to the shipwreck, but provides a longer sequence in which Stan visits his pet lobster. Titling is somewhat improved in the American edition, the original cloth-background credits making way for replacements superimposed over scenes from the film. *Atoll K* is known to have premiered under that title in Europe; British trade shows in January 1952 were as *Robinson Crusoeland*, although a 35mm UK print exists with the correct title. A further British release is said to have

been titled *Escapade*, but this is listed elsewhere as a compilation of *Oliver the Eighth*, *The Chimp* and *The Music Box* (all *qv*). A surviving publicity still from *Saps at Sea* (*qv*) bears the title on its reverse, probably used by its distributor in lieu of anything more suitable. A footnote: one of the principals, a stateless wanderer, might well be compared to assistant director John Berry, at that time an exile from America's McCarthy era.

(See also: Alternative titles; Boats, ships; France; Interviews; Marriages; Stage appearances)

AUBREY, JIMMY (1889-1983) Another of 'Karno's Speechless Comedians', Bolton-born Jimmy Aubrey took the role of 'the Terrible Turk' in the sketch *Mumming Birds* (*qv*). He was very soon a success in American films, working for various minor studios in between stints with Vitagraph, where he finally settled in 1919. From here began a two year period in which Aubrey was supported by Oliver Hardy; Laurel & Hardy scholar Leo Brooks has identified no fewer than 24 Aubrey comedies in which Hardy appears, from *Mules and Mortgages* (April 1919) to *The Tourist* (April 1921). From here, Hardy graduated to supporting Larry Semon (*qv*), Vitagraph's top comedian and a former director of the Aubrey series. In 1924, Aubrey moved to Joe Rock (*qv*), who at that time was producing comedies starring Aubrey's old Karno colleague, Stan Laurel. Supporting both comedians was Anita Garvin (*qv*), who recalled that Laurel directed some of these Aubrey films; Laurel's real training in this area was to come in later years at the Roach studio. By the end of the 1920s, Aubrey's heyday was over and he may be glimpsed playing minor roles in at least three Laurel & Hardy comedies (all *qv*): in *Their Purple Moment* he is the chef with whom Laurel & Hardy engage in a battle of soup, while it is Aubrey who pours still more soup over Ollie's head in *That's My Wife*. He is said also to be among the conventioneers in *Sons of the Desert*. In talkies, Aubrey became one of several veteran comics known for sidekick roles in 'B' westerns, eventually retiring to the Actors' Home in Woodland Hills, California. An obituary in the December 1983 edition of *Classic Images* quotes Aubrey's claim to have outlived Chaplin and Laurel through being neither a smoker nor a drinker. Aubrey had the last laugh, because accompanying the piece is a photograph of the comedian smoking a big cigar!

(See also: Belmore, Lionel; Drunks; Karno, Fred; Periodicals; Stan Laurel Productions; Solo films)

AUCTIONS (all films *qv*)

There are two notable auction scenes in the Laurel & Hardy films. In *One Good Turn*, Stan and Ollie attempt to dispose of their car by this method in order to help an old lady apparently in danger of eviction. *Thicker Than Water* pivots around these two trusting gentlemen taking at face value an auctioneer's sign claiming him to be 'giving things away today'. Once inside, they agree to keep open the bidding for a grandfather clock on behalf of a lady who has to return home for her money. They are, of course, stuck with an unwanted and (after bidding against each other) costly purchase. This routine appears again in the much later *The Dancing Masters*. In real life, certain Laurel & Hardy items (notably autographs) have been known to fetch high prices at auction, although a disappointing response greeted the bowler hats that surfaced at Christie's in December 1988. It was claimed that they had been worn in the film *Hats Off*; this is unlikely, as the team's hats were destroyed at the film's conclusion. The hats did not reach their reserve price. Another auction of this period at Nottingham brought to light 51

letters and a toy sent by Stan to a young admirer: the collection fetched £5,600.

(See also: *Fine Mess, a*; Hats; Letters)

AUSTIN, WILLIAM (1884-1975)

(Laurel & Hardy films *qv*)
Actor specializing in monocled 'silly ass' types, born in Georgetown, British Guiana (now Guyana) where his father had a sugar plantation. On his father's death, Austin and his mother moved to England, where his education was completed. Austin subsequently went into business in Shanghai before moving to America. In 1919 he took up acting. After three years in stock companies (in plays such as *A Tailor Made Man* and *Three Faces East*) he spent an unprofitable period as a freelance until gaining a five-year contract with Paramount on the strength of his work in Bebe Daniels' *Swim, Girl, Swim*. Perhaps he is best remembered for the 1927 Clara Bow vehicle *It*, where, coincidentally, he lost Clara to Antonio Moreno (*qv*), who was later to appear with Laurel & Hardy in *The Bohemian Girl*. Austin appeared in two Laurel & Hardy comedies, the very early *Duck Soup* and the talkie two-reeler *County Hospital*. In the former he is an English nobleman seeking to rent the vacant mansion in which vagrants Laurel & Hardy are hiding; in the latter, he is the patient sharing Ollie's hospital room, whose trousers are dismembered on being switched with those of his roommate. Sound gave Austin a chance to complete his characterization with a hitherto inaudible high-pitched cackle.

William Austin: 'Hardy old bean ... I have on your trousers by mistake', from County Hospital

B

BABES IN TOYLAND
(Laurel & Hardy film)
Released by M-G-M, 30 November 1934. Produced by Hal Roach. Directed by Gus Meins and Charles Rogers. Camera: Art Lloyd, Francis Corby. 80 minutes. Reissue titles include *March of the Wooden Soldiers*, *Laurel & Hardy in Toyland* (or simply *Toyland*), *March of the Toys* and *Revenge Is Sweet*.
With Stan Laurel & Oliver Hardy, Charlotte Henry, Felix Knight, Henry Kleinbach (Henry Brandon), Virginia Karns, Florence Roberts, William Burress.

In Toyland, Stannie Dum and Ollie Dee lodge with Mother Peep (Florence Roberts), whose residence is the old shoe of nursery rhymes. Toyland is an idyllic community with one grubby exception, Silas Barnaby (Henry Brandon), 'the meanest man in Toyland'. Unfortunately, Barnaby holds the mortgage to the shoe and threatens Mother Peep with eviction. Her lodgers believe they can borrow the money from their employer, the Toymaker (William Burress), but his anger with them (for persistent lateness) culminates in their dismissal after Stannie has misinterpreted an order from Santa Claus: instead of six hundred toy soldiers at one foot high, the pair have constructed one hundred soldiers at six feet high. The mortgage must be paid, but Barnaby is willing to cancel the arrangement in exchange for the hand of Mother Peep's daughter, Bo-Peep (Charlotte Henry), just as she has agreed to marry her sweet-heart, Tom-Tom the Piper's son (Felix Knight). Stannie and Ollie attempt to retrieve the mortgage document by burgling Barnaby's residence, but are caught. Sentenced to the ducking stool and subsequent exile to Bogeyland, their fate is too much for Bo-Peep, who agrees to marry Barnaby on his promise to withdraw the charge against them. The wedding goes ahead, and the mortgage is cancelled. Barnaby lifts the bride's veil for a kiss, to discover he has married Stannie. Toyland rejoices but Barnaby plots revenge. He abducts Elmer, one of the Three Little Pigs, planting evidence of apparent murder in Tom-Tom's house. Tom-Tom is exiled to Bogeyland, but Stannie and Ollie find

Ollie Dee, Stannie Dum and one of a hundred wooden soldiers in **Babes in Toyland**

the pig, alive, in Barnaby's cellar. Bo-Peep has followed her sweetheart to Bogeyland; Barnaby follows by a secret route through the town's well and is pursued by Stannie and Ollie. They apprehend Barnaby, but are forced to return on confronting the army of Bogeymen under Barnaby's control. Back in Toyland, they brag about their conquest of Barnaby and his horde, until the gates open and Toyland is under siege. The Bogeymen meet resistance but all seems lost until Stannie remembers the giant wooden soldiers he and Ollie have built. Before long, Barnaby and his Bogeymen are routed and Toyland is safe - except for Ollie, whose 'parting shot' of darts from a toy cannon has backfired on himself!

One of the most charming films ever made, *Babes in Toyland* retains a timeless appeal. Among the few genuinely effective attempts to appeal to all ages through a predominantly children's theme, *Toyland* remains a Christmas perennial on American TV and was seen fairly regularly on British television until an alleged copyright difficulty. One of the few Roach features to have passed into different ownership, *Toyland* has been reissued under several titles in varying degrees of mutilation. The best-known reissue, *March of the Wooden Soldiers*, was incomplete; the copy shown on British TV, called simply *Toyland*, was substantially intact though missing much of the original opening, with Mother Goose (Virginia Karns) introducing the tale through a

large storybook. More recently, a pristine master copy has provided new, complete material for American TV and video release, retaining the *Wooden Soldiers* title presumably to differentiate it from both the 1961 Disney version and a further remake from the 1980s. Walt Disney (*qv*) granted permission for the use of his Three Little Pigs, their theme tune 'Who's Afraid of the Big Bad Wolf?' and the Mickey Mouse character in the Laurel & Hardy version. The new copies have been rendered into colour by computer, with results considered by some to be of the highest quality yet produced by this process. This is fortunate, since *Toyland* is one of the very few Laurel & Hardy films that stands to gain from such an addition. Stan Laurel told John McCabe (*qv*) that his only regret about the film was that it had been made in black and white. In various interviews (notably with Anthony Slide in the spring 1970 edition of *The Silent Picture*), Hal Roach spoke scathingly about both the film and Stan Laurel's behaviour during its making. Roach had acquired the rights to the show but, realizing it had no plot, constructed one during the journey home. Laurel considered it unsuitable and, after an argument, was permitted to make the film his own way. Roach commented subsequently on the film's poor reception (unsubstantiated by reviews and box office receipts), mostly on the grounds of excessive horror in the Bogeyman footage. Another claim, that Laurel said 'We aren't funny without the derby hats', is not borne out in any way, as the team do not appear in even a variant of these, as they do in *The Bohemian Girl* (*qv*). What does seem certain is that the rift permanently damaged Roach-Laurel relations, to the point where Roach claimed that it was after *Babes in Toyland* that he had no further wish to produce the Laurel & Hardy films. Although their association continued on-and-off for a further six years, a break was inevitable.

(See also: Alternative titles; Animation; Brandon, Henry; Colour; Feature films; Hats; Henry, Charlotte; Knight, Felix; Operas; Our Gang; Reissues; Roach, Hal E.; Roberts, Florence; Seawright, Roy; Shoes; Teaming; Television; Titling; Video releases; Villains)

BACON GRABBERS

(Laurel & Hardy film)
Released by M-G-M, 19 October 1929. Produced by Hal Roach. Directed by Lewis R. Foster. Camera: George Stevens, Jack Roach. Story: Leo McCarey. Two reels. Silent, with synchronized music and effects.
With Stan Laurel and Oliver Hardy, Edgar Kennedy, Charlie Hall, Eddie Baker, Harry Bernard, Jean Harlow.

The Sheriff's office is a busy place but for attachment men (or 'bacon grabbers') Stan and Ollie. They are awakened from a sound sleep to deliver a summons and collect an unpaid-for radio. Their car jolts into undulating life only after a well-placed kick; it takes them straight into the back of a parked lorry. They reach the home of Collis P. Kennedy just as he is mowing the lawn. Ollie cannot find the summons, permitting Kennedy to escape into the house. Stan produces the document, but Kennedy reappears at the door with a yapping toy dog. Evidently fooled, Laurel & Hardy flee the premises; Ollie returns with a Great Dane borrowed from a small boy, who guarantees a vicious animal fed on raw beef. One sight of the toy dog and the enormous pet scurries off, dragging Ollie within inches of a

Charlie Hall offers a solution to a punctured radiator; a deleted scene from **Bacon Grabbers**

passing car. Ollie returns the dog with a recommendation to 'change his diet'. Kennedy, amused, is less pleased to see Stan blocking the doorway. By the time Ollie returns with the summons, Kennedy has vanished, leaving Stan in a one-man hammerlock. Ollie decides that Stan should remain while he chases Kennedy through from the back door. Stan, noticing it is lunchtime, munches sandwiches until Ollie calls, having apprehended Kennedy. Stan rushes around, handing Kennedy a sandwich instead of the summons. Kennedy escapes into the house, Ollie in pursuit through the open door. Stan misses Kennedy *en route* but hands the paper to Ollie. Kennedy is finally caught off-guard, and the summons served; now the boys must reclaim his radio. Noticing an open upstairs window, they borrow a ladder from a nearby construction site, leaving the unwary owner to plunge straight into a vat of white-wash. The ladder is too short, forcing Stan to balance while Ollie holds the ladder aloft. Kennedy appears through the window, pushing at Stan with a chimney brush before slamming the window on Stan's fingers. Ollie, his task complicated by falling trousers and a dog pulling at his braces, topples over after Kennedy fires a shotgun. The shot decapitates a fire hydrant, bringing over a policeman. The officer gains them entry to Kennedy's home, from which they emerge with the radio. They are halfway across the road when Kennedy rushes up to kick Ollie; the boys follow him back but Ollie has scarcely taken his vengeance when a steamroller flattens the radio. Kennedy laughs until his wife appears, having paid for the radio; Stan and Ollie's mirth vanishes when the steamroller runs over their car.

A variant on *Big Business* (*qv*), *Bacon Grabbers* is a beautifully-timed battle of wits unjustly overlooked. Part of this may be due to its absence from the Youngson compilations, a frequent starting point for those studying the Laurel & Hardy silents, although Jay Ward's *The Crazy World of Laurel & Hardy* (*qv*) incorporates several of its scenes. *Bacon Grabbers* was issued originally with music and sound effects, rediscovered late in the 1970s. This track and that for *Angora Love* (*qv*) compare unfavourably with earlier examples, orchestral accompaniment having given way to a lone theatre organ. The sound effects are quite good, particularly when the fire hydrant bursts open, while musical puns include 'The Whistler and His Dog' as a motif for the Great Dane.

(See also: Compilations; Detectives; Harlow, Jean; Kennedy, Edgar; Music; Silent films; Youngson, Robert)

BAILEY, ROBERT (1898-1983)
American actor, on stage from 1925; prolific on radio and, later, TV, in addition to appearing in films. Two Laurel & Hardy Fox films, *Jitterbugs* and *The Dancing Masters* (both *qv*) cast him as leading man.

(See also: 20th Century-Fox)

BANKS, MONTY (1897-1950)
(Mario Bianchi)
Italian-born comedian, famous in American silents ranging from marital farce to daredevil stunts. Most famous in the latter category is *Play Safe* (1923), in which Banks and his girl-friend embark on a terrifying train

Monty Banks is remembered today for the thrill comedy Play Safe

ride. Later, he worked in England (he married Britain's Gracie Fields) as actor and director; his acting credits include *Atlantic*, while his best-known directoral effort is George Formby's *No Limit*. In 1941 he was engaged by 20th Century-Fox (*qv*) to direct their first Laurel & Hardy film, *Great Guns* (*qv*).

(See also: St Clair, Malcolm)

BANN, RICHARD W.
Major film historian particularly associated with the Roach output. His Laurel & Hardy filmography has required only slight amendment since its appearance in Leonard Maltin's *Laurel & Hardy Book* in 1973; two years later it formed the framework for John McCabe's book on the films. Bann has also collaborated with Maltin on *The Little Rascals: The Life and Times of Our Gang*. Enthusiasts eagerly anticipate his biography of Hal Roach (*qv*), with whom Bann formed a lengthy and close friendship.

(See also: Maltin, Leonard; McCabe, John; Our Gang)

BARBERS (all films *qv*)
Perhaps due to their somewhat eccentric haircuts, Laurel & Hardy employed few scenes involving barbers. The main example is *Oliver the Eighth*, in which the team's living is made in just such a tonsorial parlour. The level of confidence in their own abilities is suggested by Stan going

elsewhere for a shave, though Ollie is prepared to trust his partner. Shaving scenes in other films include *The Rogue Song*, *Great Guns* and a routine deleted from *Our Relations*. The most unorthodox shave might be that carried out using a wood plane in *Busy Bodies*. One of the King Bee Comedies in which Hardy supported Chaplin imitator Billy West (*qv*), *His Day Out* (1918), sees West as an escaped lunatic posing as a barber. An extract may be seen in the compilation film *Four Clowns*, where West, in adjusting the chair with perhaps too much gusto, sends Hardy through the ceiling. It was a barber who gave Hardy his life-long nickname of 'Babe' in 1914. The actors at Lubin's studio in Florida would visit a nearby Italian barber who, in Hardy's words, 'took a great fancy to me and every time after he'd finish shaving me, he'd rub powder into my face and pat my cheeks and say, "Nice-a babee. Nice a-babee".' Hardy's colleagues started to kid him about it, calling him 'baby' and, eventually, 'Babe'.

(See also: Businessmen; Lubin, Siegmund 'Pop'; Names; Youngson, Robert)

BARRYMORE, LIONEL
(1878-1954)
Distinguished actor from a famous family, in films from earliest days. Remembered from latter days as 'Dr Gillespie' in the *Doctor Kildare* series, by which time he was confined to a wheelchair. There are two minor connections with Laurel & Hardy, both from M-G-M features (both *qv*): he played a director in *Hollywood Revue of 1929*, and was the genuine director of *The Rogue Song*.

BARTY, JACK (1888-1942)
British comedian from variety, musical comedy and pantomime who spent a brief time at Roach during 1933-4. Jack Barty appears in *Oliver the Eighth* (*qv*) as 'Jitters', the butler and at least three other Roach comedies, the

Stan and Babe met Jack Barty (top left) at the London Coliseum in 1932 By kind courtesy of Michael Pointon

Todd-Kelly *Babes in the Goods* and *Maid in Hollywood* plus Charley Chase's *Luncheon at Twelve*. In the latter film Barty refuses to empty Chase's ashcan, to be told 'That's the trouble with this country - there's too many foreigners here'. Soon after Barty runs into another Briton, Charlie Hall (*qv*). Barty's career began in 1907 as half of a variety double-act; service in the First World War intervened, but he returned to variety as a single, alternating with musical comedy and revue as in *Our Liz*. He appeared in variety across South Africa, Australia and America before his next London successes, in the musical comedies *White Horse Inn* (1931-2) and *Casanova* (1932-3). Laurel & Hardy saw the latter (co-starring Marie Löhr) at the Coliseum, and visited the cast backstage; Barty's subsequent tenure at Roach was probably at their invitation.

(See also: Chase, Charley; Englishmen; Insanity; Kelly, Patsy; Music-hall; Pantomime; Servants; Stage appearances; Todd, Thelma)

THE BATTLE OF THE CENTURY
(Laurel & Hardy film)
Released by M-G-M, 31 December 1927. Produced by Hal Roach. Directed by Clyde Bruckman. Camera: George Stevens. Two reels. Silent.
With Stan Laurel and Oliver Hardy, Noah Young, Charlie Hall, Dorothy Coburn, Ellinor Vanderveer, Anita Garvin.

The big fight is on, with ringside seats extending 'as far west as Honolulu'. Even the referee considers Canvasback Clump (Stan) the outsider in the bout against his tough opponent, 'Thunder-Clap Callahan' (Noah Young), but Canvasback is egged on by his manager (Ollie) nonetheless. Through a sheer fluke, Canvasback floors Callahan, but ruins the count by failing to go to a neutral corner; Callahan recovers and flattens Canvasback. The following day, the unsuccessful pugilist and his manager are approached by an insurance salesman (Eugene Pallette) with whom the manager takes out a policy against the fighter being injured. Attempts to cash in take the form of placing a banana skin in his path, which instead trips up a pie delivery man. A slow exchange of pie-throwing draws in passers-by until the scene is one of mass hysteria, pies and more hysteria. Ultimately a cop intervenes and the pair escape, leaving chaos behind.

The initial concept of *The Battle of the Century* was to parody what is still one of boxing's most notorious incidents, the 'long count' that took place during the Jack Dempsey-Gene Tunney fight of 1927. This satirical urge continued into the creation of a climactic sequence that is one of film comedy's most famous. Planned as 'the pie picture to end all pie pictures', the pie fight was supposed to parody what was even then a long-obsolete motif but became known instead as one of its finest examples. The reasons for this are easy to see: each pie lands in a quite different context (a dental patient's mouth, a society woman's lorgnette) with skill and originality, with the whole constructed so that an orderly exchange of indignities escalates quite logically into a frenzy that would be inexplicable out of context. Later attempts by others at such a free-for-all, lacking a similar structure, degenerate into the very incoherence that this film seeks to parody. Laurel & Hardy's skill in this sequence has, unfortunately, led many to bracket them with lesser 'pie-throwing' comedians. Only a truncated form of the film is known to survive today. The pie fight was believed to be the only extant segment until 1979 when, incredibly, the opening boxing match surfaced in an American TV package. Despite claims for the survival of the section in which Hardy takes out insurance on Laurel,

Blackhawk Films (*qv*) were forced to substitute stills and explanatory titles in their version (a not dissimilar edition was released on UK video). The pie fight itself is not complete, deriving from a version prepared by Robert Youngson (*qv*) for his 1958

The Battle of the Century *before the fight and the pie fight at its zenith. A contemporary advertisement gives this short comedy equal prominence with the feature attraction.*
Advertisement courtesy of Robert G. Dickson

compilation *The Golden Age of Comedy* (*qv*). Youngson had access to a negative already in an advanced stage of decomposition, and edited what was left into a fast-paced and admittedly very effective summary. The most severe loss is that of the arrival of a cop who, when asking Laurel & Hardy who started the fight, receives a pie himself for the film's conclusion. Youngson's version ends with the unforgettable moment in which Anita Garvin (*qv*), unaware of the chaos nearby, slips and sits directly into a stray pie. Her reaction, taken very slowly, is one of dubious speculation followed by a subtle glance to see if anyone has witnessed her fall from dignity. Arising carefully, she returns whence she came, pausing only to shake a leg in a vain attempt to dislodge whatever has sullied her person. In interviews, the actress has marvelled at being remembered for 'a nothing' done at Laurel's request; made during her lunch break

from a film with Charley Chase (*qv*), her contribution is classic mime to equal (or surpass) more celebrated talents.

(See also: Agee, James; Boxing; Compilations; *Great Race, the*; *Hoose-Gow, the*; Lost films; Miller, Henry; Names; Pallette, Eugene; Parodies; Rediscoveries; Slapstick; Vanderveer, Ellinor; Young, Noah)

BBC

See: *Cuckoo*; Documentaries;
Interviews; Radio and Television.

BE BIG

(Laurel & Hardy film)
Released by M-G-M, 7 February
1931. Three reels. Produced by Hal
Roach. Directed by James Parrott.
Camera: Art Lloyd.
With Stan Laurel and Oliver Hardy,
Isabelle Keith, Anita Garvin, Charlie
Hall.

Stan and Ollie have organized a trip to
Atlantic City with their wives. The
excited Ollie is concerned that everything is packed, even his moustache
cup. Mrs Hardy (Isabelle Keith) calms
her husband and tells him to see if the
Laurels are ready. Stan, answering the
door, is equipped for the seaside, having prepared his toy boat for the
occasion. Mrs Laurel (Anita Garvin)
arrives with the missing ingredients, a
bucket and spade. Ollie returns home
and takes a telephone call from the
local hunting lodge where he and Stan
are to be honoured with a testimonial
dinner that evening. Ollie explains
about the trip, but is lured by the
promise of various exotic delights and
the instruction to 'be big!'. Ollie
feigns illness, aided by a towel over
the head and a pallid complexion of
talcum powder. As his distraught wife
relates the news to the Laurels, Ollie
convinces the ladies to go ahead with
the trip, he and Stan will follow in the
morning. A taxi arrives and the wives
depart, whereupon Ollie removes the
towel from his head and explains the
ruse to Stan. Panic greets the return
of Mrs Hardy, who has forgotten her
fur; in the confusion, Ollie has placed
it on his head in lieu of the towel.
When she leaves, the boys change into
their hunting lodge outfits, Stan taking time out to play with an exercise
machine. Ollie has difficulty putting
on his boots, which after several minutes are discovered to be Stan's. The
problem now is to remove the undersized footwear; attempts culminate in
the boys becoming entangled in each
other's clothing and Ollie being
dragged around the room. Ollie's rear
lands on a tin-tack, which has to be
removed with a claw hammer. Ollie
pleads for a calm approach to the
problem, which lasts until Stan disappears into a folding bed. Having
extricated his friend, Ollie demonstrates the art of boot-removal on
Stan's leg, tugging at the much less
reluctant boot and flying into the
filled bathtub. Ollie emerges with his
pullover sagging to knee level. 'What
could be worse?' he asks, and discovers the answer as the wives return. He
and Stan hide in the folding bed, for-
tified with the motto 'be big'; twin
shotgun blasts send Stan, Ollie and
the bed flying into the pond outside.

Be Big is generally regarded as an
overlong exploration of a single gag.
Some idea of its pace may be gauged
from the fact that a British 8mm distributor was able to condense the
action into an effective single reel!
Although issued complete on video,
UK television copies of *Be Big* have

*Anita Garvin and Isabelle Keith make
an unexpected return in* **Be Big**

always lacked the sequence in which Stan hammers Ollie's foot into a boot-jack, a segment familiar in part from *The Best of Laurel & Hardy* (*qv*). This segment is also absent from *Los calaveras*, the Spanish version, which substitutes a gag with Ollie hanging from an upstairs window. Also unseen in English is a very funny moment where Ollie's head is caught in the belt of an exercise machine.

Unusually, there is a further extant foreign edition, the French-language *Les carottiers*, a name translating to *Be Big's* working title, *The Chiselers*. This French edition was long considered to be the only survivor of these foreign endeavours, and suggests a degree of tailoring to specific countries: French audiences enjoy a risqué alteration in Ollie's belongings when the 'moustache cup' of the English and Spanish becomes a nightshirt. Leonard Maltin (*qv*) has noted a poignant moment in *Les carottiers* where Ollie's customarily mute camera-look breaks tradition with a line translating to 'Maybe it's *me*!'. Of the supporting cast, Germaine de Néel takes over as Mrs Hardy in French; Linda Loredo (see also **Come Clean**) does the same in Spanish, but Anita Garvin and Charlie Hall (both *qv*) remain in each. Anita Garvin is obviously speaking in the appropriate language but has been dubbed; Charlie Hall speaks his own dialogue. The foreign prints are expanded into features by the addition of an extra-length *Laughing Gravy* (*qv*). Credit for these hybrids goes to *Laughing Gravy*'s director, James Horne (*qv*). Even the lesser Laurel & Hardys have their share of amusement and *Be Big* is helped by some amusing dialogue and the character comedy permeating Ollie's musical doorbell and Stan's absurd motor horn equivalent. Films such as this serve as illustration of the team's ability to carry slight material through sheer strength of characterization.

(See also: Beds; Camera-looks; Characters; Foreign versions; *Hog*

Guarding Fort Arid in **Beau Hunks**

Wild; Television; Women; Working titles)

BEAU CHUMPS
See: *Beau Hunks*

BEAU HUNKS
(Laurel & Hardy film)
Released by M-G-M, 12 December 1931. Four reels. Produced by Hal Roach. Directed by James Horne. Camera: Art Lloyd, Jack Stevens. With Stan Laurel and Oliver Hardy, Charles Middleton, Tiny Sandford, James Horne.

Ollie is at the piano, singing dreamily of his fiancée, while Stan cuts out a newspaper advertisement for fertilizer. At the song's conclusion, Stan, who has cut out the seat he was resting on, asks Ollie what he is 'getting so mushy about'. Ollie tells him of the wondrous 'Jeanie-Weanie', to whom he is to be married. This blissful mood is punctured by the arrival of a letter from the girl, announcing that all is over. Ollie arises from the mutilated armchair, taking a spring with him, announcing that he and Stan are 'going where we can forget'. Before Stan can discover why he has to go, Ollie takes the door full in the face

and bounces straight into the piano. Stan and Ollie arrive in the desert in a new draft of the Foreign Legion, only to discover that every recruit is a Jeanie-Weanie victim. Planning to leave 'before it's too late', they announce their decision to the Commandant (Charles Middleton), only to be informed that they are in the Legion for life. On being dismissed, they notice a giant picture of Jeanie-Weanie behind the Commandant's desk. Part of their training is an eight-hour route march; soon after their return, word is brought of a siege at Fort Arid, where reinforcements are urgently required. Every available man is sent, but Stan and Ollie are separated from their comrades in a sandstorm. They arrive at the besieged fort ahead of the others, and are put on sentry duty. They narrowly miss sniper bullets and are completely unaware of the intruders who climb into the fort and open the gates from within. Stan and Ollie are to defend the gateway with hand grenades, but Stan pulls the pin from one only to lose it amid the others. Once the grenade is disposed of, a knife-wielding attacker chases the boys into a storage room, where they see barrels filled with tin-tacks. Scattered over the fort, the tacks render the barefoot attackers easy meat for the approaching reinforcements. Stan and Ollie bring the 'Chief of the Riff-Raffs' to the commanding officer, and are ordered to search him. His most treasured possession is a photograph of Jeanie-Weanie.

The captured chief is none other than director James Horne (*qv*) in a cameo role. Current prints bill him as 'Abdul Kasim K'Horne' which, according to Richard Finegan in *The Intra-Tent Journal*, was mis-transcribed from 'Abul' in the 1940s reissues. Finegan also records the omission (dating from Roach's own 1937 revival) of the opening two minutes, in which Ollie sings 'Pagan Love Song' before engaging in dialogue with Stan about putting fertilizer on strawberries (a scatalogical reference doubtless forbidden after the 1934 Production Code). The opening gag title is also missing; music over the main credits has been replaced with a theme written for *Way Out West* (*qv*).This vague parody of *Beau Geste* is known as *Beau Chumps* in the UK, even on the reissue copies. The photographs of 'Jeanie-Weanie' depict Jean Harlow (*qv*) in costume for *Double Whoopee* (*qv*), a relic from her days with Roach before reaching stardom in Howard Hughes' *Hell's Angels*. The unusual four-reel format had previously been confined to some of the team's foreign language films, and would be repeated only in the shorter version of *A Chump at Oxford* (*qv*); when the team remade this film as *The Flying Deuces* (*qv*), it was in a feature-length version. The gag involving tin-tacks was borrowed for *Old Bones of the River*, a 1938 vehicle for British comedian Will Hay.

(See also: Alternative titles; Army, the; Censorship; Feature films; Foreign versions; Middleton, Charles; Reissues; Remakes; Romance; Songs)

BEDS (all films *qv*)
Stan and Ollie's ongoing war with inanimate objects extends naturally enough to beds, objects of trust which, in the world of Laurel & Hardy, waste no opportunity for betrayal. They frequently collapse, as in *Leave 'Em Laughing* or *Laughing Gravy*; they are sometimes (innocently) dampened, with a hot water bottle in (again) *Leave 'Em Laughing* or a leaking pipe in *They Go Boom*. The latter's inflatable mattress often surprises modern audiences: it is evidently not the recent innovation one might imagine. Disaster must follow when such an item is entrusted to Stan and Ollie, and the mattress of *They Go Boom* is allowed to inflate to giant proportions. Inflation gives way to contraction when they share a single bunk in *Berth Marks*, *Pardon Us* and *The Big Noise*. A sidelight: casual examination of *Unaccustomed As We Are* shows that Mr and Mrs Hardy have a double bed, unremarkable until one remembers that within five years the Hays Office insisted on twin beds, even for married couples.

(See also: Censorship; Homosexuality)

BELMORE, LIONEL (1875-1940)
British theatre actor, in films from 1911. One of his better-known roles is that of Burgomaster in *Frankenstein* (1931). He plays Ossman in *The Rogue Song* (*qv*) and appears briefly in *Bonnie Scotland* (*qv*) as the blacksmith. Laurel & Hardy shot a routine with him that was cut from the final version (see **Deleted scenes**). Belmore is known also to have worked alongside Babe with Jimmy Aubrey (*qv*).

BELOW ZERO
(Laurel & Hardy film)
Released by M-G-M, 26 April 1930. Two reels. Produced by Hal Roach. Directed by James Parrott. Camera: George Stevens.
With Stan Laurel and Oliver Hardy, Charlie Hall, Frank Holliday, Tiny

Sandford, Leo Willis, Kay Deslys, Bobby Burns.

Street musicians Stan and Ollie attempt to brighten the 'freezing winter of '29' by demonstrating their prowess on double bass and portable organ. They fare badly, largely through a poor choice of both location (a deaf and dumb institute) and repertoire - 'In the Good Old Summertime' being quite unsuitable for a blizzard. Their only earnings consist of a dollar, with the request to 'move on a couple of streets'. An irate householder (Charlie Hall) makes his own comment with some well-aimed snowballs. They drop the dollar they have earned, failing to realize their loss until a 'blind' man stoops to pick it up. When another coin seems to drop into their tin mug, it turns out to be an egg dropped by a pigeon. Stan aims a snowball at the bird, hitting a man who has just opened an upstairs window. When he retaliates, the snowball lands in a small can belonging to a sizeable lady (Blanche Payson). Blaming Stan and Ollie, she engages them in an exchange of violence that concludes with the destruction of the boys' musical instruments. Their luck changes when discovering a wallet filled with money, but a thug (Leo Willis) spots the find and gives chase. The intervention of a cop (Frank Holliday) saves the day and a grateful Stan and Ollie invite him to lunch. The cop recommends a 'great spot' where, as the boys discover, the proprietor (Tiny Sandford) deals violently with non-paying customers. They exchange pleasant chat over lunch until Stan takes out the wallet, discovering the cop's photo inside. The policeman, believing Stan and Ollie to be pickpockets, decides arrest is too good for them and leaves them instead with an unpaid bill. The lights go out, but the sounds of mayhem are all too clear. Ollie is dumped into the street, and nearly hit by a truck. Of Stan there is no sign and when Ollie returns for his friend, his beating on the door is interrupted by the sound of gurgling from a nearby rain barrel. Stan is inside, but has had to drink all the water. When he is tipped out, we see his body has been distended to giant size.

Below Zero contains very little dialogue, but what there is tends to be quoted frequently. When a lady enquires how much the boys earn per street (so that she can pay them to move two streets away), she calls Ollie 'Mr Whiteman', a direct reference to the famous bandleader and Hardy lookalike, Paul Whiteman (the similarity may be inspected in Whiteman's 1930 film *The King of Jazz*). The computer-colour edition issued on both sides of the Atlantic omits this sequence, as does the British Super-8 sound version released in the late 1970s. Subtler sound jokes depend not on dialogue but on effects and music, as when Charlie Hall (*qv*) decides not to throw a snowball when the boys switch from 'In the Good Old Summertime' to 'Sweet Rosie O'Grady' (a snowball appears from offscreen when they change back again!). Otherwise, *Below Zero* demonstrates the team's skill in presenting situation comedy through visual means; a considerable achievement and probably quite useful when refilming in different languages. The Spanish version, *Tiembla y titubea*, exists today: key differences are the addition of an incidental music track, the replacement of most of the supporting actors and a running time extended to three reels. The Spanish copy opens with additional footage of the cop receiving a cash award from a superior, thus explaining the amount of money in his wallet. Robert O'Connor replaces Frank Holliday as the officer; his superior is played by Enrique Acosta, also the police chief in the Spanish *Night Owls* and replacement for Wilfred Lucas (*qv*) in the Spanish *Pardon Us*. In this Spanish version, another policeman intervenes when Ollie attempts to

Below Zero: *with Frank Holliday in a hat-switch deleted from the English version but retained for the foreign-speaking market*

retrieve a coin he and Stan have accidentally lost to the blind man. A friendlier cop saves Laurel & Hardy from a robber; he shoots at the culprit instead of merely shouting. The thief fires back, sending Stan, Ollie and the cop into confusion and a hat-switching routine. The danger facing Laurel & Hardy in the cafe is accentuated by shots of waiters carrying knives, replacing the quick blackout. Stills suggest the filming but later deletion of these scenes from the domestic copies, which themselves have survived in varying condition. *Below Zero* is unusual in circulating with its original opening titles, probably because it was ignored in reissues. The soundtrack tends to be rather noisy in quality, although a superior master was available for the anthology *The Best of Laurel & Hardy* (*qv*).

(See also: Burns, Bobby; Colour; Deslys, Kay; Foreign versions; Home movies; In-jokes; Payson, Blanche; Policemen; Rediscoveries; Reissues; Titling; Willis, Leo)

BERNARD, HARRY (1878-1940)
(all films *qv*)
Perennial policeman, as were James C.

Morton and Tiny Sandford (both *qv*). Harry Bernard represents the law in, amongst others, *Night Owls*, *Another Fine Mess* and *Our Relations*; in both *Wrong Again* and *A Chump at Oxford* it is he who complains that he nearly had his brains blown out, before revealing a shotgun blast to the seat of his trousers. Other roles include a fight promoter in *Any Old Port*, a dissatisfied diner in *Way Out West* and the tomato-throwing lorry driver in *Two Tars*; his last Laurel & Hardy film, *Saps at Sea*, transfers him from the police to a similar post as harbour patrolman.

(See also: Policemen)

BERTH MARKS
(Laurel & Hardy film)
Released by M-G-M, 1 June 1929.
Produced by Hal Roach. Directed by Lewis R. Foster. Camera: Len Powers. Two reels.
With Stan Laurel and Oliver Hardy, Harry Bernard, Charlie Hall, Pat

Berth Marks: *one-half of a 'big-time vaudeville act' has just sat on someone's hat*

Harmon, Silas D. Wilcox, Baldwin Cooke.

'Big-time' vaudevillians Stan and Ollie meet at a railway station to catch the last train to Pottsville. First of all, they miss each other around the building; next, they find the station announcer unintelligible. Eventually they discover their train is leaving, and just scramble aboard, losing their sheet music but rescuing the bass fiddle. On board, they are shown to their berth, unwittingly causing arguments among the other passengers. In Stan and Ollie's absence, this escalates into a clothes-ripping battle. Unaware of the usual practice of changing in the cloakroom, the boys attempt to undress in their cramped, shared berth, becoming hopelessly entangled. As they finally settle down to sleep, the conductor announces that the train has reached Pottsville, whereupon his uniform is shredded by the feuding passengers. Stan and Ollie scramble from the train in their underclothes, and on dressing realize that their bass fiddle is still aboard the departing train.

The team's second talkie reverses the principle of their first, *Unaccustomed As We Are* (*qv*), by relying mostly on visuals. Exceptions include an early encounter with a garbling station announcer, the sound of an off-screen ripping of clothes and the conductor's sarcastic response to Ollie's description of Stan and himself as a 'big-time vaudeville act' ('Well, I'll bet you're *good*!'). Otherwise, dialogue is minimal with, as Leonard Maltin (*qv*) has noted, far too many instances of Ollie saying 'will you stop crowding?' Nor does the action vary sufficiently to maintain interest; the upper-berth scene (reworked in *Pardon Us* [*qv*]) is stretched beyond audience patience. The later history of

Berth Marks takes some bizarre turns: much of it was incorporated into the foreign versions of *The Laurel-Hardy Murder Case* (*qv*), made the following year; in 1936 the opening scenes were overdubbed with the Laurel & Hardy theme taken from, of all things, the Columbia 78 recorded by the team in London. When Blackhawk Films (*qv*) issued the film to collectors, they offered only silent copies (even in 16mm) until 1973. UK television has sturdily ignored the film, despite its availability on video; while the restored video master prepared for American TV in the 1980s derives mostly from the negative of the film's silent version (such alternative editions were common in early talkie days). This offers much improved quality even if some minor lip movement is lost where titles have been removed. It is this version that has been converted to colour by computer.

(See also: Beds; *Big Noise, the*; Colour; Foreign versions; Gag titles; Midgets;

Music; Records; Reissues; Silent films; Sound; Trains; Vaudeville)

THE BEST OF LAUREL & HARDY

(1971) (Laurel & Hardy films *qv*)
Not released in British cinemas, *The Best of Laurel & Hardy* surfaced on Britain's commercial TV once in December 1974 (minus one sequence) and again nine years later. Concerned entirely with sound films, *Best of Laurel & Hardy* is superior to the parallel *Crazy World of Laurel & Hardy* (*qv*) in that each sequence is permitted time to develop and is spared any frenetic cross-cutting; any abbreviation of the action is accomplished through well-placed dissolves. Its opening is actually rather discouraging: unsuitable music (seeming to be a garbled version of the Laurel & Hardy theme) covers a series of name-checks for the supporting cast, selected not in order of reputation but, one suspects, as a grab-bag of whoever else is present. It also has the

disconcerting idea of billing Hardy before Laurel. From here things improve, with footage from *Night Owls* sub-headed 'Night owls and alley cats', followed by a section of *Below Zero* retitled 'Music hath charms ...?' The makeshift auction of *One Good Turn* becomes 'The $125 misunderstanding', followed by much of *The Live Ghost* as 'A dollar a head'. 'Crime and punishment' presents a capsule version of the full-length *Pardon Us*, a segment rescued from unwieldiness by the original's episodic structure. 'Man's best friend' is *Laughing Gravy* and 'Tallyho!' derives from the middle of *Be Big*, incorporating much of the footage absent from UK television copies. 'How to visit a sick friend' might just as easily be how not to, being Stan's visit to Ollie in *County Hospital*, a sequence that is followed by the bungled elopement from *Our Wife*, retitled 'Moonlight and romance'. 'Three's a crowd' derives from *Their First Mistake* and is the last representative of the short comedies. From here we see a précis of *Our Relations* which, unlike *Pardon Us*, requires far more footage and throws the compilation off-balance. This apart, *Best of* remains pleasant viewing even if the films selected do not necessarily reflect the title. Producer: James L. Wolcott. Editorial consultant: Morrie Roizman. Production assistant: Paul M. Heller.

(See also: Compilations; Television; Youngson, Robert)

BIBLICAL REFERENCES
(Laurel & Hardy films *qv*)
Every day, people quote phrases from the Bible, often without realizing it. Even the Laurel & Hardy films employ such references, notably the opening gag title from *Big Business*: 'The story of a man who turned the

The Best of Laurel & Hardy
received theatrical release in the US but not in Britain

other cheek - and got punched in the nose'. Another example is one of Stan's classic malapropisms, from *Fra Diavolo*: 'As ye cast your bread on the water, so shall ye reap'. The highlight of *Slipping Wives* is Stan Laurel's mime of the story of Samson; this accomplished set piece has been compared favourably to Chaplin's account of David and Goliath in *The Pilgrim* (1923). John McCabe (*qv*) has described Oliver Hardy as being not formally religious, but devoted throughout his life to Masonic ideals; both McCabe and Hardy's widow confirm that he read the Bible a great deal, at least later in life.

(See also: Freemasons; Marriages)

BICYCLES (all films *qv*)
An ideal prop, the bicycle (in tandem form) provides Laurel & Hardy with a means of escape as early as *Duck Soup*. Its remake, *Another Fine Mess*, repeats the idea but uses doubles: one of the riders has been identified as one Joe Mole. A distracted cyclist in *Men O'War* plunges into a nearby lake; a telegram is delivered by Bobby Dunn (*qv*) after crashing his bike in *Me and My Pal*. Cycling students are among

those greeting *A Chump at Oxford*; while in *Air Raid Wardens*, the boys are momentarily in the bicycle business.

(See also: Stand-ins)

BIG BUSINESS
(Laurel & Hardy film)
Released by M-G-M, 20 April 1929. Produced by Hal Roach. Directed by James W. Horne. Camera: George Stevens. Two reels. Silent.
With Stan Laurel and Oliver Hardy, James Finlayson, Tiny Sandford, Lyle Tayo.

No matter how sunny California may be at Christmas time, door-to-door salesmen Stan and Ollie stick to tradition with their overcoats, gloves and stock of fir trees. One lady (Lyle Tayo) is asked if she would be interested in a tree; the reply is negative. 'Wouldn't your husband like to buy one?' asks Ollie. The shy response is that she has no husband. Stan: 'If you had a husband, would he buy one?' The door is slammed shut. The next call is even less promising: a householder whose signs forbid salesmen; he is visible only as a hand bringing down a hammer on Ollie's head. Their third call is to irascible James

Bicycles: Stan and Ollie demonstrate their cycling skills in a publicity shot for Air Raid Wardens

Finlayson, who is also unwilling to buy a tree and whose patience is exhausted when he has to answer the door a second time. The reason for this is that the boys' tree has been caught in the door; another trip is necessary when Stan's coat is trapped; another when the tree is caught again. Finlayson takes the precaution of throwing the tree out of reach, but is pestered a fifth time when Stan asks if he can take his order for next year. At first, it seems that Finlayson has succumbed to Stan's salesmanship, but on his return, he demolishes the tree with shears. In response, Stan takes out a penknife and cuts slices from the door frame. Finlayson returns, leading to a skirmish culminating in Ollie trimming the few strands of hair on Finlayson's scalp. Finlayson retaliates by reducing Ollie's watch to fragments. When his doorbell is torn out, he attempts to telephone the authorities, but Stan cuts the wire and Ollie tears out the instrument completely. Finlayson in turn amputates Ollie's shirt-tail and tie before going inside. Ollie draws him back outside with a knock on the door, where he is showered by a garden hose. Stan and Ollie have reached their car, from which Finlayson removes a headlight. The headlight is thrown through the windscreen. Stan and Ollie return to the house, followed by a growing number of spectators; Stan removes the porch light and, on Ollie's suggestion, hurls it through a window. Finlayson in turn bends up one of the car's mudguards, so the boys return to the house, taking time out to rip up an obstructive shrub. Wielding an axe, they chop up Finlayson's door from within. Their opponent sets to work destroying steering wheel, fuel tank and Christmas trees, by which time a policeman (Tiny Sandford) is surveying the action from afar. Ollie chops into a trellis as Stan tears down the

awnings; soon the incredulous cop makes a note of Ollie felling a tree. Finlayson has almost totally dismembered the car, completing the job by putting a match to it; still unsatisfied, he hammers flat the remains. A shovel-wielding Ollie digs up the lawn as Stan throws vases out of a window; Ollie forsakes the lawn in favour of smashing the vases, first on the ground then intercepting them in flight. After demolishing the chimney with a well-aimed missile, Ollie pursues a runaway vase but smashes the

Big Business: *attrition becomes contrition*

policeman's toe. Realization of their situation dawns on Ollie, but Stan, oblivious, drags Finlayson's piano into view and reduces it to fragments. Stan, noticing the cop, attempts to reassemble the instrument but this is forgotten as the law brings the combatants face to face. 'Who started all this?' asks the policeman. Finlayson points accusingly and Stan, trying to explain, breaks down in tears, joined by Ollie. The cop, visibly affected, turns to Finlayson saying 'So you started this', drawing another tearful account. Moments later the policeman and the entire crowd of onlookers are reduced to helpless sobbing, as Stan,

Ollie and Finlayson shake hands. 'Merry Christmas' says Stan, handing Finlayson a cigar. As the disconsolate policeman enters his car, Stan and Ollie look at him, then at each other, and grin. Furious, the policeman chases them into the distance, as Finlayson lights what is actually an exploding cigar.

Big Business is probably the greatest comedy ever filmed. While many enthusiasts claim the superiority of *Two Tars* or *The Music Box* (both *qv*),

Big Business is by far the more consistently acclaimed, even among critics usually unresponsive to the team. One of their strongest techniques, that of 'reciprocal destruction' (*qv*), is presented here in its most carefully-constructed and concentrated form, as the tension escalates from personal indignity into uninhibited warfare. James Finlayson (*qv*), an asset to any comedy, is at his wrathful best; Tiny Sandford (*qv*) epitomizes the studio's special breed of patient lawman, tolerant of human foibles and reluctant to take action despite overwhelming reason to do so. A famous anecdote records Finlayson launching into his 'double-take-and-fade-away' routine - in which his head would circle before jerking into a fixed position, one eye clamped into a scornful expression - performing the manoeuvre with such ferocity that his head struck the doorway, knocking him cold. *Big Business* exists today in two versions, each taken from a separate camera in order to provide negatives for home and overseas. The second (British) copy varies in both camera angles and points of detail, as when Stan grins after Ollie is hit with a hammer; titling also varies, Finlayson calling for the 'ambulance corps' rather than the patrol wagon. The second version, unused for more than half a century, offers superb quality except where decomposition has forced the reduping of a few shots from the American copy. This domestic edition was seen in excellent quality in *When Comedy Was King* (*qv*), although many TV prints are disappointing. It is the second version that has been issued on UK video; its American counterpart seems to use the same picture element but with titles lifted from the US release.

(See also: Apocrypha; Christmas; Cuckoo; *Four Clowns*; McCarey, Leo; Silent films; *Two Tars*; Video releases)

THE BIG NOISE
(Laurel & Hardy film)
Released by 20th Century-Fox, September 1944. Produced by Sol M. Wurtzel. Directed by Malcolm St Clair. 74 mins.
With Stan Laurel and Oliver Hardy, Doris Merrick, Arthur Space, Veda Ann Borg, Bobby Blake, Jack Norton, Frank Fenton, James Bush, Esther Howard.

Eccentric inventor Alva P. Hartley (Arthur Space) submits yet another idea to the Patents Office; his latest innovation, a powerful explosive called

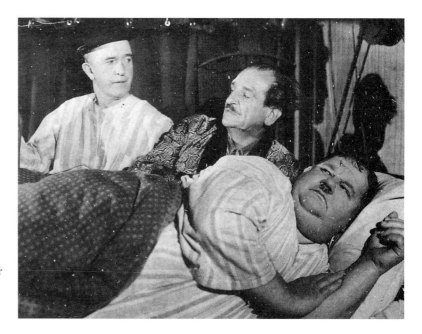

'the big noise', has some use to the war effort and is, for a change, taken seriously. Hartley's small son (Bobby Blake) fakes a telephone call from Washington requesting sight of the invention. Hartley calls a detective agency to obtain guards for the bomb. The office is empty except for the two janitors, Stan and Ollie, who take the opportunity to become detectives themselves and head for the inventor's home. There they encounter Hartley's myriad innovations, not least among these being a completely automated room. Thieves have infiltrated the house via a crooked chauffeur; their initial target, jewels belonging to Hartley's aunt Sophie (Esther Howard), takes second place when they decide a foreign power might pay a fortune for the bomb. Stan and Ollie are entertained to dinner, but are surprised when served with concentrated food pills; a bigger surprise is when aunt Sophie takes a shine to Ollie. Her five previous husbands - all deceased - bear a striking resemblance to Ollie, and each has met with a mysterious death. So, it seems, may Ollie when the sleepwalking widow roams the house wielding a carving knife. She enters the boys' room and walks off

Jack Norton shares the team's berth in **The Big Noise**

with the bomb; when Hartley retrieves it and threatens to dismiss them, Stan and Ollie decide to take turns in going to sleep. The following day Hartley and the boys take the bomb to a remote spot in order to photograph a test, Stan sits on the detonator before they are ready. Hartley then receives a genuine call from Washington, summoning him to demonstrate his invention. After the thieves try to snatch the bomb, Hartley decides to travel by air, sending the detectives by train as decoys. They are supposed to be carrying a dummy bomb inside a concertina; after they have left, Hartley discovers they have the real thing. Stan and Ollie pass an uncomfortable night in a sleeping car before receiving a telegram informing them of their dangerous cargo; unable to wait for the train connection to Washington, they thumb a lift to an aerodrome but are picked up by the thieves. Rescue seems to be at hand when a motorcycle cop stops the car. The boys reach the aerodrome and hide in a light aircraft, but find themselves airborne in a military target range. Fortunately there are parachutes on board, and they descend over the harbour. Ollie spots an enemy submarine and the bomb is duly dropped upon it. The film ends with Stan and Ollie perched upon a marker buoy, Stan playing the concertina to a group of dancing fish.

Usually acknowledged as worst of the wartime Laurel & Hardy films (and included in the book *The Fifty Worst Films of All Time*), *The Big Noise* is actually not the weakest of them. This is still not saying very much, although one critic has said how difficult it is not to smile when Stan plays concertina to an audience of fish (the tune itself, 'Mairzie Doats', was a popular hit of the day). As usual in this series, there are a number of misplaced reworkings of earlier routines: the basic idea of *Oliver the Eighth* (*qv*) is there, but thrown away, while others are under-exploited; the hand-twisting gesture denoting eccentricity in *Wrong Again* (*qv*) is resurrected, but nothing is made of it; while sheer perversity may have influenced the writers to lift a gag from *Habeas Corpus* (*qv*) before incorporating that very phrase into the dialogue. There is a further back-ward glance when Edgar Dearing (1893-1974), the motorcycle cop in *Two Tars* (*qv*), plays an identical role, and even uses the expression 'hog wild'. The best sequence is a reworking of *Berth Marks* (*qv*), enlivened by comic drunk Jack Norton (1889-1958)(who may also be seen in *Pick A Star* [*qv*]) but even this was ham-strung by studio complacency. Stan later described his wish to update the gag by constructing an inexpensive aircraft interior, an idea dismissed out of hand by a Fox employee. Trivia note: child actor Robert 'Bobby' Blake, known in adult life as the star of TV's *Baretta*, was a member of Our Gang (*qv*) after Roach sold the series to M-G-M.

(See also: Aircraft; Alcohol; Detectives; *Hog Wild*; Remakes; Songs; Trains; 20th Century-Fox; Wartime)

BIOGRAPHIES

In 1932 the Roach publicity depart-ment asked Stan to prepare an autobiographical work for their refer-ence. The result, titled *Theatrical Career of Stan Laurel*, was of course never published, nor was *Turning the Pages*, a memoir started by Stan's father, Arthur Jefferson (*qv*). When John McCabe (*qv*) first approached Laurel & Hardy with the idea of a biography, their response was less than enthusiastic; perhaps the two comedians had wearied of the fre-quency with which their marriages had featured in the press. Stan Laurel claimed that his life was of insufficient interest, consisting as it did largely of work, but McCabe was able to con-vince him of the merits of just such an account. Thus was born *Mr Laurel and Mr Hardy*, an instant success on its American publication in 1961 (a UK edition followed in 1962) and continuously in print ever since. An updated edition from 1966 incorpo-rates a further chapter describing the author's initial meeting with the team, the genesis of the book itself, Stan Laurel's latter years and the Sons of the Desert club (*qv*). A second vol-ume, *The Comedy World of Stan Laurel* (1974) permitted McCabe to explore Laurel's career further and, with the passage of time, put into per-spective some of the comedian's marital upsets. A somewhat different viewpoint dominates *Stan* (1980), in which Fred Lawrence Guiles, previ-ously biographer of Marilyn Monroe and Tyrone Power, chronicles Laurel's private affairs in even greater detail. Guiles is sometimes sympathetic, though many feel he assumes the worst of Stan in certain instances. One might add that Stan's second wife was involved in this project at the outset, but did not live to see publication. McCabe completed his biographical trilogy in 1989 with *Babe: the Life of Oliver Hardy*, followed by a revised American edition of *Comedy World* a year later. Books on the films are many, but mention should be made of an early entry from France, Borde and Perrin's *Laurel & Hardy* (1965). William K. Everson (*qv*) followed with *The Films of Laurel & Hardy* (since retitled *The Complete Films of Laurel & Hardy*) in 1967; a year later came *Laurel & Hardy* from British writer Charles Barr; 1973 saw *The Laurel & Hardy Book*, edited by Leonard Maltin (*qv*); two years later McCabe collaborated with Al Kilgore and Richard Bann (both *qv*) on *Laurel & Hardy*, a detailed account of the films; while the 1980s saw another major work, *Laurel & Hardy: the Magic Behind the Movies* by Randy Skretvedt (*qv*). A British study worthy of note is Bruce Crowther's *Laurel & Hardy: Clown Princes of Comedy* (1987); a more recent UK volume is Ronald Bergan's *The Life and Times of Laurel & Hardy* (1992).

(See also: Marriages; Publicity)

BIRDS OF A FEATHER

Also known as *The Whisky Tasters*, *Birds of a Feather* was Laurel & Hardy's sketch during their final stage tour. Written and staged by Stan Laurel, the sketch opens with Ollie walking into a street scene, consulting his watch, and leaving; Stan enters, looks around, and continues on his way. Each reappears from different ends of the stage, meeting halfway with an unconscious 'How do you do?' before doing a 'take'. Stan, it seems, has found them a trial engagement as whisky tasters; the more they drink, the more they earn. As they depart for this happy occupation, the scene changes to a hospital room where Ollie is classed as a 'mental case'. Stan visits, explaining that after a busy morning's tasting, Ollie had cele-brated an offer of permanent employment by leaping from the win-dow to 'fly around with the birds'. 'Why didn't you stop me?' asks Ollie;

'Well, I'd been celebrating, too', replies Stan, 'and I thought you could do it'. Stan has brought sustenance in the shape of onion and jam sandwiches plus some fresh eggs. These are put out of harm's way before the arrival of a nurse, one Rosie Parker, who reveals that Dr Berserk plans to remove Ollie's brains for examination. This unnerving news, compounded by the arrival of an undertaker to take Ollie's measurements, emphasizes the need to escape. Ollie ties his bedsheets together, instructing Stan to tie the end to 'something solid'. Seeing the makeshift rope tied around Stan's neck, Ollie abandons the plan in favour of sending Stan to fetch a barrister. In his absence, Ollie tells Rosie of his intention to sue everyone in the hospital. Stan returns with a bannister, asking 'What do you want me to do with this?'. 'Don't ask me', replies Ollie. Rosie departs, unimpressed. The doctor, whose operations are 'always successful even if the patient dies', enters to examine his charge. Ollie palms off Stan as the patient, but this is prevented by Rosie. Stan is now more than happy for his friend to be thought crazy, even claiming that Ollie laid the eggs he had brought in. The eggs are put away in a cupboard. Dr Berserk subjects Ollie to a final test, in which the patient consumes a cup of bird seed to determine whether he sings like a canary or a buzzard. Stan takes some, followed by Ollie, and as Stan prepares to leave they both start chirping. The frantic doctor orders Rosie to rush the eggs into dissection, but when she opens the cupboard two pigeons fly out; the sketch ends in ornithological chaos. A partial descendant of *County Hospital* (*qv*), *Birds of a Feather* resembles the absurd spirit of the comedians' film work, despite adaptation to a different medium. 'In music hall... you have to be broader, and you get more unreal', Stan explained, though maintaining the sketch still to be 'the basic kind of nonsense Babe and I love'. Indeed it is, complete with some classic Stanley

malapropisms ('Are you trying to make a mountain out of my mole?') plus ample supply of the whimsy that overtook slapstick with the passing years ('I popped in. P-o-opped in'). *Birds of a Feather*, though lost to us in performance (except for an audio recording Laurel gave to John McCabe [*qv*]), survives in scripted form and may be enjoyed thus in *The Comedy World of Stan Laurel*.

(See also: Alcohol; Biographies; Doctors, nurses; *Driver's Licence Sketch, the*; Hats; Insanity; Music-hall; *On the Spot*; Stage appearances)

BIRTHS

Stan Laurel was born in Ulverston, Lancashire (now Cumbria) on 16 June, 1890; Oliver Hardy was born in Harlem, Georgia, on 18 January, 1892. Laurel's birthdate is sometimes given erroneously as 1895, the possible result of a second christening in that year (after a difficult birth, Stan was considered unlikely to survive and given a first, hurried christening at home). In 1974, a blue plaque was placed on Stan's birthplace in Argyll Street (formerly Foundry Cottages), Ulverston; 17 years later a further plaque honouring his partner was unveiled at the City Hall in Harlem, Georgia, the house itself having been demolished. Stan is further commemorated in his home town by a museum and the Stan Laurel pub; the team made their last visit there in 1947.

(See also: Apocrypha; Biographies; Deaths; Hardy, Emily; Hardy, Oliver Sr.; Jefferson, Arthur; *Jitterbugs*; Museums; Names; *Thicker Than Water*)

BLACK, MAURICE (1891-1938)

Warsaw-born but educated in England and America, Maurice Black entered films after a screen test during the play *Broadway*. His appearances include *Little Caesar*, *The Front Page*, *Broadway Babies*, *Street of Chance*, *Runaway Bride*, and

Laurel & Hardy's *Bonnie Scotland* (*qv*), in which he plays rebel leader Mir Jutra. He died quite suddenly, after an illness lasting just two days.

BLACKHAWK FILMS

Founded in 1927 by Kent Eastin as 'Eastin Pictures', this Iowa-based company was for many years the largest distrubutor of 8 and 16mm prints for film collectors. From the 1950s until ceasing to trade some thirty years later, Blackhawk controlled non-theatrical rights to the Roach package in the US, Canada and US territories overseas, issuing a thorough Laurel & Hardy range envied by those outside the areas in question - the company's agreement with Roach Studios forbade export elsewhere. With few exceptions, Blackhawk prints were first-class, complete editions despite company policy of remaking opening titles. The Blackhawk 16mm range has been revived by a former employee, noted film historian David Shepard, who has also upgraded material where possible.

(See also: *Battle of the Century, the*; *Do Detectives Think?*; Home movies; Titling; Video releases; *We Faw Down*)

BLACK HUMOUR (all films *qv*)

A definite sense of the macabre runs through the Laurel & Hardy films, obvious in *Do Detectives Think?*, *Habeas Corpus*, *The Laurel-Hardy Murder Case* and *The Live Ghost*, to name but a few. Much of this seems to derive from Stan Laurel, whose sanguine attitude to life was countered to a degree by a laconic attitude to death. Suicide and murder (both *qv*) loom large in his films, as does a bluntness about mortality, illustrated in *Way Out West*:

Lola: Tell me about my dear, dear Daddy; is it true that he's a-dead?
Stan: Well, we hope he is, they buried him.

Another manifestation of black

humour is through freak endings (*qv*) and various forms of mutilation, such as their tying the chef's arms together in *Swiss Miss*, or, most notably, in *Block-Heads* when Stan appears to have lost a leg. The hanging scene of *Fra Diavolo* is a vivid embodiment of the term 'gallows humour', and one might include in this category an order to shoot themselves in *Bonnie Scotland*. *The Midnight Patrol* ends with the pair obviously shot dead, the last line of dialogue being 'Send for the Coroner'. *Pack Up Your Troubles* finishes with them chased off by a knife-wielding maniac; while the climactic sequence of *Our Relations* sees Stan and Ollie about to be drowned, their feet in cement. The post-Roach films follow the *noir* look of much 1940s cinema but misapply the concept of black humour: *A-Haunting We Will Go* makes no actual joke of the boys accompanying a coffin and the sleepwalking murderess of *The Big Noise* is merely a silly shadow of Mae Busch (*qv*) in *Oliver the Eighth*; *Nothing But Trouble* is morbid and humourless. *Atoll K* at least illustrates more of the proper spirit when we see that a stowaway has been consumed by a lion.

(See also: Dialogue; Graves; Hereafter, the; Letters; M-G-M; Radio; Sickness; 20th Century-Fox)

BLACKMAIL (all films *qv*)
Always a good basis for comic desperation, the concept of blackmail surfaces in Stan and Ollie's world in Laurel's solo *Eve's Love Letters* and the early *Love 'Em and Weep*. Both this film and its remake, *Chickens Come Home*, feature a businessman whose bachelor days return to haunt him in the shape of an old flame; James Finlayson (*qv*) plays the businessman in the first film, but is replaced by Oliver Hardy in the remake. Mae Busch (*qv*) plays the blackmailer on both occasions. *Come Clean* varies this theme with Mae Busch (again) as an attempted suicide

who, on being rescued by Laurel & Hardy, threatens to blame them for her brush with death unless they agree to take care of her. *Sugar Daddies* relies heavily on *Love 'Em and Weep* for plot and certain gags, with Finlayson obliged to escape the fortune-hunting family that he has married into during a drunken spree. Laurel & Hardy themselves are mistaken for blackmailers in *Pack Up Your Troubles*, when attempting to locate the family of an orphaned child.

(See also: Boxing; Risqué humour)

BLAINE, VIVIAN (b. 1921)
Actress and singer known both for stage work and films, perhaps the most famous of these being the screen version of *Guys and Dolls* (1955). 20th Century-Fox (*qv*) clearly intended her to join their dynasty of blonde musical stars, with Laurel & Hardy's *Jitterbugs* (*qv*) providing an early showcase for her talents. She retains pleasant memories of working with the team, not least because they differed from many comedians in being able to relax rather than remain 'on'.

BLETCHER, BILLY (1894-1979)
(Laurel & Hardy films *qv*)
Comedy veteran who, like Bobby Burns (*qv*), worked with Babe at Vim long before playing bit roles with Laurel & Hardy. Best known as the voice of Disney's 'Big Bad Wolf', a character who resurfaces in *Hollywood Party*; the wolf's theme tune is used in *Babes in Toyland*, in which Bletcher plays the Chief of Police. It is Bletcher's voice calling 'Car 13' in *The Midnight Patrol*, and dubbed on to a midget in the elevator scene of *Block-Heads* ('Out, please... thank you!').

(See also: Disney, Walt; Dubbing; *Hungry Hearts*; Pollard, Harry 'Snub'; Solo films)

BLOCK-HEADS
(Laurel & Hardy film)
Released 19 August, 1938 by M-G-M.

Produced by Hal Roach. Directed by John G. Blystone. Camera: Art Lloyd. 58 minutes.
With Stan Laurel & Oliver Hardy, Billy Gilbert, Patricia Ellis, Minna Gombell, James Finlayson.

In the trenches during 1917, Private Laurel is ordered to guard a trench while his colleagues advance. Stan remains at his post, a mountain of empty bean cans beside him, until 1938, when he is discovered after trying to shoot down a civilian pilot. A hero's welcome awaits Stan in the US, where his recently-married friend Oliver Hardy sees his picture in a newspaper. A visit to the Old Soldiers' Home leads to an invitation to dine at the Hardy residence, which they reach only after ample indication that Stan's talent for disaster remains unimpaired. Mrs Hardy (Minna Gombell) is unimpressed by the 'knick-knacks' her husband brings home, and is certainly unwilling to feed one. On her departure, Ollie decides to fix the meal himself but with Stan's assistance blows up the apartment. Help arrives in the attractive form of neighbour Mrs Gilbert (Patricia Ellis), whose dress is promptly soaked by a miraculously intact bowl of punch. She has been accidentally locked out of her own flat, so changes into a pair of Ollie's pyjamas while a key is sent for. This coincides with the return of Mrs Hardy and, soon, the neighbour's big-game hunter husband (Billy Gilbert). Mr Gilbert, whose wife has by now been concealed in a trunk, investigates the argument at the Hardy household and becomes conspiratorial when he realizes that the trunk contains a woman. Privately, he lectures Stan and Ollie on his own, discreet methods of philandering, until his wife emerges from the trunk. Mr Gilbert and his elephant gun send the boys scurrying from the building.

Block-Heads is a remake of *Unaccustomed As We Are* (*qv*), and the

Block-Heads: *Mrs Hardy returns just as Mrs Gilbert dons Ollie's pyjamas*

last of only two Laurel & Hardy features directed by John G. Blystone (*qv*), who died shortly after the film's completion. The last Roach production released through M-G-M (*qv*), it was announced as the final appearance of Laurel & Hardy. Contractual rifts had led to Laurel's departure from the studio and subsequent reports of a new Laurel project, *Problem Child*, about the normal-sized son of a midget couple. Perhaps fortunately, this bizarre-sounding notion remained unfilmed, and Laurel & Hardy were eventually reunited. In the intervening period, Hardy went on to co-star with Harry Langdon (*qv*) in Roach's feature *Zenobia* (also *qv*). Langdon, who had starred in a brief series of sound shorts at Roach during 1929-30, returned to the studio as a gagman on *Block-Heads*. One obvious Langdon contribution is the idea of Stan being left in the trenches, unaware of the war's end, repeated from his own *Soldier Man* of 1926. Langdon was to remain on the Laurel & Hardy gag team until *Saps at Sea* (*qv*) in 1940. The film concludes with an idea taken from Laurel & Hardy's own 1920s backlog, the final gag from *We Faw*

Down (*qv*), in which a shotgun blast is followed by men leaping from virtually every window in sight. Stan Laurel had planned to show the team's heads mounted up as Gilbert's latest trophies (with Ollie no doubt reflecting on another nice mess), but this was never filmed. One macabre gag that was used, however, takes place when Ollie visits Stan at the Old Soldiers' Home: Stan sits in a wheelchair designed for someone minus a leg, folding the limb underneath; Ollie assumes the worst and actually carries him a considerable distance before realizing the mistake. This sequence is a singularly revealing example of the way Laurel & Hardy's characterizations permitted material that with other comedians would be considered tasteless.

(See also: Aircraft; Army; Black humour; Bletcher, Billy; Cars; Ellis, Patricia; Freak endings; Gilbert, Billy; Gombell, Minna; Remakes; Risqué humour; Shotguns)

BLORE, ERIC (1887-1959)
British actor whose early UK work includes writing Tommy Handley's

famous sketch *The Dis-Orderly Room*. He became ubiquitous in Hollywood portraying valets. Appearances include the Astaire-Rogers musicals *The Gay Divorcee* (1934, released in Britain as *The Gay Divorce*) and *Top Hat* (1935), also the Preston Sturges classic *Sullivan's Travels* (1941). In Laurel & Hardy's *Swiss Miss* (*qv*) he is valet to a composer who escapes to a remote Swiss resort for inspiration.

(See also: Servants)

BLOTTO
(Laurel & Hardy film)
Released by M-G-M, 8 February 1930. Three reels. Produced by Hal Roach. Directed by James Parrott. Camera: George Stevens. Reissued 1937 with new incidental music. With Stan Laurel and Oliver Hardy, Anita Garvin, Frank Holliday, Tiny Sandford, Charlie Hall.

Stan's night out with Ollie depends on being able to escape from Mrs Laurel (Anita Garvin) and borrow the bottle of liquor she has saved since Prohibition. Ollie telephones to suggest an ingenious ruse: Stan should send himself a telegram calling him away on 'important business'. Mrs Laurel overhears on an extension line but plays along - having first replaced the liquor with a non-alcoholic mixture of such things as cold tea and mustard. At the Rainbow Club, Stan and Ollie convince themselves that a merry time is being had until Mrs Laurel arrives. Initially they laugh uproariously at the thought of having tricked her but instant sobriety results from the disclosure of the bottle's contents and of her newly-acquired shotgun, two blasts from which flatten the taxicab in which the boys attempt to escape.

Much of the humour in *Blotto* derives from situation rather than specific gags. A contemporary review in *Judge* by the future documentary-maker Pare Lorentz expressed the view that Laurel & Hardy were making the best short comedies of the day and found praise for *Blotto*'s restrained approach. *Blotto*, in Lorentz's opinion, had 'very few gags and not much of a story. But the gags were pulled so deliberately and with such finesse, I wonder that Mr Parrott does not establish a new school of movie direction'. As John McCabe has noted, Lorentz had no way of knowing that the prime influence behind the team's approach was that of Stan Laurel rather than any of their nominal directors. Today *Blotto* tends to circulate in copies unlike those seen in 1930. A 1937 reissue brought appropriate background music but also the loss (through negative damage) of an opening gag in which Mrs Laurel responds to Stan's plea for 'fresh air' by switching on an electric fan. Many copies, including that shown on BBC TV, have been cut to two reels. One of the several resulting omissions is a scene in which Laurel & Hardy are reduced to tears by club singer Frank Holliday's rendition of 'The Curse of an Aching Heart'. The longer version prepared for European TV and issued on tape in the UK bears new opening titles erroneously crediting Dorothy Christy (*qv*) instead of Anita Garvin (*qv*). The colour edition is from America and has the late 1930s reissue titles. Two foreign-language versions were shot: *Une nuit extravagante*, with French actress Georgette Rhodes replacing Anita Garvin, and *La vida nocturna*, substituting in turn Spanish-speaking Linda Loredo. Both are extant and provide both a clue to the overall look and scoring of the original English copies and an example of the way the pair's films were extended for the foreign market. Much of the extra ten minutes' running time is contained in the night-club sequence, with additional cabaret acts such as a belly dancer and another girl performing a comic dance

with balloons. Unseen in the English version is the boys' own drunken rendition of 'The Curse of an Aching Heart' and an uncomfortable moment for an elegant lady (Symona Boniface) who sits in a chair drenched in soda water. An article in the spring 1993 *Intra-Tent Journal* by Richard Finegan refers to several moments cut from the English version on its 1937 reissue: the electric fan gag is not mentioned, but described instead is some business with a soda syphon (preceding the gag with Symona Boniface, which was not in the English copy); also lost is some drunken fooling prior to Frank Holliday's song, plus Laurel & Hardy singing their own, inebriated equivalent.

(See also: Alcohol; Foreign versions; Laughing; Music; Night-clubs; Periodicals; Rediscoveries; Reissues; Reviews; Songs; Shotguns; Taxis; Telephones; Women)

BLYSTONE, JOHN G. (1892-1938)

Director of *Swiss Miss* and *Block-Heads* (both *qv*). Wisconsin-born

Blystone's experience of film comedy dated back to his experience as prop man, actor, sometime manager of L-KO comedies (*qv*) and, from 1923, director. He was the favoured director of Mabel Normand (*qv*), with whom he made *The Extra Girl* (1923). A lengthy if unremarkable career at Fox was punctuated by a few interesting departures, notably Keaton's *Our Hospitality* and *Seven Chances* for Metro, and UA's 1930 remake of the Henry King silent *Tol'able David*. Blystone's direction of Laurel & Hardy provided mixed results: although *Swiss Miss* is uneven in its interwoven sub-plot, *Block-Heads* is one of the team's most popular features. His sudden death before the latter's release brought to an end what might well have been a profitable association.

(See also: Cook, Clyde; Davidson, Max)

Foreign versions of **Blotto** *include a comic balloon dancer*

BOATS, SHIPS (all films *qv*)
Seagoing vessels appear in a number of Laurel & Hardy films. Actual footage of the US Naval fleet opens *Two Tars*, in which our heroes are described as 'two dreadnoughts from the battleship *Oregon*'. Its talkie equivalent, *Men O'War*, confines itself to the smaller craft to be found on a boating lake. The seafaring twins of *Our Relations* arrive on board the *Periwinkle*, a craft only slightly more reputable than the reputed ghost ship in *The Live Ghost*. Even more decrepit is the tiny *Prickly-Heat*, aboard which Stan and Ollie become 'Saps at Sea'. It does at least prove seaworthy, which cannot be said of the *Momus*, which founders in a storm early in *Atoll K*. When attending a convention in *Sons of the Desert*, the boys are unaware that the ship on which they are supposed to be has foundered. *Why Girls Love Sailors* survives in a French version titled *There Was Once a Little Boat*; another smaller craft is filled with water to detect leaks in *Towed in a Hole*. This unimpressive fishing boat is named *Ruth*, after Stan's soon-to-be second wife; he was to pay her a greater compliment when naming his plush yacht the *Ruth L*, used for deep-sea fishing until the US Government acquired the boat during wartime. In *Nothing But Trouble* they return by sea to a wartime America, having been released by the Japanese (who prefer ritual suicide to Ollie's cooking!). Another 1940s exploit, *Jitterbugs*, concludes with a riverboat chase. *Sailors Beware* is a tale of intrigue set aboard the cruise liner *Mirimar*, the same ship that brings Stan to America in *Putting Pants On Philip*. Other transAtlantic trips are implied in *A Chump at Oxford* and *The Flying Deuces*. Stan Laurel's first real-life journey was made with Fred Karno (*qv*) aboard the *Cairnrona*; subsequent trips home would be on famous liners, including the *Queen Mary*. A contrast to the team's cattleboat crossing in *Bonnie Scotland*!

(See also: Ireland; Marriages; Roberts, Thomas Benton; Sailors; Stage appearances)

THE BOHEMIAN GIRL
(Laurel & Hardy film)
Released by M-G-M, 14 February 1936. Produced by Hal Roach. Directed by James Horne and Charles Rogers. Camera: Art Lloyd, Francis Corby. From the 1843 opera by Michael W. Balfe. 70 minutes.
With Stan Laurel and Oliver Hardy, Jacqueline Wells, Mae Busch, Antonio Moreno, Zeffie Tilbury, James Finlayson, William P. Carlton, Darla Hood, Thelma Todd.

A gypsy band travels through Bohemia; among them are Stan and Ollie. Mrs Hardy (Mae Busch) is blatantly unfaithful with Devilshoof (Antonio Moreno), but Ollie considers himself sufficiently modern to overlook such matters. The travellers go about their business of purloining money, Stan and Ollie operating as bogus fortune-tellers. Devilshoof, apprehended in the castle of Count Arnheim, is lashed. The gypsies are ordered from Arnheim's land, and Mrs Hardy, nursing her lover, curses the Count, wishing him 'a year of woe' for each mark placed by the lash. This is fulfilled when she abducts the Count's infant daughter, Arline (Darla Hood), palming her off to Ollie as their hitherto undisclosed offspring. When Devilshoof leaves the band, Mrs Hardy follows, exchanging Ollie's jewels for a note informing him that the child is not his. Twelve years pass and Arline, now a young woman (Jacqueline Wells) occupies the caravan while Stan and Ollie sleep outside. They are on Arnheim's land once again, and Arline, travelling to the village, finds herself drawn to the castle. Stan has been left to bottle wine but, unaware of the techniques required, consumes much of it. Ollie arrives with news of Arline's imprisonment for supposed theft, dragging a sozzled Stan to the castle. They man-age to get the dungeon keys from the Captain of the Guard (James Finlayson) but are apprehended. The Captain drags the 'girl' to the lashing post, only to find it is Stan, who goes on a drunken rampage with the whip. Arline is finally caught but saved when a locket reveals her true identity; Stan and Ollie are by now in the torture chamber but Arline pleads for their release. The boys exit as the Captain observes the mutilated pair, Stan squashed into a midget and Ollie stretched like a giant.

Their last fully-fledged opera, *The Bohemian Girl* underwent considerable revision both in scripting and after previews. The comedy routines developed in the team's usual fashion (see **Scripts**) but plotting required amendment after the sudden death of Thelma Todd (*qv*) before the film's release. In the initial cut, she was cast as Queen of the Gypsies, whose love was scorned by Devilshoof in favour of Mrs Hardy. Devilshoof leaves the band for no greater reason than restlessness in the final version, an unconvincing replacement for his original banishment by the jealous Queen. Zeffie Tilbury (*qv*) was among those brought in to film additional sequences, replacing Todd as an elderly character. Thelma Todd remains in the release version, usually in crowd shots (some of them backprojected behind Zeffie Tilbury), and she retains one song, 'The Heart of a Gypsy'. Her singing voice is dubbed, but it is untrue to suggest that this was done because she had not lived to record it. Another addition was Felix Knight (*qv*) from *Babes in Toyland* (*qv*), brought in to sing 'Then You'll Remember Me'. This song, accompanying Mrs Hardy's scene with her departing lover, seems to have been intended as a duet between Mae Busch and Antonio Moreno (both *qv*). Despite extensive alteration, it seems likely that Laurel & Hardy's comedy scenes were unaffected.

CHICKENS COME HOME
(Laurel & Hardy film)
Released by M-G-M, 21 February
1931. Three reels. Produced by Hal
Roach. Directed by James Horne.
Camera: Art Lloyd, Jack Stevens.
With Stan Laurel and Oliver Hardy,
Mae Busch, Thelma Todd, James
Finlayson, Patsy O'Byrne, Norma
Drew.

Stan and Ollie are successful businessmen, having made their fortune with
fertilizer. Ollie, candidate for Mayor,
dictates a speech to Stan, who appears
from the 'sample room' holding a fly
swatter. This essential business is
interrupted by the arrival of Ollie's
former girlfriend (Mae Busch) with an
embarrassing photograph from Ollie's
bachelor days. The visitor demands
money for her silence, but arrangements are suspended due to the arrival
of Mrs Hardy (Thelma Todd). The
blackmailer is hidden in the wash-
room, where she remains
undiscovered even after Mrs Hardy
has walked in. Her fur, left in Ollie's
office, is palmed off as a surprise gift
for Mrs Hardy; this will be another
item for Ollie to settle when visiting
the blackmailer's home at seven that
evening. Ollie has to entertain at
home, and enlists Stan as emissary.
When Stan arrives in Ollie's
place, the

furious blackmailer forces him to
reveal Ollie's telephone number and
calls the Hardy home. The butler
(James Finlayson), listening to Ollie's
conversation, indulges in some blackmail of his own. When Ollie hides the
cigars as an excuse to go out for more,
the butler brings in a further supply,
earning a kick on the shins plus some
more hush money. Mrs Hardy
answers the next telephone call, and is
unconvinced by Ollie's tale of an old
school friend ('We used to room
together'). The blackmailer's next call
is interrupted by Stan, who has tried
to barricade her in the room. She
breaks free and Stan is caught by a
local gossip (Patsy O'Byrne), who
promises to report his extra-marital
antics. As Stan and the 'wild woman'
drive off, they demolish the gossip's
car. Stan and the blackmailer, introduced as 'Mr and Mrs Laurel', arrive
just as Ollie's other guests are leaving.
Stan has taken a framed copy of the
incriminating photograph from the
woman's home, which falls from his
coat and has to be concealed. As
Mrs Hardy sees her guests to the
door, Ollie tells his former girlfriend
to leave; she insists on a 'settlement',

Chickens Come Home *features Mae
Busch as the blackmailer and Thelma
Todd as Mrs Hardy; the Spanish*
Politiquerias *replaces them with Rina de
Liguoro and Linda Loredo. The outfit
suggests that Mae Busch and Rina de
Liguoro were the same size.*
Politiquerias *(left) plays Santiago.
Advertisement by courtesy of Robert G.
Dickson*

and Ollie offers a final one when producing a revolver. Mrs Hardy returns
to find that 'Mrs Laurel' has fainted,
and proceeds to arrange a room for
her to spend the night with Stan. The
only option is to get her out of the
house, something achieved with Ollie

bent double beneath the unconscious woman's coat. As Stan escorts the unwieldy figure to the door, the real Mrs Laurel appears, brandishing an axe. The boys swap roles, but Stan trips over and they are chased into the night.

A straight remake of *Love 'Em and Weep* (qv), *Chickens Come Home* is an accomplished blend of situation and slapstick with enough material to justify the third reel despite some minor padding. The extant Spanish version, *Politiquerias*, takes things to an extreme, being extended almost to an hour with a brace of superfluous if fascinating entertainers at Ollie's soirée. Robert Dickson has identified both the magician, Mexican-born Abraham J. Cantu, and the Arab-costumed regurgitator Hadji Ali. The latter displays an extraordinary ability to consume vast quantities of nuts,

water and even kerosene, expelling each alternately. Dickson has also noted Hadji Ali's presence in *Scarlet Dawn* (1932) with, coincidentally, Mae Busch (qv) as his wife. *Politiquerias* contains one comic gem unseen in the usual version: as Ollie attempts to sneak from the house, Mrs Hardy (Linda Loredo) is waiting outside the front door. After destroying Ollie's hat and overcoat, she reinforces her point with a well-aimed blow. Mae Busch is replaced by Countess Rina de Liguoro (1892-1966), a concert pianist and actress known to have given a recital in Los Angeles during February 1930. A contemporary newspaper describes her as being from 'a historic family of Italy, where she has played leading roles in moving pictures', adding that she was under contract to M-G-M. She was a major star in Italian silent films. Most copies of *Chickens Come Home* derive from the Film Classics

reissue, whose title cards reduce the poultry factor to a solitary Chicken. Fortunately the American TV restoration (marred by some poor sound and two missing words of dialogue) has unearthed the original cards, which can be seen in the colourized version. Evidently the colour artist is something of a Thelma Todd fan, for her close-ups in this and *Unaccustomed As We Are* (qv) are treated with particular care. Intriguingly, this same version treats the viewer to what is perhaps the only colour newspaper photograph of 1931! Further trivia note: the gossip is played by Patsy O'Byrne, who died in 1968 aged 82. A familiar face both in Sennett comedies and Roach's series with Charley Chase (qv), Miss O'Byrne reappeared in the Laurel & Hardy saga years later with a small role in *Saps at Sea* (qv). In *Politiquerias*, she is replaced by an obviously younger actress, Nelly Fernandez. The actress taking the role of Mrs Laurel, Norma Drew (aka Elizabeth Forrester), eluded detection by Laurel & Hardy fans until she was finally discovered living in the Los Angeles area.

(See also: Blackmail; Businessmen; Christmas; Colour; *Come Clean*; Finlayson, James; Foreign versions; Hardy, Emily; Lyn, Jacquie; Magicians; Reissues; Todd, Thelma).

CHILDREN
(Laurel & Hardy films qv)
Hal Roach insisted that the greatest comedians imitate children. There is no denying the continued popularity of Laurel & Hardy with youngsters, who obviously relate to the childlike characters portrayed by the team. They make convincing children in *Brats*, repeating the idea briefly in *Wild Poses*, one of Roach's Our Gang series (qv). Members of the Gang turn up in a few Laurel & Hardys (notably Darla Hood in *The Bohemian Girl*), though perhaps the most endearing is Jacquie Lyn (qv), reputedly signed for

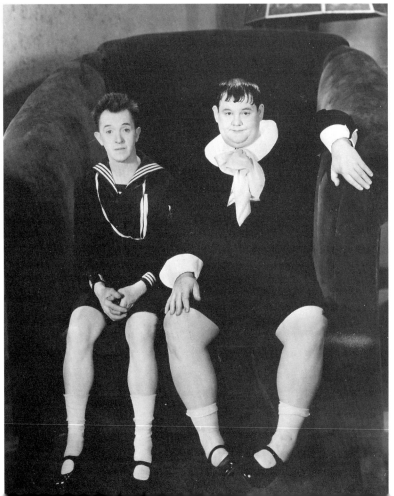

the series but present only in Laurel & Hardy's *Pack Up Your Troubles*. *Their First Mistake* entrusts a baby to Stan and Ollie's care, a position no less precarious than that of the tree-top infant in *Babes in Toyland*, and the pair look after a much older child in *Nothing But Trouble*, unaware that he is an exiled King. A stricken Ollie is visited by a polite little girl in *Saps at Sea*; less charming specimens are two more from Our Gang, Tommy Bond (*Block-Heads*) and Bobby Blake (*The Big Noise*), the latter having joined the series after its acquisition by M-G-M. Most insidious of the bunch is the apparent baby from *Sailors, Beware!* (see **Midgets**) with 'Sturgeon', the landlady's son of *You're Darn Tootin'*, running a close second.

(See also: Characters; *Days of Thrills and Laughter*; Jefferson, Stanley Robert; Laurel, Lois)

THE CHIMP

(Laurel & Hardy film)
Released by M-G-M, 21 May 1932.
Produced by Hal Roach. Directed by James Parrott. Camera: Walter Lundin. Three reels.
With Stan Laurel and Oliver Hardy, Billy Gilbert, James Finlayson, Tiny Sandford, Bobby Burns, Martha Sleeper, Charles Gemora (title role).

Stan and Ollie are working in 'Col. Finn's Big Show', a circus clearly fallen on hard times. As the two halves of a pantomime horse, they are less than effective (Ollie, claims Stan, looks better in the rear half). Poor business leads to the show's closure, each employee receiving a portion of the circus in lieu of back pay. Ollie is given 'Ethel', an educated ape; Stan gets the flea circus. Ollie plans to sell Ethel to a zoo, but first they must find lodgings for the night. They reach a boarding-house whose proprietor (Billy Gilbert) is awaiting his absent wife, also named Ethel. Convinced she is 'playing around'

again, he is at his wits' end even before seeing the boys and their anthropoid friend. The ape is refused admission, a situation complicated by the presence of another circus refugee, a lion. Ethel is dressed in Ollie's clothes and taken up to their room; Ollie, in Ethel's ballet skirt, narrowly escapes the lion. From an upstairs window, Stan drops Ollie's clothes; his trousers catch halfway down, and when Ethel tries to reach them she falls to the ground, dragging Stanley with her. Ethel is locked in a bunker as the boys retire for the night, but at three o'clock climbs through the window and joins them in bed. Stan is knocked to the floor and gets into another bed; Ollie, realizing his new companion's identity, sends her into a corner but has his bedclothes stolen. He joins Stan in the other bed, only to find they are sharing it with the flea circus. When a neighbour plays a gramophone record, Ethel begins to dance. Overhearing the boys' cries to 'Ethel', the landlord bursts in, revolver in hand, delivering the pleas of a betrayed husband. His wife walks in but departs hastily on seeing the monkey; Stan, Ollie and the landlord follow suit when Ethel gets hold of the gun.

'What in heaven's name is that?' asks Billy Gilbert. Why, it's Ethel, **The Chimp**

Although its title suggests a parody of the previous year's Jackie Cooper-Wallace Beery vehicle *The Champ*, this is instead a variant of *Angora Love* and *Laughing Gravy* (both *qv*). Described by Stan Laurel as 'one of the liveliest comedies we've done', this is certainly true although *The Chimp* is at times overstretched. William K. Everson (*qv*) considers the film undeserving of its comparative obscurity, a status it had in the UK until around 1970, despite its presence in 8 and 16mm film libraries. It was revived in extract form by BBC TV's *The Sound of Laughter*, subsequently being screened in its entirety. The BBC print is the Film Classics reissue, in which the gag titles are ruined by being placed in reverse order.

(See also: Animals; Circuses; Gilbert, Billy; Landlords; M-G-M; Parodies; Reissues; Remakes; Risqué humour; Sandford, Tiny; Sleeper, Martha; *Swiss Miss*; Titling; Working titles)

THE CHISELERS
See: *Be Big* and Working titles

CHRISTMAS
The festive season is commemorated fully in the team's classic silent *Big Business* (*qv*), which according to Stan Laurel takes place at Christmas, despite an unfounded story that it is set in July. Randy Skretvedt (*qv*) has determined that shooting took place during the Christmas week of 1928. Spurious Christmas presents are delivered in July during *Chickens Come Home* and *Babes in Toyland* (both *qv*). It has been said that Stan Laurel secretly disliked the holiday after 1908, when his father insisted on a proper family Christmas despite the death of Stan's mother earlier in the month; true or not, he dutifully wished the season's greetings to all in his correspondence around December.

(See also: Jefferson, Arthur; Letters)

CHRISTY, DOROTHY
(Laurel & Hardy films *qv*)
Actress from a stage background who planned initially to become an opera singer. Film debut 1930 in the Will Rogers vehicle *So This Is London*; among other early appearances are *Playboy of Paris* and Keaton's *Parlor, Bedroom and Bath*. Contemporary advertising suggests that she joined at least part of the pre-filming tour of the Marx Brothers' *A Night at the Opera*. She plays Mrs Laurel in *Sons of the Desert*, a part originally intended for Patsy Kelly (*qv*). She is sometimes credited, erroneously, as Mrs Hardy in *That's My Wife* and Mrs Laurel in *Blotto*; married to a Hal Christy, her own name is sometimes misspelled Christie.

(See also: Garvin, Anita; Keaton, Buster; Marx Brothers, the; Oakland, Vivien)

A CHUMP AT OXFORD
(Laurel & Hardy film)
Released by United Artists, 16 February 1940. Produced by Hal Roach. Directed by Alf Goulding. Camera: Art Lloyd. 63 minutes (Europe), 42 minutes (US: longer edition released 1941).
With Stan Laurel & Oliver Hardy, Wilfred Lucas, Forrester Harvey, Charlie Hall, Peter Cushing, James Finlayson, Anita Garvin, Vivien Oakland.

Stan and Ollie are open to offers for suitable employment. An agency needs a married couple to wait at a dinner party, and Ollie knows a couple 'who will just fill the bill' - himself and Stan. Ollie as butler and Stan as maid are insufficiently versed in etiquette (a disadvantage complicated by Stan's literal interpretation of 'serve the salad undressed'), and their next job finds them sweeping the streets. A discarded banana skin from their lunch break stops a bank robber in his tracks and, as a reward, they are provided with 'the best education money can buy' - at Oxford. They arrive dressed for Eton and are ragged by their fellow students, being sent through a maze and installed in the Dean's quarters. Innocently they betray the student culprits and are about to be run out of Oxford until a blow to the head reveals Stan to be Lord Paddington, an all-round genius who had disappeared from Oxford after a similar blow years before. Paddington is a fierce fighter and makes short work of the students; before long he is Oxford's leading scholar and athlete, with Ollie as his personal valet. Paddington is arrogance personified, prepared to fit in a visit from Einstein only when convenient, while the mistreated Ollie decides to return to America - until a further blow restores the old Stan.

First of two 'comeback' features for Roach (*Block-Heads* [*qv*] had been announced as their last) and a partial victim of Roach's unsuccessful policy of 'Streamliners' (*qv*), i.e. featurette-length subjects. The team's popularity in Europe demanded an additional sequence which was filmed separately and constituted a two-reeler that could play quite independently (and indeed did, in a British 8mm edition called *Home Helps*). The longer edition received US distribution shortly after the initial release; modern prints derive without exception from this version, although for years Blackhawk Films (*qv*) offered 8mm collectors only the abridgement (16mm users had the choice). A complete 8mm edition was available in the UK long before its US counterpart. The extra segment is a close remake of the silent *From Soup To Nuts* (*qv*), with Anita Garvin (*qv*) in her last appearance with the team, repeating her role as hostess with James Finlayson (*qv*) as her husband. As in the earlier version, Laurel & Hardy ruin the dinner party, but the humour acquires a greater edge with Stan reviving his impersonation of 'Agnes', the maid. The final gag is that of another silent, *Wrong Again* (*qv*), in which policeman Harry Bernard (*qv*), the recipient of a shotgun blast intended for Laurel & Hardy, claims that the shot has almost blown his brains out - before turning to reveal the smouldering seat of his trousers! The film's hybrid nature accounts not only for the absence of Anita Garvin and James Finlayson from the on-screen cast list, but above all for the film's unwieldy construction. Alf Goulding (*qv*), whose association with the pair dates back to the earliest Laurel one-reelers at Roach, was simply not the most brisk of directors. His style, sometimes protacted even by Laurel & Hardy standards, is typified by the lengthy travel collage representing the team's journey to England. Nevertheless,

there are some nice touches: as a parody of the 1937 *A Yank At Oxford*, the film follows its brief by parallelling certain scenes from the original, notably the shots depicting irate undergraduates in ominous pursuit of Stan and Ollie. As with certain Laurel solo parodies (such as *Mud and Sand*

Roadsweepers Laurel & Hardy have foiled a bank raid in **A Chump at Oxford**

and *The Soilers* [*qv*]), some knowledge of the earlier film is preferable but not essential. One surprising name that made the credits is that of Peter Cushing, years before his fame in Hammer horror films. In his book, *Peter Cushing: An Autobiography* (1986), he recalls his eagerness to take a minor role as a student solely for the chance to work with Laurel & Hardy. His recollections of them are as considerate men who ensured the provision of towels, blankets and hot drinks after Cushing *et al* had to fall into a pool, and as perfectionists; Stan Laurel is described as devising most of the material, which he would discuss with Hardy and Goulding. Noted also are Hardy's habit of twirling a key-chain while humming a tune and his constant consumption of doughnuts, a means of retaining his famous waistline. Perhaps the most

remarkable performance in this film is that of another Englishman: Stan Laurel. His 'Lord Paddington', held by some to be a parody of an earlier dual role for George Arliss (*qv*), is an impressive creation whose convincing upper-crust accent (lapsing only slightly) is matched by a bullying personality to shame Tom Brown's legendary adversary, Flashman. The voice at least is a clear legacy from his music-hall days and offers a rare indication of Laurel's off-screen talent for mimicry. Oliver Hardy in turn provides some effective comic pathos as his downtrodden valet, recalling a much earlier film when these roles were reversed, *Early To Bed* (*qv*).

(See also: *Atoll K*; Education; Female impersonation; Harvey, Forrester; Home movies; Lucas, Wilfred; Oakland, Vivien; Parodies; Rolin Film Co., the; Servants; Stand-ins; Streamliners; Trailers)

CIRCUSES

The circus seems an obvious setting for clowns and indeed is, at least for the conventional type. Although Buster Keaton (*qv*) adapted his talents for the prestigious Cirque Medrano in Paris, this venue is more typical of international cabaret than a circus environment. For performers used to working in everyday surroundings, the absence of a contrast with reality can be unsettling; as Joe Adamson has said of the Marx Brothers' *At the Circus*, the fact that they belong in a circus is precisely why they shouldn't be there. To an extent, the same is true of Laurel & Hardy, whose whole purpose is not to fit into the society to which they aspire; it does however make sense for them to be working in such a show as the one in *The Chimp* (*qv*), presumably the latest of their fore-doomed engagements. Oliver Hardy finds himself pursued by a circus elephant in *Zenobia* (*qv*), a tolerable experience compared to Stan Laurel's real-life nightmare of many years before: as a young comic, he had been lured out of a music-hall act called *The Rum 'Uns From Rome* (*qv*) to appear in the show *Fun on the Tyrol* in Rotterdam. The project was managed and directed by one Jim Reed, who had obtained financial backing from, oddly, a Scotland Yard detective born of a wealthy family. The venue was the Circus Variété, a wooden-roofed structure seemingly purpose-built to amplify the rain that dominated the run. As much of the show would have been inaudible, opening was delayed for a week, at the end of which Reed was reminded of a 'no play no pay' contract that forbade any salary for his cast. Sunday's weather permitted a performance, as did Monday's. Tuesday saw a return to rain, which continued into the next day. The show was cancelled and the backer was contacted for funds to transport the troupe to potential bookings in Brussels. The starving troupe resorted to stealing bread; wiry, dexterous Stan being considered the most suited to

Nat Clifford worked with Stan from the 'teens to the 1930s. This scene is from Hustling For Health *(1919). Photograph by Phil Johnson*

the task. Salvation seemed at hand with a booking in Liège, and would have been had not the undernourished Stan collapsed during a stilt routine, sending himself and colleagues crashing. The troupe was paid off, Stan and Ted Leo having enough to reach Brussels before borrowing more in order to reach London. It was a very shabby-looking Stan who visited his brother Gordon, manager of the Prince's Theatre; Gordon gave Stan various tasks around the building in addition to casting him in its then-current production of Dion Boucicault's *Ben Machree*. Stan returned to *Mumming Birds* (*qv*) for its second American run after a chance meeting with Alf Reeves (*qv*).

(See also: Jefferson, Arthur)

*Two portraits of **Nat Clifford** from music-hall and pantomime days By kind courtesy of Tony Barker*

CLIFFORD, NAT
(Laurel & Hardy films *qv*)

Comedian known to American historians as 'Frank Terry', a writer and actor with Roach from the 1910s. He appeared occasionally in the Laurel & Hardy films: as a safecracker in *The Midnight Patrol* and a butler in *Me and My Pal*, doubling up in the latter as an announcer heard from Ollie's radio. He may be glimpsed in *Fra Diavolo* as a servant who directs Lord Rocburg to San Marco's quarters, and appears with his back to camera as the owner of a lunch wagon in *Any Old Port*. Speculation also exists over the on-screen credit for a 'Marion Bardell' in *Me and My Pal*; opinions are divided over whether this refers to Clifford or (more plausibly) to the actress playing Ollie's bride. Nat Clifford has long been something of an enigma, and was once labelled 'Walter Plinge' in lieu of definite identification (a name used in British theatre as a pseudonym for an actor playing more than one part; the UK equivalent of the American 'George Spelvin'). Much of this mystery was created by Clifford himself, and with good reason: his adventurous life made necessary the use of pseudonyms, not always for professional purposes. In 1961, Stan Laurel described Clifford in a letter to John McCabe (*qv*), an account gleaned from various sources with no guarantee of veracity. Despite Stan's doubts, other references exist to confirm the man's extraordinary odyssey. Of Clifford's aliases, the letter quotes 'Frank Terry' and 'La Petit Franklin' as examples; the latter is likely to date from his time as a child performer. Stan's account begins with Clifford as a native of New York who stowed away to England in boyhood, sold newspapers in London, took up boxing and became, eventually, a very successful music-hall comedian and songwriter. Clifford's accent, the 'posh Cockney' peculiar to the music-halls, suggests at least an upbringing in London if not birth. An interview

with Clifford at the age of 24 appeared in the *Encore* of 6th December, 1895. The interview asks if he had returned to England after his first appearance (with an acrobatic team billed as the 'Brothers Melrose), thus implying English origins. This was at the age of six in South America; he remained there for two years before the act joined Monte's Circus in India, 'Asiania' and Australia; from here to Paris, where the 12 year old veteran met a new partner, Harry Mae, with whom (as 'Clifford and Mae') he performed 'tumbling and legmania acts'. The team was brought to a premature close when Mae missed a trap one evening and broke his neck. Clifford, though shocked, accepted this as an occupational hazard, and continued as an acrobat and contortionist, finally reaching England on the Livermore tour of Newcastle. It was for a benefit at the Newcastle Empire that Clifford made the switch to comic songs and patter, though retaining the 'legmania business', adding that only he and the great Little Tich did the 'draw-up'. He was taken up by an agent, Will Sley, for provincial bookings and was subsequently represented by London agents Oliver and Holmes. He had several numbers written for him by Bennett Scott and A. J. Mills and composed quite a few of his own; among the many items published are 'My Wife's Husband', 'I Thought My Luck Was In' and 'That's How I Saved My Life'. In time he would also compose songs for other artists; extant today is a 1907 contract (on Vaudeville Club notepaper) assigning the rights to 'Poodle Dog' (or 'Has Anyone Seen My Poodle Dog?') to Billy Williams, a singer best recalled for 'When Father Papered the Parlour'. The 'Nimble One', as Clifford became known, was at the peak of his profession and apparently settled domestically (the *Encore* piece refers to his marriage being due the day before publication) when disaster struck in what Stan called a 'married woman scandal'. Clifford fled to

Australia where, according to Stan, alcoholic exploits led to several bigamous marriages to barmaids; this marital multiplicity was also documented in the contemporary British press. Friends smuggled Clifford out of Australia in a meat sack aboard a ship bound for the East. Reported dead at sea, Clifford made his way to China and India, where he employed aliases to facilitate his activities in horse racing and card-sharping until choosing a Rajah as his victim. Sentenced to a prison island, Clifford somehow escaped to Cairo, where he hid in the care of an English prostitute. Making his way to the States, he entered vaudeville as writer of songs and acts, then as performer in the New York area; thence to California and picture work at Sennett (*qv*) and Roach. He has been credited as director (alternating with Roach) of some early Laurel films in 1918-19, and is among the cast of *Hustling For Health* (see **Rolin**). Also in 1919 he was involved in the accident which nearly killed Harold Lloyd (*qv*) during a stills session: Clifford innocently handed Lloyd a live bomb from what should have been harmless props; the resultant explosion blew away half of Lloyd's right hand, in addition to endangering his face and eyesight. Clifford, the upper plate of whose dentures was bizarrely split in two by the blast, hailed a passing car and took Lloyd to hospital. Stan Laurel was one of many to send Lloyd goodwill messages. Lloyd's 1928 memoir *An American Comedy* relates the incident (though without mention of the hand injury), referring to Clifford as 'Frank Terry' and describing him as an ex-Karno performer; this is unlikely but not impossible, as Karno often hired established names in addition to creating his own. By the 1930s, Clifford was on the regular Laurel & Hardy gag team. As well as playing the minor roles credited above, he is reported to have concocted the absurd marching ditty sung at a lodge meeting in *Sons of the Desert*. Given that he was probably wanted in several countries, Clifford's screen appearances seem brazen. In Britain, the *Performer* of 23 September 1931 referred to Clifford as having been able to read an account of his own death and burial, evidence that details had emerged of his escape if not of his actual whereabouts. According to Stan Laurel, Clifford suddenly acquired religion and became a missionary in Hawaii, acting for a while as Chaplain to a leper colony until opening a mission hall in Honolulu. The letter adds that Clifford retired to California, spending his remaining years with his wife and two daughters. Stan's last contact with the surviving relatives was around 1951, when they were living in Glendale. Nat Clifford's story may never be fully chronicled but it would be an understatement to say that even just a fraction of it makes for an eventful life.

Dorothy Coburn is a noise-conscious nurse in The Finishing Touch

(See also: Englishmen; Karno, Fred; Music-hall; Servants; Vaudeville; Writers)

COBURN, DOROTHY (1905-78)
(Laurel & Hardy films *qv*)
Dark-haired actress very much in the 'flapper' mould. In this guise she is pursued by Stan in *Putting Pants On Philip* and is the recipient of a painted posterior in *The Second Hundred Years* (she receives a kick in the same region during *Hats Off*). *From Soup To Nuts* offers another assault on her dignity: as dinner guest Dorothy is startled by a dog crawling between her legs, she tells the host to 'be a gentleman'! *The Finishing Touch* casts her as a fiery nurse who objects to noisy builders Laurel & Hardy; she plays another nurse in *Leave 'Em Laughing*. She has less to do in *Sugar Daddies* and *Sailors Beware*, but makes a convincing amazon in *Flying Elephants*, is among the first participants in *The Battle of the Century* and partakes in the mud bath of *Should Married Men Go Home?* As

with Edna Marian and Viola Richard (both *qv*), Dorothy Coburn disappears from the Laurel & Hardy films in mid-1928.

COLOGNE
There seems no end to the type of information sought by dedicated enthusiasts. *The Intra-Tent Journal* has a regular feature titled 'Ask John McCabe', in which Laurel & Hardy's authorized biographer answers readers' questions. Most are related to the team's work or hobbies but one rather surprising request was for details of Stan Laurel's favoured brand of cologne; for the record, it was English Leather.

(See also: McCabe, John; Periodicals; Sons of the Desert [club])

COLOUR (theatrical films *qv*)
Laurel & Hardy's first colour appearance was as comic relief in an operatic film of 1930, M-G-M's *The Rogue Song*. The film was shot in the early

two-strip Technicolor process, which offered a useful if limited colour spectrum. It is difficult to evaluate the effectiveness of their colour debut as the only available Laurel & Hardy sequence takes place at night. By the mid-1930s, Technicolor had been perfected and reportedly the team's 1938 feature *Swiss Miss* was the subject of colour tests. Further rumour insists that a complete Technicolor version was shot but printed into black and white. The make-up, set design and even grain in the image suggest a monochrome copy from colour, but this must remain conjecture. The last professionally-made colour film to feature Laurel & Hardy was a short item made for the US Department of Forestry, *The Tree in a Test Tube*. Made in 16mm Kodachrome, the quality of available prints is variable, but all give some indication of Laurel's red hair and Hardy's well-earned golfing tan. The smaller gauges preserve more colour footage in the form of home movies. A 16mm Kodachrome reel taken of Laurel & Hardy performing their *Driver's Licence Sketch* on a wartime tour is in private ownership. Other home movies record Stan Laurel in retirement, seen at home playing with a pair of Laurel & Hardy marionettes. Perhaps the most notorious is *Stan Visits Ollie*, taken after Hardy's enforced, drastic weight loss toward the end of his life and unfortunately very widely circulated. During the 1980s, video technology had advanced to the point where something approaching natural colour could be added to black and white films by computer. This process, created by a Toronto-based firm, continues to arouse much hostility both in and out of the industry but was motivated by an American survey in which it was discovered that most TV viewers would switch off anything in monochrome. As perhaps the most durable black and white series, the Laurel & Hardy films were considered ideal to demonstrate the technique. Although

Colouring: Stan's bright blue eyes are barely visible in this still from G. M. Anderson's The Egg
BFI Stills, Posters and Designs

early experiments with the shorts disappointed, sufficient work had been done by 1985 to make the colour video edition of *Way Out West* a great success in the US and, later, in the UK. Rosina Lawrence (*qv*), the heroine of *Way Out West*, has vouched for the computer colour's authenticity. The British release was in 1991, by which time several other Laurel & Hardy titles had been rendered into colour in America, among them *Babes in Toyland*. Stan Laurel told biographer John McCabe (*qv*) that his only regret about *Toyland* was that it had not been made in colour; McCabe believes that Laurel would have approved of the new technology if consulted about the colour content. There is no questioning the technical quality of computer-added colour. The main objection is that several subjects have been coloured in their abridged *Laurel & Hardy Show* editions, incorporating fades for commercials and cuts to a number of shorts and features (*Swiss Miss*, in colour at last, is among those affected). A further intrusion is the addition of Ronnie Hazlehurst's Roach music to previously unscored films; though excellent, the recordings are not the originals and are often selected without regard for mood.

(See also: *Below Zero*; Colouring; *Driver's Licence Sketch, the*; *Fighting Kentuckian, the*; Height, weight; Home movies; *Hoose-Gow, the*; *Men O'War*; Music; *Music Box, the*; *Night Owls*; Television; Video releases)

COLOURING

The team's preponderance of monochrome work makes it difficult to determine their exact colouring. For the record, Oliver Hardy had black (some say brown) hair, brown eyes and a golfer's tan. The somewhat paler Stan Laurel had red hair which, according to one source, caused the comedian genuine regret when it whitened with age. Laurel's bright blue eyes caused problems much earlier in life, as the period's orthochromatic film stock was insensitive to that colour. Extant films refute the story that he was unsuited to photography until the introduction of panchromatic stock during the 1920s, although it is noticeable that Laurel accentuated his eyes with heavy make-up until the middle of the decade.

(See also: Apocrypha; Colour; Golf; Hair; Height, weight; Make-up)

COME CLEAN

(Laurel & Hardy film)
Released by M-G-M, 19 September 1931. Two reels. Produced by Hal Roach. Directed by James Horne. Camera: Art Lloyd.
With Stan Laurel and Oliver Hardy, Mae Busch, Gertrude Astor, Linda Loredo, Charlie Hall, Tiny Sandford, Eddie Baker.

chocolate ice cream. Ollie pulls the bath plug and Stan disappears. Ollie tells Mrs Laurel that Stan has 'gone to the beach'.

Come Clean is a concise variation of *Chickens Come Home* (*qv*), released only seven months earlier, and kicks off with a scene borrowed from *Should Married Men Go Home?* (*qv*). The idea of rescuing a suicide may well have been prompted by Chaplin's then-current feature *City Lights*, but *Come Clean* has itself proved influential: an episode of the 1973 BBC series *Seven of One* presents Roy Castle and Ronnie Barker as partygoers who, dressed as Laurel & Hardy, encounter a woman given to screaming like a lunatic. The following year's documentary, *Cuckoo* (*qv*) includes out of context the scene where Laurel & Hardy stage a mock parade in order to conceal the noise from Ollie's bedroom. The idea was to convey the childlike nature of the team's characters, but the full sequence displays instead the application of a child's solution to an adult problem, a subtle but significant difference. *Come Clean* benefits from some clever set pieces, as when Ollie gets the worst of a swing door while trying to find a 'pitcher' for the ice cream (Stan brings a picture). The ice cream salesman is Charlie Hall (*qv*) at his most irascible, yet he shows commendable restraint at both their confused order and the destruction of the eggs and straws on his counter. Mae Busch (*qv*), whose menace is compounded here by a streak of apparent lunacy, is effective as ever, with a brand of screaming worthy of Fay Wray in *King Kong*.

(See also: Astor, Gertrude; Chaplin, Charlie; Doors; Foreign versions; Impersonators; Insanity; *Love 'Em and Weep*; Nudity; Remakes; Suicide; Women)

Ollie and his wife (Gertrude Astor) are settling down for a comfortable evening without 'those Laurels' when Stan and Mrs Laurel (Linda Loredo) ring the doorbell. Ollie decides they should pretend to be out, an illusion which is convincing only until Ollie takes in and returns the note Stan has slid under the door. The Laurels are welcomed with forced delight and it is not long before Stan sits on Ollie's hat. Stan wants ice cream, which means a trip to the local parlour. The list of flavours includes everything but chocolate; Stan agrees to have ice cream without chocolate. Finally, a carton is placed on the counter, containing chocolate. Outside, a woman (Mae Busch) says goodbye to the world, preparing to drown herself. 'Goodbye!' replies Stan just as she leaps into the river. Ollie takes charge, and plunges into the water after a shove from Stan. The woman is saved, but Ollie nearly drowns, particularly after being thrown a rope attached to an anchor. The woman is not only ungrateful but somewhat unhinged: insisting that the boys should 'take care' of her, she screams hysterically when they try to leave. Stan and Ollie head for home, but the woman follows, pushing past the doorman (Tiny Sandford). The doorman summons the police. Ollie asks the woman to leave them alone, but she wants money. The defiant Ollie decides to 'come clean' and tell the wives what has happened; he tries to get Stan to go, but the woman accuses Ollie of 'bluffing'. Ollie confronts the wives, but his nerve fails, all the more so when Stan pushes the woman into his bedroom. Wearing one of Mrs Hardy's robes, she switches on the radio. To mask the noise, Stan and Ollie start to bang cutlery in the fashion of a military band, parading through to the bedroom and switching off the radio. The woman has hidden in the closet by the time the boys are confronted by their wives, who are convinced their husbands are 'cuckoo'. They depart in disgust, and Ollie begs the woman to leave. She is persuaded to do so, if she can keep Mrs Hardy's fur coat. As she departs, a detective (Eddie Baker) arrives, forcing a return to Ollie's home. Soon she and Stan are locked in the bathroom. Stan takes a bath, fully clothed, as an alibi for his presence. The detective forces his way in, apprehending the woman and telling Stan of the thousand dollars' reward due him. When Ollie asks Stan what he plans to do with the reward, Stan explains that he will buy a thousand dollars' worth of

THE COMIC (1969)

Carl Reiner's portrait of a fictional silent-movie comedian has been interpreted by a few as a representation of Stan Laurel. Its star, Dick Van Dyke (*qv*), resembles Laurel to a degree, and a reconstructed beach set is in turn reminiscent of Laurel's *Half A Man* (*qv*), but the storyline offers closer parallels to Keaton's misfortunes. Considered on its own merits, *The Comic* is entertaining and evocative, but it should be emphasized that neither Keaton nor Laurel became impoverished or emotionally defeated as this film's central figure does.

(See also: Keaton, Buster)

COMPILATIONS

(Laurel & Hardy films *qv*)

The main source of Laurel & Hardy compilations has been Robert Youngson (*qv*), whose first feature-length effort, *The Golden Age of Comedy* (*qv*) was, in his own words, 'top-heavy with Laurel & Hardy' despite a brief to represent American silent comedy in general. *Golden Age* has been credited with accelerating the revival of the team's popularity; its sequel, *When Comedy Was King* (*qv*), concludes with most of *Big Business*. *Days of Thrills and Laughter* (*qv*) contents itself with solo clips. *Thirty Years of Fun* (*qv*) unveiled the recently-rediscovered *Lucky Dog*, Laurel & Hardy's first appearance together. *M-G-M's Big Parade of Comedy* (*qv*) gave Youngson access to *Bonnie Scotland* and, more interestingly, the seldom seen *Hollywood Party*. 1965 saw Youngson's first specific Laurel & Hardy anthology, *Laurel & Hardy's Laughing Twenties* (*qv*), a skilled blend of highlights and potted versions of whole films presented within the context of clips featuring talented Roach contemporaries such as Charley Chase and Max Davidson (both *qv*). The next, *The Further Perils of Laurel & Hardy* (*qv*), allows concisely abridged shorts to dominate; the last, *Four Clowns* (*qv*), divides into equal parts shared with Chase and Buster Keaton (*qv*). Other hands have been less skilful. Jay Ward's *The Crazy World of Laurel & Hardy* (*qv*) contains a surfeit of brief clips from too many films, almost all of them talkies, often ruined by unsuitable music and additional sound effects. Another talkie collection, *The Best of Laurel & Hardy* (*qv*), fares better by employing lengthy clips from fewer films, but is overbalanced by the inclusion of an overlong

abridgement of *Our Relations*. The author helped to put together a UK compilation for video release, the winner of a 1991 trade award; two further anthologies have followed from the same distributor. M-G-M's *That's Entertainment Part 2* (1976) eschews any Laurel & Hardy footage under the studio's ownership in favour of brief clips from a few Roach silents. The narration does the team little justice, implying Laurel & Hardy to have been basic slapstick 'in the beginning' of movie history (neither is true).

(See also: Documentaries; *Wild Poses*)

CONFIDENCE TRICKS

(all films *qv*)

The innocent Stan and Ollie are, sadly, prime targets for confidence men. The insurance deal of *The Battle of the Century* is rather suspect and its equivalent in *The Dancing Masters* even more so. Crime features heavily in the clichéd Fox films; they are sold a fake money machine in *A-Haunting We Will Go* and multiple fraud runs throughout *Jitterbugs*. More entertaining are the intrigues in the operas, notably Ollie's masqerade as *Fra Diavolo*, Stan as substitute bride in *Babes in Toyland* and the boys' fraudulent predictions in *The Bohemian Girl*. Stan and Ollie participate in an

Confidence tricks: a fortune-telling scam in The Bohemian Girl

elaborate game to lure a ship's crew in *The Live Ghost*, although top of the tree stands, as ever, James Finlayson (*qv*), whose 'Mickey Finn' in *Way Out West* is the most shameless double-dealer in Laurel & Hardy history.

(See also: Criminals; Eggs; Operas; Practical jokes; 20th Century-Fox)

CONTINUITY ERRORS

(all films *qv*)

The Laurel & Hardy films include several occasions when the action appears inconsistent from shot to shot. These instances have been documented faithfully over the years by alert enthusiasts. A few: 'Lord Plumtree' of *Another Fine Mess* switches forenames between

'Ambrose' and 'Leopold' until Thelma Todd (*qv*) tries to rescue matters by calling him 'Leopold Ambrose'; in *The Music Box*, an insert shot of the piano running over Ollie shows the instrument to have reversed its position; in *Brats*, Ollie Jr. emerges, drenched, from a bathtub, only to be dry moments later; while *The Midnight Patrol* sees officers Laurel & Hardy claiming to have started only that morning, despite an earlier disagreement over where they had spent their last day off. Continuity girl during the mid-to-late 1930s was Ellen Corby, known later as an actress in TV's *The Waltons*. Virginia Lucille Jones joined the team for *The Flying Deuces*, and was unimpressed by Babe's seeming arrogance. When he politely declined her advice on how he had been holding various props, she expected disaster, but she was impressed when the shot matched perfectly; so impressed, in fact, that she later married him.

(See also: Marriages)

***Baldwin Cooke** is an irate neighbour in* Perfect Day

COOK, CLYDE (1891-1984)
Elastic-limbed Australian nicknamed 'the Kangaroo Boy'. Clyde Cook's image consisted of clownish vacuity accentuated by a moustache stretching from nose to lower lip. A former dancer, he made his stage debut aged six, eventually reaching London, Paris (at the *Folies Bergère*) and New York, where he was in the *Ziegfeld Follies* prior to becoming principal clown at the Hippodrome. From here came an offer to star in Fox comedies during 1920, some of them directed by John G. Blystone (*qv*). He also worked in several features, playing a clown in Chaney's *He Who Gets Slapped* (1925). Cook joined Roach in the mid-1920s, but found the studio unsure of how to use him. Vast amounts of incoherent footage were shot by various directors, none of it useable, until Stan Laurel (with whom Cook had appeared in one-reelers) constructed a framing device in which a bizarre script is related to a film producer. This motif was repeated by W. C. Fields in *Never Give a Sucker an Even Break*. Cook, with whom Babe appeared in the Laurel-directed *Wandering Papas* (1925), was given plenty of spot gags and slapstick routines but it took

character to establish a comedian in the upper echelons and by the 1930s Cook had changed to supporting roles in dramatic films. A reminder of earlier days came when Cook was put into the *Taxi Boys* (*qv*), a series more typical of Sennett than of Roach.

(See also: Solo films)

COOK, ELISHA JR. (b. 1903)
Supporting actor famed for portraying seedy neurotics, characters either at odds with or accentuated by his babyish looks, notably as 'Wilmer' in *The Maltese Falcon* (1941). Among many other notable films is George Stevens' *Shane*. He appeared in *A-Haunting We Will Go* (*qv*) as a gangster masquerading for part of the time as an elderly lady.

(See also: Female impersonation; Patrick, Lee; Stevens, George)

COOKE, ALICE AND BALDWIN
(Laurel & Hardy films *qv*)
The vaudeville team of 'Cooke and Hamilton' were in reality a married couple, Alice and Baldwin ('Baldy') Cooke, Stan's partners from 1916-18. Alice Cooke (1881-1985) recalled their

his old friends from the early days'.

(See also: Keystone Trio, the; Marriages; Vaudeville)

CORNWALL, ANNE (1898-1980)
Often associated with silent westerns, Anne Cornwall first came to public attention appearing opposite Lionel Barrymore (*qv*) in *The Copperhead* (1922) and was voted among the 'Wampas Babies' three years later. Today she is remembered as the leading lady in Keaton's 1927 film *College*, directed by Laurel & Hardy regular James Horne (*qv*) and including Charlie Hall (*qv*) in its cast. Her contribution to Laurel & Hardy's *Men O'War* (*qv*) is equally memorable, as the girl who appears to have mislaid a vital piece of clothing.

(See also: Keaton, Buster; Risqué humour)

COSTELLO, LOU (1906-59)
The fatter half of the Abbott & Costello team, Laurel & Hardy's main rivals in the 1940s. Stan Laurel is said to have resented Costello's borrowings from his character, chiefly the cry; one might also draw attention to the similarity between *Pack Up Your Troubles* (*qv*) and Abbott and Costello's *Buck Privates Come Home*. Costello once conceded that Laurel & Hardy were 'the funniest comedy team in the world'. Coincidentally, he is visible in the fight audience of *The Battle of the Century* (*qv*), made at a time when the unknown Costello was engaged in stunt work at M-G-M.

(See also: Crying; *Great Guns*; Gilbert, Billy; Hall, Charlie; M-G-M; *Taxi Boys, the*)

COSTUME
(Laurel & Hardy films *qv*)
One of the hallmarks of lesser Laurel & Hardy impersonators is an inatten-

close relationship as 'utter fun', off-stage as well as on. Their act, *The Crazy Cracksman* (written by Stan) brought the house down but there were at least as many laughs socially. Despite a shared weekly income of $175, excellent for 1916, there were times when it wouldn't last: in the Hofbrau, a favoured spot in Troy, New York, they had precisely enough for two beers, a sandwich and a small tip when a friend of Stan's arrived and was impulsively invited to join them. The extra guest had to be financed from Alice's dime bank, constructed to open when containing $5 in coins but prised open ahead of schedule. The Hofbrau was treated to the spectacle of 40 dimes cascading over its floor, Stan and Baldy scrambling around trying to recapture them. The seemingly inseparable trio was split up when Stan made the acquaintance of Mae Charlotte Dahlberg, better known to posterity as Mae Laurel (*qv*). His parting from the Cookes was traumatic, but he redeemed himself with his suggestion of a replacement, another British comic named Billy Crackles, and his presenting *The Crazy Cracksman* to the Cookes. Soon after, the Cookes discovered that Stan and Mae were doing the same act, the result of financial desperation on Stan's part rather than from any other motive. Extant reviews prove this to have been a very temporary measure, the Cookes having asserted their right to the sketch. Alice later ascribed the

incident to Stan's infatuation with Mae; that there was no lasting acrimony is evidenced by the Cookes' reappearance in Stan's life in the 1920s, when they were supportive during his last, turbulent years with Mae, acted as witnesses for his marriage to Lois Neilson in 1926 and even started to appear in Roach comedies through Stan's influence. Vaudeville was on its way out and the Cookes were among several such displaced artists helped by Stan. Alice remembered appearing in *The Bohemian Girl*, *Our Relations* and *Babes in Toyland* (as Mother Hubbard); Baldy may be seen in several Laurel & Hardy films (notably as the neighbour in *Perfect Day* and a fellow lodge-member in *Be Big*) though he is given more to do in two-reelers with Charley Chase (*qv*). Their relationship grew even closer around the time of Stan's second marriage, when the Cookes spent a protracted time as Stan's houseguests, chaperoning the bride and witnessing the ceremony in Mexico. They were later supportive through Stan's most troubled matrimonial times, particularly with the tempestuous Illiana. The Cookes' loyalty to Stan is summed up by comments made by Alice much later, describing their friend as 'the kindest, most thoughtful, most generous and most loyal man I've ever met in my life... a lot of stars, when they get to be big, get big heads too. But never with Stan. He was always the same with us, and with all

tion to costume. They assume the team to have dressed entirely in black, perhaps with pinstripe trousers and even spats (present only on such occasions as Ollie's wedding in *Me and My Pal*). In truth, their standard costume (such as it is) usually consists of two options: in poverty, Stan wears a light, double-breasted suit (growing tattier over the years), Ollie a tight sports jacket and dark trousers, let out at the seat; in moneyed roles, Stan wears a lighter suit, an immaculate three-piece, contrasting with Ollie's darker equivalent. On a number of occasions, the grandiose Hardy figure is decorated with a cloak. Their everyman status requires mostly unexceptional clothing, even the wing collars (sometimes abandoned in the earliest and last films) being in their day only modestly formal and in keeping with the team's gentility. The ill-fitting nature of their clothing was confined to impoverished circumstances until the big studios used the idea to emphasize their contrasting builds; the scripts were just as orientated toward caricature. Certain settings dictated special outfits, their garb in various operas (*qv*) and *Swiss Miss* proving especially delightful.

(See also: Courtliness; Hats; Impersonators; Reviews; Shoes; Spectacles)

COUNTY HOSPITAL
(Laurel & Hardy film)
Released by M-G-M, 25 June 1932. Produced by Hal Roach. Directed by James Parrott. Camera: Art Lloyd. Two reels.
With Stan Laurel and Oliver Hardy, Billy Gilbert, William Austin.

Mr Hardy is enjoying a quiet hospital stay, his broken leg safely tethered aloft. Mr Laurel arrives with a present of hard-boiled eggs and nuts (candy is too expensive, and Stan has yet to be paid for the last batch). When Mr Hardy rejects the gift, his friend decides not to waste anything; as a nutcracker, he lifts the counterweight keeping Ollie's leg in place, sending Ollie to the ceiling and the doctor (Billy Gilbert) hanging from a top-floor window. Order is restored but the doctor orders Ollie from the premises. The patient's trousers do not fit over the plaster, so a leg must be trimmed: 'the leg of the pants', emphasizes Ollie. The wrong leg is removed; the second follows its companion before they realize the trousers belong to Ollie's English room-mate (William Austin). Stan drives Ollie home but has almost been rendered unconscious after sitting on a syringe. The wild ride that follows is concluded when their car emerges from between two streetcars, twisted into a semi-circle.

The finale of *County Hospital* is clearly intended to rival that of *Hog Wild* (*qv*), but suffers from inept back-projection. At this time the studio was under strict financial pressure, which marred sequences such as this as well as forcing the departure of several key talents. This aside, *County Hospital* is one of the best Laurel & Hardy shorts, its meticulous chaos blending with clever dialogue; there is also a risqué element, as when Stan thinks Ollie has given birth (he has the wrong room). Billy Gilbert (*qv*) is expert as the doctor whose unctuous manner leads Stan to address him as 'ma'am', while his eventual wrath gives Ollie the chance to reprimand his friend in a classic parental manner, evaluating, slowly, Stan's destruction of a tranquil stay. *County Hospital* is one of several shorts to have undergone amendment in the late 1930s reissues; music from *Our Relations* (*qv*) was added, and the opening gag title deleted. Main titles (themselves replaced on a further reissue) were cropped to remove director and technical credits.

(See also: Austin, William; Cars; *Dancing Masters, the*; Doctors; Eggs; Food; Gag titles; Hal Roach Studios, the; Locations; Music; Reissues; Risqué humour; Sickness; *Twice Two*)

COURTLINESS (all films *qv*)
One of the aspects that sets Laurel & Hardy apart from their contemporaries is the old-world courtesy of their characters. This element, one of the few shared between their on- and off-screen personalities, provides comic incongruity when placed within an inappropriate context: Ollie's elaborate way of signing into a posh hotel (*Double Whoopee*) is twice as funny in a less reputable establishment (*Any Old Port*). This contrast permits them to see the best in people despite evidence to the contrary: a thuggish-looking convict in *The Hoose-Gow* is

County Hospital: *Stan arrives bearing hard-boiled eggs and nuts*

COURTROOMS
See: Judges

CRAMER, RYCHARD (1889-1960)
(Laurel & Hardy films *qv*)
A Laurel & Hardy nemesis in *Scram!*,
Pack Up Your Troubles, *Saps at Sea*
and (briefly) *The Flying Deuces*,
Rychard Cramer is considered the
most humourless of Laurel & Hardy
villains. Cramer's true character is
suggested instead by his portrayal of a
Mountie who is reduced to tears by
W. C. Fields' absurd ballad in *The
Fatal Glass of Beer* (1933). Cramer's
earlier work encompassed the stage
and many films, among them *Murder
on the Roof*, *Painted Desert*, *In Line of
Duty* and *The Strange Love of Molly
Louvain*.

(See also: Censorship; Dillaway,
Donald; Prison; Villains)

CRAZY TO ACT (1927)
See: Sennett, Mack and Solo films

**THE CRAZY WORLD OF
LAUREL & HARDY** (1966)
(Laurel & Hardy films *qv*)
Executive producer Jay Ward credits
Hal Roach as the actual producer of
this anthology, although his direct
involvement seems unlikely. Historian
and distributor Raymond Rohauer
receives credit as 'associate producer',
but the final content may well have
been determined by editors Skip
Craig, Roger Donley and supervising
editor Thomas Stanford. Presumably
inspired by the success of earlier compilations by Robert Youngson (*qv*),
Crazy World differs from these in
favouring talkies over the team's silent
work (represented only by scenes
from *Bacon Grabbers* and a fleeting
glimpse of *Leave 'Em Laughing*) and
in taking editorial licence. An example: key sequences of *Beau Hunks*
have the order of events completely
and unnecessarily rearranged. A

referred to as 'that gentleman over
there', while the dockside floozies of
Our Relations are introduced as 'two
charming and refined young ladies'.
Women in particular are greeted with
profound courtesy and receive the
best of Ollie's southern manners. Ollie
makes frequent use of his full, three-
barrelled name and much of his
genteel background may be found
humorously exaggerated within his
screen work. The most extreme example is perhaps his masquerade as
'Colonel Bixby' in *Jitterbugs*. John
McCabe (*qv*) once described Babe's
real-life courtliness on an occasion
when he visited the comedian's dressing room in the company of a lady:
'The only word I can think of is "gallant"... she was no-one special, no
celebrity, but she was to him. She was
a lady. He regarded her as he regarded
all women - except floozies - as a lady,
so he treated her that way'. It is Ollie
who usually takes the lead in social
matters, introducing them to
strangers with his customary 'I'm Mr
Hardy, and this is my friend Mr
Laurel', while constantly reminding
Stanley to remove his hat. Stan would
like to be as adroit but his naïvety

forbids it, as in his inexplicable habit
of addressing gentlemen as 'ma'am'.
Both comedians favoured what was
then an only slightly dated dignity in
choice of costume, particularly the
wing collars and bowler hats. In person, they would greet friend and fan
alike with consideration.

(See also: Characters; Costume;
Hardy, Emily; Hats; Letters)

COURTWRIGHT, WILLIAM
(1848-1933) (Laurel & Hardy films
qv)
Character actor who plays the departing butler in *Duck Soup* and Ollie's
uncle in *That's My Wife*. He is less
evident in talkies, among his appearances being a 1930 Our Gang comedy,
Teacher's Pet. Other films include
Mary Pickford's *My Best Girl*. 'Uncle
Billy' was originally a Shakespearian
actor and prepared his own marble
gravestone in advance, inscribed
'William Courtwright, noted actor'.
He married his third wife when the
bride was over 70.

(See also: Our Gang)

Rychard Cramer (in trilby) is apprehended in Saps at Sea

CRYING (Laurel & Hardy films *qv*)
One of the most famous of Laurel mannerisms, the cry, is also that which he disliked the most. It remained in his repertoire partly through Roach's insistence, but it is clear that he recognized its popularity among audiences. One of the childlike qualities Roach always considered essential to the great comedians, the Laurel cry would initially accompany any great disaster, but it would in time come to represent fear and confusion. The Fox writers understood neither its underlying principle nor its necessary brevity. In *A-Haunting We Will Go* Stan is compelled to weep at great length, during both the sabre cabinet sequence and elsewhere (he should not get tearful about the leading lady, as he does here and in *Great Guns*). Children often resort to tears after committing some dreadful misdemeanour, and when chastized for drinking Ollie's share of a soda in *Men O'War*, Stan launches into instant waterworks. There are a few instances in which Ollie joins the tears: as a heart-broken bandit early in *Fra Diavolo* and when listening to night-club singer Frank Holliday (*qv*) in *Blotto*; while the Fox writers misplaced the idea once more by having them sob uncontrollably after being forced to betray their friend in *Great Guns*. Ollie rarely cries outside of these joint efforts, a notable exception being in *The Fixer-Uppers* when he is in genuine fear for his life. He is close to breaking down in *Helpmates* but Stan begins to cry instead. A few tears are shed during the solo films, as when his artist character in *Hungry Hearts* (*qv*) has to choose between love and wealth. Otherwise the childlike principle remains; in a flashback from Billy West's *Playmates*, Babe is seen bawling in best nursery fashion.

(See also: Characters; Children; Laughing; 20th Century-Fox; West, Billy)

decision to chronicle the team's repeated use of specific props (cars, doors, and so on) is fine in principle, but when applied to physical film results only in a fast intercutting that is alien to the team's methods. This surprising disregard for Laurel & Hardy's slower, subtler visual humour is suggested further by the addition of gratuitous sound effects of the type favoured by the Three Stooges, notably when a bulb horn is dubbed over an extract from *The Bohemian Girl*. Jerry Fielding's music replaces the Roach studio themes, sacrilege to some and serving in any case to date this compilation to the mid-1960s. Narrators Garry Moore and Bill Scott are at least given worthwhile comments, not least when describing Laurel & Hardy as 'two funny gentlemen - and two funny, gentle men': a pity that such sensitivity could not have been displayed elsewhere.

(See also: *Best of Laurel & Hardy, the*; Compilations)

CRIMINALS (all films *qv*)
When a criminal element surfaces in the Laurel & Hardy films, it is unlikely to be represented by the boys themselves. The most obvious of cutthroats is the title character of *Fra Diavolo*, whom they meet after becoming bandits through economic necessity. Stan and Ollie are forced into crime by a policeman in *Night Owls*, while their pocket-picking activities in *The Bohemian Girl* are again expected of them by the gypsy band. They are imprisoned in *Pardon Us* under the soon-defunct Prohibition law, and are in *The Hoose-Gow* merely for 'watching a raid'. We are unaware of their transgressions in *The Second Hundred Years* but assume them to have been minor. It is essential that archetypal good guys Stan and Ollie should at times encounter those guilty of blackmail, murder (both *qv*) or other crimes. They are plainly unable to deal with such characters, even as policemen in *The Midnight Patrol*, and are easy prey for gangsters in *Our Relations*. The gangster motif is overworked in the Fox films but at least has a twist in *Jitterbugs*. Preferable is the comic criminal typified by Walter Long (*qv*) in earlier exploits such as *Going Bye-Bye!*.

(See also: Confidence Tricks; Policemen; Prison; 20th Century-Fox)

CROSBY, BING
See: Gambling; Golf and *Riding High*

CUCKOO (Laurel & Hardy films *qv*)
A film in the BBC TV *Omnibus*
series, first screened in December
1974 with a repeat the following year.
This major project remains a key work
among Laurel & Hardy documentaries, offering constructive
examination (not analysis) of well-
chosen clips, intelligent narration
(delivered by Britain's top double-act,
Morecambe and Wise), appropriate
stills and, perhaps of the greatest
value, interviews with surviving
friends, relatives and colleagues. Many
of these are no longer with us: producer Hal Roach; Babe's widow
Lucille; composer T. Marvin Hatley;
Jean 'Babe' London; early Laurel producer Joe Rock (all *qv*); journalist
Kenneth Tynan, whose 1950s review
of their stage act remains among the
better tributes; and documentary-
maker Basil Wright (*qv*), always one of
the team's champions in the UK.
Others include actress Dorothy
Granger, biographer John McCabe,
mime artist Marcel Marceau (all *qv*),
critic Dilys Powell and comedians
Dick Van Dyke, Jerry Lewis (both *qv*),
Bob Monkhouse and Spike Milligan.
At least 40 of the Laurel & Hardy
films are incorporated, if only through
momentary fragments. Some are presented more than cleverly: *Angora
Love* and *Be Big* are intercut during a
routine common to both films, while
Ollie's request to see 'the future Mrs
Hardy' (in *Oliver the Eighth*) precedes
an interview with his widow. Footage
of *Our Wife* is mixed with home movie
film of Babe London with Stan
Laurel, seemingly watching themselves on TV. Other peripheral
footage includes colour home movies
of an older Laurel playing with Laurel
& Hardy marionettes, amateur film of
their 1932 UK trip, 1947 coverage of
the team's visit to the Romney, Hythe
and Dymchurch Railway plus a
glimpse of Laurel solo in *The Noon
Whistle* (1923). Flaws are that Laurel's

birthdate is given as 1895 instead of
1890 (common in earlier publicity)
and footage from *Come Clean*, showing the pair acting like children, is
used with the explanation for their
behaviour deleted. The post-Roach
output is treated very sweepingly,
although there are many *aficionados*
who would encourage this trend. The
programme, written and produced by
Robert Vas, attracted much favourable
attention in its day and one can only
lament its subsequent disappearance.

(See also: Births; Characters;
Documentaries; *Goon Show, the*;
Home movies; Marriages; Newsreels;
Reviews; Sawmills; Television)

CURRIER, RICHARD (1892-1984)
Head of Roach's editing department,
1920-32. He is credited on almost
every release of that period for contractual reasons, although most Laurel
& Hardy comedies were edited by
Bert Jordan (*qv*). Another victim of
Henry Ginsberg, who was probably
responsible for forcing H. M. Walker
(*qv*) out of the studio, Currier later
worked at Paramount, Monogram
plus another stint at Roach before
establishing his own editing company.

(See also: Hal Roach Studios, the)

CUSHING, PETER
See: *A Chump at Oxford* and Stand-
ins

CUSTARD PIES
See: *The Battle of the Century* and
Slapstick

D

DANCE OF THE CUCKOOS
See: Music

DANCING (all films *qv*)
There are various dance routines throughout the films with a musical angle, notably the operas (*qv*), *Pick A Star* and *Swiss Miss*. *The Dancing Masters* has the team in that very occupation but their best-known excursions into terpsichory are the saloon dance from *Way Out West* and the similarly casual steps in *The Music Box* and *Bonnie Scotland*. Mr and 'Mrs' Hardy create a disturbance on the dance floor during *That's My Wife*, but Hardy's real-life grace is more apparent in two lesser-known films, *Zenobia* and *Jitterbugs*.

(See also: Songs)

THE DANCING MASTERS
(Laurel & Hardy film)
Released by 20th Century-Fox, 19 November 1943. Produced by Lee Marcus. Directed by Malcolm St Clair. 63 minutes.
With Stan Laurel and Oliver Hardy, Trudy Marshall, Bob Bailey, Margaret Dumont, Matt Briggs, Charles Rogers, Daphne Pollard.

At the 'Arthur Hurry' School of Dancing, its proprietors, Stan and Ollie, are teaching ballet and folk dance. Gangsters arrive with 'insurance' as part of a protection racket. Ollie takes out a sizeable policy on Stan, but the crooks are apprehended on leaving the premises. Ollie has good reason to seek cash; their only

regular fees are from Trudy Harlan (Trudy Marshall) whose boyfriend, Grant (Bob Bailey) works for her father's munitions factory. Grant has secretly been working on a ray gun that could help the war effort; he is opposed not just by Mr Harlan (Matt Briggs) but by George Worthing (Allan Lane), Harlan's choice for Vice-President and son-in-law. Grant is dismissed from the factory on a flimsy pretext but accepts Trudy's invitation to visit that evening. Grant, Stan and Ollie visit the Harlan residence while George and Trudy's parents are travelling to Washington. Grant's trousers are soaked when he attempts to open a bottle of ginger ale; they are still drying when the householders return unexpectedly. Grant's trousers are returned and he is ordered from the house. Stan and Ollie have taken refuge upstairs, hiding under the Harlans' twin beds. They make their escape after the Harlans have retired for the night; Ollie drags a carpet throught the window, pulling Mr Harlan and his bed into a lily pond. The next morning, Stan and Ollie are faced with paying their school's back rent or being evicted by noon; Stan persuades Ollie to withdraw their 'nest egg' of $300. This done, they are lured into an auction room by the promise of something for nothing, but are persuaded to bid for a clock by a lady who has to return home for her money. The lady does not reappear and the boys are left with an unwanted clock for precisely $300. They depart with the clock, which is

The Dancing Masters: *'Class dismissed!'*

destroyed by a truck when Stan pauses to retrieve his hat. Trudy arrives at the boys' home, asking them to stand in for Grant when demonstrating the ray gun to her father. Stan impersonates a foreign inventor with Ollie as his representative. The display works well enough until Stan turns the gun on Harlan's house and allows the machine to overheat to the point of explosion. Grant, watching from nearby, intervenes and the ruse is discovered. Needing money to help Grant, Ollie remembers his insurance on Stan. Acquiring a banana from a street vendor, Ollie places the skin in Stan's path in the hope of his partner breaking a leg; Ollie takes the fall himself. In the meantime, George approaches Harlan with the idea of buying out Grant for a small sum or, if necessary, stealing the invention. Harlan finally realizes George's dishonesty and throws him out, determined now to finance Grant's ray gun. Trudy tells Grant the good news and they set off to find Stan and Ollie. The boys are heading for a seaside funfair, Ollie having met a man who collected his insurance after a roller-coaster accident. The bus on which they are travelling is evacuated at the sight of an apparently mad dog; Stan tries to control the runaway vehicle as Ollie is trapped on the upper deck. Stan is thrown off while Ollie remains aboard, facing a bus ride on a roller-coaster. After a mighty crash, Ollie lands in hospital with his own leg broken.

The convoluted synopsis can only hint at the tawdry miscellany that is *The Dancing Masters*. Reworkings of earlier material abound in the Fox series but this entry combines more than the others put together: elements of *Thicker Than Water*, *County Hospital*, *The Battle of the Century*, *Block-Heads* and *Dirty Work* (all *qv*) may be found, stitched together without cohesion and separated by such unsuitable (and ancient) routines as creating a mess to demonstrate a vacuum cleaner before realizing there is no power. This ragbag approach is typified by plot elements that disappear midway and a finale consisting of a throwaway verbal gag. Another pointer to the film's fragmented nature is that no fewer than four single-reel extracts were released to the home movie market without any obvious connection between them. *The Dancing Masters* is of interest mostly for the supporting cast: Robert Mitchum (*qv*), as a 'B'-picture gangster; Trudy Marshall (*qv*), who worked well with Laurel & Hardy; two Roach faces, Daphne Pollard and Charles Rogers (both *qv*); and Margaret Dumont, by then cast adrift from the Marx Brothers (*qv*) and accepting minor work such as this and Abbott & Costello's *Little Giant*. As Mrs Harlan, Miss Dumont expresses surprise at her husband's concealed bar; she would in reality have recognized the set, a leftover from her sequence with W. C. Fields deleted from the previous year's *Tales of Manhattan*. At the time of writing, *The Dancing Masters* has the distinction of being the team's only 1940s feature never to have been shown on British TV; perhaps it's just as well.

(See also: Auctions; Bailey, Robert; Buses; Criminals; Dancing; Fairgrounds; Home movies; Insurance; Remakes; 20th Century-Fox; Video releases)

DANTE THE MAGICIAN
See: Magicians

DARLING, W. SCOTT (1898-1951)
Ontario-born screenwriter whose career reaches back to the Al Christie comedies of the 'teens. William Scott Darling was brought in to script the last four Laurel & Hardy films at Fox, presumably in the belief that any comedy veteran would suit the team. He died in unusual circumstances, missing for more than a week before his body was found in the Pacific off Santa Monica.

DAVIDSON, MAX (1875-1950)
Berlin-born comedian specializing in Jewish humour who starred in his own series of silent shorts at Roach. He also supported other comedians, as in Mabel Normand's *The Extra Girl*, and, later, Charley Chase entries such as *Long Fliv the King* (which also features Oliver Hardy). Davidson's *Call of the Cuckoos* (*qv*) features Laurel & Hardy, Chase and James Finlayson as guests; the compilation *Laurel & Hardy's Laughing Twenties* (*qv*) incorporates footage from this and other Davidson films. Talkie appearances are less common; two examples are *Itching Hour* (1931) and *Roamin' Wild* (1936). Despite its essentially sympathetic approach, his characterization tends to discourage revivals; a pity, as his gags are not exclusively ethnic and

Max Davidson and an unwieldy burden in his 1928 two-reeler, Dumb Daddies. *The sack contains a store dummy*

are of a high standard.

(See also: Blystone, John G.; Chase, Charley; Finlayson, James; Normand, Mabel; Race; Sleeper, Martha; *Thirty Years of Fun*)

DAYS OF THRILLS AND LAUGHTER
(20th Century-Fox 1961)
Robert Youngson (*qv*) changed direction somewhat in his third feature compilation, incorporating action sequences as well as comedy. The former comprises highlights from serials with Pearl White, Houdini and others, plus a potted version of Fairbanks' *Wild and Wooly* (1917). The latter includes Sennett material from the 1920s, Chaplin, Charley Chase and, especially, Snub Pollard (all *qv*), the last of whom Youngson seems to have been attempting to promote as he had Laurel & Hardy in the earlier *Golden Age of Comedy* (*qv*). The 'Thrills and Laughter' elements are combined in Monty Banks' *Play Safe* (1923), in which Banks abandons his situational style in favour of an impressive locomotive chase. This sequence has since become somewhat clichéd through over-use, something attributable in part to the success of Youngson's film. Youngson's interests also extended into humour of an earlier age and from a different continent. *Days of Thrills and Laughter* breaks tradition by the inclusion of an early French

comedy, *The Bath Chair Man*, entertaining in itself, though more might have been made of the French influence upon Sennett and, by implication, American film in general. For all this adventurous spirit, certain elements are lacking, not least the fullness of orchestra familiar from earlier films. Laurel & Hardy are rather poorly represented on this occasion: Babe consuming sausages in Billy West's *The Hobo* and attempting to bathe a child in the 1926 Roach comedy *Say It With Babies*, and Stan portraying a zealous salesman in *Kill Or Cure*. This is rather a pity, as *Days of Thrills and Laughter* is one of the best-constructed of Youngson's films.

(See also: Banks, Monty; Children; Compilations; 20th Century-Fox; West, Billy)

DEAN, PRISCILLA (1896-1987)

New York-born actress, daughter of stage star May Preston Dean. She was on stage from the age of four (in *Rip Van Winkle*) and in films at 12. Early experience in Nestor comedies with Eddie Lyons and Lee Moran led to prominent roles in features, among them, *Under Two Flags*, *A Cafe in Cairo*, *The Virgin of Stamboul* and *The Speeding Venus*. By the late 1920s, her career had declined to the point where she became one of Roach's 'fading stars' (*qv*), appearing in *Slipping Wives* (*qv*), one of the first shorts in which both Laurel & Hardy featured.

(See also: Army, the; Parodies; Rawlinson, Herbert)

DEATHS

Oliver Hardy died on 7 August, 1957, at the age of 65; Stan Laurel followed him on 23 February, 1965, aged 74.

(See also: Births; Black humour; Doctors; Graves; Murder; Suicide)

DE BOTE EN BOTE

See: *Another Fine Mess* and *Pardon Us*

DELAIR, SUZY (b. 1916)

Singer, dancer and actress Suzy Delair became famous in her native France through café-concert, musical comedy and opera. Earlier films include *Le Dernier des Six* (1941), directed by her then husband, Henri-Georges Clouzot (best remembered for *The Wages of Fear* and *Les Diaboliques*); later seen in, among others, *Quai des Orfèvres*, *Lady Panama* and Laurel & Hardy's *Atoll K* (*qv*). Suzy Delair's sense of the risqué is suggested by her song 'Avec Mon Tralala', nominally about a bustle but clearly referring to the area beneath; she would be greeted with cries of 'Tra-la-la' at any public event. One evening Suzy was walking home with her husband, who jokingly suggested a display of her 'tralala' to the crowd; she quite happily obliged. This revealing episode (recorded in a 1955 anthology of *Men Only*) is in keeping with the woman who threatened a Lysistrata-type strike in the event of a future war. As the *Men Only* scribe has noted, there has not been a major war since.

(See also: France; Risqué humour)

DELETED SCENES (all films *qv*)

The process of editing and fine-tuning after previews (*qv*) would sometimes lead to the deletion of

Dentists: Stan as nervous patient in Leave 'Em Laughing

Deleted scenes: part of the jettisoned first reel of Two Tars

whole routines. Few such deletions survive from the Laurel & Hardy comedies (see **Out-takes**) but stills often exist of these lost moments. The planned midget routine from *Their Purple Moment*, is a prime example, as are the reshot segments of *Pack Up Your Troubles*. A few others: *Any Old Port* loses all its intended scenes with the team onboard ship, while both *Bonnie Scotland* and *The Bohemian Girl* are minus a routine where Ollie lands in a tub of water. English copies of *Pardon Us* dispense with an excellent sequence (fortunately extant in the Spanish copy) wherein Walter Long (*qv*) has designs on the Warden's daughter during a prison fire; Laurel & Hardy save the girl when she leaps from an upstairs window, but permit Long to hit the ground. Stills from *Two Tars* show that its deleted first reel included a routine with Laurel & Hardy at a shoeshine stand. *Bacon*

Kay Deslys on the downward slide in Their Purple Moment

Grabbers does without the 'put-the-rice-in-the-radiator' business (reportedly a true-life experience of Charlie Hall [*qv*]) used later in *The Hoose-Gow*; while for *Our Relations*, the comedians filmed an unused shaving routine as 'Alf' and 'Bert' plus a reworking of *Two Tars*.

(See also: Foreign versions)

DELFONT, LORD BERNARD
See: Salaries, Stage appearances and Television

DENTISTS
(Laurel & Hardy films *qv*)
As William K. Everson (*qv*) has observed, there is humour in pain, something obtained efficiently through the dentist's chair. Chaplin in *Laughing Gas* and W. C. Fields in *The Dentist* typify the approach, while a Laurel solo film of 1923, *White Wings*, includes Stan's attempt at sideshow dentistry. Laurel & Hardy's *Leave 'Em Laughing* incorporates a dentistry routine that was later reworked into the 1931 feature *Pardon Us*. No further dentist routines enter the Laurel & Hardy repertoire, probably as a result of the sudden death in 1933 of Laurel's brother, Teddy Jefferson, while undergoing dental treatment. It may be noted that from the early 1940s Stan Laurel suddenly acquired better dentition. Close examination of earlier films and stills reveal the absence of most of his teeth toward the back, but from this time on, they have been replaced (presumably by dentures) and his less in-character portraits reveal a greater tendency to smile with his teeth exposed. It seems possible that the familiar tight-lipped Laurel grin may have been born of a self-consciousness about his teeth. The team's friend and valet, Jimmy Murphy (*qv*) told an amusing anecdote concerning the loss and replacement of his own teeth while in their employ: when he defended Laurel in a night-club argument, Murphy's teeth were knocked out and duly replaced by a set of dentures inscribed 'Property of Laurel & Hardy Productions', which he was told should be returned if he left their service! Fortunately, Murphy kept the teeth for the rest of his life. Floyd Jackman, the team's occasional cameraman in silent days, eventually gave up the profession for a career in dentistry. One can only speculate on whether his decision was influenced by seeing *Leave 'Em Laughing!*

(See also: Cameramen; Doctors; Jefferson, Arthur; Laurel, Mae; Laurel & Hardy Feature Productions)

DERBIES
See: Hats

DESLYS, KAY (all films *qv*)
Chubby English-born actress from the stage; in films from 1923. She is one of the floozies in *Their Purple Moment* and *We Faw Down* and Mrs Hardy in *Should Married Men Go Home* and *Perfect Day*, among others. Her best-remembered scene is that in *Below Zero* when she gives buskers Laurel & Hardy money to 'move on a couple of streets'.

(See also: Women)

DETECTIVES
(Laurel & Hardy films *qv*)
Laurel & Hardy first acquired their usual costumes as the detectives of whom it was asked *Do Detectives Think?* Stan solo had in 1925 starred as *The Sleuth* and assumes the role unofficially in *Sailors, Beware*. Others are on the trail in Laurel's solo films *A Man About Town* (*qv*) and *Kill Or Cure*. Detectives of various types appear in *Forty-Five Minutes From Hollywood*, *Bacon Grabbers*, *The Laurel-Hardy Murder Case*, *The Stolen Jools*, *Pardon Us*, *Come Clean* and *Pack Up Your Troubles*. Prominent in such roles was Eddie Baker, who is reported to have taken up the profession in preference to acting; while *Murder Case* is investigated by Fred Kelsey (*qv*), archetype of police detectives. The clichéd scripts forced upon the team during wartime are full of such characters. Stan and Ollie become private eyes in *The Big Noise* and *The Bullfighters*.

(See also: Female impersonation; Judges; Policemen; 20th Century-Fox)

THE DEVIL'S BROTHER
See: *Fra Diavolo*

DIALOGUE (all films *qv*)
In his 1968 study, *Laurel & Hardy*, Charles Barr noted the team's advantage over many silent contemporaries in having at least a use if not a need for dialogue. Certainly their interaction encouraged a degree of chat that would have seemed gratuitous from such loners as Chaplin and Keaton. From the introduction of talkies, Laurel & Hardy decided to remain primarily visual, but seemed willing to intersperse more than just functional speech. Their talkie debut, *Unaccustomed As We Are*, launches almost immediately into a dialogue routine with Thelma Todd (*qv*), and is followed shortly by a very noisy lecture from Mae Busch (*qv*). Despite this, they talk with comparative infrequency though some of their exchanges have passed into legend:

Beau Hunks:
Ollie: Didn't I just tell you I was going to be married?
Stan: Who to?
Ollie: Why, a woman of course. Did

Donald Dillaway as the boys' army buddy in Pack Up Your Troubles

DILLAWAY (OR DILLOWAY), DONALD (1905-82)

Appeared with Laurel & Hardy in *Pack Up Your Troubles* (*qv*) as the boys' army buddy, Eddie Smith. According to an obituary in *The Laurel & Hardy Magazine*, New York-born Dillaway began his stage career when only 12, entered talking pictures in the 1930 Marie Dressler-Wallace Beery vehicle *Min and Bill* and remained a close friend of the Laurel family after working with the duo. Other films include *Body and Soul*, *Cimmaron* and Capra's *Platinum Blonde* starring Jean Harlow (*qv*). He also appeared in *The Strange Love of Molly Louvain*, as did Rychard Cramer (*qv*) and was later a talent scout for RKO.

(See also: Capra, Frank; Periodicals)

DIRTY WORK

(Laurel & Hardy film)
Released by M-G-M, 25th November 1933. Produced by Hal Roach. Directed by Lloyd French. Camera: Kenneth Peach. Two reels.
With Stan Laurel and Oliver Hardy, Lucien Littlefield, Sam Adams.

Chimney sweeps Stan and Ollie arrive to ply their trade at the home of Professor Noodle (Lucien Littlefield), an amiable lunatic who is about to fulfil his twenty-year quest for the secret of rejuvenation. They are admitted by the butler, Jessup (Sam Adams), a laconic wit who directs them to the chimney ('You'll find it standing against the wall'). They set to work as the Professor goes about his own eccentric business. A protective cloth is anchored to the mantelpiece with a clock and other ornaments. When the whole is deposited on Ollie, Stan is left below while Ollie climbs to the roof. Stan sets the clock chiming and must beat it into silence; next he sends the extended brush through the chimney, sending Ollie in turn through a fan-

you ever hear of anybody marrying a man?
Stan: Sure.
Ollie: Who?
Stan: My sister.

Me and My Pal:
Ollie: You know what a magnate is, don't you?
Stan: Sure, a thing that eats cheese.

The Fixer-Uppers:
Stan (answering the 'phone): Hello? (pause) It sure is.
Ollie: Well, who was it?
Stan: Oh, some fella having a joke... I said 'Hello' and the guy said 'It's a long distance from Atlanta, Georgia, and I said 'It sure is'...
Ollie: I wish there was a way to put a stop to those practical jokers!

On several occasions Stan presents a lucid idea but cannot repeat it on demand; the most famous example concerns their fish business from *Towed in a Hole*:

Stan: I know how we can make a lot more money... if we caught our own fish, we wouldn't have to pay for it; then whoever we sold it to, it'd be clear profit.

Ollie: Tell me that again.
Stan: Well, if you caught a fish... then whoever you sold it to, they wouldn't have to pay for it... then the profits would... go to the fish...

Less easy to quote but of equal reputation is the splendid moment in *Going Bye-Bye!* when Ollie, having first been handed a tin of condensed milk in lieu of the telephone, asks his caller to hold because 'my ear is full of milk'. Just as memorable is another telephone call, this time from *Helpmates*, in which Stan explains his absence from Ollie's party through having been bitten by a dog; he might even have contracted 'hydrophosphates'. Their most complex dialogue routine occurs in *Thicker Than Water*, when wife and landlord quickly regret having asked about some missing money; indicating Ollie, Stan says 'I gave it to him', from which point its travels become a baffling maze.

(See also: Black humour; *Brats*; Catch-phrases; Characters; Crying; Leno, Dan; Records; Reviews; Sound; Telephones; Walker, H. M.)

light. Ollie returns, hauling both brush and Stan to roof level. 'Don't push it up until I tell you' says Ollie, pushing Stan back down. The lowest extension is broken in his descent. Stan replaces it with a shotgun, which blows all the way through the chimney, bringing down a passing duck. Stan climbs to the fanlight, opening it just in time to launch Ollie into a greenhouse. Amid the garden sprinklers, Ollie demands re-entrance. The Professor is still experimenting, this time achieving a 'half-drop' of some bizarre fluid by means of a pair of scissors. Ollie is let in through the front door: 'I have nothing to say', he tells Stan, returning to the roof. The brush extension is poked into Ollie's eye; when he shoves it back, the still-attached shotgun sends another bullet flying. In the ensuing squabble, Ollie is pulled into the fireplace, where bricks descend on to his head, one by one. The brush has punctured the piano; the butler is covered in soot. 'Somewhere, an electric chair is waiting', says he, exiting. Further squabbling brings Ollie another torrent of bricks. They start to clean up, but Stan digs a shovel into the carpet. Chastized, he imitates Ollie's 'I have nothing to say', earning a shovel over the head. Another whack follows the disclosure that Stan has been shovelling soot into Ollie's trousers instead of a sack. The Professor, his jubilance punctuated by a chicken-like cluck, has completed his experiment; Jessup, who has gone to take a bath (Stan: 'He went somewhere to look for an electric chair') is unavailable to witness the spectacle of a duckling being returned to the egg stage. The boys look at each other with doubt as the Professor goes to find Jessup, his intended human specimen. In his absence the boys decide to try the experiment on a fish; Ollie, holding the entire beaker, leans over the vat but Stan, fetching an eye-dropper, knocks him in. After much bubbling, Ollie emerges as a chimp. Stan's plea for a response is met with the expected reply: 'I have nothing to say!'

The joint offspring of *Habeas Corpus* and *Hog Wild* (both *qv*), *Dirty Work* is one of those interesting films in which a preponderance of slapstick is tempered by the team's characters. Their alternate pushing and shoving plus Ollie's petulant refusal to speak to Stan epitomizes the childlike aspect of their portrayals. The science fiction motif, more typical of the Three Stooges (albeit much earlier), provides unusual territory for the comedians, while a hint of Babe's heritage emerges when, asked where Jessup is, he replies 'about 35 miles south-east of Augusta, Georgia'. The film's undoubted highlight is the beautifully-timed scene where Ollie, sitting in the fireplace, patiently accepts each single brick as it strikes his head; believing the assault to have finished, he looks up, only to receive still another. A small tableau recreates the scene in the fireplace of the Stan Laurel pub in Ulverston. Often overlooked, particularly when juxtaposed to *Busy Bodies* (*qv*) (its immediate predecessor in release), *Dirty Work* is one of the most rewarding Laurel & Hardy sound shorts.

(See also: Animals; Births; Businessmen; Catchphrases; Characters; Dialogue; Hardy, Emily; Littlefield, Lucien; Reissues; Seawright, Roy; Shotguns; Titling)

DISNEY, WALT (1901-66)
Animation's most famous name. Walt Disney's regard for Laurel & Hardy was such that he permitted the use of Mickey Mouse and his Three Little Pigs theme ('Who's Afraid of the Big Bad Wolf?') in the team's operetta, *Babes in Toyland* (*qv*), itself remade by Disney in 1961. Stan and Ollie caricatures appear in several Disney cartoons and both contributed to M-G-M's *Hollywood Party* (*qv*). It is said that Stan Laurel approached Disney to animate the horse for the finale of *The Flying Deuces* (*qv*), without success.

(See also: Animation; Bletcher, Billy)

DOCTORS, NURSES (all films *qv*)
Of the eccentric medics practising in the Laurel & Hardy films, perhaps the most fondly regarded is James Finlayson (*qv*) or, to be precise, Dr J. H. Finlayson, whose patent 'lung-tester' (an enormous balloon) diagnoses Ollie's 'Hornophobia' in *Saps at Sea*. The enigmatic 'Canis Delirius' (or 'nervous shakedown', as Stan puts it) is best treated in humans by a veterinary surgeon, or so it seems in *Sons of the Desert* (Ollie: 'Why did you have to get a veterinarian?' Stan: 'Well, I didn't think his religion would make any difference'). Billy Gilbert (*qv*) treats Ollie's gout in *Them Thar Hills*, despite the devastating consequences of his prior encounter with the same patient in *County Hospital* (Dr Gilbert spends part of the time hanging from a top-floor window). Another of Mr Hardy's hospital stays, in *Thicker Than Water* includes a bungled blood transfusion that leaves Laurel & Hardy 'all mixed up'. Ollie would appear in hospital again in *The Dancing Masters* and the stage sketch *Birds of a Feather* (*qv*). In real life, Stan Laurel's last joke was made to a hospital nurse. Shortly before the end, he told the nurse that he would have preferred to have been out skiing. 'Do you ski, Mr Laurel?' she asked. 'No,' replied her patient, 'but I'd rather be doing that than having all these needles stuck in me!'

(See also: Deaths; Dentists)

DOCUMENTARIES
Television has explored the topic of Laurel & Hardy on more than one occasion. In the early 1970s, Granada TV's *Clapperboard* presented a worthwhile half-hour on the team, in a quality series on cinema that deserved better than its children's slot. The programme returned to the topic in

1979, in an edition tied in to the first British convention of the Sons of the Desert society (*qv*). Another children's series, BBC TV's *Jackanory*, abandoned its storytelling format for one week during 1973 in order to profile specific comedians. Presenter for that week was the team's fellow Water Rat, Ted Ray; Laurel & Hardy appeared in the third episode. BBC TV's *Omnibus* series followed late in 1974 with an entry titled *Cuckoo* (*qv*). The very beginning of 1991 saw commercial TV's equivalent with London Weekend's *South Bank Show* somewhat belatedly commemorating the Laurel centenary with another team profile. An apparent restriction in the film footage available was countered in some measure by some informative interviews and worthwhile comments. Italy's RAI station has presented a multi-part examination of the team, while American TV's *The Laurel &*

Hardy Show has incorporated a Scrapbook section in which rarities and parallel Roach films have been presented. One major entry includes an adapted version of the team's 1954 *This Is Your Life* tribute, fleshed out somewhat by additional footage and stills. Documentaries to have appeared on video cassette include *Laurel & Hardy: The Real Story* and *Laurel & Hardy: Archive Rarities*. Despite the essentially visual nature of their humour, Laurel & Hardy have provided ample scope for radio documentaries. Arthur B. Friedman's *Turning Point* interview with Stan Laurel remains an important work, the discussion covering its subject's entire career and preserving Laurel's views on topics ranging from fan mail to the camera-speed for silent comedies. The programme was produced for the University of California, Los Angeles, whose contribution to the

preservation of film and related material has been exemplary. Tony Thomas interviewed Laurel in 1959 for the LP *Voices From The Hollywood Past*. A few years later, W. T. Rabe fashioned his extensive Laurel interview material into a programme that would later be adapted for use by Voice of America. Familiar to many overseas admirers by short-wave broadcasts, there were more priceless Laurel recollections and unique onstage recordings of the team. 1976 brought a documentary from BBC Radio 4, titled after McCabe's biography *Mr Laurel & Mr Hardy*. The programme, introduced by British entertainer (and occasional Laurel lookalike) Roy Castle, presented an effective team history combining relevant quotes with appropriate clips.

Do Detectives Think?: *our heroes face the maniacal 'Tipton Slasher'*

Michael Pointon, who wrote and compiled the programme, returned to the subject in a much later series titled *Funny That Way*. Hubert Gregg's *I Call It Genius* series for BBC Radio 2 covered similar ground in 1980, and a UK tour account called *Laurel & Hardy Slept Here* was broadcast on BBC Radio 4 in August 1987.

(See also: Biographies; Compilations; Impersonators; Interviews; Radio; Records; Rediscoveries; Stage appearances; Television; Video releases; Youngson, Robert)

DO DETECTIVES THINK?
(Laurel & Hardy film)
Released by Pathé Exchange, 20 November 1927. Produced by Hal Roach. Directed by Fred Guiol. Two reels. Silent.
With Stan Laurel, Oliver Hardy, James Finlayson, Noah Young, Viola Richard, Frank Brownlee.

Judge Foozle (Finlayson) sentences 'The Tipton Slasher' to hang, adding, indiscreetly, 'and I hope you choke'. The Slasher vows revenge and escapes, gaining entrance to Foozle's home by posing as the new butler. One of his first tasks is to greet the detectives Foozle has engaged for his protection, Ferdinand Finkleberry (Stan Laurel) and Sherlock Pinkham (Oliver Hardy). Their William Tell-style demonstration of target practice is enough to convince anyone of their incompetence, and when they retire for the night Foozle is fair game. While taking a bath, Foozle spots the butler approaching with a large scimitar. The house is awakened but the detectives are of little use until Foozle, falling from the stairs, appears with a horrible mask jammed over the back of his head. The terrified Slasher believes Foozle to be a ghost, and is led away. The police arrive to apprehend the killer, who has been locked in the cupboard where Pinkham had taken refuge. Pinkham, much the

worse for the encounter, blacks Finkleberry's eyes before they depart in a show of misplaced dignity.

Known through certain 8 and 16mm versions as *The Bodyguard*, *Do Detectives Think?* lost much of its reputation on the rediscovery of *Duck Soup* (*qv*). It had been believed that *Detectives* was the first film in which Laurel & Hardy portrayed their familiar characters, but *Duck Soup* usurped that status. This does, however, remain the earliest example of the team in usual costume, complete with bowler hats (customary for detectives of the period). Laurel's bowler is not the tall, flat-brimmed design of later films (and Hardy's moustache is a trifle large) but the hat-switching routine is present and the relationship between them is fully established. Titling in these early films retained the idea of silly character names; 'Mr Laurel and Mr Hardy' were still in the future. Some amendment to the pecking order of stupidity would also follow: *Do Detectives Think?* introduces Laurel as 'the world's second worst detective' and Hardy as 'the worst', rather than the other way around. Prints of this film can vary considerably in their quality. Older home movie copies from Britain tend to be adequate but the material available to American collectors via Blackhawk Films (*qv*) was of such a low standard that the company apologized for it on at least one occasion. When the Blackhawk range was later revived, new 16mm copies were struck from a virtually pristine original, comparable in quality to the superb footage used in the 1967 compilation *The Further Perils of Laurel & Hardy* (*qv*). The UK video edition seems to derive from a similar source. The concept of a vengeful murderer would undergo massive revision to become *Going Bye-Bye!* (*qv*). Connoisseurs of less relevant detail will savour the knowledge that 'The Tipton Slasher' is said to have been named after a character in Lincolnshire folklore.

(See also: Characters; Costume; Detectives; *Hereafter, the*; Graves; Hats; Home movies; Judges; Murder; Names; Night scenes; Race; Remakes; Teaming)

DOGS
See: Animals

DOORS (all films *qv*)
As comedy props, doors prove more than useful to Laurel & Hardy. Even a simple bell pull can bring disaster, as when in *From Soup to Nuts* Ollie rips out the whole fitting. A frequent gag consists of a door opening straight into Ollie's face, but others can be more elaborate. The long-lost silent *Hats Off* employs a routine with the team as salesmen scurrying to and fro between sets of duplex doors (its

Doors: Ollie pulls out the bell in From Soup to Nuts

descendant may be seen in the twin lift doors of *Come Clean*). Similar confusion between neighbouring houses appears in *Sons of the Desert*. Another silent, *Early to Bed*, sees a tipsy Ollie tormenting Stan by sneaking through the front doorway while Stan's back is turned, then locking Stan out. To compound the trick, Ollie reaches through a hatch in the door, ruffling Stan's hair. Best remembered is the team's inability to enter or leave a room without confusing themselves and everyone else. *Bacon Grabbers* and *Beau Hunks* share the motif of Laurel & Hardy nervously leaving a superior only to enter a cupboard, bathroom or whatever else a door can lead to before managing to make an exit. Burglars Laurel & Hardy spend much of *Night Owls* entering and locking themselves out of their victim's house, material revised in *Scram!* and for a later stage tour. More legal housebreaking takes place in *The Midnight Patrol* as policemen Laurel & Hardy batter down a door with a marble garden seat. Laurel logic insists that when transporting a wheelbarrow through a gate in *Babes in Toyland*, he must use the small door set in the gate to climb through, open the gate, wheel his load through, close the gate, then climb back in through the small door. Hardy

misfortune causes the descent of a skylight when he slams the door in *Saps at Sea*. Simple negligence means that in *Way Out West* Stan will fail to notice that Finlayson has answered the door, and continue to knock on Fin's head. Impracticality will compel Ollie to attach exercise equipment to a doorframe in *Angora Love*, bringing the entire structure down upon the landlord. The devastation of *Big Business* develops mostly from Stan's coat being jammed in Finlayson's front door. In *Blotto* Stan pauses by a doorway before continuing, taking the wrong side of the door and walking into the wall; this gag is repeated at greater speed in *Our Wife*. As hotel staff in *Double Whoopee*, Laurel & Hardy compete for tips by holding doors for guests. One of the most poignant (if absurd) moments in the team's films concludes *Helpmates* as Ollie, his house reduced to an open-air shell, asks the departing Stan to close the door: 'I'd like to be alone!'

(See also: Characters; *Goon Show, the*; Marx Brothers, the; *On the Spot*)

DOUBLE WHOOPEE
(Laurel & Hardy film)
Released by M-G-M, 18 May 1929.
Produced by Hal Roach. Directed by

Lewis R. Foster. Camera: George Stevens and Jack Roach. Story: Leo McCarey. Two reels. Silent.
With Stan Laurel and Oliver Hardy, Jean Harlow, Tiny Sandford, Charlie Hall, Rolfe Sedan, Charles Rogers, Captain John Peters.

'Broadway - Street of a Thousand Thrills' is also the location of a hotel awaiting its most distinguished visitor, a foreign Prince (Captain John Peters). As his car draws up outside, the entire lobby looks up to greet him. He is preceded by Stan and Ollie, who are taken for the Prince and his Prime Minister. They sign the register with great dignity, Ollie customarily regal and Stan characteristically inept; after much preparation Stan produces an X. Greeted by the manager, they hand him a letter introducing them as the new footman and doorman, 'the best we could do on such short notice'. The boys are quietly dispatched to get their uniforms as ceremonies divert to the correct recipient. The Prince reaches the lift but steps out to make a speech, just as a pudgy finger is seen pressing the lift button. The Prince continues on his way, straight into an empty lift shaft. Ollie descends, in doorman's uniform, taking his post oblivious of catastrophe. The vanished dignitary is retrieved, his vanity outraged and person considerably soiled. 'This would mean death in my country', he declares, in a manner suggesting it might also happen on Broadway. Another finger presses the button and the Prince returns to the lift shaft. This time Stan, an immaculate footman, makes his serene way to duty. Outside, Ollie tries out his brand new whistle. One blow summons a taxi driver (Charlie Hall) who, annoyed at the false alarm, departs. Stan goes about his task with enthusiasm, helping a guest with his overcoat but removing his shirt in the process. Ollie, meanwhile, is having trouble

Stan collects Ollie's tip in **Double Whoopee**

determining which set of doors to hold for departing guests; getting the wrong side again, he loses a tip to Stan. Annoyance grows when he inadvertently holds the door open for Stan; Ollie takes the quarter Stan has received but is forced to return it by a policeman (Tiny Sandford). The policeman departs but Ollie, having palmed the coin, throws it down a grating. The officer returns, compelling Ollie to replace the money from his own pocket. Ollie blows a raspberry, earning a nasty look. Stan discovers Ollie's whistle, producing a sound that brings back the cab driver. The irate cabbie detaches Ollie's whistle from its cord and stamps it flat. Next he tears Ollie's handkerchief in two, just as Stan bends to retrieve the whistle. Stan fears the obvious but is distracted when the cab driver tears the peak from Ollie's cap. Quarrels between himself and Ollie are forgotten as Stan rips the cab driver's hat so that its peak becomes a chinstrap. Ollie, laughing, has a button plucked from his uniform; the cabbie reaches for another but instead grabs the policeman's tunic. He departs with haste. Another cab brings a beautiful visitor (Jean Harlow), who receives Ollie's personal escort to the reception desk. Neither is aware that Stan has closed the cab door on her dress, leaving her spectacularly unclad. Stan tries to signal but has to rush to the desk. Ollie, horrified, removes Stan's coat, in which the girl scurries off; Stan is left in his longjohns. The boys begin to squabble, eye-poking and shin-kicking; this very soon spreads through the lobby, just in time for the Prince to receive a flying cake over his clean dinner jacket. Vowing to report this outrage to both the King and Queen, he plummets once more into the lift shaft just before Stan and Ollie descend, exiting with great dignity.

Double Whoopee tends to be remembered only for the sight of an undraped Jean Harlow (*qv*). Legend insists that she was even more visible on the first take, her remaining garb being so transparent that even seasoned technicians were shocked; despite the more opaque apparel of take two, her contribution is memorable. Harlow aside, *Double Whoopee* contains much of the best of Laurel & Hardy, exploring the full range of their characters from misplaced gentility to childish petulance in an environment ripe for the unwitting spread of chaos. Vanity is the chief target, some of it Ollie's, but more closely typified by the Harlow scene and the haughty lady who smears ink over her face after Stan flicks a pen into her compact. The most deflated ego of all belongs to the Prince, a Von Stroheim lookalike portrayed by the original's stand-in. His monocled Prussian aristocrat is a superb portrait, convincing even within the comic setting and a perfect counterpart to the misfortunes inflicted upon him. There is in existence a never-released version of *Double Whoopee* synchronized with dialogue in 1969. Voices are by Chuck McCann from a script by Al Kilgore (*qv*), both of them charter members of the Sons of the Desert club (*qv*).

(See also: Dubbing; *Golden Age of Comedy, the*; Lifts; Policemen; Royalty; Sedan, Rolfe; Taxis)

DOUGLAS, GORDON (1909-93)
Director, former gagman and extra at Roach. His 1936 Our Gang comedy *Bored of Education* won an Academy Award. Directed Babe in *Zenobia* (*qv*) and Laurel & Hardy in *Saps at Sea* (*qv*). Other Roach features include *Broadway Limited* and *First Yank Into Tokyo* (1942); best-known later for *Harlow* (1965) and *The Detective* (1968).

(See also: Harlow, Jean; Kelly, Patsy; Our Gang; Hal Roach Studios, the)

DREAMS (all films *qv*)
Very seldom employed by Laurel & Hardy, the dream motif serves to wrap up (rather disappointingly) *The Laurel-Hardy Murder Case* and *Oliver the Eighth*; Stan dreams of beautiful maidens after a blow in *Lucky Dog*, while another young lady in *The Bohemian Girl* has, of course, dreamt of her childhood home.

(See also: Songs)

THE DRIVER'S LICENCE SKETCH
Originally written by Stan for the team's appearance at a Red Cross benefit in 1940, this sketch was subsequently expanded for use during the 1947 tour. The opening gag, where Stan persistently interrupts Ollie's greeting to the audience (saying, eventually, 'You're standing on my foot') is preserved in at least one newsreel clip. The bulk of the action involves a cop interviewing Ollie, who wants to renew a driving licence inherited from his grandfather. The policeman, noting the name 'Oliver N. Hardy', is told the initial stands for 'Enry' ('and you spell the 'Holiver' with a 'ho'!'). 'You don't write 'Henry' with an N', insists the cop, to which Stan replies 'Of course you don't. You write it with a pencil'. Their address has recently changed, because the landlord wouldn't raise the rent ('Well we couldn't raise it, could we, Ollie?'). and it is revealed that Ollie has a driving conviction for speeding - on the pavement. The cop questions Ollie on his road sense, describing at great length a hypothetical emergency in which they must choose to hit either a train or an ambulance. Laurel & Hardy have helped themselves to the contents of his lunch box; 'Now!' declares the cop, as the startled pair spit crackers everywhere, 'which one would you hit?' Stan chooses the train, because 'we'd need the ambulance to get home in'. The cop refuses them licences, picks up a shotgun and chases them off. He trips over Ollie's cane, sending buckshot into the air; 'Why don't you watch where you're shooting?' shouts Ollie. Although rather obvious on

paper, *The Driver's Licence Sketch* took on new life in performance, as evidenced by the laughs audible in a rare sound recording. Dialogue predominates but room is still found for visual gags, mostly byplay with Ollie's cane and a splint on Stan's index finger. At one point the splint is transferred to Ollie's finger and, in retrieving it, Stan's hand jerks back into the policeman's face. Ollie replaces the cop's dislodged hat, placing it back-to-front. In all, the sketch is in keeping with Stan's music-hall roots and quite akin to the sketches devised by his former mentor, Fred Karno (*qv*). The complete text appears in *The Comedy World of Stan Laurel*.

(See also: Biographies; *Birds of a Feather*; Documentaries; Morton, James C.; Names; Newsreels; *On the Spot*; Policemen; Stage appearances)

DRUNKS
See: Alcohol

DUAL ROLES
The motif of an actor taking two or more parts is a theatrical tradition that was extended to the earlier days of trick films. Chaplin's stock company would often double up their roles as a matter of course (e.g. Henry Bergman as both an old woman and an artist in *The Immigrant*) while Chaplin portrayed twin characters in *The Idle Class* and *The Great Dictator*. Alec Guinness (*qv*) portrayed an entire family in *Kind Hearts and Coronets*, as did Fernandel in *The Sheep Has Five Legs*. More recently Bette Midler and Lily Tomlin have played sets of twins in *Big Business* (which is not a remake of the Laurel & Hardy film bearing that title!). Laurel & Hardy explored the theme in three films (all *qv*): *Brats* presents the team with small sons, each a replica of his father, by an illusion created by the construction of identical sets of differing sizes. *Twice Two* extends the idea into their having

identical twin sisters, with the result being achieved by the use of doubles, quick cutting and a small amount of split-screen, or 'matte', work. The feature-length *Our Relations*, while ambitious, again keeps matte effects to a minimum but combines cutting and back-projection with further use of doubles to produce a convincing effect, this time of twin brothers. Much earlier, Stan Laurel had appeared in *Twins*, a two-reeler produced by Joe Rock (*qv*). In *A Chump at Oxford* (*qv*), Stan assumes the identity of an English aristocrat, but this is more in the nature of an *alter ego* than a twin personage.

(See also: Maté, Rudolph)

DUBBING
(Laurel & Hardy films *qv*)
Although Laurel & Hardy's first talkies were remade in multiple-language versions, the more economic process of dubbing soon became standard. The comedians are said to have carried out the task themselves initially, reshooting minor scenes to accommodate signs translated into the appropriate language. There are stills from *Pack Up Your Troubles* in which their lunch wagon has been repainted with Spanish signwriting (this Spanish version, titled *El abuelo de la criatura*, is elusive, but is known to have been revived in Barcelona during the 1960s). Other voices were employed later, sometimes in specimens of hybrid editing similar to their own reshot versions (*Les deux legionaires* combines *Helpmates* with *Beau Hunks*). In many instances their tones were approximated quite reasonably, if somewhat caricatured, as in some German Super-8 prints. Audiences in Spain, amused by the dreadful pronunciation in the team's genuine foreign versions, demanded the withdrawal of efficiently-dubbed films in favour of editions deliberately redone in bad Spanish. Less conscious ineptitude has surfaced elsewhere, as in

the films noted many years ago by British enthusiast Malcolm Stuart Fellows on a visit to Turkey. He found Stan dubbed into high-pitched screeching and Ollie into morose growling. The international co-production *Atoll K* depends rather heavily on dubbing, its clumsiness varying in relation to the nationality of the print. Some domestic soundtracks have employed dubbing, as with the female characters from *Twice Two* and a 1932 comedy starring Our Gang (*qv*), *Choo-Choo*, in which a character yells in what is unquestionably Ollie's voice (another such dub, from *Hog Wild*, is used twice in Charley Chase's *Young Ironsides*). In *The Bohemian Girl*, Stan is heard singing in a high vocal, sounding rather like Rosina Lawrence (*qv*), followed by a bass reminiscent of Billy Bletcher (*qv*). Miss Lawrence's singing voice, apparently from a studio test of early 1936, replaces that of Jacqueline Wells (*qv*) in the film (Rosina Lawrence remained unaware of the fact until seeing the result for the first time, 50 years after its release!). An equivalent scene in *Way Out West* employs her talents once more, the bass being supplied this time by Chill Wills. Billy Bletcher's deep tones were used later for a midget in *Block-Heads*.

(See also: Chase, Charley; *Double Whoopee*; Foreign versions; Goon Show, the; Home movies; Midgets)

DUCK SOUP
(Laurel & Hardy film)
Released by Pathé Exchange, 13 March 1927. Produced by Hal Roach. Directed by Fred L. Guiol. Two reels. Silent.
With Stan Laurel and Oliver Hardy, Madeline Hurlock, William Austin, Robert Kortman, William Courtwright, Bobby Dunn.

The Sheriff (Robert Kortman) is rounding up vagrants to help fight forest fires. Two unwilling volunteers are Laurel & Hardy, whose flight from the scene takes them on a wild downhill ride on a stolen bicycle. They take refuge in a deserted mansion but the arrival of prospective tenants (Madeline Hurlock and William Austin) forces Ollie to pose as the owner and Stan as his maid. Their impersonation is barely convincing but succeeds until the unexpected return of the real owner. The pair are apprehended by the Sheriff and the final shot sees them swinging in midair at the mercy of an uncontrollable fire hose.

Considered lost for decades, *Duck Soup* resurfaced in the 1970s and in the process rewrote much of Laurel & Hardy history. Hitherto it had been assumed that their teamwork had evolved over a period of several months, but in this, their first Roach comedy together (barring *Forty-Five Minutes From Hollywood*, in which they share no scenes) they appear almost exactly in the format of their mature work. Their relationship towards each other is certainly familiar: Ollie gives the orders, Stan reluctantly takes them and neither has any brains. The key difference between this and their later films lies in their appearance, their vagrant status being perhaps overstated in costuming. As William K. Everson (*qv*) noted (in what was the first modern-day critique of this film), this applies to Hardy in particular, who in his 'gentleman tramp' role sports a top hat in lieu of a bowler, a monocle and a notably unshaven chin more typical of the villains he portrayed earlier in his career. Available copies of *Duck Soup* derive from two sources: one is a Belgian 35mm reissue with music and sound effects, the other a French 9.5mm home movie edition. No record survives of the English-language text, although translations have been made of the foreign subtitles. The Belgian text appears closer to the original than the French; the 16mm version issued by

Blackhawk Films (*qv*) derives from the latter copy and suffers from a rather literal translation. Each surviving edition of *Duck Soup* contains footage missing from the other. The opening scenes of the owner preparing for his trip and the closing shot of Laurel & Hardy with the hose are absent from the French version, while the Belgian material lacks a sequence in which a horrified Stan (dressed as the maid) has to prepare a bath for Madeline Hurlock (*qv*). A video edition issued in America during 1992 derives entirely from the Belgian material and has been translated effectively if not precisely from the foreign text. *Duck Soup* merits a further place in Laurel & Hardy history as an adaptation of a stage skit written by Laurel's father in 1908, *Home From the Honeymoon*. It proved such ideal material for the team that a talkie version was made in 1930, titled *Another Fine Mess* (*qv*). Studio supervisor Leo McCarey (*qv*) reused the title *Duck Soup* for the Marx Brothers (*qv*) in 1933; it was to be employed once more for an Edgar Kennedy short of 1940.

(See also: Austin, William; Bicycles; Courtwright, William; Dunn, Bobby; Foreign versions; France; Home movies; Jefferson, Arthur; Kennedy, Edgar; Kortman, Robert; Rediscoveries; Remakes; Servants; Teaming; Video releases)

DUELS

(Laurel & Hardy films *qv*)
The classic method of settling a dispute, duelling surfaces in several Laurel & Hardy-related films. The best is that in *The Fixer-Uppers*, where Charles Middleton (*qv*) shoots Ollie but fails to realize he has been using blanks. A prehistoric variant pits Laurel against Hardy in *Flying Elephants*, while it is Stan who accidentally finishes the sword fighting in *Fra Diavolo*.

(See also: Villains)

DUMONT, MARGARET
See: *Dancing Masters, the*

DUNN, BOBBY (1891-1966)
(all films *qv*)
Former Keystone Cop whose glass eye lent him a somewhat out-of-focus appearance. Dunn lost the eye during a stunt in which he was supposed to land in a barrel of water; unfortunately someone left a matchstick floating on top. His appearances include that of removal man in *Duck Soup*, telegraph boy in *Me and My Pal*, bartender in *The Bohemian Girl* and, best of all, the persistent pilferer who systematically denudes Laurel and Hardy's electrical store in *Tit For Tat*. He also played extra roles, as in *Bonnie Scotland*.

(See also: Hall, Charles)

DUNN, EDDIE (1896-1951)
(all films *qv*)
Actor and gagman in many Roach subjects, among them *The Hoose-Gow*, *Another Fine Mess*, *Pardon Us*, *Me and My Pal* (as the cabbie) and *The Midnight Patrol* (as the desk sergeant). Not related to Bobby Dunn (*qv*).

(See also: Taxis)

DURANTE, JIMMY
See: *Hollywood Party* and Keaton, Buster

EARLY TO BED

(Laurel & Hardy film)
Released by M-G-M, 6 October 1928.
Produced by Hal Roach. Directed by
Emmett Flynn. Camera: George
Stevens. Two reels. Silent.
With Stan Laurel and Oliver Hardy,
Buster the dog.

Stan and Ollie share their residence -
a park bench - with a dog. Fortunately
the postman knows where to locate
them, and delivers a letter to Ollie
informing him of a sizeable inheritance. Stan is heartbroken: 'What's to
become of me?' he asks. Ollie, ponder-
ing this for a moment, magnanimously
offers him the position of butler.
Wealth goes to Ollie's head, to be
joined on the night of his birthday by
a fair amount of alcohol. On arriving
home he teases Stan, locking him out
and scratching the back of his head
through a panel in the door. Once
inside, Stan is treated to an account of
his employer's wonderful evening followed by more general horseplay. A
hiccup betrays Ollie's inebriation and
a shocked Stan tries to put Ollie to
bed. His efforts culminate in losing a
wrestling match to Ollie; the
exhausted valet, abandoning the
effort, retires for the night but is
awakened when Ollie pours water into
his bed. Stan's resignation will follow
in the morning. When the moment
arrives for Stan's departure, Ollie will
not permit it. 'I'll make you fire me',
says Stan, angrily kicking his way
around the room. Ollie laughs until
Stan nearly breaks something of value.
Stan takes his chance and embarks on

a frantic round of destruction, Ollie
giving chase in a fruitless attempt to
save his valuables. His panic increases
when, after falling into a cake, Stan
appears to be foaming at the mouth. 'I
want blood, warm blood!' screams
Stan, taking a massive swing with a
poker. Ollie seeks refuge in a fountain,
decorated in a moment of vanity with
replica Hardy heads. Replacing one of
the heads with his own, he attempts to
simulate the flow of water from the
original by taking periodic mouthfuls.
Stan notices the irregular flow and
tries to beat Ollie's head back into
function. Eventually Stan's bewilder-
ment reduces Ollie to laughter and he
emerges, offering his hand in friendship. Stan accepts, and is pushed into
the fountain.

The mixed reputation of *Early to
Bed* reflects the seriousness with
which Laurel and Hardy admirers
take the team's relationship. Some
consider it disappointing while others
regard it as a major work. It is certainly unsettling to see Ollie so
thoroughly spoiled that he is willing
to destroy his friendship with Stan;
yet despite the unnecessary vindictive-
ness, his mistreatment of Stan remains
in the childlike mould expected of
their characters. Ollie's panic when
Stan turns the tables is, like a parallel
sequence in *One Good Turn* (*qv*), a
perfect reflection of a school bully
whose reign is unexpectedly terminated. *Early to Bed*'s final sequence
tends to inspire less resentment when
seen in isolation in the compilation
The Further Perils of Laurel & Hardy

Early to Bed: *Stan appears rabid after
falling into a cake*

(*qv*). William K. Everson (*qv*) has
traced the fountain gag to an earlier
Roach comedy starring Mabel
Normand (*qv*). For years, all copies of
the film in general circulation derived
from those issued by Blackhawk Films
(*qv*). Deterioration to the master is
evident (particularly at the end of reel
one), with all titles in the Blackhawk
version being replacements bearing
the company's logo. A more recent
version prepared for European video
and TV reinstates most of the originals in frozen frames, suggesting the
retention in the negative of what are
known as 'flash' titles, consisting of
one or at most a few frames of each.
Reinstated also are two shots of a cake
Stan has baked for Ollie's birthday,
bearing a written greeting to his old
friend.

(See also: Alcohol; Animals; Insanity;
Race; Servants; *Should Married Men
Go Home?*; Rebellions - by Stanley ;
Vagrancy; Video releases)

EARTHQUAKES

Despite a Californian setting, few
earth tremors disturb Laurel & Hardy
history: in *Block-Heads* (*qv*), a kitchen
explosion sends Stan hurrying from
the building, the stability of which he
tests in the mistaken belief that an
earthquake has occurred. The sudden
appearance of an island during a
storm in *Atoll K* is the nearest to a
terrestial disturbance elsewhere in the
Laurel & Hardy films. The real-life

tremor that rocked California in 1933 is commemorated by (probably faked) news film of W. C. Fields calmly leading people from the set of Paramount's *International House*: over at the Roach lot, Stan Laurel was relaxing with his stand-in, Ham Kinsey, declaring 'This is the life' just as the area began to shake!

(See also: Stand-ins)

EDITORS, FILM
See: Currier, Richard and Jordan, Bert

EDUCATION
(Laurel & Hardy films *qv*)
Both Laurel and Hardy strongly regretted their lack of formal education. To the end of his life, Stan believed he would have been a better comedian but for this lack: John McCabe (*qv*) recalls overhearing a 'phone conversation at the Laurel flat in Santa Monica, during which Stan chastized an aspiring young comic by saying 'Now listen, no argument. You came to me for advice, and I'm going to give it to you: finish your schooling, and get as much of it as you can. I didn't, and I bitterly regret it to this very day'. Stan, eager to get into show business, had left school at the earliest opportunity; Babe, despite his studio biography, had as little schooling. Stan's theatrical background, albeit with a father in theatre management, meant an education spread over various towns; variously Gainford, Bishop Auckland, Tynemouth and, eventually, Glasgow. At Bishop Auckland he attended the King James Grammar School, a boarding establishment. One of its masters, named Bates, engaged Stan as after-hours entertainer for himself and colleagues. In a tactical error, Stan interpolated his impression of a German teacher who had taken a dislike to the boy, an enmity magnified on seeing Stan emulate his habit of chewing a horizontally-placed pencil. As a favoured pupil, Stan's inadequacies in class tended to be overlooked; in Glasgow, his total

absence was disregarded. A move from Rutherglen School to Queen's Park Academy brought with it what Billy Bunter might call a 'wizard wheeze', consisting of ready-made absence notes in the form of complimentary tickets from his father's theatre. Stan had found the 'Complimentary' stamp, an item duly hidden once the ruse was discovered. Stan's father soon acquiesced to his son's aversion to school; Babe's mother was more determined. Her son's addiction to music and the stage was sufficient distraction for her to send him to a boarding school to the north of Atlanta. The 14-year-old remained for a while before escaping to Atlanta on 17 April 1906, just in time to catch a race riot of giant proportions. The affray was quelled by torrential rain and the boy, caked with mud, trudged along the railway lines to a local depot. The stationmaster cleaned him up and informed Mrs Hardy of her son's whereabouts. The contrite escapee returned on foot to his home in Milledgeville, where he convinced his mother of a desire to study music. He was sent to the Atlanta Conservatory of Music, but a preference for singing to illustrated slides in the local cinema brought a swift transfer to Georgia Military College. It had been trouble enough being fat in an ordinary environment, but at military school was even worse. It brought modest compensation on an occasion when the heavyweight pupil, weary of drilling, could not be moved when he decided to lie down. Running away from this establishment was easy, located as it was across the road from his mother's hotel. Grievance this time was inadequate food, a situation remedied by the consumption of 20 home-made biscuits. Typically, his best moment was a stage presentation by the undergraduates, a comic version of *Who Killed Cock Robin?* in which young Hardy, suitably costumed, intoned 'I am the bull!' in an incongruous high tenor. His next and last place of schooling was the lib-

eral-minded Young Harris College, Georgia, whose curriculum was much given to outdoor activity. On one trek, Hardy suggested his future career again by climbing a tree as if pursued and, once there, crying in best 'Preacher and the Bear' fashion 'Lawd, if you don't help me, don't help that bear!' From here he considered following his father's reputed profession by enrolling in law school, but was dissuaded by his eldest sister, Elizabeth, who considered him too comic. Roach publicists would later invent for him a tenure at the University of Georgia's Law School, to which the comedian adhered both from loyalty and a sense of insecurity over his scholastic neglect. At the Roach studio itself, Babe and Stan were back to basics in a schoolroom scene for *Pardon Us*, resembling Our Gang (*qv*) right down to the latter's signature tune. Much later their academic shortcomings were caricatured in dialogue for *A Chump at Oxford*, a film taking them to one of the world's most famous places of learning. During production in 1939, an unknown publicist manufactured a letter from the two comedians requesting an honorary degree from Buena Vista University, Iowa. In a polite refusal, the University expressed its belief that such honours should be earned rather than merely bestowed, a tenet since overturned by several other academic bodies. The initial request was almost certainly made without the comedians' knowledge, its literary style and signatures bearing no similarity to their own.

(See also: Hardy, Emily; Hardy, Oliver Sr.; Jefferson, Arthur; Music; Musichall; Publicity; Stage appearances; Vaudeville)

EDWARDS, RALPH
See: Television

EGGS (Laurel & Hardy films *qv*)
Leaving aside an early Laurel film titled *The Egg*, there are a number of

Laurel & Hardy sequences using this familiar comedy prop. One of their classic exchanges of violence, in the aptly-named *Tit For Tat*, culminates in shopkeeper Charlie Hall (*qv*) first sitting in a tray of eggs, before being showered with the contents of another crateful. A further exchange involving eggs may be found in *Air Raid Wardens*. An egg lands in the boys' collecting mug when they are busking in *Below Zero*; another, larger example houses a miniaturized Stan at the end of *A-Haunting We Will Go*. One of their most ingenious routines, in *The Live Ghost*, concerns a wager in which the victim proves he can place an egg in his mouth without breaking it. This done, a blow to the jaw breaks the egg. Aborted tricks in the team's magic act from *Hollywood Revue of 1929* involve a tray of eggs crushed during a squabble; a further egg is crushed before it can leave Stan's pocket. The *Revue*'s follow-up, *Hollywood Party*, has as its highlight a tit for tat egg battle between Laurel & Hardy and Lupe Velez (*qv*); this routine was later

reworked in *The Bullfighters*. Stan's on-screen diet leans heavily toward hard-boiled eggs, particularly when accompanied by nuts. These are his gifts to a stricken Ollie in *County Hospital* and when his friend rejects them, he consumes one with considerable flair, to the point of producing salt and pepper shakers from his pockets. In a sketch recorded during their 1932 tour, Stan is momentarily silenced when given an egg to eat, which is disposed of complete with shell. It was Laurel & Hardy who created the Water Rats' 'Golden Egg' award for the worst joke cracked at a meeting.

(See also: Food; Grand Order of Water Rats; *M-G-M's Big Parade of Comedy*; Records; Semon, Larry)

ELEPHANTS NEVER FORGET
See: *Zenobia*

ELLIS, PATRICIA (1916-70)
Actress who as Mrs Gilbert in *Block-Heads* (*qv*) was soaked with a bowl of

Patricia Ellis turns palmist in this publicity shot for Block-Heads

punch. She had auditioned for the role of Bo-Peep in *Babes in Toyland* (*qv*) nearly five years earlier. Active primarily in the 1930s, an early appearance was in Busby Berkeley's *42nd Street* (1933).

ENGLISHMEN
Until comparatively recently, the standard Hollywood view of Englishmen tended to be either that of a monocled 'silly ass' or a cap-touching Cockney. There are several in the Laurel & Hardy films, the former represented by William Austin (*qv*) and Charles Gerrard, the latter typified by Forrester Harvey (*qv*). Nat Clifford and Charlie Hall (both *qv*) could turn in a reasonable stage Cockney but were spared that task in the Laurel & Hardy films. Gerrard, the 'Lord Plumtree' of *Another Fine Mess* (*qv*), switches to the other stereotype as an asylum attendant in the 1930 *Dracula*. Stan Laurel, himself born in England,

contributes a 'What-ho!' type to a silent Our Gang (*qv*), while a later guest spot, *On the Loose* (*qv*), includes Claud Allister and John Loder as a brace of English gentlemen. Perhaps it was Laurel's influence that led to a large British presence at Roach; whatever the reason, the many UK talents (all *qv*) included Scotsman James Finlayson, Cambridge-born film editor Bert Jordan, Oxford-born writer Frank Butler plus British comics Charles Rogers, Jack Barty and Jimmy Aubrey. There were also several Australians, chiefly Mae Busch and Daphne Pollard.

(See also: Births; Guest appearances; Murphy, Jimmy; Music-hall; Stage appearances)

EVERSON, WILLIAM K. (b. 1929) Renowned film historian, British-born but in America for many years. He is a regular visitor to the UK, where his programmes of classic films are widely appreciated. He has been a consultant to TV series such as *Silents, Please* and *Movie Museum*, and also author of many film books, including *The Art of W. C. Fields*, *The Bad Guys* and *The Films of Hal Roach*. His *The Films of Laurel and Hardy* (1967), the first modern evaluation in English, is valuable for its perceptive analysis.

By kind courtesy of Robert G. Dickson

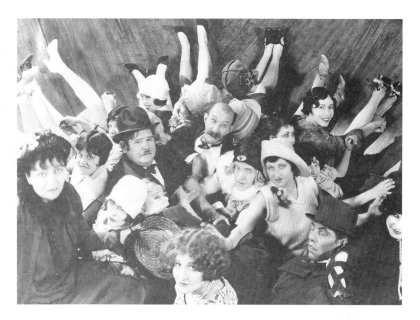

EVE'S LOVE LETTERS (1927) Stan Laurel's penultimate solo film, *Eve's Love Letters* also stars Agnes Ayres, one of the 'fading stars' (*qv*) employed by Roach when their fortunes were in decline. Miss Ayres is recalled mainly as Valentino's leading lady in *The Sheik* (1921). The letters of the title are addressed to 'Sir Oliver Hardy', though Babe is not present and his name seems to have been used as an in-house joke; this may explain in part the film's presence in earlier, less accurate Laurel & Hardy listings. Blackmail is in the air, and the butler, played by Stan, is engaged to help retrieve the letters. There is a football game over them, anticipating similar business in *The Finishing Touch*. The quick change motif of *Another Fine Mess* (*qv*) finds an ancestor in a scene where Stan and the heroine are dressed in identical vamp costumes, with Stan switching back to his own garb. Highlights are Stan wrestling an empty female costume and, on pretending to be shot, hearing angel voices and seeming to ascend into their company. Directed by Leo McCarey (*qv*), *Eve's Love Letters* is a well-paced farce, faltering only at its rather abrupt conclusion; many Roach films of the period are

Fairgrounds: tangled revellers in Sugar Daddies

similarly flawed, which is regrettable, considering the studio's superiority over most contemporaries.

(See also: Blackmail; Female impersonation; Hereafter, the; In-jokes; Servants; Solo films; Video releases)

THE EVOLUTION OF FASHION
See: *Just Nuts* and Vaudeville

'FADING STARS' (all films *qv*)
Hal Roach tried various means of attracting audiences while adding prestige to his product. One ploy was to use various big names whose fame, if not at an end, was certainly in decline. Some, such as Mabel Normand (*qv*) had made their reputations in comedy; others, notably Theda Bara, were dramatic stars whose Roach comedies tended to parody their earlier work. This frankly exploitative tactic would sometimes result in the actors receiving better offers from elsewhere, but was mostly an embarrassing indication of a faltering career. *Slipping Wives* pairs dramatic leads Priscilla Dean and Herbert Rawlinson (both *qv*) in a slapstick comedy that is frenetic even by the standards of the genre, while *Love 'Em and Weep* gives top billing to Mae Busch (*qv*), in a role far removed from the psychological dramas she had made with Erich von Stroheim. The necessity of hiring such names seems to have expired with the success of Laurel & Hardy's first comedies.

(See also: All-Star series; *Eve's Love Letters*; Hal Roach Studios, the; Finlayson, James; Teaming)

FAIRGROUNDS (all films *qv*)
The carnival atmosphere of a fairground, seemingly conducive to comedy, can just as easily prove too frivolous in itself for any humour to stand out. *Sugar Daddies* succeeds quite well as our heroes blunder their way through a cake-walk and a huge revolving drum. Laurel & Hardy make a guest appearance in the Pitts–Todd

short *On the Loose*, most of which takes the girls through what purports to be Coney Island. Ollie's most hair-raising time at a fair is in *The Dancing Masters*, where he is trapped on a roller-coaster.

(See also: Buses; Circuses)

FATTY'S FATAL FUN
See: Arbuckle, Roscoe 'Fatty' and *Laurel & Hardy's Laughing Twenties*

FEATURE FILMS
(Laurel & Hardy films *qv*)
Laurel & Hardy were exclusively in short subjects when loaned to M-G-M (*qv*) for *Hollywood Revue of 1929*; the same applied to the following year's *Rogue Song*, but they would be working on their own feature before 1930 was out. The Spanish version of *Chickens Come Home* was stretched to an hour by superfluous action and *Be Big* and *Laughing Gravy* were cobbled together as a feature for overseas. Their first real feature was *Pardon Us* which began life as a short but was expanded through financial necessity. Neither Stan nor Babe wished to enter the full-length field, and continued to regret making the move, but were compelled to do so by a growth in double-feature programmes and the growing encroachment of cartoon shorts. Indeed, from 1935 Roach confined them to full-length films, thereafter disposing of anyone deemed unsuited to features. British journalist Hannen Swaffer (in *Picturegoer*) hinted that the comedians had been goaded into *Pardon Us* by their wives, anxious to move into the Beverly Hills

district denied to those working in short subjects. This absurd notion was topped by his condemnation of the 'raspberry' noise recurrent in the film, not referred to by name (and this from a man unused to pulling punches) but noted as having occurred 27 times. This surprising prurience may explain why, in the following year's *If I Had A Million*, Charles Laughton's celebrated raspberry was replaced in Britain with a two-fingered salute, roughly equivalent to America's gesture with a solitary digit (*someone* must have considered it less offensive). *Pardon Us* received mixed notices but did well on release in 1931; later that year they made a four-reel subject, *Beau Hunks*, publicity for which encouraged exhibitors to play it as Laurel and Hardy's second feature. This hybrid format, hitherto reserved for a few foreign-language editions, provided only ungainliness and dull stretches and it is a wonder that Roach later returned to this 'streamlined' approach. The next authentic feature, *Pack Up Your Troubles*, was similar albeit with fewer favourable reviews. The main problem with both is construction, *Pardon Us* seeming like a two-reeler interrupted by two others, and its successor a brace of featurettes. *Fra Diavolo* holds together but has a 'straight' plot running parallel to the comedy, helped not at all by employing two directors. *Sons of the Desert* is the first Laurel and Hardy feature with unity, a complete story carried by the team's characters; its lessons were to some extent applied to *Babes in Toyland*, though the earlier opera's 'split' is still apparent. *Bonnie*

Scotland is a retrograde step, dividing Laurel & Hardy even further from the plot; while *The Bohemian Girl* integrates them totally but fails to sustain consistent comic invention. It was the problem of being funny for 60 minutes and more that encouraged the intrusive sub-plotting. *Our Relations* proved the best compromise since *Sons of the Desert*, involving the team in complexities of plot within which the routines could be placed; *Way Out West* is even better, allowing time for routines within a story that permits further comedy. *Swiss Miss* reverts to a sub-plot, but is more reminiscent of *Fra Diavolo* than *Bonnie Scotland*. *Block-Heads*, one of the shorter features (few are more than 60 or 70 minutes), allows good routines within no more plot than is necessary, and an amusing one at that. *The Flying Deuces*, made away from Roach, moves briskly and efficiently but the final Roach comedies (*A Chump at Oxford* and *Saps at Sea*) are structurally undermined by compromised length. For all their flaws, the above are redeemed by the team's comedy, although it is sometimes diluted by the extended length. After 1940 even this element was eroded, leaving comparatively little to praise.

(See also: Chase, Charley; Foreign versions; Guest appearances; Streamliners; M-G-M; 20th Century-Fox)

FEMALE IMPERSONATION
(Laurel & Hardy films *qv*)
Many comedians attempt female impersonation; in Britain, the comic 'dame' is a staple of pantomime (*qv*), one of the greatest practitioners being Stan Laurel's boyhood hero Dan Leno (*qv*). Laurel's own forays into drag favour this eccentric variety, especially in his 'Agnes' persona of *Duck Soup*, *Another Fine Mess* and *A Chump at Oxford*. None of these are essential to the plot, but the action in *That's My Wife* depends entirely on Stan's masquerade as Mrs Hardy. Equally necessary is Stan's female guise in

Why Girls Love Sailors, a glamorous type recalling the 'vamps' from his solo films *The Sleuth* and *Eve's Love Letters* (*qv*). By contrast, his 'Aunt Emily' from *Jitterbugs* is almost convincing despite the comic element. Female impersonation of a sort may be found in the bizarre creature from *Sugar Daddies* consisting of a female-clad Laurel perched on Finlayson's back; while confusion surrounds a kilted Stan in *Putting Pants On Philip* when a cop declares 'this dame ain't got no lingerie on'. Oliver Hardy is seen less frequently in skirts, but one of the earliest known stills from his days with Lubin (*qv*) shows him impersonating a woman. Hardy adopts female disguise in some of his films with Billy West (*qv*), that in *Cupid's Rival* (1917) being particularly convincing. *Twice Two* offers the unique sight of Laurel and Hardy portraying their own twin sisters, an illusion aided by trick photography and dubbed voices. Sometimes it is not the comedians themselves who adopt the disguise: criminals find women's clothing a suitable mask for their nefarious activities in *Forty-Five Minutes From Hollywood*, *The Laurel-Hardy Murder Case* and *A-Haunting We Will Go*.

(See also: Cook, Elisha Jr.; Costume; Detectives; Dual roles; Melodrama; Rediscoveries; Sawmills; Servants; Solo films; Teaming; Women)

FIELDS, STANLEY (1884–1941)
Beefy actor who replaced Tiny Sandford (*qv*) in *Way Out West* (*qv*). They appeared together in the 1936 version of *Show Boat*. Born Walter L. Agnew in Pennsylvania, Fields was a prizefighter until defeated by Benny Leonard. Stage work was followed by films, *Mammy*, *See America Thirst* and *Cracked Nuts* being among the earlier examples.

(See also: *That's That!*)

THE FIGHTING KENTUCKIAN
(1949)
The unlikely alliance between Oliver Hardy and John Wayne began early in 1949 when they toured in a Masquers Club production of *What Price Glory?* Hardy was subsequently offered a supporting role in Wayne's upcoming Republic feature, *The Fighting Kentuckian*, but hesitated through loyalty to his partner and a reluctance to create rumours of a split. Laurel, at that time inactive owing to a diabetic problem, gave Hardy his full blessing, reasoning that his health should not prevent both from working. Hardy contributed many fine moments to the film, his native accent serving him well in this tale of the South set in 1819. Among the highlights are an oversized brawl (a Wayne trademark), further mayhem in a bar and some gentle humour when Hardy, as 'Willie Payne', lends Wayne a hat belonging to an illustrious ancestor, Daniel Boone. A more typical 'Ollie' appears when they attempt to survey some

The Fighting Kentuckian and (inset) the long-forgotten stage production of What Price Glory? *that brought about the Hardy-Wayne association Advertisement courtesy of Robert G. Dickson; photograph BFI Stills, Posters and Designs*

The Finishing Touch: *an argument over finances with Sam Lufkin*

land, with Hardy backing away from Wayne until landing in a stream. This one gag and his reactions to it are virtually all that can be identified from his usual work, the remainder of his scenes placing him as sidekick, guide and eventual rescuer of the hero. *The Fighting Kentuckian*, though enjoyable in itself, serves primarily to suggest Hardy's eventual direction had he not teamed with Stan Laurel; his character comedy of the early 1920s would be revisited only here and in Roach's *Zenobia* (*qv*). *The Fighting Kentuckian* was converted into computer-colour in 1990; a more immediate legacy was a visit by Wayne and Republic head Herbert Yates to the set of *Atoll K* (*qv*).

(See also: Arbuckle, Roscoe 'Fatty'; Charities; Colour; Solo films; Stage appearances; *Stolen Jools, the*)

FILM CLASSICS
see: Reissues and Titling

FILM FUN
British comic paper, ostensibly for children but read by many adults. Published between 1920 and 1962, *Film Fun* specialized in strip-cartoon portrayals of famous stars. During 1920 its sister publication, *Kinema Comic*, had run a short-lived 'Babe Hardy' strip, but Laurel & Hardy remained in *Film Fun*, usually

occupying both front and back covers, from 1930 until a few weeks after Hardy's death in 1957. When the team visited England, editor Frederick George Caldwell forbade artist Bill Wakefield to visit them, fearing they would ask for money (*Film Fun* paid no royalties for the use of characters). Wakefield's son, Terry, eventually took over the job and received honorary membership of an early UK branch of the Sons of the Desert club (*qv*), known as the Film Funsters. The comic's history is detailed in a book by Graham King and Ron Saxby, *The Wonderful World of Film Fun* (1985); it should not be confused with a similarly-titled American humour magazine, which sometimes employed photos of Laurel & Hardy.

(See also: Caricatures; Periodicals)

A FINE MESS (1986)
Much press speculation preceded the release of this Blake Edwards film, to the effect that it would be some kind of *hommage* to Laurel & Hardy or, more likely, a specific remake of their Oscar-winning *The Music Box* (*qv*). Cited as potential stars were names redolent of a somewhat different brand of comedy (among them Richard Pryor), but in the end top billing went to Ted Danson (of *Cheers* fame) and Howie Mandel. Although much of the publicity attempted to identify these as the duo following in the wake of Laurel & Hardy and others, the most identifiably Laurel & Hardy-like behaviour belongs to Richard Mulligan (from *Soap*) and Stuart Margolin. Mulligan seems to be doing his best to imitate Stan Laurel while Margolin at least reacts at times in the appropriate manner. The plot, concerning gangsters amid a scheme to dope racehorses, is alien to Laurel & Hardy except when compared to the inappropriate scenarios burdening the Fox films; of the gags, very few relate to Laurel & Hardy except a bungled auction modelled on *Thicker Than Water* (*qv*), and the

heroes' disposal of a player-piano acquired there. The piano-moving scene is virtually thrown away, odd for an announced remake of the Laurel & Hardy equivalent. *A Fine Mess* is difficult to distinguish from the numerous 1980s *Blues Brothers* clones in which hysteria, car chases and selected expletives substitute for style. There is, at the time of writing, word of a further modern-day feature intended to honour and/or emulate Laurel and Hardy; we shall see.

(See also: *Goon Show*, *the*; *Great Race*, *the*; Remakes; 20th-Century-Fox)

THE FINISHING TOUCH
(Laurel & Hardy film)
Released by M-G-M, 25 February 1928. Produced by Hal Roach. Directed by Clyde Bruckman. Camera: George Stevens. Two reels. Silent.
With Stan Laurel and Oliver Hardy, Edgar Kennedy, Dorothy Coburn, Sam Lufkin.

'Professional Finishers' Laurel & Hardy are promised $500 to complete the building of a house for its owner (Sam Lufkin). Requested to finish by noon the following Monday, Ollie rashly promises the job for noon that very day. They set to work but, being near a hospital, create sufficient noise for a nurse (Dorothy Coburn) to complain to the local policeman (Edgar Kennedy). The policeman's request for quiet is heeded, but the silence ends with Ollie's plunge through a board linking the porch to a trestle. The nurse arrives, demanding to know who the 'big cheese' is: Stan indicates Ollie, who receives a smack in the nose. As the nurse leaves, she steps on a board which flips up, smacking her on the behind. Assuming Ollie to be the culprit, she returns, punches him in the stomach and does the same to Stan (who has to be stopped from returning the blow). Spotting a hammer lying nearby, the nurse bends to pick it up; to create the illusion of rending fabric, Stan tears a piece of sandpaper in two. Embarrassed, the nurse backs her way out. Returning to work, Ollie sets about the task of affixing roof slates while Stan, having made too much noise fitting a window, is sent to arrange another plank bridging the gap between trestle and porch. Stan, needing a longer plank, cuts through the one which is supporting Ollie. The slates promptly descend, attaching themselves to the policeman, whose uniform is reduced to a collage of slates, glue and rags. Ollie tests the bridge Stan has made and reaches the porch, which collapses. Later on, the owner arrives and, delighted with the finished house, pays the two builders. His delight ends when the chimney collapses under the weight of a small bird, followed by the disintegration of roof, windows and pillars. Retrieval of the money involves the householder in a game of catch, developing quickly into a variant of American football. Recovering his cash, the owner adds further injury by giving Stan a violent kick. Stan responds by daubing paint in the man's face, causing Ollie to laugh heartily. The householder punches Ollie in the stomach, but ducks when Ollie retaliates with a bucket of whitewash, which instead ruins the policeman's new uniform. The nurse, having given up her protests, leaves the hospital, which bears a sign saying FOR RENT. By now Stan, Ollie and the householder are aiming rocks and bricks at each other: one knocks over the sign, while another sends the nurse into a vat of whitewash. Seeking another missile, Stan grabs the rock that is keeping their lorry immobile on a slope and the vehicle trundles unfettered into the house. For the fade-out, Stan drops the rock on Ollie's toe.

A descendant of two solo comedies, Laurel's *Smithy* and Hardy's *Stick Around* (qv), *The Finishing Touch* is enjoyable despite an over-reliance on slapstick. Repetition features strongly, as in Ollie's periodic attempts to reach the porch prior to the collapse of a supporting plank and the several occasions on which he swallows a mouthful of nails. One ingenious sight gag, in which Stan appears to be supporting both ends of a lengthy piece of timber, was to resurface much later in *Great Guns* (qv). *The Finishing Touch* is one of the few Laurel and Hardy silents where elements of both American and British versions are known to exist. As with *Big Business* (qv), the second negative offers different camera angles plus some variations in action. In *The Finishing Touch* this is most obvious in close-ups of the nurse, which in the British version are presented from a different perspective and with some dissimilar facial reactions to the American equivalent. An amendment in sub-titling tells us that nine years of schooling took Laurel & Hardy to the 'First Reader' for American audiences, and the 'Infants' for the British. It seems likely that today's American edition, originating from Blackhawk Films (qv), combines footage from both versions.

(See also: Animation; Coburn, Dorothy; Doctors, nurses–; *Eve's Love Letters*; Gag titles; Kennedy, Edgar; *Laurel and Hardy's Laughing Twenties*; Policemen)

FINLAYSON, JAMES
(James Henderson Finlayson)
(c. 1887-1953)

Scottish comedian considered by many an almost indispensable part of the Laurel & Hardy team. Born in Larbert, near Falkirk in 1881, 1884 or 1887 (Finlayson gave varying birth dates) he was apprenticed as a panel-beater before a repertory company took him to the United States in Bunty Pulls the Strings. Early film experience included time with Mack Sennett (qv), L-KO (qv) and others. He first appeared with Stan Laurel in Roach comedies during 1923. The mid-1920s saw a failed attempt by Roach to build Finlayson into a star, producing such interesting hybrids as Yes, Yes, Nanette! (qv), starring Finlayson with

James Finlayson lends an ear in a posed shot from Big Business

Hardy in support and co-directed by Laurel. Finlayson's roles in the early Laurel & Hardy comedies were of sufficient prominence for much contemporary publicity to consider them a trio. By the time Laurel and Hardy were established as a double-act, Finlayson had started to find other work (notably in features at First National) before drifting back into the regular company toward the end of 1928. Although not star material, his balding, popeyed irascibility (and enormous prop moustache) brought memorable support in a total of 33 Laurel and Hardy films, notably Big Business and Way Out West (both qv). During the promotion of Fra Diavolo (qv) he returned to Britain, remaining for a period to appear in films such as What Happened to Harkness? and Oh, No, Doctor!, an early picture directed by Michael Powell. Both were released in 1934, and by the following year Finlayson was back with Laurel & Hardy. His final appearance with them was the team's last for Hal Roach, the 1940 release Saps at Sea (qv). Finlayson continued in occasional minor roles (among them that of a slapstick old-timer in 1947's fictionalized account of Pearl White's career, The Perils of Pauline) until his death in 1953.

(See also: Academy Awards; Freemasons; *Man About Town ,a*; *Soilers, the*; Solo films; Teaming)

FIRE-RAISERS
See: Practical jokes

FISH (Laurel & Hardy films *qv*)
As a rule, fish have about as pleasant a time with Laurel & Hardy as they do in real life. Stan and Ollie sell them in *Towed in a Hole* and catch them in both *The Laurel-Hardy Murder Case* and *The Live Ghost*. The latter instance is all the more pointed for their supposed profession of gutting them, as they do also in *The Flying Deuces*. Caveman Stan clubs fish into submission in *Flying Elephants* but in the solo film *Bears and Bad Men*, his best catch is a pair of corsets. Stan and Ollie attempt to grill a fish over bedsprings in *Bonnie Scotland*, a film where snuff induces a Hardy sneeze sufficient to drain a river, leaving its finned inhabitants in dry dock. Another unfortunate specimen is confined to a small tank in the laboratory of Professor Noodle in *Dirty Work*. Bigger fish stand more of a chance, notably the shark in *The Flying Deuces*. Another resilient breed, shellfish, are represented by the runaway crab from *Liberty* and Stan's pet lobster in *Atoll K*. One of the early Warner Brothers cartoons caricatures Laurel & Hardy as fish, something that clearly failed to diminish Laurel's off-screen fondness for deep-sea angling. On a postwar visit, one journalist noticed Stan's lapel badge, earned in 1935 after landing a 256lb tunny.

(See also: Animation; Food; Hobbies; Stage appearances)

THE FIXER-UPPERS
(Laurel & Hardy film)
Released by M-G-M, 9 February 1935. Produced by Hal Roach. Directed by Charles Rogers. Camera: Art Lloyd. Two reels.
With Stan Laurel and Oliver Hardy, Mae Busch, Charles Middleton, Arthur Housman

Stan and Ollie travel from door to door peddling greeting cards. Their first customer, a drunk (Arthur Housman) is reduced to tears by Stan's tender verse; the second, an artist's wife (Mae Busch) is already in tears because her husband, Pierre (Charles Middleton) is neglecting her. She engages Ollie to pose as her lover in order to make the artist jealous. Ollie does too good a job and is challenged to a duel. In a café, Ollie ponders imminent doom until Stan reminds him that the artist does not have their address, and there is no reason for Ollie to go through with the duel. Ollie telephones Pierre, contemptuously refusing to attend. Pierre sets out after him. The pair meet up with their former customer, who has been refused a drink. An agreement is made for the boys to order drinks for him, and they finish unconscious after an alcoholic binge. The police find the artist's card in Ollie's pocket and dump the unconscious pair at that address. Pierre returns home and is

The Fixer-Uppers: *card salesmen Laurel & Hardy with their best customer (Arthur Housman)*

persuaded not to kill Ollie; that is until he and Stan are discovered in his wife's bed. The duel is on but Pierre's bullets have been replaced with blanks. Ollie plays dead, but he and Stan must escape when Pierre makes plans to cut up the remains. They take refuge in dustbins. Once Pierre has gone, Stan climbs out and looks for Ollie, only to see him disappear around the corner in a dustcart.

A remake of the very early *Slipping Wives* (*qv*), *The Fixer-Uppers* is one of the low-key efforts characterizing their final shorts. Best known for a famous telephone conversation sequence (see **Dialogue**), it is also remembered for a necessarily well-timed scene in which Mae Busch (*qv*) demonstrates a lengthy, passionate kiss on a most dispassionate Stan, who collapes, only to return with a powerful kiss of his own. Charles Middleton (*qv*) is a reasonably volatile artist in a setting which was clearly undecided between French and American locales; authentically plastered as usual is Arthur Housman (*qv*), whose tearful reaction to a Christmas card verse is one of the film's highlights.

(See also: Alcohol; Artists; Crying; Duels; France; Policemen; Scripts; Tashlin, Frank; Telephones; Young, Noah)

FLOWERS (all films *qv*)
A hallmark of the team's gentility is remembering flowers for a lady. In *Going Bye-Bye!* they bring a bouquet for Mae Busch but never actually

relinquish it, passing the flowers to each other throughout the ensuing mayhem. Stanley is aware of floral niceties but is hampered by his customary naïvety, as when in *Me and My Pal* he orders a wreath for Ollie's wedding. In their *Wedding Night* sketch for radio, Ollie's bride is wearing real oranges in lieu of their blossom. Stan visits Ollie in hospital in *Thicker Than Water* bearing a

The Flying Deuces: *Ollie 'forgets'*
with a mountain of laundry (below)

bouquet of lilies, the centres of which provide Stanley with a snack.

(See also: Characters; Courtliness; Food; Radio)

THE FLYING DEUCES
(Laurel & Hardy film)
Released by RKO-Radio, 20 October 1939. Produced by Boris Morros. Directed by A. Edward Sutherland. Camera: Art Lloyd. 67 minutes. With Stan Laurel and Oliver Hardy, Jean Parker, Reginald Gardiner, Charles Middleton, James Finlayson, Rychard Cramer.

Stan and Ollie are staying in Paris when Ollie falls for innkeeper's daughter Georgette (Jean Parker). Ollie proposes marriage but is refused grace-fully; he is unaware that Georgette is married to François (Reginald Gardiner), a Foreign Legion officer. Ollie decides to jump in the Seine, persuading Stan to come along; they pause to discuss the possibility of reincarnation, Ollie deciding to return as a horse. Further delays ensue until they meet François, who suggests the Legion as an alternative. The suicide is abandoned but Ollie still lands in the river, narrowly missing an escaped shark. In the Legion they disrupt a parade, while their familiarity with François is taken as insubordination. They rebel when the Commandant (Charles Middleton) tells them how little they will be paid, but are soon washing a mountain of laundry. Ollie conveniently 'forgets' Georgette, which they think entitles them to leave. On their way out they meet Georgette, who has arrived to be with her husband. François is enraged to see Ollie kissing his wife; worse still, they are arrested for desertion and sentenced to be shot at sunrise. A note arrives telling them of an escape route via a trap door, but they are pursued. The tunnel leads into a wine cellar, from which they enter the main building. Unwittingly they stumble into Georgette's bedroom; she faints, and François arrives just as they try to revive her. The chase continues into an aircraft hangar, and they are soon airborne in a runaway craft. They crash, Stan emerging unscathed as he watches Ollie's angelic figure float skyward. The scene dissolves to Stan as a carefree wanderer, his attention caught by a whistle and Ollie's voice; Stan is overjoyed to see his old friend, who has been reincarnated as a horse.

Despite a minimal budget, *The Flying Deuces* is virtually the only non-Roach Laurel & Hardy feature worthy of attention; producer Boris Morros (*qv*) operated a small independent unit, affording Laurel something of his usual control. Laurel & Hardy were then under a new, non-exclusive contract with Roach, having recently signed as a single entity for the first time; their final Roach films, *A Chump at Oxford* and *Saps at Sea*, were released after *Deuces* but Randy Skretvedt (*qv*) has ascertained that the four-reel version of *Chump* was completed prior to this film. The apparent public-domain status of *Flying Deuces* makes it a common title on home video. American copies tend to be complete but UK material (including TV and 8mm film) usually derives from an abridgment, losing several moments from the film's first third, including chunks of the hotel sequence, all reference to a shark loose in the Seine and a cartoon portrait of Laurel & Hardy drawn by Harry Langdon (*qv*). Longer versions have begun to appear but remain in the minority.

(See also: Aircraft; Army, the; Feature films; Gardiner, Reginald; Langdon, Harry; Parker, Jean; Reincarnation; Records; Romance; Songs; Stage appearances; Suicide; Video releases)

FLYING ELEPHANTS
(Laurel & Hardy film)
Released by Pathé Exchange, 12 February 1928 (completed 1927). Produced by Hal Roach. Directed by Frank Butler. Two reels. Silent. With Stan Laurel, Oliver Hardy, James Finlayson, Viola Richard, Dorothy Coburn.

In the Stone Age (so named because men had the choice of marriage or work on the rock pile) King Ferdinand orders all eligible men to marry on pain of 'death, banishment or both'. Little Twinkle Star (Stan Laurel) considers himself exempt, his mother not having told him everything as yet; the Mighty Giant (Oliver Hardy) is rather more experienced. Each has to follow the decree but decide upon the same girl (Viola Richard), daughter of aged wizard Saxophonus (James Finlayson). Saxophonus has a terrible toothache; the Giant finds favour when disposing of it with his club. Twinkle Star does battle with the Giant, attempting to trick him into a position where he can be kicked over a cliff; a goat does the job instead. Twinkle Star is united with his future bride and father-in-law, plus a grizzly bear who chases them under Saxophonus' wagon.

Best known in Britain from an 8mm edition titled *Stone Age Romance*, *Flying Elephants* derives its name from an animated shot actually showing these bizarre creatures. The remaining action is sufficiently unreal to pass for a cartoon (one critic has accurately compared this film's matching of Laurel & Hardy to that of Popeye and Bluto!), not least Hardy's battle with a female wrestler and Laurel's grabbing fish from a stream. Given the promise shown in earlier

Pathé shorts, the two are given surprisingly few scenes together; more remarkable is that *Kinematograph Weekly* described a reissue of this film as featuring them both, but believed the far more typical *Do Detectives Think?* (*qv*) to be a Laurel solo film! *Flying Elephants* is one of a few Laurel & Hardy silents that seem to exist only in mediocre prints. Superior material was found for the 1967 compilation *The Further Perils of Laurel & Hardy* (*qv*), but picture quality remained inferior to that in other clips.

(See also: Animation; Cavemen; Fish; Locations; Pathé Exchange; Reissues; Seawright, Roy; Teaming)

FLYNN, EMMETT
See: *Early to Bed* and *Two Tars*

FOOD (all films *qv*)
The respective figures of Laurel and Hardy suggest Ollie to have been the gourmet of the two, implied further when he orders food in *Below Zero*, *Any Old Port* and *Swiss Miss*; oddly, it is usually Stan who appears to be munching, echoing accounts of real-life gatherings at which Babe would exchange his heavily-laden plate for Stan's much smaller portion. This may have happened during Babe's periodic attempts to reduce, for he was known otherwise as *bon viveur* and master chef. Lucille Hardy had high praise for Babe's Caesar Salad, and the famous story of his teaming with Stan depends upon an accident sustained in the kitchen. In *The Bohemian Girl* Stan consumes the entire breakfast prepared for himself and Ollie; lesser repasts include the wax apple from *Sons of the Desert* and a banana (eaten in the manner of corn on the cob) in *Saps at Sea*. Stan's diet echoes that of the goats in *Saps* and *Angora Love* when extending to the stamens of a flower (*Thicker Than Water*) and a disgusting chocolate sandwich (*The Flying Deuces*). Ice cream looms large, as in *Come Clean*

and *Twice Two*, but his native diet, in keeping with his eccentric character, consists primarily of nuts, requested whenever a meal is offered and consumed in tandem with eggs in *County Hospital*. Despite surviving for 20 years on baked beans in *Block-Heads*, Stan's taste still has limitations, as when he objects to the lunch of strong cheese and spring onions belonging to a fellow soldier in *With Love and Hisses* (there is nonetheless room for some 'horse's radish' in *Twice Two*). Several films use food as a slapstick weapon. *The Battle of the Century* is the prime example, while cakes are splattered rather ignominiously in *From Soup to Nuts*, *That's My Wife*, *Hollywood Revue of 1929*, *Twice Two* and *Our Relations* amongst others. Other misused comestibles include soup (*From Soup to Nuts*, *Their Purple Moment*, *You're Darn Tootin'*, *That's My Wife*, *The Hoose-Gow*), sandwiches (*Perfect Day*, *One Good Turn*) and a hambone which is dumped in Stan's bed in *Early to Bed*. In *Unaccustomed As We Are*, Ollie's lap is decorated with spaghetti, a dish that features in the synthetic meal they serve a killer in *Saps At Sea*. The *Midnight Patrol* by officers Laurel and Hardy is punctuated by a dive into

sauerkraut. Perhaps the most notorious food joke in the Laurel & Hardy repertoire concerns their arrival at Oxford University in unsuitable garb: when told they are 'dressed for Eton', Stan replies 'That's swell - we haven't eaten since breakfast!'

(See also: Characters; Eggs; Fish; Height, weight; Marriages; *Nothing But Trouble*; Slapstick; Teaming; West, Billy)

FOREIGN LEGION
See: Army, the

FOREIGN VERSIONS
(English editions *qv*)
The international market for silent films required only two concessions, one being replacement sub-titles, the other a separate negative prepared by having two cameras turning simultaneously. Talkies presented a new set of difficulties, which in time would be overcome by the twin techniques of dubbing and sub-titling. Before either became the norm, industry practice favoured the unwieldy, expensive process of shooting separate editions. There seems to have been a particular traffic between Great Britain and Germany: BIP's *Atlantic* (1930) was

completely recast for a German edition, while Germany's *The Blue Angel* (also 1930), while retaining Emil Jannings and Marlene Dietrich as stars, was remade simultaneously in English. In American comedy, Laurel & Hardy remade several films in this way, as did Charley Chase and Buster Keaton (both *qv*). The stars spoke their dialogue parrot-fashion, aided by language coaches and off-screen prompting boards. Supporting casts tended to change except among key artists; of the performers virtually unique to the overseas editions, special mention should be made of Spanish-speaking Robert O'Connor, who functioned also as interpreter. Linda Loredo, an ideal screen wife in the Spanish versions, appeared also in the English-language film *Come Clean*; Robert G. Dickson has discovered that she died just a few months after the latter film's completion, aged only 23. Stan Laurel later recalled that no reshooting would take place until the domestic version had been completed, so that no unnecessary scenes would be taken. *Pardon Us* was evidently re-shot after the event but nonetheless contains scenes absent in English. Of the shorts, which also incorporate scenes deleted from domestic release, records suggest earlier subjects to have been shot simultaneously (*Variety* of 13th November 1929 describes *Night Owls* as being made thus) but that *Be Big* and *Chickens Come Home* were filmed in English before commencing the overseas editions. For many years the only available foreign Laurel & Hardy remake was a French release, *Les carottiers*, a feature-length compilation of *Be Big* and *Laughing Gravy*. Subsequent discoveries include its Spanish equivalent, *Los calaveras*, and six other Spanish films, *Ladrones* (*Night Owls*), *La vida nocturna* (*Blotto*), *Tiembla y titubea* (*Below Zero*), *Noche de duendes* (*Berth*

Marks/*The Laurel-Hardy Murder Case*), *Politiqueiras* (*Chickens Come Home*) and *De bote en bote* (*Pardon Us*). More recently the French *Blotto* has been located in Europe. A 'scrap-book' section of America's *The Laurel & Hardy Show* has used a sequence unique to the foreign versions of *Pardon Us*; the others have been seen in their entirety on Spanish television. Rumours circulate of further discoveries, one of them a mute copy of the German *Spuk um Mitternach* (*Murder Case*), but none have been seen. Other known remakes are *Brats* in German, *Hog Wild* in French and Spanish and *The Laurel-Hardy Murder Case* (incorporating *Berth Marks*) in French. A reported German edition of *Be Big/Laughing Gravy* is now thought not to have been made; Robert Dickson has examined a Roach Studios list of each alternative version which, along with Laurel's own listing, confirms the precise number of remakes. The foreign editions are usually longer than their domestic counterparts, partly the result of Laurel & Hardy's greater popularity overseas. A further explanation lies in Roach's domestic distribution arrangement with M-G-M, which restricted the price of a given subject to that of a two-reeler irrespective of final running time. M-G-M persuaded Roach to discontinue these special versions by mid-1931, the alleged result of overseas exhibitors having preferred them to the larger studio's dubbed features. They were, as they say, fun while they lasted: one unnamed foreign release is said to have included an inadvertent and decidedly vulgar expression! Problems aside, these versions were effective to the point where overseas fans did not realise the team to have been monolingual. Regardless of technique, worldwide fame extended to local nicknames (often based on 'fat' and 'thin'), 'El Gordo y El Flaco' in Latin America and Spain, 'Helan' and 'Halvan' (Sweden), 'Dick und Doof' (Germany), 'Flip e Flap' (Poland) and 'Dikke' and 'Dunne'

(Holland). Italy prefers the 'Stanlio' and 'Ollio' of *Fra Diavolo*; one of the games in Eurovision's eccentric *Jeux Sans Frontières* was entitled 'Stanlio and Ollio Break Out of Jail'. John McCabe (*qv*) has recorded the celebration of Laurel & Hardy even in remotest China, where in pre-Communist days their picture was witnessed on a Buddhist altar, symbolizing a fat Mandarin and an undernourished peasant; noted also is a post-revolution building bearing their picture for no apparent purpose except decoration.

(See also: *Another Fine Mess*; Dubbing; France; Granger, Dorothy; Mexico; *That's That!*; Unfilmed projects)

FORTY-FIVE MINUTES FROM HOLLYWOOD
(Laurel & Hardy film)
Released by Pathé Exchange, 26 December 1926. Produced by Hal Roach. Directed by Fred Guiol. Two reels. Silent.
With Glenn Tryon, Theda Bara, Our Gang, Stan Laurel, Oliver Hardy.

Orville (Glenn Tryon) and his family travel from their rural home to pay an urgent bill at a Hollywood office. A sightseeing bus affords views of strange goings-on, not least of which is a genuine bank raid. Orville asks a woman if he can get into pictures; as she is one of the robbers, Orville is soon pursued by the law. Orville and the woman escape into the 'Hollywood Hotel' (where directors are forbidden to run in the corridors), taking refuge in, of all places, a room occupied by the house detective (Oliver Hardy). The detective is in the bath; the robber is in fact a man, who knocks Orville unconscious before stealing Orville's clothes - and bankroll. Orville is left in the robber's female disguise, creating complications when the detective's wife returns to find an unconscious 'woman' on the bed. Before long, both the towel-

clad detective and the police are chasing Orville, who in turn is pursuing the robber. When Orville catches him a struggle ensues in a room occupied by a 'starving actor' (Stan Laurel), who takes the worst beating. The police and detective are outside; when they break down the door, the film ends in chaos.

Forty-Five Minutes From Hollywood deserves notice solely as the first Roach comedy with both Laurel and Hardy on-screen. This is only just the case, as they do not appear together but are visible as intercut characters separated by a door. Many audiences fail to recognise Laurel at all, identifying him instead as James Finlayson (*qv*), whom he is made up to resemble. One writer has suggested this to be the result of a then-current dispute between Laurel and Joe Rock (*qv*), whose terms forbade on-screen work elsewhere. This might explain Laurel's reluctance to step before the cameras in *Get 'Em Young*. *Forty-Five Minutes From Hollywood* is considerably below the standard of much contemporary Roach product, being altogether more frenzied and less coherent (especially in current European TV and video release, where all sub-titling has been deleted). It is probable that the film's creators enjoyed it rather more, with the frequency of jokes about directors and their assistants, and the incorporation of clips featuring Roach contractees ranging from Theda Bara to Our Gang.

(See also: *Laurel and Hardy's Laughing Twenties*; Teaming; Tryon, Glenn; Video releases)

FOSTER, LEWIS R. (1900-74)
(Laurel & Hardy films *qv*)
Director and screenwriter, with an Academy Award for 'Best Original Story' for *Mr Smith Goes To Washington*. Lewis Foster worked briefly with Charley Chase (*qv*) before joining the Laurel & Hardy unit for *Double Whoopee*, *Bacon Grabbers*,

Angora Love, Unaccustomed As We Are, Berth Marks and Men O'War. He subsequently directed Roach's series with Harry Langdon (qv).

(See also: Academy Awards)

FOUR CLOWNS (1969)
(Laurel & Hardy films qv)
This last silent-comedy anthology from Robert Youngson (qv) is in a sense the victim of its successful predecessors, relying for its Laurel & Hardy scenes upon hitherto-unused segments from films covered elsewhere. The single exception is the treatment of *Their Purple Moment* which, presented here in an efficient abridgment, manages to outshine minor sequences from the otherwise superior *Big Business*, *Two Tars*, *Double Whoopee* and *Putting Pants on Philip*. The Laurel and Hardy solo appearances are as derivative, the extract from Laurel's *Kill or Cure* being virtually the only segment remaining after prior use in *Days of Thrills and Laughter* and *Laurel & Hardy's Laughing Twenties* (both qv). Clips representing Hardy's supporting work for Billy West (qv) in *His Day Out* and *The Hobo* once more overlap with previous compilations, although ample compensation is provided by some choice Hardy villainy from Roach's 1927 feature *No Man's Law*. Babe appears as a scarred, unshaven fiend whose eyepatch lifts to reveal a perfecty functional eye, useful when surveying Barbara Kent's nude swimming scene. Despite its derivative nature, the Laurel & Hardy section remains very enjoyable, suffering only in comparison with Youngson's prior selections. *Four Clowns* concludes with an abridgment of Keaton's *Seven Chances*, but the real honours are carried off by the middle section which displays the considerable talents of Charley Chase (qv). Hardy reappears in *Fluttering Hearts* (1927), as a speakeasy drunk whose attention is diverted by the female store dummy manipulated by Chase; best of all is the potted version of *Limousine Love* (1928), in which Charley, driving to his wedding, discovers a naked woman in the back of his car. Youngson often described Chase as 'master of the comedy of embarrassment', and *Limousine Love* provides a fine example of this. Interviewed by Leonard Maltin (qv) prior to *Four Clowns*' release, Youngson made it plain that

he wanted to promote Chase in the way that he had Laurel & Hardy in earlier years. The Chase revival has still to gain proper momentum, although *aficionados* are increasing in number.

(See also: Compilations; Keaton, Buster; Nudity; Richard, Viola; Solo films)

FRA DIAVOLO
(Laurel & Hardy film)
Released by M-G-M, 5 May 1933. Produced by Hal Roach. Directed by Hal Roach and Charles Rogers. Camera: Art Lloyd, Hap Depew. Adapted by Jeanie MacPherson from Auber's opera *Fra Diavolo* (1830). 90 minutes.
With Stan Laurel and Oliver Hardy, Dennis King, Thelma Todd, James Finlayson, Lucile Brown, Arthur Pierson, Henry Armetta.

In early eighteenth-century Italy, the countryside lives in fear of a notorious outlaw named Fra Diavolo, or 'the Devil's Brother' (Dennis King). Diavolo's methods consist of masquerading as the decadent Marquis de San Marco, infiltrating the aristocracy before making off with their valuables and, sometimes, their women. Both seem likely results when he turns his attention to the aged and cynical Lord

San Marco's 'retinue' in **Fra Diavolo**

Rocburg (James Finlayson), whose interests tend more toward wealth than his young, beautiful wife (Thelma Todd). Sharing part of a stagecoach journey with the Rocburgs, Diavolo charms the neglected lady and discovers the hiding place of her jewels. His band hold up the coach, take the Rocburgs' jewels but do not find their money; another attempt will be required. Meanwhile, vagabonds Stanlio and Ollio have planned to retire on their hard-earned savings but are set upon by bandits. Deciding to recoup their losses in like fashion, they are moved to tears by their first victim. The village panics at hearing the theme song of the notorious Diavolo; Ollio adopts both his name and the song, but picks on none other than Diavolo. The would-be thieves are surrounded and about to be hanged until Stanlio's tears win him a reprieve - providing he can hang Ollio. The attempt fails, but both are spared as Diavolo needs two henchmen who would not be recognised by the Rocburgs. Consequently, Diavolo, in his Marquis disguise, arrives with 'retinue' at the Tavern del Cucu, where the Rocburgs are staying. The boys take away his sedan chair, which is destroyed when Stanlio attracts a bull by waving a red handkerchief. The impoverished innkeeper, Matteo (Henry Armetta) plans to marry off his daughter, Zerlina (Lucile Browne) to the wealthy Francesco (Matt McHugh). Her sweetheart, Lorenzo (Arthur Pierson) is Captain of the Guard and hopes to finance their wedding with the reward offered for Diavolo. Lady Rocburg is delighted to renew acquaintance with the Marquis, her husband less so. Rocburg forges a letter inviting his wife to the Marquis' suite, but it goes astray. Rocburg waits in his rival's place but is captured by Stanlio and Ollio, themselves aware of the reward. Diavolo meets Lady Rocburg by chance before discovering the plot against him; he ensures future loyalty with a threat to cut out Ollio's gizzard. Diavolo asks Matteo for

sleeping draughts, pouring them all into a glass of wine for his servants to deliver to Rocburg; when he declines, Stanlio drinks it. The boys are ordered to await Diavolo's signal in the courtyard. By the time it arrives, Stanlio is barely conscious, rendering their ascent to the upper balcony all the more hazardous. Diavolo searches the Rocburgs' quarters as the boys watch Zerlina, who is outside. She leaves her post on hearing the soldiers, who have returned from a raid on Diavolo's encampment. Diavolo, who has stolen Lady Rocburg's medallion, watches knowingly as Lorenzo climbs to Zerlina's room. The following morning, Zerlina is to marry Francesco. Stanlio and Ollio are despatched to draw wine, but once the jug is full Stanlio can think of no other receptacle than his throat. The medallion is reported stolen but Diavolo plants it on Lorenzo, concocting a story of the medallion financing Lorenzo's marriage to Zerlina; neither is prepared to explain Lorenzo's climb to the balcony the previous night. Lady Rocburg decides not to press charges; Lorenzo promises to deliver the real thief. Alone with Lady Rocburg, Diavolo persuades her to change back into her dress of the preceding evening; he locates the money in her petticoat. Stanlio and Ollio are watching preparations for the wedding when Stanlio begins to laugh drunkenly. Ollio joins in, but Zerlina notices Stanlio repeating a song she had sung when outside the Rocburgs' room. Lorenzo questions them, but Stanlio threatens to tell Diavolo. 'He doesn't mean Diavolo, sir,' says Ollio, 'he means the Marquis de San Marco'. The inn is surrounded and Diavolo spreads panic with his theme song. Lorenzo faces him in a duel, acquitting himself well but emerging as victor only through Stanlio's clumsiness. Zerlina and Lorenzo ask Rocburg for the reward, but he claims not to carry sufficient funds. Diavolo provides the sum, hurling the petticoat at the nobleman. Matteo accepts

Lorenzo as son-in-law. Lord Rocburg confronts his wife as Diavolo, Stanlio and Ollio are to be shot. Stanlio blows his nose, the red handkerchief attracting the bull once more. Diavolo escapes on horseback; his servants clamber up a roof, slide down and disappear atop the runaway bull.

A favourite of both comedians, *Fra Diavolo* was released under that title everywhere except the US, where M-G-M decided upon a last-minute translation to *The Devil's Brother*. Roach later explained that his distributor regarded the title as incomprehensible in most areas, though aware himself that Laurel & Hardy fans would attend irrespective of title, and that a potentially large opera audience was lost by the renaming. The author has seen two British copies bearing the correct title, a 1974 35mm revival and a 16mm library print. European copies follow suit though unfortunately, UK television screenings are from American prints. Original US preview copies were also called *Fra Diavolo*, the title favoured by its stars. One of the most successful Laurel & Hardy features, *Fra Diavolo* received excellent reviews though some critics were bored with the Roach-directed plot footage. Pare Lorentz in *Vanity Fair* considered the 'narrative stupidity' to have been rescued by Laurel & Hardy's 'first rate music-hall pantomime', while the British *Film Weekly* said that 'Messrs. Laurel and Hardy are not going to let any singer get away with their picture'. William K. Everson (qv) reports many critics, aware probably only of the team's features, to have considered Laurel the funnier of the two; *Film Weekly* qualified this somewhat, believing it 'impossible to praise one without incidentally praising the other'. The film was considered 20 minutes too long, and this after losing half an hour following previews; it seems unlikely that any Laurel & Hardy scenes were lost. Their routines here are excellent, particularly a rickety ascent on stacked tables, the drinking scene and Stan's childlike tricks, commonplace among British youngsters but unknown elsewhere. One consists of placing the palms together with both middle digits folded, creating the illusion of one long, pivoting finger; the other is an elaborate routine ('kneesie-earsie-nosie') involving an alternate slapping of knees, pulling of nose and ear, and fluttering of hands. Special praise should be reserved for LeRoy Shield (*qv*), whose arrangement of the score is a masterful achievement. His baroque version of the Laurel & Hardy theme may be heard also in *Them Thar Hills* and *Wild Poses* (both *qv*). *Fra Diavolo* is one of the Roach films of which M-G-M retained ownership; in UK video release, it has been ignored in favour of other (inferior) studio-owned titles, *Bonnie Scotland*, *Air Raid Wardens* and *Nothing But Trouble* (all *qv*). There have been video editions in the US and Europe.

(See also: Alcohol; Armetta, Henry; *Blotto*; *Bohemian Girl, the*; Browne, Lucile; Feature films; Finlayson, James; King, Dennis; Laughing; M-G-M; Morton, James C.; Operas; Previews; Reviews; Television; Todd, Thelma; Video releases)

FRANCE
Laurel & Hardy have always been popular in France. In the 1930s, a large society devoted to the team flourished and during the filming of *Our Relations* (*qv*), Stan and Babe received a giant postcard, some six feet in length, from them. On their first visit to Paris in 1932, they passed through the crowd-filled Champs Elysées in a car supplied by the President. A later occupant of the Presidency, Vincent Auriol, honoured the team with a lunch when they arrived to film *Atoll K* (*qv*) in 1950 (newspaper photographs show the team being greeted by fans wearing Laurel & Hardy masks). The making

of this film proved an unhappy experience, as was their attempt to perform in the Lido, Paris, in 1947. They were unhappy with the restrictive microphone placing, a preponderance of drunks and too many unclad chorus girls, an embarrassment when receiving children among their backstage visitors. That aside, Laurel & Hardy always retained great affection for a country where they were so greatly appreciated.

(See also: *Fixer-Uppers, the*; *Flying Deuces, the*; Foreign versions; Marceau, Marcel; Rediscoveries; Stage appearances; Video releases)

FRATERNALLY YOURS
See: *Sons of the Desert*

FRAUDS AND FRENZIES (1918)
See: Semon, Larry

FREAK ENDINGS (all films *qv*)
A recurrent method of concluding the team's adventures is to leave them in some state of physical distortion. Hal Roach is said not to have cared very much for the idea, and the deletion of such an ending from *Block-Heads* has been attributed to him. There are nonetheless numerous examples, including *Going Bye-Bye!*, with Stan and Ollie seated, legs tied around their necks; *The Live Ghost*, in which their heads are twisted around 180 degrees; *Thicker Than Water*, which presents a mixed-up pair after a bungled blood transfusion; *Dirty Work*, when a scientific formula turns Ollie into a chimp; a similar transformation in *The Flying Deuces*, with Ollie reincarnated as a horse; *The Bohemian Girl*, after a spell in the torture chamber leaves Stan squashed and Ollie stretched; and from the later films, Stan miniaturized into a prop egg in *A-Haunting We Will Go* and the pair 'skinned alive' down to bare bones in *The Bullfighters*. Distortions occuring elsewhere in the films include the distended stomach endured by Ollie in *They Go Boom* and *Be Big* (*Below Zero*

concludes with a similarly inflated Stan), Ollie's stretched neck in *Way Out West*, Stan's stretched ear in the same film (and in *The Bohemian Girl*) and Ollie's huge, pulsating toe after a collision in *Habeas Corpus*.

(See also: Black humour)

FREEMASONS
One of the least-discussed aspects of Hardy's life is his keen interest in Freemasonry, shared by his long-time colleague James Finlayson (*qv*). The meticulously-kept Masonic archive preserves Hardy's Petition for Membership of Solomon Lodge no. 20, F.A.M. (Free and Accepted Masons), Jacksonville, Florida; dated 20 March 1916, it describes his address at that time as having been 725 May Street and place of employ (Vim Comedies) as 750 Riverside Drive. He had been at the May Street address for six months, and a Florida resident for two years. His occupation is given as Actor, Motion Pictures (his membership was proposed by Garry Hotaling, a studio colleague). Shortly afterwards, location work for a film required Hardy to appear drunk in a public parade, and he was spotted by members of his Lodge in this apparent condition. The professional nature of this conduct was obscured by the concealment of the camera in a nearby truck; as a result, an extraordinary meeting of the Lodge was called the next day for Hardy to explain this inappropriate public behaviour! Despite this early mishap Hardy attained the position of Master Mason later in 1916 and was awarded life membership of his Lodge in October 1948, a comparatively rare honour. His final resting place is in the Masonic section of the Garden of Valhalla Memorial Park, North Hollywood, where his ashes were placed in a Masonic service. Freemasonry traces its origins back to King Solomon's Temple, something which may have influenced the announcement in 1918 of a comedy

Anita Garvin keeps her dress in the release version of **From Soup to Nuts**

with Babe supporting Chaplin imitator Billy West (*qv*) titled *King Solomon.* Informed word suggests that the lodge meeting attended by Laurel and Hardy in *Sons of the Desert* (*qv*), though unlike Masonic proceedings, is humorously reminiscent of the spirit of such gatherings. It might be pleasant to speculate on Hardy's unofficial role as Technical Advisor!

(See also: Alcohol; Graves; Homes; Lubin, Siegmund 'Pop'; Solo films)

FRENCH, LLOYD A. (1900-50)
(Laurel & Hardy films *qv*)
He began in 1919 as actor at Roach Studios, where his father, Lewis A. French, was assistant production manager before assuming total responsibility for the Laurel & Hardy unit. The younger French turned to directing, as assistant until attaining full status in 1933 (he had previously received credit for directing *That's My Wife*). He co-directed *Me and My Pal* with Charles Rogers (qv) and is credited alone on *The Midnight Patrol, Busy Bodies, Dirty Work* and *Oliver the Eighth.* For *Sons of the Desert* he returned to the role of assistant director. Later, he worked on shorts at other studios, including a lengthy stint with Vitaphone in New York. He directed Edgar Kennedy (*qv*) in several of his RKO two-reelers, *Drafted in the Depot* (1940), *Two For the Money*

(1942) and *Hold Your Temper* (1943).

FROM SOUP TO NUTS
(Laurel & Hardy film)
Released by M-G-M, 24 March 1928. Produced by Hal Roach. Directed by E. Livingston Kennedy (Edgar Kennedy). Camera: Len Powers. Two reels. Silent.
With Stan Laurel and Oliver Hardy, Anita Garvin, Tiny Sandford, Edna Marian, Otto Fries, Ellinor Van Der Veer.

Newly-rich Mrs Culpepper (Anita Garvin) is anxious to impress at her smart dinner party. Less than impressive are her butlers for the evening, Stan and Ollie, whose arrival by the front door is a bad enough start even before they destroy the doorbell. They are waiters experienced only at railroad eating houses and have brought with them some robust attitudes: Mr Culpepper (Tiny Sandford) is unimpressed when Ollie describes his wife as 'some wiggler'. The waiters befriend the maid (Edna Marian) but Stan antagonises the chef when, having been told to remove his hat in the house, he tries to ensure that the chef does not wear his cap. Ollie intervenes and the pair set about the business in hand. Mrs Culpepper has been having difficulty coaxing a cocktail cherry away from the dish, and on finally capturing the rogue

titbit with her spoon, she falls victim to a tiara over her eyes. Stan and Ollie serve the soup, much of it pouring over Ollie's foot. The Culpeppers' dog has a strange taste for bananas, the discarded skin proving disastrous when Ollie carries in a cake. Stan solves Mrs Culpepper's problem with the elusive cherry by inverting the glass and permitting the cherry to fall in. Mrs Culpepper's tiara descends once more as Stan pats her on the back. An order to serve the salad 'undressed' results in a Stan clad only in long underwear; once her tiara is dislodged, Mrs Culpepper screams at the sight. Ollie covers Stan's top half with a jacket, asking his hostess 'How's that - perfect?' Mrs Culpepper finally abandons all pretence at decorum and knocks Ollie into the tea trolley.

Best known from its inclusion in *Laurel & Hardy's Laughing Twenties* (*qv*), *From Soup to Nuts* is familiar also through having been remade as the first two reels of *A Chump at Oxford* (*qv*). Although unsubtle, *From Soup to Nuts* is full of good gags in addition to showcasing the considerable talents of Anita Garvin (*qv*). *From Soup to Nuts* was the first of two occasions on which the comedians were directed by their fellow-actor, Edgar Kennedy (*qv*). After one more effort, *You're Darn Tootin'* (*qv*), Kennedy returned to the front of the cameras. Today's prints display signs of decomposition in certain scenes, particularly around the sub-titles (which have been replaced completely in the first reel). An employee of the Library of Congress in Washington has expressed heartbreak at having to dispose of the original negative of this film; fortunately new master material had been made before the damage became severe.

(See also: Compilations; Food;

Preservation; Remakes; Servants; Slapstick)

FUN ON THE TYROL
See: Circuses

THE FURTHER PERILS OF LAUREL & HARDY
(20th Century-Fox 1967)
(Laurel & Hardy films *qv*)
The success of *Laurel & Hardy's Laughing Twenties* (*qv*) guaranteed a further selection from writer and producer Robert Youngson (*qv*). As in the preceding effort, Laurel & Hardy are supported by extracts from other Roach comedians, on this occasion Snub Pollard, Charley Chase and Jean Harlow (all *qv*). The Harlow footage is from *The Unkissed Man* (1929), starring Bryant Washburn, a film misidentified by at least one source as a Laurel & Hardy comedy; Chase's *The Way of All Pants* (1927) typifies his adroit handling of otherwise commonplace material, turning the repeated loss and exchange of trousers into precision-timed farce. Just as

Laughing Twenties complements the Laurel & Hardy films with examples of their solo work, *Further Perils* in turn presents Laurel's 1918 Roach comedy *Just Rambling Along*; Hardy's days with Chaplin imitator Billy West (*qv*) are commemorated by *His Day Out* and *The Hobo* (both familiar from other Youngson films) plus West's shameless theft of Chaplin's *Tillie's Punctured Romance*, titled *The Villain*. *Further Perils* chronicles the team's development through *Flying Elephants* and *Sugar Daddies*, but takes considerable artistic licence when claiming Laurel & Hardy to have been a permanent team after *Do Detectives Think?* Later silents, presented either as abridgements or in lengthy extracts, are *The Second Hundred Years*, *Leave 'Em Laughing*, *You're Darn Tootin'*, *Habeas Corpus*, *That's My Wife*, *Angora Love*, *Should Married Men Go Home?* and *Early to Bed*. *You're Darn Tootin'* surfaces on two occasions, and special mention must be made of John Parker's skill in synchronising music to the film's opening bandstand scene.

The Further Perils of Laurel & Hardy *opens with the team as bandsmen*

Although much of the scoring is over-typical of 1960s methods, this section rivals the adroit dubbing of *Big Business* in Youngson's earlier *When Comedy Was King* (*qv*). Narration is in Youngson's customary style, effective if overburdened by witticisms (a *Punch* reviewer found praise for everything but the 'over-facetiousness' of the commentary). *Further Perils* is recommended for buff and general viewer alike.

(See also: Compilations; Dubbing; *Golden Age of Comedy, the*; Music; Rolin Film Company, the; Teaming; 20th Century-Fox)

111

G

GAGMEN
See: Writers

GAG TITLES (all films *qv*)
The art of title-writing for silent films extended far beyond conveying essentials of plot and dialogue. The best silents provided a minimum of titling with the maximum of wit, turning a cumbersome necessity into a positive contribution. At Roach these titles were usually the province of H. M. ('Beanie') Walker (*qv*), whose terse observations enliven even lesser comedies. A fair measure of Stan's character in *Sailors Beware* can be drawn from a title telling us that 'he bought a grandstand seat to see the world come to an end'. An impatient would-be homeowner in *The Finishing Touch* is 'looking for a quick finish - he'll get it'. Best of all are those setting the scene following the main credits: *Big Business* relates 'the story of a man who turned the other cheek - and got punched in the nose'; *Should Married Men Go Home* poses the question 'what is the surest way to keep a husband home? Answer: break both his legs'. *Leave 'Em Laughing* opens with another pertinent query (this time by Reed Heustis): 'What's worse than an aching tooth at three in the morning? Two of them'. Subtitling was redundant with the coming of sound but these introductory jests remained for a while. Matrimonial comment remained as in *Be Big* ('Mr Hardy is a man of great care, caution, and discretion - Mr Laurel is married too'), as did apt descriptions of the team's characters, notably *The Hoose-*

Gow's 'Neither Mr Laurel nor Mr Hardy had any thoughts of doing wrong - as a matter of fact, they had no thoughts of any kind'. The practice ceased after 1932, presumably the result either of Walker's departure from the studio or a growing awareness of the motif's archaic nature. In several instances gag titles were removed on reissue, losing comic introductions to such as *Brats*, *County Hospital* and *Blotto*, to name a few.

(See also: Reissues; Romance; Titling; Women)

GAMBLING
Modest wagering takes place in the Laurel & Hardy films, as when Ollie puts money on Stan losing a boxing match in *Any Old Port* (*qv*). On-set and other informal surroundings would sometimes see a quiet poker game, evidenced by a cheque that once surfaced at auction by which Stan settled a $25 gambling debt with Babe. This modest success typifies

Gambling: Mr. Hardy's luck runs true to form

Babe as gambler rather less than does his cameo role in *Riding High* (*qv*), where he blows a substantial sum on a hopeless horse. *Riding High* stars Bing Crosby, a golfing buddy of Babe's, who shared with him also a love of the racetrack. Babe often lost considerable amounts, not just at the track but on roulette and cards. This tapered off with time, but his luck with horses remained unchanged. At one time, with customary enthusiasm, he initiated a stable of his own, complete with animals and staff. Most of the horses were, to quote his widow, 'clinkers', but he bet on them loyally except once, delayed *en route* to the track. He then discovered his horse had won and been claimed by someone else.

(See also: Auctions; Golf; Hobbies)

Reginald Gardiner as a Foreign Legion officer in The Flying Deuces

GARDINER, REGINALD
(1903-80)
British actor in many Hollywood films. One of his most oddball successes is the comedy record *Trains*, an eccentric classic in which he impersonates various railway noises before concluding with 'back to the asylum!' He plays the Foreign Legion officer in *The Flying Deuces* (*qv*), and is remembered also from Chaplin's *The Great Dictator*.

(See also: Chaplin, Charlie)

GARVIN, ANITA (1906-94)
(Laurel & Hardy films *qv*)
New York-born actress who landed a job in a Sennett stage show, *Seeing Brooklyn*, when only 12. Her height and make-up enabled the young hopeful to pass for 16. Later, she was a Ziegfeld Girl, but, always more interested in films, she left a touring company of *Sally* while in California in order to seek picture work. Supporting roles in features were interspersed with short comedies at Christie and Educational; she first met Stan Laurel when both worked for Joe Rock (*qv*). Her work in these films (such as *The Snow Hawk* and *The Sleuth*) led to Stan asking Roach to hire the young actress, but to no avail. By coincidence, she was cast in *Raggedy Rose*, starring Mabel Normand (*qv*) and directed by Stan. In the Laurel & Hardy silents, Anita Garvin plays the Captain's wife in *Why Girls Love Sailors*, one of the officers' ladies in *With Love and Hisses*, a jewel thief in *Sailors, Beware!*, one of the boys' unresponsive customers in *Hats Off*, a night club floozie in *Their Purple Moment*, snooty Mrs Culpepper in *From Soup to Nuts* and, most famously despite the role's slightness, the girl who sits on a pie during *The Battle of the Century*. In talkies, she is best known as Mrs Laurel in *Blotto* and *Be Big*; she appears also in *Swiss Miss* and *A Chump at Oxford*, this last recreating her role in *From Soup to Nuts*. A filmography for Anita Garvin is difficult to compile, as she worked frequently with virtually everyone in film comedy, not just at Roach but elsewhere: feature credits include Garbo's *The Single Standard*, Trent's

*A publicity portrait of **Anita Garvin***

Last Case with Raymond Griffith and Universal's *Modern Love*, a 1929 feature with Charley Chase (*qv*). Miss Garvin's work with Chase deserves particular mention, especially *Whispering Whoopee* (1930), *His Silent Racket* (1933) and *Never the Dames Shall Meet* (1927), the last-named showing them in a male-female scrap anticipating similar moments in the screwball comedies of a decade later. Her aloof, disdainful character in this film (excerpted in *Laurel & Hardy's Laughing Twenties* [*qv*]) typifies the on-screen Garvin, whose dignity would regularly be forced to succumb to events. Her timing and reactions place her in comedy's top echelon, inspiring descriptions such as 'magnificent' and 'the uncrowned queen of slapstick'. She married bandleader 'Red' Stanley in 1930, family life taking precedence as the decade progressed. Later films include RKO shorts with Leon Errol, another Ziegfeld veteran; in *Truth Aches* (1939) her icy screen persona thaws somewhat as Errol's distraught wife, reduced to tears by her husband's disappearance. Miss Garvin retired during the 1940s, and to all intents and purposes vanished, despite maintaining contact with Stan. In 1973, Leonard Maltin (*qv*) (in *The Laurel & Hardy Book*) said how wonderful it would be to locate the actress, something that finally happened four years

later. Subsequently she was honoured by film societies, not least amongst them the Sons of the Desert (*qv*), among whom she was perhaps the most popular celebrity. Her interviews revealed a friendly, humorous and genuinely modest lady who seemed pleasantly surprised at the interest taken in her. Toward the end of his life, Stan Laurel told her that he intended to have a star placed for her on the Hollywood Walk of Fame; he did not live to do so but shortly before her death, the Sons of the Desert attempted to fulfil this wish.

(See also: Aubrey, Jimmy; *Pair of Tights, a*; Sennett, Mack; Shotguns; *Tit For Tat*)

GEMORA, CHARLES
See: Animals, *Chimp, the* and *Swiss Miss*

GET 'EM YOUNG
See: Rediscoveries and Teaming

GHOSTS
See: Hereafter, the

GILBERT, BILLY
(William Gilbert Baron) (1893-1971) (Laurel & Hardy films *qv*)
A stage actor who turned film comedian on Laurel's recommendation, Billy Gilbert blustered his way through several Laurel & Hardy

films, among them *The Chimp*, *The Music Box*, *County Hospital* and *Pack Up Your Troubles*. In *One Good Turn*, he is cast against type, playing a drunk who accidentally places a wallet in Stan's pocket; *Towed in a Hole* presents a benign Billy, from whom the boys acquire an ageing boat, while in *Them Thar Hills* the kindly Dr Gilbert examines Ollie's gout. In a sense Gilbert served as a replacement for Edgar Kennedy (*qv*) in roles demanding frustrated anger rather than straightforward menace; his character in *Block-Heads* is a direct parallel to Kennedy's part in the film's prototype, *Unaccustomed As We Are*. Gilbert joined Roach as actor and gagman after Stan Laurel saw him on stage. Other Roach appearances include shorts with Our Gang (*qv*), Pitts and Todd, and co-starring status in the *Taxi Boys* series (*qv*). The latter films, pairing Gilbert with slimline comic Ben Blue, were unworthy of his considerable talent; similar teamings would recur throughout his career, notably with Vince Barnett at Educational, with whom he made such genuinely funny comedies as *Two Lame Ducks*. Feature work includes the Marx Brothers' *A Night at the Opera* and more surprisingly, the Alice Faye musical *Tin Pan Alley*. He also provided the voice of 'Sneezy' for Disney's *Snow White and the Seven Dwarfs*. Later in life, the comedian was honoured by the Sons of the Desert club (*qv*). A year before his death he wrote an introduction to the book *Movie Comedy Teams*, recalling his work with many of its subjects, revealing that it was he who introduced Bud Abbott to showbusiness.

(See also: Burton, Richard; Costello, Lou; Doctors; Maltin, Leonard; Marx Brothers, the; Shotguns)

Billy Gilbert holds a press conference – and Patricia Ellis – in Block-Heads

GLASSES
See: Spectacles

GODDARD, PAULETTE
(1911-90)
Actress officially 'discovered' by
Chaplin (*qv*) and subsequently
his third wife. After appearing
with him in *Modern Times* and
The Great Dictator, they separated both personally and
professionally, the actress proving
her worth in *The Ghost Breakers*
(1940), directed by George
Marshall (*qv*). She entered films as
a crowd extra with Hal Roach, and
has been identified in *Young
Ironsides*, a 1932 short with Charley
Chase (*qv*). That same year she
appeared in Eddie Cantor's *The Kid
From Spain*, directed by Leo
McCarey (*qv*). Miss Goddard is said
to be visible in Laurel and Hardy's
Berth Marks (*qv*); a European
TV/video edition makes the bold step
of billing her on the opening titles.

GOING BYE-BYE!
(Laurel & Hardy film)
Released by M-G-M, 23 June 1934.
Produced by Hal Roach. Directed by
Charles Rogers. Camera: Francis
Corby. Two reels.
With Stan Laurel and Oliver Hardy,
Walter Long, Mae Busch.

'Butch' Long (Walter Long) has been
convicted for murder largely through
evidence provided by Stan and Ollie.
He accepts his fate with resignation
even when sentenced to life imprisonment; the balance is upset when Stan
asks 'Aren't you going to hang him?'
Long swears to escape, break off the
boys' legs and, as crowning indignity,
tie the limbs around the owners'
necks. Ollie is sceptical until Long,
breaking free from a straitjacket,
causes panic in court. Outside, they
are advised to leave town. To finance a
trip East, they advertise for a travelling companion, receiving an answer
from a lady (Mae Busch) who is as
unaware of their identity as they are of

her status as Long's girlfriend. Long
escapes, taking refuge in the woman's
flat just before her new travelling
companions arrive. Fearing a visit
from the police, Long is hidden in a
trunk when the doorbell rings.
Discovering her callers to be Stan and
Ollie, the woman tries to open the
trunk but finds it jammed. Telling the
boys that her friend 'accidentally fell
in', she enlists their help in opening
the trunk before setting off to fetch a
more qualified friend. Their efforts
contribute mightily to Long's discomfort; in boring holes to provide air,

they puncture Long's posterior.
Looking through one of the holes,
Long recognizes Ollie. He suggests a
blowtorch to melt the lock, but Stan
sends a jet of flame into the trunk.
The smouldering occupant is doused
by a fire hose, which also loosens the
sides of the trunk. The police have
intercepted Long's girlfriend, but
arrive after Long has taken his
promised revenge. Stan and Ollie
make a bizarre sight on the sofa, their
legs tied neatly around their necks.

Another of the 'freak endings' (*qv*)
favoured by Stan concludes this variation of *Do Detectives Think?* (*qv*). The
funniest moments are, untypically,
verbal: Ollie's repetition of the phrase
'Aren't you gonna hang him?' (imitating Stan's grin), Stan's remark 'It
could happen' when told about the
man in a trunk and, above all, Ollie
excusing himself from a telephone call
because his 'ear is full of milk'.
Among the rather savage (but very
funny) visual gags are Stan sitting
atop the trunk, happily sawing into it
without noticing the blade heading
toward his groin, and the inadvertent
shredding of Ollie's jacket.

(See also: Busch, Mae; Cars;

Going Bye-Bye!: *if they only knew
what was in the trunk*

Dialogue; Flowers; Judges; Locations; Lufkin, Sam; Murder; Remakes; Telephones; Working titles)

THE GOLDEN AGE OF COMEDY
(DCA/Fox 1958)
(Laurel & Hardy films *qv*)

The first feature-length compilation written and produced by Robert Youngson (*qv*), presented at a time before interest in silent films had become widespread. It might fairly be claimed that this film did more than any other to foster that interest. American audiences had begun to rediscover Laurel & Hardy through TV, but serious critical attention was only drawn to the pair when *The Golden Age of Comedy* offered an extensive survey of their best silent work. Youngson admitted (when interviewed for *Film Fan Monthly*) that the selection was 'top-heavy with Laurel & Hardy'. Evidently he had something of a point to prove and his decision was vindicated by excellent reviews and a brace of Oscars. *Golden Age* was released overseas by 20th Century-Fox (*qv*) but reached US cinemas via a small independent company, DCA. Every major distributor had considered the project uncommercial; its enormous success guaranteed distribution for Youngson's subsequent efforts. The film opens with a collage of highlights (concluding with Laurel & Hardy's *Angora Love*) before dividing into a series of 'acts', the first dealing with Sennett's work of the 1920s. The second, sub-titled 'Nobody liked them but the public', presents Laurel & Hardy in extracts from *Habeas Corpus*, *The Second Hundred Years*, *We Faw Down* (identified by its British title, *We Slip Up*) and the pie fight from *The Battle of the Century* which, as noted, owes its survival to this anthology. Act three is devoted to Will Rogers, concentrating chiefly on his film parodies (*Uncensored Movies* and, unnamed, *Big Moments From Little Pictures*) made at Roach. The fourth section, 'Two unforgotten girls', refers

Golf: Stan's head makes a useful tee

to Carole Lombard (supported by Daphne Pollard [*qv*]) and Jean Harlow (*qv*); the latter appears with Laurel and Hardy in *Double Whoopee*. Next is Ben Turpin (*qv*), followed by act six, 'a comedy classic', comprising all but the opening of Laurel & Hardy's *Two Tars*. Harry Langdon (*qv*) dominates the next part in scenes from *The Luck of the Foolish*; act eight, 'Animal comedy', permits trained creatures to get the better of Charley Chase (*qv*), Billy Bevan, Andy Clyde and others. The finale belongs to Laurel & Hardy, employing the final third of *You're Darn Tootin'*, in which passers-by are drawn into a trouser-tearing battle.

(See also: Compilations; Hall, Charles; Maltin, Leonard; M-G-M; Periodicals; Television)

GOLF
The dominant interest of Babe's leisure hours was golf, a sport to which he had been introduced by Larry Semon (*qv*). In 1922 they appeared in a two-reeler titled simply *Golf*, lampooning the game in a fashion that was repeated by the Laurel & Hardy duo in their *Should Married Men Go Home?* (*qv*). A regular at the

Lakeside Country Club in San Fernando Valley, Babe regularly won the Roach Studio's annual tournament; he took on most of the industry in the Motion Picture Golf Tournament, defeating Adolphe Menjou in the final. Stan Laurel's double work load forbade many trips to the links, although he was known to join his screen partner on occasion.

(See also: Gambling; Seiter, William A.; Solo films; *Topper*)

GOMBELL, MINNA (1892-1973)
Broadway actress who migrated to Hollywood in 1930, achieving early success supporting Sally Eilers in *Bad Girl* (1931). She played Mrs Hardy in *Block-Heads* (*qv*); her many other films include *The Thin Man* (1934), *The Hunchback of Notre Dame* (1939) and *Pagan Love Song* (1951). Her date of birth is given sometimes as 1900, but at her death she was reported to have been 81 years of age. Also known as Winifred Lee and Nancy Carter.

(See also: Women)

THE GOON SHOW

In discussing his taste in humour, Stan Laurel expressed dislike for the 'rough type of nut humour' practised by the Marx Brothers (*qv*), favouring the quieter craziness of Dan Leno (*qv*). He considered *The Goon Show* typical of that brand of British craziness. Anarchic and innovative, *The Goon Show* ran on BBC radio between 1951 and 1960, redefining absurdist and satirical humour while influencing the generation that produced Monty Python. The principals were Peter Sellers (1925-80), Harry Secombe (b. 1921), Spike Milligan (b. 1918) and Michael Bentine (b. 1922). On the surface, Laurel's interest seems surprising, yet the Goon style shares many elements with that of Laurel & Hardy, not least when the pace slows to allow the dim-witted characters Eccles (Milligan) and Bluebottle (Sellers) a chance to engage in rambling duologues, each of them building to the conclusion of an absurd premise. Eccles sometimes has dialogue that could just as easily suit the Stanley character: 'I may not say much, but what I do say, don't make sense!'; while the aged and monumentally decrepit Henry and Min (Sellers and Milligan) are as inept as Stan and Ollie when required to open and close doors, each continuing to lock out the other. In one of the 1950s shows, there is a jokey saxophone rendition of 'On To The Show', the Roach studio melody considered by many to be a second Laurel & Hardy theme tune. In a 1972 show reuniting the Goons for the BBC's 50th birthday, Sellers, in his best Laurel voice, claims that 'anyone with a name like Hitler can't be all that bad'. Milligan's response, in a thick German accent, is obvious: 'This is another fine mess you've got us into'! Michael Bentine, who left after the second series, was then known for a variety act (preserved in the Goons' 1952 film *Down Among the Z Men*) in which a solitary prop, a chair back, could be made to represent every item referred to in his monologue. In an autobiography, *The Long Banana Skin* (Wolfe, 1975), Bentine recalls meeting Laurel and Hardy, who praised the originality of the routine. Many years later Bentine would present clips of the two comedians, together and solo, in BBC TV's *Golden Silents*. Harry Secombe, who in 1981 became one of comedy's very few knights, has frequently emphasised his rotund figure in a creditable imitation of Oliver Hardy. In addition to performing, Spike Milligan dominated the scripting of the show. In 1974 he was among those to share his thoughts on Laurel & Hardy in the BBC documentary *Cuckoo* (*qv*). Peter Sellers is said to have kept a picture of Laurel & Hardy wherever he travelled: particularly prized was a photograph of himself with Stan during a visit to the Laurel home in 1964, an occasion commemorated in Laurel's visitors' book (the Sellers character in *Being There* is based to a large degree on Stan Laurel). Sellers and director Blake Edwards made no secret of the debt owed to Laurel & Hardy in the visual comedy of their *Pink Panther* films, although the style in these latter-day efforts is broadened considerably. Sellers' long-time friend and auxiliary member of the Goon team, Graham Stark, has recorded an occasion early in their careers when he and Sellers were required to dub voices on some silent Laurel & Hardy comedies. Titles selected are unknown, but it would be intriguing to know if these survive. Each considered it a labour of love and one can imagine Sellers to have been responsible for the Laurel & Hardy poster visible in his 1968 film *I Love You, Alice B. Toklas*.

(See also: Catch phrases; Doors; *Fine Mess, a*; Impersonators; Music)

GORDON, MARY (1882-1963)

(Laurel & Hardy films *qv*)
Scottish-born actress, remembered chiefly as 'Mrs Hudson' to Basil Rathbone's Sherlock Holmes. She played 'Mrs MacTavish' in *Pack Up Your Troubles*, 'Mrs Bickerdike' in *Bonnie Scotland*, an unnamed (but Scottish) kitchen hand in *Way Out*

Peter Sellers of **The Goon Show** *liked to carry a picture of Laurel & Hardy wherever he went. Here is a notable example on the set of* I Love You, Alice B. Toklas *(1968)*

West and the boys' neighbour in *Saps at Sea*.

GOULDING, ALFRED (1896-1972)

It was Alf Goulding who first recommended Stan Laurel to Roach. At the time (1918) Goulding was one of Harold Lloyd's regular directors. He did not direct Laurel & Hardy until their penultimate Roach film, *A Chump at Oxford* (*qv*), but was conveniently placed some years later when *Atoll K* (*qv*) ran into trouble at its location near Cannes. An Australian, Goulding was directing minor films in Britain (such as *Dick Barton, Special Agent*) when Stan Laurel brought him over to tidy up the directing. Goulding's widow, Betty, told Randy Skretvedt (*qv*) that Stan Laurel thought highly enough of the director to accept his word on certain things rather than assume his usual total control; Goulding was however unable to exert too much influence over the crew of *Atoll K*.

(See also: Lloyd, Harold; Rolin Film Company, the)

GRAND MILLS HOTEL

See: Unfilmed Projects

GRAND ORDER OF WATER RATS, THE

British society organised somewhat on Masonic lines and composed mainly of variety comedians. Noted for its charity work, the Order was born during an informal outing in 1889 and given its constitution the following year. The name derives from a trotting pony compared, rather unkindly, to a water rat; another reason is that 'rats' is the reverse spelling of 'star'. The Order survives to this day and virtually every major talent in British comedy has been a member. Laurel & Hardy were initiated into their number on 30 March 1947 and wore their GOWR lapel badges on almost all subsequent public appearances. One of the features at Lodge meetings is the award of a 'Jester's Medal' to who-

ever makes the best joke, retained by the wearer until succeeded by a comparable quip. Stan Laurel introduced an opposite award, the 'Golden Egg', presented for the worst joke and accompanied by a fine. In 1955, Stan and Babe contributed a filmed greeting to a BBC TV programme about the Order, entitled *This is Music-Hall*. On Babe's death two years later, fellow-Water Rat Charlie Chester composed a eulogy which was later reprinted in Chester's book *The World Is Full of Charlies*. Stan received a copy and wrote to Chester in appreciation. As Chester has noted, it was not too long before he was to write a similar eulogy for Stan Laurel. Stan's widow subsequently gave his Water Rats memorabilia to Tom Sefton, Grand Sheik of the San Diego Tent of the Sons of the Desert (*qv*), who has showcased the material.

(See also: Freemasons; Leno, Dan; Music-hall; Stage appearances; Television; Unfilmed projects)

GRANGER, DOROTHY (b. 1912)

(Laurel & Hardy films *qv*)
Actress best remembered today as a frequent wife to Leon Errol in his RKO two-reelers. Short comedies with other stars include Clark & McCullough (*Jitters the Butler*, *The Gay Nighties*), W. C. Fields (*The Dentist*) and the Three Stooges (*Punch Drunks*). Although identified chiefly with shorts, she may be seen in comedy features such as Wheeler & Woolsey's *Hips, Hips, Hooray* and Danny Kaye's *The Secret Life of Walter Mitty*; indeed, a 1969 profile in *Film Fan Monthly* lists no less than 77 full-length films. Roach appearances include the *Boy Friends* series, *The King* with Harry Langdon (*qv*), at least six films with Charley Chase (*qv*) plus *The Laurel-Hardy Murder Case*, *One Good Turn* and *Hog Wild*, playing Ollie's maid and a girl crossing the road, with her back to camera. Inexplicably, her photo is used to represent the landlord's wife in *The*

Chimp, a role actually played by Martha Sleeper (*qv*). She told *Film Fan Monthly* that she had an 8mm print of *Murder Case*; elsewhere she recalled having played in the film's three foreign versions, her linguistic skill permitting the studio to pay off her replacements.

(See also: Foreign versions; Home Movies; Periodicals)

GRAVES

Oliver Norvell Hardy's last resting place is in the Masonic section of the Garden of Valhalla Memorial Park, North Hollywood. He had requested cremation, a Masonic service and to be interred anywhere but Forest Lawn. Stan Laurel was in poor health and forbidden by his doctor to attend the funeral. When Stan followed his partner, his remains were also cremated in keeping with his belief that the dead should not occupy space needed by the living. Stan's ashes were placed in the Court of Liberty, the new Hollywood Hills Forest Cemetery. A memorial plaque describes him as 'a master of comedy – his genius in the art of humor brought gladness to the world he loved'. The funeral eulogy was read by comedian Dick Van Dyke (*qv*), a text later reprinted in an updated edition of *Mr Laurel and Mr Hardy*; the book's author, John McCabe (*qv*) accepts the spirit of Stan's epitaph but favours instead the comedian's first billing in music-halls: 'Stan Jefferson - He of the Funny Ways'. Nothing can compare with the somewhat eccentric ambition Stan conveyed to a *Daily Herald* reporter in 1932: when surveying the team's neon-lit billing at the Empire, Leicester Square, he was reminded of a lighthouse built in the graveyard of his home town, Ulverston, taking the form of a 'tombstone with a light on top'. He added, quite seriously, that his ambition was to have just such a monument.

(See also: Biographies; Births; Black

humour; Deaths; Freemasons; Radio; Stage appearances)

GRAVES, STAX (1882-1969)

Head still photographer for Roach until starting his own business in 1929, Chester Lee Graves was known as 'Bud' but preferred the designation 'Stax' for his work. The famous 'Stax' portrait of Laurel & Hardy from 1929 has become almost standard.

GREAT GUNS

(Laurel & Hardy film)
Released by 20th Century-Fox, 10 October 1941. Produced by Sol M. Wurtzel. Directed by Montague (Monty) Banks. Director of Photography: Glen MacWilliams. 74 minutes.
With Stan Laurel and Oliver Hardy, Sheila Ryan, Dick Nelson, Edmund MacDonald, Russell Hicks, Ludwig Stossel, Mae Marsh, Alan Ladd.

Young millionaire Dan Forrester (Dick Nelson) leads a sheltered life thanks to his doting aunts and a physician adept at inventing allergies. Dan is pleased when his draft notice arrives and surprises his devoted retainers, Stan and Ollie, by passing the medical. Still believing him fragile, Stan and Ollie join up in order to take care of him. They arrive at the 10th Cavalry accompanied by their pet blackbird, Penelope, a creature unwilling to fly home. Dan and the boys make an immediate enemy of Sgt. Hippo (Edmund MacDonald), particularly when failing to recognize a General during inspection. Dan's rivalry with the Sergeant escalates when making friends with Ginger (Sheila Ryan), who runs the camp's photo shop. At a rodeo, Hippo plans revenge by putting Dan on a particularly wild horse; Stan and Ollie are at first horrified then delighted as Dan proves an able rider. Hippo takes over but humiliates himself by being thrown. Stan and Ollie laugh a little too hard and are given the job of exercising horses, miles from camp. They

lose the horses and hop a lift back, straight into a target range. Later they cause trouble when Penelope the blackbird joins them at inspection, all the more so after she is concealed in Ollie's trousers. As Dan's romance with Ginger flourishes, so does Stan and Ollie's belief in his frailty. Determined to end the relationship, they visit the girl posing as financiers willing to buy her off. Ginger recognizes them from a photo with Dan and launches into a melodramatic rejection of their offer. As a last resort, they have Dan put in the guardhouse. Dan is left behind as the platoon engages in manoeuvres. Stan and Ollie are captured after a wild jeep ride and are put to work constructing a pontoon bridge. Hippo hears of this and informs Dan, who escapes custody and sends Penelope to find Stan. On horseback, Dan follows the bird, leading the platoon straight to the enemy bridge and victory. Dan joins the platoon on parade, followed

by his retainers and a uniformed Penelope aboard that most prestigious of vehicles, a sanitation wagon.

First in the team's series for 20th Century-Fox (qv), Great Guns sets the trend of providing Laurel & Hardy with unsuitable and derivative material in its aping of Abbott & Costello's recent Buck Privates and its disregard for their characterizations. Randy Skretvedt (qv) has noted a scene where Stan derides a flour-coated Ollie instead of trying to help, while one might add the moment when an infantile Stan claims to 'play soldier'. Scriptwriter Lou Breslow clearly failed to comprehend the difference between child-like and child-ish, erasing their dignity further with contemptuous references in the dialogue. Heroine Sheila Ryan (qv) should be in sympathy with them, yet compares their physiques to a fire hydrant and observation balloon. There is even a racial joke, usually avoided by the team, as Stan, in the unaccustomed role of wisecracker, describes a smoke-blackened Sergeant as 'Old Black Joe', and so on. Characteristic touches exist, but are placed arbitrarily: a 'white magic' gag, using a lightbulb that functions only outside of the lamp, works well enough, but the best moment is a revived gag from *The Finishing Touch* (*qv*) in which Stan appears to support both ends of a lengthy plank. The supporting cast provides some interest, among them future star Alan Ladd in a walk-on and former Griffith heroine Mae Marsh. Another veteran was cameraman Glen MacWilliams, a friend of Babe's from solo days. His career was in the doldrums after many years in Britain, but the comedian used his influence to make MacWilliams director of photography on this and their next Fox picture, *A-Haunting We Will Go* (*qv*).

(See also: Army, the; Banks, Monty; Barbers; Censorship; Costello, Lou; Crying; Race; Reviews; Video releases; Wartime; 'White magic'; Writers; Wurtzel, Sol M.)

THE GREAT RACE (1965)
Blake Edwards' much-imitated comedy spectacular bears the dedication 'for Mr Laurel and Mr Hardy', presumably as *hommage* both to visual comedy and Laurel himself, who died earlier the same year. This story of a turn-of-the-century car race abounds in period trappings and full-blooded performances, the most obvious parallels to Laurel & Hardy being the oversized battles in a saloon and, especially, a bakery. Echoes of Stan and Ollie permeate the comic business between villains Jack Lemmon and Peter Falk, particularly in an exchange of soakings and the moment where Lemmon's frozen moustache snaps off. While flawed by an overlong pastiche of *The Prisoner of Zenda*, *The Great Race* is very entertaining but not quite in the Laurel & Hardy spirit; as noted elsewhere, the

team's few excursions into out-and-out slapstick earned them an unjust reputation for basic knockabout. (See also: *Battle of the Century, the*; *Fine Mess, a* ; Goon Show, the; Slapstick)

GREENE, GRAHAM
See: Reviews

GREY, ANNE (1907-?)
Born Aileen Ewing in London, Anne Grey began as a journalist but switched to film acting, mostly in Britain (*The Runaway Bride*, *The Nipper*) but sometimes in Hollywood. In *Bonnie Scotland* (*qv*) she plays Lady Violet Ormsby, whose scheming separates young lovers Lorna MacLaurel and Alan Douglas. Other American films include Paramount's *Too Many Parents*.

GUEST APPEARANCES (all *qv*)
Laurel & Hardy were considered welcome additions to other people's films from their earliest days as a team. A 1927 Roach comedy starring Max Davidson (*qv*), *Call of the Cuckoos*, includes Laurel & Hardy clowning with Charley Chase, James Finlayson and Charlie Hall (all *qv*). One of the shorts pairing ZaSu Pitts with Thelma Todd (*qv*), *On the Loose*, finishes with an unbilled appearance of Laurel & Hardy as the girls' prospective suitors. A charity short, *The Stolen Jools*, includes a memorable moment involving Stan and Ollie with a collapsing car. The long-running Our Gang series (*qv*) was enhanced by a few appearances of the two in their solo days plus a brief shot of them both (as babies) in the 1933 comedy *Wild Poses*. Charley Chase contributed excellent support to the Laurel & Hardy feature *Sons of the Desert*; in turn Laurel & Hardy are to be glimpsed in the 1936 Chase short *On the Wrong Trek*. The team's contributions to *Hollywood Revue of 1929*, *The Rogue Song*, and *Hollywood Party* are of sufficient weight to lift them out of the 'guest' category but their two sequences in

Pick A Star, despite totalling some ten minutes, seem to exist solely as a means of bolstering a pleasant but unremarkable Roach feature.

GUILES, FRED LAWRENCE
See: Biographies

GUINNESS, SIR ALEC (b. 1914)
Distinguished British actor whose achievements on stage, film and television range between Shakespeare, the Ealing comedies and John le Carré's espionage tales, via *Bridge Over the River Kwai* and *Star Wars*. In 1961, Guinness wrote to Stan Laurel after reading *Mr Laurel and Mr Hardy*, congratulating Stan on his recent Academy Award and recalling that in youth he had played Shakespeare's Sir Andrew Aguecheek (from *Twelfth Night*) as per the Stanley character. Contemporary critics noted this perhaps unconscious imitation, which Guinness considered evidence of the degree to which he had absorbed Laurel's work. A little more may be detected in Guinness' *The Card* (1952).

(See also: Biographies; McCabe, John; *Our Relations*)

GUIOL, FRED L. (1898-1964)
(Laurel & Hardy films *qv*)
Director of Laurel & Hardy films in the formative period of 1926-7. Originally with Griffith, Guiol joined Roach as a cameraman in 1919, graduating to director four years later. His studio nickname, 'Chilli', derived from a fondness for chilli con carne, then very much in vogue. Guiol later collaborated with another ex-cameraman, director George Stevens (*qv*), on the screenplays for *Gunga Din* and *Shane*; he was also associate director of the latter film. Other directoral credits include Wheeler and Woolsey's *The Nitwits*.

GYPSIES
See: *The Bohemian Girl* and Censorship

HABEAS CORPUS

(Laurel & Hardy film)
Released by M-G-M, 1 December
1928. Produced by Hal Roach.
Directed by James Parrott. Camera:
Len Powers. Two reels. Silent, but
released with music and sound effects.
With Stan Laurel and Oliver Hardy,
Richard Carle, Charles Rogers.

Professor Padilla (Richard Carle)
needs a body in order to prove his theory that the human brain is,
sometimes, 'practically flat'. The task
of grave-robbing goes to Stan and
Ollie, who have stopped at his house
to beg for food. The Professor's state
of mind may be gauged from such
eccentric habits as flicking ash into his
waistcoat pocket. His butler (Charles
Rogers) is an undercover police detective; Padilla will be looked after while
Laurel and Hardy are followed to the
graveyard. En route, Stan and Ollie
try to obtain directions from a street
sign; unable to see it in the dark, Ollie
climbs to the top, to find it reads
WET PAINT. Ollie is left with white
handprints on his bottom and what
resembles disembodied limbs
imprinted on his suit (evidently building up to a gag cut before release).
They find the graveyard, where the
detective, draped in a sheet, is already
hiding. Stan is sent in through the
open gates but, hearing the detective
sneeze, scurries out again. Ollie sends
him back, but this time Stan attracts

Richard Carle engages the boys as
grave-robbers in **Habeas Corpus**
A UK billing for this 'synchronised'
film co-stars the enigmatic 'Olivier' Hardy

the attention of a graveyard official
who, investigating the disturbance,
trips over the detective. Panic ensues,
with Stan's exit followed quickly by
that of the official, who locks the
gates. Re-admittance means scaling
the wall, something achieved after
great difficulty and with Stan falling
into an open grave. Stan sets to work,
Ollie observing from afar, unaware
that he has placed his lamp on the
back of a moving tortoise. A fluttering
bat causes Stan to clap his hands; the
detective does likewise. Stan tries
again; another clap from the detective.
Ollie insists it to be an echo until
Stan, deliberately missing a clap, still
hears an 'echo'. The bat resumes flying around Stan just as the tortoise
reaches the detective. His sheet set on
fire by the lamp, the detective runs
through the graveyard; exit Stan once
more. Ollie decides to climb the wall,
demolishing it in the process. As Stan
digs, Ollie nurses a sore foot. Noticing
his toes in the soil, they assume them
to be something from the grave and
smash them. After yet another exit,
Ollie examines his pulsating toes
before Stan is sent in again. The
detective, wrapped in his sheet (curiously unsinged), hides in the grave,
rising to his feet as Stan digs. Stan,

terrified, escapes the apparition, who
returns to the grave. Ollie brings out
the 'body' in a sack, giving Stan the
job of carrying him through the
street. The detective's feet pop
through, enabling him to walk behind
Stan. Suspicious, Stan pauses, calling
Ollie back. The detective frees an
arm, first lifting Ollie's hat then
putting his hand over Ollie's face;
instant flight culminates in Ollie and
the detective plunging into a deep
puddle. As Ollie surfaces, he asks Stan
where the body has gone: Stan points
to the moving sack, and the boys disappear down the street.

Habeas Corpus, a descendent of the
graveyard sequence in their earlier *Do
Detectives Think?* (*qv*), is easily their
most extensive foray into black
humour (*qv*). This macabre aspect
does much to offset the unusual pro-
ponderance of obvious slapstick,
usually balanced in their films by situation and character. It is no
coincidence that films given too much
to comic panic tend not to be their
best; *The Laurel-Hardy Murder Case*
(*qv*), even with its horror-parody
basis, suffers in this way. One particularly frustrating sequence in *Habeas
Corpus* is that in which the team
spend far too long attempting to scale
a wall. Laurel later admitted to occasional 'over-milking', although this
example may perhaps be explained by
the film's having been released initially with music and sound effects.
Today this soundtrack is unavailable,
but the action seems timed to fit a
musical beat. Although Randy

Skretvedt (*qv*) has ascertained that editing took place before Roach made arrangements for sound, it is possible that such accompaniment was either anticipated or allowed for in subsequent re-editing. The climbing sequence becomes less tiresome when dubbed in similar fashion for *The Further Perils of Laurel & Hardy* (*qv*). Another frustration in today's copies derives from the absence of at least one sub-title in the opening scene; the boys' motive for visiting the scientist's home is rendered unclear (they have in fact called to request 'a slice of buttered toast'). Some modern prints retain the original cloth-background titles, but in most these are replaced with white-on-black. Some sources have credited Leo McCarey (*qv*) as director of this film. McCarey was certainly involved in his usual capacity as writer and supervisor, but the official director was James Parrott (*qv*).

(See also: Animals; Black humour; *Big Noise, the*; Compilations; Graves; Insanity; Night scenes; Policemen; Sound; Titling; Vagrancy)

HAIR (all films *qv*)

The team's rather distinctive appearance is topped by eccentric hairstyles. Stan Laurel kept his hair long on top in order to facilitate a comic 'fright wig' that could be pulled up while scratching the head. Oliver Hardy favoured a forward-combed fringe, conveying both grandeur and the possibility of his barber owning a pudding basin. Off-duty, they kept their hair slicked down in the fashion of the period; this was also true of the on-screen Stan until he and Babe had their heads shaved for *The Second Hundred Years*, after which his hair grew into a vertical mess that drew sufficient laughter to ensure its retention. The Hardy fringe took a little longer to develop, still being combed more laterally until mid-1929; as the fringe progressed, so the bald spot at the top of his head developed. Longer hair was provided in the form of wigs

for the operas (*qv*) and other costumed roles, such as the female impersonation of *Twice Two*. Facial hair tended to be avoided, as it would obscure their range of expression, although Ollie's miniscule moustache serves to complete his cherubic face. Larger prop moustaches form part of an unconvincing disguise in *Swiss Miss*, while deleted scenes from *Bacon Grabbers* and *Pardon Us* show them in false beards of similar credibility.

(See also: Barbers; *Bullfighters, the*;

Hair: the prison haircuts and the aftermath

Call of the Cuckoos; Colouring; Deleted scenes; *Duck Soup*; Female impersonation; *Hats Off*; Villains)

HAL ROACH STUDIOS, THE

Begun as the Rolin company (*qv*) with D. Whiting as Roach's partner, the Hal Roach Studio became just that from 1919 when construction began at Culver City, near Los Angeles. The mainstay series which starred Harold Lloyd (*qv*) (who would soon graduate to features), continued at Rolin until the short comedies were handed to a supporting player, Snub Pollard (*qv*), often under the direction of Charley Chase (*qv*). After an amicable split between Roach and Lloyd, the studio's big series were those with Chase and Our Gang (*qv*), branching out into occasional features and employing declining stars for short comedies. Lloyd's departure had left Roach without a major star: Lloyd had begun as a conscious Chaplin imitator and Roach wanted a figure who would become comparable to both, attempting to build Pollard, James Finlayson (*qv*) and Clyde Cook (*qv*) into the role. A single such figure never emerged but the Laurel & Hardy films eventually provided the answer, in turn spawning various inferior double-acts, in-house and out. It is generally held that Roach provided the best and only environment in which Laurel & Hardy could have met, developed and flourished as they did. An informal structure and communal enthusiasm meant that good ideas were encouraged and shared and the studio attracted comedy's best with its friendliness and incentive. As boss, Roach functioned not merely as figurehead but often as writer and director, in later years making a point of piloting special projects or the first of a new series. Roach had the sense to experiment and would be prepared to lose money on a worthwhile comedy; the expensive set for *Brats* (*qv*) seems today a remarkable luxury for any short subject, while *Beau Hunks* (*qv*) was permitted to run double the planned length despite an agreed sum for a two-reeler. Studio atmosphere was threatened somewhat when the depression really bit, mostly through economies personified in one Henry Ginsberg. Reportedly imposed upon the studio by Roach's creditors, Ginsberg was acquainted with figures but not with the methods that earned the money. His regime as General Manager saw the abandonment of some promising ideas and, more seriously, the departure of several key

personnel. Those who remained soldiered on, the familial air surviving until Roach bowed to the relegation of short comedies to the minor league. Chase and Our Gang were gone while Laurel & Hardy's features commanded less of Roach's attention, his ambitions having diverted to the prestigious *Topper* (*qv*) or *Of Mice and Men* (*qv*). During the war, Roach served as a lieutenant-colonel while his studio was occupied by the US Government for the making of training films. On his return, Roach found that his guests had worn out the studio equipment but he continued, moving into TV while most of his contemporaries quaked in its presence. Hal Roach Jr. eventually took over, but bad business deals hastened the studio's demise. The premises themselves succumbed to demolition in 1963. The building's loss is justly regretted, though its survival might not have been a good thing: as a shrine, the mere husk could do little to represent the studio's real body, the unique assembly of creative people whose work continues to delight an audience of millions.

(See also: All-Star Series; Currier, Richard; 'Fading stars'; Feature films; Jones, F. Richard; Marshall, George;

The Hal Roach Studios *provide the backdrop for this publicity still*

McCarey, Leo; M-G-M; Pathé Exchange; Roach, Hal E.; Short films; *Taxi Boys, the*; Teaming; Television; United Artists; Walker, H. M.; and numerous others)

HALE, ALAN (1892-1950)

Silent film veteran whose good humour and impressive figure (6' 2") was perfectly suited for Little John in Fairbanks' *Robin Hood* (he appears also in the 1938 version plus a 1950 variant, *Rogues of Sherwood Forest*). The same applies to his role as

Alan Hale *as the irate Groagan in* Our Relations

'Groagan', the beer-garden proprietor of *Our Relations* (*qv*). Also a prolific director; not to be confused with his near-lookalike son, Alan Hale Jr., whose chief claim to fame is the 1950s *Casey Jones* TV series.

HALF A MAN (1925)

Last of the 'Stan Laurel Comedies' produced by Joe Rock (*qv*) and directed by Harry Sweet. *Half a Man* presents the story of Winchell McSweeny (Stan), a sheltered son of impoverished fisherfolk who is sent on his way in the world. He takes seriously a warning to avoid women, but meets a crew largely composed of

them when boarding a yacht. After leaving port, Winchell is pursued by the girls and caught by one very large specimen (Blanche Payson). Winchell is sat down to join the crew for lunch, where he sees a young lovely whose charms outweigh his fear of women. The giantess feeds him on pork, inducing seasickness; before long most of the crew share his nausea. For some unknown reason Winchell prepares to photograph the ship's company, using a magnesium flash despite the strong sunlight. When the flash fails to work, Winchell takes it below decks, causing an explosion that sets the ship afire. They abandon ship, the ladies aboard a boat, the men entrusting themselves to the waves. Winchell, being 'half a man', spends a considerable period deciding whether to jump. The girls reach an island, where they languish on the beach, surveying the horizon. Winchell scrambles to dry land, and is immediately chased by the lonely women. Reaching a cliff, he threatens to jump off unless the girls abandon their pursuit. They acquiesce, Winchell establishing his supremacy until the giantess resumes her interest in him. Winchell once more threatens to jump from the cliff, but the ruse succeeds only until the remaining men appear on the beach. The giantess throws Winchell over the edge as the girls chase the new arrivals. The men escape back into the ocean while Winchell, unharmed by his fall, skips away with the young girl he met at lunch. *Half a Man* is an uneasy mixture of energy, absurdity and gags ranging between the funny and the tasteless. Seasickness can be funny, but it requires wit and comparative discretion (as in Chaplin's *The Immigrant*). Stan's longtime dilemma of characterization leads him here into a pastiche of Harry Langdon (*qv*), at that time a recent success in films. The Laurel of *Half a Man*, sporting frock coat, sou'wester and enormous pince-nez spectacles, shares Langdon's naivety but not his passiveness, and overdoes the latter's

child-like indecision. Titles for this and others in the series are the work of Tay Garnett, who as a director is perhaps best known for *Mrs Parkington* (1944) and *The Postman Always Rings Twice* (1946). In his book *Light Your Torches* and *Pull Up Your Tights*, Garnett recalls a time when he and Stan were observing a group of swimsuited lovelies around the set. Stan, deadpan, said 'That's the trouble with the picture business; you look at filet mignon all day, then go home at night to cold hash!'

(See also: Payson, Blanche; Solo films; Spectacles; Walker, H. M.)

HALL, CHARLIE (1899-1959)
(Laurel & Hardy films *qv*)
A British-born character comedian, the diminutive (5'3") Charlie Hall worked as a carpenter in and around his native Birmingham before making his way in show business. He worked for Fred Karno (*qv*) but remained in Britain when the company toured America. He made the trip Stateside late in 1915 to visit his sister in New York and found work in pictures as a stagehand. According to a later interview, Hall was introduced to acting by

a chance conversation with Sennett comedian Bobby Dunn (*qv*). By 1924 he was appearing in Roach comedies, among them Will Rogers' *Big Moments From Little Pictures* and Stan Laurel's *Near Dublin* (*qv*). Hall continued to work at various studios (he can be seen in Keaton's 1927 film *College*), but by 1926 he was a near-permanent fixture at Roach where he formed a close friendship with Mabel Normand (*qv*). His work with Laurel & Hardy begins with *Love 'Em and Weep*, in a minor role as a butler. Before long, he was given more interesting things to do, being the catalyst of *The Battle of the Century*. He portrayed the first of a string of landlords (*qv*) in *Leave 'Em Laughing*. Another such character, from *Laughing Gravy*, is one of Hall's major contributions; as is his antagonistic colleague in *Busy Bodies*. Above all, he will be remembered as Stan and Ollie's nemesis in *Them Thar Hills* and *Tit For Tat*, two of the best Laurel & Hardy shorts. Charlie Hall had the best moments of his career at Roach, acting in various series in addition to contributing

Charlie Hall plays the cabbie in Double Whoopee

gags; elsewhere he was given modest roles in short comedies (for example RKO's series with Clark and McCullough) and little more than walk-ons in feature films, such as *Sherlock Holmes and the Secret Code*. When Edgar Kennedy (*qv*) co-starred with Will Hay in a British film, *Hey! Hey! USA!* (1936), Hall was included in the cast. He crops up briefly in a 1950s *Abbott and Costello Show*, but his last public appearance may well have been an edition of Groucho Marx's quiz show *You Bet Your Life*; Stan saw the show and wrote congratulating Hall on the performance. Charlie Hall is one of cinema's neglected stalwarts, though there is a valuable biography written and published by British enthusiast Ray Andrew. *On the Trail of Charlie Hall* was written with the co-operation of the Hall family in England; Charlie Hall's brother, Frank Hall, subsequently became active in the UK's Sons of the Desert club until his death in 1993. Among rare photographs and documents in his family's possession were Hall's own copies of two early scripts for *The Bohemian Girl*. Hall is absent from the film itself (apart from a brief voice-over), but contributed to the scripting. Charlie Hall is not to be confused with another Englishman born in the same year, Charles D. Hall, an art director whose credits include Laurel & Hardy's *Swiss Miss*, *A Chump at Oxford* and *Saps at Sea*.

(See also: Costello, Lou; Deleted scenes; Englishmen; *Golden Age of Comedy, the*; Keaton, Buster; Marx Brothers, the; *Pair of Tights, a*; Practical jokes; Stage appearances; Writers)

HALL, HENRY
See: Television

HANCOCK, TONY (1924-68)
Britain's top post-war comedian who, like Laurel & Hardy, turned desperation into humour, but with an edge of

despair rather than optimism. His writers, Alan Simpson and Ray Galton, developed with Hancock a comic figure built upon truth, human frailty and, one suspects, many of the man's own inner conflicts. His profound insecurity (aided by some poor luck) led to problems with alcohol and, eventually, suicide, but at his peak, he was a talent second to none. Enormously successful in radio and TV, Hancock saw greater possibilities as an international comedian in film but his first starring vehicle, *The Rebel* (1960) fared badly in the US (due in part, it has been suggested, to its somewhat inflammatory American title, *Call Me Genius*). In the film, office worker Hancock is more preoccupied with his extracurricular painting and sculpting. When his landlady (Irene Handl) enquires as to the subject of his 'self-portrait', Hancock replies, sarcastically, 'Laurel and Hardy!'. Hancock visited Stan Laurel for advice on adapting to a world audience, but Laurel could only suggest that Hancock eliminate any slang. In their book *Hancock* (William Kimber & Co., 1969), Freddie Hancock and David Nathan suggest that Laurel's viewpoint was restricted by having been a 1930s film comedian, but in truth Hancock had posed an impossible question. His characterization pinpointed the British outlook so succinctly that he was virtually unex-

'That,' says **Tony Hancock**, *'is a self-portrait'. 'Who of?' asks Irene Handl; 'Laurel and Hardy!'* replies Hancock. The Rebel *(1960)*

portable. The meeting with Laurel is mentioned in a play presenting Hancock's final moments as a fictionalized soliloquy. Laurel's specific advice is mentioned, as is a fabricated account of Laurel attending Hardy's funeral (he did not in fact attend), which serves as an excuse for a fairly ancient gag to which the payoff is 'Hardly worth your going home, is it?'. In later years Stan Laurel accumulated an impressive collection of tape recordings. One that survives in private hands is a copy of what is perhaps Hancock's best radio episode, known officially as *A Sunday Afternoon at Home* (on this occasion retitled *A British Sunday*). The show, which explores the profound boredom of such an occasion, may well have reminded Laurel of his homeland's less appealing aspects.

HARBAUGH, CARL (1886-1960)
Roach's top gagman of the 1920s, Carl Harbaugh also played occasional bit parts, one of them cut from the final version of *Fra Diavolo* (*qv*). From all accounts a colourful character, he would arrive for the morning script conference dreadfully hungover but still possessed of a fertile imagination

and robust attitude. When asked by a relative newcomer how a certain prop came to appear during the action, he replied 'because the goddam propman *put* it there!' This direct philosophy is endearingly typical of silent comedy and must have served him well; other credits include two features with Buster Keaton (*qv*).

(See also: Hal Roach Studios, the; Writers)

HARDY, EMILY (1860–?)
Born to a Scottish family that had emigrated to America in the eighteenth century, Emily Norvell, Babe's mother, had been married to one T. Sam Tant (sometimes amended to 'Tante') prior to wedding Oliver Hardy Sr. (*qv*) in 1890. She had borne Tant four children, Elizabeth, Emily, Sam and Henry. Norvell, her only shared offspring with Hardy, was 11 months old when Mrs Hardy, herself only 32 years of age, was widowed for a second time. A living had to be earned, despite Mrs Hardy's dismissal from the hotel she had been managing with her husband. She took the family to a similar establishment, the White House, near to the Georgia and Central Railroad depot in Madison. She later managed the Delancey Hotel, Covington, before moving on to Atlanta. Mrs Hardy, known to all as 'Miss Emmie', anticipated better times there, which eventually materialized when her eldest child, Elizabeth, married into a wealthy family. They soon moved to Milledgeville, Georgia, where Mrs Hardy took over its best hotel, the Baldwin. Her busy life meant little time for the children and Norvell was thus rather fussed over by the two daughters. Much of his time was occupied in observing the various guests, which he called 'lobby watching'. This lifelong interest enabled him to capture their foibles and mannerisms in his character. Norvell was very close to each of his half-siblings, and was badly affected when Sam drowned in the

Oconee River, aged 12. Norvell and another boy tried to rescue Sam, to no avail. Many years later, when Norvell was known to the world as Oliver Hardy, he was delighted when Henry (known to the family as 'Bardy') adopted his famous brother's surname. Norvell himself had adopted his father's forename on the advice of a numerologist; his mother in turn once consulted a fortune-teller, who told her that her son's name would one day be known throughout the world. Once this had come true, her famous son tried to set her up in a comfortable California residence, but this 'true Georgian' returned to her native territory soon after. She is commemorated somewhat in *Chickens Come Home* (*qv*) by an enormous copy of the Norvell family crest in Ollie's dining room.

(See also: Characters; Courtliness; Education; Names; Superstition; Tattoos)

HARDY FAMILY, THE
See: Unfilmed projects

HARDY, LUCILLE
See: Continuity errors, Food, Marriages and Stage appearances

HARDY, MADELYN
See: Marriages

HARDY, MYRTLE
See: Marriages

HARDY, OLIVER SR.
(1841/2–1892)
Babe's father, often described as a lawyer, was in fact a line foreman for the Georgia Southern Railroad, one of his tasks being to lay new track between Augusta and Madison. No extant documentation suggests any connection with the law, though he may possibly have worked for a solicitor's office at some time. Even less specific is the family claim of descent from the Hardy who served with Nelson (novelist Thomas Hardy

claimed the same lineage); what is known is that the Hardy family had a distinguished service heritage in Great Britain. This heritage continued with Babe's father into the 16th Georgia Regiment during the American Civil War, where he received several mentions in dispatches and incurred serious wounds at Fredericksburg. Hardy was married three times: his last marriage was to Emily Norvell Tant, widow of another railroad employee. They were married on 12 March 1890, Hardy by then 48 years of age. His health was not good, possibly a legacy of his wounding many years earlier; their only joint offspring, Norvell, was born scarcely eleven months before his father's sudden death on 22 November 1892. By this time Mr and Mrs Hardy were managing the Turnell Butler Hotel in Madison, Georgia; despite evident financial problems, Mrs Hardy continued in the hotel management business. Young Norvell later adopted the name Oliver as a tribute to the father he resembled so strongly but never knew.

(See also: Education; Hardy, Emily; Names)

HARLOW, JEAN (1911–1937)
The archetypal movie blonde (and sometime redhead), Jean Harlow (born Harlean Carpenter) tends to be remembered today for her own early death (from complications of uremic poisoning) and that of her husband Paul Bern; lost amid considerable myth is a remarkable comic talent. Harlow's early film career was spent in extra roles until Howard Hughes put her into his aviation epic *Hell's Angels* (1930). There followed a contract with M-G-M who, after several loan-outs to other studios (notably for Capra's *Platinum Blonde*) placed her in hard-boiled but good-natured roles, often in exotic settings such as in *China Seas* (1936). Her strong flair for comedy manifested itself in *Bombshell* (1933) and *Libeled Lady* (1936). The

Jean Harlow moments before her cele-brated disrobing in Double Whoopee

comedy influence is perhaps easily explained: Harlow's pre-*Hell's Angels* work was primarily with comedians (she can be spotted in Chaplin's *City Lights*), including a stint with Hal Roach. At the Roach lot, she appeared with Bryant Washburn in *The Unkissed Man* (sometimes miscredited to Laurel & Hardy), with Edgar Kennedy (*qv*) in *Why is a Plumber?* and *Thundering Toupées* plus three 1929 Laurel & Hardy comedies (all *qv*), *Liberty*, *Double Whoopee* and *Bacon Grabbers*. In *Liberty*, it is she who, with her boyfriend, attempts to enter a cab already occupied by Stan and Ollie. Her contribution to *Double Whoopee* is the famous sequence in which she leaves another cab, only to have Stan close the door on her dress. *Bacon Grabbers* concludes with her returning home to husband Edgar Kennedy, with the news that she has paid for the radio set which Stan and Ollie have just repossessed (and which by this time has been splintered under a steamroller). Even after departing for loftier things, Harlow continued to appear by proxy: stills for *Brats* (*qv*) reveal her portrait decorating a man-telpiece, while a photograph of Harlow in her *Double Whoopee* cos-tume is used to represent the faithless 'Jeanie-Weanie' who sends Ollie (and

countless others!) to the Foreign Legion in *Beau Hunks* (*qv*).

(See also: Capra, Frank; Dillaway, Donald; Douglas, Gordon; M-G-M)

HARMON, LARRY
American producer whose Laurel & Hardy caricatures have appeared as toys, comic books and television car-toons since the 1960s.

(See also: Animation; Caricatures)

HAROLDE, RALF (1899-1974)
Gangsterish-looking actor who plays just that type in *Our Relations* (*qv*); many other films include *Farewell My Lovely* (1944).

(See also: Criminals; Night-clubs)

HARVEY, FORRESTER
(1890-1945)
Character actor who, despite apparent Irish origins (some sources quote a London birthplace) portrayed Cockney stereotypes in American films depicting Britain. *The Invisible Man* (1933) is a famous example; another is *A Chump at Oxford* (*qv*), in which he plays Meredith, valet to 'Lord Paddington'. His employer's amnesia was induced by a window that, in Meredith's words, ' 'it you on the 'ead as 'ard as an 'eavy 'ammer'! Originally in British theatre and films, Harvey achieved an early success in the Betty Balfour vehicle *Somebody's Darling* (1925).

(See also: Englishmen; Servants)

HATLEY, T. MARVIN (1905-86)
(Laurel & Hardy films *qv*)
Multi-talented musician and com-poser, whose 'Happy-Go-Lucky Trio' played regularly on a radio station located at Roach's premises. Hatley joined the studio after his 'cuckoo' theme was adopted by Laurel & Hardy, becoming musical director until the end of the decade and scor-ing most of Roach's late feature product. Despite this great responsi-bility and three Oscar nominations, Hatley was to earn more in his

T. Marvin Hatley (playing bass and cornet) with his 'Happy-Go-Lucky Trio' and two guests

subsequent occupation as cocktail pianist. Hatley appears briefly in *Bonnie Scotland* as an accordion-playing soldier; he provides the off-screen music supposedly played by *The Music Box*; he is believed to be leading the musicians in *Sons of the Desert* and at least the Spanish version of *Chickens Come Home*. Other reputed 'bits' include *Our Relations*; he receives on-screen credit for *Midsummer Mush*, starring Charley Chase (*qv*).

(See also: Academy Awards; *Cuckoo*; Music; Radio; Records; Shield, LeRoy; Songs)

HATS (all films *qv*)
The bowler hat, or 'derby' in America, is for many people Laurel & Hardy's trademark. It was used by comedians on the variety stage and in early films almost as a matter of course. Chaplin (*qv*), with whom it is similarly identified, did not pioneer the bowler among comedians but instead followed a trend. Laurel and Hardy had sometimes worn them in solo days, but assumed them regularly as a team, probably after recognizing their suitability in *Do Detectives Think?* At that time, bowlers represented tough guys in America and the middle classes in Britain. Laurel & Hardy took them up in the first guise but retained them for the second, representing as they did aspirations to gentility. The hats on this first appearance were normal, curved-brim types: in keeping with their physiques and personalities they later selected distinct styles, Ollie's hat staying rounded and grandiose, Stan's becoming tall-crowned and flat-brimmed. Stan's is usually worn back-to-front, not obvious until one notices the position of the bow in the hatband. Impersonators (*qv*) very seldom obtain the correct type. *Do Detectives Think?* also introduced what is known as the 'hat-switching routine', a creation of Leo McCarey (*qv*) that consists of one, then both, losing his hat, from which point the hats are passed back and forth without either regaining his own headgear. Quite early on, this device became the basis of an entire two-reeler, *Hats Off*, combining at its conclusion with a giant street battle. The hat-switching routine remained with them throughout their working lives, except when circumstances compelled them to

adopt different headgear (even *The Bohemian Girl* starts with them in elongated versions of the bowlers). Other types of hats include the eighteenth-century models of *Fra Diavolo*; the pixie-style caps in *Babes in Toyland*; Romany designs in the carnival scenes of *Swiss Miss*; their various adventures in uniform; and the masquerades of *Jitterbugs*.

(See also: Army, the; Costume; Marshall, Trudy; Policemen; Sailors)

HATS OFF

(Laurel & Hardy film)
Released by M-G-M, 5 November 1927. Produced by Hal Roach. Directed by Hal Yates. Two reels. Silent.
With Stan Laurel & Oliver Hardy, James Finlayson, Anita Garvin, Dorothy Coburn, Ham Kinsey, Sam Lufkin.

Stan and Ollie are fired from their jobs as dishwashers but seek parallel employment selling Kwickway washing machines. Despite drenching the proprietor (James Finlayson) in suds, they get the job and proceed to haul a sample machine from door to door. One port of call causes confusion with a quadruple set of doors; another brings disappointment when the lady who has summoned them (Anita Garvin) only wants the boys to post a letter. The lady's residence is atop a vast flight of stone steps, making it an arduous trip with a washing machine. When she calls them back for a second trip, it is only because she has forgotten to put a stamp on the letter. During their return to street level, Stan and Ollie meet another lady, this time a potential customer (Dorothy Coburn) who would like to see the machine demonstrated - back at the top of the hill. Stan, his patience exhausted, kicks her in the behind. She hits Ollie in retaliation, then leaves the boys to squabble. In another of the hat mix-ups that have plagued them throughout the

proceedings, Stan and Ollie's bowlers are kicked along the street. Before long a group of passers-by are engaged in a fierce battle, destroying each other's hats. The washing machine is demolished by a passing steamroller and the crowd of battling pedestrians arrested - except for Stan and Ollie, who pick up their battered hats, only to get them switched once more.

At the time of writing *Hats Off* holds the dubious distinction of being the only lost Laurel & Hardy short. Certain others exist only in fragmented form but no trace whatever can be found of this, one of their earliest major works. Its influence is clear, both on the later silents with a 'battle' format and, above all, on the Oscar-winning sound short *The Music Box* (*qv*). The staircase common to both films still exists, and is a place of pilgrimage for *aficionados*. The idea of using such a location is said to date back to a 1925 comedy with Charley Chase (*qv*), while the idea recurs in a much later Three Stooges short, *An Ache in Every Stake* (1941). The director of *Hats Off*, Hal Yates (*qv*) also used stairs, a washing machine and several *Hats Off* gags in a two-reeler of 1945, *It's Your Move*, starring Edgar Kennedy (*qv*). The genesis of the washing machine idea is recounted in an early 1930s profile by British journalist Margaret Chute: Stan is said to have called Babe after receiving a visit from a man 'travelling in washing machines'; Babe needed no prompting as to their next roles. The likelihood of this film's rediscovery grows more remote with the passage of time but reported sightings continue. Three occurred during the 1980s alone, none of which produced any results, but collectors hope the law of averages will one day pay dividends.

(See also: Auctions; Hats; Locations; Lost films; Race; Rediscoveries; Remakes; *We Faw Down*)

HAY WIRE

See: *Hog Wild* and Working titles

HEALY, BETTY

Scatterbrained comedienne, somewhat reminiscent of the later Lucille Ball character, who played Mrs Laurel in *Our Relations* (*qv*). Her estranged husband, Ted Healy (1886-1937), was the original employer of the Three Stooges; 'Ted Healy and his Stooges' are among the myriad talents on view in *Hollywood Party* (*qv*).

HEIGHT, WEIGHT

There is a popular misconception that Stan Laurel was tall and thin while Oliver Hardy was short and fat. This illusion was perpetuated somewhat by the team's own notepaper, bearing a cartoon drawing of them in these proportions. For the record, Stan Laurel was 5' 9" (some sources claim an inch taller) while Oliver Hardy was 6' 1". Many people were surprised to learn how tall Babe was (the *Times* obituary made a point of saying 'he was tall as well as fat'); sensitive about his weight, the comedian would often secretly misinterpret this as a reference to obesity. In his youth, he was considerably larger than in the films with Stan Laurel; there was at least one occasion when he was contractually encouraged to gain weight. In 1932 he was reported to be over 300lb. This seems an exaggeration, though he certainly attained this before slimming down in the mid-1950s. Periodic dieting is evident, as in *Tit For Tat* (*qv*), where he appears little heavier than his partner, but for the most part he felt obliged to maintain his role in the 'fat-and-thin' image. The enormous frame associated with his later career seemed to appear suddenly in 1938; Stan Laurel gained several pounds during the same period. The angular Laurel of the solo films was never really evident in the Laurel & Hardy series but his jacket started to tighten noticeably in about 1934. The reduced contrast in the team's physiques is commemorated in a 1935 edition of the newspaper feature *Seein' Stars*, referring to orders from Roach for the team to restore the status quo. Stan was reported to be 150lb in the early 1930s, but was rather more than that before the end of the decade. A severe illness during *Atoll K* (*qv*) brought him down to 115lb; his proper weight was eventually restored but photographs from the 1952 tour show a Laurel still noticeably emaciated by the experience. To paraphrase H. M. Walker (*qv*), 'for much of the time neither Mr Laurel nor Mr Hardy demonstrated an extreme in weight; they were much more a contrast in personalities'.

(See also: Apocrypha; Colour; Colouring; Stage appearances; West, Billy)

HELPFUL HENRY

An early newspaper strip, 'Helpful Henry' was recalled by Oliver Hardy as an influence on his screen character, its titular hero being big, important and fussy, trying to help but 'always making a mess of things'. Hardy described the strip as having appeared in Georgia papers of his boyhood, but this is unlikely; it is probable that he had confused the name with one of several bearing similar titles.

(See also: Animation; Caricatures)

HELPMATES

(Laurel & Hardy film)
Released by M-G-M, 23 January 1932. Two reels. Produced by Hal Roach. Directed by James Parrott. Camera: Art Lloyd.
With Stan Laurel and Oliver Hardy, Blanche Payson, Robert Callahan, Bobby Burns.

Ollie is delivering a stern lecture to the man who has 'pulled a wild party' in his wife's absence. The culprit is Ollie himself, looking into a mirror. A telegram brings panic at the news of his wife's return, to a house bearing all the signs of a recent riotous gathering. Ollie's only recourse is to telephone Stan, who is at home in bed. Once he realises that it is not the alarm clock he can hear, Stan answers the telephone and explains why he missed the previous night's festivities ('I was bitten by a dog... the doctor said I might get hydrophosphates'). Summoned to Ollie's residence, Stan appears moments later, fully dressed, and is persuaded to help clean up. Ollie, putting his 'best foot forward', slips on a carpet sweeper. As Ollie dresses upstairs, Stan finishes the washing-up. When Ollie reaches the living room, a further slip on the carpet sweeper sends him into the pile of crockery. Ollie opens the back door to fetch a rubbish bin; the door is attached to the flue by a small washing line, and Ollie is covered with soot. Ollie reaches for the soap but grabs some butter Stan has left nearby. Opening a cupboard in search of a towel, Ollie is turned from black to white by a tin of flour. Ollie returns upstairs to change, and drops a collar stud under the dresser. Stan arrives, takes a handkerchief from the dresser, and leaves the drawer open. Ollie's head plunges through the drawer. Back in the kitchen, Stan tries to unblock the sink and jabs the handle into Ollie's eye. Stan tries to dispose of the water through a window, which closes, nearly soaking Ollie's last suit. Ollie goes outside to prop up the window, and is drenched. The bucket, aimed at Stan, travels through the house and knocks over a neighbouring gardener. Ollie turns on the gas oven in order to dry his jacket. Before lighting the gas, he retrieves his trousers from Stan, who has put them through a wringer then straight into a bucket of water. Ollie returns to the oven, where a single match reduces the scene to devastation. Worse still, Mrs Hardy (Blanche Payson) calls with a demand to be met at the station. Stan is left to clear up while Ollie finds another suit of clothes. Once the room is tidy, Ollie returns in an Admiral's uniform, obviously left over from a party. In Ollie's absence, Stan prepares a welcoming fire, unaware that the logs in the fireplace are artificial. A little petrol is applied... and a battered Ollie returns to what was once his house. Stan tries to explain but a calm Ollie merely wants to be left in peace. As Stan departs, Ollie asks him to close the door: 'I'd like to be alone'. Ollie sits resignedly as the rain starts, too late to extinguish the house but

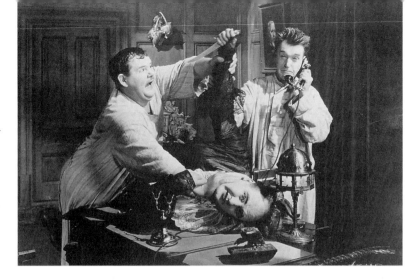

right on cue to give him yet another drenching.

The excellent reputation of *Helpmates* has been supported by various critics, not least William K. Everson (*qv*), comparing it to their best silent work. There are those for whom *Helpmates* is over-reliant on slapstick, but this is to ignore the skill by which such elements are constructed, each disaster contributing not just to the next but to Ollie's total downfall. For a comedy thus geared, there is a surprising amount of first-class dialogue, notably in the extended nonsense of Ollie's telephone call to Stan. It would be interesting to learn if Ollie's division of 'im-possible' into two words predates Samuel Goldwyn's identical utterance.

(See also: Dialogue; Dubbing; Payson, Blanche; Slapstick; Telegrams; Telephones; Women)

HENDERSON, DEL (1883-1956)
(Laurel & Hardy films *qv*)
Ontario-born actor from the stage, George Delbert Henderson is the millionaire owner of 'Blue Boy' in *Wrong Again*, the culprit in *The Laurel-Hardy Murder Case* and a sympathetic judge in *Our Relations*. Among other films are *The Crowd*, *Hit the Deck* and *The Champ*; further Roach shorts include several with Charley Chase and *Our Gang* (both *qv*). Later worked with W. C. Fields in *It's a Gift* and *You're Telling Me*.

HENRY, CHARLOTTE (1914-80)
The heroine of *Babes in Toyland* (*qv*); of her few other appearances, her title role in *Alice in Wonderland* (1933) is best remembered. The preceding year she had portrayed the 'Pioneer Girl' in Goldwyn's *Arrowsmith*, starring Ronald Colman and Helen Hayes.

HERBERT, VICTOR
See: *Babes in Toyland* and *The Red Mill*

Del Henderson caught in the act in The Laurel-Hardy Murder Case

HEREAFTER, THE (all films *qv*)
Laurel & Hardy's often rather black humour would sometimes extend into speculation on the next world; *Near Dublin* sees Stan taken for a ghost after his 'murder'. In *The Live Ghost*, Laurel & Hardy believe they have shot a drunken shipmate. In preparing to dump the 'corpse' (actually a trunk) overboard, Stan asks Ollie if he thinks the man has gone to heaven. 'I'm afraid not,' replies Ollie, sadly, 'I guess probably he went to the *other* place. Get me a large piece of coal.' Stan asks if one is required to bring one's own coal, but is told that it is to weight down the sack containing their apparent victim. The drunk returns after a coat of whitewash and is taken for a ghost. A more positive view occurs when in *Bonnie Scotland* they are ordered to blow out their brains. Stan: 'I'll see you when you get to heaven!' Ollie: 'But how will I know you?' Stan: 'I'll have wings and a harp in my hand.' Ollie: 'But so will the rest of the angels.' Stan: 'I'll keep my hat on, so you'll know me!' After the team crashes an aircraft in *The Flying Deuces*, Ollie is seen ascending skyward, bearing wings and a harp. For

Charlotte Henry, as Bo-Peep, receives the unwelcome attentions of Barnaby (Henry Brandon) in Babes in Toyland

The hereafter: Stan will have 'ghost trouble all night long' in The Live Ghost

the finale he is reincarnated as a horse. *Do Detectives Think?* contains a sequence with Laurel & Hardy in a graveyard, from which they make a hasty exit after seeing the sinister shadow cast by a goat (of the sort that just happens to wander into silent comedies!). Persistent rumour suggests there to have been a closing shot for *The Midnight Patrol* showing the team as angels. No such scene is known to have been filmed and a probable explanation is that BBC TV's copy has an 'end' title transplanted from *Oliver the Eighth* retaining its final frames showing Laurel & Hardy in white barbers' outfits. *Oliver the Eighth* is a partial remake of *The Laurel-Hardy Murder Case*, itself chock-full with supposed apparitions.

(See also: Animals; Black humour; *Eve's Love Letters*; Murder; Reincarnation)

HICKORY HIRAM
Character name adopted by Stan Laurel in 1918 for his first series of films, after his debut in *Just Nuts* (*qv*). Produced by Universal chief Carl Laemmle for Nestor release, none of the films are available today and probably did little business at the time. Stan described their release as being to 'all the first-run comfort stations'. Known titles are *Hickory Hiram* and *It's Great To Be Crazy*.

(See also: Names; Solo films; Vaudeville)

HILL, THELMA
See: *Two Tars*

HIS DAY OUT
See: West, Billy

HOBBIES
The team's off-screen activities are documented here and there; Babe's love of golf dominated his leisure hours although he spent much time at the racetrack. His widow, Lucille, believed her husband considered himself better represented by his many hobbies than through his career. His love of sport first manifested itself at school and in Lubin days, where he played football. He was later a keen follower of the USC team. He was similarly interested in basketball and baseball, playing the latter with Vitagraph's team. This aside, he was interested in people: 'in a way, *people* were his hobby', said Lucille. Stan Laurel spent too many hours at the studio to be much of a hobbyist, though he loved deep-sea fishing and took an interest in strange forms of horticulture. One interest has been described as 'chemical gardening', while a syndicated news feature, *Seein' Stars*, once reported his attempt to produce an onion-flavoured potato. In retirement, Stan devoted many hours to answering fan mail, creating new gags for the sheer pleasure of it and watching TV. He owned a tape recorder and spent much time making up tapes for his friends, not of his own voice but drawing instead upon a collection of music-hall records. A much-repeated quote to the effect that Stan had *married* all of his 'hobbies' is said to have been a cruel fabrication.

(See also: Apocrypha; Boats, ships; Fish; Gambling; Golf; Hancock, Tony; Letters; Lubin, Siegmund 'Pop'; Marriages; Music-hall; Vitagraph)

HOG WILD
(Laurel & Hardy film)
Released by M-G-M, 31 May 1930. Two reels. Produced by Hal Roach. Directed by James Parrott. Camera: George Stevens. British title: *Aerial Antics*, although UK reissues revert to the American original.
With Stan Laurel and Oliver Hardy, Fay Holderness, Dorothy Granger.

Ollie cannot find his hat: neither Mrs Hardy (Fay Holderness) nor the maid (Dorothy Granger) tell him to look on his head. Seeing himself in the mirror, Ollie bluffs it out and declares his intention to meet Stan. Mrs Hardy insists - violently - that their radio aerial must first be installed. Stan drives to Ollie's house, nearly causing an accident when distracted by a pretty girl (Dorothy Granger again, with her back to camera). He *does* cause an accident at Ollie's house, sounding his motor horn just as Ollie is climbing a ladder. Ollie accepts Stan's help dubiously ('I don't mind – that is, if you'll *help* me'), an uneasiness that is justified when his behind is set on fire by Stan's car exhaust. A bucket of water misses the smouldering portion and instead hits Ollie's face. When Ollie hurls the bucket through a window, Mrs Hardy hits him with a frying pan. Ollie places a board over Stan's car, as support for the ladder. On the roof, the boys attempt to fix poles for the aerial, but Ollie slips on one and plummets into a pond below. Climbing back, he gives Stan a wire to attach, on which he is tripped once more into the pool. On his third ascent, Ollie hammers nails into the roof, sending plaster all over his wife. More entanglements with the wire send Ollie, Stan and half the chimney into the pond. Mrs Hardy looks out, asking them to stop their 'playing'. This time Ollie climbs alone, leaving Stan to catch the lead and attach it to the radio. Connecting it to the wrong terminal, Stan electrocutes Ollie, who falls down the chimney. One more

determined attempt sees Ollie climbing the ladder, still perched on the car, but Stan, catching the starter, sends them on a nightmare journey through the town. The ride concludes with the ladder resting on an open-topped bus, where Ollie greets the passengers as best he can. Ollie falls in the vehicle's path, and just scrambles clear as his heartbroken wife appears. Ollie

assures her he is unharmed, but her tears are because the radio has been repossessed. They retire to Stan's car which, parked on the streetcar tracks, stalls. An off-screen crash leaves the trio in a crushed Model T.

Hog Wild has long been praised by critics, not least by the British documentary film maker Basil Wright (*qv*). Although available prints do not verify Wright's description of an off-screen splash accompanied by a flight of birds, his review captured the spirit of the sequence if not its precise detail (there

The final scene of **Hog Wild** *with Fay Holderness in the English version and Yola D'Avril (above) in the French*

is also the remote possibility that original UK prints varied the action somewhat). No foreign version of *Hog Wild* is known to be extant, though rumours once circulated of a home-movie edition of the Spanish *Radiomania*, in which Fay Holderness is replaced by Linda Loredo. When questioned many years later, Dorothy Granger (*qv*) could not recall being in the foreign versions of this film. Stills exist both of *Radiomania* and the French *Pêle-Mêle*, with Yola D'Avril as Mrs Hardy. Born in Lille, France, Yola D'Avril trained for the stage in Paris, Lisbon, Barcelona and Brussels before travelling to America. Other films include *The Right of Way*, *All Quiet On the Western Front* and *The Scarlet Dawn*. Post-production continuities suggest that neither foreign edition of *Hog Wild* varies significantly in content.

(See also: Alternative titles; *Big Noise, the*; Buses; Cars; *Dirty Work*; Foreign versions; Home movies; Radio; Women)

HOLLIDAY, FRANK (all films *qv*) Gagman and actor who plays the cop in *Below Zero* and a prison officer in *Pardon Us*. 'Mr Holliday' is referred to by that name as a dinner guest in *Chickens Come Home*. Longer prints of *Blotto* feature him as a night-club singer.

(See also: Crying; Night-clubs; Writers)

HOLLYWOOD PARTY
(Laurel & Hardy guest appearance)
Released by M-G-M, 1 June 1934. Produced by Harry Rapf and Howard Dietz. Directors (all uncredited): Allan Dwan, Richard Boleslawski, Roy Rowland and (for Laurel & Hardy) George Stevens. Camera: James Wong Howe. 68 minutes. Black and white, but with animated sequence in colour provided by Walt Disney.
With Stan Laurel and Oliver Hardy, Jimmy Durante, Lupe Velez, Charles

Disney (*qv*) supplied a Technicolor *Silly Symphony* titled *Red Hot Chocolate Soldiers*, prefaced by monochrome footage of Mickey Mouse with the live-action cast. For many years Britons had few opportunities to reappraise the film. Aside from a few obscure revivals, *Hollywood Party* vanished until Channel Four presented it on television in 1990. Until then, most UK *aficionados* had to content themselves with the egg-breaking scene, excerpted in the compilation *M-G-M's Big Parade of Comedy* (*qv*) and remade in *The Bullfighters* (*qv*).

(See also: Animation; Flowers, Bess; Guest appearances; Healy, Betty; Marx Brothers, the; Reincarnation; Remakes; Velez, Lupe)

THE HOLLYWOOD REVUE OF 1929

(Laurel & Hardy guest appearance) Released by M-G-M, 23rd November 1929. Produced by Harry Rapf. Directed by Charles F. Riesner. 115 minutes approx. Photographed partly in two-strip Technicolor. Camera: Maximilian Fabian, John M. Nickolaus, John Arnold, Irving G. Ries.

With Jack Benny and Conrad Nagel (Masters of Ceremonies), John Gilbert, Norma Shearer, Joan Crawford, Bessie Love, 'Ukelele Ike' (Cliff Edwards), Stan Laurel and Oliver Hardy, Anita Page, Nils Asther, Brox Sisters, Sistova and Company, Marion Davies, William Haines, Buster Keaton, Marie Dressler, Charles King, Polly Moran, Gus Edwards, Dane and Arthur, Gwen Lee, Albertina Rasch Ballet, The Rounders. Dances and Ensemble by Sammy Lee.

Around 40 minutes into this revue film, Laurel & Hardy contribute a sketch of approximately six minutes' duration. Co-host Jack Benny, who

Butterworth, Polly Moran, June Clyde, Eddie Quillan, Jack Pearl, George Givot, Richard Carle, Edwin Maxwell, Ted Healy and his Stooges, Tom Kennedy, Mickey Mouse.

Fading jungle-film star Schnarzan (Jimmy Durante) is advised to revive his reputation by replacing his decrepit lions with a more savage variety. At his plush Hollywood party, the lions arrive as planned, courtesy of explorer Baron Munchausen (Jack Pearl). They are followed by the lions' owners, Laurel & Hardy, who have been given by the Baron a cheque for '50,000 Tiddleywinks'. Stan and Ollie want to reclaim their lions (Stan: 'We'll get by without his old Piddleywinks!'). After some difficulty in getting past the burly doorman (Tom Kennedy), they roam the premises in search of the Baron but meet instead Schnarzan's temperamental co-star, 'Jungle Woman' Lupe Velez. Her volatile nature inflamed by an order to serve her no more drinks, Lupe is soon occupied in an exchange of egg-breaking indignities with Laurel & Hardy. The doorman reappears and the retreating Laurel & Hardy unleash the lions. In the ensuing chaos, Schnarzan, wrestling a lion, wakes up to find he has been

dreaming, and that his wife is waiting for him to take her to a real party at Lupe's.

Planned as a belated follow-up to *The Hollywood Revue of 1929* (*qv*), the protracted genesis of *Hollywood Party* has been related in some detail by Randy Skretvedt (*qv*), who describes 12 months of agony before the film's best scenes, with Laurel & Hardy, were dashed off in just a few days. Directed by their former cameraman, George Stevens (*qv*), Laurel & Hardy were on one of their brief loans to Roach's distributor, M-G-M. Despite a poor reputation, *Hollywood Party* is at times engagingly silly, while Jack Pearl's radio character of 'Baron Munchausen' is greeted in a fashion clearly inspired by the Marx Brothers' *Animal Crackers*. Critical reception tended to the view that Laurel & Hardy (who received top billing) were the best thing in it, although London's *Times*, despite being unnerved by the trend of providing arbitrary collections of comic talent (such as Paramount's *International House*), considered the blend of comedians acceptable. Reservations were expressed at the inclusion of Disney material, which was considered best 'untouched by any exterior influence'.

has had several outfits ruined so far, announces the end of the 'low comedians', but gets little further before the curtains part to show Stan and Ollie preparing their magic act. Ollie is loading Stan with props, reminding him not to remove his hat. Stan is first to notice the open curtains, something he is able to convey to Ollie only at length. They greet Benny, and a dove flies out from beneath Stan's raised hat. Exit Benny as the boys squabble, which finishes with Ollie's hand pushed into a bowl of eggs. Ollie wipes his hands on Stan's coat-tail before hurling the bowl off-stage. Benny, surprisingly unscathed, reappears protesting at Ollie's carelessness. A contrite Ollie asks the orchestra for music. To the 'Skaters' Waltz', Ollie transforms a candle into a bouquet, Stan covering the manoeuvre with a cloth. As Ollie prepares to turn a banana into an egg, Stan is visibly returning both bouquet and candle to their home in the candlestick. This earns him a kick in the pants, with disastrous consequences for the egg located in his back pocket. 'The egg trick is out', declares Ollie, announcing instead a trick involving a vanishing cake. As Stan gives Ollie the

Hollywood Revue of 1929: *a master illusionist and his assistant*

cake, he clears the table, sending to the floor the abandoned banana from their last trick. Inevitably, Ollie and cake slide to the floor. 'I faw down - and go 'blop'', says Ollie, in impeccable 1920s baby-talk. Ollie hurls the cake into the wings; also inevitably, Benny returns, covered in cake. The failed magicians exit sheepishly, allowing Benny to introduce the next item.

The Hollywood Revue of 1929 was M-G-M's contribution to the rash of mostly awful revue films mounted by the big studios at this time. The intention seems mostly to have been to display the maximum number of contract players within a small amount of studio space, displaying their abilities (or lack of) in the new talking pictures. Technicolor had been available for several years, but acquired more point within the greater realism provided by sound. Universal's *The King of Jazz*, based around bandleader (and Hardy looka-like) Paul Whiteman, was made entirely in the process; most, *Hollywood Revue* among them, were content to restrict colour to a few scenes. Reports that *Hollywood Revue*'s colour footage no longer exists may be true in the US, but since 1960 the British Film Institute has had complete material. Their viewing copy has included the colour sequences since its first screening, although these scenes were replaced in more satisfactory quality late in the 1970s. The soundtrack on this copy derives from disc; the image itself is reduced from the full 35mm frame of silent days, minimizing the loss of picture area common in prints of this and other early talkies. The Laurel & Hardy sketch, in black and white, easily outshines the remainder of the film, although some of today's critics have additional praise for Charles King (in the finale, 'Orange Blossom Time') and Joan Crawford's energetic song-and-dance number, 'Gotta Feeling For You'. The growing plight of Buster Keaton (*qv*) in the studio's hands is

suggested by his inappropriate - and silent - piece in what appears to be the guise of an Egyptian dancing girl. Keaton resurfaces with most of the cast (Laurel & Hardy conspicuously absent) for a Technicolor rendition of 'Singin' in the Rain'.

(See also: Academy Awards; Colour; Eggs; Food; Guest appearances; *Hollywood Party*; Magicians; M-G-M; Slapstick; Sound; *We Faw Down*)

HOME FROM THE HONEYMOON
See: *Duck Soup* and Jefferson, Arthur

HOME MOVIES
Except in the hands of more skilled amateurs, home movies tend to be little more than modest records of family life. They take on additional interest when they are either made by or of those whose living is in film, and there are several such items recording Laurel and Hardy on and off-duty. The 1932 tour is preserved chiefly by two excellent 16mm reels, fully titled and expertly shot, covering the team's visit to Tynemouth and Edinburgh. The two films have been widely circulated in 16mm and Super-8. Less often seen are the 16mm reels from Stan Laurel's own collection, which include moments with Babe and Stan's daughter Lois, some of them made between takes of *The Chimp* (*qv*). Of a later vintage is the 9.5mm reel of Laurel & Hardy in a theatre dressing room, taken in Britain by Stan's cousin Nancy Wardell; another privately-held reel offers a Kodachrome glimpse of *The Driver's Licence Sketch* (*qv*) as performed early in the 1940s. The 1974 documentary *Cuckoo* (*qv*) incorporates colour film of Stan Laurel in retirement, in addition to monochrome footage of him with Babe London (*qv*). The last film taken of Laurel & Hardy together is a colour item known generally as *Stan Visits Ollie*, a rather notorious item showing Babe after his drastic loss of weight. The film, taken by a fan who

Home movies: Stan and Ollie graced French living rooms even in the 1930s. Oui, c'est merveilleux!
Blotto archives
Reproduced by kind permission of Kodak Ltd.

was killed in a motor accident soon after, has been duplicated on numerous occasions. The team's professional films, together and solo, have long been distributed on the smaller gauges. Most of the team's work circulates in 16mm sound and silent prints. Early on, the Kodascope library issued 16mm copies of various silent films, a number of which have since been lost in their original 35mm form. It is probable that *With Love and Hisses* and *Sailors, Beware!* (both *qv*) owe their existence to this source. In America, 8 and 16mm prints were released by various companies although Blackhawk Films (*qv*) controlled most of the Roach package from the 1950s onwards. Some of the peripheral names were Coast, Atlas and Carnival; a pre-Blackhawk selection was issued by Official Films. The 8mm gauges went into sound in a big

way during the 1960s, usually favouring magnetic sound on film. A bizarre exception appeared in the mid-1960s from a subsidiary of Columbia's 8mm division, calling itself 'Americom' and offering 'sound movies for silent projectors'. Extracts were issued from the Laurel & Hardy Fox films *A-Haunting We Will Go*, *The Dancing Masters* and *The Big Noise* (all *qv*). Americom supplied silent prints with superimposed sub-titles, enclosing a flexible disc of the soundtrack. Start marks were supplied, but a problem arose over the company's decision to 'stretch' the sound to synchronize with silent projection speed. The speed actually required was somewhere in between (about 20 frames per second) and few enthusiasts achieved satisfactory results. Magnetic sound versions were supposedly available, but these were confined to a few non-Laurel & Hardy

items. In Britain, 9.5mm editions of the Roach films appeared from Pathéscope, whose parent organization in France also released several titles. British 8mm distribution was fairly widespread, most notably from Walton and Portland Films. Between them the two firms issued most of the team's Roach films, though too often in abridgments. Portland's copies of the silents tended to lose footage, although the features were mostly uncut. Walton favoured selected sound shorts and features, but rarely in unmutilated form. At least two shorts, *County Hospital* and *Tit For Tat* (both *qv*), were first issued uncut but abridged later on. Absurdities abound: Walton's feature version of *Pack Up Your Troubles* (*qv*) was missing segments that were included in the company's extracts, even the three-minute, mute editions. Another oddity is *Below Zero* (*qv*), long available only in a silent version of reel one (with its second reel transformed into another three-minute fragment); when finally released as a sound two-reeler, it was minus a gag that was retained in the packaging's synopsis, left over from the one-reeler. Older, mute editions of the sound shorts deriving from Peak and Capitol films are often prized by collectors; among many others, dealing primarily with the silents, were Arrow, Collectors' Club and Vintage Films, the last-named offering Standard-8 prints of an exceptionally high standard. Although old prints continue to circulate, the field has been almost totally eclipsed by video releases (*qv*); recent reports suggest that contractual matters forbid the release of Laurel & Hardy on 8mm film in Britain.

(See also: *Duck Soup*; Newsreels; *One*

Good Turn; Stage appearances; *That's That!*)

HOMES

In researching various Laurel & Hardy locations, Robert Satterfield of the Sons of the Desert club (*qv*) has pinpointed most of the homes occupied by the team over the years. Stan's earliest known Hollywood home was in West 69th Street, Los Angeles, during 1922; next were flats in the Sommerset Apartments, Hollywood Boulevard, then at Stoneleigh Apartments, Franklin Avenue. From 1924 until the end of the decade, he was at 3716 S. Van Ness. Also in 1924, Babe is known to have lived at 1719 Talmadge Street, Hollywood; from 1926 he was at Fredonia, near Universal City. His next home was 621 Alta Drive, Beverly Hills; Stan had by then moved into his own Beverly Hills mansion, 718 N. Bedford Drive. Both were printed in *The World Film Encyclopaedia*, a British publication of 1932 for which most stars preferred to give studio addresses. When Stan's marriage broke up he moved elsewhere in Beverly Hills, to 304 S. Palm; with his second wife he shared 10353 Glenbar, Cheviot Hills. The story goes that Stan wanted a sunken bathtub and converted one of its bedrooms to contain a raised sunken bath, accessible by steps. Next was the imposing Canoga Park residence, designated 'Fort Laurel'; Stan moved there around 1940, the same year that Babe moved into his final home on Magnolia Boulevard, an address perhaps reminiscent of his native South. Two other addresses separate Fort Laurel from Stan's later homes, 1111 Franklin in Santa Monica, a beach house in Malibu and, finally, the Oceana, a residential hotel also in Santa Monica. His last move is known to have been through the poor TV reception at Malibu; in turn, Fred Lawrence Guiles has suggested hotel life to have been more in keeping with the ex-vaudevillian's style

than any mansion he might have owned.

(See also: Biographies; Freemasons; Hobbies; Locations; Periodicals)

HOMOSEXUALITY (all films *qv*)

At the time of Laurel & Hardy's greatest popularity, homosexuality was seldom discussed openly and carried considerable shock value. It should be said that stereotyped male effeminacy was more usually the target than homosexuality itself, though Laurel's solo film *The Soilers* includes an unmistakably gay cowboy. The pre-teaming Laurel and Hardy *With Love and Hisses* makes a lot of Stan's misinterpretation of the hand-on-hip pose required by 'right dress'; *The Second Hundred Years* sees a misunderstanding over the French custom of ceremonial kissing; and the Scottish hero of *Putting Pants On Philip* is unaware of the impression caused by linking arms with his uncle. A seventeenth-century dandy in *The Bohemian Girl* is often taken to be gay, yet an unfilmed segment of the script makes it plain that he is something of a ladies' man. The motif fell

into disuse partly through stricter censorship imposed by the 1934 Production Code but also from the development of the team's characters into a pre-sexual, childhood attitude: when a fearful Stan awaits the dentist in *Pardon Us*, he clings to Ollie in a childlike need for security. The team's frequent sharing of a bed reflects further this pre-pubescence; in addition, this was often an economic necessity in the depression years. The device was later copied by British comedians Morecambe and Wise. Indeed, it was not until a feminist critic of the 1970s described male comedy duos, Laurel & Hardy included, as 'latently homosexual' that the matter was broached at all. There followed other suggestions of homosexuality in their screen characters, one writer inappropriately citing *Liberty*, thereby missing the point of a gag in which Stan and Ollie are repeatedly discovered attempting to exchange trousers. A much later source declared the same for the comedians themselves, a ludicrous

Homosexuality: a misunderstanding in Liberty

James Finlayson joins Laurel & Hardy for coffee and rice between takes of **The Hoose-Gow**

notion when one considers a still-current press interest in their relationships with women.

(See also: Beds; Censorship; Melodrama; Risqué humour)

HONOLULU BABY
See: Songs and *Sons of the Desert*

THE HOOSE-GOW
(Laurel & Hardy film)
Released by M-G-M, 16 November 1929. Produced by Hal Roach. Directed by James Parrott. Camera: George Stevens. Story editor: H.M. Walker. Two reels.
With Stan Laurel and Oliver Hardy, Tiny Sandford, James Finlayson, Leo Willis, Dick Sutherland, Ellinor Vanderveer, Retta Palmer.

A prison wagon delivers some new arrivals. Last out are Stan and Ollie, who protest their innocence to the guard (Tiny Sandford), explaining that they were only 'watching the raid'. Instant escape lies in their having been given two apples to throw over the wall, as a signal to friends outside; when the guard confiscates the apples and throws them out, a rope ladder descends and the guard pursues the culprits. Distracted, the guard leaves Stan and Ollie outside the gates, but their escape is terminated by two gunshot blasts. The boys are put to work on a road gang, where Stan's pick spends less time digging than in jabbing Ollie and tearing his clothes. Stan and Ollie are nearly lost in the rush when the time comes to eat, and are unable to find a place at the table. Another convict directs them to a small table nearby, where they settle until the table's intended occupant, the guard, returns to kick them out. Ollie asks the cook for some food, and is told to fetch some wood, with the promise of the more wood, the more food. Stan and Ollie chop down an entire tree, at the top of which is a prison guard; both tree and guard land neatly in the cook tent. At this chaotic moment the Governor (James Finlayson) and his entourage arrive to inspect the camp. Two ladies in the party inspect Stan and Ollie with disdain; Stan and Ollie inspect them with greater interest. When Stan gets his pickaxe caught in Ollie's clothing once more, Ollie hurls it straight through the radiator of the governor's car. They stem the flow of water by filling the radiator with rice from the cook tent, which creates a bubbling mess when the governor prepares to leave. The guard, knowing who to blame, kicks Stan into the pool of rice; before long the entire scene has degenerated into rice-throwing chaos. The Governor and the guard leave to fetch the militia, but back the car into a truck loaded with white-wash. Its contents pour into the back seat, from which Stan and Ollie appear, coated in white.

The Hoose-Gow combines ingenious ideas with a baser form of slapstick than is usual for Laurel & Hardy. Although still very funny, it typifies many early talkies in that unduly slow cutting reduces the impact of certain sequences, especially its rice-throwing variant of *The Battle of the Century* (*qv*). Its outdoor locations serve to minimize the stilted result, however, and the film at least compares favourably with much contemporary product. Since the late 1940s, *The Hoose-Gow* has circulated in muddy dupes from Film Classics. The 1980s saw a version restored for American TV, reinstating the original title cards (illustrated with prison bars) and offering virtually pristine picture quality. It is this restoration to which colour has been added.

(See also: Colour; Prison; Reissues; Sandford, Tiny; Slapstick; Television; Titling; Vanderveer, Ellinor)

HOP TO IT (1925)
See: *Stick Around*

HORNE, JAMES WESLEY
(1881-1942)
Director from silent days, starting with the Kalem company. 1920s credits include Keaton's *College* (1927). He worked on many first-class Laurel & Hardy films, notably *Big Business* and *Way Out West* (both *qv*). William K. Everson (*qv*) has noted the team's indelible influence on Horne's style, the director's later serials having

inherited the comic sense and expressions of his Roach work. He appears in *Beau Hunks* (*qv*) under a pseudonym.

(See also: Cornwall, Anne; Hall, Charlie; Keaton, Buster)

HOSPITALS
See: Doctors, nurses

HOUSMAN, ARTHUR
(1890-1942)
Comic drunk who supported (and was supported by!) Laurel & Hardy in *Scram!*, *The Live Ghost*, *The Fixer-Uppers*, *Our Relations* and *The Flying Deuces* (all *qv*). While comedians specializing in drunken roles are often teetotallers in real life, Stan Laurel remembered Housman as an exception. He took care to emphasize that Housman's screen antics derived entirely from talent but noted a genuine alcohol problem. This condition may account for Housman's decline after a position of some eminence in silent films, starting with the Edison Company in the 1910s and continuing through some 40 appearances during the 1920s. At one stage he took star billing in a series of feature-length 'Housman Comedies', at least one of which (1923's *Male Wanted*) is known to exist today. Later 1920s films include Murnau's *Sunrise*. Housman made his way through the 1930s playing bits in various shorts and features,

some quite prestigious (*The Merry Widow*), others less so (*Blondie Takes a Vacation*). He may be seen in Harold Lloyd's 1932 release Movie Crazy. One of his last appearances is in the Marx Brothers' *Go West*. There is some confusion regarding the spelling of his surname: originally 'Hauseman', the name was anglicized first to 'Housman' then, on occasion, 'Houseman'. The middle version is the most commonly employed.

(See also: Alcohol; Lloyd, Harold; Marx Brothers, the; *Taxi Boys*, *the*)

HUNGRY HEARTS (1916)
A Vim comedy directed by Jerold T. Hevener, *Hungry Hearts* is one of a series pairing Babe with the diminutive Billy Ruge as 'Plump and Runt'. Vim took over what had been the Lubin premises at Jacksonville. Formed in 1915 by Louis Burstein, Bobby Burns and Walter Stull, Vim starred the latter pair as 'Pokes and Jabbs', with Babe supporting in at least ten of these films. He receives co-star status in 'Plump and Runt' which, according to historian Leo Brooks, overlapped with rather than followed the Stull-Burns series. Other Hardy appearances for Vim included several with chubby comedienne Kate Price (1872-1942), who worked again with Babe in Semon's *The Perfect Clown* and turned up later in *The Rogue Song* (*qv*). *Hungry Hearts* opens

Babe as a disconsolate 'Plump' in the 1916 comedy **Hungry Hearts**

with Plump and Runt as artists, bereted and, Babe's physique notwithstanding, starving. Plump is painting a portrait of his girlfriend when a rich man enters the studio. He takes an immediate (and lecherous) interest in the girl, offering to buy her portrait. Plump offers him a picture showing only his model's upper half, but there is no interest until Runt adds a section depicting the girl's legs. Plump, furious, slashes the painting, despite Runt's pleas for him to take the money. The erstwhile customer is ejected, and Plump leaves the studio for the park, where he meets a widow whose inheritance has attracted Runt's interest. She requests a portrait and Plump sets to work, only to flee when the sitter becomes amorous. Plump is forced to choose between his true love and the financially secure widow. Runt has no such qualms and rushes into marriage for wealth. Plump's girlfriend receives a letter naming her as the true heiress instead of the widow. She and Plump are married immediately, barring the loveless, impoverished Mr and Mrs Runt from their home with a notice that reads 'closed for disinfection'. *Hungry Hearts* provides Babe with the type of leading man role he would soon abandon in favour of comic villainy. His best scene shows him attempting to capture the widow's likeness, at the same time inadvertently daubing her face with paint.

Arthur Housman joins Stan and Ollie for a night out in Our Relations

Madeline Hurlock appeared in the first recognizable Laurel & Hardy film, Duck Soup
Photograph by courtesy of Michael Pointon

(See also: Artists; Burns, Bobby; Lubin, Siegmund 'Pop'; Semon, Larry; Solo films; Villains)

HURDY GURDY
See: Sound

HURLEY, EDGAR
See: Keystone Trio, the

HURLOCK, MADELINE
(1899-1989)
Leading lady and comedienne, mostly in Sennett comedies of the 1920s, where she contrasted splendidly with that peculiar leading man, Ben Turpin (*qv*). Her most famous appearance is that with a lion in *Circus Today*. She is seemingly absent from films after 1928, though some claim she retired as late as 1935. New York film publicist-cum-songwriter Howard Dietz introduced her to the Algonquin literary set via Marc Connelly, who became her second husband; this brief match was followed by a more permanent marriage to playwright Robert B. Sherwood. Miss Hurlock appeared with Laurel & Hardy in their first recognizable team film, *Duck Soup* (*qv*).

(See also: Publicity; Sennett, Mack)

HUSTLING FOR HEALTH
See: Rolin Film Company, the

I

IMPERSONATORS

Laurel & Hardy are among the most impersonated people in history. Although the level of accuracy varies, each attempt conveys profound affection rather than the degree of satire usually inherent in the impressionist's art. Nor are such impersonations the strict domain of professionals; Dick Van Dyke (qv), whose Laurel imitation on TV was seen by Stan himself, once said how easy it is to find someone who does a good imitation of Stan Laurel. They are just as easy to locate among sitcoms ranging from Lucille Ball's shows to *Happy Days*, the British *Hi-De-Hi!* and numerous others. A complete half-hour, in the BBC's 1973 series *Seven of One*, cast Ronnie Barker and Roy Castle as two men who, clad as Ollie and Stan for a fancy dress party, are involved *en route* in an authentic Laurel & Hardy dilemma. Roy Castle repeated his Laurel impersonation on several occasions, frequently in partnership with Sir Harry Secombe. In 1967 they were considering a major biographical project on the team, but were dissuaded when a similar idea was announced in America with Van Dyke and Jackie Gleason (which was also never made). In 1976, Castle narrated a BBC Radio documentary on the team. Perhaps the best Laurel impressionist is Jim MacGeorge (the voice of 'Ollie' in the TV cartoons). He is often seen in TV commercials with Chuck McCann, a charter member of the Sons of the Desert club (qv). In 1992 the British Opposition leader referred to the Prime Minister and his Chancellor as 'the Laurel & Hardy of British Politics', hardly original though the press loved it. They were similarly amused when a team of Laurel & Hardy lookalikes were primed to attend the Party's next conference. Not all the impersonators have post-dated the comedians' lives: William K. Everson (qv) has noted a purely unintentional Hardy lookalike in Kewpie Morgan, whose presence in many Sennett comedies has often led scholars to misattribute them to Babe. In the late 1920s, several contemporary double-acts imitated Laurel & Hardy to varying degrees: a 1930s reel of *Carroll Levis Discoveries* presents a further brace of lookalikes and press books would sometimes encourage theatres to engage bogus Laurel & Hardys. In a 1959 interview for *Films in Review*, Stan describes a Chinese comedy team actively remaking the Laurel & Hardy subjects. He was also aware of someone claiming to be his brother, 'Joe Laurel', who was touring the world as a comedian. Graeme Bell's 1988 memoir *Australian Jazzman* (Child & Associates) describes the spurious sibling arriving in Australia with several ancient cuttings; Bell arranged an audition for the comedian and his wife in Bondi, which concluded amid 'embarrassed silence'. In 1964, a British paper published a photo of the man visiting Genoa, believing him to be Stan; the genuine Stan Laurel wrote correcting the piece and an apology was published. Several UK admirers had sent him the cutting, and in his reply to one he said 'I can never understand who would ever desire to look like ME!' Stan did not in fact approve of impersonators, believing instead that a true artist should want to *be* impersonated. He may well have recalled his days as a Chaplin lookalike which, despite his expertise, presented an artistic blind alley.

(See also: Advertising; Costume; Documentaries; *Goon Show, the*; Interviews; Keystone Trio, the; Sennett, Mack)

IN-JOKES

(Laurel & Hardy films qv)
Laurel & Hardy's realistic approach seldom permits self-conscious inside references. In this respect their films differ radically from, for example, the Marx Brothers (qv) or the Crosby-Hope 'Road' series, in which the stars' irreverence could extend to an awareness of the totally fictional nature of their exploits. The few exceptions in the Laurel & Hardy films tend toward the strategic but obvious placement of names: the bank raid foiled by the team in *A Chump at Oxford* is at the Finlayson National Bank; a fight billing in *Pack Up Your Troubles* refers to one 'Kid McCarey', a reference to Leo McCarey's younger brother Ray, co-director of the film; while a bottle of Sloan's liniment in *Brats* has been rechristened in honour of studio manager Warren Doane. A more general theatrical reference occurs in *Why Girls Love Sailors*, when Stan finds a trunkful of women's clothes marked 'Jules Eltinge Theatre', an obvious nod toward renowned female

impersonator Julian Eltinge. Stan and Ollie's electrical shop in *Tit For Tat* bears the notice 'Open for big business', presumably as a tribute to their greatest 'tit-for-tat' film, *Big Business*. Elsewhere in the film Charlie Hall tells Mae Busch 'No beating around the bush with me'. James Finlayson features in a further inside reference toward the conclusion of *The Bohemian Girl*, when his popeyed persona receives a jab to his 'good eye'! *Beau Hunks* contains a linking title that is meaningless outside of the US, referring to 'not a chirp in a carload'; it would be interesting to know if this film was made before or after Laurel & Hardy's appearance in advertisements for a cigarette whose slogan was 'not a cough in a carload'. Among the most pleasant back-references in Laurel & Hardy takes place in *Babes in Toyland*: Ollie attempts to emulate

Stan's expertise with the phrase 'Anything you can do, I can do'; Stan disagrees, miming the feats of dexterity that had baffled Ollie in *Fra Diavolo*. Curiously, the most obvious cross-reference in the Laurel & Hardy films is totally accidental: in *Bonnie Scotland*, Stan suggests that he and Ollie travel 'Way, way out west' - two years before the film in which they did precisely that!

(See also: Advertising; Busch, Mae; Butler, Frank; *Eve's Love Letters*; Finlayson, James; Hall, Charlie; McCarey, Leo; Vanderveer, Ellinor)

INDIA
See: *Bonnie Scotland*

INSANITY
(Laurel & Hardy films *qv*)
In this perhaps more compassionate

Insanity: Stan froths at the mouth

age, mental illness tends to be treated more sympathetically than in the heyday of visual comedy. The level of understanding during this period may be gauged from a title card in Chaplin's *Modern Times* which declares blithely that the Tramp has been 'cured of a nervous breakdown'. Laurel & Hardy pursued this topic less frequently than some of their contemporaries, although stereotypes remained common early in their careers. *His Day Out* (*qv*), one of the comedies in which Hardy supports Billy West (*qv*), concerns West's antics during a day's escape from his whitecoated guardians. Soon after their initial teaming, Laurel & Hardy appeared as guests in Max Davidson's *Call of the Cuckoos*, in which Davidson objects to his lunatic neighbours.

Early to Bed, which sees Ollie tormenting Stan to the point of rebellion, includes a moment where Stan falls face-first into a cake, making Ollie think he is frothing at the mouth. In *Habeas Corpus*, a crazed scientist engages the boys as grave-robbers; there is a further example of the breed in *Dirty Work*. Stan impersonates an eccentric inventor in *The Dancing Masters*, while they meet yet another, albeit less outrageous, specimen of the same in *The Big Noise*. The latter contains a sequence where the boys are menaced by a knife-wielding madwoman, clearly inspired by similar business with Mae Busch (*qv*) in *Oliver the Eighth*. There is also some question over the sanity of her character in *Come Clean*, an attempted suicide who screams her deafening way through much of the film. *Oliver the Eighth* also features some notable lunacy from British comedian Jack Barty (*qv*) as Jitters, the butler who lays the table without cutlery then rebukes diners for using the wrong fork. A more lethal manservant is the escaped killer posing as a butler in *Do Detectives Think?* The maniacal 'Tipton Slasher' is played by Noah Young (*qv*), whose crazed expressions in this and certain other films convey more than mere comic villainy. In *Sons of the Desert* Ollie feigns a nervous breakdown in order to permit a recuperative trip (in fact a jaunt to a lodge convention); *Saps at Sea* brings a genuine collapse with 'Hornophobia', an ailment seemingly common to those who test motor horns. Ollie considers the millionaire in *Wrong Again* to be somewhat eccentric, a status he demonstrates with a twisting gesture of the hand (a motif repeated in *The Big Noise*). Other unusual types appear in *Hollywood Party*, while in *Night Owls*, James Finlayson (*qv*) is accused by his employer of being 'nutty'. Laurel & Hardy's stage sketch during their final tour, generally known as *Birds of a Feather* (*qv*), is dominated by a scene in which Ollie has been taken into hospital after

attempting to fly among the birdies. The illusion is short-lived (being the result of enthusiastic whisky-tasting) and the hospital staff seem more in need of treatment than their patient.

(See also: Black humour; Criminals; Henderson, Del; *Just Nuts*; Murder; Servants; Sickness; Suicide)

INSECTS (all films *qv*)

When Laurel and Hardy met for the first time in *Lucky Dog*, a title card had Babe describe his future partner as an 'insect'. In *A Chump at Oxford*, one of the chief attractions of the Dean's quarters is, to quote Stan, 'no flies or nuthin'; he might well have recalled the disastrous fate of Ollie's wedding cake in *Our Wife*, which is covered in flies until Stan sprays it with Flit. Ollie doubtless retained memories of the flea circus which found its way into their bed in *The Chimp*, but it is their military exploits which bring them into more regular contact with the insect world. *With Love and Hisses* concludes with a platoon of swollen posteriors, the legacy of some outraged hornets; while *Bonnie Scotland* draws to a chaotic close amid numerous upset beehives. The customary state of the trenches during the First World War may be gauged from a title in *Pack Up Your Troubles* ('the cannons boomed all day and the cooties boomed all night') plus the nickname 'Cootie Avenue' for their dugout in *Block-Heads*.

(See also: Animals; Army, the)

INSURANCE

More a subject for drama such as *Double Indemnity* than comedy, insurance may sometimes provide its share of laughs. Eddie Cantor fashioned a one-reel comedy around an insurance medical, while Laurel & Hardy had Stan covered against injury in *The Battle of the Century* and *The Dancing Masters* (both *qv*). In real life, a form of insurance provided Stan Laurel with a healthy income for his

retirement, the comedian having wisely invested in annuities after the crash of 1929. Reprinted in the winter 1987-8 issue of *Blotto* magazine is a 1932 life insurance policy taken out on Oliver Hardy by the Roach studio; detailed within are particulars of the comedian's own annuity arrangements.

(See also: Apocrypha; Periodicals)

INTERVIEWS

Laurel & Hardy gave surprisingly few one-to-one interviews; among the most interesting of these is a post-war item from Denmark. Another was recorded for Belgian radio. Oliver Hardy's relatively early death robbed latter-day interviewers of many valuable recollections, although there are three minutes of film in which Hardy, about to leave for France to make *Atoll K* (*qv*), speaks of the new film, his early career, the genesis of the team, its longevity (denying rumours of a split), and the decline of visual comedy. In 1933 he visited Panama and was interviewed there at the Hotel Tivoli by Raphael Ades, a student at Panama High School. Published in the *Panama American* of 28 May, the piece consists largely of chat about his visit but includes reference to *Fra Diavolo* (*qv*) being made in five languages (only one was made), Babe's opinions on the Depression and his naming of Chaplin as his favourite star. When asked if he would like to appear in 'serious' pictures, Babe replied 'No, life is too serious itself'. The interviewer considered his subject to be more like a statesman than a comedian, noting his seriousness throughout. Their cordial discussion concluded, the young student took his leave, Babe saying 'Come over to Hollywood sometime, and I'll be glad to see you'. An important interview from 1954 is transcribed in the book *Mr Laurel and Mr Hardy*, conveying much of Hardy's gentle good humour. The conversation records much of Hardy's history, his views on their characterizations and, almost parenthetically, society in general. Exactly one week after Hardy's death in 1957, Stan Laurel was interviewed by Arthur B. Friedman for *Turning Point*, a radio series produced in association with the University of California. In approximately 75 minutes Laurel gives a concise, detailed history ranging from his music-hall beginnings to the recent death of his partner. Two years later saw a shorter but comparable interview with Tony Thomas, first released on the LP *Voices From the Hollywood Past*. Another interview, with Boyd Verb, was published in *Films in Review* that same year. The extensive Laurel interviews conducted by W. T. Rabe in 1961 reached a wide audience when broadcast by Voice of America. A transcript later appeared in a University of Michigan publication, *The Woods-Runner*.

(See also: Biographies; Foreign versions; Impersonators; *Lucky Dog*; Radio; Records; Semon, Larry; Teaming; Television; *Yes, Yes, Nanette!*)

IRELAND

The Irish gift for humorous fantasy is much acknowledged, and it may be significant that both Hal Roach and Mack Sennett (*qv*) were of Irish stock. A small Irish village is the scene of considerable mayhem in Laurel's solo film *Near Dublin* (*qv*), something evidently forgiven for Laurel & Hardy were very popular throughout the island. *The Belfast Telegraph* for 10 June 1952 refers to these 'favourites for a generation' whose sketch, *On the Spot* (*qv*), was then playing at the Grand Opera House. Better known is their arrival in Cork Harbour, just outside Cobh, on 9 September 1953. The visit, reconstructed for *The Laurel & Hardy Magazine* by local enthusiast Trevor Dorman, began with Stan, Babe and their wives looking over the rail of the S.S. *America* to see a fleet of small boats heading in their direction; on board were people waving, shouting and blowing whistles, as the crowds lining the harbour chanted 'Laurel and Har-dy' over and over. The distinguished visitors had intended no fuss and were genuinely surprised, the more so when local traffic was halted by the presence of countless children (truants all!). The team responded instantly and autographs were given all round. 'We were absolutely overwhelmed', Babe said, 'there scarcely ever was a film scene like it. They are grand children and Stan and I are grateful to them'. Babe was then drawn into good-natured argument with heavyweight Cobh celebrity Harry Deane over whose frame was the heaviest (Deane won by four ounces). Sean O'Brien, Irish manager for the American line by which they had travelled, escorted the visitors to St Colman's Cathedral whose bells began to play the Laurel & Hardy theme. In recounting the story to John McCabe (*qv*), Stan said 'Babe looked at me, and we cried... I'll never forget that day. Never.' Their wives turned to each other and wept also. Next was a trip to the Blarney Stone, Stan being held over the parapet to kiss the stone. Babe could not manage the steps, but joked that 'Nobody would hold me; I'm too big'. There followed lunch at the Cork City Hall with Alderman P. McGrath, Lord Mayor of Cork, and Mr A. A. Healy, where Stan and Babe were photographed signing the Lord Mayor's visitors book. In press interviews, Babe cited *Fra Diavolo* (*qv*) as his favourite among the Laurel & Hardy films. From here, they took the train to Dublin, where they rehearsed their sketch *Birds of a Feather* (*qv*) before departing for Liverpool.

(See also: Biographies; Height, weight; Periodicals; Reviews; Stage appearances)

Grand Theatre of Varieties
CORPORATION STREET, BIRMINGHAM.
Acting Manager .... Mr. CROSSLEY TAYLOR
MONDAY, SEPT 6th, 1915
(A) TWICE NIGHTLY AT 6·50 and 9·5.

1 **OVERTURE** ... ... Orchestra
2 **WILL HAY** - The Schoolmaster
Comedian of "Bend Down" Fame
3 **KRICK & KROCK**
Eccentric Comedians
4 **ARTHUR JEFFERSON**
And his Company in a Mirth-
Provoking Playlet—with a Plot—
written and produced by himself,
entitled—**"A NIGHT IN SOCIETY"**
Scene—DRAWING-ROOM IN A LONDON MANSION.

5 The World's Celebrated Parisienne
Actress, **Mdlle. GABY DESLYS**
and **MR. HARRY PILCER.**
Supported by **Mr. Bolingbroke** in a scene from "Racy Rapture" from the Duke of York's Theatre, London.
By **J. M. BARRIE**
And a Sketch entitled **"FLIRT"** by
C. H. BOVILL.

6 **LATEST NEWS & WAR FILMS**
7 **HAROLD MONTAGUE**
Entertainer at the Piano
8 **FRANK VAN HOVEN**
The American Dippy Mad Magician

JAILBIRDS
See: *Pardon Us*

JANNEY, WILLIAM (1908-92)
New York-born actor, on stage at 11. His first films include *Salute*, *Coquette* (with Mary Pickford), *Mexicali Rose* and the 1930 version of *The Dawn Patrol*. Among later appearances are *I Am A Fugitive From A Chain Gang* and Laurel & Hardy's *Bonnie Scotland* (*qv*) where he played 'Alan Douglas', with whom Stan and Ollie join a Highland regiment.

JEFFERSON, ARTHUR
(1856 or 1862-1949)
Stan's father, known to all as 'A. J.', was a prominent theatrical figure in the northern part of the UK. Arthur Jefferson's early career in repertory served both as apprenticeship and opportunity to display his varied skills; George Arliss (*qv*) later wrote of Jefferson's adept way with stagecraft, make-up and even wig-making. His talents extended also to that of play-wright, many of his sketches and melodramas providing the principal fare in the theatres he managed. By the 1880s he was actor/manager in a small wooden theatre called Spencer's Gaff, in Ulverston, Lancashire. Across the road in Foundry Cottages, later renamed Argyll Street, lived George and Sarah Metcalfe, whose daughter Margaret ('Madge') sang in a choir. Jefferson fell for her immediately and they were married on 19th March 1884. Madge continued to work with her husband on and off-stage for the rest of her life. Their first child was a

A latter-day Arthur Jefferson company precedes legendary beauty Gaby Deslys, complete with her ragtime anthem 'The Gaby Glide'; comedian Will Hay later proposed Babe Hardy's membership of the Water Rats.
Mark Newell collection.

son, Gordon; the second, Arthur Stanley, known always as Stan; there followed a daughter, Beatrice Olga; another son, Sydney Everett, who died in infancy; and last, Everett ('Teddy'). Gordon, who like his father went into management, later rescued Stan after a disastrous engagement. He followed Stan to America in 1915. Teddy joined them later, working as Stan's chauffeur until his bizarre death in 1933 during dental treatment. Olga, her name deriving probably from her mother's stage success as 'Olga Snake' in *Bootblack*, tried a stage career but settled instead in the licensed trade; her pub, the Bull Inn, Bottisford (near Nottingham), displays photographs of Laurel & Hardy visiting the premises in 1953 (an event commemorated in a radio programme of 1987, *Laurel & Hardy Slept Here*). Stan's resemblance to his father, both in features and colouring, is well documented; less recognized is an equal similarity to his mother, from whom he inherited a long jaw and sloping nose (it is not an unkindness to say that in one extant portrait Madge resembles one of Stan's later female impersonations!). Alone of the Jefferson children, Stan spent his first six years living with his maternal grandparents, returning for school

holidays. His schooling was then in Bishop Auckland, where 'A. J.' had been managing the Eden Theatre which had been revamped by the Jeffersons from the old Theatre Royal. His business extended rapidly: on 13 August 1899 the theatrical paper *Entr'acte* carried an advertisement for Jefferson companies at the Theatre Royal, Blyth, Theatre Royal North Shields and Theatre Royal, York. Theatres Royal elsewhere included those at Wallsend, Hebburn and Jarrow; among further enterprises was an interest in the North British Animated Picture Company. Stan later recalled one of his father's publicity stunts: 'I can remember he once had a lion cage hauled around the streets with a real lion in it mauling a body. The body wasn't real, of course – just a fully dressed dummy with a big piece of meat inside. When crowds would gather around the wagon, canvas signs would drop down reading "Tonight! At The Theatre Royal!".'. Other such stunts took the form of placing an immaculately-dressed actor in a hansom cab, its driver seemingly unaware that his passenger had a large, bloodied knife through his chest, and the launching of a balloon that would billow smoke before dropping its advertising banner. The full-blooded nature of his plays reflects more of the man's spirit, with titles such as *The Orphan Heiress* and *A Royal Divorce*. Their influence on Stan manifested itself in his first childhood attempt at entrepreneurism, a production staged in an attic theatre on top of the family home in North

Shields. He starred in a self-composed melodrama building up to a fight lifted bodily from a more famous example, John Lawson's *Only a Jew*. The climactic struggle sent the oil lamps flying, ending the performance prematurely as the curtains blazed. Within a year or two Jefferson faced disaster: grateful to the people of Blyth for their consistent patronage, the ever-benevolent A. J. had built a new theatre for the town at a then-astronomical cost of £14,000; used to less plush surroundings, audiences stayed away and Jefferson's fortunes plummeted. Forced to give up his various theatres, in August 1901 A. J. took over the Metropole, Glasgow. The hall, formerly the old Scotia, had been Lauder's starting-place in the business. Jefferson's excellent reputation was enhanced further by his drastic improvements to the facilities, maintaining at the same time touring versions of his plays. Madge died in Glasgow in December 1908, aged 50. Young Stan, by then making his own way, returned home immediately prior to her death. A. J. continued in Glasgow until the 1920s, when he was persuaded back to run the Eden in Bishop Auckland. By the time Laurel & Hardy visited in 1932, A. J. and his second wife, Venitia, had moved to London; their Ealing address, 49 Colebrook Avenue, is mentioned on-screen by Stan in *Pack Up Your Troubles* (*qv*). Much lionized in his day, A. J. was by now sought after as the father of a world-famous comedian, contributing interviews to *Picturegoer* and other magazines. He later visited Stan in California. His views remained outspoken: when his sketch *Home From the Honeymoon* became a Laurel & Hardy short called *Another Fine Mess* (*qv*), he was less than complimentary about the results. A. J.'s last years were spent with Olga in Bottisford.

(See also: Biographies; Births; Christmas; Circuses; Colouring; Dentists; Documentaries; Education; Home movies; In-jokes; Lauder, Sir Harry; Melodrama; Music-hall; Pantomime; Radio; Stage appearances)

JEFFERSON, MARGARET
(Madge Metcalfe)
See: Jefferson, Arthur

JEFFERSON, STANLEY ROBERT
Stan Laurel's second child, from his marriage to Lois Neilson, was born in May 1930 but lived only a few weeks.

(See also: Children; Laurel, Lois; Marriages)

JIGSAW PUZZLES (all films *qv*)
In *Me and My Pal*, Stan distracts everyone from Ollie's wedding with his gift of a jigsaw puzzle. Another such puzzle so engrosses Edgar Kennedy (*qv*) in *Air Raid Wardens* that he is reluctant to follow blackout regulations. A charming (though incomplete) 1930s jigsaw puzzle graces London's Museum of the Moving Image, depicting scenes from Laurel and Hardy's *Bonnie Scotland*, *The Bohemian Girl*, *Our Relations* and *Way Out West*. The museum has given the relic a wider audience by reproducing it in postcard form.

(See also: Museums)

JITTERBUGS
(Laurel & Hardy film)
Released by 20th Century-Fox, 11 June 1943. Produced by Sol M. Wurtzel. Directed by Malcolm St. Clair. Camera: Lucien Andriot. 74 minutes.
With Stan Laurel and Oliver Hardy, Vivian Blaine, Robert Bailey, Douglas Fowley, Noel Madison, Lee Patrick, Robert Emmett Keane, Anthony Caruso.

Travelling two-man band Laurel and Hardy are stuck in the desert due to an empty fuel tank. Eventually a car

Jitterbugs peddling 'gas pills'

stops, from which emerges Chester Wright (Bob Bailey), a con-man claiming to have invented 'gas pills', guaranteed to turn water into petrol. He fills the boys' tank with genuine fuel before noticing their profession. He then suggests they join him in nearby Midvale to make some money. Stan and Ollie's ingenious remote-control instruments start the crowd dancing and, more importantly, attract attention for a sales pitch. Chester makes the acquaintance of a local girl, Susan Cowan (Vivian Blaine). As unwitting con-men, Stan and Ollie do a good job until one purchaser staggers back from an exploding car. Chester, posing as a detective, hustles the boys out of town. *En route*, he discovers a bag left in the car by Susan, but is saved the job of returning it, Susan having hitched a lift on the back of Stan and Ollie's trailer. Susan tells Chester of a property deal involving her family; Chester recognizes a 'financier' as a crooked gambler, and determines to recover the cash invested by Susan's mother. Back in

Midvale, the family solicitor discovers the money placed in his safe to be newspaper cuttings, switched using twin marked envelopes. The New Orleans racetrack opens the following week; Ollie, as 'Colonel Bixby', checks in at the hotel with Chester as his secretary and Stan as 'Potts', the valet. The 'Colonel' establishes himself as a ladies' man by approaching Susan, who identifies Corcoran (Robert Emmett Keane), one of the swindlers. When Chester mentions the Colonel's fierce wife, Corcoran arranges a compromising meeting with the seductive Dorcas (Lee Patrick). She adopts her best southern accent but snares Stan by mistake; a knock on the door, and the woman claims it is her husband. Ollie arrives instead, charming the would-be vamp as Stan hides beneath the couch, finishing off the drink. They are in a clinch when the 'husband', Corcoran, arrives, agreeing not to name the Colonel in a divorce case in exchange for $10,000. Ollie then assumes another character, that of Sheriff of Midvale with a warrant for the man's arrest. Corcoran turns over his share of the swindle, naming his partner, Bennett, as holder of the remaining sum. Bennett owns a riverboat, where Susan arrives to try out as a singer. Bennett could stage a show but cannot persuade a local gangster, Tony Queen (Noel Madison), to put up the money. Susan has a rich aunt in Boston; Stan impersonates her, ostensibly visiting her sweetheart, Colonel Bixby. Negotiations with 'Aunt Emily' proceed, with Bennett obviously planning a switch of envelopes; the boys plan to do the same. Bennett arrives with Queen, from whom he has borrowed much of his share (with considerable interest), and the double switch of envelopes is made. Stan and Ollie nearly escape but are caught when the crooks check their envelope; Chester has left with the money. The villains catch up with Susan, and it seems that Chester has deserted

them. Queen decides to take over the riverboat, with Susan as resident singer; Stan, still taken for an authentic 'aunt', is taken below with Ollie. In the boiler room, Ollie is made to stoke the furnace; an attempt to knock out their guard leaves Ollie buried in coal. Ollie drops the 'gas pills', exactly what the indigestion-ridden gangster needs. He takes one and inflates, drifting to the ceiling as Stan and Ollie escape. Queen is forcing his attentions on Susan, but a gas pill in his drink turns the crook into a balloon. Stan and Ollie are pursued through the dance hall. In the boiler room, the inflated gangster grabs the main switch and sends the riverboat off at full speed. Amid the panic, Ollie assumes the helm just as Chester returns in a police launch. The money has been wired to Susan's mother and Bennett is arrested. The young couple leave, but Queen and his men still have a score to settle with Stan and Ollie, who dive into the river.

Though over-plotted in the manner of the Fox series, *Jitterbugs* has long been regarded as the best of a poor lot. Its con-men *v* con-men principle has been considered an anticipation of *The Sting*, though a better explanation for its superiority lies in a concentration on the boys' acting skills instead of an attempt to rehash their earlier successes. Indeed, *Jitterbugs* only takes off after jettisoning the forced knockabout of its opening scenes. A new talent, Vivian Blaine (*qv*), was clear incentive for the studio to boost budget and morale, while Roach days were recalled somewhat by the presence of Noël Madison (*qv*), repeating his gangster role from *Our Relations* (*qv*). Though still below-par Laurel & Hardy, *Jitterbugs* usually draws modest praise from critics otherwise hostile to the team's post-Hal Roach releases.

(See also: Bailey, Robert; Boats, ships; Confidence tricks; Patrick, Lee;

Songs; 20th Century-Fox; Video releases)

JOANNON, LEO
See: *Atoll K*

JONES, F. RICHARD (1894-1930)
Production supervisor at Roach until late 1927, formerly with Mack Sennett (*qv*) where he directed the Mabel Normand feature *Mickey* (1918). Stan Laurel trained under Jones as a director, and recalled his indefatigable nature and expert guidance: '[Dick Jones] taught me a lot of tricks about the use of the camera... he was a man with a brilliant mind and with greatly advanced ideas... I'm sure that overwork killed him'. Frank Capra (*qv*) ranked Jones alongside Hollywood's greatest geniuses, considering him the 'brains' of the Mack Sennett comedies with a total understanding of construction, timing and the building of gags. Despite his tragically early death, the influence of F. Richard Jones on film comedy is inestimable.

(See also: Langdon, Harry; McCarey, Leo; Normand, Mabel)

JORDAN, BERT (1887-1983)
British-born film editor, former actor and cameraman. Experience with Griffith and Vitagraph (*qv*) before joining Roach in 1921. He was the actual editor of the Laurel & Hardy series, though uncredited until the departure of Richard Currier (*qv*) in 1932. He gained an Oscar nomination for editing *Of Mice and Men* (*qv*) and later worked in TV. Jordan's skill was greatly appreciated by Stan Laurel who oversaw the editing in any case but needed a technician familiar with his methods.

JUDELS, CHARLES (1881-1969)
Amsterdam-born character actor in American films. He provided comic support on many occasions as in *Hot For Paris, Fifty Million Frenchmen* and Laurel & Hardy's *Swiss Miss* (*qv*), as

the wily cheeseshop proprietor who buys Stan and Ollie's business with worthless currency.

JUDGES (all films *qv*)
There are times when Stan and Ollie's misadventures lead them into court. They are faced with a particularly vicious judge in *Scram!*, who is even less friendly later on when discovering them (innocently) cavorting with his wife. Another unsympathetic justice is described by title card in *The Second Hundred Years* as having taken one look at Stan and 'instructed the jury', in the same way as another judge, refusing to believe that Laurel & Hardy were 'watching the raid', sent them straight to *The Hoose-Gow*. Mercy is shown the boys' twin brothers, 'Alf' and 'Bert', when a judge in *Our Relations* takes them to be his fellow lodge members, Stan and Ollie. Hardy himself plays a judge in *Love 'Em and Weep*. The latter's remake, *Chickens Come Home*, sees Ollie entertaining a judge among his dinner guests, while Stan and Ollie assist the course of justice as witnesses in *Going Bye-Bye!*. They refuse to act as witnesses when a judge arrives to marry Walter Long (*qv*) to the heroine of *Any Old Port*; a like dilemma in *Babes in Toyland* is solved by substituting Stan for the bride. Ben Turpin (*qv*) officiates in *Our Wife*, Edgar Kennedy (*qv*) doing likewise in one of Laurel & Hardy's radio sketches. Detectives Stan and Ollie discover they have sent an innocent man to prison in *The Bullfighters*, a miscarriage that pales alongside the kangaroo court of *Atoll K*.

(See also: Burns, Bobby; Cramer, Rychard; Detectives; Henderson, Del; Policemen; Prison; Radio; Vagrancy)

JUST NUTS
In his later years, Stan Laurel cited as his first film a 1917 short, *Nuts in May*; examination of his personal film listings suggests his debut to have been made a year later, in either *The Evolution of Fashion* or, more probably, *Just Nuts* (a possible working title for *Nuts in May*), a seemingly lost item financed by Adolph Ramish, owner of the Los Angeles Hippodrome. Short, stocky and unpretentious, Ramish watched Stan and his partner Mae from the wings before summoning Stan to his office. 'It's my personal opinion that you're funnier than Chaplin', said Ramish, who was prepared to back his words with an offer of $75 a week for the young comedian to star in two-reel comedies. The deal was made on a handshake and took the form of leasing studio space in Royle, Los Angeles plus the hiring of Bobby Williamson from Kalem to serve as director and Stan's co-writer. Although only one film was definitely produced, its preview at the Hippodrome brought along Stan's old colleague Charlie Chaplin (*qv*) and Universal chief Carl Laemmle.

Mixed Nuts *offers a clue to the action in* **Just Nuts**

Chaplin promised to call Stan with an offer of work, but failed to keep his word. Laemmle came through instead, Stan's next picture work being for Universal as 'Hickory Hiram' (*qv*). Stan remembered the Ramish film depicting himself as an escapee from an asylum, wearing a Napoleon hat. Its precise content may never be determined, but a surviving film, titled *Mixed Nuts*, bears a remarkable similarity both in title and action. Stan described *The Evolution of Fashion* as having been a live shadow-show, albeit 'like a movie', making its inclusion on his film list all the more puzzling.

(See also: Insanity; Laurel, Mae; Rolin Film Company, the; Solo films; Streetcars; Vaudeville)

JUST RAMBLING ALONG
See: Rolin Film Co., the

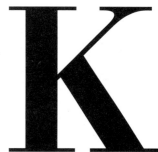

KARLOFF, BORIS (1887-1969)

British-born actor (real name William Pratt), in numerous American silent and early talkie films before *Frankenstein* (1931) established his career in macabre fantasy. One of his last appearances before this was the French version of Laurel & Hardy's *Pardon Us* (*qv*), though his scenes may have been cut prior to release; sadly, this edition is not known to have survived. Still extant is a Roach comedy with Mabel Normand (*qv*) titled *The Nickelhopper*, with Babe playing a jazz drummer and Karloff appearing as a would-be seducer.

(See also: Foreign versions; Night scenes)

KARNO, FRED (1866-1941)

Britain's leading comedy impresario in music-hall days, Fred Karno (born Westcott) created sketches such as *Jail Birds* and *Mumming Birds* (*qv*), performed on tour by his various companies. His name entered popular slang to mean anything ramshackle or chaotic, while British troops of the First World War described themselves, with heavy irony, as 'Fred Karno's Army'. Stan Laurel was one of many comics to have achieved fame as a direct result of working for Karno; Charlie Chaplin (*qv*) was the star of Karno's troupe touring America between 1910 and 1912. His headquarters, the 'Fun Factory', consisted of two houses in Camberwell knocked into one. From here he masterminded an enormously lucrative business that only began to fail as the

Fred Karno (left) on the set of Night Owls. *James Parrott (right) seems less than impressed*

1920s progressed. His downfall is attributed mostly to a failed enterprise, the 'Karsino', on Tagg's Island in the Thames. At this point, Karno decided to try his luck in America, visiting Chaplin but finding greater response from Stan Laurel who, delighted to see 'the Guv'nor', made sure his former employer was taken on as 'associate producer' or, in practice, gagman. Karno's stay with Roach was brief and unhappy, probably through clashing methods and personalities: a photograph taken during *Night Owls* (*qv*) shows Karno on-set, Stan looking on approvingly, Babe seeming dubious and director James Parrott (*qv*) glaring at Karno with outright hostility. Some idea of Karno's failure to fit in may be gathered from a *Film Weekly* item of 16th December 1929 headed 'Fred Karno's Interpreter'. Karno, it seems, had requested just such an assistant on receiving his first scenario (for a Charley Chase comedy), filled with such baffling expressions as 'He horns in on them', 'They take it big', 'He does a Brodie' and 'They neck'. Roach told the author that the only thing Karno did during his stay was to get into a legal row over some tyres, damaged while driving near the studio. Karno left Roach with a generous bonus. It is pleasant to note that Karno staged a reasonable comeback with his show *Real Life*, which was attended by none other than Hal Roach when he visited London. Roach

arrived at the packed theatre and was unable to obtain a seat, but Karno was able to oblige after the manager persuaded two of his regular patrons to postpone their visit until the following evening. Roach witnessed the triumphant performance and praised Karno at a subsequent press conference. Later on, Karno operated a small off-licence. His reputation, tarnished by revelations of his private life, recedes into history but a giant legacy to humour is undeniable. Stan Laurel recalled him thus: 'He had no equal. His name *was* box-office. He was a great boss, kind and considerate - and I hate to remember how he turned out eventually.'

(See also: Aubrey, Jimmy; Clifford, Nat; Hal Roach Studios, the; Keystone Trio, the; Music-hall; Reeves, Alf; Vaudeville; Writers)

KAYE, DANNY (1913-87)

Eccentric comedian noted for dialect, patter and songs. He is remembered chiefly for his Goldwyn features, stage work and considerable aid to UNICEF. Kaye was a particular hit in London, following the precedent for Hollywood visitors set by Laurel & Hardy in 1947. When poor health prevented Stan Laurel from collecting his special Oscar, Kaye accepted it on his behalf and delivered it personally to Stan's home. He autographed Stan's visitors' book with a description of his host as 'a giant among giants'.

(See also: Academy Awards; Stage appearances)

KEATON, BUSTER (1895-1966)
Top-echelon silent comedian, raised in vaudeville (*qv*). As with Chaplin (*qv*), Keaton's story need not be documented here except to say that after his 1920s heyday his career plummeted through difficulties with sound, his marriage, alcohol and the studio (to be placed in order at the reader's discretion). By the early 1930s, M-G-M had the bright idea of teaming him with Jimmy Durante and emphasized the strange pairing by photographing them with an altogether happier partnership, Laurel & Hardy. Though eventually restored to health and professional respect, Keaton spent many years accepting whatever film work was available. This was largely undistinguished but at least plentiful; gag-writing at M-G-M included one of the last Laurel & Hardy features, *Nothing But Trouble* (*qv*). Offscreen, Keaton and Laurel & Hardy were on excellent terms, the Keaton-Laurel friendship remaining firm until the latter's death. At the funeral, Keaton was heard to say that Laurel was the greatest, with Chaplin second. Trivia note: Joe Franklin's *Classics of the Silent Screen* includes a still from *Sherlock Jr.* in which Keaton plays the projectionist at a cinema where one of the attractions is Stan Laurel's *Mud and Sand*.

(See also: Anderson, G. M.; Arbuckle, Roscoe 'Fatty'; Bruckman, Clyde; Christy, Dorothy; *Comic, the*; Cornwall, Anne; Hall, Charlie; *Hollywood Party*; *Hollywood Revue of 1929*; Horne, James W.; Marx Brothers, the; M-G-M; Parodies; *Stolen Jools, the*; Todd, Thelma; Unfilmed projects)

KELLY, PATSY (1910-81)
Archetypal wise-cracking comedienne of many 1930s and 1940s films, Patsy Kelly joined Roach as co-star of two-reelers with Thelma Todd (*qv*). Feature work for the studio includes *Kelly the Second* (the title role) in 1936, *Pick A Star* (*qv*), *Topper Returns* (1941) and *Broadway Limited* (1941). The last pairs her with ZaSu Pitts, Thelma Todd's original partner; in one sequence they echo Laurel & Hardy when sharing a bed with a baby – and a leaking hot water bottle. Miss Kelly later concentrated on other media but may be spotted in occasional 1960s TV segments (such as *The Dick Van Dyke Show*) and the film *Rosemary's Baby* (1968). The actress retained fond memories of the Roach studio, describing the producer as 'the best boss I've ever had', and recalling how Laurel & Hardy would visit to suggest material for the two-reelers.

(See also: Chase, Charley; Lawrence, Rosina; Maltin, Leonard; Hal Roach Studios, the; *Topper*)

KELSEY, FRED (1884-1961)
Ohio-born actor somewhat typecast as policemen, occasionally in uniform but mostly as the archetypal plain-clothes man in bowler hat. He plays such a part in *The Laurel-Hardy Murder Case* (*qv*), a parody of his customary milieu. The satirical element followed him to Busby Berkeley's *Dames* (1934), where he plays an actor specializing in detectives; he was even caricatured as a canine sleuth in a 1943 Tex Avery cartoon, *Who Killed Who?*

(See also: Animation; Detectives; Policemen)

KENNEDY, EDGAR (1890-1948)
(Laurel & Hardy films *qv*)
Comedian noted for his large build, bald head and 'slow burn', Edgar Kennedy's early career ranged from vaudeville to boxing, on one occasion fighting Jack Dempsey. For over 30 years he portrayed everyday frustration, starting in Keystone comedies of the 'teens. In these the younger, hirsute Kennedy is barely recognizable but his swiftly denuded scalp identifies him in 1920s comedies with Charley Chase (*qv*) and others. He is a frequent nemesis for Laurel & Hardy in films made up to the end of 1929, often as a policeman. Notable appearances include *The Finishing Touch*, *Leave 'Em Laughing*, *Angora Love*, *Perfect Day* and *Night Owls*. As 'E. Livingston Kennedy', he directed *From Soup To Nuts* and *You're Darn Tootin'*. He joined RKO in the early 1930s, where his own starring two-

Edgar Kennedy has not noticed his fallen trousers in Leave 'Em Laughing

Tom Kennedy escorts the boys in
Hollywood Party

reelers continued until his death.
Feature work includes the 1937 ver-
sion of *A Star Is Born* and Harold
Lloyd's 'comeback' film *Mad
Wednesday*. He was reunited with
Laurel & Hardy twice in the 1940s,
joining them in a radio skit and in the
film *Air Raid Wardens*.

(See also: Hall, Charlie; *Hats Off*;
French, Lloyd; Kennedy, Tom; Lloyd,
Harold; Marx Brothers, the; *Pair of
Tights, a*; Policemen; Radio; Sound;
Unaccustomed As We Are; Yates, Hal)

KENNEDY, TOM (1885-1965)
(Laurel & Hardy films *qv*)
Brother of Edgar Kennedy (*qv*) and,
more visibly marked by their shared
pugilistic experience, in which he was
once America's amateur heavyweight
champion. Prolific in comedy supporting roles (sometimes with his
brother), entering the world of Laurel
& Hardy as the recruiting sergeant in
Pack Up Your Troubles and the
obstructive footman in *Hollywood
Party*. Other feature work includes
M-G-M's *The Big House*, a film parodied by Laurel & Hardy as *Pardon Us*.

KEYSTONE STUDIOS
See: Sennett, Mack

KEYSTONE TRIO, THE
The departure of Chaplin from
Mumming Birds (*qv*) led to the swift
demise of the company's American
tour. Among those electing to remain
in the US was Stan, who with Karno
colleagues Edgar and Wren Hurley
formed a new trio called *The Three*

*Stan mimics Chaplin in his **Keystone
Trio** days*

English Comiques. Stan wrote a sketch, *The Nutty Burglars*, with the intention of playing Chicago and the Midwest before taking it to New York. This lightweight piece, reminiscent of one of Karno's turns, took the form of Stan and Edgar as noisy housebreakers, their ruthless ineptitude suggested by a toolbag inscribed 'Waffles & Co, Berglars - Merders Dun'. They are discovered by the maid (Wren), a gullible type willing to accept their claim to be icemen. One burglar flirts with the maid as his colleague continues the burglary; a bomb designed to blow the safe is passed from hand to hand before being thrown out of the window. An off-stage explosion follows, and a smoke-blackened policeman (usually played by the local stage manager) appears to arrest the two thieves. The act did reasonably well around Chicago for a few months until Kalma, an illusionist sharing the bill in Cleveland, suggested they meet his agents, Gordon and Claude Bostock. Gordon Bostock was willing to advance the trio from small-time to big-time vaudeville, but with a few changes: first, they acquired the snappier name Hurley, Stan and Wren; more significantly, they were costumed after Chaplin, Chester Conklin and Mabel Normand, the current raves in Sennett's Keystone comedies. Before very long the costuming dictated a final rechristening, *The Keystone Trio*. Stan's impersonation of his former Karno colleague predates the flurry of Chaplin lookalikes who would soon appear in films; in addition, his version was confined to the stage and therefore not in competition with the original. As Chaplin's understudy, he combined a modest entitlement with unique knowledge of his subject's style, enhanced further by his own talents. Long after the event, Stan demonstrated his Chaplin to John McCabe (*qv*):

He did a bit of his Keystone Trio act and it made me, one of those perhaps very singular people who almost never laugh at Chaplin, simply roar aloud... what I saw was not only Chaplin but Laurel as well: two great comedians interfused. Stan was doing more than imitating the balletic grace of the Tramp; he was imposing upon it his own wild and wonderful comedic charm... it was then I knew, if indeed I really needed proof, that Stan was capable of being as great, and indeed a greater, comedian than Charlie Chaplin.

The Keystone Trio tried out at New York's Columbia Theatre before a group of big agents and were accepted on the Proctor Circuit. The act's eventual demise is generally supposed to have been brought about by Hurley's misguided wish to play the Chaplin role, though Stan is known to have confided professional dissatisfaction with The Hurleys at an earlier date. He had stated his misgivings to another couple, Alice and Baldwin Cooke (*qv*), with whom he wanted to team though loyalties on both sides intervened. The split finally came, and by 1916 Stan and the Cookes had become *The Stan Jefferson Trio*, by this time under the management of Claude Bostock. The Chaplin imitation and burglar theme remained, but a new sketch had to be written, Hurley having copyrighted the original (*The Keystone Trio* met a swift end soon after). *The Crazy Cracksman* begins with an actress (Alice) being advised by a press agent (Baldwin) to stage a fake burglary as a means of generating publicity; a real burglar (Stan) enters, bedecked with kitchen utensils, but is spotted by the actress. He claims to be a piano tuner but the actress, taking him for the hired thief, reacts with familiarity. Knockabout gags with flypaper and soda syphon are followed by the arrival of another burglar, actually the press agent who has been unable to hire anyone else. A policeman, spotting the agent's unpro-fessional break-in, arrests both intruders. Stan's later comment on this opus was 'You honest to God had to be there', words borne out by a successful two-year run around the US, elevated all the time to more prestigious circuits. Alice Cooke retained memories of Stan's expertise in a hilarious but potentially dangerous stunt requiring him to slide down a ladder, arms and legs akimbo; she remembered also the trio's lengthy list of props, a selection guaranteed to provoke dismay on their arrival at the theatre. Propmen everywhere would object, with the exception of one man who, on being told how much each prop enabled the act to reach its full potential, responded by providing everything without argument. *The Stan Jefferson Trio* remained inseparable until its nominal leader was led away by one Mae Charlotte Dahlberg, soon to become known as Mae Laurel (*qv*).

(See also: Chaplin, Charlie; Criminals; Karno, Fred; Marriages; *Night Owls*; Vaudeville)

KILGORE, AL (1925-83)
American cartoonist, considered one of the finest. Stan Laurel favoured Al Kilgore's Laurel & Hardy caricatures over all others; sadly, these were not chosen for the US commemorative stamp in 1990. A PBS TV series, *The Dawn of Laurel & Hardy*, was written, produced and directed by Kilgore. His career as illustrator also includes the *Bullwinkle* comic strip, innumerable book and record jackets, a regular movie-star crossword and an escutcheon for the Sons of the Desert club (*qv*), of which he was a charter member.

(See also: Caricatures; Dubbing; McCabe, John; Records; Stamps)

KILL OR CURE
See: Solo films

Dennis King, as the bandit Fra Diavolo, charms Lady Rocburg (Thelma Todd)

KING BEE COMEDIES
See: West, Billy

KING, DENNIS (1897-1971)
Coventry-born opera singer who played the title role in Laurel & Hardy's *Fra Diavolo* (*qv*). Famous in both his native Britain and the US, King started as call-boy in Birmingham Repertory Theatre. War service intervened but King subsequently returned to the stage, working in London and America. Best known as D'Artagnan in *The Three Musketeers* and for *The Vagabond King*, starring also in the latter's 1930 film version. Later appearances include the 1960 American TV version of Gilbert & Sullivan's *The Mikado*, starring Groucho Marx. King's visit to Stan Laurel around this time is commemorated by an inscription in the comedian's visitors' book.

(See also: Marx Brothers, the; Operas; Todd, Thelma)

KING, WALTER WOOLF
(1896-1984)
Remembered as composer 'Victor Albert' in *Swiss Miss* (*qv*), Walter Woolf King was among the many talents to forsake Broadway musicals for the early talkies, beginning with *Golden Dawn* (1930). King later played villainous roles, not all of them serious, notably with the Marx Brothers (*qv*) in *A Night at the Opera* (1935) and *Go West* (1940). Towards the end of his life, King attended various gatherings of the Sons of the Desert club (*qv*), even taking time out to film a special greeting for the UK membership.

KINSEY, HAMILTON 'HAM'
See: Earthquakes, Practical jokes and Stand-ins

KLEINBACH, HENRY
See: Brandon, Henry

KNIGHT, FELIX (b. 1916)
(Laurel & Hardy films *qv*)
The leading man in *Babes in Toyland*, playing Tom-Tom the Piper's son. Knight also performed a song in Laurel & Hardy's next operetta, *The Bohemian Girl*, titled 'Then You'll Remember Me'. More recently, Knight has been a guest at various functions organized by the Sons of the Desert (*qv*).

KORTMAN, ROBERT (1887-1967)
Philadelphia-born actor of stern features, often in westerns; he pursued vagrants Stan and Ollie in *Duck Soup* (*qv*). Later visible whenever tough guys congregate: *Pardon Us*, *Beau Hunks* and *On the Wrong Trek* (all *qv*). In *The Midnight Patrol* (*qv*) he attempts to steal the spare tyre from Laurel & Hardy's police car. Kortman's feature work includes *Trader Horn*, *Blood Will Tell*, *The Big Killing*, *Conquering Horde*, *Twenty-Four Hours* and *Branded*.

KUZNETZOFF, ADIA (1890-1954)
One of Hollywood's Russian colony, as was Mischa Auer of *Pick A Star* (*qv*). Kuznetzoff brought his exotic accent to the role of chef in *Swiss Miss* (*qv*). Other films include *Bulldog Drummond's Bride*, *For Whom the Bell Tolls* and Bob Hope's last Goldwyn vehicle, *The Princess and the Pirate*.

L

LACHMAN, HARRY (1886-1975)

Director, originally a successful painter, whose work earned him the French Legion of Honour. He entered movies collaborating with Rex Ingram on *Mare Nostrum* and *The Garden of Allah*. He is best remembered in partnership with cameraman Rudolph Maté (*qv*) for *Dante's Inferno* (1935); a year later they were director and photographer of Laurel & Hardy's *Our Relations* (*qv*). Lachman's film work was divided between the US and Britain and he had many UK credits in early talkies, such as Gertrude Lawrence's *Aren't We All?* (1932). Later examples include *They Came By Night* (1940), a dramatic film with veteran Scottish comedian Will Fyffe.

(See also: Moreno, Antonio)

LADRONES

See: Foreign versions and *Night Owls*

LANDLORDS (all films *qv*)

In the often impoverished world of Laurel & Hardy, the landlord is a natural enemy. Charlie Hall (*qv*) takes the role most frequently, in *Leave 'Em Laughing*, *They Go Boom* and *Laughing Gravy*. Edgar Kennedy (*qv*) plays the dreaded figure in *Angora Love* while Billy Gilbert (*qv*) is the irascible proprietor of a cheap hotel in *The Chimp*. James Finlayson (*qv*) is in his element parodying the landlords of Victorian melodrama in *One Good Turn*, a character not unlike Barnaby from *Babes in Toyland*. Landladies,

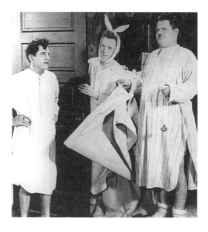

Landlords: Charlie Hall in Leave 'Em Laughing

though less in evidence, are represented efficiently by Mary Gordon (*qv*), the hotel keeper in *Bonnie Scotland*. She tolerates much from the team before turning them out into the street, but Agnes Steele ejects the boys when they owe a mere 14 weeks' back rent in *You're Darn Tootin'*. The team's relationship with landlords often owes less to financial problems than to their own conduct. Nocturnal disturbances during *Leave 'Em Laughing*, *Angora Love*, *They Go Boom* and others draw inevitable complaints, although audience sympathy remains entirely with Laurel & Hardy when they keep a forbidden pet in *Laughing Gravy*. The inspiration behind these exploits may perhaps be traced to Laurel's days as room-mate to Charlie Chaplin (*qv*), when they would break the rules by frying food. Significantly, *Bonnie Scotland* incorporates a sequence in which Laurel and Hardy fry fish in their hotel room.

LANG, JUNE (b. 1915)

Leading lady of the 1930s and 1940s, a former dancer. She is the heroine of *Bonnie Scotland* (*qv*) and appeared with Babe in *Zenobia* (*qv*). Other films include *Chandu the Magician*, a 1932 thriller with Edmund Lowe and Bela Lugosi, Eddie Cantor's *Ali Baba Goes to Town* (1937) and the episodic *Flesh and Fantasy* (1943). She has recently

attended gatherings of the Sons of the Desert club (*qv*).

LANGDON, HARRY (1884-1944)

Baby-faced comedian of minimalistic style, discovered by Sennett in vaudeville playing a chauffeur. After the early entries *Picking Peaches* (his debut) and *Smile Please* (both 1924), Langdon developed a child-like character, wholly dependent on fate to see him through life. His persona was developed by director Harry Edwards and scriptwriter Frank Capra (who

Harry Langdon poses with Babe in costume for their film together, Zenobia

took over direction from Edwards), resulting in a series of successful shorts (notably *All Night Long*, *Feet of Mud* and *Boobs in the Woods*) before graduating to features at First National. *The Strong Man* (1926), *Tramp, Tramp, Tramp* (1926) and *Long Pants* (1927) confirmed Langdon's status as a comedian to rival Chaplin, Keaton and Lloyd. From here Langdon decided to direct himself, with instant disaster: *The Chaser* (1928), an interesting but ill-executed idea about an errant husband forced to adopt his wife's role, was followed by *Three's A Crowd* (1928). Clearly inspired by Chaplin's *The Kid* (1921), only this time with mother in attendance as well as the child, *Three's A Crowd* is overburdened with pathos and ridiculously drawn-out in places, even given the slow pacing which had served him well under Capra. *Heart Trouble* is believed lost but would seem comparable to *Three's A Crowd*. Within a year, Langdon's fall was complete. He signed to appear in sound shorts for Hal Roach, but comedies such as *The King* and *The Fighting Parson* created no excitement. Langdon continued to find supporting roles throughout the 1930s (most effectively in the 1933 Al Jolson vehicle *Hallelujah, I'm A Bum*), until Stan Laurel found him work as a gagman. Langdon had been a strong influence on Laurel's solo work (particularly in the 1925 comedy, *Half A Man*) and it seems probable that Laurel welcomed both a suitable colleague plus the chance to repay a debt. Langdon's name appears on the Laurel & Hardy features from *Block-Heads* in 1938 until *Saps at Sea* two years later. The former's celebrated gag concerning Stan being left in the trenches after the war's end originates in Langdon's 1926 *Soldier Man*. When Laurel was absent from the Roach payroll for much of 1939, Langdon and Hardy were paired in the feature *Zenobia* (*qv*). Despite a fall from the top echelon, Langdon at least remained busy, albeit in shorts for Columbia and

RKO, B-features like the 1940 Monogram release *Misbehaving Husbands* and co-scripting such things as Roach's *Road Show*. As comedian, gagman or even cartoonist, he worked consistently until his sudden death from a brain haemorrhage at the age of 60.

(See also: Astor, Gertrude; Capra, Frank; Caricatures; Foster, Lewis R.; Granger, Dorothy; *Half a Man*; Sennett, Mack; Writers)

LAUDER, SIR HARRY (1870-1950) Scottish music-hall singer, composer and all-round ambassador, from 1919 the variety profession's first knight. Laurel and Hardy visited him at the palatial Lauder Ha' in 1947, donning tam o'shanters and strolling around the estate, aided by two fine specimens from a collection of gnarled walking-sticks (a Lauder trademark). Lauder is mostly applauded, though some are uncomfortable with his promotion of the miserly Scottish stereotype. Colin MacInnes (in the book *Sweet Saturday Night*) expressed dismay at Lauder's transformation of music-hall into a 'respectable' area, though admitting that the man's records did much to temper such reservations.

(See also: Music-hall; Stage appearances)

Laughing: 'Wait'll my wife finds out we drank her liquor!'; *Blotto*

LAUGHING (all films *qv*) Stan Laurel's laugh has been described as a 'refined horse laugh', a joyous, unrestrained expression of merriment. Its contagion is exploited to the full in several Laurel & Hardy sequences where the boys are reduced to hysterics: the first, *Leave 'Em Laughing*, is remarkable in achieving the effect despite being silent (cast and crew broke up so much that shooting had to be suspended!), while its next use, in the early talkie *Blotto*, brings a new audial dimension. Alcoholic settings are usually a good excuse for the giggles, which continue through *Scram!* into *Fra Diavolo*. Stan's most prolonged laughing fit is provoked by a different stimulus, tickling, in *Way Out West*, bringing the hysterical shriek to apotheosis. Ollie's laughter, altogether more restrained, serves often to cover moments of embarrassment, a coy titter complementing admirably his gesture with the tie. Sometimes it is in reaction to a less discreet cackle, as again in *Scram!* but particularly from the silly-ass English stereotypes of *Another Fine Mess* and *County Hospital*. There are also very occasional instances of the supporting cast having obvious difficulty in maintaining a straight face.

(See also: Crying; Englishmen; Ties)

HP-L39

LAUGHING GRAVY
(Laurel & Hardy film)
Released by M-G-M, 4 April 1931.
Two reels. Produced by Hal Roach.
Directed by James Horne. Camera:
Art Lloyd.
With Stan Laurel and Oliver Hardy,
Charlie Hall, Harry Bernard.

On a snowy night, the boys are asleep
in their run-down lodgings when Stan
begins to hiccup. The noise disturbs
not just Ollie but Stan's dog,
'Laughing Gravy', whose presence is
forbidden by the landlord (Charlie
Hall). A drink of water alleviates the
problem only until an even louder hiccup sets the dog barking. Ollie soothes
the animal but the landlord is awakened by the sound of the boys'
collapsing bed. He investigates, and
on finding the dog concealed in a cupboard throws him into the snow. Stan
decides to fetch him, but Ollie goes
instead. Outside, Ollie finds Laughing
Gravy but is locked out. Stan lowers a
string of knotted bedsheets, hauls up
his pet and, forgetting Ollie, closes the
window. When the landlord looks outside, Ollie takes cover and makes
yapping sounds; the landlord throws a
shoe at him. Stan returns to the window and drops the knotted sheets to
Ollie, but they cannot take his weight
and he is dropped into an icy rain barrel. Stan risks a trip to the front door
to rescue his frozen pal, and all is well
until the bed collapses once more,
bringing back the landlord. Once Stan
and Ollie have hidden the dog up the
chimney, the landlord charges the
door. Stan opens it just in time for the
landlord to rush straight through their
room, smashing into the kitchen. The
boys are ordered to leave in the morning. A more immediate problem is the
retrieval of Laughing Gravy, who has
made his way to the roof; Stan follows
him up the chimney, intending to pass
him to Ollie through the window.
Ollie becomes trapped on the window

Laughing Gravy: *Ollie, immediately
post-rain barrel*

ledge, and has to join Stan on the roof.
As they climb back through the chimney, the landlord looks outside and is
knocked unconscious by some bricks
they have dislodged. Back in their
room, the boys decide they need a
bath, and start with Laughing Gravy.
After much difficulty filling the tub,
they begin to scrub the dog until
interrupted by a knock on the door.
Laughing Gravy is hidden and Stan's
head thrust into the suds. Their visitor is a drunk who has called at the
wrong room. The next caller is their
now-conscious landlord; too late, Stan
removes the dog and pushes Ollie's
head into the water. Unaware of the
reason, Ollie hurls the water at Stan,
who ducks and allows the landlord to
be soaked. The boys' eviction notice is
brought forward to precisely 15 minutes. They are escorted out by the
shotgun-toting landlord, who opens
the door to find a policeman nailing
on a sign. An outbreak of smallpox has
quarantined them for two months.
Sadly, the landlord walks off, two separate gunshots indicating his painful
suicide.

   The official remake of *Angora Love*
(*qv*), *Laughing Gravy* gains from a
greater variation of action and the
charm of its canine centrepiece. The
same dog resurfaces in several other
Roach films, including Laurel &
Hardy's *The Bohemian Girl* and the
extended version of *Pardon Us* (both
qv). Charlie Hall (*qv*), giving one of
his best performances, is a splendidly
malicious landlord and extends
Laughing Gravy into a parody of
Victorian melodrama. Two foreign-
language versions were made, the
French *Les carottiers* and the Spanish
Los calaveras. Each is combined with
Be Big (*qv*) to make a feature of
approximately one hour, with the
Laughing Gravy section following a
title describing Laurel & Hardy's
poverty after being divorced. Charlie
Hall remains in the foreign versions,
and the sharp-eyed will notice that he
appears as the bellboy in *Be Big* in

addition to playing the landlord. He
speaks his own dialogue in the *Be Big*
footage but is obviously dubbed later
on. *Laughing Gravy* proceeds along
similar lines in each version until the
finale, where the foreign editions jetti-
son the quarantine ending in favour of
an additional ten-minute section. In
this extra reel, Stan receives a cheque
for $10,000, an inheritance dependent
on his parting from Ollie. The proviso
is based on the belief that Ollie is
responsible for Stan's 'deplorable condition', something Stan prefers to
keep secret from his friend. Ollie, who
has blamed Stan for their circumstances, is delighted when he finally
learns of the bequest, but chastened
when he reads the conditions. Ollie
insists that Stan's best interests lie in
going his own way, but when Stan
reaches the door, Ollie insists on keeping the dog. Stan pauses, tears up the
cheque and returns. Ollie's delight
turns to fury on learning that Stan's
loyalty is to the dog rather than his
friend. This ending was thought
unique to the overseas prints until an
English language copy surfaced in
1985. Differing accounts suggest that
it was found either in Britain or the
US. It seems to have been edited
(though unscored) at the time of production, its deletion having probably
been decided very shortly before
release. The general opinion is that
the sequence was deleted as it was of a
much slower tempo and darker mood.
The American TV restoration
includes both this and the quarantine
ending, a clumsy arrangement but of
great academic interest. When the
film was converted to colour by computer, the extra reel was given
background music but the choice of
themes was unsuitable. Better results
might have been achieved by following
the scores in the foreign versions.

(See also: Animals; Beds; *Chimp, the*;
Deleted scenes; Foreign versions;
Landlords; Melodrama; Music;
Remakes; Sickness; Snow)

THE LAUREL-HARDY MURDER CASE

(Laurel & Hardy film)
Released by M-G-M, 6 September
1930. Three reels. Produced by Hal
Roach. Directed by James Parrott.
Camera: George Stevens, Walter
Lundin.
With Stan Laurel and Oliver Hardy,
Fred Kelsey, Del Henderson, Tiny
Sandford, Frank Austin, Dorothy
Granger.

Stan and Ollie are on a jetty, Stan
fishing with string and a hook, Ollie
attempting to doze despite interrup-
tions from flapping fish and a need to
retrieve his hat. A newspaper blows
into Ollie's face, advertising the reading of a will, that of the late
Ebeneezer Laurel. Questioning Stan
about his lineage, Ollie learns enough
for him to set off with Stan to claim
an estate of $3,000,000. The Laurel
mansion is particularly spooky on this
stormy night; all the spookier is that a
police detective (Fred Kelsey) suspects murder and forbids anyone to
leave the house. Stan and Ollie are
given the room where the murder was
committed, and on retiring are sus-
ceptible to frights over anything from
a cat to a gruesome painting. The butler (Frank Austin) informs another
guest of a telephone call in the library.
As he lifts the receiver, the lights go
out and he disappears, screaming. The
various Laurels investigate the disturbance, but are sent back to bed. An
elderly couple are summoned for their
telephone call, and disappear in the
same manner. This time the butler has
an accomplice, a seemingly harmless
old lady. Ollie decides to investigate,
with Stan following. Stan borrows
Ollie's trousers, with the braces
wrapped around a lamp stand. The
lamp follows Ollie to the landing,
where a collision sends Ollie, Stan and
the lamp rushing downstairs. They
return to a bed which is now occupied
by a bat; apparently pursued by a flying bedsheet, they rush downstairs,
sending the police scurrying away.

**The Laurel-Hardy
Murder Case:** *Our heroes
spend a terrifying night. Its
German counterpart,* Spuk
Um Mitternacht, *opened in
Berlin during May 1931
Advertisement by courtesy of
Robert G. Dickson*

When the bat and Ollie are
released, the suspicious detective asks Stan and Ollie some
questions, until more screams
indicate the disappearance of the
remaining relatives. The butler
announces a telephone call for Stan,
but a uniformed officer (Tiny
Sandford) goes in his place. This time
the lights stay on, revealing a chair
that dumps its victim through a trap-
door when the telephone is lifted. The
policeman vanishes, followed by the
detective. Stan is about to take his
'call' when Ollie decides to go instead.
Ollie sits in the chair, lifts the receiver
and vanishes, only to reappear because
his weight has jammed him in place.
The old lady appears, carrying a knife,
and in being fought off is revealed as a
man in disguise. As he and Ollie
struggle, the scene dissolves to the
jetty, where Ollie, dreaming, wrestles
Stan and himself into the water.

The dream
device was hackneyed even in
1930, let alone four years later when it
was repeated in *Oliver the Eighth* (qv).
The hyphenated title (often misquoted
as *The Laurel and Hardy Murder
Case*) emphasizes the satirical intent, aimed
at a genre inspired by real-life's Hall-
Mills case, but the result is stilted.
There is certainly too much yelling,
some of it to avoid specific dialogue in
shots reused for the French, German
and Spanish versions. There seems no
trace of the French copy (*Feu mon
oncle*), but the German edition is said
to exist in at least mute form while the
Spanish, called *Noche de duendes*, survives complete. The best moments
are, as in the original, contained in the
few stretches of dialogue: the opening
retains a gag deleted from the English
version, to the effect that Stan has an
uncle at university - in a glass jar. The

foreign editions were extended to five reels by reworking *Berth Marks* (*qv*) into a sequence where Laurel & Hardy take an overnight train to the mansion. The train sequence of *Noche de duendes* combines new scenes with material duplicated from the release version of *Berth Marks* plus what seem to be out-takes from that film. At least one UK critic has claimed this to be among the team's most popular films, thanks to its intriguing title: this may have been verified in 16mm rental figures but not among the general public, to whom this subject was virtually unknown until surfacing on TV in 1974.

(See also: Foreign versions; Granger, Dorothy; Hereafter, the; Kelsey, Fred; Murder; Parodies; Television; *That's That!*; Trains; *Wrong Again*)

LAUREL, IDA
See: *Atoll K*, Marriages and Stage appearances

LAUREL, ILLIANA
See: Marriages

LAUREL, LOIS
Stan Laurel's first child was born in 1927 from his marriage to Lois Neilson. Married to British writer Tony Hawes, whom she met at a Sons of the Desert convention (*qv*).

(See also: Children; Home movies; Jefferson, Stanley Robert; Lyn, Jacquie; Marriages; *One Good Turn*; Shops; *That's That!*)

LAUREL, MAE
(Mae Charlotte Dahlberg)
(1888-1969)
A vaudevillian who toured with Cissy Hayden as half of the 'Hayden Sisters', Australian-born Mae teamed with Stan Jefferson in 1918 after they had appeared on the same bill at a theatre in Philadelphia. George Burns has recalled them portraying gossipy old women, but available reviews describe a routine in which Stan is a

burglar who practises dentistry on Mae. The act was variously called *Raffles the Dentist*, *No Mother To Guide Her* and variants thereon; billing in turn varied between Stan and Mae Jefferson and simply Stan Jefferson but was amended permanently to Stan and Mae Laurel when Mae chose the new surname. Their fortunes improved somewhat, but domestic arrangements remained complicated. Mae was unable to obtain a divorce from her husband in Australia, but she and Stan were in every other sense a married couple. Mae was later to regret the often tempestuous nature of their alliance, admitting to a considerable temper that damaged them professionally as well as romantically. Mae's presence in Stan's early films tended to frighten off producers, who expressed wariness at her temperament and fondness for

dubious gags. Joe Rock (*qv*) recalled Mae's insistence on playing Stan's girlfriend despite being too old for an *ingénue*, though she does not seem to take such roles in available films. Scenes such as those illustrated here (see **G. M. Anderson**) depict her not as leading lady but as character actress. There is no doubt that Mae's influence damaged Stan's work, as

filming with Rock deteriorated amid Stan's weariness and increased drinking. Rock eventually conspired with director Percy Pembroke to send Mae back to Australia, arranging the ocean voyage, passport and even the retrieval of Mae's jewels from a pawnshop. Mae exited in 1926, just as Rock introduced Stan to a new partner, actress Lois Neilson. Mae evidently did not stay long in Australia: *Blotto* magazine reproduced an Amsterdam theatre programme for October 1928, billing her with a 'Jimmy Jiggs' as 'eccentric dancers'. Mae resurfaced after a decade to sue for property rights as former 'common-law wife'; the matter was settled out of court.

(See also: Cooke, Alice and Baldwin; *Just Nuts*; *Keystone Trio, the*; Marriages; Names; Periodicals; Plays; Superstition; Vaudeville)

Mae Laurel (left) looks on as Stan is in trouble: The Pest *(1922)*

LAUREL & HARDY FEATURE PRODUCTIONS
A successor to Stan Laurel Productions (*qv*), Laurel & Hardy Feature Productions was incorporated in 1939 with Stan as President, Babe

as Vice-President and Ben Shipman (*qv*) as Secretary-Treasurer. The company lacked production capital but formed instead a negotiating body (i.e. Ben Shipman) in dealing with studios.

(See also: Dentists; Murphy, Jimmy; Salaries; 20th Century-Fox)

LAUREL, VIRGINIA RUTH
See: Biographies and Marriages

LAUREL & HARDY'S FABULOUS FABLES
See: Pantomime, Television and Unfilmed Projects

LAUREL & HARDY'S LAUGHING TWENTIES
(M-G-M 1965)
(Laurel & Hardy films *qv*)
Several feature-length successes enabled compiler Robert Youngson (*qv*) to assemble his first full-scale examination of Laurel & Hardy. *The Golden Age of Comedy* (*qv*) had bordered upon this status and in itself assisted the revival that made this later collection possible. Having helped to re-establish critical interest in Laurel & Hardy, Youngson clearly set out to do the same for others, Snub Pollard (*qv*) receiving much attention in *Days of Thrills and Laughter* (*qv*). *In Laughing Twenties*, he punctuates the Laurel & Hardy footage with Charley Chase (*qv*) in *Never the Dames Shall Meet* and *Snappy Sneezer*, and Max Davidson (*qv*) in *Dumb Daddies* and *Pass the Gravy*. Excerpts from Davidson's *Call of the Cuckoos* separate the plot footage from a gag sequence where Laurel, Hardy and Chase clown with James Finlayson and Charlie Hall (both *qv*). Other early team footage incorporates moments from *Sugar Daddies*, *Putting Pants On Philip* plus the brief intercutting between the two in *Forty-Five Minutes From Hollywood*. Still earlier are solo clips of a phenomenally young Babe in *Fatty's Fatal Fun* (1916), a more seasoned Hardy in *Along Came Auntie*

and further glimpses of Laurel in *Kill Or Cure*, a film employed by Youngson both before and subsequently. Of the mature Laurel & Hardy work, potted versions are presented of the following: *From Soup to Nuts*, *Wrong Again*, *The Finishing Touch* and *Liberty*. Brief excerpts from *Leave 'Em Laughing*, *Double Whoopee* and *Habeas Corpus* accompany similar fragments reprising sequences from *The Golden Age of Comedy*, including the fights from *Battle of the Century* and *You're Darn Tootin'*, the finale of *Two Tars* and the famous gag from *The Second Hundred Years* in which Stan unwittingly daubs paint over a young lady's bottom. *Laughing Twenties* was very successful in its day, inspiring a direct sequel, *The Further Perils of Laurel & Hardy* (*qv*); Youngson's approach had been refined, allowing individual sequences to build rather than be subject to the rapid cutting obligatory to a more general compilation. The narrative style retained in turn a blend of necessary information with witty counterpoint to the action, a balance which was not always maintained. As both a convenient Laurel & Hardy sampler and a display of the compiler's art, *Laurel & Hardy's Laughing Twenties* is difficult to beat.

(See also: Arbuckle, Roscoe 'Fatty'; Coburn, Dorothy; Compilations; Finlayson, James; Garvin, Anita; M-G-M; Richard, Viola; Risqué humour; Sleeper, Martha; Solo films; Teaming; *That's My Wife*)

LAWRENCE, ROSINA (b. 1912)
Actress, singer and dancer born in Canada to British parents, Rosina Lawrence was first taught dancing as a means of overcoming a childhood injury. That childhood was spent variously in Canada, Great Britain and, finally, Los Angeles, where her father had obtained work as a set-builder. Picture work was the logical progression, Miss Lawrence beginning as a child actress in a Universal film

starring Virginia Valli, *Lady of Quality* (1923). There followed stage musicals and a dancing role in the 1927 film *Angels of Broadway*; another, unofficial contribution was doubling for star Leatrice Joy in close-ups of her hands, something she would later do for several other stars. (In earlier years, Leatrice Joy had worked with Babe in Billy West's comedies.) Subsequent pictures include the revue film *Paramount On Parade* (1930), Will Rogers' *A Connecticut Yankee* (1931), *Dance Team* (1932) with Sally Eilers, *Disorderly Conduct* (1932) with Spencer Tracy and *Reckless*, a 1935 vehicle for Jean Harlow (*qv*). While in vaudeville during 1934, she made the acquaintance of a father-daughter act known as 'The Dancing Cansinos', the younger member of which achieved fame as Rita Hayworth. Both were spotted by a talent scout for Fox pictures, Rosina appearing in five films there until a merger with 20th Century put an end to existing contracts. From here she moved to Roach, following an appearance in M-G-M's *The Great Ziegfeld*: though visible in the final cut, her two production numbers fell victim to drastic editing. At Roach, she was given the finest opportunities of her career, billed alongside Patsy Kelly (*qv*) and Lyda Roberti in trade ads such as that declaring 'Meet Hal's Gals!'. She appeared with both in *Nobody's Baby* and again with Patsy Kelly in *Pan Handlers* and *Kelly the Second*. Our Gang (*qv*) acquired a new schoolteacher in Miss Lawrence, who was with them for eight films, including the Oscar-winning *Bored of Education* and the feature-length *General Spanky*. She supported Jack Haley in a Roach film, *Mr Cinderella*, and became screen wife to Charley Chase (*qv*) for *Neighborhood House* and *On the Wrong Trek* (*qv*). Laurel & Hardy's *Way Out West* (*qv*) provided her with the role of heroine, while *Pick A Star*

*A beautiful portrait of **Rosina Lawrence**, inscribed to the author*

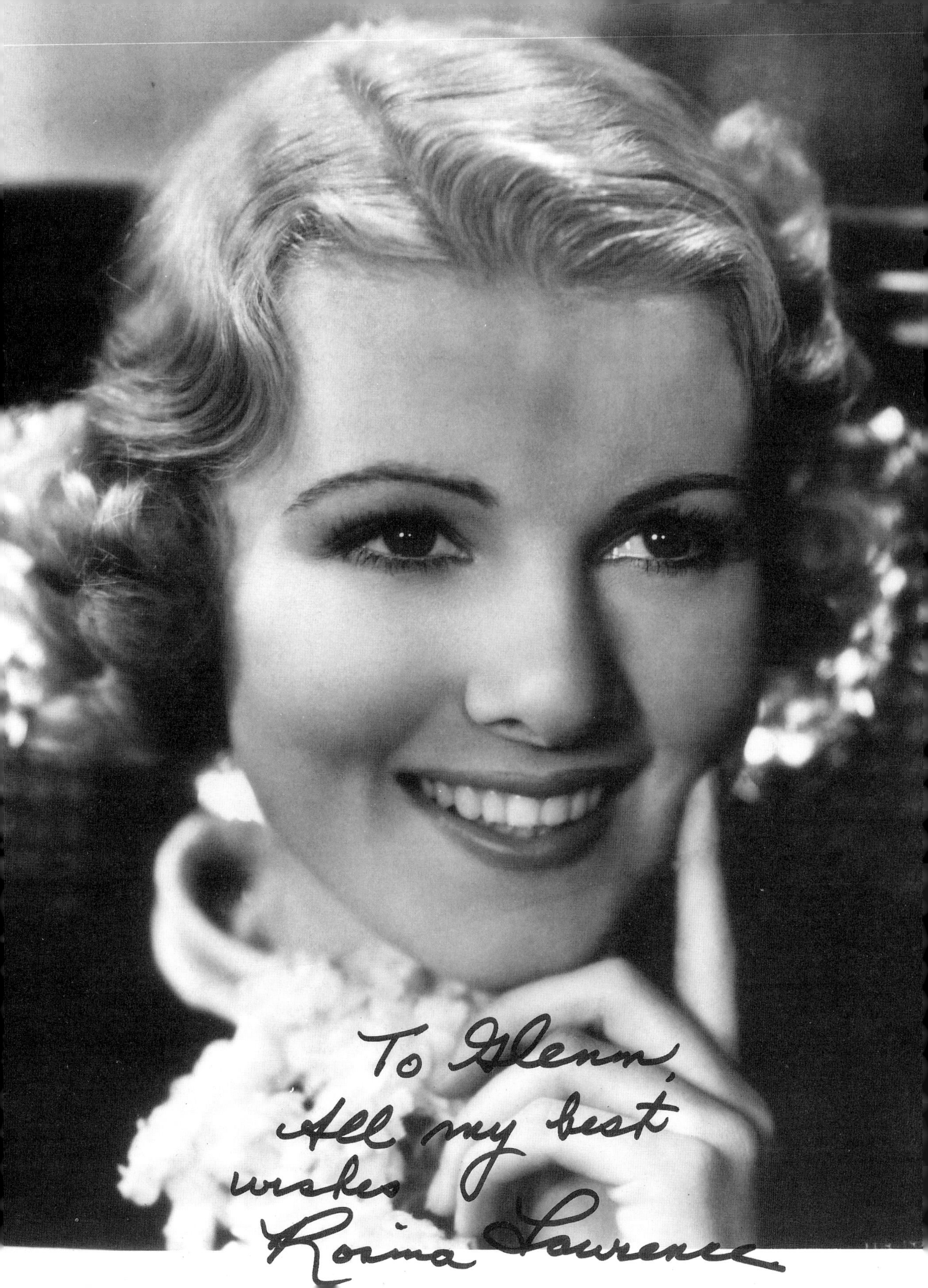

To Glenn,
All my best
wishes
Rosina Lawrence

(*qv*) reunited her with Patsy Kelly, Jack Haley and Laurel & Hardy. Roach's plan to star her in an Italian co-production of *Rigoletto* fell through but another Italian company offered her the role of an American girl visiting Italy in the film *In Compagna e Caduta Una Stella* (*In the Country Fell a Star*). The film was completed in 1939, just in time for her to return home before war broke out. She later retired to family life but was delighted when the Sons of the Desert club (*qv*) invited her to attend its meetings. In 1984 she was among the honoured guests at the society's convention in England, where another such guest, John McCabe (*qv*), was in attendance; by this time they were, respectively, widow and widower, their relationship leading to marriage on 8 June 1987.

(See also: Dubbing; Guest appearances; Hal Roach Studios, the; *Hollywood Revue of 1929*; Songs; West, Billy)

LEAVE 'EM LAUGHING
(Laurel & Hardy film)
Released by M-G-M, 28 January 1928. Produced by Hal Roach. Directed by Clyde Bruckman. Camera: George Stevens. Two reels. Silent.
With Stan Laurel and Oliver Hardy, Edgar Kennedy, Charlie Hall, Otto Fries, Jack V. Lloyd, Viola Richard, Dorothy Coburn, Tiny Sandford.

Stan's toothache means sleep for neither him nor Ollie. Stan disrupts Ollie's peace even when he is confined to the kitchen, so attempts are made to extract the offending tooth. Use of a doorknob and string succeeds only in detaching the doorknob. The landlord (Charlie Hall) investigates the noise, with the message 'Tomorrow, you move'. He is stunned by a blow from Stan's fist; a similar blow from Ollie puts Stan to sleep, but their bed collapses beneath them. The following morning, the boys witness scenes of carnage as Stan awaits the dentist's

attention. Stan's turn for the chair arrives, but the application of gas sends him into a panic. Ollie asks the dentist (Jack V. Lloyd) to leave him with Stan, with the idea of coaxing him into the chair so the dentist can sneak up on him. Ollie demonstrates how easy it is to sit in a dentist's chair, while the dentist, exhausted, sends his brawny colleague (Otto Fries) to finish the job. Before he can explain, Ollie is both anaesthetized and minus a tooth. He regains consciousness to discover Stan holding his missing tooth in the dentist's pliers. Forcing Stan into the chair, he tries to give Stan some of the laughing gas, but soon both are under its influence. Unwisely, they start to drive home in this condition and, after one minor accident, the boys meet a traffic cop (Edgar Kennedy). He waves them on but they are immobilized with laughter. With the traffic held up, the cop orders them to move, but is asked to crank their car. He loses his belt, and his trousers fall to the ground. Eventually he commandeers their vehicle, driving it around the corner and straight into a

Leave 'Em Laughing: it's not Officer Kennedy's day

deep puddle. Stan and Ollie continue to laugh as they sink into the mud.

Leave 'Em Laughing provides something of a bridge between the subversive edge of the team's earlier work and the greater innocence of their mature characters. The concluding scene is in line with the anarchy of, among others, *The Battle of the Century* and *You're Darn Tootin'* (both *qv*), but the opening section anticipates several future concentrations on Stan and Ollie in their lodgings, notably *They Go Boom* and *Laughing Gravy* (both *qv*). Stan as patient and Ollie as amateur dentist reflect the child-like traits that would become more pronounced in their work after the introduction of sound; these characteristics are particularly noticeable in a revival of the dentistry sequence in their feature-length comedy *Pardon Us* (*qv*).

(See also: Beds; Cars; Characters; Compilations; Dentists; Gag titles; Hall, Charlie; Kennedy, Edgar; Landlords; Policemen)

LEDERER, OTTO (1886-1965)
Czech-born actor, in American films from the 'teens. He plays the band-

master in *You're Darn Tootin'* (*qv*). Other films include Colleen Moore's talkie debut, *Smiling Irish Eyes* (1929).

LELAND, DAVID (c.1932-87)
American actor who as a youth played the role of an exiled boy-king in Laurel & Hardy's *Nothing But Trouble* (*qv*). Other films include *The Hour Before the Dawn* (1944) and *I Want To Live* (1958). He was for many years road manager for Robert Goulet and later acted in TV series. Not to be confused with the British director of the same name.

LENO, DAN (1860-1904)
Premier artist of British music-hall, born George Galvin in Somers Town, London. The slightly built Leno turned from the championship clog-dancing of his youth to a comedy of nervous energy tempered with whimsy, desperation compensated by defiance and a personal presence that won over the nation. The type of comedian often funnier in himself rather than through his material, Dan's eccentric ways permeated the various characters he portrayed, either in music-hall songs such as 'The Grass Widower' or in Drury Lane pantomime. For a while he was known as 'The King's Jester', after performing for King Edward VII at Sandringham. Leno's immense popularity, early death and reputed spiritual guidance to later performers have perpetuated his memory more than his many gramophone records (primitive even for the time) and one surviving film, none of which communicate what it was that made him so special. His legacy to the comic art is difficult to define, except to say that he served as a prototype for the modern stand-up comedian in addition to influencing the great mimes who were to follow. One of those mimes was Stan Laurel, who revered Leno throughout his life despite not having seen him. Leno's reputation was such that nobody in music-hall (or perhaps outside it) was unaware of his status,

David Leland learns finger-tricks from the master

and young Stan learned much of Leno from his many imitators. The similarities between Laurel and Leno extend even to photographs of Leno with the tight-lipped grin, upraised hair and outstretched arms familiar from Laurel's mature work, while portraits of Stan in his earliest music-hall days show him imitating Leno both in expression and make-up. The broad, toothy smile and triumphant drum-roll jig of Laurel's solo films were Leno's, but with Leno they suggested a desperate triumph rather than mere self-congratulation. A more effective adaptation involved Leno's technique of describing something so intricate that he would lose himself mid-way; Stan refined this so that he could present a lucid idea but mangle it when Ollie asks 'tell me that again...'. Coincidentally, Leno's success in pantomime was in partnership with another heavyweight comedian, Herbert Campbell, though the relationship between their characters differed from that of Stan and Ollie. Leno was a founding member of the Grand Order of Water Rats (*qv*), serving as King Rat on several occasions; Laurel and Hardy joined the lodge in 1947.

(See also: Female impersonation; Goon Show, the; Music-hall; Pantomimes; Solo films)

LET GEORGE DO IT
See: Working titles

LETTERS
(Laurel & Hardy films *qv*)
As spokesman for the team, Stan tended to write most of their correspondence. He was in any case a prolific letter-writer, unlike his partner. Numerous Laurel letters survive today, varying widely in purpose, content and recipient. Many of those written on tour relate to social occasions, either as acceptance or thanks after the event. Often they are in Stan's own meticulous handwriting, though later correspondence is usually typed. Common to each is a warm-hearted courtesy typical of both comedians, indicated by such closing remarks as (to a fellow professional) 'continued success always, sincerely and fraternally' or, with intimates, a 'God bless!' in the manner of British theatre's older generation. Many such examples were collected by the magazine *Bowler Dessert* in a series titled 'The Laurel Letters', another collection graced *Blotto* magazine, and still another (available for inspection at the Newcastle Central Library) appeared in the book *Laurel Before Hardy*. These courteous notes might be punctuated by Stan's self-effacing and often macabre wit, as when John McCabe (*qv*) enquired about *Putting Pants On Philip* and *The Battle of the Century*: Stan mentioned their

director, Clyde Bruckman (*qv*), reflecting sadly on the man's recent suicide before jokingly ascribing the tragedy to Bruckman having found and screened *Battle*. Stan's wit and modesty permeate his communications to British writer Michael Pointon: having been told of the loud audience reaction to *When Comedy Was King* (*qv*), Stan suggested that it might not have been *enjoyment*; when asked if he could be addressed as 'Stan' rather than "Mr Laurel", he replied 'You can call me 'Maggie' if you want to!'; and when told of an erroneous British newspaper item listing him among the greats in the forthcoming *It's A Mad, Mad, Mad, Mad World* he reacted with some anger, perhaps through suspected misuse of his name but more probably because of his decision to retire out of respect to Babe's memory. After Babe's death Stan was of course the prime source for information on the team. Fan mail, amplified by the compilations and McCabe's *Mr Laurel and Mr Hardy*, reached giant proportions, Stan doing his best to answer each personally despite failing eyesight and, one would imagine, considerable expense. He would often hear from youngsters who had discovered his work through television. One of these, Dean Kaner, later published his collection of Laurel correspondence as *The Stan Laurel Scrapbook*. Letter-writing became one of Stan's chief occupations in his retirement and at least gave him plenty of excuse to indulge a favoured pastime, visiting stationery stores. The orderly fashion of such establishments appealed to him and he once said that he would have become a stationer had he not gone into the theatre. He would be meticulous about his personalized letterheads, cards and envelopes, the latter printed in distinctive colours that would vary between yellow or blue, contrasting with the letter itself. A general correspondent at this busy time might receive a card in return for every two or three letters, though

the average seems to have been rather more frequent; he particularly enjoyed hearing from British fans, taking a genuine interest in their lives and news of his native country. There would be lengthy exchanges of reminiscence with friends, relatives and colleagues on both sides of the Atlantic, and he also wrote consistently to collectors of his films, feeling he had a responsibility to them. He would circulate jokes even to people known to him only by mail (one survivor of these, a two-page item called 'Getting it Right', purports to represent a series of letters from the owner of a second-hand typewriter, each message becoming more obscured by the machine's escalating shortcomings). His genial spirits could be tempered when the occasion demanded: during the preparation of McCabe's first book, Stan recommended a friend of Babe's from Florida days, only to be told that the gentleman in question would supply recollections and stills only in return for substantial remuneration. Stan's comments were 'we can get along without his information and am sure he knows what to do with his stills'. As he once wrote to a fan who

had recently seen *The Big Noise*: 'Nuff said'.

(See also: Auctions; Biographies; Black humour; Courtliness; Periodicals; Wood, 'Wee' Georgie)

LEWIS, JERRY (b. 1926)

Manic comedian and director whose name was made in partnership with Dean Martin. He was in solo work from 1957, in films often considered an acquired taste though revered in France. His work in *King of Comedy* (1981) enhanced his reputation somewhat though many remain unconverted. Stan Laurel liked Lewis both as a person and a talent, but found his style somewhat alien. It is known that Stan Laurel turned down a lucrative offer to work as Lewis' script consultant, preferring to keep their friendship on a non-professional basis. There is a Laurel lookalike in *The Bellboy* (1960). Jerry Lewis spoke of Laurel in some detail for the 1974 BBC film *Cuckoo* (*qv*).

(See also: Tashlin, Frank; *Wild Poses*)

Perilous perching in **Liberty**

LIBERTY
(Laurel & Hardy film)
Released by M-G-M, 26 January 1929. Produced by Hal Roach. Directed by Leo McCarey. Two reels, silent with music and sound effects. With Stan Laurel and Oliver Hardy, James Finlayson, Tom Kennedy, Jean Harlow, Jack Hill.

Prison officer Tom Kennedy is in hot pursuit of escapees Stan and Ollie. The fugitives are picked up by friends, changing into civilian clothes in the back of the car. To elude a policeman on a motorcycle, Stan and Ollie leap from the moving car, quickly adopting a nonchalant pose beside a parked vehicle. Their hasty dressing has left each wearing the other's trousers and in seeking various places to make the exchange, the boys are repeatedly caught lowering their trousers. Although soon followed by a suspicious policeman, they eventually make the necessary switch in a building-site lift. Ollie accidentally catches a lever which sends them to the top of a partly-constructed skyscraper. As the lift has returned to ground level without them, Laurel and Hardy make their way around the girders. The danger to their lives is complicated by a runaway crab acquired from an attempt to exchange trousers outside a fishmonger's. Stan and Ollie make it back to the lift, which on descent squashes the pursuing policeman into a midget.

Randy Skretvedt (qv) has mentioned that *Liberty* owes its existence to the drastic cutting necessary to bring *We Faw Down* (qv) down to length. The film's best sequence, in which Laurel & Hardy have to exchange trousers, was also the only one that could be removed while maintaining continuity, and *Liberty* provided the means of salvaging the routine. Despite being made in order to preserve a single segment, *Liberty* is considered one of their finest shorts, and is familiar to modern

Della Lind *pretends to be caught off-guard*

audiences through inclusion in the compilation *Laurel & Hardy's Laughing Twenties* (qv). The hair-raising skyscraper footage was achieved by the studio's usual means of constructing a set on a high point overlooking the city (a technique dating back to the similar comedies starring Harold Lloyd [qv]), although some element of risk remained. When director Leo McCarey (qv) appeared on Laurel & Hardy's *This Is Your Life* in 1954, he remembered Hardy comforting a nervous Laurel by demonstrating the effectiveness of a safety net provided some 20 feet beneath; the net proved ineffective and Hardy continued to fall a further 20 feet to a safety platform. Fortunately Hardy escaped with a few bruises. *Liberty* survives with an orchestral accompaniment and sound effects from its original release. At least two earlier subjects were issued with similar tracks, but the discs have yet to be found. Some copies of the film have surfaced bearing titles suggesting a post-war reissue by Film Classics (in a package consisting primarily of talkies), but it is not known if the 1929 soundtrack accompanied that issue. An American video release incorporates the original track but not its European counterpart.

(See also: Criminals; Homosexuality; Prison; Reissues; Sound; Skyscrapers; Television)

LIFTS (Laurel & Hardy films qv)
Lifts, or 'elevators' in America, offer plenty of opportunity for comic confusion. In *Come Clean* the boys continue to miss each other as they travel up and down; in *Double Whoopee* they send a foreign prince down a lift shaft; while a Laurel solo film, *Pick and Shovel* (1924) makes much of a lift designed for miners. In *Pack Up Your Troubles*, a dumb waiter serves as a makeshift version, as does the perilous harnessing of their mule in *Way Out West*. In *Block-Heads* the lift in Ollie's department building varies between inactivity and the bumpiest of rides.

(See also: Apocrypha; Doors)

LIGHTING
See: Lachman, Harry and Lloyd, Art

LIND, DELLA (b. c.1912)
Austrian-born actress in American films, the leading lady of *Swiss Miss* (qv). Miss Lind's vocal talents are ample evidence of her background in Viennese musical-comedy. Also known as Grete Batzler.

LITTLE RASCALS, THE
See: Our Gang

LITTLEFIELD, LUCIEN
(1895-1960)
Texas-born actor prolific from silent days to the 1950s, Lucien Littlefield is known to Laurel & Hardy fans for his splendid eccentrics from two 1933 films, *Dirty Work* and *Sons of the Desert* (both qv). In the former he is 'Professor Noodle', crackpot genius with a formula for rejuvenation (qv); the latter casts him as 'Horace Meddick, M.D.', a veterinary surgeon who diagnoses Ollie's malaise as *Canis Delirius*. Students of 1930s comedy will recall him in W. C. Fields' *The Man on the Flying Trapeze* (1935).

(See also: Doctors; Insanity)

THE LIVE GHOST
(Laurel & Hardy film)
Released by M-G-M, 8 December
1934. Produced by Hal Roach.
Directed by Charles Rogers. Camera:
Art Lloyd. Two reels.
With Stan Laurel and Oliver Hardy,
Walter Long, Arthur Housman, Mae
Busch, Charlie Hall, Harry Bernard,
Leo Willis.

Sea captain Walter Long cannot get a
crew for his supposedly haunted ship.
Turned down by every prospective
mariner in a waterfront bar, he
chances upon two fish cleaners, Stan
and Ollie, whose day off is spent fishing. They are just as reluctant to join
his ship but agree to help him shanghai a crew at a dollar a head. They
return to the saloon where Stan
engages their victims in a practical
joke: 'I'll bet you a dollar you can't
put this egg in your mouth without
breaking it', says Stan, bringing a fist
up to the man's jaw once he accepts
the challenge. Stan is chased out only
for his pursuer to be knocked cold
with Ollie's frying pan. Long thus
builds up a sizeable crew until Ollie
decides to take Stan's place; unfortunately his first target is a man (Charlie

An atmospheric set for **The Live Ghost**

Hall) who has seen the trick in action,
and reverses the move. His mirth is
curtailed when Ollie places an egg in
the man's mouth and breaks it, whereupon Ollie is chased into the street as
planned. Stan, his aim impaired by
the saloon door, knocks out Ollie
before hitting his target; when he
strikes the Captain he too is knocked
cold. At sea, Stan and Ollie wake up
alongside the shanghaied crew. They
are about to be lynched when the
Captain intervenes, guaranteeing their
safety providing they remain on
board. The crew vows revenge on
Stan and Ollie; Long vows revenge on
anyone who mentions ghosts. His specific threat is that he will twist the
culprit's head so that 'when you're
walkin' north, you'll be lookin' south'.
Ten ports later, Stan and Ollie have
still not been ashore. Another,
drunken crew member (Arthur
Housman) is ordered to remain on
board, and is placed in the boys'
charge. He escapes, leaving a trunk
under his bedclothes. As Stan and
Ollie prepare for bed, Stan finds a
concealed revolver which Ollie quickly
grabs; a bullet is sent flying into what
they believe to be the drunk. Ashore,
their wavering shipmate falls into a
vat of whitewash; by the time they
prepare to dump the 'corpse' overboard, he has sneaked back aboard and
climbed into his bunk. Stan and Ollie
dump their sleeping comrade into a
sack, consign him to the briny and
return to bed. The drunk climbs back
aboard, his luminously-white figure
sending Stan into a panic. Ollie is
sceptical until he sees the apparition
himself. The boys' terror is shared by
the gang who have returned to 'fix'
them, and they decide instead to jump
overboard. The Captain returns with
a dockside floozie (Mae Busch) who,
recognizing the drunk as her
estranged husband, gives vengeful
chase. Unthinkingly, Ollie tells Long
of the 'ghost'; Long reaches offscreen
to Ollie's neck. 'Did you see it, too?'
he asks Stan. 'Uh-huh', replies Stan.
'What did you see?' continues Long.

'I saw a ghost' admits Stan, caught
off-guard. For the fade-out, Stan and
Ollie have their heads mounted back-
to-front: another nice mess.

Complex in plot but compact in
execution, *The Live Ghost* is one of
the author's favourite Laurel & Hardy
shorts. Very atmospheric, aided by
detailed sets and judiciously-placed
mist, the film presents their stock
company at its best while offering
Laurel & Hardy a pleasant blend of
visual humour and some memorable
dialogue. Mae Busch (*qv*), the movies'
perennial streetwalker, for once is
presented in such a role without a
shred of ambiguity, while Arthur
Housman and Walter Long (both *qv*)
are seen to best advantage. The contrived notion of falling into
whitewash is rendered credible by
Housman's skill, while the aggrieved
Captain is Long at his roguish best.
Diminutive comic Charlie Hall (*qv*)
has a particular highlight when he
and his shipmates plot revenge
against Stan and Ollie: 'I want the big
guy', he claims. This, along with several other moments, was omitted from
the 8mm version released in Britain
by Walton Films; fortunately the
BBC TV print is uncut.

(See also: Alcohol; Boats, ships;
Censorship; Characters; Confidence
tricks; Dialogue; Eggs; Fish; Freak
endings; Hereafter, the; Home
Movies; Practical jokes; Risqué
humour; Television)

L-KO COMEDIES
A studio formed by ex-Keystone
director Henry 'Pathé' Lehrman in
direct competition with, and imitation of, his former employers. L-KO
(or 'Lehrman Knock-Out') released
at least two Laurel films in 1918,
Phoney Photos and *Whose Zoo*, neither
of which is known to exist today.
Oliver Hardy worked for them the
following year in *Freckled Fish*, *Hop
the Bellhop*, *Lions and Ladies*, *Hello
Trouble* and *Painless Love*, all of which

seem to have followed the Laurel films into oblivion.

(See also: Sennett, Mack; Solo films)

LLOYD, ART (1896-1954)

Regular Laurel & Hardy cameraman following the departure of George Stevens (*qv*), Art Lloyd first joined Roach in 1923. He later served with US Signal Corps and photographed the Bikini Atoll explosion; his early death has been attributed to radiation exposure. Stan Laurel so appreciated Lloyd's work that he insisted on taking him over to RKO to photograph *The Flying Deuces* (*qv*). The comedian preferred colleagues who were used to his requirements, in this case a type of lighting designed to emphasize the blank look of the team's faces; in addition, Lloyd was obliged to keep the whole set evenly lit to facilitate extemporized action.

(See also: Jordan, Bert; Maté, Rudolph; Unfilmed projects)

LLOYD, HAROLD (1893-1971)

In common with Chaplin and Keaton (both *qv*), there is no need here to describe Lloyd's great success. He was Roach's first comedy star when setting up in production and would remain so until departing in the early 1920s. Roach and Lloyd had begun together as extras and would make their reputations in tandem. Stan Laurel worked at the studio in its days as Rolin (*qv*) and became acquainted with Lloyd just before his 'glasses' persona moved from single reel comedies into two-reelers. Lloyd's comedy of perilous heights (actually a small part of his repertoire) would be revived by Laurel & Hardy in *Liberty* (*qv*). Stan Laurel admitted that Lloyd hardly ever made him laugh but admired his inventiveness: 'The best of the straight comedians', was Laurel's evaluation.

(See also: Bruckman, Clyde; Clifford, Nat; Pollard, Harry 'Snub'; Roach,

Hal E.; Skyscrapers; Taylor, Sam)

LOCATIONS

(Laurel & Hardy films *qv*)
Most of the Roach comedies were filmed either on the studio lot or in the area surrounding its Culver City location. Sometimes an excursion was necessary, as with the desolate Nevada scenery required for *Flying Elephants*, but when possible they stayed close to home. Despite inevitable change, much remains familiar to Laurel & Hardy buffs, many of whom have visited the actual sites. This task was made easier by Bob Satterfield's *Laurel and Hardywood*, a special edition of *Pratfall* magazine devoted to his findings. The magazine identifies (among numerous others) the staircase used in *Hats Off* and *The Music Box* (located in the Silverlake area of Los Angeles), the houses used in *Big Business*, *Perfect Day*, *Hog Wild* and others, plus areas such the old Santa Fe depot used in *Berth Marks* and Laurel's early solo *Hustling For Health*. Sadly, the local City Hall, which served as the *County Hospital* and a courtroom in *Going Bye-Bye!* has since been declared unsafe and demolished, though the survival rate continues to be encouraging.

(See also: Apocrypha; Homes; Periodicals; Rolin Film Co., the)

LONDON, JEAN 'BABE' (1901-80)

Born Jean Glover in Des Moines, Iowa, Babe London travelled to California with her family when still a child. At 17 she answered a newspaper advertisement for a film company, playing in a one-reeler for them before following the company to Los Angeles. She met Stan Laurel during a stint with Vitagraph, where Laurel was supporting Larry Semon (*qv*). London quickly established a reputation as a comic 'fat girl', an early important role being that of a switchboard operator in Fairbanks' *When the Clouds Roll By* (1919). In Chaplin's *A Day's Pleasure* (1919) she may be seen becoming very seasick; in 1972 she told Anthony Slide that she had 'quite a nice scene with him, close-ups and stuff', and that Chaplin had said 'Babe, if you stick by this, you're going to make it'. Make it she did, featuring in numerous comedies, notably with producer Al Christie.

*Captain **Walter Long** sends the boys into a saloon to shanghai a crew in* The Live Ghost

London recalled Christie's fondness for putting her in blonde curls as a 'bum Mary Pickford'. She obtained work in features at First National, as did James Finlayson (*qv*), appearing with Colleen Moore and in the 1927 Langdon film *Long Pants*. Other late 1920s features included the W. C. Fields-Chester Conklin remake of *Tillie's Punctured Romance* (1928). Film work continued well into talkies, notably Laurel & Hardy's *Our Wife* (*qv*), in which she played Ollie's fiancée. She later turned to vaudeville, but retained contact with her movie contemporaries. When attending Sennett's funeral in 1960, she realized how their number was dwindling and produced a series of oil paintings commemorating the great stars. The collection, titled 'The Vanishing Era', is now on display at the University of Wyoming. Babe London's adventurous spirit never dimmed; a slimmer but recognisable London took part in the 1974 BBC documentary *Cuckoo* (*qv*), and the following year saw her third marriage, to composer and musician Phil Boutelje. Toward the end of her life Babe London was a frequent and honoured guest of the Los Angeles 'Tent' of the Sons of the Desert club (*qv*).

(See also: Chaplin, Charlie; Darling, W. Scott; Langdon, Harry; Romance; Sennett, Mack)

LONG, WALTER (1879-1952)
(Laurel & Hardy films *qv*)
Bullet-headed character actor whose double-edged comic menace was employed by Laurel & Hardy in *Pardon Us*, *Any Old Port*, *Going Bye-Bye!*, *The Live Ghost* and *Pick A Star*. Long's film career dates back to D. W. Griffith (he plays 'Gus' in *The Birth of a Nation*), while 1920s credits include *The Yankee Clipper* (1927) and *King, of the Khyber Rifles* (1929). Long may also be seen as 'Plumitas', the bandit in Valentino's *Blood and Sand*, a film parodied at the time by Stan Laurel.

(See also: Anderson, G. M.; Freak endings; Villains)

LOOKING FOR TROUBLE
See: *On the Spot*

LOREDO, LINDA
See: *Chickens Come Home*, *Come Clean*, Foreign versions and *Hog Wild*

LOST FILMS
The survival rate of most silent and many early sound films is dismaying. Industry neglect, combined with the unstable, inflammable nitrate base usual for 35mm film stock until 1951, has caused the loss of countless films. Given the odds against their survival, relatively few Laurel & Hardy subjects are missing today. Constant revivals have ensured the existence of most of their sound films and many silent Laurel & Hardy subjects are said to owe their existence to the last-minute work of Robert Youngson (*qv*), who in the 1950s copied much footage just before decomposition set in. Blackhawk Films (*qv*) made great efforts to obtain optimum material, sometimes upgrading their releases when superior copies were discovered. High on the Laurel & Hardy 'wanted' list is *Hats Off* (*qv*), a silent two-reeler regularly reported extant without anything more being heard. The last definite sighting was in the 1950s before its rarity was appreciated. By one of those irritating quirks of fortune, the print was supposed to have been delivered to a private collector, who had screened it prior to purchase; he received instead a 1930 musical short of the same title. Leading the search for this missing item is Danish historian Peter Mikkelsen. On the list of virtually every archive is *The Rogue Song* (*qv*), M-G-M's all-Technicolor vehicle for Metropolitan Opera star Lawrence Tibbett (*qv*). Laurel & Hardy contributed several scenes and although the soundtrack, trailer and sections of the film itself have surfaced, the complete subject remains elusive; California-based enthusiast

Robert Stowell continues his exhaustive detective work on the film. Many of the foreign versions (*qv*) re-shot by the team continue to be unavailable. These apart, the majority of missing Laurel & Hardy footage is in the solo category, their pre-teaming efforts being represented today by a fraction of the total output. Even today there remains hope, with rediscoveries continuing as collectors and archives co-operate in the search.

(See also: Foreign versions; Rediscoveries)

LOVE 'EM AND WEEP
(Laurel & Hardy film)
Released by Pathé Exchange, 12 June 1927. Produced by Hal Roach. Directed by Fred Guiol. Two reels. Silent.
With Mae Busch, Stan Laurel, James Finlayson, Oliver Hardy, Charlotte Mineau, Vivien Oakland, Charlie Hall, Gale Henry.

Businessman Titus Tillsbury (James Finlayson) receives a visitor from his bachelor days, an old flame (Mae Busch) who has memories of 'a wild day at Coronado' and an incriminating photo. Her blackmail scheme is postponed by the arrival of Mrs Tillsbury (Charlotte Mineau), but a meeting is arranged for that evening. Tillsbury sends his aide, Romaine Ricketts (Stan Laurel) to use his 'power over women' to keep her at bay while Tillsbury entertains visitors at home. Ricketts arrives (bearing a bouquet of 'California Puppies') but the blackmailer, unimpressed, calls Tillsbury, who promises to meet her at a nightclub. *En route*, a gossip (Gale Henry) spots Ricketts with the woman; she spots them again at the nightclub, from which Ricketts and his companion head for the Tillsbury home. Tillsbury introduces them as 'Mr and Mrs Ricketts', while the real Mrs Ricketts (Vivien Oakland), alerted by the gossip, is also heading for the *soirée*. As Tillsbury's guests begin to leave, his old flame demands

Wilfred Lucas finds his living quarters invaded in A Chump at Oxford

money but faints when her victim puts a gun to his head. Attempts to remove her are interrupted by the furious Mrs Ricketts: the blackmailer, awakened, makes her escape while a chase ensues around the house.

Fairly typical of pre-teaming Laurel & Hardys, *Love 'Em and Weep's* chief interest today lies in being the prototype not just of a literal remake, *Chickens Come Home* (*qv*) but of an entire Laurel & Hardy sub-genre. Most ingredients for their depiction of women can be traced to this film, be they wives, gossips or less respectable types. The latter variety is represented here by Mae Busch (*qv*), who in this, her first appearance with them, receives top billing. This was a time when Roach was still attempting to add prestige by engaging major stars who were in decline; Mae Busch had recently entered that category. Another major talent, but from the short comedy field, was Gale Henry, a former starring comedienne who was by then in supporting roles: she contributes memorably to *His Wooden Wedding*, a 1925 Roach film with Charley Chase (*qv*). Angular to the point where some have considered her a possible model for Popeye's sweetheart Olive Oyl, Gale Henry's career had reached its zenith in the Joker comedies of a decade before. The casting of *Love 'Em and Weep* provokes further interest when compared with its remake: Stan Laurel and Mae Busch remain in their original roles, but James Finlayson (*qv*) becomes the businessman's butler, excelling in a part previously underexploited by Charlie Hall (*qv*). Finlayson is replaced by Oliver Hardy (an incidental dinner guest in the earlier version), whose greater range brings a necessary blend of over- and under-playing, combining panic, cunning and a complacent dignity. In 1930, *Love 'Em and Weep* was part of a UK reissue

package from Wardour Films, who offered music and sound effects on disc. In 1983, the London branch of Sons of the Desert (*qv*) screened a print with part of the soundtrack restored.

(See also: Blackmail; Businessmen; Fading stars; Names; Our Gang; Reissues; Remakes; Risqué humour; Sound; Sugar Daddies; Women)

LUBIN, SIEGMUND 'POP' (1851-1923)

German-born film pioneer who emigrated to the US at the age of 25. Siegmund (not Sigmund) Lubin attempted various trades until settling down in Philadelphia as an optician. His interest in such work extended to the infant cinema, and by 1896 Lubin was producing his own films. Even within the buccaneering world of movie pioneers, Lubin may be considered somewhat adventurous: early releases included faked boxing matches, imitations of others' successes (e.g. emulating Porter's *The Great Train Robbery* with *The Bold Bank Robbery*) and outright piracy, as in the notorious tale of Lubin trying to sell a bootlegged print of *A Trip to the Moon* to its maker, Georges Méliès. Although an early legal threat was sufficient to send Lubin temporarily

back to Germany, he was to conceive or acquire enough patents of his own for Edison to invite him into the Patents Trust that sought to control the industry. With this status came a greater respectability, later work featuring an established stock company and a second studio at Jacksonville, Florida. It was at the latter premises that Oliver Hardy began his film career in 1913. Lubin's fortunes dwindled as government intervention emasculated the Trust, but Lubin was probably unworried; he was a wealthy man whose empire had embraced films, cinema equipment and even a theatre chain. In 1984 the Philadelphiabased National Museum of American Jewish History celebrated his career in the form of an exhibition, film screenings and a detailed book, *Peddler of Dreams*.

(See also: Anderson, G. M.; Arbuckle, Roscoe 'Fatty'; Rediscoveries; Reeves, Alf; Solo films; Vitagraph)

LUCAS, WILFRED (OR WILFRID) (1871-1940)

(Laurel & Hardy films *qv*)
Canadian character actor, educated in London and Paris. He began his career on the stage, entering films in 1907 with Vitagraph and later with D. W. Griffith. Played the Warden in *Pardon Us* and the Dean in *A Chump*

at Oxford; is credited with the role of 'Alessandro' in *Fra Diavolo* despite the deletion of his footage prior to its release.

LUCKY DOG
(Laurel & Hardy film)
Filmed circa 1920. Produced by G. M. Anderson. Directed by Jess Robbins. Two reels. Silent.
With Stan Laurel, Oliver Hardy, Florence Gillett.

Stan is ejected by his broom-wielding landlady, whose blows send him into a trance. He imagines himself surrounded by beautiful girls in classical

'Stick 'em both up, insect'; Hardy's first words to Laurel in **Lucky Dog**
BFI Stills, Posters and Designs

costume, until he recovers sufficiently to realize that he is kissing a stray dog. Another rude awakening comes with the realization that he is sitting on the streetcar tracks. After a near miss, Stan packs the dog in his suitcase, only to be caught on the front of another streetcar. Evasive tactics place him in the path of a passing limousine occupied by a young lady and her well-to-do boyfriend. Stan and the girl exchange friendly chat before the car moves off; the dog-laden suitcase walks away. Stan follows it straight into the path of a hold-up artist (Oliver Hardy). The thief inadvertently places the takings from his last robbery into Stan's pocket; Stan is amazed to discover that he actually has money for the thief to take. Stan manages to escape with the money, but is pursued, first through a hole in a nearby fence (in which the much larger thief becomes jammed) and eventually into a café, where the presence of a policeman ensures the robber's departure. The café has a strict 'no dogs' ruling and Stan leaves with the idea of disposing of the pooch. Attempts to dump the animal in a dustbin are thwarted by the watchful policeman. Around the corner are the girl and her boyfriend, who are entering their poodle for a dog show. Stan's dog makes the poodle's acquaintance, entwining their leads and ensuring another meeting of

their owners. As the show stipulates 'thoroughbreds only', the dog must be sneaked in; Stan and friend are thrown out, but are followed by the other dogs, ending the show. Stan and the girl are chatting when a policeman arrives, telling them to move the car from a hydrant. Stan drives the girl home, leaving behind her boyfriend who, engaging the thief as paid assassin, follows on. At the house, Stan is enjoying the family's hospitality until confronted by the thief, who once more aims a gun at Stan's head. When the gun jams, Stan offers to help but instead sends a bullet flying toward the boyfriend. The thief runs off but still receives the second shot. He is despatched to kidnap the girl while the boyfriend plants dynamite under the sofa where Stan and the girl's father are sitting. The dog retrieves it, chasing boyfriend and thief outside. The dynamite is left under a bush where they have taken refuge; one explosion later, they emerge, defeated.

Lucky Dog owes its place in history to the chance appearance of Oliver Hardy in what is otherwise a Stan Laurel comedy. They would not work together again for several years, by which time each had developed a quite different niche in the industry. Mythology insists that Babe's contribution is restricted to the moment where he first encounters Stan, probably the result of this being the only sequence used by Robert Youngson (qv) in his 1964 compilation *Thirty Years of Fun* (qv). Until Youngson's discovery of a print, *Lucky Dog* was known to have been made but could not be located. A further error concerns the film's production date, long presumed to have been 1917 due to a description of dynamite as 'Bolsheviki candy' and a joke about its uses in Russia. Others have considered this a reference to the 'Red Scare' of 1919 rather than the Russian revolution of two years before. When interviewed for *Turning Point*, Stan quoted a pre-1920 production date, but this may not have been accurate. Release is believed to have been in or around 1922, the year *Lucky Dog*'s producer, G. M. Anderson (*qv*), started making Stan Laurel comedies. It is evident that Anderson had been awaiting acceptance of this as a pilot for the series. Laurel remembered that director Jess Robbins made this film between pictures with Larry Semon (*qv*), with whom Stan had worked two years before. Most of the subsequent Anderson-Laurel comedies were directed by Gil Pratt.

(See also: Animals; Apocrypha; Interviews; Solo films; Teaming; Villains)

LUFKIN, SAM (1892-1952)
(all films *qv*)
Supporting player who remained mostly inconspicuous through approximately 40 Laurel & Hardy films. He is seen more prominently in silents (*Two Tars* uses him twice), notably as the fight referee in *Battle of the Century* and the house owner in *The Finishing Touch*. Occasional dialogue appearances tend to be meaningful: in *Going Bye-Bye!* it is he who advises Stan and Ollie to put space between themselves and 'Butch' Long; while *Block-Heads* allows him to say 'C'mon lug, get out of that chair!'

(See also: Long, Walter; Periodicals)

LUNDIN, WALTER
See: Cameramen

LYN, JACQUIE (b. 1928)
Aside from her role as the little girl who contributed so much to *Pack Up Your Troubles* (*qv*), nothing else was known of Jacquie Lyn for many years other than a reputed London birthplace (contradicted by an entry in the 1932 *Picturegoer's Who's Who and Encyclopaedia*), the fact that she had appeared in *Prosperity* with Marie Dressler and Polly Moran (*qv*) and a brief home movie taken by Stan Laurel of Jacquie playing with his daughter, Lois (*qv*). *The Motion Picture Almanac* mentions two other films, *Wicked* and *The Strange Love of Molly Louvain*. A lengthy search for the missing Jacquie (including an appeal on British television by London-based enthusiast Malcolm Stuart Fellows) brought nothing until 1992, when an American video release of *Pack Up Your Troubles* included the home movie and an appeal by Lois for any news of Jacquie's whereabouts. By a fortunate coincidence, Jacquie's son, who knew of his mother's appearance in the film, decided to buy her the tape as a present. Jacquie responded by contacting Dwain Smith of the New York Sons of the Desert (*qv*). She was reunited with Lois and soon after was an honoured guest at the Sons' 1992 convention in Las Vegas. Jacquie Lyn (now Mrs Jacquelyn Dufton) was found to be living just a few miles from Lois. Jacquie Lyn is not to be confused with Jackie Lynn Taylor of *Our Gang* (*qv*).

(See also: *Chickens Come Home*; Cramer, Rychard; Dillaway, Donald)

LYNNE, SHARON
(1904 or 1908-63)
Born D'Auvergne Sharon Lindsay in Weatherfold, Texas, Sharon Lynne (or Lynn) worked as a singer in nightclubs and on stage, appearing in a New York run of *Sunny Side Up* and in the 1929 film version. She was also a composer of songs, the most successful being 'Monte Carlo Moon'. Later films included *Hollywood Nights*, *The Big Broadcast* and Laurel & Hardy's *Way Out West* (*qv*), in which she plays villainous songstress Lola Marcel.

(See also: Smoking; Songs)

Jacquie Lyn has to choose which hand contains the sweets in Pack Up Your Troubles. *Stan saves her the trouble*

MADISON, NOEL
(1898-1975)
Actor whose looks typecast him in gangster roles (such as 1935's *G-Men*, and *Crackerjack*, a British picture with Tom Walls), in which capacity he was engaged for *Our Relations* and *Jitterbugs* (both *qv*).

(See also: Criminals)

MAGICIANS
(Laurel & Hardy films *qv*)
Laurel & Hardy contributed a brief sketch to *M-G-M's Hollywood Revue of 1929* in which they appear as inept conjurers. The Fox feature *A-Haunting We Will Go* incorporates the stage act of Harry A. Jansen, known professionally as Dante the Magician (1883-1955). Dante was an important international talent whose film appearances include a 1950s RKO feature, *Bunco Squad*, a 1930s short made in Sweden and possibly others made on his global travels; he was also much on TV in America. The Spanish version of *Chickens Come Home* incorporates two entertainers, Mexican-born magician Abraham J. Cantu (1896-1949) and the 'Egyptian Enigma', Hadji Ali (c. 1892-1937). Both have been documented by Los Angeles-based scholar Robert Dickson, who reveals the latter to have been the subject of considerable interest among physicians, justly intrigued by Ali's ability to swallow and independently regurgitate quantities of various bizarre items. Hadji Ali cannot really be classified as a magician but his abilities were nonetheless extraor-

dinary; he died after being taken ill during a tour of the UK. Among more peripheral marvels, the silent *Flying Elephants* casts James Finlayson (*qv*) as 'Ye Aged Saxophonus', a Stone-Age wizard; another wizard, from Oz this time, takes the form of Charlie Murray in the 1925 version of the story.

(See also: Semon, Larry; 'White magic')

MAIDS
See: Female impersonation and Servants

MAKE-UP
Laurel & Hardy's child-like characters required a blanking-out of facial details with light make-up. This applied particularly to Stan although Babe's golfing tan needed to be subdued. Stan accentuated his apparent dimness by creating the illusion of small eyes, a feat accomplished by lining the inner lids. 20th Century-Fox (*qv*) decided to make them more 'real' (a purely relative term) by amending their make-up to a recognizable flesh tone, undermining their image while simultaneously making them appear older.

(See also: Characters; Colouring; Golf; Lachman, Harry; Lloyd, Art)

MALTIN, LEONARD
Author, historian and broadcaster whose reputation was established as a teenager with his magazine *Film Fan Monthly*. Many books since then, of which *The Great Movie Shorts* (*aka Full Supporting Program*), *Movie*

Comedy Teams and *The Great Movie Comedians* are of particular interest to Laurel & Hardy buffs. In 1973 Maltin edited *The Laurel & Hardy Book*, one of a paperback series expanding on *Film Fan Monthly*; this remains one of the key reference works, prized by collectors (particularly in Britain, where it was not widely distributed). Another in the series, *The Real Stars*, is a useful anthology of profiles and interviews. American TV viewers know Maltin from *Entertainment Tonight*, while his annual *Movie and Video Guide* is a consistent best-seller.

(See also: Burton, Richard; Periodicals)

A MAN ABOUT TOWN (1923)
A Man About Town, directed by George Jeske, begins with Stan on a streetcar, barely visible between two large ladies. He asks the conductor where to change cars, and is advised to follow a girl sitting nearby. He does so, but is soon following a different girl in an identical dress. He is taken further from his path when a third similarly-dressed girl appears, whom he follows into a clothier's. Supervising the premises is a detective, James Finlayson (*qv*), an alert type who challenges a suspected shoplifter only to discover the bulge under his coat to be a hunched back. He becomes very suspicious of Stan who, waiting for the girl to complete her business, tries on various hats, the last of them unwittingly taken from a midget. When the girl leaves, Stan follows with Finlayson in pursuit; Stan takes refuge in a barber's shop, where he is

A Man About Town: *a posed shot. In the film itself, the girl does not enter the barber shop*

joined by Finlayson. Each decides to have a shave, an unnerving decision as both barbers (George Rowe and Mark Jones) turn out to be cross-eyed. They exit when the original girl walks past the shop, the two men following her aboard a streetcar. The girl alights, is followed once more and reports the fact to a policeman, who arrests Finlayson by mistake. Finlayson shows the cop his detective's badge, and the two look on as Stan, thinking he is boarding another streetcar, waves to them while climbing into a police van. Despite an over-reliance on gags relating to physical deformity, *A Man About Town* is very funny and among the slickest early Laurel films. Finlayson is a definite asset, his wary gaze as effective here as in the Laurel & Hardy comedies, while the predominance of streetcars lends considerable period charm.

(See also: Barbers; Black humour; Detectives; Midgets; Solo films; Streetcars; Video releases)

MANDY, JERRY (1893-1945)
Supporting actor in Roach roles, including a hungry soldier in *With Love and Hisses* (*qv*) and a convict in *Pardon Us* (*qv*).

MANNERS
See: Courtliness

MARCEAU, MARCEL
(b. 1923)
Comparatively few people know Marcel Marceau to have been a Stan Laurel discovery. When Laurel & Hardy were in France making *Atoll K* (*qv*), Marceau invited Laurel to see his small theatre company, a group dedicated to the revival of traditional French mime. Laurel was sufficiently impressed to call an immediate press conference, announcing Marceau's genius to the world. They were reunited when, early in 1961, Marceau visited the Laurel home in Santa Monica. The press were in attendance as Marceau, describing Stan as 'the master', amused his host with impressions of the Laurel walk and crying routine. When notice was taken of the immense volume of fan mail, Stan remarked on the team's popularity overseas, adding 'we once had a fan club in Europe that numbered two million members'; Marceau, it seems, was among them.

(See also: France; Letters; Sons of the Desert [club])

MARCH OF THE WOODEN SOLDIERS, THE
See: *Babes in Toyland* and Reissues

MARIAN, EDNA (1908-57)
(Laurel & Hardy films *qv*)
Blonde, petite Chicagoan from the stage, in film comedies from 1926; a 'Wampas Baby' star of that year. She is remembered from the earlier Laurel & Hardy silents, appearing in *Sugar Daddies*, *From Soup to Nuts* and *Should Married Men Go Home?*. Stills from *Flying Elephants* suggest her presence in a sequence cut before release. Other Roach films include several with Charley Chase (*qv*); she is known also to have appeared in mid-1920s features for Columbia and Fox. A contemporary filmography lists *Still Alarm*, *Sinner's Paradise*, *Skinner*

Edna Marian joins in a musical break on the set of From Soup To Nuts

Steps Out, *Romance of the West* and *To-day*. According to Randy Skretvedt (*qv*), Edna Marian's Roach contract was abruptly terminated in mid-1928, for reasons unclear. Some sources spell her surname Marion; the original family name has been given variously as Mannen and Hannam.

(See also: Coburn, Dorothy; Richard, Viola)

MARLOWE, JUNE (1903-80)
Actress of great charm, among the 'Wampas Baby' stars of 1925. She achieved modest fame the following year after playing Trusia in Warners' *Don Juan*. Subsequent feature work at Universal (*Alias the Deacon*, *Wild Beauty*, *Grip of the Yukon*) preceded a move to the studio's operation in Germany; she was fluent in the language, having been raised in a German-American community. Miss Marlowe's career declined somewhat when she returned to the US. She worked with canine star Rin-Tin-Tin before joining Roach in 1930 as 'Miss Crabtree', schoolteacher in the Our Gang series (*qv*). Other Roach films include *Fast Work* (1930) with Charley Chase (*qv*) and Laurel & Hardy's *Pardon Us* (*qv*). Her contribution to the film is a brief bit as the Warden's daughter, in a scene where escaped convicts Stan and Ollie attempt to repair her father's car. She receives top billing after Laurel & Hardy, perhaps in deference to former starring status but more likely the relic of a part much diminished after previews. Miss Marlowe's acting career gave way to married life as the 1930s progressed. The June Marlowe in Latin-American films of the 1940s seems to have been a different actress.

MARRIAGES
The only really adverse publicity the team ever received was in connection with their marital misfortunes. Stan Laurel was a particular target although Oliver Hardy occasionally received such attention. Why the two

Marriages: Stan and Babe with Ida, the last Mrs Laurel, during a stage tour of 1947-8

comedians were singled out more than most is a matter for conjecture; perhaps certain commentators enjoyed contrasting such matters with the simplicity of their screen characters (in person, each was good-looking when not made up for comedy roles). There has been much mythology published about their marriages, and this section exists primarily to record fact with, it is hoped, a measure of perspective. Oliver Hardy married three times, first to Madelyn Saloshin in 1913; this youthful match lasted seven years. From 1921 to 1937 he was married to Myrtle Lee Reeves, a relationship that gradually deteriorated amid Myrtle's alcohol problem. Babe endured much emotional pain in addition to spending considerable sums on his wife's medical care. For much of the 1930s he sought companionship with Viola Morse; far from being a casual dalliance, this parallel relationship provided Babe with

something of a refuge. The association with Viola ended when Babe met and married Virginia Lucille Jones, script girl on *The Flying Deuces* (*qv*); the marriage endured until Babe's death. Stan's first 'marriage' could not be legalized owing to his partner's inability to obtain a divorce; Mae Laurel (*qv*) shared Stan's life from 1918 to 1925, bringing turbulence in her wake. This pattern would be repeated later, but Lois Neilson (or Neilsen), to whom Stan was legally married from 1926 to 1935, was an astute, even-tempered, agreeable woman who incidentally handled many of Stan's financial dealings. As a film actress (including roles in some of Stan's Joe Rock films), Lois understood the demands of the profession. Roach later expressed genuine regret at the couple's divorce, believing subsequent events to have damaged Stan's career. The reasons for their split seem varied, though based in part on the strain imposed by Stan's long working hours. Stan said that they no longer shared a sense of humour, reasonable in itself though more likely a contributory factor to a period of restlessness. Stan himself probably regretted abandoning the marriage, at least until settling happily in later life. His next love was Virginia Ruth Rogers, a Los Angeles widow more given to the gregarious life than Lois; their relationship began late in 1932 and explains the name 'Ruth' painted on the boat in *Towed in a Hole* (*qv*). She moved in with Stan late in 1933 prior to marriage but, with a prudence virtually unknown in Hollywood, chaperoned by Stan's old friends Alice and Baldwin Cooke (*qv*). This adherence to decency, though instigated by Ruth, characterizes Stan's attitude to women: Frank Butler (*qv*), a close friend, once stated that Stan's honourable nature compelled him to marry one or two women who might better have been kept as mistresses; one of Stan's wives described him as 'a good boy but he has a marrying complex'. An exception to the marital rule was Alyce (or Alice) Ardell, a dedicated bachelor girl who formed an equivalent to Viola Morse as Stan's refuge. Alyce, who appeared in some of the contemporary Stan Laurel Productions (*qv*), remained in Stan's life for most of the 1930s. The years with Ruth, a blend of laughter and discord, began badly as Stan mistimed his divorce from Lois: the first ceremony with Ruth predated the final decree and had to be repeated. The marriage had broken down by 1938, when Stan married Vera Ivanova Shuvalova, a Russian expatriate known as 'Illiana'. Her extravagance and volatile temper brought trouble at home and with the police. Again, the couple went through two legal ceremonies through Stan's fear (groundless this time) that his divorce

from Ruth was not final. Illiana's background dictated a further, Russian Orthodox ceremony. They were divorced in 1940, and a year later Stan remarried Ruth. The short-lived reconciliation ended legally in 1946, when Stan found marital contentment with a second Russian, Ida Kitaeva, widow of famed concertinist Raphael. Ida (pronounced 'Eda', the way Stan would often spell it as emphasis) was in Hollywood for a role in Harold Lloyd's *The Sin of Harold Diddlebock* (later released as *Mad Wednesday*) when she met Stan at one of the Russian bar-restaurants Stan had known since his time with Illiana. A complete contrast to her tempestuous predecessor, Ida's love, appreciation and care made Stan's last two decades happy despite diminution of health and finances, much of Stan's fortune having evaporated in alimony payments. Babe's marriage to Lucille and the touring of 1947-54 brought about a close foursome by the time of Babe's death; Stan remained in contact with Lucille until the end of his days. The above should make it clear that Stan was variously married to four women, though circumstances dictated a total of eight ceremonies; exaggerations to the contrary may be discounted. Stan was to some extent dogged by circumstance: Fred Lawrence Guiles phrased it well by describing Stan as 'a man of decent instincts to whom a number of devastating and amusing things happened'. He was certainly pained by his misfortunes and would discuss them only with intimates, John McCabe (*qv*) among them. It is significant that Stan discouraged biographical works until assured of a concentration upon his work.

(See also: Apocrypha; Biographies; Boats, ships; *Cuckoo*; Hal Roach Studios; Jefferson, Stanley Robert; Laurel, Lois; Lloyd, Harold; Rock, Joe; 20th Century-Fox; Women)

Trudy Marshall and her instructors in The Dancing Masters

MARSHALL, GEORGE
(1891-1975)
(Laurel & Hardy films *qv*)
Director who took small roles in two of the three Laurel & Hardy films bearing his name. His tough-guy looks proved useful when substituting for a missing actor in *Pack Up Your Troubles*, in which he plays an irate army cook. He may also be seen as a neighbour who congratulates Stan and Ollie on the adoption of a child in *Their First Mistake*. Marshall's work with the team ended with *Towed in a Hole*, after which he fell victim to a studio economy drive. Marshall's career dates back to acting roles in the 1910s (he is visible in the 1916 Arbuckle short *The Waiter's Ball*), from which he graduated to director of westerns and Ruth Roland serials. Subsequent directing work includes W. C. Fields' *You Can't Cheat An Honest Man* (1939), the Marlene Dietrich-James Stewart vehicle *Destry Rides Again* (1939), 1940's *The Ghost Breakers* (the first in a long association with Bob Hope), *Murder He Says* (1944) and *The Blue Dahlia* (1946). In 1962, Marshall was among three directors (with Henry Hathaway and John Ford) credited in the Cinerama epic *How the West Was Won*. An autobiography is said to have been written, but has yet to appear.

(See also: Arbuckle, Roscoe 'Fatty'; Goddard, Paulette; Hal Roach Studios, the)

MARSHALL, TRUDY (b. 1922)
Leading lady in *The Dancing Masters* (*qv*), seen often in Fox's second features of the period (such as *Sentimental Journey*, *The President's Lady*). Quoted by Randy Skretvedt (*qv*) in *Laurel & Hardy: the Magic Behind the Movies* (1987), she spoke of Laurel & Hardy's great professionalism and of their encouragement when she expressed a desire to work in light comedy. Laurel & Hardy asked her to join them in their hat-switching routine, which she completed without retakes, after which Laurel playfully nicknamed her 'One-take Marshall'. She further recalled a charming piece of advice from Hardy, to the effect that Miss Marshall should stand to one side of him in order to remain visible!

(See also: Hats; 20th Century-Fox)

MARX BROTHERS, THE
(Laurel & Hardy films *qv*)
Anarchic comedy trio (originally a quartet), rivals to Laurel and Hardy though not in the direct fashion of other duos. The main trio, Groucho (1890-1977), Harpo (1888-1964) and Chico (1887-1961), who employed the respective styles of fast-talker, non-speaking mime and Italian dialect, began in vaudeville (*qv*) and continued through three Broadway shows, 13 feature films and various work elsewhere. One of the last appearances of Charlie Hall (*qv*) was on Groucho's TV show *You Bet Your Life*. The Marxes were true originals, but like most comedians, Laurel & Hardy included, shared elements of style and material with their contemporaries. Comparisons have been made between the cramming of three people into a small car in *Our Wife* and some later Marx routines, although these latter sequences differ radically in scale, approach and intent. A few specific Laurel & Hardy gags trickled into the Marx repertoire. In *The Fixer-Uppers*, Ollie orders 'two beers', only to have Stan say 'I'll have two beers, too', a remark repeated in the Marxes' 1935 comedy *A Night at the Opera*. A joke confusing 'burning bridges' with 'britches' (from *Unaccustomed As We Are*) recurs in the Marxes' *Room Service*, while Stan's inability to recall his birthplace on the grounds of having been too young (in *The Laurel-Hardy Murder Case*) is shared by Chico Marx in *Duck Soup* (1933). *Duck Soup* is a title borrowed from one of the first Laurel & Hardy films by its director, their early mentor Leo McCarey (*qv*). Some of the routines in the Marx film are more typical of the Laurel & Hardy style than their own, if adapted in execution and specific gags. The 'tit-for-tat' motif recurs, involving none other than a veteran of several Laurel & Hardy comedies, Edgar Kennedy (*qv*), while Chico and Harpo try their skills at housebreaking in a manner reminiscent of *Night Owls*. The key difference, as Marx chronicler Joe Adamson has observed, is that Laurel & Hardy's disasters derive from sheer incompetence, whereas with the Marxes they are the deliberate product of their own perversity. The Marxes were also among those to try a comedy western in the immediate wake of *Way Out West*, and their *Go West* (1940) has a similar plotline to the Laurel & Hardy film, though once again approach and specific gags do not duplicate. The Marx Brothers provide an interesting gauge for the differing personalities and tastes of Laurel & Hardy in real life. Stan Laurel did not care for their approach but Oliver Hardy enjoyed their work and came to know Chico Marx quite well through their shared love of the racetrack. Chico and Groucho are known to have toured with Laurel & Hardy at various times during the war. In both a 1970s BBC TV interview and his book *The Groucho Phile*, Groucho's chief recollection was of Laurel & Hardy being 'pleasantly sloshed', admitting with comparative grace that he still could not outshine them. Groucho's memory of the tour may have been influenced by crowd reaction: it is said that out of his costume and customary make-up of painted moustache and eyebrows, the unrecognizable Marx drew less instant acclaim than the readily identifiable stars such as Laurel & Hardy. On another occasion, Groucho told a story at his own expense concerning a motorcycle cop who, on recognizing the famous comedian, decided not to issue him with a ticket, but felt obliged to ask him why there weren't more Laurel & Hardy films on TV!

(See also: Gambling; Gilbert, Billy; Housman, Arthur; Reciprocal destruction; Romance; Stage appearances; Todd, Thelma; Wartime)

MASQUERS CLUB, THE
See: Charities, *Fighting Kentuckian, the* and *Stolen Jools, the*

MATÉ, RUDOLPH (1899-1964)
Cinematographer best known for his effects work in the 1935 *Dante's Inferno*. The following year Maté was required to simulate twin Laurel & Hardys in *Our Relations* (*qv*), employing matte work, doubles and intercutting. Maté's work is impeccable: the illusion fails only at the editing stage, which produced one rather abrupt switch between the two. Camerawork here is superior to most Laurel & Hardy films, being the result of Maté's skilled blend of his own techniques with Laurel's preference for the generalized, flat lighting suited to the team's make-up and improvisational methods.

McCABE, JOHN C. (b. 1920)
Writer, actor and university lecturer John McCabe is the authorized biographer of Laurel & Hardy. He first met the team while in England as a doctoral candidate at the Shakespeare Institute of the University of Birmingham. This was in 1953, when Laurel & Hardy were touring in their sketch *Birds of a Feather* (*qv*). McCabe

John McCabe visits Ida and Stan Laurel at Malibu in 1957
By kind courtesy of John McCabe

saw the show and visited the two comedians backstage. From here developed a friendship that led to McCabe's pioneering biography, *Mr Laurel and Mr Hardy* (1961), a volume available in numerous editions ever since. Later volumes on the subject are *The Comedy World of Stan Laurel* (1974), *Babe: the Life of Oliver Hardy* (1989) and *Laurel & Hardy* (1975), the latter in collaboration with Al Kilgore and Richard W. Bann (both *qv*). Other books: *George M. Cohan: the Man Who Owned Broadway*, *Charlie Chaplin*, *The Grand Hotel* and (with G. B. Harrison) *Proclaiming the Word*. He was in addition the true author of James Cagney's ghostwritten autobiography. John McCabe was the prime force behind the creation of the Sons of the Desert club (*qv*); at the society's 1984 convention in England he met actress Rosina Lawrence (*qv*), whom he subsequently married.

(See also: Biographies; Stage appearances)

McCAREY, LEO (1898-1969)
(Laurel & Hardy films *qv*)
Though justly famed for his Academy Award-winning films *The Awful Truth* (1937), *Love Affair* (1939) and *Going My Way* (1944), Leo McCarey's earlier days with Roach merit at least equal attention. Taking over as supervising director from F. Richard Jones (*qv*) in 1927, McCarey was first to decide that Laurel and Hardy should work together. With Stan Laurel he devised the team's format and receives story credit on the films into 1930, though

this may in some cases have been a contractual requirement. His usual role as supervisor made way for a director's credit on three Laurel & Hardy films, *We Faw Down*, *Liberty* and *Wrong Again*. Many of the team's regular motifs were created by him, notably the 'tit-for-tat' exchanges dominating *Two Tars* and *Big Business*. After his departure from Roach, McCarey's younger brother Ray (1904-48) worked at the studio, directing Laurel & Hardy in *Scram!* and receiving co-director credit on *Pack Up Your Troubles*.

(See also: Butler, Frank; Chase, Charley; *Habeas Corpus*; Marx Brothers, the; Reciprocal destruction; Teaming; Television; Writers)

ME AND MY PAL

(Laurel & Hardy film)
Released by M-G-M, 22 April 1933.
Produced by Hal Roach. Directed by Charles Rogers and Lloyd French.
Camera: Art Lloyd. Two reels.
With Stan Laurel and Oliver Hardy, James Finlayson, Nat Clifford/Frank Terry, Bobby Dunn, Eddie Dunn, James C. Morton, Charlie Hall.

Successful businessman Mr Hardy is

Me and My Pal: *Mr Cucumber wants to see the groom*

about to crown his achievements in the International Horsecollar Corporation by marrying the boss's daughter, a move carrying with it instant promotion to general manager. Mr Laurel, the best man, arrives with a bag of rice and a wedding present: it is a jigsaw puzzle. He also has the ring plus tickets for the honeymoon, which are to Chicago rather than Ollie's intended destination, Saskatchewan ('the man said there was no such place as Suskatch - Susquash...'). The taxi is ordered but the boys become engrossed in the puzzle; they tear themselves away on the cab's arrival, but the driver (Eddie Dunn) is also drawn into its intrigues. A policeman walks in to give the cabbie a ticket for parking by a hydrant. He joins the puzzlers. The bride's father, Mr Peter Cucumber (James Finlayson) telephones to ask where the bridegroom has gone. Stan takes the call, primed with an excuse but accidentally making it plain that Ollie has yet to leave. The party starts out but Stan has a puzzle fragment instead of the ring; they return to the house. Meanwhile, the tearful bride hears the doorbell but is let down when discovering it to be a man delivering a wreath (ordered by Stan). Mr Cucumber sets off for the Hardy residence, wreath in hand ('I may have some use for this'). A telegraph boy brings an urgent message, pocketed by Stan as its bearer joins the puzzle team. Mr Cucumber appears, demanding Ollie's immediate departure; the policeman forbids anyone to leave, as there is a piece missing from the puzzle. Everyone is to be searched, but the cabbie takes a spill. A scuffle breaks out, escalating to riot proportions. The police break up the fight, arresting everyone except Stan and Ollie, who emerge from their respective hiding places when Stan remembers the telegram; Ollie is to sell all his stock at a handsome profit. He starts to telephone but is interrupted by a radio newsflash, confirming him to have been wiped

out. Having eradicated Ollie's future wedding, career and fortune, Stan makes to leave; he pauses to resume the puzzle after finding the missing piece, and is thrown out.

The jigsaw motif is typical enough of misplaced preoccupations for *Me and My Pal* to have etched a place in the public memory. Though a lesser short, it retains the power to absorb audiences just as the jigsaw proves irresistible to everyone in the film. Nat Clifford (*qv*) (alias Frank Terry), doubling as Ollie's butler and the voice emitting from a radio, delivers a remarkable news broadcast describing not just Mr Hardy's impending nuptials but the views of Mr Laurel, including among various irrelevancies a reference to 'Technocracy', a theory much-discussed during 1933. This and a similar moment in *Busy Bodies* (*qv*) are among the few topical items in the team's normally timeless repertoire.

(See also: Businessmen; Dialogue; Dunn, Bobby; Dunn, Eddie; Flowers; Jigsaw puzzles; Morton, James C.; Names; Policemen; Radio; Scripts; Taxis; Telegrams; Weddings)

MELODRAMA
(Laurel & Hardy films *qv*)
Melodrama was very much the province of Stan's father Arthur Jefferson (*qv*); Stan followed by composing a melodrama of his own, but an early professional experience, from 1909, took him on tour in *Alone in the World*. He later recalled having contributed only briefly as a pseudo-American tramp, attempting to fish before uttering the deathless line 'Wal, I guess 'n' calculate I cain't ketch no fish with that tarnation mob a-singin'... Gee whizz!' According to *Bowler Dessert* magazine, Stan returned in a second role as a comic policeman, but on-stage drama paled when the manager disappeared without paying the cast. This type of theatre was already becoming parody

material: Keystone lampooned the tied-to-a-track tradition as early as 1913's *Barney Oldfield's Race For Life*, while the finest send-up must be W. C. Fields' often misunderstood *The Fatal Glass of Beer*. Billy West's *The Villain* (itself inspired by Chaplin's *Tillie's Punctured Romance*) presents its star as top-hatted baddie in the great tradition, sending up the genre to the point of using a sawmill in order to dispose of a victim. Laurel & Hardy's *One Good Turn* allows James Finlayson (*qv*) to twirl his moustaches during a play rehearsal, in a manner similar to his stern parent of *Our Wife*. Much of *Way Out West* is in like vein and in *The Bohemian Girl* he actually says 'me proud and haughty beauty'! *Any Old Port* is Griffith revisited; Charlie Hall (*qv*) as a wicked landlord in *Laughing Gravy* is a meanie of the old school (the extra reel in turn parodies the idea of old friends having to part); so is Henry Brandon (*qv*) of *Babes in Toyland*. The genre is revived in Stan's parody of ruin in *Putting Pants On Philip* and through his abandonment of Ollie (and baby) in *Their First Mistake*.

(See also: Female impersonation; *Further Perils of Laurel & Hardy, the*; Periodicals; Sawmills; West, Billy)

MEN O'WAR
(Laurel & Hardy film)
Released by M-G-M, 29 June 1929. Produced by Hal Roach. Directed by Lewis R. Foster. Camera: George Stevens, Jack Roach. Two reels. With Stan Laurel and Oliver Hardy, Anne Cornwall, Gloria Greer, James Finlayson, Harry Bernard, Charlie Hall.

Sailors Stan and Ollie visit a park while on shore leave. They meet two girls (Anne Cornwall and Gloria Greer) and find a pair of bloomers, which have fallen from a laundry basket. Assuming that they belong to one of their new acquaintances, the boys engage them in vague enquiries as to

whether one of the girls has 'lost' anything. As one girl has mislaid her gloves, the conversation becomes confused, assuming embarrassing proportions when she claims to have just cleaned them with gasoline. The boys realize their mistake when a cop returns the lady's gloves, and dispose of the stray garment as they take the girls to the soda fountain. A budget of 15 cents will not finance four drinks: Ollie instructs Stan to refuse a soda. The proprietor (James Finlayson) becomes increasingly annoyed as their order is interrupted by Stan's inability to comprehend the ruse. Eventually the message takes hold and the boys share a drink, which Stan drains because his half was 'on the bottom'. Ollie is surprisingly forgiving, leaving Stan to pay the bill - which comes to 30 cents. Stan risks his meagre funds on a fruit machine which, after an agonising pause, provides enough

money to cover the bill and a trip on the boating lake. For professional mariners, Stan and Ollie prove remarkably inept at rowing; a series of collisions culminate in a battle with everyone on the lake boarding Laurel & Hardy's boat, which sinks with all hands.

A variant of *Two Tars* (*qv*), *Men O'War* resembles their silent comedies in its three-part structure and the re-use of a routine from *Should Married Men Go Home?* (also *qv*). This third talkie is easily the best they had made up to that time, benefiting from attractive locations (at Hollenbeck Park) and a comfortable blend of action with dialogue. The still-primitive state of talkies is evident, both in editing and the soundtrack itself: William K. Everson (*qv*) has noted the sometimes audible whirring of cameras, while one might remark further

Men O'War: *'Did either one of you ladies lose anything?'*

upon the absence of any music from the bandstand visible at the beginning. Apparently the original track had a popular hit, 'Runnin' Wild', under the titles and bandstand footage; this recording is unavailable at present although a 1929 soundtrack disc for reel one has been reported in private hands. At least three attempts have been made to bolster the audio content, first when Film Classics reissued the film (mistitled *Man O'War*) having redubbed the titles with music from *Busy Bodies* (*qv*), complete with the sound effect of a circular saw. This unsatisfactory version was adapted by the BBC, who combined an unadorned recording of the 'Cuckoo' song with modern library music and the Roach theme 'Here We Go'. The latter presumably was lifted from the titles of *Any Old Port* (*qv*), while part of the same library music introduces Walton's 8mm compilation *Laurel & Hardy's Musical Moments*. Curiously, Walton's Super-8 version of *Men O'War* is dubbed identically to the BBC copy. The 1980s restoration from American TV solves the problem simply and effectively by adding title music from *One Good Turn* (*qv*), permitting it to run past the credits into the bandstand sequence. This version, vastly superior to the poor quality prints of other reissues, has since been converted to colour.

(See also: Boats; Cornwall, Anne; Reissues; Remakes; Risqué humour; Sailors; Sound; Television; Titling)

METCALFE, MADGE
See: Jefferson, Arthur

METROPOLE THEATRE, GLASGOW
See: Jefferson, Arthur

M-G-M (all films *qv*)
The studio with 'more stars than there are in heaven', Metro-Goldwyn-Mayer was an amalgam of Metro Pictures (owned by Loew's, Inc.) with Sam Goldwyn's old company and Louis B. Mayer. Goldwyn himself had no connection with the enterprise; Mayer was supreme, though Irving Thalberg had as much say until his early death in 1936. From 1927 M-G-M acquired distribution of Roach's product, in a deal quite advantageous to the producer. He explained that 'while I had agreed to finance my own product, it was only a few years before they financed me for less money than the banks'. The initial agreement was made with Nick Schenck of Loew's rather than Mayer. Schenck was also studio President, but was not connected with production as was Mayer. Said Roach: 'Louis Mayer always resented the fact that I made my deal with Schenck... we were still friends up until the day he died, but he was in charge of production so he was always

mad that I hadn't made the deal with him'. There could have been no better distributor, as M-G-M's features had an assured market and were block-sold with the Roach shorts, permitting an early forecast in profitability. Roach explained that M-G-M went to all of the big circuits, saying 'You pay this much for the Hal Roach comedies; you can use them as many times as you want or as few times; but you don't get any unless you buy 'em all, and the price of all is so much'. There were further hints that supply of the studio's features depended somewhat on acceptance of the Roach product. Not surprisingly, Roach described his years with Metro as 'very pleasant'. The first Laurel & Hardy film thus distributed was *Sugar Daddies*; the last, *Block-Heads*, after which the producer switched to United Artists (now ironically merged with M-G-M). During this period Laurel & Hardy were often featured as M-G-M stars in studio publicity, and appeared on loan to them in *Hollywood Revue of 1929*, *The Rogue Song* and *Hollywood Party*. Two of their Roach features, *Fra Diavolo* and *Bonnie Scotland*, remained M-G-M's property though most others reverted to Roach. During the 1940s, Laurel & Hardy had parted from their old home and were forced to work at the major studios. Most of their wartime films were made at 20th Century-Fox (*qv*), but their non-exclusive contract permitted two features at M-G-M, *Air Raid Wardens* and *Nothing But Trouble*. Neither contains much to commend, the big studio conditions virtually duplicating those at Fox. Although Metro offered a greater budget, they had no room for independent workers and foisted upon the team directors past their peak and scripts that were unsuitable.

(See also: Anderson, G. M.; Compilations; Hal Roach Studios, the; Keaton, Buster; *Laurel & Hardy's Laughing Twenties*; *M-G-M's Big Parade of Comedy*; Our Gang; Pathé

Exchange; Sedgwick, Edward; Shipman, Ben; Taylor, Sam; Wartime; Youngson, Robert)

M-G-M'S BIG PARADE OF COMEDY
(M-G-M 1964)
Known also by such variants as *The Big Parade of Comedy* and *M-G-M's Big Parade of Laughs*, this is a star-filled collection of the studio's comic highlights, assembled for them by Robert Youngson (*qv*). Although Youngson's native territory was silent film, he had compiled earlier works from talkies and this anthology displays his usual skill. A greater problem lay in the source material: the result displays M-G-M's comedic strengths and weaknesses, the crux being that such a prestigious studio scored heavily with the light, romantic comedy of the *Thin Man* series but tended not to know what to do with the visual humour of, for example, Buster Keaton (Youngson uses footage from *The Cameraman*, almost the last film Keaton created without undue interference). It is significant that the Laurel & Hardy scenes in this film avoid their later days under M-G-M itself, concentrating instead on the dance sequence from Roach's *Bonnie Scotland* (*qv*) and the egg-breaking routine from *Hollywood Party* (*qv*), a film made under M-G-M's banner but without direct supervision. Contemporary studio awareness of such limitations is suggested by Roach's long-term distribution arrangement with them, with his stars often promoted in M-G-M's publicity. Many comedy names in this collection (Abbott & Costello, W. C. Fields, the Three Stooges) are those who made infrequent appearances at M-G-M, their reputations being made elsewhere. One notable exception is that of the Marx Brothers (*qv*), whose film work might well have ended had M-G-M's Irving Thalberg not shown interest. The climactic train ride of their *Go West* is among the highlights of this collection; nonetheless, it may

be significant that *Big Parade* ends not with a clip from a studio feature but footage from one of the *Pete Smith Specialties*, produced by a small unit within M-G-M. One particular advantage of a big studio is that Youngson's participation in this project guaranteed distribution for his later anthology, *Laurel & Hardy's Laughing Twenties* (*qv*).

(See also: Costello, Lou; Compilations; Guest appearances; Keaton, Buster; M-G-M; *Tree in a Test Tube*; Wartime)

MEXICO

The success of Laurel & Hardy outside the United States was helped considerably by the foreign-language editions, particularly those in Spanish. They developed a huge following in Mexico, and were promoted heavily; when the team's career was in hiatus during 1941, there was talk of producing films in Mexico, but nothing came of it. They did attend Mexico City's Motion Picture Industry Festival that year, appearing in person at the Olimpia theatre. Their film career resumed soon after with 20th Century-Fox (*qv*); the last in that series, *The Bullfighters*, is set in Mexico but was filmed in Hollywood.

(See also: Cooke, Alice and Baldwin; Foreign versions; Stage appearances; Unfilmed projects)

MIDDLETON, CHARLES
(1884-1949)
(Laurel & Hardy films *qv*)
Gaunt, often menacing actor whose austerity contrasted neatly with Laurel & Hardy's comedy. He portrayed the commandant in both of Laurel & Hardy's Foreign Legion adventures, *Beau Hunks* and *The Flying Deuces*, in addition to playing a sour-faced orphanage official in *Pack Up Your Troubles* and a volatile artist in *The Fixer-Uppers*. Originally a stage actor, Middleton's best-known

Charles Middleton lays down the law in The Flying Deuces

film work elsewhere is as 'Ming, the Merciless' in Republic's *Flash Gordon* serials; other appearances include the Marx Brothers' *Duck Soup*, the 1932 Paul Muni vehicle *I Am A Fugitive From A Chain Gang*, the 1934 version of *Mrs Wiggs of the Cabbage Patch* and John Ford's Oscar-winning *The Grapes of Wrath* (1940).
Coincidentally, among Middleton's earlier credits is an M-G-M film titled *Way Out West*, subsequently the title of a Laurel & Hardy feature released through the same company.

MIDGETS
(Laurel & Hardy films *qv*)
The exploitation of certain physical characteristics has, perhaps fortunately, declined since Laurel & Hardy's time, but midgets continue to feature in modern-day productions (e.g. *Time Bandits*), albeit mostly in a less negative fashion. Gags involving midgets crop up several times in the Laurel & Hardy canon, perhaps the most famous being that in *Liberty* where a policeman is crushed to a fraction of his former height. Stan Laurel himself is squeezed to these proportions at the end of *The Bohemian Girl*, and reduced to an even smaller size in *A-Haunting We Will Go*. He accidentally sits on a midget in *Berth Marks*, while Ollie meets a diminutive man with a

booming voice in *Block-Heads*. Both encounter a midget dance troupe in *Their Purple Moment*, a film originally intended by its creators to finish with Laurel & Hardy disguised among the midgets. One of the troupe, Harry Earles, played a prominent role in Laurel & Hardy's *Sailors Beware*, as a midget criminal who operates disguised as a baby. During a contractual split with Roach in 1938, Stan Laurel announced his association with Mack Sennett (*qv*), for whom he would star in *Problem Child*, as a normal-sized son born to midget parents. Associate producer was to have been Jed Buell, remembered today for producing Columbia's rather tasteless midget western, *The Terror of Tiny Town* (1938); given the latter film's subsequent reputation, it is probably as well that the project did not come to fruition.

(See also: Black humour; Freak endings; Teaming; Unfilmed projects)

THE MIDNIGHT PATROL
(Laurel & Hardy film)
Released by M-G-M, 3 August 1933. Produced by Hal Roach. Directed by Lloyd French. Camera: Art Lloyd. Two reels.

With Stan Laurel and Oliver Hardy, Nat Clifford/Frank Terry, Frank Brownlee.

Policemen Laurel & Hardy interrupt night duty for a snack, which they have concealed inside a police telephone. Back in their car (number 13) they receive a radio message to the effect that their tyres are being stolen. The robbers disposed of, they are summoned next to investigate a burglary. As the car refuses to start, Ollie examines the engine, receiving a faceful of petrol. Once they are mobile again, they cannot remember the address. As Stan has unwittingly cut off the police telephone, another must be found; Stan locates one in a jeweller's, where a safecracker (Nat Clifford/Frank Terry) is at work. Stan takes him to be the owner, but Ollie arrives and makes an arrest. Having agreed a mutually convenient date for him to appear in court, he goes on his way. Stan has called the station for the address, but the street has been written on a second piece of paper. Ollie calls the station, gets the full address, and they set off to investigate the burglary. On reaching the car, they find the safecracker at the wheel, asking for a push; just for that, he can appear tomorrow. They drive away, minus tyres. They arrive at the house just in time to see a man gaining entrance via the storm cellar, unaware that he is the householder. They follow the same route, but halt at a locked door. The next ploy is to charge the front door, Ollie backing up into a lily pond. Ollie decides they should use a marble bench seat as a battering ram; the run-up sends Ollie back into the pond, this time pinned underwater by the bench. The next attempt breaks down the door but the boys continue through the staircase, into the basement and ultimately into a barrel of sauerkraut. The owner, investigating the disturbance, falls through the gap in the stairs and is knocked out cold by the two officers. Stan and Ollie proudly haul their cap-

tive into the station, where he is recognised as being Chief of Police. The boys excuse themselves from their now-conscious charge, but their exit becomes a permanent one when the Chief borrows a revolver. Stan and Ollie's offscreen demise is evident when fellow officers remove their caps; 'Send for the Coroner', says the Chief.

The Midnight Patrol has been considered a reversal of *Night Owls* (*qv*), in that the boys' inept housebreak is on the side of the law rather than against it. William K. Everson (*qv*) in turn considers it a parallel to Chaplin's policeman role in *Easy Street* (1917). Either way, Stan and Ollie contribute nothing to law and

Officers Laurel and Hardy agree to charge the door rather than a lily pond in **The Midnight Patrol**

order irrespective of their occupation. This is not through any perfidy on their part but the result instead of sheer naivety. For many years there have been rumours of a missing postscript to the film (see **Hereafter, the**), the probable legacy of a replacement 'end' title on the BBC print; the playout music on unmutilated copies runs continuously through the last scene over the closing title. One of the British 8mm editions replaces the opening titles, rechristening the subject *Crazy Cops*; its counterpart on video crops off the Chief's closing remark, ruining the finish.

(See also: Bletcher, Billy; Clifford, Nat; Continuity errors; Criminals; Home movies; Policemen; Telephones; Television; Titling; Video releases)

MILLER, HENRY (d. 1980)

Writer associated rather more with his books *Tropic of Cancer* and *Tropic of Capricorn* than with an essay called 'The Golden Age', which was published in a collection called *The Cosmological Eye*. Speaking of Laurel & Hardy's *The Battle of the Century* (*qv*), Miller overstates the case in describing it as following 'thousands of slap-stick, pie-throwing Mack Sennett films', but not in recalling 'thousands and thousands of pies'. He also makes an arguable point in describing it as 'the greatest comic film ever made' and 'the ultimate in burlesque'.

(See also: Slapstick)

MITCHUM, ROBERT
(b. 1917)

Actor whose greatest fame was preceded by several low-budget westerns and a villainous role in Laurel & Hardy's *The Dancing Masters* (*qv*). His subsequent and distinguished career includes *The Big Steal* (1949), *Night of the Hunter* (1955), *Ryan's Daughter* (1971) and *Farewell, My Lovely* (1975). He later starred in *The Winds of War*, a TV mini-series set in the 1940s, which at one point shows the principals attending a screening of *Saps at Sea* (*qv*).

(See also: 20th Century-Fox)

MIXED NUTS
See: *Just Nuts*

MORAN, PATSY (1905-68)

Comedienne of the wise-cracking school, Patsy Moran appears in two Laurel & Hardy films (both *qv*), *Block-Heads* and *Saps at Sea*. In the first, she is an old flame of Ollie's who, unaware of his recent marriage, has sent a torrid note to the Hardy residence; in the second she is switchboard operator at the boys' apartment building. She is present also in one of the team's rare excursions into radio (*qv*), playing Stan's fiancée. Not to be confused with Polly Moran (*qv*).

MORAN, POLLY (Pauline Moran) (1884-1952)

(Laurel & Hardy films *qv*)
Comedienne from vaudeville and Sennett comedies, once described as 'the most travelled vaudeville performer in the world'. She is best recalled as partner to Marie Dressler, both in M-G-M features and in an earlier short, Christie's *Dangerous Females* (1929). Both actresses are present in *Hollywood Revue of 1929* though not in the Laurel & Hardy sequence; Polly Moran appears in *Hollywood Party*, again sharing no screen time with Laurel & Hardy. In *The Stolen Jools* she is seen with Our Gang (*qv*) in scenes overlapping with Laurel & Hardy's contribution. Buster Keaton (*qv*) planned to cast her as Ollie's lover in *Grand Mills Hotel*, a project that did not come to fruition. She should not be confused with Patsy Moran (*qv*).

(See also: Lyn, Jacquie; Sennett, Mack; Unfilmed projects; Vaudeville)

MORELAND, MANTAN (1901-73)

Black American actor in mostly comic roles, remembered primarily as chauffeur 'Birmingham Brown' in the *Charlie Chan* series. Mantan Moreland's career took him from circus beginnings through vaudeville into films. Stage work included appearances at New York's Apollo theatre with Redd Foxx, and a 1957 black production of *Waiting For Godot* (*qv*). Moreland was a major star in comedies made for black audiences, but tended to play minor roles in mainstream product; his contribution to *A-Haunting We Will Go* (*qv*), where he plays a waiter on a dining car does at least allow him to function as a comedian.

(See also: Race; Toler, Sidney)

MORENO, ANTONIO (1896-1967)

Born in Madrid but long resident in America, where he was educated, Antonio Moreno entered films in 1914 and appeared in many prestigious 1920s features, among them *Mare Nostrum* (1926) and the 1927 Clara Bow film *It*. In Britain, he appeared with Dorothy Gish in *Madame Pompadour*; early talkie days saw him directing Spanish-language films in between acting roles, mostly for Fox. His career in sound films was hampered somewhat by a strong Spanish accent, but he was given the role of Mrs Hardy's lover in *The Bohemian Girl* (*qv*). Many years before, while in Vitagraph serials, Moreno had applauded Stan Laurel's work in *Frauds and Frenzies*; it may be that Moreno was hired as an act of loyalty to an old friend.

(See also: Austin, William)

MORGAN, KEWPIE
See: Impersonators

MORROS, BORIS (1891-1963)

Independent producer who made one Laurel & Hardy film, *The Flying Deuces* (*qv*). His memoirs, *Ten Years a Counterspy* were published in 1957 and revealed his work as a double agent during the Second World War;

Antonio Moreno portrays Mrs Hardy's lover in The Bohemian Girl

three years later Ernest Borgnine played the producer in a screen adaptation, *Man On a String* (released in Britain as *Confessions of a Counterspy*).

MORSE, VIOLA
See: Marriages

MORTON, JAMES C. (1884-1942)
(Laurel & Hardy films *qv*)
A familiar face in two-reel comedies, James C. Morton made an ideal policeman, especially in *Me and My Pal*, *Tit For Tat* and early performances of *The Driver's Licence Sketch* (*qv*). When a period-costumed lawman was required for *The Bohemian Girl*, Morton was an obvious choice. Other characters include the role of barman in *Way Out West*, dealing with Harry Bernard (*qv*), himself taking time out from the force as a dissatisfied customer. A barely recognizable Morton has an amusing sequence in *Fra Diavolo* as an old man whose tale of woe reduces would-be bandits Laurel & Hardy to tears. He is undisguised but less prominent in *Block-Heads*, playing the caretaker who draws Ollie's attention to a newspaper shot of Stan. Morton was also busy elsewhere on the Roach lot: for example, a Taxi Boys comedy, *Hot Spot* casts Morton as an over-hearty type who is pushed around after a tactless remark. One of Morton's last films, again in uniform, is *The Boogie Man Will Get You* (1942), a horror spoof with Boris Karloff (*qv*).

(See also: Policemen; Taxi Boys, the)

MOVIE STRUCK
See: *Pick a Star* and Reissues

MUD AND SAND (1922)
See: Anderson, G. M., *Bullfighters, the* and Parodies

MUMMING BIRDS
The stage sketch favoured by Karno's company in America (where it was retitled *A Night in an English Music-Hall*), *Mumming Birds* took the

ingenious form of a show within a show. Within the set was a miniature variety theatre with stage and boxes, presenting a series of deliberately hopeless turns facing a rough audience. Leading the hecklers was Charlie Chaplin (*qv*), playing 'Archibald', a drunk whose patrician attire was at odds with his conduct. On arrival the drunk attempted to light a cigarette from an electric light bulb; a young boy, laden with food (his ammunition for the night) offered a match but the drunk, leaning too far, landed on the stage. The first act, a comic singer and patter comedian, was so bad that the drunk chased him from the stage. Next was a woman singer at whom, according to eye-witness Groucho Marx, the drunk 'was alternately spitting a fountain of dry cracker crumbs... and beaning her with overripe oranges' (Groucho refers to this as occurring in *A Night at the Club*, actually called *A Night in a London Club*; this sketch combined elements of *Mumming Birds* and another sketch, *The Wow-Wows*). The soprano thus disposed of, there followed a dismal magic act, a quartet and one of that long-extinct brand of vocalist dedicated to accounts of Britain's glory (Chaplin's mother was once seduced by such a character, one Leo Dryden; one can only speculate on Chaplin's glee in pelting a fictional counterpart). Last in line was the 'Terrible Turk', an underweight wrestler who scrambled for a bun hurled by the boy. The management offered £100 to anyone willing to challenge the emaciated Turk, drawing a response from a 'plant' who instead found himself fighting the drunk. The challenger gone, the drunk, stripped to his elaborate underwear, faced the wrestler, who succumbed to the drunk's tickling; the subsequent riot ended the sketch amid total disintegration. *Mumming Birds* served the troupe during both tours of the US; John McCabe (*qv*) has recorded that Stan Laurel, while understudying the Chaplin role, never

took the star part but played virtually all the others at various times. A surviving bill for *London Club* describes him as 'Percy Swoffles (a Dude)'. He is recorded elsewhere in the role of the boy whose foodstuffs were liberally spread about the stage. McCabe considers this essentially visual routine vital to the development of Laurel and Chaplin as film comedians; Chaplin had no difficulty in adapting it to the silent screen, in the 1915 Essanay comedy *A Night in the Show* (known as *Charlie at the Show* in Britain). The use of this sketch seems to have been tolerated by Karno, who otherwise enforced the copyright in his material; it is known that he dealt swiftly with those pirating the routine on stage. Such unauthorized use was sufficiently common to warrant the added precaution of periodic changes to the internal stage acts. The edition of *Film Weekly* for 19th August 1929 reported the disappearance of Chaplin's brother Sid, amid rumours that he had left for America to help Charlie with a sound-film version of *Mumming Birds*. Athough this was never made, there remains fascination in the idea of such a project being contemplated by the talkies' chief opponent. Oddly, an identical production was mentioned when Roach contemplated filming in Britain during 1933.

(See also: Anderson, G. M.; Karno, Fred; Marx Brothers, the; Music-hall; Sketches; Unfilmed projects; Vaudeville)

MURDER
(Laurel & Hardy films *qv*)
Foul play is either attempted or carried out in the plots of several Laurel & Hardy films, prime example being of course *The Laurel-Hardy Murder Case*. Homicidal maniacs of varying types may be found in *Do Detectives Think?*, *We Faw Down*, *Pack Up Your Troubles*, *Oliver the Eighth*, *Going Bye-Bye!*, *The Big Noise* and *The Bullfighters*. Policemen Laurel &

Hardy are murdered by their own chief for the finale of *The Midnight Patrol*, and are very lucky to survive in *Fra Diavolo*, *Our Relations*, *Saps at Sea*, *Nothing But Trouble* and *Jitterbugs*, while another Fox film, *A-Haunting We Will Go*, seems preoccupied with little else. The frustrated anger of Billy Gilbert (*qv*) brings him close to murder in *The Music Box*, *The Chimp*, *Pack Up Your Troubles* and *Block-Heads*, while Tom-Tom, the Piper's Son is wrongly accused of the crime in *Babes in Toyland*. Even Oliver Hardy seemed a potential killer before officially teaming with Stan Laurel; he spends much of *Lucky Dog* trying to despatch his future partner, with whom he is also engaged in mortal combat in *Flying Elephants*. Another pre-teaming film, *Why Girls Love Sailors*, closes soon after Anita Garvin (*qv*) shoots her philandering spouse; yet another, *Sailors, Beware!* offers Stan the choice of being murdered or working as a ship's steward. Even earlier, in *Near Dublin*, James Finlayson (*qv*) believes he has done away with Stan. In real life, the shadow of murder hangs somewhat over *The Bohemian Girl*, extensively recut after the death of Thelma Todd (*qv*), a tragedy many insist was neither accidental nor self-induced.

(See also: Busch, Mae; Hereafter, the; King, Dennis; Long, Walter; Marshall, George; Shotguns; Suicide; Young, Noah)

MURPHY, JIMMY (1910-86)

Lancashire-born (in Newton-le-Willows) but long resident in America, Jimmy Murphy was a variety artist who later became both valet and close friend to Laurel & Hardy. Although they later lost touch, Stan traced Jimmy through Joan Crawford, for whom Jimmy had been working. Jimmy Murphy was in turn rediscovered by the Sons of the Desert club (*qv*) when a British enthusiast, Jack Stevenson, met him in New York; they remained firm friends until Jimmy's death. Interviewed by Stevenson for *Helpmates News* (now *The Laurel & Hardy Magazine*) Murphy recalled having been brought to America by Bert Wheeler and introduced to Stan Laurel by Morton Downey; he worked officially for Laurel & Hardy Feature Productions (*qv*) but mostly took care of Stan. This reached an extreme when Jimmy defended Stan in a nightclub argument (see **Dentists**). Jimmy was present during the making of *Great Guns* and *A-Haunting We Will Go* (both *qv*) prior to being conscripted for war service; he rejoined Laurel & Hardy post-war but had to return home from the 1947 tour after it was discovered that Jimmy, by now an American citizen, had no work permit. Late in life he attended several Sons gatherings, including the 1984 International Convention held in his native Britain. Always happy to share his memories, Jimmy made friends wherever he went and was a character in the very best sense.

(See also: Chaplin, Charlie; Periodicals; Practical jokes; Stage appearances)

MUSEUMS

At the time of writing the best-known Laurel & Hardy archive accessible to the public is that in Laurel's home town of Ulverston. Though not based at the house itself, the Laurel & Hardy Museum dates back to the time of its clearance in 1974, some of its contents forming the display's nucleus. The museum, which attracts visitors from around the world, is operated by Bill Cubin, who keeps very busy amid civic activities in addition to organizing the local branch of the Sons of the Desert club (*qv*).

(See also: Births; Jigsaw puzzles; Stage appearances)

MUSIC
(Laurel & Hardy films *qv*)

When talkies arrived, Roach lost no time in adapting to the new trend. Many of his last silent comedies were released with synchronized music and sound effects, initially using an orchestra but subsequently reduced to a theatre organ. Choice of themes was generally designed to comment on the action: for example, when the horse in *Wrong Again* is seen drinking from a fish tank, the music switches to 'How Dry I Am'. The studio's first talkies featured no incidental music, though opening titles would normally be adorned with a hit of the day (the 1928 song 'That's My Weakness Now' may still be heard over the titles of *The Hoose-Gow*). The team's 'Cuckoo' theme, written by T. Marvin Hatley (*qv*), made its debut early in 1930; copyrighted as 'Ku-Ku' and known generally as 'The Dance of the Cuckoos', it is often said to have been used first on *Brats*, an opinion current until it was heard in the rediscovered Spanish version of *Night Owls*. It has since been confirmed as having opened the original English prints of this and *Blotto* (several earlier comedies had the theme added on reissue). As with the title music, incidental scoring of 1930 releases favoured popular song; one, 'Smile When the Raindrops Fall' (by Alice K. Howlett and Will Livernash), seems to have been purpose-written and had a minor vogue. Charley Chase (*qv*) may be heard singing it in *Whispering Whoopee* and *What A Bozo!*, while Laurel & Hardy fans will recall the tune from its use in *Hog Wild* and for the car 'radio' of *Busy Bodies*. The latter part of the year saw the arrival of background melodies written mostly by Le Roy Shield (*qv*), again reminiscent of the period's 'hot' dance music and endlessly recycled throughout the studio's product (modern British audiences, familiar only with the Laurel & Hardy films, are often surprised to hear these tunes as accompaniment for other comedians). Though employed in each Roach series, a tune aptly titled 'Gangway

casualty was the cuckoo theme, reinstated for *Atoll K* and stage appearances (*qv*) but absent from the Fox/M-G-M releases. The most prestigious name associated with any of these is Alfred Newman, who scored *A-Haunting We Will Go*. None has the charm of Shield and Hatley, whose work was prized by Stan Laurel as a way of adding momentum. Today their music is appreciated both because of its association with Laurel & Hardy and as pleasant compositions in their own right. There have been orchestras working on this material in both the US (Vince Giordano's *Night Owls*) and Europe (the Amsterdam-based *Beau Hunks Orchestra*).

(See also: Colour; *Further Perils of Laurel & Hardy, the*; *Goon Show, the*; M-G-M; Records; Reissues; Songs; Sound; 20th Century-Fox; *When Comedy Was King*)

THE MUSIC BLASTERS
See: Working titles and *You're Darn Tootin'*

THE MUSIC BOX
(Laurel & Hardy film)
Released by M-G-M, 16 April 1932.
Three reels. Produced by Hal Roach.
Directed by James Parrott. Camera:
Walter Lundin, Len Powers.
With Stan Laurel and Oliver Hardy,
Billy Gilbert, Charlie Hall, Gladys
Gale, Lilyan Irene, Sam Lufkin.

The Laurel & Hardy Transfer Co. ('foundered 1931') has to deliver a player-piano. The address is at the top of a huge flight of steps. They prepare to unload the piano from their wagon but Susie, the horse, deliberately moves and the crate falls on Ollie. They struggle half-way up the huge staircase until meeting a nursemaid with a pram. They try to make way for her, but the piano slides to the pavement. When the nurse laughs at their misfortune, Stan kicks her in the rear. Ollie's own mirth is quelled when the nurse breaks the baby's

Charlie' was used as title music for most of the Chase talkies. Thelma Todd (*qv*) and ZaSu Pitts were introduced by 'Beautiful Lady', while Our Gang (*qv*) had 'Good Old Days' as its theme, which is used punningly during the schoolroom scene of *Pardon Us*. The lilting tune opening *Laughing Gravy* is called 'Candy, Candy'; *One Good Turn* and *Helpmates* are introduced by 'The Moon and You'; the chime-dominated theme of numerous films is called 'Bells'; the stentorian introduction of *Scram!* is known as 'Cops'; the flowing prelude to *Our Wife* and *Any Old Port* is 'Here We Go', and the cascading composition often considered a second Laurel & Hardy theme is called 'On to the Show'. These and many others were first identified for Laurel & Hardy

fans by Ronnie Hazlehurst, director of music for BBC TV and avowed Laurel & Hardy admirer. Hazlehurst had employed these tunes for *The Generation Game* before recording a first album in 1980. This and the second volume are much enjoyed by enthusiasts; when Marvin Hatley received a copy of the initial LP he expressed both joy and his full approval. The selection of material extends into the later Shield/Hatley scores for the features of 1936-7, much of which was added to contemporary reissues of earlier short subjects. Titles here include 'We're Out For Fun', 'Change My Clothes', 'On a Sunny Afternoon' and 'Up in a Room'. The post-Roach Laurel & Hardy films were scored in the house style of the appropriate studio: first

bottle over his head. As Stan and Ollie resume their task, the nurse tells a cop that she has been kicked, 'right in the middle of my daily duties'. The cop calls the boys from the street; Stan climbs down to investigate. The cop, however, wants 'that other monkey' 'He don't want me,' calls Stan, 'he wants the other monkey!' Ollie makes his way down, followed by the piano, which runs over him. The cop reprimands Ollie, but Stan considers it unjust ('Don't you think you're bounding over your steps?'); he receives a light blow to the head. Back on the staircase, the boys meet Professor Theodore von Schwarzenhoffen, M.D., A.D., D.D.S., F.L.D., F., F., F., and F. (Billy Gilbert), a gentleman whose dignity forbids his walking around the piano. In the struggle, Stan knocks the Professor's hat downstairs, where it is flattened by a truck. Exit the Professor, screaming threats. The boys finally reach the top of the steps, but keep going up a further flight, where Ollie is dumped into an ornamental pond. Once out, Ollie rings the door-bell but the piano slides toward the staircase; a futile grab for the crate results in Ollie being dragged back to street level. A title card saying 'That afternoon' leads into the boys once more at the top of the steps. The post-man (Charlie Hall) explains that all they had to do was drive up to the house by a side road. Stan and Ollie take the piano downstairs and drive it up the correct way. As they prepare to unload the cart, Ollie makes sure Susie has been detached. Ollie pushes the piano to the front door, unaware that Stan has hitched a ride. There being no answer at the front door, they prepare a block and tackle to haul the piano through an upstairs window. Having done so (the piano supported by a surprisingly resilient awning), Stan drops the block and tackle on Ollie, who is perched on a ladder below; both ladder and Ollie push the front door open. Ollie walks upstairs, but is summoned by Stan. Having

explained the footsteps to be his own, Ollie throws his hat in anger; Stan returns the wrong hat. Ollie is summoned back to exchange hats, but gets the wrong one again. Reluctant to call his friend yet again, Stan clips the too-large bowler into a trilby. Ollie arrives upstairs, is smashed in the face by the door then asks where Stan found the hat. Stan sheepishly restores its usual shape and the task is resumed. They are carrying the piano downstairs to the living room when Ollie and their cargo slide out of a window, landing in the pond. Stan watches from the window until Ollie once more throws his hat in fury. Stan, retaliating, falls into the pond. In the living room, the crate is opened but water cascades everywhere. The boys squabble, Ollie treading on a nail protruding from one of the boards. Stan tries to plug the instrument into a chandelier, ripping it from its moorings, before Ollie finds the wall socket. As the machine starts to play 'a medley of patriotic songs', the boys begin to dance until interrupted by the householder, Professor von Schwarzenhoffen. As he surveys the mess, the boys explain that they have delivered his piano. 'Piano? Piano?' he shouts, 'I hate and detest pianos!

They are mechanical blunderbusses!'. They attempt to remove it but, creating even more damage, are saved the task when the Professor takes an axe to the machine. After a pause to salute when the National Anthem is played, the piano is reduced to matchwood just as the Professor's wife enters; she had ordered the piano as her husband's birthday surprise. Contrite, the Professor feigns a love for such instruments and agrees to sign the delivery docket. Stan hands him a pen, which shoots ink into the Professor's face; the householder is restrained as Stan and Ollie beat a hasty retreat.

Stan Laurel's personal favourite of the films, *The Music Box* was recognized in its day by an Oscar for 'Best Live-Action Short Subject'. Some admirers find the repetition wearying (particularly at three reels) but this tends to be after several screenings. This said, most agree with the film's high reputation, rivalled only by the silent *Two Tars* and *Big Business* (both *qv*), or the talkie short *Helpmates* (*qv*). *The Music Box* is itself based on another silent, *Hats Off* (*qv*). As an

Billy Gilbert is an unwilling recipient of **The Music Box**

example of subtle slapstick, *The Music Box* displays how violent gags can acquire intelligence: when Stan brings a ladder into shot, the far end disappears behind the piano, from which we hear a dull thud and a yell followed by the sight of Ollie standing up, nursing his eye. The boys' unintelligent adherance to procedure is typified when they take the piano back to the street in order to bring it up by the correct route. A subtle, cinematic gag (often taken as technical carelessness) occurs when Stan's descent into the pond is punctuated by the obvious throwing of two buckets of water from different directions. Another such challenge to audience credulity appears in *The Midnight Patrol* (*qv*). Despite this apparent unreality (crowned by the perversity of a strong-willed piano), *The Music Box* parallels human behaviour quite realistically: interviewed for the BBC documentary *Cuckoo* (*qv*), Kenneth Tynan recalled having unconsciously duplicated Ollie's painful treading on an exposed nail. In the same programme, Jerry Lewis (*qv*) considered the film's very subject matter to be an extension of Stan's spirit, the outlook of a man less interested in the aesthetic joys of music than in the tribulations of whoever had to deliver the instrument. This might be considered a little fanciful but there is no denying *The Music Box* its place in legend. When the computer-colour process had achieved acceptable results, this short received the treatment in a restored version complete with its original titling. Unfortunately, the whole was marred somewhat by the addition of music (there was no incidental score on this and several other films of the period) and a number of background effects (such as dogs barking), designed presumably to exploit a remixed stereo soundtrack.

(See also: Academy Awards; Colour; Continuity errors; Gilbert, Billy; Hatley, T. Marvin; Locations; Pianos; Remakes; Short films; Slapstick)

MUSIC-HALL

Britain's mass entertainment in the pre-cinema and broadcasting age, music-hall developed from the tavern concerts of the early nineteenth century via pub extensions, supper rooms and finally purpose-built theatres. Folk memory insists that its performers were exclusively working-class types making good with robust humour, perpetuated in part by the repertoires of several top names. Less recalled are the satirists and gentle songstresses, or the fact that many artists (Robey among them) were very much from the middle classes. For decades, music-halls differed from orthodox theatres in terms of licence, permitting the consumption of alcohol in the auditorium (a practice that survives in London's Players' Theatre) but forbidding spoken sketches, each act requiring music of some sort even if interrupted by patter. A change in the law in 1912 permitted speech to dominate but removed alcohol from the audience; from here music-hall is correctly termed variety, though the two were often interchanged. Cinema and radio took much of music-hall's business from the 1920s on (many halls were converted to cinema use); television finished it off during the 1950s. Stan Laurel saw the last three stages of the halls, making his debut in its peak period, leaving just as variety took over and returning during its dying days. A famous story concerns Stan's debut as a comedian in a Glasgow hall (the Panoptikon, in 'Pickard's Museum', during May 1906). A month short of 16, Stan took to the stage with an act compiled from those of other 'boy' comedians, unaware that his father was at the back. Stan spotted him during his turn, panicked and kicked his hat into the orchestra, topping the manoeuvre by ripping his coat. The audience chose to see it as deliberate and he 'finished big'. Stan's father took the lad's ambitions with magnanimity, even after discovering the wardrobe to have been his own. Music-hall's

legacy is precarious if considered to reside in its occasional films and the often unrepresentative discs of its luminaries; more tangible is its influence on American film comedy and consequently the world, as spread by the many British expatriates in silent comedy, Chaplin and Laurel among them.

(See also: Aubrey, Jimmy; Barty, Jack; *Birds of a Feather*; Chaplin, Charlie; Clifford, Nat; *Driver's Licence Sketch, the*; Grand Order of Water Rats, the; Karno, Fred; Leno, Dan; *Mumming Birds*; Newsreels; *Night Owls*; *On the Spot*; Reeves, Alf; Plays; *Rum 'Uns From Rome, the*; Stage appearances; Vaudeville)

MUSSOLINI
See: Unfilmed projects

MYERS, HARRY
See: Teaming

NAMES

(Laurel & Hardy films *qv*)

Stan Laurel was born Arthur Stanley Jefferson but known always as 'Stan'. The surname 'Laurel' dates from 1918 when his partner, Mae, saw a picture of a Roman general, Scipio Africanus, wearing a laurel wreath. The name was adopted immediately but not legally changed until the early 1930s. Oliver Hardy was originally given the Christian name of Norvell, his mother's maiden name; the 'Oliver' had been his father's, added later as a mark of respect and to create what he considered an impressive three-barrelled effect. Quite often he uses this full name in the Laurel & Hardy films, with genuine pride and no sense of ridicule; in *Pardon Us* it appears on a wanted poster, but his middle name is mis-spelt (deliberately?) as 'Norval'. To friends he was 'Babe', a nickname acquired in his days with Lubin (*qv*). He was billed by that name in many 1910s appearances, but seldom used it professionally by the 1920s. The team's unusual habit of retaining their genuine names on-screen spread to the supporting cast (all *qv*): James Finlayson, Charlie Hall, Mae Busch et al are often referred to by those very titles. Hardy told John McCabe (*qv*) the reason for this practice: quite often a comedian would portray a character whose name belonged to the studio, which could not be used if the comic in question worked elsewhere. Babe Hardy's early career included stints in series titled 'Pokes and Jabbs', 'Plump and Runt', 'Bungles', and so on, while Stan Laurel spent time as 'Hickory Hiram' (*qv*). The tendency toward facetious character names persisted even into their early team films: in *Do Detectives Think?* they are 'Ferdinand Finkleberry' and 'Sherlock Pinkham'; *The Second Hundred Years* casts them as 'Little Goofy' and 'Big Goofy'; prizefighter Stan is labelled 'Canvasback Clump' in *The Battle of the Century*; while even as late as *Their Purple Moment*, Stan masquerades as a 'Mr Pincher'. Before long their own names were established with the buffoons they portrayed, although talkies (starting with *Perfect Day*) brought Hardy the screen nickname 'Ollie'. In the silent *Habeas Corpus* and *Big Business*, Stan can be lip-read calling him 'Babe'. Fortunately, the comedians had no objection to such close identification with their screen equivalents.

(See also: Barbers; Characters; *Hungry Hearts*; Laurel, Mae; Solo films; Superstition; *Yes, Yes, Nanette!*)

NAZIS

See: Censorship and Wartime

NEAR DUBLIN (1924)

One of the Laurel solo films made at Roach, *Near Dublin* takes place in an Irish village of the eighteenth century. Stan is a postman whose girlfriend (Ena Gregory) is much admired by the town's villain, a wealthy brick merchant played by James Finlayson (*qv*). Finlayson threatens to evict the girl's family unless she complies with his wishes, but Stan intervenes with a wad of money. The girl's father takes all of Stan's cash, pays Finlayson with part of it, steals it back and keeps the entire bankroll. Stan accepts the loss with grace. The villagers are celebrating their annual holiday at a barn dance, an occasion dominated by the local sport of brick-throwing. Stan's participation is sufficient excuse for Finlayson to have him arrested, leaving the girl easy prey. Stan makes his escape, rescues the heroine but is promptly struck by a chair. Stan is unharmed but conspires with the girl to play dead. Finlayson is put on trial for murder, but the appearance of Stan's 'ghost' sends the villagers running. Finlayson, imprisoned in the stocks, is ordered to leave as Stan and his girlfriend embrace. Directed by Ralph Cedar, *Near Dublin* is violent even by contemporary standards but maintains what John McCabe (*qv*) has described as 'fulsome comic gusto'. Typical is the moment wherein a blindfolded Stan tries to catch a suspended apple in his teeth, only for the apple to be replaced by a brick. Stan's energetic style is effective in a Chaplinesque fashion despite a tendency to try too hard. Mae Laurel (*qv*) is present as one of the villagers, but contributes little to the available copies of the film, which have been cut to half the original two reels.

(See also: Hereafter, the; Ireland; Murder; Solo films)

NEILSON, LOIS

See: Marriages

NEWMAN, ALFRED
See: Music

NEWSREELS
Perhaps the most important category of peripheral Laurel & Hardy footage, newsreels of the team survive from relatively early days. Their rather sparsely covered 1932 tour is represented in the UCLA archive by M-G-M news film of Laurel & Hardy visiting Broadway; extant in the UK is a clip from Universal Talking News. Also at UCLA are three glimpses of Babe Hardy at race meetings, from 1937 and 1939. Present in each is Bing Crosby, who shared with Hardy the twin pursuits of horse-racing and golf; Babe would later appear in Crosby's horse-racing adventure *Riding High* (*qv*). Film of Laurel & Hardy on a wartime tour appears in a 1977 TV documentary, *The Movies Go To War*, but most available material dates from after the hostilities. The 1947 visit is recorded variously by British Movietone (a visit to the Romney, Hythe & Dymchurch Railway) and an extensive array of Pathé News items. These include an interview after arriving on the Queen Mary, their train journey from Southampton to London, a visit to that year's *Daily Mail* Film Awards and a formidable gathering of comedians at the Apollo theatre. In this last item, Laurel & Hardy join Sid Field, George Robey, Tommy Trinder and most of the Crazy Gang in rustic attire as they collect for a farmers' charity. Another item records their meeting Tessie O'Shea and Vera Pearce at the Ideal Home Exhibition. The team's arrival in France is preserved at UCLA and elsewhere in a brief Metro Journal clip. Again at UCLA is the Gaumont-British film of Laurel & Hardy returning to Britain in January 1952, this time in the company of Winston Churchill. Pathé News recorded their clowning at the New Theatre, Northampton during the final visit in 1953; from the same source is film of them attending a lunch at the Variety

Night-clubs: our heroes succumb to the lure of the Pink Pup in Their Purple Moment

Club of Great Britain. An interview with Eamonn Andrews, screened on British TV in the mid-1970s, seems to date from the same occasion. Many of these brief items afford genuinely amusing bits of business; they should not be confused with the fake newsreel in which Laurel & Hardy ham it up with the Sons of the Desert!

(See also: Charities; Gambling; Home movies; Grand Order of Water Rats, the; *Sons of the Desert* (film); Stage appearances; Unfilmed projects; Video releases; Wartime)

NICKELHOPPER, THE
See: Karloff, Boris

NIGHT-CLUBS
(Laurel & Hardy films *qv*)
Among the most familiar buildings in Roach's back lot is a night-club called The Pink Pup, visible in several Laurel & Hardy silents (*Love 'Em and Weep, Putting Pants On Philip*) in addition to being pivotal to the action of *Their Purple Moment* and *That's My Wife*. *Blotto* brings a change of venue, this time to the elaborate Rainbow

Club. Even more lavish is the Pirate Club set for *Our Relations*, a vast construction that contributes significantly to the film's prestigious look. Less impressive is the Mexican night-club set for *The Bullfighters*, where a floor show serves to occupy rather too much footage. Although Laurel & Hardy were in real life occasional clubgoers, likelier places of amusement tended to be hotels, restaurants or (in Hardy's case) country clubs.

(See also: Dentists)

NIGHT IN A LONDON CLUB, A
See: *Mumming Birds* and Vaudeville

NIGHT IN AN ENGLISH MUSIC-HALL, A
See: *Mumming Birds*

NIGHT OWLS
(Laurel & Hardy film)
Released by M-G-M, 4 January 1930. Two reels. Produced by Hal Roach.

Directed by James Parrott. Camera: George Stevens. Story editor: H. M. Walker.
With Stan Laurel and Oliver Hardy, Edgar Kennedy, James Finlayson, Anders Randolph.

The newspapers declare a public outcry over the number of unsolved burglaries, something the Chief (Anders Randolph) considers the responsibility of Officer Edgar Kennedy. An ultimatum is issued: any more burglaries without arrests, and Kennedy is fired. In fun, Kennedy's fellow officers suggest he should frame an arrest, an idea that reaches fruition when Kennedy discovers vagrants Stan and Ollie asleep on a park bench, and promises to let them go providing they burgle the Chief's house, allowing themselves to be caught. Ollie asks, not unreasonably, 'what's going to become of us?', to be told that 'Kennedy will fix it'. Armed with this ambiguous promise, they set to the task with their customary expertise, creating the maximum of noise climbing over walls, avoiding cats and, at length, gaining entry and locking themselves out again. The butler, James Finlayson, becomes suspicious, but his employer considers him 'nutty'. The butler is vindicated when Stan and Ollie set a player-piano going at full blast. The police are summoned, but not Kennedy, who has been knocked cold with a brick discarded by Ollie. Kennedy recovers his senses and arrives at the house just in

time to pick up the loot left by his fleeing accomplices. Kennedy is arrested. Laurel & Hardy escape over the wall, a feat accomplished at the cost of Ollie's trousers. Ollie throws tin cans at Stan, who is wedged in a dustbin like an enormous hermit crab.

Night Owls echoes in part Stan Laurel's music-hall and vaudeville days, owing a little to one of Karno's sketches and rather more to the burglar routines he performed around the time of *The Keystone Trio* (*qv*). Another reminder is in the choice of music issuing loudly from the player-piano, namely 'Down at the Old Bull and Bush' considered by many to be music-hall's official anthem. It seems probable that Stan Laurel was responsible for the inclusion of this and similar music in the films. Laurel & Hardy were now presented with a challenge unnecessary in silent days: to satisfy an international audience, the team had to produce multiple versions in different languages. *Night Owls* was the first of these, labelled simply *Ladrones* ('Thieves') for the Spanish and for Italy *Ladroni*, the latter probably dubbed from the Spanish edition. Each was expanded to double the length, something of which Stan Laurel might have approved, to go by

Night Owls: *Stan takes direct action to free Ollie's head from a vase. This scene is unique to the foreign versions; inset is a contemporary advertisement for the Spanish edition,* Ladrones

a contemporary press interview quoting him about the difficulty he had experienced in cutting *Night Owls* to the customary two reels. The foreign editions include an ending unseen in the English-language prints. Stan and Ollie are apprehended and taken away in a police car; they attempt to escape by grabbing an overhead tree limb, only to be dumped into the Chief's car behind. At the end, the car runs into a river. Stills exist suggesting that this was also shot, but deleted from the domestic version. Kennedy and Finlayson are retained but the Chief is played by Enrique Acosta, a Mexican actor who died in 1949, aged 79. The Spanish version is extant and offers a minor surprise over the main titles in the form of Laurel & Hardy's 'cuckoo' theme, officially launched in *Brats* nearly four months later. Available English-language copies (including the 1980s restoration) derive their soundtracks from the reissues, opening with an instrumental section of the song 'Honolulu Baby', dubbed from the feature *Sons of the Desert*.

(See also: Criminals; Foreign versions; Karno, Fred; Kennedy, Edgar; Marx Brothers, the; McCarey, Leo; *Midnight Patrol, the*; Music; Music-hall; Night scenes; Policemen; Randolph, Anders; Reissues; Songs; Vaudeville)

NIGHT SCENES
(Laurel & Hardy films *qv*)
It is usual to film night scenes in daylight, darkening the image with filters or in the grading (hence Truffaut's *Day For Night*). Laurel & Hardy's *Do Detectives Think?* and *Habeas Corpus* were genuinely shot after dark, and look all the better for it. Other such scenes, as in *Night Owls* and *Way Out West*, are done in studio (the set of *Night Owls* is recognizable elsewhere in the Roach output, one example being Mabel Normand's *The Nickelhopper*).

(See also: Karloff, Boris; Normand, Mabel)

Mañana Carrera
Estreno de la ultra hilarante comedia METRO GOLDWYN MAYER
LADRONES
Laurel y Hardy

NO MAN'S LAW (1927)
See: *Four Clowns* and Solo films

NOCHE DE DUENDES
See: Foreign versions and *The Laurel-Hardy Murder Case*

NORMAND, MABEL (1894-1930)
Often regarded as the silent screen's greatest comedienne, Mabel Normand began at Vitagraph then worked at Biograph prior to joining another ex-Griffith talent, Mack Sennett (*qv*) for the first of his Keystone Comedies in 1912. She worked with Charlie Chaplin (*qv*) during 1914, and was frequently dubbed his female equivalent. Their early association suffered from a measure of artistic conflict, Normand being the nominal director of her own films; this was soon resolved and the two became firm friends. She was in any case better-humoured and more talented than the 1992 film *Chaplin* would suggest. Miss Normand's long-term romance with Sennett ended owing to the producer's involvement with Mae Busch (*qv*), but she continued to appear in Sennett films for several years, including the feature-length *Mickey*. She later starred in features for Goldwyn. Her career was damaged in 1922 through having been the last person to see director William Desmond Taylor before his murder, an unfortunate coincidence similar to that which befell her former co-star, Roscoe 'Fatty' Arbuckle (*qv*). It is untrue to suggest that she never again appeared in films (a major Sennett feature, *The Extra Girl*, followed a year later), but her career certainly spiralled downward; in 1926 she joined the 'fading stars' working at Roach, making comedies including *Raggedy Rose*, directed by Stan Laurel. Her health was in a similar state of decline to her career and morale; a marriage to actor Lew Cody seemed to provide a measure of contentment but she died from tuberculosis in February 1930.

(See also: Blystone, John G.; Davidson, Max; *Early to Bed*; 'Fading stars'; Hall, Charles; Karloff, Boris; Reciprocal destruction)

NOTHING BUT TROUBLE
(Laurel & Hardy film)
Released by M-G-M, March 1945.
Produced by B. F. Zeidman. Directed by Sam Taylor. Camera: Charles Salerno Jr. 70 minutes.
With Stan Laurel and Oliver Hardy, Henry O'Neill, Mary Boland, Philip Merivale, David Leland, John Warburton, Matthew Boulton, Connie Gilchrist.

Stan and Ollie are descendants of a long line of butlers and chefs, whose proud heritage suffers when the latest generation - and the dish 'Steak à la Oliver' - are ejected from restaurants around the world. The Japanese prefer ritual suicide to the culinary efforts of their two captives. They return to a wartime America to find the labour situation vastly changed from when they last saw it; employment exchanges are now crammed with potential employers rather than the jobless. They are engaged by a society couple, Mr and Mrs Hawkley (Henry O'Neill and Mary Boland) who are entertaining exiled boy-King Christopher (David Leland) and his uncle, Prince Saul (Philip Merivale). The young monarch is adept at affairs of state but preoccupied with American football and democracy at home, in that order. Prince Saul, believing his people unready for such niceties (especially the democracy),

Nothing But Trouble: *the crockery's days are numbered*

tries to arrange Christopher's demise by permitting him out of the hotel without a bodyguard. The arranged murder is averted when Christopher joins some local youngsters in a game of football. Stan and Ollie, returning to the Hawkley home laden with groceries, are persuaded to act as umpire and referee. Christopher scores the winning touchdown (with a little help from referee and umpire) and the boys go on their way, only to realize they have forgotten to buy a steak. Nearby is a zoo, where a hungry lion is being fed a sizeable slab of meat. Stan and Ollie try without success to steal it, but Christopher manages to get the meat away while the lion takes a leap at Stan. The lad accompanies Stan and Ollie to the Hawkleys' and is permitted to stay when fabricating a tale of starvation in an unhappy home. He is introduced to the wonders of American food, chiefly salami. Evening, and Prince Saul arrives excusing the King's absence. In the kitchen, Stan and Ollie practice etiquette for the dinner, but Stan displays such ignorance that Christopher is concealed beneath the table to act as prompt. The meal is a disaster, particularly when the horsemeat steak has to be cut with a saw. Saul receives word that Christopher has vanished, and leaves; Mrs Hawkley discovers the boy and orders all three from the house. They take refuge in a mission hall, where Laurel & Hardy tell the boy of their sadness in letting down their ancestors. The boy is recognized from a newspaper photograph and the authorities alerted; Stan and Ollie are arrested for kidnapping. Back with his uncle, Christopher pleads for Stan and Ollie to be given a job; Saul agrees, believing them the perfect cover for a poisoning. Stan and Ollie are released and given an address to visit; on arrival they recognize the boy but are dismayed to learn of his exalted position. Saul offers them the job of serving at the King's afternoon tea; the boys accept happily, declining a return engagement from one guest, Mrs Hawkley. A poisoned canapé intended for the King is lost when Stan and Ollie confuse the dishes; once found, it is taken to the kitchen. Ollie notices the damaged dish and unwittingly places the poison capsule on a cracker. Saul corners Stan, Ollie and the boy in the kitchen, forcing them at gunpoint to jump from a high window. Aware that decorators have placed boards at the window beneath, Stan and Ollie climb to the ledge. Christopher goes first, and escapes to summon help; by the time Stan and Ollie are ready, the boards have vanished; they are given a count of ten to jump, which is never reached because Saul has eaten the poisoned cracker. Ollie discovers the dead Prince but has to rescue Stan; both are hanging from the ledge when Christopher arrives with the police. Back in the kitchen, Stan, Ollie, Christopher and the officers join in a rousing football song.

Slow-moving and mawkish, *Nothing But Trouble* is fairly typical of the team's work for the big studios and one of the weakest entries. The pathos and sentiment hinted at in *Air Raid Wardens* (*qv*), typical of M-G-M's homey approach, is evident while the comedy scenes are either unsuitable (the football game) or hackneyed, especially when a tree saw is needed to cut the steak. Even allowing for the team's often macabre edge, the melo-dramatic emphasis on murder is too much. Character comedienne Mary Boland (*qv*) gets most of the genuine laughs, pinpointing a fundamental problem: the studio could (and often did) produce classic comedy using actors in a society setting, but was poorly equipped to deal with such specialized star comedians as Laurel & Hardy.

(See also: Black humour; Keaton, Buster; Leland, David; M-G-M; Royalty; Skyscrapers; Taylor, Sam; Trailers; Zoos)

NOW I'LL TELL ONE
(Laurel & Hardy film)
Released by Pathé Exchange, 9th October 1927. Two reels. Produced by Hal Roach. Directed by James Parrott. Silent.
With Charley Chase, Edna Marian, Lincoln Plumer, Stan Laurel, Will R. Walling, Oliver Hardy.

Now I'll Tell One stars Charley Chase (*qv*) and only technically qualifies as a Laurel & Hardy comedy. The Chase filmography published in 1969 by *Film Fan Monthly* lists Stan Laurel in the supporting cast, Hardy's contribution being unknown until an incomplete copy of the film was recovered by British collector David Wyatt in 1989. Reports from *The Laurel & Hardy Magazine* and *The Intra-Tent Journal* describe Stan as playing Chase's lawyer, with Babe in a separate section as a policeman. Until the reappearance of this comedy, the official Laurel & Hardy tally had been considered 105 films, not counting newsreels and other peripheral material; the expected '106' had been *The Rent Collector* (*qv*), but this was not to be.

(See also: Periodicals; Rediscoveries)

NUDITY
(Laurel & Hardy films *qv*)
One would not expect any nudity in the Laurel & Hardy films. This opinion was certainly held by an advertising agency who, in the 1980s, ran a magazine advertisement showing Stan Laurel sitting fully-clothed in a bath (from *Come Clean*), claiming that he would not do a nude scene. It may surprise those responsible to learn that he and Hardy had done just that, in *With Love and Hisses*. Though necessarily careful to maintain decency, the footage of them bathing and making their way back to their army camp (after the loss of their clothes) qualifies as an authentic nude scene, as does the fleeting glimpse of an unclad Max Davidson (*qv*) in his collapsing bath from *Call of the Cuckoos*. One of Hardy's solo films, the Roach feature *No Man's Law*, has his villainous character leering at heroine Barbara Kent while she is swimming in the nude (those who care to investigate will notice her flesh-coloured bathing costume!). This scene is incorporated into the compilation *Four Clowns* (*qv*). In *Duck Soup*, Stan, posing a housemaid, is shyly aghast at the thought of seeing a naked Madeline Hurlock (*qv*) after her decision to take a bath (she appears instead dressed in a bathrobe). Jean Harlow's scene in *Double Whoopee*, in which her dress is torn off, is said to have required a retake owing to her transparent underwear making her appear nude. Other scenes of undress, be they through violence (e.g. *Berth Marks*, *You're Darn Tootin'*) or accident (as with Thelma Todd in *Unaccustomed As We Are*, or Ollie's several trouserless moments) are firmly outside the category of nudity; often those concerned are wearing more than is today required for street wear!

(See also: Advertising; Harlow, Jean; Risqué humour)

NURSES
See: Doctors, nurses

NUTS IN MAY
See: *Just Nuts*

OAKLAND, VIVIEN
(1895-1958)
(Laurel & Hardy films *qv*)
Former child star and Ziegfeld girl whose association with Laurel & Hardy predates their teaming; *Forty-Five Minutes From Hollywood* shows her picture in a fan magazine. In *Along Came Auntie* she portrays the former wife of Oliver Hardy; *Love 'Em and Weep* casts her as the current Mrs Laurel. She is Mrs Hardy again in *We Faw Down*, a status she relinquishes once more in *That's My Wife*. By the 1930s, she had acquired a somewhat mature figure, emphasized in the 1935 short *Keystone Hotel* in which she resorts to a reducing machine. She appears thus as wife to a judge (*Scram!*) and Sheriff (*Way Out West*). Her contribution to *A Chump at Oxford* is confined to the additional segment intended only for overseas audiences, in which she works at an employment agency. Other films include *Madonna of the Streets*, *Uncle Tom's Cabin* and *The Tenderfoot*. Vivien Oakland was among the many colleagues with whom Stan maintained contact during his retirement. During 1958 he became aware of the cancer treatment the actress was then undergoing; shortly thereafter she was dead.

(See also: Garvin, Anita; Risqué humour; Women)

O'CONNOR, BOB
See: Foreign versions

Vivien Oakland shares a stagecoach in Way Out West

OF MICE AND MEN (1939)
Many years after its release, Roach spoke of this, his only great dramatic film, as having been an idea for Laurel & Hardy. The producer said that he had always wanted to make a serious film with the team, suggesting how well he appreciated the depth of their characterizations. It is, however, unnerving to picture the two comedians as Steinbeck's George and Lenny.

OLIVER THE EIGHTH
(Laurel & Hardy film)
Released by M-G-M, February, 1934. Produced by Hal Roach. Directed by Lloyd French. Camera: Art Lloyd. Three reels.
With Stan Laurel and Oliver Hardy, Mae Busch, Jack Barty.

Barbers Stan and Ollie are tempted by an advertisement placed by a 'wealthy young widow' (Mae Busch) in search of marriage. Ollie posts his letter of enquiry but deliberately misplaces Stan's. Ollie receives a reply, not knowing the woman to be a murderess who, jilted long ago by an Oliver, has sworn revenge on every man bearing that name. Ollie, an unwitting number eight, arrives at the mansion to be greeted by Jitters (Jack Barty), a retainer just as cracked as his employer. The widow makes her entrance; so does Stan, who has found the hidden letter. 'I want half of everything you're going to get', he says, adding that he has disposed of the barber shop in exchange for a gold brick and some nuts. Dinner at the mansion is a strange affair, consisting of invisible food. Eventually Stan can take no more, telling the butler 'You're nuts!' Jitters takes them aside and tells them that the widow is the crazy one, revealing also her plan to sneak in later to cut the sleeping Ollie's throat. Escape is impossible, so the boys retire with a plan to keep vigil, each taking turns to sleep. As Stan cannot keep awake, Ollie provides incentive by suspending the gold brick over Stan's head, secured with string placed over a candle; Stan must remember to move the candle at intervals. Ollie has barely settled before his toes are taken to be a hand grabbing at the foot of the bed; one shotgun blast later, Ollie is hopping around the room. The brick, forgotten amid the panic, knocks Ollie cold, just as the widow approaches with a sharp knife. Stan, trapped in a cupboard, tries to aim the gun, the resultant shot waking Ollie from the dream he has had while sitting in the barber's chair.

A reworking of *The Laurel-Hardy Murder Case* (qv), *Oliver the Eighth* is generally disappointing. The earlier film is flawed by its dream ending and padded length of three reels; this version inherits both, and may perhaps explain why the team's remaining shorts were two-reelers. There are still

though the Film Classics reissue barely carries the title at all, their opening plaque obliterating 'Oliver the Eighth' until it is ready to wipe into the next title. For many years BBC TV used an original print with full titling, but later showings both on the BBC and commercial channels have favoured a reissue, of noticeably inferior quality.

(See also: Barbers; Barty, Jack; *Big Noise, the*; Black humour; Busch, Mae; Dreams; Hereafter, the; Insanity; Murder; Reissues; Servants; Shotguns; Television; Ties; Titling)

'Goodbye, Oliver the Eighth; I hope you have a nice, long sleep!'

highlights, some of them described above but these are mostly confined to the beginning, especially when Stan once again mangles a once-lucid idea (informing us that beauty is only knee deep). The film's title is sometimes quoted as *The Private Life of Oliver the Eighth* for British release, and is referred to as such in reissue publicity. This reference to the previous year's *The Private Life of Henry the Eighth* is missing from all prints in circulation,

ON THE LOOSE
(Laurel & Hardy guest appearance)
Released by M-G-M, 26 December 1931. Produced and directed by Hal Roach. Camera: Len Powers. Two reels.
With ZaSu Pitts and Thelma Todd, Claud Allister, John Loder, William (Billy) Gilbert, Charlie Hall, Stan Laurel and Oliver Hardy.

Thelma and ZaSu arrive home at midnight after yet another wearying date at Coney Island; numerous dolls and other novelties bear witness to the

frequency of their visits. The following morning they are splashed by a passing car whose occupant, a polite Englishman (John Loder), takes them to a salon for new outfits. The couturier (Billy Gilbert) fixes them up with clothing while the Englishman arranges a date with the girls for the following Saturday. When the day comes around he and a fellow-Englishman (Claud Allister) take them to a 'smart and original' place - Coney Island. The girls do their best to seem keen but are obviously old hands at everything from the shooting gallery to that contraption designed to blow skirts in the air. Another girl, clearly unused to it all, is thrown repeatedly into the arms of ZaSu's boyfriend. The day ends with the foursome completely submerged in a water chute. Next Saturday, the girls are contentedly at home until two visitors (Laurel & Hardy) arrive, suggesting a trip to Coney Island; the would-be escorts are chased from the premises amid a hail of fairground memorabilia.

Directed personally by Roach, *On the Loose* is one of the series pairing Thelma Todd (qv) with ZaSu Pitts (1900-63), an actress whose career was then in hiatus between dramatic pictures of the 1920s (notably Von Stroheim's *Greed*) and prominent roles in sound features. Their films range from delightful to disappointing but this is one of the best, enlivened further by one of Laurel & Hardy's occasional guest appearances. Billy Gilbert (qv) is excellent as a dress designer whose accent switches from polite to gruff when dealing with staff (to say nothing of his 'hands on' method of taking measurements), while Charlie Hall (qv) is almost as amusing playing the proprietor of a shooting gallery.

ON THE SPOT
(Laurel & Hardy films qv)
Billed also under such variants as *A Spot of Trouble* and *Looking For Trouble*, *On the Spot* is the stage

sketch written by Stan Laurel for the team's personal appearances of 1952. Although he enjoyed performing it at the time, Stan was later dissatisfied with the sketch and destroyed his copy; for this reason it was unavailable for the first edition of *The Comedy World of Stan Laurel*, a book in which other such material is transcribed in full. Fortunately, the comedian's daughter, Lois, unearthed a further copy in time for the centenary reprint in 1990. The rediscovered script, though incomplete, confirms that plot and action duplicate the 1930 two-reeler *Night Owls*, in which a luckless policeman persuades vagrants Laurel & Hardy to burgle the Chief's house in order to provide him with an arrest. Theatre programmes had suggested the original locale, a small-town railroad station in the US, while publicity stills convey certain of the gags, among them Stan pouring coffee from a hot water bottle. This last is reworked from *Pack Up Your Troubles*, while other films provide inspiration for the dialogue: expanded from *Our Relations* is a gag based on the expression 'before you can say Jack Robinson', which turns out to be the name of the cop; borrowed in turn from *Way Out West* is Stan's remark 'Ups-a-daisy', to which Ollie replies

On the Spot was the team's stage sketch for the 1952 tour. Note that Stan's cuffs are fastened with string

'Now, don't get fancy'. The idea itself is credited to Leo McCarey in the original 1930 version, although its similarity to one of the Karno sketches should be noted.

(See also: Biographies; *Birds of a Feather*; Criminals; *Driver's Licence Sketch, the*; Karno, Fred; Laurel, Lois; Stage appearances; Vagrants)

ON THE WRONG TREK
(Laurel & Hardy guest appearance)
Released by M-G-M, 18 April 1936. Produced by Hal Roach. Directed by Charles Parrott (Charley Chase) and Harold Law. Camera: Art Lloyd. Two reels.
With Charley Chase, Rosina Lawrence, Bonita Weber, Stan Laurel and Oliver Hardy.

Charley arrives back at work from a disastrous vacation; he explains how with his wife (Rosina Lawrence) and mother-in-law (Bonita Weber) he headed for California rather than Michigan (because 'Mother knows best'), passing on the way a number of hitch-hikers. Two of them are Stan

and Ollie, each thumbing in different directions. Charley thinks they look like 'a couple of horse thieves', imitates Stan's expression and keeps moving. Charley and family stop to help the apparent victims of a road accident, who turn out to be criminals who steal their car and leave Mr and Mrs Chase dressed in rags. Driving the crooks' old car, they borrow some fuel from a well-to-do couple; in the process, Charley sends the couple's car over a cliff. Police are busy preventing vagrants crossing the Californian State Line, and consider the shabby-looking family unsuitable visitors; they turn back and spend the evening at a hobo gathering, Charley and his wife contributing a song and dance in exchange for food. The following day they are back on the road, but the car breaks down with the family still 200 miles from home. Hitch-hiking brings them as much success as it had Stan and Ollie, the only vehicle to stop being a fertilizer truck. They decide to try the fake accident ploy themselves but the police, wise to the trick, arrest them. Charley concludes his tale just as the new boss arrives, the same man whose car was wrecked by Charley. Summoned into the office, Charley is delighted not to be recognized; he walks straight in but is sent back through the plate-glass door. Charley Chase (*qv*) was at this time nearing the end of his association with Roach. He would make two more films at the studio (*Neighborhood House* and *Kelly the Second*) before moving to Columbia. *Aficionados* believe the fleeting appearance of Laurel & Hardy to have been their way of bidding farewell to an old friend and colleague.

(See also: Guest appearances; Kelly, Patsy; Lawrence, Rosina; *Sons of the Desert*)

ONE GOOD TURN
(Laurel & Hardy film)
Released by M-G-M, 31 October 1931. Two reels. Produced by Hal

Roach. Directed by James Horne. Camera: Art Lloyd.
With Stan Laurel and Oliver Hardy, Mary Carr, James Finlayson, Billy Gilbert, Snub Pollard.

Stan and Ollie are 'seeing America' with a total inventory of one 1911 Ford, one 1861 tent, one set of long underwear, two shirts and three socks. Stan is tasting the soup they are cooking on an open fire; Ollie, doing the laundry by a stream, insists Stan would be better employed hanging out the washing. Soon their tent is on the fire, which Stan extinguishes with the soup. 'What could be worse?' asks Ollie, before noticing their shrunken laundry. The only option is to beg for food, something they achieve at the home of a kind old lady (Mary Carr). She declines to accept anything in return, but responds to Stan's suggestion that Ollie chop wood. Ollie tells Stan to cut it, a single swing of the axe sending a solitary log down on Ollie's head. The boys are summoned to the kitchen, where they squabble over coffee and sandwiches until overhearing dark deeds: the landlord (James Finlayson) is about to evict the old lady, whose mortgage money has been stolen. Stan and Ollie are unaware that they are hearing rehearsals for a play, and, deciding that 'one good turn deserves another', set off to raise money for the mortgage. In town, Ollie declares his intention to auction their one possession, the car, as a means of helping the 'poor old lady'.

A drunk (Billy Gilbert) bids $100, accidentally placing his wallet in Stan's pocket. An old man asks Stan the time: as he is hard of hearing, Stan shouts 'One-twenty-five' and in the process closes the bidding. As the crowd disperses, Ollie discovers both the mistake and the wallet protruding from Stan's pocket. Blaming Stan for the theft, a scuffle breaks out, during which the car collapses. Back at the house, Ollie tells the old lady that his 'one-time friend' has a confession to make. The lady tells Ollie that no money has been stolen, explaining about the play and watching aghast as Stan hits Ollie, chasing him from the house. Ollie, cornered in the shed, can only watch as Stan begins to chop at the woodwork; when the shed collapses on Ollie, Stan deliberately repeats the trick of chopping wood so that it lands on Ollie's head. The final log hits Stanley, who is chased off by an angry Ollie.

This surprising wrap-up was designed for a specific purpose. In 1980, Stan Laurel's daughter Lois attended a British convention of the Sons of the Desert club (qv), bringing with her some of her father's 16mm home movies. The films were handed to the author for screening, and had evidently not been handled since Laurel's lifetime. After a few quick repairs, the films were duly shown and included a scene where the very young Lois pulled away from her 'Uncle Babe', in reaction to the treatment meted out to her father on-screen. Lois explained that they resolved the problem by including a scene where Stan showed his ability to stand up to Ollie, and it became obvious to the assembled crowd that this was from One Good Turn. Stan's rebellions were few but devastating, this example rivalling his frenzied revenge in Early to Bed (qv).

One Good Turn: *a drunken Billy Gilbert bids for the boys' car*

(See also: Auctions; Carr, Mary; Cars; Characters; Food; Home movies; Laurel, Lois; Melodrama; Rebellions (by Stanley); Titling)

OPERAS (all films *qv*)
To the uninitiated, opera seems an unlikely setting for Laurel & Hardy. However, despite the pair's usual twentieth-century context, they are at heart the traditional clowns that have been present in theatre since its birth. Three of Laurel & Hardy's starring features were based upon operatic works. The first, *Fra Diavolo* was among their greatest successes and remained a personal favourite of the team, as did the next, *Babes in Toyland*. *The Bohemian Girl* is a pleasant but obvious imitation of *Fra Diavolo*; some prefer the later film, objecting to the clear division between plot and Laurel & Hardy's comedy. This same applies to *Bonnie Scotland* and *Swiss Miss*, the latter of which has sufficient musical content for some to categorize it among the operas. Among Roach's unfilmed projects (*qv*) was an intended version of Verdi's *Rigoletto*, but this was probably not intended for Laurel & Hardy. It is generally accepted that the Laurel & Hardy operas were inspired by their appearance in M-G-M's *The Rogue Song*. Reputedly a book summarizing the plots of famous operas, belonging to Stan Laurel, survives with *Fra Diavolo* and *The Bohemian Girl* marked for reference.

(See also: Feature films)

ORANGES AND LEMONS
See: Solo films

OUR GANG
(Laurel & Hardy films *qv*)
Roach series starring children, beginning in 1922. Sixteen years later M-G-M, Roach's distributors, bought out the series and continued it until 1944. This acquisition included the series title, forcing reissues of the Roach comedies to go under the name

'Little Rascals', reportedly the intended banner until an early entry, titled *Our Gang*, caught on with the public. In common with a few other Roach series, Our Gang overlaps with Laurel & Hardy on several occasions. Both Laurel & Hardy contributed moments in their early days: Stan Laurel is in 1927's *Seeing the World*, seen with Frank Butler (*qv*) in a cut-away supposedly in London (behind them is a fish and chip shop, visible also in *Love 'Em and Weep*); Oliver Hardy is in *Thundering Fleas* (1926), *Baby Brother* (1927) and *Barnum & Ringling, Inc.* (1928). Babe's voice may be heard momentarily in a much later Gang short, *Choo Choo* (see **Dubbing**). As a team, Laurel & Hardy contribute a brief gag appearance to *Wild Poses*. The Gang supply an overlapping segment with the Laurel & Hardy footage in *The Stolen Jools*, and are among the celebrities on view in *Forty-Five Minutes From Hollywood*. Several of the youngsters are present in Laurel & Hardy's *Babes in Toyland*, while one of their number, Darla Hood, plays the younger incarnation of *The Bohemian Girl*. Tommy Bond, resident Gang bully of the latter 1930s, is the football-playing child of *Block-Heads*. When interviewed by Anthony Slide for *The Silent Picture* magazine in 1970, Hal Roach explained the genesis of the series. A child had been brought to his office displaying the customarily artificial song-and-dance abilities shared by so many stage-struck youngsters; a bored Roach found his attention drawn to the genuine antics of children visible from his window. The concept of depicting the natural humour of children (albeit in exaggerated circumstances) proved a worldwide success with audiences of all ages.

(See also: Children; Englishmen; Guest appearances)

OUR RELATIONS
(Laurel & Hardy film)
Released by M-G-M, 30 October

1936. Stan Laurel Productions for Hal Roach. Directed by Harry Lachman. Photographed by Rudolph Maté. With Stan Laurel and Oliver Hardy, Daphne Pollard, Betty Healy, Sidney Toler, Alan Hale, James Finlayson, Iris Adrian, Lona Andre, Noel Madison, Arthur Housman, Harry Bernard, Tiny Sandford.

Respectable married men Stan and Ollie receive a note from Ollie's mother reminding them of their identical twins, 'Alf' and 'Bert', who had run away to sea years before. The twins are believed dead, hanged after becoming involved in a mutiny. Stan and Ollie decide not to tell their wives (Betty Healy and Daphne Pollard). Alf and Bert are not only alive but heading for their locality aboard the *Periwinkle*. Before going ashore, a wily shipmate, Finn (James Finlayson) persuades them to part with their wages, on the pretence of helping them save. Alf and Bert make for Denker's Beer Garden, where they have been asked to deliver a pearl ring for their captain (Sidney Toler). There they meet 'two charming and refined young ladies', Alice and Lily, (Iris Adrian and Lona Andre) who run up a huge bill. The

Our Relations: a deleted scene with 'Alf' and 'Bert' aboard ship

sailors need finances and prepare to leave for Finn's lodgings. The proprietor (Alan Hale) requires some guarantee of their return, so they leave him the pearl ring. Finn is unwilling to return their money, so they steal and pawn his clothes. Returning to Finn's lodgings, they discover their money has been sewn into the suit's lining, so Finn insists on borrowing their clothes, wearing one suit while pawning the other to pay interest on the first ticket. Stan and Ollie meet their wives in town and, coincidentally, walk into Denker's Beer Garden. Mistaken for their twins, they are surprised to receive both such a huge bill and a pearl ring on settlement. The attentions of the two girls are as great a surprise, this evidence of apparent philandering being complicated by the arrival of Finn. The girls depart in disgust; so do the wives, planning divorce. Stan and Ollie have Finn ejected and decide to punish their intolerant spouses by staying out all night. They meet a drunk (Arthur Housman) who had befriended the sailors earlier, and head for the plush

Pirate Club. Alf and Bert arrive at the Beer Garden dressed in clothes improvised from blankets (in the manner of 'Singapore Eskimoes'). The proprietor insists that he has returned the ring and the resultant scuffle lands Alf and Bert in an overnight court. A neighbour, witnessing their arrest, telephones Stan and Ollie's wives; the distraught women collect what they believe to be their husbands, promising the judge that they will keep the boys out of trouble. Alf and Bert, believing them to be social workers, are happy to go along with their plans in exchange for freedom and a change of clothes. To avoid further trouble, they visit a 'high class' establishment, the Pirate Club, where Stan, Ollie and the drunk are living it up. Alf and Bert meet the girls, who want to know why they have been rejected for two 'old cronies'. Exit the wives, after Mrs Hardy dumps a cake on Bert's head. As Bert goes to clean up, Stan and Ollie meet the Captain, who demands the pearl ring. After a fight, Stan is sent to fetch the manager. Alf hears Ollie's voice, thinking it to be Bert; he meets Ollie who, taking him for Stan, puts the ring in Alf's pocket and tells him to 'beat it'; the Captain pursues Alf but is ejected after Stan returns with the manager. Ollie asks Stan for the ring, but he does not have it; Ollie thinks Stan is double-crossing him but the club's owners, who saw Ollie place the ring in Alf's pocket, offer to scare Stan into handing it over. They leave, followed by the Captain and the police. Bert rejoins Alf and the girls, and is horrified to hear of the Captain's arrival; worse still, Finn arrives with two thugs. Alf and Bert escape from the club as their twins arrive at the waterfront. The clubowners are genuine crooks, and the boys are left with a choice between handing over the ring or being drowned, their feet in round bowls of cement. Stan and Ollie are beside the dock when Ollie is punched; they start to teeter and push the gang into the water. They struggle to stay upright but are soon over the side; Alf and Bert finally lose Finn but, spotted by the Captain, hide in a dark warehouse. The Captain sees Stan and Ollie and winches them up, only to let them go when they deny having the ring. In the warehouse, Alf searches for a match and finds the ring; they hand it to the Captain, who sees both sets of twins and flees. Alf and Bert haul their brothers to safety and all is explained.

Complex in plot but high in production values, *Our Relations* is one of the finest Laurel & Hardy features. Laurel receives on-screen credit as producer (for Roach Studios), a reputedly cosmetic affair that may nonetheless explain the superiority of this and their next feature, *Way Out West* (qv). Another credit identifies *Our Relations* as an adaptation of *The Money Box* by short-story writer W. W. Jacobs (whose work as essayist includes a 1929 piece, *Are Film Comedians Funny?*), though the notion of mixed-up twins goes back to Shakespeare's *The Comedy of Errors* and further. Charles Barr considers this film 'a son of *Sons of the Desert*' (qv) in the sense of Laurel & Hardy in domesticated affluence. The idea of lodge ritual resurfaces when 'Alf' and 'Bert' meet a judge and, presumably, in Stan and Ollie's business of placing a finger on each other's nose (with cries of 'Shakespeare!' 'Longfellow!') when they happen to use the same phrase simultaneously. Some critics rightly comment on a lack of set-pieces within the fast-moving framework, though the gags are excellent and the film again echoes *Sons* by creating a story entirely dependent upon Laurel & Hardy. Unusually for their work, *Our Relations* almost always circulates in excellent copies, though there are exceptions; the BBC print was superb until a temporary stay with commercial TV (who once screened a barely comprehensible abridgment), after which it reappeared minus a scene in which Laurel &

Hardy burn Finlayson's nose with a lamp socket. Responsibility for the cut is unknown but it is tempting to assume that someone thought children might copy the gag. American TV's *Laurel & Hardy Show* version reduces the film to an hour, as with other Laurel & Hardy features running over that length; this is the edition to which colour has been added by computer.

(See also: Adrian, Iris; André, Lona; Biographies; Characters; Colour; Dual roles; Feature films; Finlayson, James; Hale, Alan; Healy, Betty; Henderson, Del; Pollard, Daphne; Stan Laurel Productions; Royalty; Sailors; Television; Toler, Sidney; Women)

OUR WIFE
(Laurel & Hardy film)
Released by M-G-M, 16 May 1931.
Two reels. Produced by Hal Roach.
Directed by James Horne. Camera: Art Lloyd.
With Stan Laurel and Oliver Hardy, Jean 'Babe' London, James Finlayson, Charles Rogers, Blanche Payson, Ben Turpin.

Prospective bridegroom Ollie is rehearsing the words 'I do' with the aid of a throat spray. Stanley, the best man, is arranging the wedding breakfast. After smashing most of the crockery, Stan, noticing the flies that have descended upon the cake, fills the throat spray with Flit and renders the cake inedible. Ollie's chubby fiancée, Dulcy (Babe London) has problems of her own, as her father (James Finlayson) has forbidden their marriage, locking her in the bedroom. A telephone call to Ollie brings the promise of an elopement, but when Ollie returns to his throat spray he receives a liberal dose of fly killer. His throat is soothed with a chunk of ice, which causes him to trip into the cake. Ollie arrives at Dulcy's house ready for a discreet exit. The *in*discreet Stan rings the front doorbell and tells the butler (Charles Rogers) of Ollie's

plans. The girl's father is alerted just as Ollie, perched on a ladder, plummets through a downstairs window. Dulcy throws down her suitcase, and the contents scatter. Her father enters the room, but Dulcy tricks him by standing behind the door and making a quick exit. Outside, Stan throws some premature confetti over the couple before they make for the 'limousine' he has brought. The car is scarcely big enough for a midget, let alone a sizeable trio and their protracted efforts to squeeze in culminate in Stan's head protruding through the roof. At the home of William Gladding, Justice of the Peace, Stan is greeted by a large lady (Blanche Payson) who, on asking what he wants, is told 'We want to get married'. 'Not we', says Ollie, 'us'. 'Not we', repeats Stan, 'us'. After a little more of this, she hits Stan but summons her 'Paw' to officiate. The judge is none other than cross-eyed Ben Turpin, whose garbled version of the ceremony concludes with Ollie married to Stan.

Our Wife is one of the few talkie appearances of comedy veteran Ben Turpin (*qv*); it is also the only Laurel & Hardy comedy with Babe London (*qv*), who worked prolifically in silent comedy, later sharing her memories in the TV documentary *Cuckoo* (*qv*). *Our Wife* is overlooked among Laurel & Hardy shorts but has much to recommend it: minor touches include Ollie looking skyward after wedding cake has blemished his hat, and Stan curiously examining the contents of Dulcy's suitcase. The elopement itself recalls *Night Owls* but with greater momentum and the admittedly protracted business of crowding into an undersized car offers some amusing moments. Further comedy of frustration occurs when Stan meets Blanche Payson (*qv*), who can take only a little of Stan's confused questioning before punching him on the nose. Stan returns to the car and resumes the conversation with Ollie, who quickly gives up the effort. 'C'mon, honey, let's get out', he tells his fiancée, his resignation illustrating amply the difference between his attitude to Stan and that of the outside world.

(See also: Cars; Finlayson, James; Food; Gag titles; Insects; Marx Brothers, the; Melodrama; Weddings)

OUT-TAKES
(Laurel & Hardy films *qv*)
Regrettably, very few out-takes survive from the Laurel & Hardy films.

The ill-fated wedding to **Our Wife**

During the 1980s, deleted footage from *Pardon Us* and *Laughing Gravy* was unearthed and reinstated in certain versions. Prior to this, the main source for such material was the gag reel *That's That!* There seems no truth in the assumption that out-takes from M-G-M's *The Big House* appear in Laurel & Hardy's *Pardon Us*, but it is reasonably certain that the team's 1945 Fox film *The Bullfighters* incorporates fragments of the studio's 1941 remake of *Blood and Sand* (the original of which, coincidentally, was parodied by Stan Laurel in 1922). It has been suggested that the team's contribution to the 1933 Our Gang short *Wild Poses* may have been an unused test shot from their own *Brats*, but this is pure speculation.

(See also: Deleted scenes; Home Movies; Television; Video releases)

OUTWITTING DAD
See: Solo films

OWEN, CATHERINE DALE
See: *Rogue Song, the*

P

PACK UP YOUR TROUBLES
(Laurel & Hardy film)
Released by M-G-M, 17 September
1932. Produced by Hal Roach.
Directed by George Marshall and
Raymond McCarey (despite this
credit, George Marshall is said to have
directed the film unassisted). Camera:
Art Lloyd. 68 minutes.
With Stan Laurel & Oliver Hardy,
Donald Dillaway, Mary Carr, James
Finlayson, Billy Gilbert, Rychard
Cramer, Grady Sutton, Jacquie Lyn.

When America enters the First World
War in 1917, Stan and Ollie try
unsuccessfully to dodge the recruiting
officer and are soon disrupting military drill. Their efforts are rewarded
by a job emptying bins. On asking the
cook (director George Marshall in a
cameo role) where the bins should go
they are told, sarcastically, to take
them 'to the General'. This they do,
landing themselves in a cell with the
cook, who vows revenge - with a carving knife. In France, they distinguish
themselves by the accidental capture
of a German platoon, with the aid of a
runaway tank caught in barbed wire.
Their army buddy, Eddie Smith
(Donald Dillaway), has been killed
and following the Armistice, they
return to seek his infant daughter
(Jacquie Lyn) who, with her mother
long since vanished with another man,
has been left in the care of strangers.
The child's guardian (Rychard
Cramer) is a layabout whose prime
interest in keeping her derives from
the money he receives. Stan and Ollie
take the little girl into their own care

and set about locating her grandparents, armed only with the knowledge
that their name is Smith. After a
series of embarrassing mistakes,
Laurel & Hardy's pursuit of the
world's Smiths is interrupted by the
arrival of orphanage officials, who
have been alerted by the former
guardian. Needing money to flee the
State, Stan and Ollie approach a bank
manager for a loan, using their lunch
wagon as security. He tells them he
would have to be 'unconscious' to
agree to such an arrangement, and
when he is rendered thus by an accident with a falling ornament, Stan
and Ollie feel entitled to take the
required sum. The police soon capture them and they are taken to the
bank manager's home, where he and
his wife recognize their son in a photograph found with the boys' stolen
money. Stan and Ollie explain their
search and are freed, their future

Pack Up Your Troubles: *a deleted
version of the wedding sequence, showing
Laurel & Hardy in uniform and Frank
Brownlee in lieu of Billy Gilbert*

assured - until they meet their host's
chef, an ex-army cook wielding a carving knife!

Seldom seen intact since 1932, the
American reissue copies of *Pack Up
Your Troubles* were censored owing to
a sequence in which the child's
'guardian' is guilty of wife-beating. A
further section, in which Laurel &
Hardy escape from the man and his
cronies by pouring hot kettles of water
over them, was cut for similar reasons.
The first sequence is the most serious
loss, since it justifies Laurel & Hardy's
taking of the child and their subsequent violent treatment of the man,
some of which remains in the
abridgment. The 8mm and 16mm
copies from Blackhawk Films (*qv*) are
said to be from this version.
Fortunately the copy shown on British
TV (both BBC and, earlier, Channel
4) retains this scene although the second has been physically removed from
the print. An earlier TV copy, shown
on BBC TV during the 1970s, derives
from the cut reissue, with its first title
replaced by the Film Classics 'plaque'.

Despite superior quality to most copies, it proved a disappointment to British enthusiasts, who were used to seeing the deleted segments in the 8mm version (and extracts therefrom) distributed in the UK by Walton Films. Although slightly abridged (with their extracts often including moments trimmed from the feature edition), Walton's material seems to derive from a post-war reissue by UK distributor New Realm, who clearly did not share the qualms of their US contemporaries. It should be noted, however, that UK copies always omit the opening gag title, to the effect that America's entry into the war 'caused crowns to rattle'; perhaps the British censors objected to any gags about royalty. Today's British TV copy resembles this edition, although a version supplied to European TV and UK video release suggests origins in the abridged 16mm Blackhawk print. It was therefore with surprise that British enthusiasts heard that American collectors had unearthed what was believed to be the only copy of the censored scenes, dubbed into French. Happily the 16mm copies issued in the revived Blackhawk range are from complete material. The American reissue also lacks a few opening shots of printing presses and newspapers being sold on a street corner, plus a rear view (in long-shot) of Laurel & Hardy sitting on a park bench; a more serious loss was approximately one-half of a charming scene in which young Jacquie Lyn (*qv*) sends Stan to sleep while telling him a bedtime story. Reportedly this scene was written with Hardy in mind, but with characteristic unselfishness he insisted that his partner was better suited to the sequence. Stills survive suggesting preview versions of *Pack Up Your Troubles* differing somewhat from the final cut. A sequence in which Laurel & Hardy disrupt a wedding seems to have been shot at least three times, first with Laurel & Hardy wearing army uniform rather than the civilian clothes of subsequent takes, with

Frank Brownlee (*qv*) (the drill sergeant in the finished film) as the bride's father. In the second version, he has been replaced by Billy Gilbert (also *qv*), with Laurel & Hardy in civilian garb; while these changes are familiar from the released version, the action is not, being a reworking of the pie fight from *The Battle of the Century* (*qv*).

(See also: Army; Blackmail; Boxing; Businessmen; Carr, Mary; Censorship; Children; Deleted scenes; Dillaway, Donald; Feature films; Home movies; In-jokes; Marshall, George; McCarey, Leo; Reissues; Risqué humour; Royalty; Slapstick; Sutton, Grady; Video releases)

PAINTINGS (all films *qv*)
Wrong Again is all about the confusion between Gainsborough's famous 'Blue Boy' and a horse of the same name; the painting is eventually dumped over a servant's head. Mae Busch (*qv*) portrays an artist's wife who is seen both in person and in oils in *The Fixer-Uppers*, a remake of the early *Slipping Wives*. Another early entry, *Duck Soup*, opens with a painting dropped on its owner's head. Later on, the owner's framed likeness betrays his identity to Stan and Ollie, as it does in the remake, *Another Fine Mess*. A police detective is unconvinced when in *The Laurel-Hardy Murder Case* Ollie tries to establish a likeness between Stan and a portrait of General Grant, while a portrait of Hitler has an apple shot into its mouth in *Air Raid Wardens*. The portrait of the Dean in *A Chump at Oxford* is replaced by the real thing just in time to be sprayed with soda. Stan and Ollie absently discuss a landscape as soot is shovelled into Ollie's trousers in *Dirty Work*, but the best gag with a portrait (possibly a photograph) is from *Their Purple Moment*, where Stan

has constructed a hinged flap in a portrait in order to conceal his money.

(See also: Artists; Caricatures; Remakes; Wartime)

A PAIR OF TIGHTS (1928)
A silent Roach two-reeler starring Anita Garvin, Marion Byron, Edgar Kennedy and Stuart Erwin. *A Pair of Tights* is an excellent film with a punning title referring to tightwads Kennedy and Erwin, whose reluctance to spend means the loss of a free

Babe with Marion Byron, co-star of **A Pair of Tights,** *and (inset) contemporary publicity for the film. The faint autograph is that of Anita Garvin, whose punning message of 'love and hisses' echoes both her spirited portrayals and the title of one of her Laurel & Hardy films*

dinner to the starving girls. When the foursome are out in Stuart's car, Marion spots an ice-cream parlour; Kennedy is willing to stump up for four cones when Anita cunningly suggests that ice-cream might spoil their appetites for dinner. From here, much of the action concerns Marion's difficulty in retaining several orders of ice-cream despite opposition from swinging doors, a dog and a bratty kid

(Spec O'Donnell). Her friends, meanwhile, have their own problems with a cop who insists on them moving their double-parked car. Ultimately a street fight develops, with passers-by knocked into a sitting position. William K. Everson (*qv*) has described this short as 'a minor classic', suggesting that it might have been intended for Laurel & Hardy but was recast owing to its similarity to *You're Darn Tootin'* (*qv*) (which was, incidentally, directed by Kennedy); equally plausible is that a female equivalent to Laurel & Hardy was sought as early as 1928. Anita Garvin worked in many Roach comedies of the period, creating a formidable line of tough ladies; petite Marion Byron is recalled mostly as Keaton's leading lady in *Steamboat Bill, Jr.*. The film's family likeness to Laurel & Hardy is understandable, with Hal Yates and Leo McCarey (both *qv*) as, respectively, director and supervisor, plus the customarily witty titles of H. M. Walker (*qv*). The supporting cast includes Laurel & Hardy stalwarts Charlie Hall and Harry Bernard (both *qv*). *A Pair of Tights* was revived by Robert Youngson (*qv*) in his 1960 compilation *When Comedy Was King* (*qv*): a fuller edition was issued by Blackhawk Films (*qv*) on 8 and 16mm but lacked the concluding moments of the first reel, which are present in Youngson's version.

(See also: Garvin, Anita; Keaton, Buster; Kelly, Patsy; Kennedy, Edgar; Todd, Thelma)

PALLADIUM, LONDON
See: Stage appearances

PALLETTE, EUGENE (1889-1954)
(all films *qv*)
Portly, growling actor in films from 1913 but familiar mostly in comic supporting roles of the 1930s and 1940s. He appears in the finale of *Sugar Daddies* as the man taken for Oliver Hardy by a suspicious cop and is also the insurance salesman who in *The Battle of the Century* persuades

Ollie to take out a policy on Stan. Sadly, Pallette's contribution to the latter is missing from available prints. Pallette is present among the dinner guests in *The Second Hundred Years*, while also contributing to *The Stolen Jools* in a sequence separate from that with Laurel & Hardy. In a 1963 letter to Leo Riemens of Holland, Stan remembered Pallette's fondness for playing such roles as a change of pace between his feature commitments; 'he was very well liked on the Roach lot', the comedian added.

(See also: Insurance; Letters; Lost films)

PANCHROMATIC FILM
See: Colouring

PANTOMIME
The British tradition of pantomime has its roots in the Harlequinade but jettisoned this influence late in the nineteenth century with the introduction of talents from the music-hall (*qv*). Earlier in the century, Grimaldi had been the major pantomime talent at the most prestigious venue, Drury Lane; by the 1890s, Dan Leno (*qv*) and Herbert Campbell reigned supreme. Pantomime's appeal is not readily explained, with its young girls thinly (*very* thinly) disguised as young men, and comedians portraying old women, but no matter: its broad humour survives endless Christmas seasons (seemingly extending by months each year) to the delight of youngsters and, whether they admit it or not, the adults accompanying them. Stan Laurel saw his first panto at the age of three and remained charmed by the experience. The nearest to such entertainments in the Laurel & Hardy films is *Babes in Toyland* (*qv*), although the aborted Laurel & Hardy TV films of the 1950s were designed to approximate the spirit even more closely.

(See also: Female impersonation; Television; Unfilmed projects; Wood, 'Wee' Georgie)

PAPERHANGER'S HELPER, THE
See: *Stick Around*

PARDON US
(Laurel & Hardy film)
Released by M-G-M, 15 August 1931 (UK première, July 1931). Produced by Hal Roach. Directed by James Parrott. UK title: *Jailbirds*.
With Stan Laurel and Oliver Hardy, Walter Long, Wilfred Lucas, James Finlayson, June Marlowe.

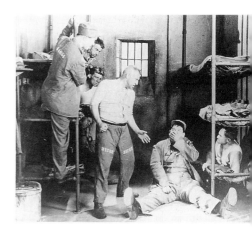

Pardon Us: *Ollie learns that Walter Long will tolerate a 'raspberry' only from Stan*

Stan and Ollie take up home brewing during Prohibition, an activity quite legal until they attempt to sell the surplus. Stan's inability to distinguish a policeman from a streetcar conductor lands them in prison. Stan has a loose tooth that punctuates each sentence with a raspberry sound unless plugged with his finger; this antagonizes first the Warden (Wilfred Lucas), then the prison's toughest convict, the Tiger (Walter Long). Fortunately the Tiger, impressed by this apparent courage, befriends Stan, although Ollie's deliberate raspberry earns him a punch in the nose. In the prison schoolroom, they become involved in an inkblot fight, and when one missile hits the teacher (James Finlayson) they are placed in solitary. On their return from the 'hole', they become involved in the Tiger's escape plan. All the escapees are captured except Stan and Ollie, who hide out in blackface amid a community of cotton-pickers. Their life in this tranquil setting comes to an end when the Warden and his daughter (June Marlowe) arrive, needing help with their car. The blackface disguise is sufficient to fool them, but Stan's loose tooth gives them away. Back in jail, a visit to the dentist means only the loss of some of Ollie's teeth but more important matters loom: another break, which they unwittingly quell with a mishandled machine gun. When the boys are pardoned, the Warden asks if he can help them resume where they left off. Stan asks if the Warden would like to order some cases of beer!

M-G-M's *The Big House* did sufficient business during 1930 for a parody to be in order, and Laurel & Hardy decided to do just that in their customary two-reel format. The story goes that Roach asked Metro's permission to use the original set, a request granted only on the proviso that Laurel & Hardy do a film for them in return. Roach refused, surprising given other such loan-outs of the team, and built a prison set that required feature-film earnings to recoup its cost. In this way, *Pardon Us*, at triple its intended length, became Laurel & Hardy's first full-length vehicle. Today its padding is obvious and approach clumsy, but in its day it generated a fair mixture of reviews and did excellent business. The comedy scenes hold up well for the most part, even an unnecessary but hilarious bit in the prison schoolroom, presided over by James Finlayson (*qv*). Walter Long (*qv*) is at his best as the rebellious convict leader and the notion of Stan's illmannered tooth is among the team's more engaging devices. Babe's delightful tenor is given one of its regrettably few outings, accompanied by Stan in a soft-shoe dance. A version of *Pardon Us* was actually

previewed during 1930, bearing their pet working title of *The Rap* and differing somewhat from the finished item. Key deletions seem to have been a fire sequence and a finale presenting Stan and Ollie as old men. Others are unclear, but a restored 1980s copy incorporates an additional ten minutes, probably from one of the last preview prints although the incidental music stops at each 'new' segment. The scenes described above are not present, but other footage illustrates a general tightening of the action. Certain trims are evidently to reduce some overacting by Wilfred Lucas (*qv*), whose performance in the final cut has been honed to a model of controlled irony; a scene where they are placed in solitary is duplicated, shown first as in the usual copy (following the schoolroom scene) then once more after their recapture from the plantation. The repeated section, from which Stan's dialogue with the guards has been removed, concludes with the sound of Stan's terrified weeping instead of his conversation with Ollie. The lengthier plantation sequence (matched in the extant foreign version) gives Laurel & Hardy more time with their puppies (the offspring of bloodhounds sent to catch them!), Stan getting a look when announcing his intention to name one 'Oliver'. The black community have an extra song. Ollie's song is as per the release copy but Stan's subsequent fall into a pond is punctuated by his reappearance, minus blackface disguise. The next sequence, where the Warden arrives in his car, repeats a shot used when we first see Laurel & Hardy on the plantation (Ollie is delicately picking cotton as Stan rips up entire plants!); the entire routine is missing the incidental music of the release version. This extended edition, inferior artistically but an archival treasure, is that rendered into colour for video release. Also present is an otherwise deleted moment in which Stan asks for copies of their prison photographs, intended to facilitate an unused finale:

outside the prison gates, Ollie asks Stan for a light; in searching through his pockets, he produces the photographs and is chased offscreen. This gag concludes the Spanish version, which today is the only known survivor of the four foreign editions; there are however post-production continuities for the French, German and Italian copies, which have been examined in detail by Robert G. Dickson. Each refers to the domestic edition as *Their First Mistake*, a second working title used instead for a later two-reeler. In French, the film is titled *Sous les verrous*; in German, *Hinter Schloss und Riegel*; in Italian, *Muraglie*; while the Spanish is called *De bote en bote*. In Mexico at least, the last-named played as *Los Presidiarios*, emphasizing it as a parody of *The Big House* (known in Mexico as *El Presidio*). It has been said that the foreign editions replace the prohibition theme with a tale of Laurel & Hardy's arrest while placing money into a bank vault; the idea probably was considered but it is known that each edition explains the prohibition law with an opening title card. The foreign versions match each other closely, rearranging a few sequences and containing most of the scenes added to the extended English version; minor variations include the boys' game of 'choose a hand', which seems present only in English and French. Otherwise, each runs between 61 and 63 minutes, similar to the longer English copy. The schoolroom routine is omitted, but the otherwise lost fire scene is incorporated. In Spanish at least, this has been dubbed rather than re-shot. It is likely that Walter Long and June Marlowe (*qv*) are retained in each version, Long probably being dubbed. June Marlowe was fluent in German, and would have had no difficulty in adapting to each edition. Other supporting actors are changed, principally Wilfred Lucas (*qv*) who in Spanish is replaced by Enrique Acosta; Boris Karloff (*qv*) appears in a still attributed to the French edition but no such scene can be traced in the continuity. This was probably shot but deleted, as was a sequence filmed for each edition in which the boys unwittingly give the warden a package filled with explosives. Extensive tinkering and consequent delay suggest a desire to make the most of Laurel & Hardy's feature debut, at least in America. Costa Rica, Mexico and Chile are known to have screened the Spanish version between early March and May of 1931. In Britain the film (retitled *Jailbirds*) opened on 10 July, 36 days before the American release.

(See also: Alcohol; *Another Fine Mess*; Deleted scenes; Dentists; Education; Feature films; Foreign versions; Guest appearances; M-G-M; *Night Owls*; Parodies; Previews; Prison; Race; Songs; Smoking; *Their First Mistake*; Video releases; Working titles)

PARKER, JEAN (b. 1915)
Leading lady of Laurel & Hardy's 1939 film *The Flying Deuces* (*qv*); earlier in the same year she had appeared with Babe in *Zenobia* (*qv*). Other films include Capra's *Lady For A Day* (1933), *Little Women* (1933), *The Ghost Goes West* (1936) and *Bluebeard* (1944).

(See also: Busch, Mae; Capra, Frank)

Jean Parker (third from left) with Babe in Zenobia

Parodies: Stan mimics Valentino vanity in Mud and Sand
BFI Stills, Posters and Designs

PARODIES
(Laurel & Hardy films *qv*)
Laurel & Hardy's rather insular screen environment still permits the occasional nod toward the rest of filmdom. *Pardon Us* and *Sons of the Desert* have their sights on recognizable contemporaries, while *Beau Hunks* does as much for *Beau Geste*. *Bonnie Scotland* parallels *The Lives of a Bengal Lancer* and the team's last Roach features, *A Chump at Oxford* and *Saps at Sea* are, respectively, deliberately reminiscent of *A Yank at Oxford* and *Souls at Sea*. In the latter instance, the satirical intent extends no further than the title, a commonplace device characterizing much comedy of the period (the Taxi Boys' *Call Her Sausage* has nothing to do with Clara Bow's *Call Her Savage*). To a great extent, the 'official' Laurel & Hardy parodies tend more toward customary farce within the original's setting. *Way Out West*'s target is westerns in general rather than any specific title. The Laurel solo parodies of the 1920s are clear in their intent: *The Soilers* (*qv*) is one of the best. The sequence from *Mud and Sand* illustrated here makes barbed comment on Valentino's dressing scene in *Blood and Sand*. Another Valentino film, *Monsieur Beaucaire*, became *Monsieur Don't Care*, and so on. It is said that Stan's parodies provided a framework at a time when finding a character proved difficult; the results were mostly good and the films still generate laughs, even among audiences unfamiliar with the originals.

(See also: Anderson, G. M.; Rock, Joe; Solo films; *Taxi Boys, the*)

PARROTT, CHARLES
see: Chase, Charley

PARROTT, JAMES (1897-1939)
(Laurel & Hardy films *qv*)

A prolific director in Laurel & Hardy's formative years, James Parrott had once starred in Roach comedies under the name 'Paul Parrott', a persona often erroneously taken to be Parrott's brother, Charley Chase (*qv*). He directed some Laurel & Hardy classics, among them *Two Tars*, *Brats* and *Hog Wild*. A contemporary review suggests Parrott to have joined Laurel & Hardy on stage in San Francisco in 1929. Randy Skretvedt (*qv*) has said that Parrott's early death, officially from a heart attack, was more likely to have been a drug-related suicide.

(See also: *Blotto*; Stage appearances)

James Parrott (left) tries a different form of directing as his brother, Charley Chase, harmonizes with Laurel & Hardy. Note the absence of Babe's moustache, probably removed at this time for his child role in Brats

PARROTT, PAUL
See: Parrott, James

PARSONS, LOUELLA
See: Radio

PARVIS, TY
See: *Sons of the Desert*

PATHÉ EXCHANGE
Roach's distributor from early days with Rolin (*qv*) until moving to M-G-M (*qv*) in mid-1927. The parent company was French: Roach described the New York office as containing no more than two people who spoke English, adding 'Many times I was talking to the people there through an interpreter'. Pathé was nonetheless a major US outlet, almost monopolizing 1920s comedy with the twin product of Sennett and Roach on its books. Roach severed his connection with Pathé at the birth of the Laurel & Hardy team, with the result that Pathé's embryonic Laurel & Hardy titles were often withheld to coincide with the mature M-G-M comedies. The company was absorbed into RKO-Radio within a few years.

(See also: Sennett, Mack; Teaming)

PATRICK, LEE (1906-82)
Actress known to many as the scatter-brained spouse in the 1950s *Topper* TV shows, themselves based on the

Lee Patrick tempts 'Potts' in Jitterbugs

earlier features made at Roach. A prolific film career was highlighted by her role as Humphrey Bogart's secretary in *The Maltese Falcon* (1941), and in 1975 she was persuaded out of retirement to repeat the task in George Segal's parody *The Black Bird* (Elisha Cook Jr. [*qv*] was also recruited from the 1941 version). She appeared with Laurel & Hardy in *Jitterbugs* (*qv*), an experience she enjoyed although she later expressed surprise at the team's reputation for improvisation: it should be remembered that the Laurel & Hardy Fox films were made from scripts permitting few departures.

(See also: Brandon, Henry; Scripts; *Topper*; 20th Century-Fox)

PAYSON, BLANCHE
(1881-1964) (all films *qv*)
Amazonian Blanche Payson lends her imposing presence to several of the boys' films. In Laurel's *Half a Man* she is the giantess who carries Stan around on her shoulders, forming an unwieldy creature some ten feet tall. Stan and Ollie's busking in *Below Zero* is ended when she destroys their musical instruments. She displays greater tolerance in *Our Wife*, enduring perhaps a minute's worth of Stan before hitting him. Her brief contribution to *Helpmates* is a telephone call sufficient to send Ollie into a panic. Miss Payson's pre-movie career is said to have been that of women's prison officer, no great surprise to anyone who has seen her in films.

(See also: Women)

PEMBROKE, PERCY
See: Laurel, Mae and Rock, Joe

PERFECT DAY
(Laurel & Hardy film)
Released by M-G-M, 10 August 1929. Produced by Hal Roach. Directed by James Parrott. Two reels. With Stan Laurel and Oliver Hardy, Edgar Kennedy, Isabelle Keith, Kay

Perfect Day: *Edgar Kennedy looks ready to exclaim*

Deslys, Harry Bernard, Baldwin Cooke.

Plans for a Sunday picnic go awry when the sandwiches are spread over the floor and the dog attacks Uncle Ed's gouty foot. Uncle, the dog and the boys' wives are crammed into the back of their Model T as Stan and Ollie attempt to get the car moving. Prolonged 'goodbyes' with the neighbours lead to nothing when the car gets a flat tyre. This fixed, the car remains immobile, the jack still being in place. When Stan removes the jack, the tyre flattens again. Ollie hurls the jack at Stan, but misses and smashes a neighbour's window. An exchange of violence is terminated by the arrival of a parson, whose presence sends the neighbourhood scurrying indoors. Returning to the car, they find it unwilling to start:. As Ollie tries the crank handle, Stan lets out the choke, producing an explosion that sends Ollie into the road. Ollie tells Stan to 'throw out the clutch', an instruction he obeys rather literally. The car is eventually started, and despite the need to extinguish an exploding engine they exit, amid more 'goodbyes', around the corner into a deep mud puddle.

One of the team's best short comedies, *Perfect Day* is a surprisingly adroit talkie for its period and drew praise at the time for its use of sound.

John McCabe (*qv*) has quoted a review from the *Film Exhibitor's Herald* which describes as 'the funniest sound effect yet recorded' the moment where a blow to Stan's head produces the sound of a bell. As McCabe noted, this now-commonplace technique was then a complete innovation. *Perfect Day*'s soundtrack has been kept up-to-date by the polished music score added on its 1936 reissue. It would be interesting to see how fresh the film would be in its original form, but it seems probable that only this later version survives. Perhaps the most surprising piece of sound occurs when the picnickers scramble away from an approaching clergyman. In 1985 the author received a telephone call from a fellow enthusiast mentioning Kennedy's use of a notorious word during this scene: inspection of a print confirmed this, barely audible in the general confusion but most obvious to an alerted listener. This word has eluded censors through several reissues, frequent TV screenings, home movie editions and even soundtrack LPs, only to be discovered more than 50 years after being uttered. If you want to know *which* word, the author recommends watching *Perfect Day*!

(See also: Animals; Cars; Censorship; Cooke, Alice and Baldwin; Deslys, Kay; Food; Kennedy, Edgar; Music; Reciprocal destruction; Reissues; Sickness; Sound)

PERIODICALS
One of the outstanding publications for film collectors is the newspaper-format *Classic Images*, published from Iowa. Begun in 1962 as *8mm Collector* (with a lengthy interval as *Classic Film Collector* before acquiring its present name), *Images* has published much of value to the Laurel & Hardy enthusiast, even compiling an all-Laurel & Hardy 'special' to coincide with the 1982 International Convention of the Sons of the Desert (*qv*). During the late 1960s and early 1970s, *Film Fan Monthly* flourished under the editor-

ship of Leonard Maltin (*qv*), providing interviews, filmographies and much more. The magazine fostered the Curtis series of film paperbacks; of these *The Real Stars* and, especially, *The Laurel & Hardy Book* are of immediate interest. Magazines devoted exclusively to Laurel & Hardy tend to derive from the Sons of the Desert club. There are numerous magazines, pamphlets and newsletters originating with its various branches, or 'Tents', and a few of the major examples are worth detailing here: the 'Way Out West' Tent of California provided the first major entry with *Pratfall*, a high-quality publication exploring all manner of related material. Started in 1969, *Pratfall* surfaced at irregular intervals until vanishing in the mid-'80s. Since 1974 *The Intra-Tent Journal* has provided the Sons with a unifying link, in latter years revising its format while assuming to a certain extent some of *Pratfall*'s former role. Britain arrived with its own regular journal in 1977 with the Scottish-based *Bowler Dessert*, followed in 1979 by *Helpmates News* from the south-east of England. The latter changed its name after three years to become *The Laurel & Hardy Magazine*, one of the most widely distributed Sons journals. Both are high-quality in presentation and are devoted to collecting any relevant (and sometimes obscure!) information. Another high-quality European entry, *Blotto*, derived from Holland; while mostly in Dutch, an English-language synopsis was provided in each issue (its final edition was entirely in English).

(See also: Biographies; Homes; Locations)

PHILLIPS, CHARLIE
See: Stand-ins

PIANOS (all films *qv*)
The most famous Laurel & Hardy piano routine is their delivery of such an instrument up a flight of stairs in

The Music Box. Another piano delivery, this time in *Swiss Miss*, takes them across a mountain rope bridge. In *Way Out West*, they hide in a grand piano owned by James Finlayson (*qv*), whose more modest upright is reduced to matchwood in *Big Business*. A further piano is splintered in *Beau Hunks*, and still another in *Dirty Work*. No less murderous is Ollie's rendition of 'Chopsticks' in *Another Fine Mess*, though Thelma Todd (*qv*) seems to make a creditable pianist in *Chickens*

Pianos: the boys and their fabled burden in The Music Box

Come Home. The team's attempted burglary in *Night Owls* is interrupted by an uncontrollable player-piano, another specimen of which contributes to the party spirit of *Scram!* The most bizarre application of a piano must be that from *Wrong Again*, where Stan and Ollie manage (with understandable difficulty) to perch a horse on its lid.

(See also: Academy Awards; Agee, James; Animals)

PICK A STAR
(Laurel & Hardy guest appearance) Released by M-G-M, 21 May 1937. Produced by Edward Sedgwick for Hal Roach. Directed by Edward Sedgwick. Camera: Norbert Brodine and Art Lloyd. 70 minutes. Reissue title: *Movie Struck*.

With Patsy Kelly, Jack Haley, Rosina Lawrence, Mischa Auer, Lyda Roberti, Stan Laurel and Oliver Hardy, Walter Long, James Finlayson.

Cecilia Moore (Rosina Lawrence) wins a contest entitling her to a cash prize, a trip to Hollywood and a film role. The prizes do not materialize, but organizer Joe Jenkins is determined Cecilia should become a star, and is prepared to sell his garage to finance a trip to Hollywood to obtain film work for her. A visiting film star, Rinaldo Lopez (Mischa Auer), takes a lecherous interest in Cecilia and persuades her to travel to the film capital; Cecilia's sister Nellie (Patsy Kelly) decides to accompany her. On reaching Hollywood, Cecilia contacts Joe, not realizing he is working

as a nightclub waiter; she also contacts Lopez, who takes the girls to the night-club where Joe is employed. When the truth emerges, the girls leave, Joe following them outside where he is struck by a producer's car. Joe is unhurt but given a letter of introduction to the studio in lieu of a settlement. He had intended obtaining work for Cecilia but is instead given a job as chauffeur. Lopez takes the girls to visit the studio, where they see a musical in production before being introduced to Laurel & Hardy. Lopez takes Cecilia away in a car, unaware that Joe is driving, while Nellie remains to watch Laurel & Hardy shoot a comedy sequence. At the Lopez residence, Cecilia avoids seduction by breaking down in tears; Joe has fetched Nellie and the two confront Lopez. Joe gets the worst of a fist fight until Nellie cracks a vase over the actor's head. When the girls have departed, Lopez admits having been in the wrong and promises to arrange a screen test for Cecilia. At the studio, Cecilia is being made up when she is distracted by music. It is Stan Laurel, annoying his partner by playing on a toy trumpet. During their squabble the trumpet is thrown into a mirror. Cecilia considers the shattered mirror bad luck. Nerves ruin her test as a singer until Joe suggests she sit at the piano and join him in a duet. As there is no improvement, Joe tells her to imagine an orchestra playing. Cecilia overcomes her nerves, the studio is impressed and the young couple embrace. Lopez finds another starlet to chase while Nellie cringes at his technique.

The plot of *Pick A Star* may be traced back to the 1920s, a time when many would-be actresses were taken in by fraudulent 'trip to Hollywood' contests (Colleen Moore's *Ella Cinders* has exactly that premise). The Laurel & Hardy scenes

were shot concurrently with *Way Out West* (qv), evidenced in part by the patched denims Babe wears in both films; neither contribution is necessary to the story, but served to magnify contemporary box office potential. One problem is that exhibitors have always drawn considerable attention to their contribution, overshadowing the film's other merits; many Laurel & Hardy admirers have seen nothing but an extract titled *A Day at the Studio*, varying in length between one and two reels. The first sequence shows them as comic Mexican bandits, complete with elastic-tied moustaches and what appear to be (in the parlance of the time) marijuana cigarettes. They enter a cantina where everyone quakes but Walter Long (qv), with whom they take turns in breaking props over each other's heads. The take completed, Patsy Kelly (qv) asks the director, James Finlayson (qv) if she can talk to the boys; 'I would be very glad if you would', he replies. She asks if the routine hurt, and they explain the nature of 'breakaway' props; Ollie asks a propman for a bottle, but Patsy is given the real thing and accidentally knocks the boys unconscious. The second scene is less formal business with Stan playing first a toy trumpet, then a harmonica, Ollie competing with a tune from a much smaller example. Stan takes the tiny instrument and plays it with even greater skill. Ollie's last attempt to outshine him is by playing with the harmonica under his tongue; he swallows it and Stan finishes by playing 'Pop Goes the Weasel' by pressing Ollie's stomach.

(See also: *Big Noise, the*; Hal Roach Studio, the; Knight, Felix; Lawrence, Rosina; Reissues; Sedgwick, Edward; Smoking; Superstition; Trailers)

Pick A Star: *Laurel & Hardy's two guest sequences.*

PIE FIGHTS

See: *Battle of the Century, the*; *Hoose-Gow, the* and Slapstick

PITTS, ZASU

See: *On the Loose*, Kelly, Patsy and Todd, Thelma

PLAYS

There have been several plays based on the lives of Laurel & Hardy, such as *Laurel & Hardy* by Tom McGrath, *Stan and Ollie* by Ron Day and Nicky Paule and *Block-Heads* by Arthur Whitelaw and Mike Landwehr. McGrath's play, described in 1986 by the *Stage* as a 'blessing', has been revived on several occasions; *Block-Heads*, a musical staged at London's Mermaid Theatre in 1984, drew mixed comment from admirers, partly through the inaccurate depiction of Babe as casual philanderer. Stan in turn was shown as insanely jealous of Chaplin (*qv*), not true at all but unfortunately now gaining in currency (Milton Shulman of the London *Evening Standard* was given both this impression and the belief that Laurel & Hardy led uninteresting private lives). Reaction to its songs is typified by the *Daily Mail*'s comment of 'lamentably unmemorable', though critics had much praise for the performances of Mark Hadfield (Laurel) and Kenneth H. Waller (Hardy). Greater comment followed an earlier drama, David Allen's *Gone With Hardy*. This is reported to describe his relationship with a 'Kate Laurel', whom he abandons after taking her surname. In reality, there was neither a 'Kate Laurel' nor any deliberate theft of a name, the story suggesting a heavily fictionalized account of Stan's turbulent years with a quite different lady, Mae Laurel (*qv*). A more pleasing (if also somewhat fictionalized) dramatization of Stan's youth came from Scottish TV in 1987: titled *Stan's First Night*, it reconstructs his debut in a Glasgow music-hall as a teenager.

(See also: Apocrypha; Music-hall;

Names; *Red Mill, the*; *Waiting For Godot*)

PLINGE, WALTER

See: Clifford, Nat

'PLUMP AND RUNT'

See: *Hungry Hearts*, Names and Solo films

POFF, LON

(Laurel & Hardy films *qv*)
A minor supporting player who appeared with Babe Hardy at least as early as 1925, in the Charley Chase comedy *Isn't Life Terrible?* He is visible as a motorist in *Two Tars* and among the Laurel relatives in *The Laurel-Hardy Murder Case*; his role as a graveyard keeper in *Habeas Corpus* was deleted before release. His somewhat unusual name serves to intrigue Laurel & Hardy scholars, some of whom have suspected it to be a pseudonym; not so, the quite genuine Poff having been born in Bedford, Indiana, on 8 February 1870. He was 6' 2" in height, had blue eyes and was fond of fishing. Early stage work led to films from 1914, among them *The Old Swimming Hole*, *The Three Musketeers*, *Wheels of Chance*, *The Iron Mask*, *Lone Star Ranger*, *Behind Office Doors*, *Caught*, *Stepping Sisters*, *I Take This Woman* and *Tom Sawyer*. Poff died on 8 August 1952; an impressive filmography suggests his bit parts at Roach to have been mere postscripts to an altogether more distinguished career.

(See also: Chase, Charley)

POLICEMEN

(Laurel & Hardy films *qv*)
Officers of the law are by definition opposed to any subversive influences; Stan and Ollie are quite unintentional renegades but the giant conflicts of *Two Tars*, *The Battle of the Century*, *You're Darn Tootin'* and others are prime candidates for police intervention. As vagrants, the boys are quite content to occupy a park bench until moved on; as tradesmen, they can be

sure of uniformed interference. William K. Everson (*qv*) has identified the 'typical Hal Roach policeman' in the character who tails prison escapees Laurel & Hardy in *The Second Hundred Years*, unwilling to apprehend until sure of the facts. Others appear in *Liberty* and, most notably, *Big Business*, where Tiny Sandford (*qv*) halts the devastation only after a prolonged survey. Sandford appears in several comedies as a policeman and other regulars (all *qv*) include Harry Bernard, James C. Morton and Edgar Kennedy. Oliver Hardy's build meant that he would sometimes portray cops in his solo days, while both he and Stan Laurel join the force in *The Midnight Patrol*.

(See also: *Another Fine Mess*; *Below Zero*; Detectives; *Driver's Licence Sketch, the*; *Night Owls*; *Scram!*; Prison; *Unaccustomed As We Are*; Vagrancy)

POLITICIANS

The nearest Laurel & Hardy get to political status is Ollie's mayoral candidacy in *Chickens Come Home* (*qv*) and the ramshackle island government of *Atoll K* (*qv*). Real-life politicians have been known to express a fondness for the team, including Presidents Kennedy and Carter; other world leaders, of varying reputation, to have expressed similar appreciation have been Churchill, Stalin, Tito and Mussolini. The last-named is even said to have modelled his public image somewhat on that of Oliver Hardy, but that is a matter for conjecture. Politicians are often caricatured as Laurel & Hardy in order to belittle them; to quote only a few examples would be unfair, but the author retains pleasant memories of an early 1970s editorial cartoon in which two British leaders, whose policies were considered indecisive, were depicted carrying a piano up and down a flight of steps.

(See also: Impersonators)

POLITIQUERIAS
See: *Chickens Come Home* and Foreign versions

POLLARD, DAPHNE
(1890-1978)
(Laurel & Hardy films *qv*)
Melbourne-born Daphne Pollard was, at 4' 9", the tiniest of Ollie's screen wives, a role she has in *Thicker Than Water* and *Our Relations*. In *Bonnie Scotland* she plays a cockney ladies' maid. According to Randy Skretvedt (*qv*) she later toured in a vaudeville act based on her Laurel & Hardy appearances. She was also among the welcome veterans in *The Dancing Masters*. Daphne Pollard's stage debut was made in the 'Pollard Lilliputian Opera Company'; later success included a New York run of *Mr Hamlet of Broadway* (1908-9), vaudeville tours and musical comedies including *A Knight for A Day*, *The Candy Shop* and *The Passing Show of 1915*. There followed a 1917 London revue, *Zig-Zag*, starring George Robey. She recorded at least two songs from *Zig-Zag* (issued on Columbia L 1141), 'I Want Someone To Make A Fuss Over Me' and 'I'm A Ragtime Germ' (composed by 'Murray, Pollard and Downing'), the latter combining a musical trend with her diminutive stature. Subsequent London revues (*Box O'Tricks*, *Joy-Bells!* and *Jig-Saw*) were followed by *After Dinner* at the Lyric, then film work in America. One of her silent comedies for Mack Sennett (*qv*), *Run, Girl, Run* (1928), was used in the compilation film *The Golden Age of Comedy* (*qv*).

(See also: Women)

POLLARD, HARRY 'SNUB'
(1886-1962)
Australian-born comedian (real name Harold Fraser) who supported Harold Lloyd (*qv*) in his early shorts before taking over the series as star. Pollard's trademark was a moustache often described as an inverted Kaiser

Daphne Pollard with Babe behind the scenes of Our Relations *and (inset) as a rising stage star*

Wilhelm type. His heyday was at Roach from around 1920 to 1925, where he often benefited from the direction of Charley Chase (*qv*). He later moved to Weiss Brothers; a filmography by Richard W. Bann (*qv*) in *The Laurel & Hardy Book* refers to Pollard appearing with Marvin Lobach (1898-1938) in a remake of *Putting Pants on Philip* (*qv*). Later he was in bit roles, one of them a crowd scene in Laurel & Hardy's *One Good Turn* (*qv*). The Chief of Police in *Babes in Toyland* resembles Pollard but is in fact Billy Bletcher (*qv*).

(See also: *Days of Thrills and Laughter*;

Impersonators; Turpin, Ben)

POSTMEN (all films *qv*)
In the Laurel & Hardy world, postmen are sometimes permitted to

deliver information outside of the mail: Charlie Hall (*qv*) in *The Music Box* tells Stan and Ollie (a) where to deliver a piano and (b), much later, the easy way to reach it. Another of the breed in *Beau Hunks* delivers a 'goodbye' note from Ollie's beloved and still another brings news from Ollie's mother in *Our Relations*. Stan plays a postman, of the informal pre-Penny Post variety, in his solo comedy *Near Dublin*, while Ollie repairs to Stan's aid on the pretence of hearing the postman in *Another Fine Mess*.

(See also: Telegrams)

POWERS, LEN
See: Cameramen

PRACTICAL JOKES (all films *qv*)
Stan and Babe were fond of practical joking on-set. Something of this spirit is evident in *Busy Bodies*, when they allow their car to coast silently up to an unsuspecting Charlie Hall (*qv*) before sounding the horn. Hall once described a personal appearance with the team during which Babe thought Charlie looked perhaps a little too self-satisfied: Hall's brand-new suit was systematically destroyed by the team, to the delight not just of the audience but of the theatre manager, who requested the same routine at every performance. A practical joke in *The Live Ghost* goes awry when Ollie chooses Hall as his victim, unaware that Hall has seen Stan try the same trick; another on-screen practical joker, Charley Chase (*qv*) in *Sons of the Desert*, comes to grief when he in turn picks the wrong man. Today's club of the same name maintains something of that spirit with its periodic 'April Fool' items: one of the society's British members concocted what seemed a transparently bogus 'discovery', a non-existent film called *Fire-Raisers*, only to find the spurious item reprinted in some foreign newspapers. Jimmy Murphy (*qv*) once described various devices installed at Stan's home in Canoga Park, 'Fort

Laurel', such as a toilet seat that would sink into the floor. Over Stan's bar there hung a portrait equipped with eye-holes, through which Murphy could roll his eyes at the perplexed guests. Some of Stan's on-set foolings brought problems: during shooting of *Babes in Toyland* Stan and his regular stand-in, Ham Kinsey, threw a young extra into the film's medieval ducking-pond and were subsequently sued. Kinsey himself bore the brunt of Laurel's humour when he was left hanging from the studio ceiling in the harness used for *Way Out West*. Stan used such humour to maintain a happy working atmosphere but, as with all practical jokes, it would sometimes get out of hand; Kinsey was badly shaken and might have echoed Ollie's sentiment, quoted under **Dialogue**, regarding such pranksters.

(See also: Confidence tricks; Sons of the Desert club; Stand-ins)

PRESERVATION
The film industry's neglect of its backlog is well known, and is in some quarters still current. Established film archives have existed for the larger part of this century but there is only so much they can do, their problems including time, access, and above all finance. Fortunately a greater consciousness during the past two or three decades has improved matters somewhat, though much remains to be done. Of the Laurel & Hardy films, relatively few are lost completely but significant gaps remain (see **Lost films**). There are safety negatives and/or fine grain masters of all the English-speaking talkies in archives such as the Library of Congress, the British Film Institute and so on, though too many seem to reach TV or other revivals in muddy prints with poor sound. A worldwide comparison of each archive's holdings is at least a pleasant fantasy, providing the opportunity to compare 35mm dupe negatives with the originals, some of

Practical jokes: Leo Willis is willing to take a bet in The Live Ghost

which seem to have lost frames which could be restored without undue loss in quality. Often the Laurel & Hardy comedies are seen from 1940s reissues, distributed by a company best described as less than fussy. A Roach Studio restoration programme of the 1980s uncovered superior material to many of the duped versions normally circulated. These seem to have been reprinted on safety film despite fears of a video-only programme. Most Laurel & Hardy silents exist in good 35mm, either from negatives caught before decomposition became advanced or from first-generation positives; Blackhawk Films (*qv*) offered most of the silents in decent quality though some, such as *With Love and Hisses* (*qv*) seem to exist only in mediocre dupes from 16mm. The rediscovery of alternate material continues and we may one day see the entire Laurel & Hardy catalogue restored to satisfactory condition.

(See also: *Battle of the Century, the*; *Do Detectives Think?*; Rediscoveries; Reissues; Solo films; Television)

PREVIEWS
It remains customary for a new film to be previewed before going into release. The Laurel & Hardy films benefited enormously from such advance showings, in which the average duration of each laugh could be measured and the

editing amended to suit. Ollie's 'camera-looks' (*qv*), an ideal means of holding the action during a laugh, could be extended or abbreviated. Each laugh was timed by members of the production team placed at strategic points in the audience, using 'clicker' devices, each of their timings being compared to produce an average figure. It was usual for Stan to be in attendance but Babe avoided previews, not through any lack of interest but the result of a reluctance to watch himself on screen. He attended such occasions in earlier days when developing his character, but later preferred to let Stan relay any details. The audience-tailoring achieved through previews is a key reason for the films' greater effectiveness in a theatre. Good as they are on television, nothing can compare with seeing the films in a packed auditorium, where the laughs build and carry an audience along. The all-too-few theatrical revivals demonstrate this, transforming even the more deliberately-paced subjects that seem to drag somewhat on TV.

(See also: Television; Working titles)

PRISON
(Laurel & Hardy films *qv*)
Stan and Ollie's motives are never less than excellent, a fact commemorated in the famous introduction to *The*

Prison: Tom Kennedy and his elusive charges from Liberty

Hoose-Gow (see **Gag titles**). As suggested by its title, the film places our heroes into custody, a position often associated with the inevitable (albeit inadvertent) renegade status of the comedian. An earlier prison comedy, *The Second Hundred Years*, provided a useful means of launching them as a team; still earlier, Stan had worn prison uniform in *No Place Like Jail*, *Frauds and Frenzies* and *Detained*. *Liberty* begins with the boys escaping from prison; *Pardon Us* opens soon before their arrival. They are supposed to have absconded from jail to visit *Bonnie Scotland*, and later exploits land them in an army equivalent. Other military prisons are occupied by Stan and Ollie in *Pack Up Your Troubles* and *The Flying Deuces*, while they return to a civilian cell in *Nothing But Trouble*. The team's recurrent vagrancy motif (*qv*) often leads either to jail or at least the threat of it, as in *Scram!* and *A-Haunting We Will Go*. In *Night Owls* they are faced with a choice of imprisonment or participating in a staged burglary. Prison escapees cause havoc in *Do Detectives Think?*, *Going Bye-Bye!* and *Saps at Sea*, the last of which concludes with Stan and Ollie as reluctant guests of the Harbor Patrol. The most bizarre prison scene in the entire Laurel & Hardy repertoire ends *The Bohemian Girl*, where Stan and Ollie are released from a torture chamber as, respectively, squashed and stretched victims of Count Arnheim's henchmen.

(See also: Criminals; Freak endings; Policemen; Semon, Larry)

PROBLEM CHILD
See: Sennett, Mack and Unfilmed projects

PROHIBITION
See: Alcohol

PROSTITUTES
See: Risqué humour

Publicity: a pilgrim pose, Thanksgiving 1930

PUBLICITY
Show business, the film industry in particular, thrives on publicity. The Roach publicists issued weekly newsletters, describing anything from the progress of a new feature to the fact that swallows had invaded the premises. Like all such releases they must be viewed with a degree of scepticism, though they have their uses in tracing the development of various projects. It was quite usual for extensive press books to be issued even for the short comedies, containing illustrative ads, pre-written reviews and anecdotes. Early in Laurel & Hardy's career these would be the responsibility of Howard Dietz, better known as a songwriter but at that time making a living at M-G-M's New York office (Dietz later received co-producer credit on *Hollywood Party* [*qv*]). Press books for the features would be even more elaborate, suggesting local promotions on the intelligence level of advertising *Block-Heads* (*qv*) by having someone walk around with a cardboard block over his head. Some of the more appealing remnants of publicity material are gag shots unrelated to any of the films, particularly those tied into seasonal greetings. One of the best Christmas releases shows Marion Byron standing under some mistletoe, Ollie asserting his right to

kiss Marion before Stanley is permitted to do the same. Another set, presumably for Thanksgiving, presents the team disguised as a Pilgrim couple.

PUTTING PANTS ON PHILIP
(Laurel & Hardy film)
Released by M-G-M, 3 December 1927. Produced by Hal Roach. Directed by Clyde Bruckman. Camera: George Stevens. Two reels. Silent.
With Stan Laurel and Oliver Hardy, Dorothy Coburn, Sam Lufkin, Harvey Clark.

Young Scotsman Philip (Stan Laurel) arrives in the US in full kilted splendour. On the quayside he attracts much attention from the crowd; among those laughing loudest is the Hon. Piedmont Mumblethunder (Oliver Hardy), whose face drops on learning that Philip is the nephew he is supposed to meet. Philip's eccentric appearance draws unwelcome followers through the city streets, an embarrassment amplified by his scissor-like leap before each of his several attempts to pursue a passing flapper (Dorothy Coburn). Philip's kilt is easy prey to the gusts issuing from ventilator shafts opening into the street. When his underpants descend after a snuff-induced sneeze, a further gust is sufficient to cause mass fainting among the female onlookers. A cop intervenes, claiming 'This dame ain't got no lingerie on'. Piedmont decides it is time to put pants on Philip. At the tailor's shop, Philip is reluctant to submit to the measurement of his inside leg which, after a struggle, Piedmont succeeds in obtaining. Philip escapes, once more in pursuit of the girl, with whom he catches up shortly before she attempts to cross a puddle. In a gesture worthy of Raleigh, he places his kilt over the puddle, but the girl leaps over the kilt, imitates his scissor-leap and, laughing, continues on her way. Piedmont joins the laughter, and insists on crossing the puddle using Philip's kilt as stepping-stone. He disappears completely, returning to the surface to discover a gathered crowd now laughing at *him*.

Despite there being no in-series designation or even artistic precedent, *Putting Pants On Philip* has long been described as 'the first Laurel & Hardy film'. Both Roach and the comedians themselves tended to make this claim, ignoring the earlier films in which they appear in rather more typical form; opinion is that each considered the teamwork official from this point. Although temporarily jettisoning their newly-established characters (as they seemed determined to do throughout their earliest films), the team provides some treasured moments, not least Philip's panic at the tailor's shop and subsequent reproach of his Uncle as some kind of seducer. Several critics have compared this to a parallel sequence in their much later *Their First Mistake* (*qv*), in which the roles of betrayer and victim are reversed.

(See also: Boats, ships; Buses; Coburn, Dorothy; *Four Clowns*; Homosexuality; *Laurel & Hardy's Laughing Twenties*; Melodrama; Names; Pollard, Snub; Risqué humour; Teaming)

Putting Pants On Philip: *Uncle keeps Nephew from chasing Dorothy Coburn*

R

RACE (all films *qv*)
Humour based on ethnic or national origins was commonplace on the variety stage and in early films. This was an age when stereotypes of almost every group were portrayed without malice and accepted thus, and may perhaps be accepted in this context. It must be said that there were also exceptions that are quite unacceptable today. Larry Semon (*qv*) employed several examples, typified when in *Frauds and Frenzies* he is alarmed to discover himself in pursuit of a black girl. Less harmful is the Jewish characterization of Max Davidson (*qv*), whose portrayal leans more toward an affectionate caricature, seldom related to the gags. 'Chinamen' seem to have been considered amusing during the 1920s, there being brief, out-of-context references to them in the titling of both *Do Detectives Think?* and *Hats Off*. The reinstatement of *Early to Bed*'s original subtitles brought a moment where Stan, as Ollie's butler, is crestfallen to learn that 'a wonderful maid' is Chinese; available copies had amended this to the girl being married. Otherwise the Laurel & Hardy films are refreshingly devoid of such material, in keeping with most of the better silent comedies; Stan Laurel is in any case on record as describing racial discrimination as 'sinful'. A few exceptions creep in during earlier days: in *The Second Hundred Years* a black passer-by is accidentally painted white. Among the few racial references in talkies are the blackface scenes in *Pardon Us* and one of several

Race: June Marlowe meets a disguised Stan and Ollie in Pardon Us. *This still is from the French version, in which a foreign actor replaces Wilfred Lucas as June's father.*

cases of mistaken identity in *Pack Up Your Troubles*.

(See also: *Call of the Cuckoos*; Censorship; *Great Guns*; Moreland, Mantan)

RADIO

Many Hollywood stars found a secondary career in radio, either in formats unique to the medium or in adapted versions of their screen successes. Laurel & Hardy, less frequently on the airwaves, seldom contributed more than a few minutes of chat. Their earliest known broadcast dates from 17 January 1930, relayed 'live'

from the foyer of Grauman's Chinese Theatre during the première of *The Rogue Song* (*qv*). Ten days later, Laurel & Hardy joined Charley Chase, Thelma Todd, Harry Langdon and Our Gang (all *qv*) for KHJ's *Voices of Filmland*. This period of radio consciousness extended to the acquisition of the team's 'cuckoo' theme from KFVD radio (located on the Roach lot) and the classic short *Hog Wild*, in which Stan and Ollie try to install a rooftop aerial. Stills exist of Laurel & Hardy at the KFVD microphones but no further appearances can be traced until the UK visit of 1932 when the comedians gave a four-minute interview on the BBC's National programme. Nothing survives of this occasion, although that morning's *Daily Herald* speculated on the show's possible content, based on Laurel's remarks to a reporter the

The boys broadcast from KFVD, based on the Roach lot ...as Ollie tunes in

previous evening concerning, of all possible subjects, the graveyard in his native Ulverston. Their next radio work was back in the US, again relayed from an outside event. On the 8 December 1933 the Roach Studios' 20th birthday dinner was covered by NBC, featuring Roach stars past and present along with Louis B. Mayer, head of M-G-M. Later in the decade, Laurel & Hardy were 'invited' by gossip columnist Louella Parsons to appear on her Hollywood Hotel show. According to Stan's friend Booth Colman, Stan raised the subject of a fee, something never paid to Miss Parsons' guests, thus establishing a permanent vendetta against the comedians. Colman believed the resultant negative publicity to have damaged the team's subsequent film opportunities. It was indeed during a fallow period in their film work that Laurel & Hardy returned to the British Isles, where they broadcast for BBC North's *Morecambe Night Out* on 29 May 1947. On their last visit in 1953, they

were interviewed by Philip Garston-Jones for *What Goes On*, recorded in Northampton on 22 October and broadcast the following day. Although several US sponsors expressed interest in a Laurel & Hardy series, none ever came through and the most circulated Laurel & Hardy radio item remains a sketch known variously as *The Wedding Party*, *The Marriage of Stan Laurel* and *The Wedding Night*, this last confirmed by the more complete copies featuring an introduction by Lucille Ball. Sometimes dated as early as 1938, the sketch is more likely to have been performed in 1943, as a part of the series *Mail Call*. Taking part in the sketch are Laurel & Hardy plus Patsy Moran and Edgar Kennedy (both *qv*); cast listings crediting Patsy Kelly (*qv*) and Donald McBride may be disregarded.

(See also: Births; *Busy Bodies*; *Come Clean*; Graves; Documentaries; Interviews; M-G-M; Marriages; *Me and My Pal*; Music; Newsreels; Records; Stage appearances; Television; Weddings)

RAGUSE, ELMER (1901-?)
Sound technician who started with the Marconi company in 1919; later with Western Electric, AT&T, Bell and Victor. He arrived at Roach with the talkies or, to be more specific, with the equipment that made them and headed Roach's sound department from 1928, interrupted by a two-year stint (1932-3) in the same capacity at Fox. He later served as a director of the Motion Picture Research Council. Several (but not all) Film Classics reissue titles mis-spell his name 'Roguse', typical of the company's apparent carelessness.

(See also: Reissues; Sound; Titling)

RAIN (all films *qv*)
Yes, it even rains in sunny California and Stan Laurel's battle with James Finlayson (*qv*) in *The Soilers* is preceded by a massive downpour.

Inclement conditions dominate *Scram!* and provide a nasty moment in *Sons of the Desert* when our heroes are trapped on the roof in a rainstorm. Another thunderstorm concludes *Helpmates*, too late to extinguish Ollie's burning house but just in time to drench him through the open roof. The storm sequences of *The Rogue Song*, *The Laurel-Hardy Murder Case* and *Atoll K* offer their own precipitation; several other films circulate in prints that only *seem* to depict rain.

(See also: Preservation; Snow)

RAMISH, ADOLPH
See: *Just Nuts*

RANDOLPH (OR RANDOLF), ANDERS (1876-1930)
Character actor from the Broadway stage who plays the Police chief whose house is burgled by Laurel & Hardy in *Night Owls* (*qv*). Twenties features include *Peacock Alley*, *Moriarty*, *The Bright Shawl*, *Dorothy Vernon of Haddon Hall*, *Seven Keys to Baldpate*, *The Loves of Sunya*, *Four Devils*, *The Jazz Singer*, *A Son of the Gods*, *The Kiss*, *Noah's Ark* and *The Climbers*. He is known also by the names Rudolph Anders, Rudolf Ament and Robert O. Davis amongst others.

(See also: Policemen)

Anders Randolph gets dunked as a horrified Charley Chase looks on. From Chase's Snappy Sneezer *(1929)*

THE RAP
See: *Pardon Us* and Working titles

RAWLINSON, HERBERT
20th Century-Fox (1885-1953)
Leading man of the silent screen,
born in Britain. His American films
from 1911 include shorts, features and
a number of serials. He turned to
character roles in talkies, his last
appearance being in *Gene Autry and
the Mounties* (1951). Evidence of a faltering career is suggested by his
appearance in *Slipping Wives* (*qv*), one
of the Roach films dependent on
declining stars.

(See also: Dean, Priscilla; 'Fading
stars'; Teaming)

RAY, BOBBY
See: *Stick Around*

REBELLIONS (BY STANLEY)
(all films *qv*)
Although Ollie takes the dominant
role in the team's on-screen relationship, there are moments when Stan
feels it appropriate to rebel. These
transcend their momentary squabbles
(as in *Men O'War*, *Below Zero*, etc.) by
reversing their positions so that Ollie
is totally at Stan's mercy, so reminding us that the balance of their
relationship, like so many real-life
counterparts, depends largely on
mutual acceptance. Stan first fights
back in *Early To Bed*, having been tor-
mented by a *nouveau-riche* Ollie to the
point where he is willing to be
thought rabid. *One Good Turn* is
interesting because Ollie's reactions
are that of a playground bully on
whom the tables have been turned.
Helpmates defines a contained rebellion, in that Stan, having done his best
to assist his friend, objects to Ollie's
manner but is routed by mere words:

Stan: If I had any sense I'd walk out
on you!
Ollie: Well, it's a good thing you
haven't any sense.
Stan: It certainly is!

Such defiance is therefore only temporary. The status quo is restored
usually by some act of Stan's that puts
him in the place he expects to be, as
when in *One Good Turn* the logs he
sends crashing down on Ollie's head
are followed by another landing on his
own. This is entirely in keeping with
their established characters, which
cannot be said of an example from the
20th Century-Fox series (*qv*), *The
Dancing Masters*, when a trivial incident leads to them squaring up for a
fist fight.

(See also: Characters; Dialogue)

RECIPROCAL DESTRUCTION
(Laurel & Hardy films *qv*)
The ordered exchange of violence,
defined by Stan Laurel for John
McCabe (*qv*) as 'reciprocal destruction', owes its origin to Leo McCarey
(*qv*). Quoted by Peter Bogdanovich in
his book *Picture Show*, McCarey
recalls visiting New York with Hal
Roach, Mabel Normand, Charley
Chase (all *qv*) and others, all of them
aware of McCarey's inability to master
a bow tie. When they prepared to visit
a nightclub, Mabel suggested that
nobody should help McCarey with his
tie, forcing him to stay behind. The
desperate McCarey telephoned
California hoping to locate friends
who could give him instructions.
They were finally traced to a New
York number and were able to help.
McCarey caught up with the party,
explained what had happened then
had his tie pulled loose by Mabel.
Amid the laughter, McCarey pulled
Roach's tie loose, then Roach pulled
someone else's tie loose; once the ties
were exhausted, collars became the
next target until someone realised how
easy it was to pass a knife up the back
seam of a dinner jacket. 'That,' said
McCarey, 'was the basis of at least a
dozen Laurel & Hardy films'. The
rules of reciprocal destruction are
roughly as follows: an initial misunderstanding leads to the infliction of
an indignity; the recipient reacts,

slowly, before responding with a like
indignity; this in turn brings a further
indignity, the pace quickening gradually each time. Ultimately the
exchanges of violence are quite frenzied, and may continue to alternate (as
in *Tit For Tat*) or work in parallel (*Big
Business*). In either case an onlooker
familiar with only the latter stage
should find the result inexplicable.
Sometimes, as in *Perfect Day*, the
game is aborted prior to the final
stage; many others go no further than
preliminaries, as with Laurel & Hardy
versus Finlayson in *Our Relations*.
These preliminaries are often no less
savage than the concluding stage, this
example including the burning of
Finlayson's nose in a lamp socket. As
a team sport, reciprocal destruction
should spread to passers-by in the
manner demonstrated by the
McCarey prototype. *Two Tars*, *You're
Darn Tootin'* and *The Battle of the
Century* escalate in this way and are
more effective if most additional participants are kept ignorant of how the
game started. Eventual prize for all
concerned is serious loss of dignity,
property or both. On no account must
the activity be initiated with the idea
of enjoyment, although the infliction
of indignities must be savoured to the
full.

(See also: Chase, Charley; Finlayson,
James; Hall, Charlie; *Hoose-Gow, the*;
Normand, Mabel; Slapstick)

RECORDS (all films *qv*)
Gramophone records feature in a few
of the team's gags. Stan brings home a
Chinese record in *Their Purple
Moment* and wants to hear 'The
Maiden's Prayer' in *Should Married
Men Go Home?* The boys wreck a
gramophone and discs owned by
James Finlayson (*qv*) in *Liberty* and
Mae Busch (*qv*) breaks a disc over
Ollie's head in *Unaccustomed As We
Are*. *The Chimp* in the film of that
name dances to a record being played
in an adjoining room; while a gramo-
phone serves as car radio in *Busy*

Bodies. Stan and Babe made only one commercial record, a 78 from their visit to London in 1932. *Hal Roach and Metro-Goldwyn-Mayer present Laurel & Hardy* (Columbia DX-370) is a 12" disc consisting of a sketch (written by Stan) followed by a dance arrangement of their 'cuckoo' theme by Van Phillips. This record has been reissued on a few compilation albums, sometimes in abridged form. One of these, *The Golden Age of Comedy* (distributed in Britain by Charisma) has a sleeve illustrated by Al Kilgore (*qv*). A 10" 78, one of the annual *Voice of the Stars* records sold for charity (Regal-Zonophone MR 1234) incorporates a brief clip from *Sons of the Desert*. Coinciding with the tour were several disc versions of the Laurel & Hardy theme, some by dance bands and one by comedian Leonard Henry. Much later microgroove collections of soundtrack highlights appeared: pioneer in the field was Douglas Records' *Laurel & Hardy: Naturally High*, a title betraying somewhat its 1970 release date (as does its psychedelic sleeve design). Five years later, the British end of United Artists records issued as a single *The Trail of the Lonesome Pine* (from *Way Out West*), making an unexpected Christmas hit (at around the same time Spark records issued the Laurel & Hardy theme played by the Band of the Black Watch). The disc (UP 36026) remained at second place in the UK charts for several weeks, being held back from Number One by Queen's *Bohemian Rhapsody*. UA's attempted follow-up, *Another Fine Mess* (UP 36107), is a song by the Boston Barbers interspersed with soundtrack excerpts; it didn't sell. More successful were UA's album collections, *Laurel & Hardy: the Golden Age of Hollywood Comedy* and (inevitably) *Another Fine Mess*. EMI have since reissued both in a double-cassette pack. Contemporary American albums explored similar territory: *No U-Turn* and *In Trouble Again!* offered more clips while there were also whole LPs

devoted to *Sons of the Desert* and *Babes in Toyland*. The recovery of *The Rogue Song* soundtrack in 1980 resulted in a Pelican Records LP (LP 2019); a few years later Columbia (UK) released a single of *The Flying Deuces* song 'Shine On Harvest Moon' (DB 9145), punctuated with dialogue from both the film and the 1932 disc. Still later, another British firm began to issue soundtrack selections on singles, LPs, cassettes and compact discs. Among the odds and ends are *Voices From The Hollywood Past* (Delos DEL F25412) with the 1959 Tony Thomas-Stan Laurel interview, and Radiola's *Laurel & Hardy On The Air*. One pleasant footnote: a Harry Nilsson album titled *A Little Touch of Schmilsson in the Night* includes a version of 'Lazy Moon'; Nilsson,who was reportedly a great Laurel & Hardy admirer, is shown on the cover lighting his thumb as Stan does in *Way Out West*. Original copies have sleeve notes stating that the publishers knew of no earlier recording. The note adds: 'but we know Oliver Norville [*sic*] Hardy sang it in a movie in the 1930s. Harry found it. It is most certainly 70 years old. Now... guess... *which* movie?' The answer is of course *Pardon Us*, though an even older version may be found on a British HMV disc, *Minstrel Show of 1929*. Students of chart music may also recall Wayne Fontana's 'Pamela, Pamela' (1966) with its reference to Laurel & Hardy in the lyrics, and the Equals' 1968 hit 'Laurel & Hardy'. In 1983 British admirers were variously amused or annoyed to learn of a single called 'Clunk Click' credited to a young duo billed as 'Laurel & Hardy'.

(See also: Interviews; Music; Radio; Songs; Stage appearances; 'White magic')

REDISCOVERIES

(Laurel & Hardy films *qv*)
Although much early cinema has vanished, discoveries continue to be made: the importance of *Duck Soup* (*qv*), was not realized until it resurfaced

during the 1970s. A lesser work, but one much referred to anecdotally, is *Why Girls Love Sailors*. After persistent rumour, the film was finally located in the mid-1980s. One of the most famous Laurel & Hardy silents, *The Battle of the Century*, was thought to exist only in the climactic pie-fight sequence preserved in *The Golden Age of Comedy* (*qv*) until its first reel was recovered in 1979. *The Rogue Song* has reappeared in fragments, starting with a complete soundtrack, followed by three minutes of film. During 1992-3 a mute trailer and a reel of 'plot' footage were traced. Many of the foreign versions (*qv*) remain elusive, but several Spanish titles were located in the M-G-M vaults. There have been a mumber of rediscovered solo appearances. At the end of 1984, two Yorkshire-based members of the Sons of the Desert (*qv*) located a unique, privately held copy of the 1915 Hardy solo film *Something in Her Eye* which was passed to the National Film Archive early the following year. It had been thought that comedienne Billie Rhodes was leading lady, but she is not present and the unidentified actress (believed by some to be a female impersonator!) bears an appropriate question mark under her eye. The film may be seen complete in the documentary *Laurel & Hardy: Archive Rarities*. Among the more recent solo finds are *Get 'Em Young* and the '106th' Laurel & Hardy film, *Now I'll Tell One*.

(See also: Buses; Documentaries; Lost films; Solo films; Teaming)

THE RED MILL

Stan Laurel considered adapting Victor Herbert's 1906 operetta *The Red Mill* (book and lyrics by Henry Blossom) for a stage run in the early 1940s. The team had satisfactorily filmed the same composer's *Babes in Toyland* (*qv*) but it is harder to see how they might fit into this tale, concerning fleeing lovers who echo an old legend by hiding in a mill. Perhaps

Stan saw himself and Babe assisting the unfortunate couple, in servant roles reminiscent of *Fra Diavolo* (*qv*). The idea was in any case abandoned in favour of touring with *The Laurel & Hardy Revue* (*qv*), using a driving-licence sketch first performed by Laurel & Hardy at a Red Cross benefit.

(See also: *Driver's Licence Sketch, the*; Herbert, Victor; Operas; Stage appearances)

REEVES, ALF (1876-1946)
Business manager for Fred Karno (*qv*) who supervised the tours of America, and later took up a similar administrative post with Charlie Chaplin (*qv*). It has been said that Reeves unofficially kept Chaplin and Laurel informed of each other's activities. His wife, Amy Minister, was the unfortunate woman pelted by Chaplin in *Mumming Birds* (*qv*). Chaplin had taken over the role of Drunk from Reeves' brother Billie (1866-1945),

BILLIE REEVES,
The Original Drunk,
Fred Karno's 'Mumming Birds'

REVUE:
"Folies Bergeres Paris"
Principal Comedian, Xmas Run.

All Coms.—Reeves & Lamport,
18, Charing Cross Rd., W.C.2

Billie Reeves recalls earlier glories in a 1920s trade ad
By courtesy of Michael Pointon

who anticipated Chaplin further through having been 'discovered' by the Americans on an earlier Karno trip. He appeared in several editions of the Ziegfeld *Follies* from 1908 and from 1915 made film comedies for Lubin. Attempts were made to put Reeves into a Chaplin costume but he refused. Kalton C. Lahue and Sam Gill (in *Clown Princes and Court Jesters*) have compared Reeves' facial qualities to those later associated with Keaton. Film proved less than satisfying to the comedian, who returned to the stage.

(See also: Circuses; Keaton, Buster; Lubin, Siegmund 'Pop')

REINCARNATION
The belief in returning after a previous life was one that Stan Laurel considered a possible explanation for child prodigies. The concept was used as the final gag in *The Flying Deuces* (*qv*) when Ollie, having failed to survive their airborne escape from the Foreign Legion, reappears as a horse. A non-Laurel & Hardy segment of *Hollywood Party* (*qv*) incorporates a song, descriptively titled 'Reincarnation', in which Jimmy Durante sings of his past lives; the equine aspect of *Deuces* may perhaps be traced back to Durante's claim to have been Paul Revere's horse!

(See also: Disney, Walt)

REISSUES (Laurel & Hardy films *qv*)
Laurel & Hardy's films have been kept in public view almost continuously since the 1920s. During production of the series, reissues of the short films were unnecessary and in a sense undesirable, given the frequency with which storylines and gags were reworked. The silent films were of course unsuitable for 1930s audiences and their oblivion seemed assured. When Roach abandoned production of the shorts in the later 1930s, several earlier talkies were updated with new credits omitting the gag titles (themselves a relic of silent days) together with added scores from the team's then-current features. Films treated in this way include *Perfect Day*, *Blotto*, *Brats* and *County Hospital*. *Berth Marks* emerged as a hybrid, retaining the full titling of its 1929 release but with the 'cuckoo' theme as intro, outro *and* incidental music during the first scene. *Beau Hunks* lost its gag opening and was re-scored only over the main titles. Most of the scored versions benefited from the experience and the title deletions may be considered minor, though footage was deleted from *Blotto* and *Beau Hunks*.

Greater damage was to be inflicted in the 1940s by a company known as Film Classics. On acquiring the Roach backlog for reissue, Film Classics replaced some or all of the credits on each subject, sometimes committing errors along the way. Most of the films were otherwise uncut, though the heavily abridged versions of *Blotto* and *Pack Up Your Troubles* seem to date from this period. On occasion, the material used was not of optimum quality: until recently copies of *Men O'War* and *The Hoose-Gow* derived exclusively from the muddy Film Classics editions. The new, clean copies are the result of a restoration campaign from the 1980s, in which American video masters were taken from camera negative or, when necessary, first-generation prints. Most of the Roach titling was reinstated and quality restored to something approaching the original release. These restorations formed the basis of *The Laurel & Hardy Show* in the States but several were abridged for this package; they have so far reached Britain only in computer-coloured form, some of them similarly abridged. There has yet to be a comparable revival of the team's silent output, although Film Classics distributed prints of at least two such subjects (*Liberty* and *Double Whoopee*). The nearest so far has been a 1980s package of Laurel & Hardy silents touring the US, in new 35mm prints. Quality of each was excellent, with the single exception of *Duck Soup*, which survives only in material duped from old prints. It is to be hoped that most of the silent shorts may be restored to pristine condition and made available for screening.

(See also: Alternate titles; *Babes in Toyland*; Blackhawk Films; Censorship; Colour; Compilations; Music; Television; Titling; Video releases)

REMAKES
(Laurel & Hardy films *qv*)

It is a tradition among comedians, especially those from the variety stage, to rework and polish material over the years. The film industry itself has always displayed a tendency to remake its successes, sometimes inadvisedly. The necessary tailoring of vehicles for star comedians tends to mean that even acknowledged remakes require substantial revision (it takes some foreknowledge to identify Eddie Cantor's *Whoopee* as the model for Danny Kaye's *Up in Arms*). Remakes of Laurel & Hardy subjects by others are difficult to specify although Abbott & Costello's *Buck Privates Come Home* is reminiscent of Laurel & Hardy's *Pack Up Your Troubles*. Many of the Three Stooges' shorts owe something to Laurel & Hardy subjects (perhaps prompting Laurel's comment that the trio were 'hardly original') and *Hats Off* was the clear inspiration behind the 1945 short *It's Your Move*, starring Edgar Kennedy. Perhaps the most obvious *hommage* of recent years has been Blake Edwards' *A Fine Mess* (*qv*). Many Laurel & Hardy comedies are interlinked with their earlier films, together and solo: Laurel's *Smithy* provided the basis for a Laurel & Hardy silent, *The Finishing Touch*, while his *Detained* (1924), itself reminiscent of the earlier *Frauds and Frenzies*, contains elements that resurface in Laurel & Hardy's *The Second Hundred Years*. Pinpointing comparable descendants of Hardy's early work is more difficult, although William K. Everson (*qv*) has drawn comparison between *Brats* and a scene from *Playmates*, a 1918 comedy in which Billy West (*qv*) and Oliver Hardy appear as infants. This clip has been shown in Paul Killiam's TV series *Silents Please*. Less specifically, Hardy himself traced much of his conception of the team's style to his work with Bobby Ray, particularly in the 1925 two-reeler *Stick Around* (*qv*). *We Faw Down*'s plot is a simplified version of what became the feature-length *Sons of the Desert*, and *Block-Heads* is an expansion of their first talkie,

Unaccustomed As We Are. One particularly fruitful source was their last silent comedy, *Angora Love*. Closely remade as *Laughing Gravy*, the basic situation appeared once more as *The Chimp* with isolated routines being revived in *Be Big* and *Beau Hunks*. Other individual routines from silent days would recur: the dentistry scenes from *Leave 'Em Laughing* found a new home in *Pardon Us*, while a sequence in *Should Married Men Go Home?* was reused in *Men O'War*. This revival in *Men O'War* (itself suggested by the silent *Two Tars*) provides a representative example of the way such repetition would improve on the original: the scene, involving Laurel & Hardy entertaining two girls at a soda fountain despite insufficient funds, requires Stan to refuse a drink. In each version Stan is left with a bill he cannot pay, but while the earlier silent abandons the idea with a title card explaining that Stan's watch covered the thirty-cent bill ('It was that kind of watch'), the talkie equivalent develops the notion of his gambling what money they have in a fruit machine, winning enough not merely to settle the bill but also to facilitate the next scene by financing their trip on the boating lake. Sometimes minor plot elements would resurface in later films: *Do Detectives Think?*, with its motif of a convicted murderer out for revenge, is a vague ancestor of *Going Bye-Bye!*, while a complete remake of *From Soup To Nuts* formed the first two reels of *A Chump at Oxford*. Among other remade silents are *Duck Soup*, which became *Another Fine Mess*; *Slipping Wives*, protoype of *The Fixer-Uppers*; *Love 'Em and Weep*, reworked as *Chickens Come Home*; and *Hats Off*, inspiration for both a succession of street battles and, later, their Oscar-winning *The Music Box*. Recalling this for a *Film Weekly* reporter in 1935, Stan explained that the steps in *Hats Off* 'produced such roars of laughter that we remembered it when the piano story cropped up, and we adapted it without apologies.

Why not? It fitted the story perfectly'. Stan did not believe in reworking material simply because it was good, but had no qualms about adapting and improving suitable routines. The 1940s films for 20th Century-Fox and M-G-M (both *qv*) are filled with reworked sequences inserted at random by often unsympathetic writers: *The Dancing Masters* throws together material lifted from *Thicker Than Water*, *The Battle of the Century* and *County Hospital*. Objection to these reworkings derives chiefly from their inappropriate context plus a reluctance to update and improve. The best-known example concerns the writers' decision to incorporate the shared upper-berth routine from *Berth Marks* into *The Big Noise*. Stan Laurel suggested an airline setting, with consequent opportunity for gags, rather than the earlier railroad idea. He was ignored.

(See also: Costello, Lou; Kennedy, Edgar; Sequels)

THE RENT COLLECTOR (1921)
For a while there was speculation on the possibility of an undocumented Laurel & Hardy appearance, a wish probably based on an enthusiastic desire for more footage but which involved much genuine and meticulous research. Such a film was indeed unearthed, the 1927 release *Now I'll Tell One* (*qv*), but a long-standing contender was *The Rent Collector*, a Vitagraph comedy starring Larry Semon (*qv*). Although Hardy's appearance in the film was known, many believed that Stan Laurel might also be present in the cast, based on the comedian's personal film listings. His acrimonious parting with Semon in 1918 rendered such an appearance unlikely, but the film was not known to exist and thus found its way into at least one Laurel & Hardy filmography. When copies began to resurface, *The Rent Collector* was confirmed as another Hardy solo effort. The plot is a fairly direct lift from Chaplin's *Easy*

Street, except that Semon enters a tough neighbourhood to collect rent and evict defaulters rather than enforce the law. Babe parallels Eric Campbell as the unshaven bully who terrorizes neighbours and officialdom alike. Larry arrives, throwing the villain's furniture into the street; ordered to take it back inside, Larry breaks a wooden dresser over Babe's head. A chase follows and the leading lady is abducted; she is rescued, in a car driven by Larry as Babe gives chase. *The Rent Collector* is Semon's usual slapstick, the finest moment being one of Babe sitting in a barber's chair as an enormous quantity of tar covers his face.

(See also: Chaplin, Charlie; Rediscoveries; Slapstick; Solo films; Vitagraph)

REVIEWS

(Laurel & Hardy films *qv*)
It is generally held that Laurel & Hardy were, in their day, unappreciated by critics, at least in the US. Outside the trade press, where even the shorts were evaluated independently and often appreciatively, there is evidence of hostility. Many offered but condescending praise: Bosley Crowther is enthusiastic about *Swiss Miss*, but when he admits to becoming a 'convert' to their humour of 'the best two-reeler tradition', and refers to the need to ward off 'accusations of a bias toward infantilism', his defence becomes implied condemnation. This is also partly true of Frank S. Nugent's view of a 'little slapstick' called *Way Out West*, which concentrates more on the inherent funniness of their physiques than on construction and nuance. Nugent's comment that 'too many books are being written on the anatomy of humor and none on the humor of anatomy' doubtless appealed to Stan, but their most perceptive defender was Pare Lorentz, whose remarks on *Blotto* and *Fra Diavolo*

are cited elsewhere. Richard Watts, Jr. liked them, yet viewed *Sons of the Desert* with the belief that 'they never quite manage to seem really hilarious humorists'. He did admit that the screening was crowded with those of a different opinion. The *Herald-Tribune* attributed the merits of *Block-Heads* to a co-writing credit for Harry Langdon (qv), describing him at his best as 'a greater comedian than either the sad-faced man or the fat fellow ever could be'. This preposterous statement is rivalled only by the consistently bad reviews from *Variety* which, as noted by Rick Greene in *The Intra-Tent Journal*, may not be an entirely objective source. Even today, it maintains a stance and vocabulary inherited from a tough, vaudeville-minded mentor, Sime Silverman, who during 1915 sneered consistently at the Essanay films that made Chaplin a world-wide celebrity. There was little praise for the Laurel & Hardy comedies, perhaps because they avoided undue chat; to reviewers accustomed more to rapid cross-talk acts, the methodical, visual duo must have seemed incomprehensible. One might query *Variety's* review of *Way Out West*, which refers to the team's retention of their standard costumes regardless of setting: Victorian frock-coats and denim trousers were not exactly 'standard costume', even if the comedians could be said to have had such a thing. *Variety* had occasional kind words (for *Babes in Toyland* and *Our Relations*) but reserved a complete turnabout in opinion until Laurel & Hardy's debut at 20th Century-Fox (qv), *Great Guns*. This invites the assumption that obvious slapstick and unsuitably barbed dialogue conformed more to vaudeville's notion of an ideal double-act. British sources would publicize Laurel & Hardy heavily: the shorts, often ignored in the States, won praise and would frequently share

billing with the feature attraction. Even the weaker 1940s entries drew favour, *The Cinema* having commented on the 'hilarious craziness' of *A-Haunting We Will Go* and the 'rollicking' story of the often morbid *Air Raid Wardens*. Each Laurel & Hardy feature would be considered a major event, as when *Bonnie Scotland* dominated most of *Film Weekly* on 28 June 1935. Among the best-known British reviews is that by Graham Greene, the novelist and critic. In the *Spectator* he greeted *A Chump at Oxford* as 'better news than anything the papers print', evaluating Laurel & Hardy's films as 'more agreeable than Chaplin's; their clowning is purer; they aren't out to better an unbetterable world'. This echoes Crowther's stance rather less than John Grierson's comment of 1931, where he considered them to be 'perhaps the Civil Servants of comedy' who, like the rest of us, have to function within a sometimes intolerable environment.

(See also: Agee, James; *Angora Love*; Feature films; *Perfect Day*; Short films; Sound; Stage appearances; Wright, Basil)

REX, THE KING OF WILD HORSES
See: Solo films

RICHARD, VIOLA

(Laurel & Hardy films *qv*)
Lively brunette in many of the early Laurel & Hardy silents. She is the heroine of *Why Girls Love Sailors*, one of the passengers in *Sailors Beware*, Finlayson's wife in *Do Detectives Think?*, his daughter in *Flying Elephants*, a nurse in *Leave 'Em Laughing* and Ollie's girlfriend in *Should Married Men Go Home?*. Along with Dorothy Coburn and Edna Marian (both *qv*), Viola Richard vanished from the Roach lot in the summer of 1928, presumably the victim of one of the studio's periodic economy drives (though she has been

Viola Richard hitches a lift in this publicity shot. Note the film crates marked for Eastman's 'ortho' stock, the type insensitive to Stan's blue eyes

reported as an extra in *Tit For Tat*). William K. Everson (*qv*) has remarked upon her vivacity, looks and timing, and suggests that her career may have been handicapped by a close resemblance to Clara Bow; her abrupt dismissal is nonetheless one of Roach's less explicable moves. Viola Richard was perhaps used to best advantage in some of the Charley Chase comedies, particularly *Never the Dames Shall Meet* (1927) and *Limousine Love* (1928). The latter, presented almost intact in *Four Clowns* (*qv*), is the memorable occasion wherein Chase drives to his wedding with a naked Miss Richard in the back of his car.

(See also: Chase, Charley; Garvin, Anita)

RIDING HIGH (1950)
Babe Hardy made his last solo appearance in Frank Capra's remake of his own *Broadway Bill* (1934). He contributes a small section as a luckless racetrack gambler who is persuaded to back the hopeless 'Doughboy' as part of a scam. Superficially 'Ollie', wearing his bowler hat but with a checked suit more reminiscent of *Jitterbugs* (*qv*), he spreads the news of a hot tip through an increasingly hysterical crowd. 'Doughboy' comes nowhere and Hardy is carried out of the stadium, repeating the horse's name over

and over. Capra's autobiography, *The Name Above the Title* (1971), describes the necessity for such efficient, sure-fire talent in a tightly-budgeted film. He had seen Hardy in *The Fighting Kentuckian* (*qv*) and thought him ideal. In 1980, Capra told British documentary-maker Michael Pointon of his long-standing admiration for Laurel & Hardy, adding how pleased he was to direct Hardy: 'I was such a fan of his... that helps a lot, you know, when's he's funny to you - and he was just as funny as ever'. Additional incentive came from the film's star, Bing Crosby, a golfing pal of Babe's who pointed out to him the similarity of the role to Hardy's own racing disasters. 'Unfortunately,' admitted Babe, 'that character does sound like this particular Southern gentleman'.

(See also: Animals; Gambling; Golf; Langdon, Harry; McCarey, Leo; Solo films; *Wrong Again*)

RIGOLETTO
See: Lawrence, Rosina, Operas and Unfilmed projects

RISQUÉ HUMOUR (all films *qv*)
Many Hollywood films of Laurel & Hardy's period employ a degree of risqué humour. The Production Code of 1934 brought film censorship the power to eradicate anything of this nature, although the more skilled film-makers could often defeat the

Babe as the luckless gambler in Capra's **Riding High** *BFI Stills, Posters and Designs*

censor by subtle tactics. The Laurel & Hardy films are not often associated with such material. John McCabe (*qv*) encapsulated it neatly when, in describing *Scram!*, he considered it 'a great tribute to the essential decency of the Laurel & Hardy films that a scene showing two men and a woman all in pajamas laughing and bouncing drunkenly on the same bed does not have even a faint touch of suggestiveness about it'. That this decency is automatically accepted derives partly from the fact that, in common with most major talents, Laurel & Hardy had no need to employ anything of a risqué nature. This they believed important, being particularly aware of their popularity with audiences of all ages. In addition, scenes such as that quoted above demonstrate that even potentially outrageous events would be robbed of any salacious interpretation by the basic innocence of their characterizations. We know instinctively that they have no dishonourable intentions toward the woman they have (unwittingly) filled with gin, just as they are laughing and singing quite innocently with a similarly intoxicated Mae Busch (*qv*) in *Them Thar Hills*. This same innocence makes acceptable the few authentic examples of relative daring in their films, notably the fairly blatant representations of prostitutes (usually, though not exclusively, portrayed by Mae Busch). Most of these examples belong to the earlier days, when silent comedy abounded in gags that sometimes startle modern viewers who think their age has some sort of monopoly. A Hardy solo film, *Along Came Auntie*, shows Babe beating a drum until seeing Vivien Oakfield (*qv*), whereupon he suffers an instantly wilting drumstick. This surprising gag may be seen in *Laurel & Hardy's Laughing Twenties* (*qv*). *Slipping Wives* concerns a neglected wife employing a man (Stan) to pose as her lover in order to rekindle the husband's interest. Through a complicated and ingenious series of accidents, the two are caught momentarily in bed. Innocuous enough in print, but the speed of the action (especially when combined with an existing knowledge of movie censorship) still produces a startling moment. Justly famous is the finale of *We Faw Down*, in which the blast of a shotgun is sufficient to bring forth countless, often trouserless, men from the apartments nearby. This gag was repeated in their later film *Block-Heads*. Another of the better-known examples is *Putting Pants On Philip*, about the hopeless efforts of an American host (Hardy) to amend the conspicuous wardrobe of his kilted Scottish nephew (Laurel). The nephew's panic at attempts to measure his inside leg is solely that of affronted innocence, but the audience is aware of the implications. This straightforward vulgarity reached its zenith in *With Love and Hisses*; today's audiences may also be surprised when in the latter film Laurel, Hardy and comrades appear seemingly nude. Some of the sound films include a gentler sauciness, as when in *Men O'War*, Stan and Ollie discover a pair of bloomers just as Anne Cornwall has lost her gloves. The inevitable confusion results, with coy exchanges such as 'Good thing it's warm weather' and, to the boys' amazement, 'I just cleaned them with gasoline, too!'. Further misunderstandings plague the team in their attempts to trace the grandparents of a young orphan in *Pack Up Your Troubles* as many of those approached misconstrue the enquiry as being an accusation of paternity; a similar matter is suggested in *The Laurel-Hardy Murder Case* when Stan claims to be a Laurel only on his 'mother's side'. *Their First Mistake* is perhaps their most risqué moment in talkies. Stan has suggested that Ollie adopt a baby in order to ease Mrs. Hardy's wrath; they return with the child, only to find Mrs. Hardy to have left seeking a divorce in which Stan will be taken 'hook, line and sinker'. Ollie: 'Why, I'll be ostracized!' Stan: 'Well, I'm going to lose

my hook, line and sinker!' Such *double entendres* make but few appearances. The dialogue in *Another Fine Mess* between Stan (dressed as a maidservant) and prospective tenant Thelma Todd (*qv*) includes the latter's surprise at the unmarried householder maintaining a nursery: 'He has that in case of accidents', she is told. In *The Music Box*, a nurse complains of having been kicked in the middle of her 'daily duties', while another nurse in *Thicker Than Water* tells a visiting Stan that Mr. Hardy is 'convalescing': 'All right,' says Stan, 'I'll wait 'til he gets through'. In *County Hospital*, Stan is directed to 'room 14', only to watch a baby being taken from the room. Stan is relieved to learn that Ollie may be found in room 14 on the *top* floor. A parallel gag occurs in *Saps at Sea*, when Ollie is suitably alarmed at hearing a concealed 'mama' doll during the sounding of his chest. The inappropriate scripting for their 1940s films at the big studios is manifest in a segment from *Nothing But Trouble*, where a series of unwitting *double entendres* from Mary Boland (*qv*) provoke worried reactions from Laurel & Hardy concerning the nature of their new employment.

(See also: Dialogue; Homosexuality; Nudity; *That's My Wife*)

ROACH, HAL EUGENE
(1892-1992)
Among the few movie people to reach a century, Hal Roach was born in Elmira, New York on 14 January 1892 (four days before Oliver Hardy). He left home at 16, travelling between Seattle and Alaska before working in construction in the Mojave Desert. While in Los Angeles he auditioned for a film company that would later become Universal, and on set, his Seattle experience paid off when he was the only actor present who knew how to operate a roulette wheel. This was 1912, when $5 a day as an actor was infinitely preferable to the construction business. His big moment

was playing 'heavy' to J. Warren Kerrigan: 'I was supposed to age from 20 to 60 in the picture; when I finally saw the picture in a theatre, I looked the same... except I had lines in my face that I'd put on myself and I had talcum powder in my hair'. Around this time Roach met Harold Lloyd (*qv*) and Frank Borzage (1893-1962), later a famous director; their claim to fame was playing the three eunuchs who witnessed the birth of Samson. Lloyd was to become Roach's star when starting up his first studio, Rolin (*qv*). When Roach's partner was bought out, the enterprise became known as the Hal Roach Studios (*qv*). The studio's history is detailed elsewhere but Roach himself outlived his business, its major stars and in a sense the industry he helped to create. He was also pre-deceased by his wives and children: his first wife, former screen actress Margaret (or Marguerite) Nichols, died in 1941, aged 41; their son, Hal Roach Jr., died in 1972, aged 53; their daughter Margaret, whose screen career was as 'Diane Rochelle', died in 1964 at the age of 43. Another daughter, Elizabeth (from Roach's second marriage) was born in 1946 but lived only eight months. Margaret Jr.'s career was not assisted by her father: the *Film Weekly* of 22 October 1938 mentions this and her recent engagement as cabaret singer at a nightclub called La Conga.

Hal Roach visits the set of Angora Love

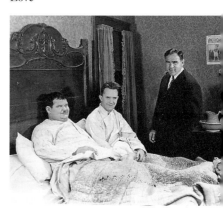

Her film appearances include a walk-on in Laurel & Hardy's Fox film *A-Haunting We Will Go* (*qv*). Hal Jr. took over his father's studio and may be seen in Laurel & Hardy's *This Is Your Life* (see **Television**). Toward the end of his life, Hal Roach visited the UK on two occasions (the last shortly before his hundredth birthday), his wit, energy and perception unimpaired. Though necessarily ruthless, Roach permitted his employees a mostly free hand within an agreeable environment; most agree that there was no finer boss.

(See also: Sound; Unfilmed projects; and, for that matter, most of the entries in this book)

ROACH REVUE, THE
See: Unfilmed projects

ROB 'EM GOOD
See: Anderson, G. M.

ROBBINS, JESS
See: *Lucky Dog*

ROBERTS, FLORENCE
(1861-1940)
Veteran actress who took over the role of Mother Peep from Margaret Seddon during the production of *Babes in Toyland* (*qv*). It is reasonable to suggest that the film may have influenced 20th Century-Fox (*qv*) to cast her as the grandmother of their *Jones Family* series, itself a parallel to M-G-M's *The Hardy Family* (no relation!). Miss Roberts' earlier films include *Eyes of the World*, *Bachelor Apartments*, *Top of the Hill* and *Daring Daughters*.

(See also: M-G-M)

ROBERTS, THOMAS BENTON
(Laurel & Hardy films *qv*)
Propman responsible for the mutilated cars so often seen in the Laurel & Hardy films, plus such extraordinary feats as constructing the regular and large-scale sets for *Brats*. Bob

Satterfield in *The Intra-Tent Journal* describes Roberts' reputation as 'The Admiral of Hollywood', the man who would supply boats whenever required by a movie studio (his last for Laurel & Hardy is believed to have been *Saps at Sea*'s *Prickly Heat*). Roberts was brought into the cast of *Two Tars* as an irate motorist, disguised in sunglasses borrowed from director James Parrott (*qv*). Always busy with various enterprises, Roberts found time to attend several gatherings of the Sons of the Desert club (*qv*) before his death in 1987.

(See also: Boats, ships; Cars; Periodicals)

ROBIN HOOD
See: Newsreels and Unfilmed projects

ROBINSON CRUSOELAND
See: *Atoll K*

ROBINSON, DAVID (b. 1930)
Prominent film historian whose 1954 *Sight and Sound* article, titled 'The Lighter People', remains one of the most important essays on Laurel & Hardy. Written when the two comedians were making their last tour of Britain, the piece examines in some detail their work in silent films, sound shorts and features, while exploring both the team's origins and, to a degree, influence. Further perceptive comment on the team may be found in Robinson's book *The Great Funnies* (1969). In more recent years Robinson has produced an exhaustive survey of Chaplin's life that seems likely to remain the standard reference.

(See also: Chaplin, Charlie; Sound; Stage appearances)

ROCK, JOE (1891-1984)
Screen comedian who started as a stunt double for Mary Pickford. During the 'teens he was partner to Earl Montgomery in Vitagraph comedies (*qv*). Later, he turned producer,

sometimes appearing on-screen, releasing material to the independent market. In 1924 Rock signed Stan Laurel to appear in twelve two-reelers for Standard Cinema-Lewis J. Selznick, on the strict condition that Mae Laurel (*qv*) was not to appear. She made trouble and the tactful Rock invited her to the studio, ostensibly to be fitted for her costume but actually to receive a stern lecture about her hampering Stan's career. The series commenced (without Mae), mostly under the direction of Percy Pembroke, with whom Stan and Mae were living. The films stand up well today: one considerable bonus was access to the sets of Universal's features, permitting a convincing Chinatown for *Mandarin Mix-Up* while the sets for Chaney's *Hunchback of Notre Dame* provided backdrop for a *Dr Jekyll* parody, *Dr Pyckle and Mr Pryde*. All went smoothly until the spring of 1925, when the distributor went bankrupt, forcing Rock to transfer release to Film Booking Office (F.B.O.). At this time a resumption of Mae's interference rendered Stan, amid a dangerous combination of alcohol and sleeplessness, unfit for work. Rock provided a generous solution by offering Mae the chance to return to her native Australia. She was offered boat fare, cash and the retrieval of her jewellery from the pawnshop. Mae accepted but Rock was clever enough to ensure that all valuables were to be withheld by the ship's purser until the voyage was underway. Stan, under the care of Joe's brother Murray, was introduced to Rock's former girlfriend, Lois Neilson, whom he married the following year. The films were completed ahead of schedule but Stan remained contractually tied to Rock, a complication, since he had been paid an advance on completing each film but would receive none of his agreed 15 per cent until all receipts were in. Stan needed to earn a living, so he and Lois consulted Pembroke for advice. All three became convinced that the percentage would never arrive, and it was agreed with Rock that Stan could accept an offer from Hal Roach, providing he remain essentially a writer and director, confining any acting to supporting roles. Stan surprised Rock by expressing a wish to abandon picture work for the stage, and provided a letter to that effect to pacify Rock's bankers. Rock was even more surprised when Stan was reported working for Roach, and reminded all concerned of his contract with Stan. A court battle followed between the Roach Studio and Rock, whose capital was frozen and studio rendered idle. Stan eventually asked for the case to be dismissed, enabling Rock to resume production; Rock in turn allowed their friendship to override other matters and was prepared to relinquish his claim. Joe Rock continued as a successful independent for many years after, winning an Oscar for his 1933 film *Krakatoa* though neglecting to claim it until 40 years later. He spent many years in Britain, producing films at Elstree, such as George Formby's *Much Too Shy*. Despite the unfortunate circumstances of his break with Stan, Rock retained pleasant memories of his former star and spoke well of him; he contributed letters to *Pratfall* in the 1970s and in his last years impressed *aficionados* with his good humour and gentlemanly demeanour.

(See also: *Forty-Five Minutes From Hollywood*; Marriages; Parodies; Periodicals; Solo films; Teaming)

ROGERS, CHARLES A.

(all films *qv*)

Not to be confused with actor Charles 'Buddy' Rogers, British comedian Charlie Rogers appeared on stage both at home and in America before joining Roach in 1928; he became Stan Laurel's closest friend until the later tours brought Laurel & Hardy together socially. Acting roles in the films range from comparatively early

Charles Rogers looks suitably aghast as Stan announces an elopement in Our Wife

things such as Finlayson's valet in *Pack Up Your Troubles* to some very late appearances, notably another valet in *The Dancing Masters*. He became a regular director of Laurel & Hardy films, though the received view is that Rogers served as figurehead while Laurel did the actual directing. Such credits include *Them Thar Hills*, *The Fixer-Uppers*, *Tit For Tat* and co-directorship of the feature-length *Fra Diavolo*, *Babes in Toyland* and *The Bohemian Girl* plus one short, *Me and My Pal*. He also served on the writing team and was drafted back in by M-G-M (*qv*) for the much later *Air Raid Wardens*. He later worked before and behind the cameras with Laurel & Hardy associates Edgar Kennedy and Harry Langdon (both *qv*); and died in a road accident on 20 December 1956, aged 58. When John McCabe (*qv*) was researching his book *Mr Laurel and Mr Hardy*, Stan Laurel particularly recommended a visit to Rogers. McCabe duly contacted him and when stating his intention to hire a car for the trip was told, 'No, don't do that, I'll come in to Santa Monica and see you'. In the subsequent three-hour interview Rogers displayed all the wit, courtesy and skill with anecdote one might expect from a man so valued by Stan Laurel.

(See also: Biographies; Directors; Marriages; Stage appearances; Writers)

THE ROGUE SONG

(Laurel & Hardy guest appearance)

Released by M-G-M, 10 May 1930. Produced and directed by Lionel Barrymore. Assistant director: Charles Dorian. Laurel & Hardy directed by Hal Roach. Camera: Percy Hilburn, C. Edgar Schoenbaum. Photographed in two-strip Technicolor. 115 minutes. Based on Franz Lehar's *Gypsy Love*. With Lawrence Tibbett, Catherine Dale Owen, Nance O'Neil, Judith Vosselli, Ulrich Haupt, Elsa Alsen, Florence Lake, Lionel Belmore, Wallace MacDonald, Kate Price, H. A. Morgan, Burr MacIntosh, James Bradbury Jr., Stan Laurel and Oliver Hardy, Harry Bernard.

Old Russia is under Cossack rule: their chief adversary is Yegor (Lawrence Tibbett), a Robin Hood-like bandit. Yegor falls for Princess Vera (Catherine Dale Owen), whose brother, Prince Sergei (Ulrich Haupt) is the Cossack leader. His efforts to woo her attract instead the Countess Tatiana (Judith Vosselli), who attempts unsuccessfully to seduce Yegor. Spurned, she arranges Yegor's betrayal but is foiled by Princess Vera, who by now returns Yegor's love. Later, Yegor learns that his sister, Nadja (Florence Lake) has committed

The Rogue Song: *Ali-Bek and Murza-Bek*

suicide, having been abducted and violated by Prince Sergei. Yegor kills Sergei in revenge but Vera will not accept his reasons for doing so. The bandit takes Vera to his mountain hideout, where she eventually consents to sharing his tent during a storm. Ultimately Yegor is captured and flogged. Vera rushes to comfort him, but each realises that her royal status forbids their marriage. Word has reached Yegor's outlaw band that their leader is no more; all seems lost until his voice is heard over the mountains.

Metropolitan Opera star Lawrence Tibbett (*qv*) was given an auspicious film debut in this ambitious, all-Technicolor production. Laurel & Hardy appear as comic relief in several sequences, although reports vary as to whether they were employed from the outset or added after production had been completed. What remains clear is that their presence was intended to guarantee interest overseas, where Tibbett was not yet known. Although their bandit roles are described in cast lists as 'Ali-Bek' and 'Murza-Bek' respectively, Laurel & Hardy retain their own forenames in the dialogue. Their sequences serve mostly as interludes to the plot: in one, Ollie tries to mount his horse but is plunged into a rain barrel; in another, Stan gives Ollie a shave but finishes by dropping the razor down the back of Ollie's shirt. Still another diverts us from the romantic leads during the storm sequence, when Laurel & Hardy, their tent blown away, seek shelter in a cave that is home to a grizzly bear. Only once do they contribute to the story: hearing that their leader is dead, they convey the news to others in the outlaw band, Ollie fabricating a quote from Yegor handing leadership over to him. The others laugh even before Yegor's return. *The Rogue Song* has been the subject of a worldwide search for years. Despite such tantalizing notions as a reputed appearance in a 1950s TV distribution list, no copy is

known to survive, although fragments have appeared at intervals. Recovered so far is a complete disc soundtrack plus a three-minute clip of the storm sequence (with the Laurel & Hardy gag), a mute trailer and one reel of non-Laurel & Hardy footage. Until the film's complete recovery, evaluation remains difficult: William K. Everson (*qv*) has pointed out that Laurel & Hardy's sequences may have been underrated by critics resentful of such a low-brow intrusion. Envy may have influenced the female correspondent who, in a letter to a contemporary fan magazine, suggested that Tibbett should not continue to appear opposite 'blinking beauty' Catherine Dale Owen! Miss Owen (1903-65) enjoyed a relatively brief career as leading lady, retiring in 1931.

(See also: Belmore, Lionel; Colour; Guest appearances; *Hungry Hearts*; Operas; 'Lost' films; Records; Rediscoveries)

ROLIN FILM COMPANY, THE

A forerunner of the Hal Roach Studios (*qv*), Rolin was owned by Roach in partnership with one D. Whiting. The first films consisted of dramas acquired for release by Universal, and a series of one-reel comedies with Harold Lloyd (*qv*). Several reports claim that none of these early Lloyds saw release, but one, entitled *Just Nuts* (not to be confused with the reported Laurel film of this title) is believed to have been issued by Pathé Exchange (*qv*) in April 1915. In a 1986 interview, Roach told the author that six comedies were sent to a company that was later to become Warner Brothers, who sold the films to Pathé. Whatever the facts, the series was suspended when finan-

cial disagreements took Lloyd to Keystone. Roach joined Essanay as a director, working alongside Charlie Chaplin (*qv*) at the Bradbury Mansion studio (the exterior of which may be seen in Chaplin's *Work*). 'They sold my pictures to Pathé', said Roach, 'but they wouldn't tell Pathé who made the pictures'. Whiting contacted Pathé, who explained that they wanted

*Two early close-ups of Stan from his **Rolin** days. From* Hustling For Health *(1919) Photographs by Phil Johnson*

more, but had no idea who was making the films. Roach was pleased, but unwilling to relinquish a lucrative Essanay salary in order to return to producing. 'We kept getting a better contract so that I couldn't refuse',

Roach claimed, 'then I started with Pathé'. Lloyd, meanwhile, had been unhappy at Keystone and returned to Roach. His original character, 'Willie Work', was replaced by a Chaplinesque figure named 'Lonesome Luke' which, though derivative, gave Lloyd sufficient experience to develop the bespectacled character for which he is remembered. Unfortunately, few of the 'Lukes' are available today, most of the negatives having succumbed to a vault fire in 1943. In 1918, Rolin acquired the services of Arnold Nobello, a famed circus clown known professionally as 'Toto'. Although an adept comedian, Toto grew restless and returned to the circus before completing the series. A replacement was found by director Alf Goulding (qv), who had seen Stan Laurel in vaudeville at Santa Barbara. Goulding's recommendation was enough for Roach to hire Laurel, production resuming on Pathé's acceptance of the first one-reeler. A total of five were reported to have been made, directed alternately by Roach and Nat Clifford (qv), titled *No Place Like Jail*, *Just Rambling Along*, *Do You Love Your Wife?*, *Hustling For Health* and *Hoot Mon*. Two are known to exist today. *Just Rambling Along* (1918) sees Stan in a café, where an incredibly young Charley Chase (qv) grabs Stan's hat and places it on a hook before Stan picks up a second hat for Chase to remove (this gag turns up in a 1919 Harold Lloyd film *Spring Fever*). Stan sits alongside a pretty girl, who switches her cheque with Stan's, leaving him with a heftier bill than expected. Blackhawk Films (qv) identified the girl as Clarine Seymour, who died two years later aged only 20; she had just been cast for a prominent role in Griffith's *Way Down East*. *Hustling For Health* (1919) begins with holidaymaker Stan arriving at the Santa Fe station (seen again in Laurel & Hardy's *Berth Marks* [qv]), only to miss the train. A friendly stranger (Nat Clifford) invites Stan home to enjoy some peace and

quiet. Stan accepts, but finds anything but tranquility. Both films pit Stan against former Chaplin foil Bud Jamison and future Laurel & Hardy nemesis Noah Young (qv). The informal, gag-orientated structure of these films should explain why Laurel could tell John McCabe (qv) very little of the plots. He recalled only that 'a basic situation was necessary... most of the time you ad-libbed your comic bits as the camera was turning'. On completion of the series, Laurel departed for supporting work with Larry Semon (qv). By his next visit, Rolin had become the Hal Roach Studios; Roach explained that 'Pathé did not like Whiting, so they loaned me the money to buy his interest out, and I owned the whole thing'.

(See also: Anderson, G. M.; *Further Perils of Laurel & Hardy, the*; *Just Nuts*; Locations; Roach, Hal E.; Rock, Joe; Solo films; Vaudeville; Video releases;)

ROYAL VARIETY SHOW, THE
See: Royalty and Stage appearances

ROMANCE
(all films qv)
Affairs of the heart have long dominated film in the way they have popular song. Chaplin used the motif more frequently as time progressed and by the 1930s it was considered almost indispensable as a means of luring a female audience. The Marx Brothers' films made more money with a love story added, even though posterity takes a different view of their worth. Fortunately Laurel & Hardy were mostly spared such intrusions, though exceptions such as *Bonnie Scotland*, *Swiss Miss* and (to a lesser extent) *Fra Diavolo* make today's audiences restless during the romantic scenes. Far better are Ollie's occasional dalliances, as in *Our Wife*, *Beau Hunks* and *The Flying Deuces*. Original prints of *Beau Hunks* carried an opening card that said 'Mr Hardy is at last conscious of the grand passion - Mr.

Laurel isn't even conscious of the Grand Canyon'. While we can accept that Ollie is sufficiently mature to have an at least naïve interest in women, it is important that Stanley's somewhat arrested persona should remain pre-pubescent in outlook. Among the many unsuitable elements in the Fox films is a tendency to make Stan vaguely interested in the leading lady. In many cases, these later films seem to concentrate more on the romantic leads than on Stan and Ollie. One cannot chronicle romance in Laurel & Hardy lore without mentioning Ray Bradbury's short story *The Laurel & Hardy Love Affair* (1987), about a couple whose relationship begins with an exchange of Stan and Ollie impressions at a party.

(See also: Crying; Marx Brothers, the; M-G-M; 20th Century-Fox; Women)

ROYALTY
(Laurel & Hardy films qv)
The opening gag title of *Pack Up Your Troubles* tells us that America's entry into the First World War 'caused crowns to rattle'; *Bonnie Scotland* brings the startling news that Stanley McLaurel's father had married a queen - of the burlesque kind. Royalty's bumpiest ride in the history of Laurel & Hardy is provided by *Double Whoopee*, in which a visiting Prince repeatedly falls into a lift shaft in addition to being splattered with cake. These are just three of the occasional regal references in the world of Laurel & Hardy, earlier examples being Babe's presence in the foreign courts of *The Wizard of Oz* and Charley Chase's *Long Fliv the King* (1926). In *Nothing But Trouble* Stan and Ollie befriend an exiled boy-king; also in exile by that time was a real-life British monarch, the former King Edward VIII, who during his brief reign enjoyed a private screening of *Our Relations* at Balmoral. His successors, King George VI and the present Queen Mother, saw Laurel & Hardy perform in the 1947 Royal Variety

Show at the London Palladium. Comedian Tommy Trinder was also on the bill and later recalled that those in the stalls considered Laurel & Hardy's sketch somewhat low-brow and remained mostly silent. A nervous Babe asked the Production Chief, Charlie Henry, what was wrong and was told 'Don't worry - they're always tough here on a Monday!'

(See also: Chase, Charley; *Driver's Licence sketch, the*; Semon, Larry; Stage appearances)

RUGE, BILLY
see: *Hungry Hearts*

RUM 'UNS FROM ROME, THE
A British music-hall sketch conceived by Stan Laurel after his first trip to America. It was performed in 1912 with Karno colleague Arthur Dandoe; the pair were billed as 'The Barto Bros.', portraying the ancient eccentrics 'Barmicuss' and 'Sillicuss'. *The Rum 'Uns From Rome* was a fast-paced bit of absurdity considered important by John McCabe as an early example of Laurel as comic character and gagman. The Roman setting permits Stan to enter riding a two-man pantomime horse, drawing a chariot ostensibly carrying Dandoe (who in fact propels the vehicle with his feet). Dandoe, mounting a dais, prepares to deliver a speech: 'Gather around!', he orders, and his one-man crowd, Stan, walks around him until halted by a stern look. The two subsequently set about each other with axes, Dandoe escaping through the trap in a nearby column. A dummy head, ostensibly Dandoe's, reappears and Stan's axe plunges into it; the head withdraws, and is replaced by Dandoe with an identical axe in his head. Stan attempts to make amends, removing the axe, bandaging the wound and securing the dressing with a nail. Battle resumes, but the enemies are united by the arrival of a lion, played by one-half of the horse. The animal is fed a railway sandwich and carried

off, dead. The fifteen-minute routine was popular with audiences, but came to an abrupt halt when Dandoe left to pursue another job. Stan found a new partner, Ted Leo, then filling in with one Charles Baldwin in a touring sketch called *The Wax-Works*. The act's most prestigious booking was at London's Old Vic, where they were spotted by Jim Reed, Leo's former partner, who invited them to Rotterdam for a new show called *Fun on the Tyrol*. In 1994 *The Laurel & Hardy Magazine* ran a photo from the team's visit to Southend in the early 1950s. The picture shows Stan with his old partner from *The Rum 'Uns*, Teddy Desmond (alias Ted Leo), who was by then manager of a local amusement arcade.

(See also: Circuses; Karno, Fred; Music-hall; Periodicals; Sketches; Stage appearances; Vaudeville; Waxworks)

RYAN, SHEILA (1921-75)
Born Katherine McLaughlin in Topeka, Kansas, Sheila Ryan was leading lady of Laurel & Hardy's first two Fox films, *Great Guns* and *A-Haunting We Will Go* (both *qv*). Other appearances include *Something For The Boys* (1944), *Caged Fury* (1947) and *Street of Darkness* (1958).

(See also: 20th Century-Fox)

S

SAILORS

(Laurel & Hardy films *qv*)
Maritime life is one of several recurrent occupations in the Laurel & Hardy films. In *Why Girls Love Sailors* Stan is a fisherman whose fiancée is abducted by a sea captain. *Sailors Beware* takes place aboard a cruise liner, with Ollie as Purser and Stan as a shanghaied steward. Both he and Ollie are shanghaied in *The Live Ghost*, *Any Old Port* chronicles their adventures ashore after a whaling voyage, while *Our Relations* presents the boys' seafaring twins, Alf and Bert. Stan and Ollie take to the high seas accidentally in what is supposed to be a moored boat in *Saps at Sea*. They join the US Navy in *Two Tars* and *Men O'War* (Stan had also worn naval uniform in his 1925 solo film *Navy Blues Days*). Another representative of that service crops up in *Angora Love*. The systematic destruction of Ollie's suits in *Helpmates* obliges Ollie to meet his wife in an Admiral's costume. This is the most prestigious moment in the team's nautical career, unless one counts the time in 1947 when Stan joined the crew of HMS *Dolphin* in queueing up for the rum ration.

(See also: Boats, ships; Risqué humour; Stage appearances)

SAILORS, BEWARE!

(Laurel & Hardy film)
Released by Pathé Exchange, 25 September 1927. Produced by Hal Roach. Directed by Hal Yates. Two reels. Silent.

Sailors: Alfie Laurel and Bertie Hardy aboard the Periwinkle

With Stan Laurel, Oliver Hardy, Anita Garvin, Frank Brownlee, Lupe Velez, Harry Earles.

Cab driver Chester Chaste (Stan Laurel) is taking Madame Ritz (Anita Garvin) and her baby to a quayside rendezvous with the SS *Mirimar*. Madame Ritz is an international jewel thief and the baby is really her midget husband, Roger (Harry Earles) in disguise. Chester's cab is mistakenly loaded aboard ship, an error that leads to Chester becoming a reluctant steward under the Captain (Frank Brownlee) and Purser Cryder (Oliver Hardy). Cryder's favourite passengers are 'blondes and brunettes', but his attempts to make conversation with such lovelies as Baroness Behr (Lupe Velez) are interrupted by the new steward. Chester becomes involved in gambling with the disguised midget, whose obviously loaded dice make it a one-sided contest. Later, Chester, having foiled Madame Ritz's crooked card game, has the job of bathing the bogus child. When he discovers the truth from the midget's hairy chest, he alerts Purser Cryder and the two share a reward - but the midget takes revenge by beating up Cryder!

Superior to most early Laurel & Hardys in terms of sets and costuming, *Sailors, Beware!* also benefits

Sailors, Beware!: *Purser Cryder greets Mme. Ritz and her 'infant'; Chester Chaste is less welcome. Note that Stan still receives solo billing*

comedically from a concentration upon Laurel & Hardy, though not in their mature characters. We can recognize Hardy's charm with the ladies but not his lechery, while his brusqueness toward male passengers is more in line with his heavy villain roles. This attitude permeates his treatment of Stan, who in turn is the more assertive brand of dimwit from his solo work (although his protests at being shanghaied soon degenerate into tears). He is cunning, too, not just in the way he tips off Madame Ritz's card opponents but through his setting up Hardy for a soaking. It is this sequence that Hardy probably had in mind when he credited *Why Girls Love Sailors* (*qv*) with the birth of his 'tie-twiddle'. Laurel's poolside antics have the bathers ready to douse him with water on his return, but he is wise enough to send Hardy through first. The soaking caught him genuinely unprepared, and he had to think of a reaction; planning to blow his nose on his wet tie, he decided to replace this potentially offensive move with a dainty gesture of embarrassment. No tie-twiddle appears in the final version of *Sailors, Beware!* although it may have succumbed to editing. What is present is an authentic stare at the audience, of the type Hardy also attributed to *Why Girls Love Sailors*. Anita Garvin (*qv*) is excellent as the elegant criminal, conveying cool disgust at the idiot steward who intrudes upon her scheming; Lupe Velez (*qv*), soon to become a major star, would later join Laurel & Hardy among those attending M-G-M's *Hollywood Party* (*qv*). Available copies of *Sailors, Beware!* seem to derive from 16mm material rather than the original 35mm. Though watchable, the quality is grainy, and most 8 and 16mm prints have lost the final gag. This is present in the old TV print titled *Ship's Hero*, but this has been cut to one reel. Fortunately a complete version was issued on UK video in 1987.

(See also: Boats, ships; Camera-looks; Children; Gambling; Midgets; Names; Sailors; Stanton, Will; Teaming; Television; Ties; Video releases; Villains; Yates, Hal)

ST CLAIR, MALCOLM
(1897-1952)
Los Angeles-born director who began with Mack Sennett (*qv*). He later collaborated with Buster Keaton (*qv*) on script and direction for *The Goat* and *The Blacksmith* (Keaton and St Clair would be reunited in 1939 for *Hollywood Cavalcade*). Director of many 1920s features, including *Gentlemen Prefer Blondes* (1928) and *The Canary Murder Case* (1929), he continued through the 1930s and was engaged during the following decade as Laurel & Hardy's director at 20th Century-Fox (*qv*). The studio seemed to believe that 1920s veterans would suit the team's style. This was not necessarily true, but Vivian Blaine (*qv*) has remarked on the close friendship between Laurel & Hardy and St Clair during the making of *Jitterbugs* (*qv*). Others in the series directed by St Clair are *The Dancing Masters*, *The Big Noise* and *The Bullfighters* (all *qv*).

(See also: Banks, Monty; Taylor, Sam)

SALARIES
'We were always well paid', admitted Stan Laurel of the team's Roach days, even if they might have earned more from a better bargaining position. Both comedians became millionaires during the 1930s, and neither was ever poor despite a later decline in fortunes. Randy Skretvedt (*qv*) has recorded that in 1928 Stan was paid $500 a week, Babe $400. By 1930, Stan's earnings totalled $74,716.67, Babe's $52,716.67, evidence of their growing popularity; the next year they earned, respectively, $104,333.33 and $77,333.33, an especially healthy income for a depression year. Increases continued through the 1930s although each was docked, incredibly, for the 1932 tour that generated so much publicity. Finch and Rosenkrantz's *Gone Hollywood* (1980), quoting film star salaries as recorded by America's Internal Revenue Service, gives Stan's 1935 earnings as $156,366, Babe's as $85,316; for 1936, $135,000 and $88,600; and for 1937, $75,000 and $101,200. Stan's sudden fall behind Babe's income may perhaps be the result of being paid via Stan Laurel Productions (*qv*). Stan usually received more money than Babe for one simple reason: he spent far more hours in the studio than did his partner, in his role as writer and unofficial director/editor. Both comedians considered this a fair arrangement and there was never any acrimony over money or, it should be emphasized, anything else. There was dissent between Laurel and Roach, although finances were not usually the prime concern. Stan's 1938 Roach deal was to pay him $2,500 per week over a period of two years, plus $25,000 per film. The contract ended prematurely owing to Stan's absence from the studio and his personal problems, both of which were connected with the most disastrous of his marriages, to the tempestuous Illiana. Both this unhappy match and the 1938 deal were things of the past when he and Babe signed to Roach for a twelve-month period in 1939. Prior to this their contracts had been due for renewal at different times, enabling Roach to bargain with each independently. The new-found strength was purely temporary, as future work at the big studios offered comparatively small sums, especially for Stan, who was now paid only for acting. Their company, Laurel & Hardy Feature Productions (*qv*), was paid $50,000 for each feature made at Fox. This was hardly upper-bracket, though preferable to the unemployment they faced in 1945. Financial rescue came in 1947 when Bernard Delfont brought them back to Britain for a second tour. Interviewed on BBC Radio in the 1980s, he recalled paying each comedian £1,000 per week (verified in a

news cutting of the period) a figure they feared might not be justified until packed houses proved them wrong. This in turn encouraged two further visits.

(See also: Apocrypha; Cooke, Alice and Baldwin; Hal Roach Studios, the; Marriages; Stage appearances; Teaming; *Zenobia*)

SALUTE TO STAN LAUREL, A
See: Television

SANDFORD, STANLEY J. ('TINY')

(1894–1961) (Laurel & Hardy films *qv*) Burly actor who appeared in 23 films with Laurel & Hardy. 'Tiny' Sandford usually represents benign but forceful authority, invariably a policeman or prison officer. *Big Business* presents Sandford at his best, as the cop who watches Laurel, Hardy and Finlayson create devastation before he finally intervenes. As a prison officer in *Pardon Us* he persuades convicts Laurel & Hardy not to go on hunger

Tiny Sandford displays unaccustomed haughtiness in From Soup To Nuts

strike with a humorous list of the delights awaiting them in the mess hall. *The Hoose-Gow* features Sandford once more as a prison guard, who suffers various indignities before becoming involved in the climactic rice fight. He is a plausibly intimidating headwaiter in *Their Purple Moment* but his underlying humour makes him an unconvincing thug in *Our Relations*. This last film was Sandford's final appearance with Laurel & Hardy; he was cast as the Sheriff in *Way Out West* but subsequently replaced by Stanley Fields (*qv*). Sandford's other work has been said to include some of Chaplin's Mutual shorts: however, the rather shorter actor identified as Sandford resembles instead a Chaplin 'regular', Frank J. Coleman. Sandford did appear with Chaplin later on, in *The Circus* (1928) and *Modern Times* (1936). His good-natured beefiness made him an ideal Porthos in Fairbanks' *The Iron Mask* (1929).

(See also: Chaplin, Charles; Finlayson, James; Policemen; *That's That!*)

SAPS AT SEA

(Laurel & Hardy film) Released by United Artists, 3 May 1940. Produced by Hal Roach. Directed by Gordon Douglas. Camera: Art Lloyd. 57 minutes. With Stan Laurel & Oliver Hardy, Rychard Cramer, James Finlayson, Charlie Hall, Ben Turpin.

Stan and Ollie work as testers for the Sharp and Pierce Horn Co., an occupation noted for creating nervous wrecks. Ollie is the latest victim, and after he goes berserk at the factory is sent home to the attentions of Stan and Dr Finlayson. The diagnosis is 'Hornophobia', an ailment treatable with sea air and a diet of goat's milk. The pair acquire a goat (which turns out to be male) and rent a small vessel that is considered safe only if kept to its moorings. It remains tethered only

Saps at Sea: 'Doesn't this noise bother you?' asks Ollie; Stan is unconcerned

until the goat chews through the rope. Drifting out to sea overnight, they are at the mercy of an escaped murderer, Nick Grainger (Rychard Cramer), who has taken refuge aboard. The stowaway demands food: having none to give, Stan and Ollie prepare a 'sympathetic' meal (fabricating bacon from a lampwick and baking biscuits with talcum powder). The killer, catching on, makes them eat the meal until Stan has an idea. He has been learning to play the trombone, and has brought the instrument with him, despite Ollie's condition. A few notes send Ollie into a fury, and he attacks the murderer, but Stan must keep playing. Fortunately the police, who have been looking for the missing boat, arrive just as Ollie finishes off the killer. Unfortunately, Stan demonstrates how his playing sent Ollie into such ferocity, and the battered policeman leads them off to share a cell with the murderer!

The team's last film for Hal Roach is clumsily constructed, presumably the result of having been planned as a 'Streamliner' (*qv*) which was extended into the feature category. There are plenty of good gags but the loose assembly suggests something of a contractual 'quickie'. Charles Barr sees a broadening of style in this and its immediate predecessors, true enough in the sense of gag-for-gags' sake though infinitely preferable to the films that were to follow at other studios. One of these, *Jitterbugs* (*qv*), employs what had been a working title for *Saps at Sea*; perhaps the team had been consulted somewhat on this project, often regarded as the best of their post-Roach features.

(See also: Biographies; Boats, ships; Cars; Insanity; Roberts, Thomas Benton; Turpin, Ben)

SAWMILLS (Laurel & Hardy films *qv*)
A surprisingly frequent question about Laurel & Hardy is 'What was the name of the film where they worked in a sawmill?'. The answer is *Busy Bodies*, a 1933 film whose classic status needs no greater tribute than this oft-asked query. In addition, Laurel solo worked in such a business in *The Noon Whistle* (1923) with James Finlayson as the foreman, and Hardy supported Larry Semon in a comedy from the previous year unambiguously titled *The Sawmill*. Still earlier is a Billy West comedy, *The Villain*, in which Babe, as the heroine (!), rescues 'her' father from a sawmill.

(See also: Female impersonation; Melodrama; West, Billy)

SCHOOLS
See: Education

SCOTT, FRED
See: Stan Laurel Productions

SCRAM!
(Laurel & Hardy film)
Released by M-G-M, 10 September 1932. Produced by Hal Roach. Directed by Raymond McCarey. Two reels.
With Stan Laurel and Oliver Hardy, Rychard Cramer, Arthur Housman, Vivien Oakland.

Stan and Ollie are in a night-time court, where they plead not guilty to vagrancy. 'On what grounds?' asks the judge (Rychard Cramer). 'We weren't on the grounds,' explains Stan, 'we were sleeping on a park bench'. The judge wants to give them 180 days' jail, but as the premises are full gives them just one hour - to leave town. Outside in the rain, they meet a drunk (Arthur Housman) who has lost his car keys down a grating. The keys are retrieved and the boys invited home. The drunk has mislaid his house keys, requiring a forced entry; once inside, Stan and Ollie change into pyjamas while their host fixes a drink. He pours a large jar of bootleg gin into a water jug before discovering he is in the wrong house. As he leaves, the butler informs the lady of the house (Vivien Oakland) of the intoxicated intruder's presence. Her husband is not home, a fortunate circumstance as he hates drunken people. She faints on seeing Stan and Ollie, but is revived with the 'water' and comforted with the news that they are friends of her husband. She is already tipsy from the gin and becomes playful. She and the boys are giggling on the bed when her real husband returns, the judge who had ordered Stan and Ollie to leave town. As he confronts his drunken wife and the two vagrants, Stan switches off the light and the soundtrack conveys the judge's wrath.

Among the team's most underrated shorts, *Scram!* is a well-paced and plotted farce incorporating some good gags. The motif of breaking into the house, reworked from *Night Owls* (*qv*), improves on its predecessor and Arthur Housman (*qv*) is at his best, particularly with a seeming ad lib about having his pockets indexed. Rychard Cramer (*qv*) never glowered so effectively as in the menacing close-ups intercut with a side-view of the bed on which Stan, Ollie and the drunken wife are seated. Ollie sees the judge, stops laughing, and alerts the others, but Stan has to look twice before his face suddenly drops; a masterful scene that should be required viewing in film schools.

(See also: Alcohol; Judges; Oakland, Vivien; Risqué humour; Vagrancy)

SCREEN ACTORS' GUILD, THE
Professional body who in 1963 gave a special award

Stan, Ollie and a customarily intoxicated Arthur Housman in **Scram!**

to Stan Laurel, presented by Dana Andrews and Charlton Heston. Stan was genuinely pleased by the honour, though his sense of humour compelled him to describe the award as 'like an eyewash bowl grown up'.

(See also: Academy Awards)

SCRIPTS (all films *qv*)
At the Roach studio, Laurel & Hardy's scripts were necessary only as a guideline that would make way for considerable on-set revision. In *The Laurel & Hardy Book* Leonard Maltin (*qv*) describes unused segments, such as the planned opening of *Any Old Port* and the boys' disruption of the parade in *Sons of the Desert*. Randy Skretvedt (*qv*), with access to many of the scripts, has pinpointed numerous such changes, ranging from

minor segments of dialogue to the abandonment of whole sequences. Further evidence surfaces in *That's That!*, the gag reel offering a lengthy alternate take from *The Laurel-Hardy Murder Case*. Dialogue at least could vary due to the practice of encouraging players to phrase matters in their own way, resulting very occasionally in clumsiness but amply compensated by the enhanced realism and evident ease of the cast. Copies of a few scripts circulate among collectors but these are sometimes confused with continuities. The latter is a written record of the final cut, detailing action, dialogue, camera angles, music and even titling (such a record proved invaluable when reconstructing *Hats Off* through stills). Texts for *The Fixer-Uppers* and the reissue version of *Beau Hunks* exist in this fashion,

although there is more to be gleaned from the actual scripts of others. That for *Me and My Pal* is a recognizable blueprint, although some of the dialogue is placed at different points in the action and there are several improvements. As scripted, Stanley takes a telephone call thus:

Stan: Oh, Ollie - it's for you.
Ollie: Can't you see I'm busy?
Stan: He's busy. (hangs up)

In the film, Ollie's butler takes the call, which is delegated to Stan. The result:

Finlayson (on telephone): Where is Mr Hardy?
Stan: He's right here, and he told me to tell you that we just left - ten minutes ago.

Scripts: A routine scripted and shot for the boys' first sequence in The Bohemian Girl *but deleted before release*

In typical Laurel & Hardy fashion, the script underwent simplification in shooting. Some of the characters were dropped, among them a detective who fears the worst when Stan, referring to a jigsaw puzzle, says 'we got her body together, but we can't find her head'. The sleuth is enlightened and joins their search for the missing piece, and it is he rather than the cop who, in the final version, insists that nobody should leave until the missing piece is found. In a series for *The Intra-Tent Journal* called 'The Laurel & Hardy Papers', Alex Bartosh evaluated the differences, noting a greater emphasis on the team after revision and comparing the script's altogether broader humour with that of the sketches they employed on stage. Of the other films examined in the series, *Their First Mistake* comes out as better-constructed in script form, with an extended opening scene (for which stills are extant). More importantly, it provides a proper conclusion: in the film, Mrs Hardy vanishes early on to sue for divorce; in the script, she consults her parents for advice and reappears at the marital home with adopted twins, leaving them with *three* babies to care for. *Their Purple Moment*, being silent, is more of an action script and demonstrates the way a deleted gag might be employed later: in the film, Stan arrives home with a Chinese gramophone record, an item quickly forgotten although the script details more. Stan tries to play the disc, but Ollie takes over and the turntable pops out on its spring. This idea was dropped but used later in *Should Married Men Go Home?* Never repeated was the deleted conclusion, in which our heroes escape from a night-club disguised as midgets (see **Deleted scenes**). There was a greater need for scripting in the feature-length films, though on-set improvisation remained the norm within individual sequences. Two early scripts for *The Bohemian Girl* survive, and were examined by Leonard Maltin (*qv*) in *The Laurel & Hardy Book*. Copies of the scripts belonging to Charlie Hall (*qv*), discovered by biographer Ray Andrew, subsequently received evaluation in *Blotto* magazine and, by the author, in *The Laurel & Hardy Magazine*. They prove valuable in determining amendments to the plot made necessary by the sudden death of Thelma Todd (*qv*) after the film's previews. The second script, dated 14 October 1935, is a slim work detailing mostly plot and action. The first, of 9 October, conveys more of the routines. The film's opening montage of gypsy caravans is present, as is the idea of Laurel & Hardy sitting beside a cooking pot. Such eventual refinements as the peel-

ing of potatoes, their heckling by a mynah bird and some dialogue (Mrs Hardy calling Stan 'woodpecker') have been added in longhand, replacing a potentially tasteless idea of spitting cherry seeds into the pot. Some clumsiness of phrasing is also corrected, chiefly Ollie's declaration that 'No wife of mine can so belittle me'. Another reference, to Stan's 'hot Corsican blood', derives from a title card in *Bacon Grabbers* and points to the difference in writing dialogue for silent and sound films. This scene concludes with a gag extant only in stills, wherein Ollie plunges into a tub of soapy water. The team's set-piece as pickpockets is more elaborate in scripting: Stan and Ollie pause at a sign warning of pickpockets, and ask a passer-by what it says. In attempting to lift his purse they are robbed not just of their own money but that taken earlier from the Town Crier. Another victim is a cross-eyed man played by Bobby Dunn (*qv*), who thus is given motive for vengeance when reappearing as an innkeeper. Scripted but unused is the scene where he supplies them with drinks quite literally 'with a wallop' (a line retained in the film) from which they awaken stripped of money and clothes. In the finished film, their change of costume remains unexplained. The scene in which they attempt to rob a dandified nobleman loses some pleasant dialogue when their victim, producing a pistol, tells Ollie that he'll 'shoot out your feather-brains and blow them to the four winds'; Stan fetches a gendarme, claiming 'He's going to blow his wind out with four feathers'. Absent from the script is the nobleman's taking of Ollie's valuables, a significant touch justifying his arrest in lieu of Stan and Ollie. Surprisingly, the script places James Finlayson (*qv*) among the gypsy band, which offers more than his eventual role as a palace guard. A deleted element regarding an obvious thief in their midst provides a scene where Stan has taken a chicken belonging to Finlayson; the bird is

concealed in Ollie's trousers, producing squawking noises and, more embarrassingly, an egg. Ollie's adopted daughter sends the egg into Finlayson's face, using a slingshot pilfered by Ollie. A second insert suggests similar business with a duck, while the main text has a scene in which Stan produces croaking noises, having swallowed a frog. Other deletions include reworked material from *Them Thar Hills*, *Bonnie Scotland* plus a second rather tasteless motif based on the aftermath of eating dried apples. Script and film part significant company in an unused sequence of the boys attending a ball disguised as aristocrats; Stan, in drag once more, attracts the interest of the nobleman they had robbed earlier. This may have been considered too costly to stage, for the second script offers an alternative version wherein Ollie and his long-absent wife are summoned to the castle, Stan making an ersatz spouse in the manner of *That's My Wife*. Both were jettisoned in favour of an even less elaborate segment, in which Stan gets drunk while alone in the caravan. While budgetary limitations may have precluded a very funny sequence, most of the deletions were probably for the best. Like Chaplin, Laurel & Hardy were willing to experiment and, if necessary, reject promising material for the sake of pace and simplicity, one of several luxuries denied them after a move to the big studios in the 1940s.

(See also: Brandon, Henry; Female impersonation; Patrick, Lee; Periodicals; *Way Out West*; Writers)

SEAWRIGHT, ROY
(1905-91) (Laurel & Hardy films *qv*) Head of Roach's optical department, Roy Seawright was taken on as office boy in 1920. Roach wanted to take care of the lad, whose father had been killed the preceding year while supervising construction of the new studio. Seawright provided animated sections (as in *Flying Elephants*, *The Finishing*

Touch), special effects such as the bisection of a car in *Busy Bodies* and clever titling effects, as with (again) *Busy Bodies*, *Dirty Work* and *The Midnight Patrol*. The animated toy soldiers in *Babes in Toyland* were his, as were the musical soap bubbles in *Swiss Miss*. He received Oscar nominations for *Topper Takes a Trip*, *Topper Returns* and *One Million BC*. When the Roach studio was turned over to making films for the war effort, Seawright ran the US Army Air Force First Motion Picture Unit; postwar activities were in the making of commercials.

(See also: Academy Awards; Apocrypha; Cavemen; Hal Roach Studios; Reissues; Titling; *Topper*)

THE SECOND HUNDRED YEARS

(Laurel & Hardy film)
Released by M-G-M, 8 October 1927.
Produced by Hal Roach. Directed by
Fred L. Guiol. Two reels. Silent.

The Second Hundred Years:
Dorothy Coburn pauses to paint her face, but Stan offers an interesting alternative

With Stan Laurel and Oliver Hardy, James Finlayson, Tiny Sandford, Ellinor Van Der Veer.

Convicts Little Goofy (Stan) and Big Goofy (Ollie) divide their time between the rockpile and various means of escape. Just how much time they have can be gauged when Stan asks another con how long he has to serve: 'Forty years', he is told. Stan gives him a letter, with the request to 'mail this for me when you get out'. One attempt at escape concludes with them tunnelling into the Warden's office; another failure follows when, marching in lockstep, they try backing out of the line only to meet an armed guard. Next time they back into a cactus: 'This one's got a bayonet' says Ollie, and they abandon the effort. A golden opportunity arrives when visiting painters break for lunch. The boys turn their uniforms inside out, borrow paint and brushes, and stroll calmly to freedom. When a policeman becomes suspicious they set out out to prove their assumed identities, painting everything in sight including a car, shop windows and (by accident) the rear end of a girl standing nearby. Exiting from the scene, Stan and Ollie leap into a passing limousine, ejecting the occupants minus their clothes. Unwittingly, they have taken the place of two French VIPs and are soon inspecting the prison from which they have escaped. At a reception, their meagre social skills somehow fail to give them away, but when touring the cells they are recognized by their fellow convicts, among them the French visitors, who have been arrested for indecent exposure. The boys, accepting recapture philosophically,

march along saluting their comrades.

Despite the absence of any in-series designation, *The Second Hundred Years* is often described the first 'official' Laurel & Hardy film, probably due to contemporary publicity announcing the arrival of the team in a 'super-comedy'. Billing remains confused, with Hardy's name before Laurel's and the press book referring to Laurel, Hardy and James Finlayson (*qv*) as a trio. Nonetheless, *The Second Hundred Years* pinpoints the moment of acceptance both of the Laurel & Hardy team and their now-familiar characterizations. Elements of the film may be traced to earlier appearances: a prison comedy from Laurel's solo days, *Detained* (1924), provides the gag where a tunnelling Ollie finds his posterior burned by the candle Stan is holding. The business of backing into a cactus dates back even further, to Laurel's 1918 *Frauds and Frenzies*, itself a source of inspiration for *Detained*. Although the silly character names typical of their pre-teaming days persist, there is no doubt that these two convicts are 'Stan and Ollie'. From here, those personalities would develop from mere dimwits into a more profound denseness, but their basic relationship would remain unchanged. Surviving material on *The Second Hundred Years* is marred slightly by decomposition, affecting several title cards (replaced in new copies) and the tunnelling scene. It remains unclear whether a still showing a cop doused in paint represents lost footage or is merely posed.

(See also: *Call of the Cuckoos*; Coburn, Dorothy; Criminals; Hair; Names; Prison; Publicity; Race; Remakes; Rock, Joe; Semon Larry; Teaming)

SEDAN, ROLFE (1896-1982)

Supporting actor, ubiquitous for well over half a century. Often remembered as the mailman in *The Burns and Allen Show*. Amid numerous films were several at Roach, including Laurel &

Hardy's *You're Darn Tootin'*, *Double Whoopee* and *Fra Diavolo* (all *qv*). In the first, he is a drunk who helps buskers Stan and Ollie by giving them a 'start'; in the second, a hotel desk clerk; in the last, a customer at 'La Taverne Del Cucu'.

SEDGWICK, EDWARD
(1893-1953)

Former comedian who as director was responsible for most of Keaton's M-G-M features. These started quite promisingly with *The Cameraman* and *Spite Marriage* before descending into the likes of *The Passionate Plumber* and *What, No Beer?* He directed *Pick A Star* (*qv*) for Hal Roach and at M-G-M six years later directed Laurel & Hardy in *Air Raid Wardens* (*qv*), repeating the downhill trend established with his Keaton films.

(See also: Keaton, Buster; M-G-M)

SEITER, WILLIAM A.
(1892-1964)

He directed Laurel & Hardy in *Sons of the Desert* (*qv*), his only such connection with the team despite a long-term friendship. Randy Skretvedt (*qv*) has recorded that Stan Laurel first met his second wife during a trip with the director. Seiter began as an artist and writer before entering films with Selig. Early work included a brief stint directing Ray Hughes in a series that has been described as imitating Billy West's imitations of Chaplin. Billy West (*qv*) used Oliver Hardy as his regular foil; another parallel between Seiter and Hardy concerns their enthusiasm for sport, each being noted for his expert golfing. During the 1920s, Seiter directed numerous feature-length light comedies, sometimes starring his wife, Laura La Plante. Others include the Colleen Moore vehicles *Synthetic Sin*, *Happiness Ahead* and *Why Be Good?* Shortly before *Sons of the Desert*, his name appeared among the directors of Paramount's *If I Had A Million* as well as on Wheeler and Woolsey's best

film, *Diplomaniacs*. Later directed the Marx Brothers (*qv*) in *Room Service*. His experience in these and other comedies would suggest an ideal Laurel & Hardy director and the brevity of his association with them remains a mystery.

(See also: Golf; Marriages)

SEMON, LARRY (1889-1928)

Knockabout comedian, a former newspaper cartoonist who entered movies as director for Vitagraph (*qv*). He directed Jimmy Aubrey (*qv*) among others before starring in his own series of comedies. He was supported by Stan Laurel in three 1918 films, *Huns and Hyphens*, *Bears and Bad Men* and *Frauds and Frenzies*. In the last-named, Semon and Laurel are convicts who escape a 'stone-breakers convention', acquire civilian clothes and set off in pursuit of a pretty girl. At the girl's house, they discover her father is warden of the prison they have just vacated. Stan is captured, but Larry manages to retain his liberty until the finale. *Frauds and Frenzies* ended Laurel's days with Semon. Stan had quickly progressed from minor roles to virtual co-starring status until Antonio Moreno (*qv*) attended the rushes and declared Laurel to be the funnier of the two. Stan was written out of the final chase as a result. Stan recalled the film as *Scars and Stripes*, but this was probably a working title. It is difficult to comprehend why Semon took so long to notice Stan's constant attempts to gain audience attention; perhaps Semon viewed rushes solely to evaluate his own performance. He would later permit Babe to steal almost every scene when Hardy supported him from 1921 to 1925. Babe recalled that Semon worked harder at his gags than anyone he knew, with the possible exception of Stan. The most famous Semon-Hardy film (though by no means the best) is the 1925 version of Frank L. Baum's *The Wizard of Oz*, adapted for the screen by Semon and

Larry Semon *escapes from a club-wielding Babe in* The Perfect Clown *(1925); Kate Price wields the rolling-pin*
BFI Stills, Posters and Designs

Frank L. Baum Jr. Despite frequent claims to the contrary, this was not the first film version and in turn probably owes its fame to the 1939 remake, from which it differs in several respects. Dorothy, for example, is represented as the exiled queen of Oz, while the Scarecrow (Semon), Tin man (Hardy) and the Cowardly Lion are human characters who adopt these guises during the story. Dorothy is played by the aptly named Dorothy Dwan, alias Mrs Larry Semon. Semon's immense popularity of the early 1920s rivalled that of Chaplin (*qv*). By the time of *The Wizard of Oz* he had parted with Vitagraph and had begun the decline in fortunes which doubtless hastened his early death from tuberculosis. Historians have tended to be dismissive, partly through the unavailability of many key Semon comedies. This situation has been remedied somewhat by a number of rediscoveries over recent years.

(See also: Carr, Mary; Fishing; Golf; *Hungry Hearts*; Magicians; *Race*; *Rent Collector, the*; Sawmills; Solo films; Villains)

SENNETT, MACK (1880-1960)

Canadian-born of Irish parents, Sennett (real name: Michael Sinnott) learned film construction from

Griffith and interpolated his own gag content with that of the Pathé comedies of France. From 1912, his Keystone comedies delighted the world with improvised, uninhibited knockabout. Stars who worked for Sennett at various times include Charlie Chaplin, Mabel Normand, Harry Langdon, Roscoe 'Fatty' Arbuckle, Ben Turpin and Charley Chase (all *qv*). Later he made sound shorts with, among others, W. C. Fields and Bing Crosby. Stan Laurel made no films at the studio, although a project was announced in 1938. Oliver Hardy made only very occasional Sennett appearances, the last being *Crazy to Act* . During the 1920s, Sennett comedies (no longer 'Keystone') were supreme, but by the following decade Roach had usurped the position and Sennett was in financial trouble. The usual belief is that Sennett had failed to adapt to sound; Roach told historian Anthony Slide that Sennett's downfall was due in part to losing his best people through a reluctance to put them under contract. Whatever the reason, Sennett's reputation survives to the point where almost any silent comedy is often attributed to him, irrespective of origin; ample illustration of the nickname used as the title for his 1955 memoir, *King of Comedy*.

(See also: Hurlock, Madeline; *Keystone Trio, the*; Midgets; Pathé Exchange; Slapstick; Unfilmed projects)

SEQUELS (all films *qv*):
Despite Hollywood's legendary fondness for supplying a 'son of' anything even remotely successful, Laurel & Hardy displayed their customary restraint by indulging in only one deliberate sequel throughout their association: *Them Thar Hills* was such a success that a specific continuation in the form of *Tit For Tat* was considered appropriate. The second film works quite adequately in isolation from its predecessor, although one or

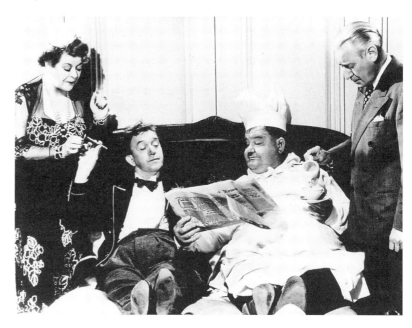

two minor references to *Them Thar Hills* may prove puzzling to the uninitiated. A more subliminal back-reference occurs in the sign gracing the team's electrical store in the film, which reads: 'Open for Big Business'. This obvious nod toward one of their other concentrated explorations of the 'tit-for-tat' theme is clearly intended for in-house amusement rather than public consumption; those involved in the films' creation considered them to be amusement for the moment rather than the subject of eventual documenting. A less formal line of succession marks the appearance of *Babes in Toyland* and *The Bohemian Girl* in the wake of the very successful *Fra Diavolo*. Although certain elements recur (notably the wine-drinking routines in *Fra Diavolo* and *The Bohemian Girl*), no continuation is evident except in a contemporary UK advertisement for *The Bohemian Girl* (proclaiming 'remember *Fra Diavolo*') and one obvious back-reference in *Babes in Toyland*.

(See also Feature-films; In-jokes; Remakes; Operas)

Servants: taking care of the servant problem in Nothing But Trouble

SERVANTS (Laurel & Hardy films *qv*)
For centuries, servants have provided comic relief in otherwise serious productions. Laurel & Hardy assumed this traditional role as reluctant aides to *Fra Diavolo*. Twentieth-century equivalents are to be seen in *From Soup To Nuts*, when Laurel & Hardy's task of waiting at a dinner party is fulfilled with their customary success. A remake of this short was incorporated into *A Chump at Oxford*, with the variation of Stan posing as 'Agnes' the maid. 'Agnes' appears on three prior occasions: in the early silent *Duck Soup*, its talkie remake, *Another Fine Mess* and in embryonic form, in a 1925 solo effort titled *The Sleuth*. Much of the confusion in *Another Fine Mess* between Stan's alternation as maid and butler echoes another solo comedy, *Eve's Love Letters* (*qv*). *Nothing But Trouble* depicts the team as chef and butler, whose services are unwanted worldwide until a wartime shortage of manpower puts them in demand. Other comic butlers (all *qv*) include James Finlayson in *Night Owls*

and *Chickens Come Home*, Charles Rogers in *Our Wife*, *Pack Up Your Troubles* and *The Dancing Masters*, Charlie Hall in *Love 'Em and Weep*, Nat Clifford in *Me and My Pal*, Jack Barty in *Oliver the Eighth* and Forrester Harvey, valet to 'Lord Paddington' in *A Chump at Oxford*. The most poignant view of a servant's life is when Ollie takes Harvey's place and is reduced to being Stan's lackey; revenge perhaps for *Early to Bed*, where Stan becomes butler to a newly-rich Ollie.

(See also: Female impersonation; Granger, Dorothy; Lubin, Siegmund 'Pop'; Murphy, Jimmy; Sleeper; Martha)

SHAVING
See: Barbers

SHIELD, LE ROY (1893-1962)
Former pianist, Le Roy Shield was the Victor Talking Machine Company's top arranger until the company sent him to Roach as part of their deal to supply the studio with sound equipment. Shield composed most of Roach's incidental themes over a two-year period. From mid-1931, he turned to NBC radio, owned by Victor after its merger with RCA. He reappeared briefly in 1936 to score *Our Relations* (*qv*).

(See also: Hatley, T. Marvin; Music; Reissues; Sound)

SHIPMAN, BENJAMIN WILLIAM (1892-1975)
Born in Warsaw, Ben Shipman obtained his law degree at the University of Southern California in 1915 and was a practising lawyer from 1914 until his death. That Shipman was permitted to practise a year before obtaining his degree (a 'para-legal' in today's parlance) is testimony to his skills. He was studio business manager for Roach during the late 1920s and later became personal attorney and business manager for both Stan

Laurel and Oliver Hardy. He became their business partner with the incorporation of Laurel & Hardy Feature Productions (*qv*). It was Shipman who represented the team when they signed with Fox and M-G-M in the 1940s; he was also of considerable help in sorting out Stan's marital misfortunes. The general view of Shipman is that he was too nice a man to function as a tough negotiator, but he was a valued friend to both comedians. In later years he and Stan would communicate daily by telephone, if only to exchange the latest jokes. He may be seen in Laurel & Hardy's *This Is Your Life* tribute.

(See also: Hal Roach Studios, the; Marriages; M-G-M; Television; 20th Century-Fox)

SHOES (all films *qv*)
A seemingly minor part of costuming, shoes contributed somewhat to Stan's screen character through being the army variety, minus heels. In August 1939, *Picture Show* spoke of the device as giving Stan 'a strange rolling gait' and a 'woebegone appearance', adding 'he's hard at work when he's 'down-at-heel'.' The flat-footed walk has the additional effect of Stan misjudging the distance in his step; when he walks across a room in *Unaccustomed As We Are*, he seems almost to be floating. Gags employing shoes include the excision of a Hardy toecap in *Them Thar Hills*, the damaged footwear being replaced by a satchel. Stan's impersonation of Mrs Hardy in *That's My Wife* necessitates the rapid mastery of high heels, and one can only marvel when Legionnaire Laurel in *Beau Hunks* pours from his boot a pile of sand plus a sizeable rock. His worn footwear contains a deed in *Way Out West*, which has developed a gap corresponding with that in the sole. Most impressive of all is the giant shoe in *Babes in Toyland*, housing Mother Peep, her daughter and lodgers Stannie Dum and Ollie Dee.

(See also: Costumes)

SHOPS (all films *qv*)
Stan and Ollie's myriad, doomed business ventures sometimes take them into shopkeeping. Best-known is their electrical business in *Tit For Tat*, destroyed while doing battle with neighbouring grocer Charlie Hall (*qv*). He is also the shopkeeper with whom they do battle in *Two Tars* while James Finlayson (*qv*) has his own altercation with them outside his shop in *Liberty*. A escapee from a pet shop forms the basis of *Angora Love*, while every shopfront on the Roach lot is painted white in *The Second Hundred Years*. A tailor's shop bears too close a proximity to the army recruitment office in *Bonnie Scotland*, and the military camp in *Great Guns* seems to have as many retailers as recruits. Another wartime film, *Air Raid Wardens*, begins with Stan and Ollie having tried to run shops of varying kinds, but they are more successful with a mobile lunch wagon in *Pack Up Your Troubles*. Door-to-door salesmanship seems more their territory, as in *Big Business*, *Towed in a Hole* and *The Fixer-Uppers*. In real life, Laurel & Hardy sometimes made personal appearances at shops: when Stan's daughter opened a shop in the mid-1950s, her father and 'Uncle Babe' attended its inauguration. In 1953 Laurel & Hardy drew publicity when visiting a jeweller's in Hull; extant today is a private tape recording made by Stan the following year, intended to introduce a display of electrical equipment in Brighton.

(See also: Bicycles; Businessmen; Laurel, Lois; Stage appearances)

SHORT FILMS
While feature-length subjects began to dominate programmes by the late 'teens, the short subject was to remain important well into the 1930s. It was certainly comedy's main outlet during this period and many key names worked almost exclusively in the format. Standard length gradually settled at two reels, about 2,000 feet in

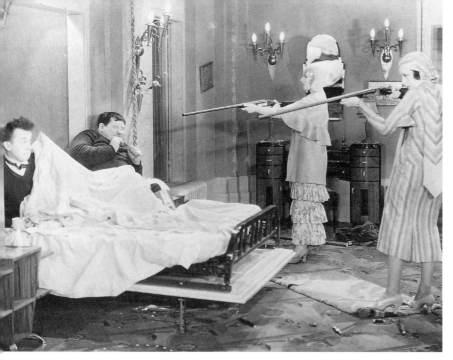

lack of incidental music), but these are interspersed with genuine classics such as *Busy Bodies* and *Them Thar Hills*. There is little doubt that the comedians retained enthusiasm for the format until its demise was assured. Even then, demand ensured the reissue of earlier shorts; later on, American TV would create its own out of dismembered feature films.

(See also: Feature films; Reissues; Reviews; Sound; Television)

SHOTGUNS (all films *qv*)
Laurel & Hardy's screen wives seem able to produce weaponry at a moment's notice: *Be Big* and *We Faw Down* conclude with the boys' vengeful spouses taking pot-shots, though it should be said that the Mrs Laurel of *Blotto* has to buy a gun for the occasion, while her counterpart in *Sons of the Desert* keeps one for the purpose of duck-hunting. Other shotgun owners are the landlord in *Laughing Gravy*, the millionaires from *Wrong Again* and *A Chump at Oxford* and Billy Gilbert (*qv*) in *Pack Up Your Troubles*. Another of Gilbert's gun-toting characters, from *Block-Heads*, has the excuse of being a big-game hunter, but the effect is the same. A blast at Stan and Ollie tends to produce anything but the expected result, be it a simple over-reaction like a collapsing taxi or an exploding wall, or dire consequences for the firer (hitting a policeman by mistake or, as in *Laughing Gravy*, a decision to turn the weapon on himself). Stan and Ollie are themselves best kept from firearms. Prime example here is Ollie's instruction to 'shoot to kill' (in *Oliver the Eighth*) at what turns out to be his own foot.

(See also: *Dirty Work*; Landlords; Risqué humour; Suicide; Women)

SHOULD MARRIED MEN GO HOME?
(Laurel & Hardy film)
Released by M-G-M, 8 September

35mm film or approximately 30 minutes of screen time at the original projection speed. By the late 1920s, this had been increased, a two-reeler by then occupying about 20 minutes. Two reels, sometimes extended to three, proved ideal for Laurel & Hardy; they were happy to continue thus until marketing dictated otherwise, as they had sufficient space for construction, gags and characterization without the need to hold audience attention for a prolonged period. Stan at least believed their best work to have been in short comedies, fully aware of the uneven nature of most of the team's features. Within their seventy-odd shorts, there are two dividing lines, both difficult to define but present nonetheless. The first distinguishes their official teaming from the earlier, chance appearances, while the second delineates the arrival of sound. When asked for a preference between their talking and silent shorts, Stan chose the silents, conceding that sound could enhance effects but believing primarily that 'action speaks louder than words'. Silent or sound, the Laurel & Hardy shorts were pre-eminent in the field and recognized as such by informed critics. There is a

tendency to assume all comedy shorts of the period to have been great, because most revivals tend to favour those worthy of reappraisal. In truth, there was (as in any period) a fair percentage of dross, particularly in the early days of sound. Many commentators were aware of a decline in comedy amid oceans of chatter, among them British journalist David Fairweather in the *Theatre World* for December 1930:

[Laurel & Hardy] will go down to film history as the justification of that witless and tedious form of torture, the 'talkie short.' On the talking screen brevity, far from being the soul of wit, usually consists of inanity beyond the dreams of mortal filmgoer. But Laurel & Hardy are a gallant exception to the rule. Long may they continue to enliven a far from lively screen.

The team's last short comedies overlap with the production of feature films, though there seems no continued loss of momentum until the last two, *The Fixer-Uppers* and *Thicker Than Water*. Some of the shorts of 1933-4, *Oliver the Eighth* in particular, are slow (suffering particularly from a

1928. Produced by Hal Roach. Directed by James Parrott. Camera: George Stevens. Story: Leo McCarey, James Parrott. Two reels. Silent. With Stan Laurel and Oliver Hardy, Edgar Kennedy, Kay Deslys, Edna Marian, Viola Richard, John Aasen.

Mr Hardy's plans to spend a peaceful day with his wife (Kay Deslys) are interrupted by the arrival of Mr Laurel. They pretend to be out but betray their presence by taking the note Stan has pushed under the door. Stan wants Ollie to play golf, but Ollie prefers to remain at home. The Hardys tolerate their guest until he decides to put on a record of 'The Maiden's Prayer', a manoeuvre that wrecks a window blind, chair and the gramophone itself. 'Go on an' golf!' orders Mrs Hardy, but before they leave Ollie swaps Stan's bowler for a golfing cap, so large that it repeatedly falls over the wearer's eyes. Stan vaults the gate outside; Mrs Hardy watches her husband as if to say 'Well?', but Ollie succeeds only in demolishing the entire fence. The golf course is restricted to foursomes, a problem solved when meeting two

Should Married Men Go Home?:
Stan disturbs a peaceful morning

girls, Edna Marian and Viola Richard. Stan and Ollie take them for a soda, on a 15-cent budget requiring Stanley to refuse a drink. When Stan fails to grasp the idea, Ollie demonstrates but is left without a soda. Out of sight, Ollie drains Stan's glass before examining the bill. As it comes to 30 cents, he leaves it with Stan. Having left his watch to square the 30 cents (!) Stan joins Ollie and the girls on the links, picking up golf balls and leaving confusion in his wake. Stan's attempts to hit the ball are concluded when an exasperated onlooker, Edgar Kennedy, plays through. Kennedy loses his toupée on the first swing and hits Stan with the second, but nonetheless hits the ball. Later Stan finds Kennedy in the rough, where his toupée makes another flight; Stan unwittingly hands him a divot instead. Kennedy's ball becomes trapped in a mud puddle, from which the rule-conscious Stan insists it must be played. Mud flies, landing on a girl's behind. She turns, catching a second batch in the face. She arrives to protest, just in time for a third splattering. The girl throws a handful of mud, hitting Viola by mistake. From here the mud battle spreads quickly, although Stan and Ollie keep clear. 'There's a right way and a wrong way

to keep out of mud' observes Stan, moments before Ollie receives a faceful. 'You're going in', says Ollie, 'You started this', but the struggle sends Ollie flat into the mud. Aiming for Stan, Ollie sends even more mud into the face of a golfer sitting nearby (John Aasen). The other golfer is a giant who dumps Stan into the pothole already occupied by Ollie. The boys surface from the mud, but notice something beneath them; they reach down, bringing up a triumphant Kennedy, holding his missing golf ball.

The genesis of *Should Married Men Go Home?* was Babe's love of golf; also commemorated here is the beginning of Laurel & Hardy's own series, rather than being considered 'All-Star Comedies'. This in-house distinction meant nothing to contemporary audiences but told the industry that Laurel & Hardy were to be a definite fixture of the new 1928-29 season. Comparatively overlooked (despite inclusion in *The Further Perils of Laurel & Hardy*[*qv*]), *Should Married Men Go Home?* proved valuable inspiration for later comedies, notably *Come Clean* and *Men O'War* (both *qv*). The climactic sequence, obviously inspired by *The Battle of the Century* (*qv*), gains interest with the presence of John Aasen, the 8' 9" Norwegian who befriended Harold Lloyd (*qv*) in *Why Worry?* (1923). Today *Should Married Men Go Home?* suffers from damage to its titling, each card obviously retained as only one or two frames in the negative. The worst casualty is an old TV edition retitled in primitive home-movie style, adding the 'fine mess' catchphrase without regard either for context or period. More interesting is the European video/TV material in which most of the originals are reinstated in freeze-frame, though some are indecipherable. At least one (describing Stan's golf system as 'metric') remains missing entirely.

(See also: All-Star series;

Catchphrases; Deslys, Kay; Golf; Kennedy, Edgar; Marian, Edna; Preservation; Records; Remakes; Richard, Viola; Slapstick; Television; Video releases)

SICKNESS (all films *qv*)

The often macabre nature of Laurel & Hardy's humour sometimes extends into sickness. Minor ailments such as Ollie's cold in *They Go Boom* or even suspected indigestion (*Block-Heads*) must inevitably pale against nervous breakdowns, be they genuine (*Saps at Sea*), bogus (*Sons of the Desert*) or unbelievably fleeting (*Tit For Tat*). Ollie feigns more nervous strain in *Be Big*. Most spectacular is the outbreak of smallpox resulting in quarantine for themselves and

Skyscrapers: a deleted scene with a mudsplattered Tom Kennedy

Laughing Gravy. Altogether more comic (though in truth unjustifiably so) is the gout endured by Ollie in *Them Thar Hills* and by Edgar Kennedy (*qv*) in *Perfect Day*. When Ollie needs a blood transfusion in *Thicker Than Water*, he mixes personalities with donor Stan.

(See also: *Birds of a Feather*; Black humour; *County Hospital*; Deaths; Dentistry; Doctors; Insanity)

SILENT FILMS
See: Short films

SKRETVEDT, RANDY

Historian whose book *Laurel & Hardy: The Magic Behind The Movies* is required reading for Laurel & Hardy admirers. He is co-author (with Jordan R. Young) of *The Nostalgia Entertainment Sourcebook*, an adjunct to their *Past Times: The Nostalgia Entertainment Newsletter*. Skretvedt is also a familiar voice on KSPC radio, Los Angeles, for whom he presents *Forward Into the Past*. He was among those interviewed for UK TV's *South Bank Show* tribute to Stan Laurel.

(See also: Documentaries)

SKYSCRAPERS

Harold Lloyd (*qv*) established the trend for 'high and dizzy' scenes on skyscrapers with *Look Out Below* (1918), carrying it on through more famous examples such as *Never Weaken* (1921) and *Safety Last* (1923). These occasional forays remain so effective that Lloyd's reputation is, unjustly, that of stunt comedian. The scenes are in any case illusory, created by carefully-placed sets. Laurel & Hardy's *Liberty* (*qv*), employs a similar illusion, though with an element of risk for the actors remaining. By the time of Lloyd's 'comeback' film, *The*

Sin of Harold Diddlebock (aka *Mad Wednesday*), the now-standard back projection method served to obliterate any thrills. The same may be said of Laurel & Hardy's *Nothing But Trouble* (*qv*), an example of M-G-M putting the team through yet another out-moded routine.

(See also: M-G-M; Marriages)

SLAPSTICK
(Laurel & Hardy films *qv*)

The term 'slapstick' applies correctly to the instrument consisting of two pieces of wood so fixed that a loud slapping sound is made, but it has become synonymous with a robust brand of humour based on violence. Many people associate Laurel & Hardy exclusively with this genre, but this is to do them something of a dis-service. They employ much physical humour, but seldom gratuitously in the manner of, say, the Three Stooges and always as punctuation to their comedy of character. In *Towed in a Hole* Ollie gets a laugh through being covered with paint, but a bigger

Slapstick: Billy Gilbert amid an embryonic pie fight deleted from Pack Up Your Troubles

reaction follows Stan's puzzled examination of his friend and the query 'What'd you put that stuff on your face for?' One of the reasons for this mis-classification is the pie-fight from *The Battle of the Century*, conceived as conscious exaggeration of a cliché but taken later as a prototype. A more authentic practitioner was Roscoe 'Fatty' Arbuckle (*qv*) who, before feature work took him into situation comedy, relied heavily on his maxim of 'the plant must be as close as possible to the gag'. This was thinking acquired under the auspices of Mack Sennett (*qv*), whose methods depended heavily on speed, violence and bizarre events. Arbuckle developed beyond this but remained loyal to the basics. Laurel & Hardy's physical gags would instead build: a suitable example may be drawn from *They Go Boom*, one of several 'two-men-in-a-room' routines concentrating mostly on the team's interaction. During Stan's attempts to care for an ailing Ollie, a nail is driven into the wall to secure a picture that has fallen on Ollie's head. The nail punctures a water pipe, soaking their bed. Much later, Stan trips while carrying a bowl of hot water, scalding Ollie; to add further discomfort, the picture descends upon Ollie's head once more, permitting the water pipe to resume its sprinkler impersonation. One of the best shorts, *Helpmates*, has been accused of undue slapstick (oddly, since it has a parallel reputation for excellent dialogue) but is another demonstration of escalating disaster. Ollie's home needs a post-party facelift before Mrs Hardy's return. Stan is recruited but Ollie's first suit of clothes is blackened by a dislodged stovepipe. He washes up, but gets butter instead of soap; in search of a towel, he opens a jammed cupboard door and is covered in flour. Ollie is soaked when helping Stan dispose of washing-up water. This set of clothes is dried by an oven, which explodes. His one remaining suit is a fancy-dress costume, which he wears

to collect his wife from the train. The humiliation costs him his marriage while, on returning home, he discovers that Stan's assistance has cost him his house. Laurel & Hardy take things slowly and seriously, going about their business in an everyday manner, the difference between their world and reality being chiefly a greater incidence of misfortune. One of the team's strengths is a mastery of the anticipated gag, seldom used to double-cross the audience but serving instead to allow audience appreciation twice, drawing a laugh first from expectation then from the sheer skill in execution. This technique explains also the films' resilience to repeated showings, which tend to erode the element of surprise essential to most comedy. The finale to *Brats* is preceded by several cutaways to the slowly-filling bathroom, building expectation to the moment when Ollie, fetching a glass of water, tells Stan 'you might spill it' before opening the door to a deluge. There is also subtle, unseen violence, notably when in *The Music Box* Ollie is hit in the eye with a ladder while crouched out of vision. The humour is conveyed by sound and Ollie's subsequent reaction. The Laurel & Hardy approach to slapstick elevates so-called 'low comedy' to a level unmatched by most contemporaries, something usually overlooked by their occasional detractors. A footnote: Kurt Vonnegut's book *Slapstick, or Lonesome No More* (1976) is 'Dedicated to the memory of Arthur Stanley Jefferson and Norvell Hardy, two angels of my time'.

(See also: Miller, Henry)

SLEEPER, MARTHA (1907-83)
Comedienne who joined the Roach studio when only 12 years old. She became leading lady to Charley Chase (*qv*) in films such as *Crazy Like A Fox* (1926). She was among the 'Wampas Babies' of 1927. As a star talent she was often cast into over-frenetic items, an example being *Sure Mike* (1926)

with James Finlayson (*qv*). Supporting roles were better chosen, notably her disgruntled housemaid in *Along Came Auntie*, in which she unwittingly displays her legs to a parrot, who cries 'Perfect!'. The highlight of Max Davidson's *Pass the Gravy* (1928) is when she tries to convey to Max that the meal he is sharing with a neighbour is in fact his guest's prize fowl. Regrettably, this is not among the scenes from the film included in *Laurel & Hardy's Laughing Twenties* (*qv*). Martha Sleeper appears briefly in Laurel & Hardy's *The Chimp* (*qv*) as the landlord's wife, although a portrait purporting to be her is in fact that of Dorothy Granger (*qv*). Other films include *The Scoundrel, A Tailor-Made Man, Lady of the Night* and *Rhythm on the Range*.

(See also: Davidson, Max; Rolin Film Co., the; Risqué humour; Servants)

THE SLIPPERY PEARLS
See: Alternate titles and *Stolen Jools, the*

SLIPPING WIVES
(Laurel & Hardy film)
Released by Pathé Exchange, 3 April 1927. Produced by Hal Roach. Directed by Fred L. Guiol. Camera: George Stevens. Two reels. Silent. With Priscilla Dean, Herbert Rawlinson, Albert Conti, Stan Laurel, Oliver Hardy.

A 'drifting husband and wife' are having breakfast. Leon (Herbert Rawlinson) is an artist preoccupied more with his work than with his wife (Priscilla Dean). At the studio, Leon speaks to his friend, the Hon. Winchester Squirtz (Albert Conti), who nearly leaves with an artist's pallette stuck to his top hat. Squirtz calls on his friend's wife, finding her in tears. When she explains her husband's neglect, Squirtz recommends arousing his jealousy with the hiring of a man to pose as her lover. Such a man appears at the door, Ferdinand

Flamingo (Stan), a paint delivery man clad in artist's costume. When the butler, Jarvis (Babe) insists he should use the tradesmen's entrance, Ferdinand engages him in a scuffle that ends with the butler in a pool of paint. Ferdinand is invited in, engaged as bogus paramour but takes Squirtz to be the husband. Jarvis has the job of grooming him, the reluctant Ferdinand taking a bath fully-clothed. Evening, and Leon is at home. Ferdinand is introduced as a writer, who when asked to detail his latest work mimes the story of Samson, going quite literally weak-kneed after the cutting of his hair and demonstrating in gruesome fashion Samson's blinding by the 'Philadelphians' (a moment punctuated by a poke in the eye from Jarvis). The wife cuddles Ferdinand, but Leon fails to notice. Still believing Squirtz to be the husband, Ferdinand panics whenever he sees him in the wife's arms. Squirtz takes Ferdinand aside and fills him with drink. The dazed Ferdinand, seeing Leon and his wife smooching, takes Leon aside with comments about this 'red-hot mamma' and her 'sap' of a husband. Ferdinand is put to bed, where he wakes up beside Jarvis. In the corridor outside, he sees Leon and wife in their bedroom. Still believing Squirtz to be the husband, he rushes in to warn them of his approach. Leon is told of the plot and pursues Ferdinand with a pistol, taking his quarry aside to explain that he is only putting on a show for his wife. Jarvis has a shotgun and, shooting to kill, chases Ferdinand from the house; he is returned by a policeman who, it seems, has almost had his brains blown out, as evidenced by the smouldering gap in the seat of his trousers.

An embryonic version of the much later *The Fixer-Uppers* (*qv*), *Slipping Wives* is one of several Roach comedies employing major dramatic stars whose fortunes had slipped, in this instance Priscilla Dean, Herbert Rawlinson and Albert Conti. One of

the first appearances of Laurel & Hardy at the Roach studio, the film shows none of the promise of their preceding effort, *Duck Soup* (*qv*), reducing them instead to the unrelated roles that would dominate most subsequent Pathé releases. It is too frenetic for the subject matter (itself a relic of 1920s emancipation), though redeemed more than somewhat by Stan's version of Samson, Babe's plummet into paint and a superbly-timed moment where Stan and Priscilla Dean are caught accidentally sharing a bed. *Slipping Wives* often circulates in mediocre prints; material from European TV and video is barely comprehensible, having lost all sub-titles after the opening gag card.

(See also: Biblical references; *Chump at Oxford*, a; Dean, Priscilla; 'Fading stars'; Rawlinson, Herbert; Remakes; Risqué humour; Teaming; *Wrong Again*)

SLOCUM, CY
See: Stand-ins

SMITHY (1924)
See: Army, the; *Finishing Touch, the*; Solo films and Video releases

SMOKING (all films *qv*)
Laurel & Hardy worked in a period before health warnings made smoking a less universal activity. In the 1920s and 1930s, virtually every adult smoked (witness the full ashtrays in *Helpmates*) although Laurel & Hardy rarely did so on screen. Rolling a cigarette in *The Second Hundred Years* proves futile and Stan clearly sees his maturity being measured by permission to smoke a cigarette in *Sons of the Desert*. Ollie's discarded cigarette in *With Love and Hisses* leaves our heroes without clothing. Seldom seen is the Spanish version of *Pardon Us*, which concludes with Ollie asking Stan to light his cigarette, something forgotten on learning that Stanley has kept copies of their prison photos. Pipes often serve to facilitate individual

Smoking: Stan, Ollie and the weed

gags, as in *Way Out West* and *Block-Heads*. Cigars often accompany a celebration (*Their First Mistake*, *The Bohemian Girl*) or round off a good meal, their lack providing Ollie with an excuse to sneak out in *Chickens Come Home*. Cigars offer a measure of status: Laurel & Hardy grab a handful from the Commandant when leaving the Legion in *Flying Deuces* (with some dialogue based on the expression 'he can put that in his pipe and smoke it'), while the bank manager in *Pack Up Your Troubles* is supposed to receive a good Havana instead of a frankfurter. Ollie is amazed to see Stan betraying him by handing a cigar to Charlie Hall (*qv*) in *Busy Bodies*, only to be reassured when Hall receives a beating for lighting up in a 'no smoking' area. Most audiences expect the payoff to be an exploding cigar, something given to James Finlayson (*qv*) as a final gesture in *Big Business*. In *Bonnie Scotland* they demonstrate snuff and, later, an unfamiliarity with the hookah pipe. No less exotic is the sight in *Way Out West* of Sharon Lynne (*qv*), an obviously wayward woman, drawing shamelessly on a cigarette holder. Mae Busch (*qv*) played enough shady ladies for smoking to be expected of her. When in *Chickens Come Home* Stan asks her if he can smoke, she replies 'I don't care if you burn up!' Perhaps the team's most disgusting encounter with nicotine is the 'sympathetic' meal of *Saps at Sea*, washed down with coffee made from tobacco.

(See also: Advertising; In-jokes; *Stolen Jools, the*; 'White magic')

SNOW (all films *qv*)

Frozen weather can often lend itself to comedy situations, prime examples in the Laurel & Hardy films being *Below Zero* and *Laughing Gravy*. In *Below Zero* their busking of 'In the Good Old Summertime' proves inexplicably unpopular, while *Laughing Gravy*'s icy setting provides extra incentive for them to conceal their pet dog, whose discovery would mean his instant eviction. The dog himself, the 'Laughing Gravy' of the title, reappears in another snowy setting when sleeping outdoors with Laurel & Hardy in *The Bohemian Girl*. Less central in terms of plotting is the wintry background to *The Fixer-Uppers*, although the heavy snow adds poignance to Ollie's final disappearance aboard a dustcart. There is snow in plentiful supply in the alpine setting of *Swiss Miss*, although the only gag relating to it concerns Stan's fabrication of the real thing using feathers: a means of persuading a St Bernard to part with his brandy. Earlier encounters with snow are suggested in the titles of Laurel's solo films *Frozen Hearts* and *The Snow Hawk*.

(See also: Duels; Rain; Songs)

THE SOILERS (1923)

One of Stan Laurel's funniest film parodies, *The Soilers* is a burlesque of Rex Beach's much-filmed western saga, *The Spoilers*. Stan's chief target would have been the 1922 version starring Milton Sills and Noah Beery, but the fight sequence at least resembles its counterpart in the 1914 Selig production. Stan portrays the hero, Bob Canister ('Roy Glenister' in the original) who is sworn to rid his fellow prospectors of the villainous Smacknamara (formerly

'MacNamara'), played by James Finlayson (*qv*). The protracted, no-holds-barred fist fight between the two is arranged as effectively as in any serious film and is punctuated by an effeminate cowboy who, flitting in and out of the scene, pays no heed to the bloodshed nearby. The combatants slug their way around the saloon, ultimately into the bar area where their struggle continues to be ignored. When Canister declares victory for himself and consequently the community, he is met with supreme indifference except from the cowboy, looking down from an upstairs window. 'My hero', he proclaims, kissing a flower which he drops, still in its

pot, on Canister's head. The dazed hero is duly collected by the local garbage wagon. *The Soilers* depends less than usual on familiarity with its original, being described by William K. Everson (*qv*) as 'satire of an entire *genre*'.

(See also: Homosexuality; Parodies; Solo films; Westerns)

SOLDIERS
See: Army, the

Solo films: A Lenoesque Stan in Oranges and Lemons
By kind courtesy of John McCabe

SOLO FILMS

Though often revived in compilations (*qv*), the early films made individually by Laurel and Hardy remain a surprise to most of the general public. Above all the surprise is in their characterizations, different in most cases from their mature work and, for that matter, from film to film. Of the two, Stan remained the more consistent, being at least nominally a star comic. His persona embodied the contradictory ingredients of brashness, whimsy and outright silliness, a wised-up child somewhere between Chaplin and the eventual Laurel image. The results can be engaging, as in *Kill or Cure* (1923), or sometimes irritating. Another 1923 Roach film, *Oranges and Lemons*, has plenty of gags but Stan's aggressive disruption, punctuated by Ford Sterling-type leaps, grows wearisome. Stan's debut was in an independent venture, *Just Nuts* (*qv*); from here followed stints with Nestor, L-KO (*qv*), Vitagraph (*qv*) and Roach, sandwiched between prolonged touring. It was of course Roach that would provide a permanent home, but Stan would make films for G. M. Anderson (*qv*) and still another series for Joe Rock (*qv*) before receiving a long-term contract. Many of Stan's 'middle period' Roach films were directed by George Jeske, a former Keystone Cop who graduated to directing for Sennett, RKO and others. Jeske, who also managed the Aladdin Theatre in Indio, California, died in 1951, aged 60. Survival rate of the Laurel solos is fairly high and many stand up well today, particularly his parodies of feature films. Babe, the character actor, functioned variously as villain, stooge, and sometimes lead. His journey to Roach was more complex, having embarked on a specific film career in 1913 at the Jacksonville premises of Siegmund Lubin (*qv*). In this he was unlike Stan, for whom pictures were a break from vaudeville. His first film, *Outwitting Dad*, released in 1914, is lost along with most of his work for the studio. There are a few survivors

from Babe's tenure with Vim, successors to Lubin in Jacksonville (see **Hungry Hearts**). As a long-time freelance, Babe worked for several studios, though he spent lengthy periods with Billy West, Larry Semon and Jimmy Aubrey (all *qv*). A clear prototype of his 'Ollie' may be seen in a comedy of 1925, *Stick Around* (*qv*), though many of his trademarks (notably the looks to camera) can be traced further. Babe recalled earning a long-term Roach contract after a 1924 release titled *Rex, the King of Wild Horses*, (detailing a scene in which, on horseback, he sank into the mud beneath), but he had probably confused this with a 1927 film featuring the same equine hero, *No Man's Law*. His freelancing after 1924 casts further doubt on the claim, as does a 1926 clipping unearthed by Randy Skretvedt (*qv*), in which Hardy's contract is announced formally. After 1928, Laurel & Hardy worked together exclusively except for Babe's three feature films (all *qv*), *Zenobia*, *The Fighting Kentuckian* and *Riding High*.

(See also: Arbuckle, Roscoe 'Fatty'; Army, the; Buses; Camera-looks; Chase, Charley; Children; Clifford, Nat; Colouring; Compilations; Cook, Clyde; *Days of Thrills and Laughter*; Detectives; *Finishing Touch, the*; *Four Clowns*; Freemasons; *Further Perils of Laurel & Hardy*, the; Garvin, Anita; Golf; Goulding, Alf; Hal Roach Studios, the; *Half a Man*; Hickory Hiram; Karloff, Boris; *Laurel & Hardy's Laughing Twenties*; Laurel, Mae; Leno, Dan; *Man About Town, a*; Marriages; Names; Normand, Mabel; Our Gang; Parodies; Rediscoveries; Remakes; *Rent Collector, the*; Risqué humour; Rolin Film Co., the; Sailors; Sennett, Mack; Servants; Sleeper, Martha; *Soilers, the*; Superstition; Teaming; *That's My Wife*; Vaudeville; Video releases; Westerns; *Yes, Yes, Nanette!*)

SONGS (all films *qv*)

Stan and Babe shared a love of music, blending their respective heritages of music-hall (*qv*) and Southern ballads during impromptu vocalizing between takes. Often they would be joined by any like-minded person nearby, such as Marvin Hatley (*qv*), whose song 'Honolulu Baby' forms a production number in *Sons of the Desert*. On occasion this would spill over into the films, as with the informal rendering of 'The Old Spinning Wheel' in *Them Thar Hills*, or the naturally developed but consciously placed 'You Are the Ideal of My Dreams' in *Beau Hunks*, a song performed by Hardy early in his stage career. Another Hardy song, 'Lazy Moon', appears in *Pardon Us*. Sung with great feeling, it is one of the few recorded versions of this number. *Way Out West* has four musical

highlights: a saloon song written by Hatley, 'Will You Be My Lovey-Dovey', performed here by Sharon Lynne (*qv*); Laurel & Hardy dancing to the Ragtime-era 'At the Ball', 'That's All', sung by the Avalon Boys; a unique Laurel & Hardy duet, 'The Trail of the Lonesome Pine' (much recorded around 1913); and finally an early Irving Berlin song (with Ted Snyder), published as 'I Want to be in Dixie', in which the boys are joined by Rosina Lawrence (*qv*). Another Berlin song, 'Somebody's Coming to My House', forms a gag in *Chickens Come Home* and its prototype, *Love 'Em and Weep*, as does another popular song, 'You May Be Fast, But Your Mamma's Gonna Slow You Down'. In stage appearances (*qv*) 'The Trail of the Lonesome Pine' would alternate with 'Shine On, Harvest Moon', sung by Babe in *The Flying Deuces*. The team's opera films were naturally filled with songs from the original scores, not sung by Laurel & Hardy and somewhat reduced in number. This is especially true of *The Bohemian Girl*, though it retains the celebrated 'I Dreamt I Dwelt in Marble Halls'. Similarly, *Swiss Miss* has a yodelling song plus two notably silly numbers, 'The Cricket Song' and the punning 'I Can't Get Over the Alps'. Items from *The Rogue Song* were released on 78s, though none were connected with Laurel & Hardy. Of the later films, *Jitterbugs* is the most obviously musical, with three production numbers by Charles Newman and Lew Pollack plus Stan and Ollie entertaining a crowd with a jazz standard, 'That's A-Plenty'. A popular hit of 1944, 'Mairzie Doats', is played on Stan's concertina in *The Big Noise*, bringing a welcome smile to a tepid film. As noted by William K. Everson (*qv*), the team's vocal performances grew naturally from the action, as though they wanted to stop being funny for a moment, and probably benefited from being infrequent rather than an expected set-piece.

(See also: *Below Zero*; Dubbing; Music; Operas; Records)

SONS OF THE DESERT
(Laurel & Hardy film)
Released by M-G-M, 29 December 1933. Produced by Hal Roach. Directed by William A. Seiter. British title: *Fraternally Yours*.
With Stan Laurel and Oliver Hardy, Mae Busch, Dorothy Christy (aka Christie), Charley Chase, Lucien Littlefield, Harry Bernard.

Stan and Ollie are pledged to attend the Chicago convention of their lodge, the 'Sons of the Desert'. Mrs Laurel is willing to let Stanley go but Mrs Hardy has plans for a trip to the mountains, forcing Ollie to feign illness. The boys engage a doctor (actually a veterinary surgeon) who is willing to prescribe an ocean voyage to Honolulu, a trip designed to exclude the seasick-prone Mrs Hardy. Stan and Ollie have a wild time in Chicago, unaware that the ship on which they are supposed to be has succumbed to a storm. While awaiting news of survivors, their wives seek temporary escape in a cinema, where they see news of a different kind: film taken at the Chicago convention, complete with footage of their husbands cavorting in the parade. Returning home, the boys hear of the shipwreck just as their wives arrive by cab. Taking refuge in Ollie's attic, they make the best of a night in exile until disturbed by a thunderstorm. Mrs Laurel investigates the noise, shotgun in hand, forcing Stan and Ollie up to the roof. Climbing down, they are discovered by a policeman who insists on checking their identity with the occupants. They are welcomed indoors, and allowed to tell their own wild version of what took place. Mrs Hardy and Mrs Laurel have a wager as to who has the most honest husband. A tale of 'ship-hiking' home is followed by the collapse of Stanley, who confesses he is pampered by his wife while Mrs Hardy

Charley Chase joins the other wise monkeys at the Chicago convention of the **Sons of the Desert**

buries her husband amid pots and pans.

Often considered the team's best feature, *Sons of the Desert* elevates the premise of *We Faw Down* (*qv*) to an adroit blend of domestic farce and social document. The comedians are integrated totally into the story rather than running in parallel to an unrelated plot, while the comedy aspect, by necessity eschewing identifiable routines, explores instead the team's characterizations. The boys are given wives who, despite the accustomed shrewishness, are at times vulnerable and sometimes display genuine concern. A definite plus is the appearance of Charley Chase (*qv*), as an obnoxious conventioneer who turns out to be Ollie's brother-in-law. Though cast against type, Chase has some very effective moments and contrasts well with the Laurel & Hardy style. As an affectionate lampoon of national lodges, *Sons of the Desert* scores unerringly. The satirical element extends also to a Marvin Hatley (*qv*) song, 'Honolulu Baby', sung by Ty Parvis in precisely the manner of crooner Dick Powell. *Sons of the Desert* itself is a likely parody of *Convention City*, a risqué comedy in which Powell had starred earlier that year. *Convention City* has sometimes been given as an alternate title for the Laurel & Hardy film, but this is probably in error (as is *Sons of the Legion*, a probable mis-

nd here he comes again! You're dashed if you'll laugh this time. Your
ibs feel bruised as it is. It isn't that there's anything really funny in what
e says. But the way he says it. That absurd slow squeaky voice. That —
ut it's no good. Off you go again, *Western Electric sound reproduction is the*
pluttering, giggling, laughing, till it hurts, *greatest invention since radio and television.*
ll you hardly dare listen any more — *It has brought to the talkie such a marvellous*
NCE AGAIN WESTERN ELECTRIC AND A *clearness and accuracy of sound that the*
OOD TALKIE HAVE GOT YOU IN THEIR SPELL! *"illusion" does literally take you "right out of yourself." Every day more and more theatres are putting in this amazing system. Look for the Western Electric sign in the vestibule.*

Sound: Western Electric advertise their sound system with a shot of Ollie from the silent *film* Two Tars!

quote based on memories of the team's Foreign Legion exploits). British prints carry the working title, *Fraternally Yours*, but a video edition reverts to the American. Today there is a real-life Sons of the Desert club (*qv*), dedicated to preserving the comedians' memory.

(See also: Alternate titles; Aubrey, Jimmy; Boats, ships; Busch, Mae; Chase, Charley; Doctors; Christy, Dorothy; Feature films; Freemasons; French, Lloyd; Littlefield, Lucien; Newsreels; Parodies; Practical jokes; Records; Remakes; Seiter, William A.; Shotguns; Sickness; Songs; Women; Working titles; Video releases)

SONS OF THE DESERT (club)
An international society aiming to preserve and celebrate the memory of Laurel & Hardy, the group derives its name from the film of that title (*qv*). There were two earlier societies, one in France (*qv*) and another in Duarte, California, some of whose membership later joined the Sons. The group exists in principle to satirize regular social organizations (as did the original), with grandiose titles for those

with no authority whatsoever. In practice, it forms a point of contact for enthusiasts, functioning also as an unofficial information centre. The Sons have done much in the field of charity work, the recovery and preservation of material and the tracing of 'lost' colleagues. The group was conceived, given shape, texture, spirit and purpose by John McCabe (*qv*), who as founder defined it through a tongue-in-cheek constitution to which Stan Laurel contributed two emendations. The constitution earned Stan's full approval for the embryo society, as it allayed his fears of the Sons being merely a purposeless fan club. His insistence on maintaining a 'half-assed dignity' produced a crest, on quasi-British lines, drawn by Al Kilgore (*qv*). Stan's suggested name for the club, 'Boobs in the Woods', was put to McCabe, but he and Kilgore thought it best to explain to Stan that the word 'boobs' had changed meaning by the 1960s. Stan agreed that a reversion to 'Sons of the Desert' was appropriate. The first official gathering was a banquet at the The Three Lions Pub, Hotel Tudor, New York City, on 14 May 1965, with McCabe and fellow charter members Kilgore, Chuck McCann, Orson Bean and John Municino. McCabe was elected 'Grand Sheik', later becoming 'Exhausted Ruler' of Sons everywhere. Before long additional branches, or 'Tents', were formed elsewhere in the US and overseas. Each Tent assumes the name of a Laurel & Hardy film, as with the 'Helpmates' Tent of south-east England. Among the few exceptions are Detroit's 'Dancing Cuckoos' (adapted from the Laurel & Hardy theme) and the 'Hal E. Roach' Tent, located at the producer's birthplace of Elmira, New York. One Tent rather bravely calls itself 'Boobs in the Woods' (actually the title of a Harry Langdon short). The original branch became known eventually as the 'Founding Tent' or, on occasion, simply 'Sons of the Desert'. Membership

worldwide is difficult to calculate but enormous; there are 'Tents' through much of the Americas, Europe and further afield; special mention should go to the work done by Brian Clarry in Australia. The group attracts people from all walks of life, including the entertainment profession. A diversity of approach between Tents is a major strength, there being something, as they say, for everyone. One of the most unusual was in an American prison named, appropriately, after *Pardon Us* (*qv*).

(See also: Grand Order of Water Rats, the; Homes; Langdon, Harry; Locations; Periodicals)

SOUND (Laurel & Hardy films *qv*)
Following years of abortive experiment, the film industry adopted synchronized sound late in the 1920s. Surprisingly (in retrospect) certain important studios delayed entry into the new medium; M-G-M, Hal Roach's distributor, was in that category but Roach himself was not. In 1986 Roach told the author that he had sound equipment (courtesy of the Victor company) six months before M-G-M, with the added bonus that short sound films, having no real precedent on the market, could command as much in rentals as feature-length productions. Certainly

Roach had wasted no time: several months into 1928 his silent comedies had started to appear with synchronized music and sound effects. Of the Laurel & Hardy films, *Habeas Corpus, We Faw Down, Liberty, Wrong Again, That's My Wife, Bacon Grabbers* and *Angora Love* were provided with such scores on disc. The possibility of other, undocumented, scored versions is suggested by a trade advertisement for *Two Tars* bearing the message 'with sound'. During 1930, some of the team's earlier Pathé shorts were reissued in the UK by Wardour Films with similar disc accompaniment. During spring 1929 the studio was refitted for sound-film production. Roach's sound equipment arrived with Elmer Raguse (*qv*), who became head of the new department; later technicians credited for sound recording include James Greene and W. B. Delaplain. The studio's first talkie, *Hurdy Gurdy*, presented a problem for burly Edgar Kennedy (*qv*), whose voice recorded at a high pitch. Another Roach anecdote of this period describes his watching the first sound rushes, with a growing annoyance at a voice which said 'that's good' after each take. Demanding to know whose voice it was, Roach was told (eventually) that it was his own. Charley Chase (*qv*) made a successful sound début with *The Big Squawk*; Our Gang (*qv*) participated in some *Small Talk*; Laurel & Hardy combined the punning with an admission of uneasiness in *Unaccustomed As We Are*. The team's misgivings were unjustified. Prior stage experience had given them an advantage, as had an existing format ideally suited to dialogue. Their status as an interactive team provided a reason for talking, something that would remain a problem with many solo contemporaries. Their voices recorded well, although there is a discernible toughening in Laurel's delivery after the first few months. Hardy's Southern accent would prove a perfect complement to the developing gentility of his character; Laurel's

nondescript (but surprisingly undulating in pitch) hybrid of Lancashire, music-hall 'posh cockney' and American twang seemed ideal for a bland-faced innocent. Providing the sound brought complications: rivalry between technical methods, mostly between disc and film recording, meant that prints had to be available either with optical sound-on-film, separate sound on discs or, to accomodate the remaining silent theatres, with sub-titles cut into the action. Stan later denied claims that these silent versions were made separately, but it is clear that the selection of specific shots could vary in order to accomodate titling, visible in the restored edition of *Berth Marks* (*qv*). Stan also recalled the inferior sound quality of the disc versions, borne out by tracks obviously transferred from this material. A further difficulty arose through the need to retain the full 35mm frame. Optical sound takes up what had been the extreme left of the image, which would remain visible in a silent screening. The customary ratio is retained on 35mm sound by reducing the picture height, which is why the originally full-framed *Perfect Day* now seems slightly 'cropped', both to the left and at the tops of heads (in early talkie days, projection would often retain the original height, resulting in a rather square-shaped picture). Some prints of *Berth Marks* lose picture in this fashion, while those deriving from Blackhawk Films (*qv*) have been reduced from the full image. Having acquired sound, the team decided not to talk unduly, a rare economy in 1929. *Unaccustomed As We Are* breaks the rule somewhat, but retains much visual humour, sound effects forming an extension to this rather than mere accompaniment. The best of several off-screen effects occurs at the finale, when Stan bids his friend good-night before disappearing downstairs. The camera remains still as Stan's painful descent is recorded in a series of exaggerated crashes. In this first

effort, the team demonstrate an immediate grasp of sound at a time when most in the industry had little idea of its application. Pacing would suffer in a few subsequent entries, but their future in talkies was secure from the outset.

(See also: Dialogue; Foreign versions; Hatley, T. Marvin; Music; Shield, Le Roy; Short films; Teaming; Walker, H. M.)

SOUS LES VERROUS
See: *Pardon Us*

SPECTACLES (all films *qv*)
Off-duty photographs and the 1932 tour film reveal that Oliver Hardy wore spectacles for much of his adult life. He rarely used them on screen, although in *Our Relations* his reading glasses are more effective *after* Stanley has broken the lenses. Stan occasionally uses reading glasses, losing them on his forehead in *Beau Hunks* and needing them to answer the telephone in *Saps at Sea*. Attempting to read a newspaper advert in *Going Bye-Bye!* requires much preparation of lamp, chair and newspaper, culminating in Stan sitting down on his glasses. 'It serves you right', says Ollie, before discovering the broken spectacles to be his own. In earlier films Stan often employs outsize pince-nez spectacles to enhance his comic appearance, as in *Half A Man* and *Sugar Daddies*. Ollie adopts a similar pair as 'Colonel Buckshot' in *Another Fine Mess* but contents himself with a monocle in the story's silent prototype, *Duck Soup*. The aristocratic Lord Paddington from *A Chump at Oxford* sports another solitary lens, but the foppish nobleman of *The Bohemian Girl* favours a lorgnette. Another lorgnette complements the tiara worn by Anita Garvin (*qv*) in *From Soup To Nuts*, neither of which proves much of an aid to vision.

(See also: Colouring; *Tree in a Test Tube, the*)

SPOT OF TROUBLE, A
See: *On the Spot*

STAGE APPEARANCES
Laurel & Hardy were film comedians whose roots were in live performance. While many movie stars were called upon to make personal appearances, Laurel & Hardy were better suited than most, and would in time concentrate primarily on the theatre. Their first stage experience as a team was in an all-star charity show in March 1928, designed to help victims of the St Francis Dam disaster. A more formal engagement was a week at the Fox Theatre, San Francisco, during November 1929. Laurel & Hardy topped the bill, supported by a film programme consisting of a Fox feature and newsreel plus their own *They Go Boom* (*qv*); a contemporary review makes it plain that it was 'Laurel & Hardy in the flesh that everybody waited for and howled over', adding:

They are funny fellows... when they finish Rube Wolf is in his union suit; their director, James Parrish (*sic*) is minus coat, shirt, porus (*sic*) plaster and waistcoat; a man in the audience is stripped of his clothes in the aisle and thrown into the orchestra pit, and both Stan and Ollie have barely enough clothing to keep within the law.

It is likely that the man in the audience was a 'plant', probably Charlie Hall (*qv*), given the similarity of this to an account quoted elsewhere (see **Practical jokes**). The review goes on to describe the routine, clearly inspired by *You're Darn Tootin'* (*qv*), as 'a riot of laughs', though conceding that they seemed funnier in *They Go Boom*: 'Maybe it was a mistake to play them against themselves' added the reviewer. By the San Francisco trip they were billed as the 'screen's greatest comedians'. Confirmation of this status came with a prolonged overseas visit in 1932. This was planned as an informal trip home for Stan (he had

returned briefly in 1927), with Babe coming along to try out the Scottish golf courses. As word got around, they were faced with a fully-fledged tour, detailed in a Roach press release of the time:

Those popular screen comedians, Stan Laurel and Oliver Hardy, left Los Angeles last week aboard a special car for New York, where they embark July 16 for England [on the *Aquitania*]... They will go direct to London, where Mr Laurel will visit his parents for several days before making a tour of the key cities and provinces. Their itinerary includes Birmingham, Manchester, Leeds, Sheffield, Newcastle, Glasgow, Edinburgh, Hull, North Shields, Blackpool and Whitehaven. The comedians plan to fly from London to *Paris*, visiting Deauville and from there to Berlin, Antwerp and Brussels. If time permits they also plan to visit Madrid. They will return aboard the *Paris*, arriving at the Hal Roach Studios late in September, where they start a new comedy immediately.

The 'special car' was in a train bound for Chicago, where they were mobbed while changing for New York; more crowds greeted them there during M-G-M's publicity farewell. Stan remembered it as 'unbelievable', and that they were 'actually frightened by seeing so many people... in New York there were newsreel cars following us down Broadway'. It is probable that M-G-M's publicists (if not Roach's) were sufficiently in touch with the market to have anticipated the response. Stan and Babe, who had seldom ventured far from the studio since their teaming, were genuinely amazed, all the more so when reaching England. They docked at Southampton on 23 July, and were met by Stan's father and stepmother as expected. What they didn't expect

was an army of fans at the quayside, whistling the team's 'cuckoo' theme. The disruption forced an hour's delay in their train to Waterloo, where they were totally inundated by the crowds. Babe found time to be photographed with a London policeman but was absorbed into the crowd along with Stan. The pair eventually made their way to a car and then to sanctuary at the Savoy, where a press conference was held in the afternoon. The next evening was spent seeing Noël Coward's *Cavalcade* at Drury Lane, taking a bow from the Royal Box. They saw at least one other London show during this period, the Coliseum presentation of *Casanova* with Marie Löhr and Jack Barty (*qv*). On 26 July they broadcast live over the BBC's National Programme; an unnerving scene greeted their appearance at the Empire, Leicester Square, to accompany a screening of *Any Old Port* (*qv*), when spectators surrounded their car and tore off one of its doors. At Glasgow Central, the crowds equalled those in London, several people needing hospital treatment after the collapse of a stone balustrade to one side of the hotel. From Glasgow, they proceeded to Blackpool, via Preston; there was a brief respite as they travelled by car unannounced and unnoticed except by a few holidaymakers at Central Beach, despite a run through Lytham St Anne's with policemen travelling on the car's running boards. 'We came here on vacation,' Stan told a reporter, 'but it's turned out to be the hardest work we've ever had in our lives. But we don't mind that'. 'It's a 1000 per cent more than we ever dreamed of', added Babe. The hard work resumed when arriving at the Metropole Hotel, where the nervous comedians tried to evade the crowds by using a side entrance, only to run into a further crowd in the lounge. The assembled gathering outside was satisfied only when the team appeared on the balcony; 'See you tonight' called Babe, which they did at the Winter Gardens (after police had cleared the way), first at dinner then in the ballroom, crammed with 9,000 people. One-third that number packed the next venue, the Palace Variety Theatre, where they joked on-stage with Arthur White; next was the Tower Ballroom before returning to the Metropole. Stan, who had been unable to see friends in the town, stayed up until two in the morning, determined to manage a quiet walk around. The next day, 2 August, they arrived in Manchester, bound for the Midland Hotel and bearing umbrellas (which proved unnecessary). They were able to sneak into the New Oxford Cinema unnoticed, but were mobbed inside and were forced back when trying to leave. Yorkshire was next, including Hull and Leeds, where Stan met an aunt, uncle and cousin; at Leeds' Majestic Cinema, the reception was so noisy that the team had to greet the audience primarily through mime. The Hull trip resulted in an interesting memento: the proprietor of a local radio and record shop, a Mr Sydney Scarborough, is reported to have suggested to them the idea of making a commercial record, which they duly cut at Columbia's London studio on 18 August (eyewitness accounts of the Hull performance describe the team as sitting on a park bench, engaging in banter similar to that on the 78). Sheffield brought the same reaction as elsewhere; Tynemouth, regarding itself as Stan's home town, laid on a civic reception headed by Mayor J. G. Telford. The occasion, captured on film by an amateur cameraman (see **Home movies**) gives some idea of the crowds but in a controlled fashion; more typical is the film of their arrival at Edinburgh's Waverley station, which records also a sightseeing trip around the Castle and on-stage footage at the Edinburgh Playhouse. They expected quieter times in Paris, travelling by the Golden Arrow to the Gare Saint-Lazare, but the fans could not even wait for them to pass through customs, clambering over

desks as an official tried in vain to prevent the taking of photographs. The French President sent his car and they were taken along the Champs Elysées to accommodation provided free by Claridge's. Overwhelmed once again, they abandoned further European plans in favour of a return to London. Exhausted, the comedians boarded the *Paris* on 24 August, finally reaching Los Angeles 19 days later. Stan had seen a fraction of those he had intended visiting, and had found no time for fishing. Babe had managed a little golf, but at Gleneagles walked into a downpour during what seems to have been a mostly dry summer. This first tour made them aware both of their status and the perils it can bring. Stan did not consider returning to Britain until 1939, by which time the outbreak of war made such a move inadvisable. Occasional personal appearances continued, one of them in September 1933 at the California Theatre, Los Angeles, the showcase for Spanish-language films made in Hollywood: Laurel & Hardy had been invited by the manager, Frank Fouce, who had directed Stan in *When Knights Were Cold*, produced by G. M. Anderson (*qv*). The team had broken with Roach by 1940, and in August of that year Stan and Babe appeared for the Red Cross in a charity show at Treasure Island, San Francisco, part of the Golden Gate International Exposition (a variation of the World's Fair). The intention was, according to the *San Francisco Chronicle*, to benefit 'the War sufferers of Europe'. Stan was appointed 'Acting Mayor of Treasure Island' and his partner 'Acting Chief of Police'. The skit, known usually as *The Driver's Licence Sketch* (*qv*) was well enough received to reject plans for a revival of Victor Herbert's *The Red Mill* (*qv*) in favour of taking this new routine on the road. *The Laurel & Hardy Revue* played 12 cities between September and December 1940, consisting of variety acts and a chorus, concluded by the Laurel &

Hardy sketch. After completing their first picture for a new studio, 20th Century-Fox (*qv*), they went on a USO tour of the Caribbean. The driving-licence sketch served again for a tour called *Hell-a-Balloo*, which visited five cities before Babe developed laryngitis, so forcing the cancellation of the show in Boston. The second Fox picture completed, they embarked on the hectic Hollywood Victory Caravan, a three-hour show presenting some 70 stars. 'If you think you are busy,' claimed a newspaper of the time, 'try to keep up with that Hollywood Victory Caravan'. Its schedule took them to 12 cities in about six weeks. Dispirited though they were by their dismal Fox films, there was considerable solace in being the stars most vociferously greeted by onlookers. When those same films ended the team's Hollywood career, they were delighted to accept an offer from Bernard Delfont (later Lord Delfont) to appear on Britain's Moss Empires circuit. There had been no precedent for such visits, the offer predating even the much-publicized triumph enjoyed by Danny Kaye (*qv*). Though anxious about their reception, the resultant tour ensured not merely their own return but similar engagements of other Hollywood names. On 11 February 1947, they arrived in Southampton on the *Queen Mary* and described their plans to the waiting spectators, reporters and newsreel cameramen. Some of these, such as making a film in England, were unfulfilled, but the tour itself exceeded all expectations. An initial Palladium booking from 10-29 March in a revised version of the old *Driver's Licence Sketch*, was extended to a further period at the Coliseum from 14 April to 10 May. This was the first time a variety show had played both theatres within such a short space of time. Of the Palladium visit, the *Times* felt that 'unlike other visitors from the screen, they hold the stage by merit, not merely by association'. The critic found amusement in their dialogue but maintained 'it is the dumbshow that counts'. 'Eric' of *Punch* conceded the team to have 'survived incarnation... more satisfactorily than I expected', and considered them better suited to '[giving] one another a whitewash shampoo or pretend to be moving a piano, but nevertheless, here were our old friends **Stan** and **Oliver**, looking curiously like themselves and as felicitously inarticulate as ever. And very nice it was to see them'. At the Coliseum, a *Times* reviewer mused upon whatever it was that distinguished true music-hall from 'radio turns and importations from revue and musical comedy', deciding that Laurel & Hardy possessed the requisite 'combination of character with healthy vulgarity, of accomplishment with a humorous sort of charm'. That their filmic approach remained intact is suggested by a description of their 'highly cultivated farce... unemphatic without seeming thin'. While in London they maintained a high profile, attending the *Daily Mail* Film Awards and posing for gag photos at Madame Tussaud's, Simpson's the tailors at Piccadilly and at the Ideal Home Exhibition, Olympia, where Babe matched *avoirdupois* with 'two-ton' Tessie O'Shea and the comparably-built Vera Pearce. On 21 March they visited a famous miniature railway, the Romney, Hythe and Dymchurch. The provincial tour, booked for a period of four weeks, was extended to ten and ultimately to nine months, the limit to which Babe could stay as an alien citizen. In May, they visited Stan's birthplace in Ulverston; other visits included the Winter Gardens, Morecambe, where they were interviewed for BBC radio; Blackpool, where they recalled being 'lucky to leave the place in one piece' 15 years before; the New Theatre, Hull, taking time out to visit the Dixon's Arms at Woodmansey; a civic reception at Grantham and another pub, the Red Lion; the Hippodrome, Coventry; Skegness, judging a beauty contest at Butlin's; and Bolton, where

a stage doorman complained of the smell made by Stan's fish and chips (Stan: 'They'll be like perfume to the air floating around here'). Post-war austerity made Britain less than appealing, but they made the best of it, even when queueing for ration cards by candlelight at the Caxton Hall, Westminster. In Newcastle the theatre was unheated, while at the hotel Stan placed the last piece of coal on the fire, intoning gravely 'There'll always be an England!' From Britain they toured Denmark, appearing at the Tivoli Gardens, Copenhagen, then on to Aarhus and Odense; thence to Sweden, opening in Stockholm at the Uppsala University Concert Hall before moving on to Gothenburg and Malmo; then a return to Copenhagen for a radio show and social engagements, including a visit to the Carlsberg brewery. A six-week engagement at the Lido, Paris was interrupted on 3 November by an overnight trip to appear at the Royal Variety Show. The Lido engagement was followed by two weeks in Brussels, continuing through Belgium via Liège (where Stan had endured great poverty in 1912), Charleroi, Ghent, Bruges, Antwerp and Arnhem. When the tour concluded in January 1948, Stan and his wife Ida left Belgium to spend a few days in England with relatives. Babe and Lucille Hardy remained for a week as guests of the theatre manager and his wife. Stan had developed diabetes and was unable to work for much of 1948 and 1949. Babe, with Stan's full blessing, appeared in a stage revival of *What Price Glory* and two films, *The Fighting Kentuckian* and *Riding High* (both *qv*). He and Stan made their final cinema film, *Atoll K* (*qv*), over 1950 and 1951, a disastrous production that more than reversed the improvement in Stan's health. It would be 1952 before the team could accept Delfont's return invitation, for which Stan wrote a new sketch, *On the Spot* (*qv*). Once again they spent nine months in Britain, arriving in

Southampton on 28 January and concluding at the New Theatre, Cardiff, in late September. BBC Television caught up with them on 20 February, when they were interviewed by Leslie Mitchell for *Picture Page*. The *Yorkshire Post* of 8 April describes them in Leeds as 'up to all the silly tricks that made them famous', believing them as funny in person as in films, despite the limitations of the stage. Liverpool's *Daily Post* of 20 May observed that 'while in real life celebrities often disappoint us, [Laurel & Hardy] effortlessly maintain the familiar... perseverance against a background of adversity', while the *Belfast Telegraph* of 10 June spoke in turn of 'the hilarious technique so familiar on the screen'. Audiences continued to welcome them, often with a sense of awe. Harry Worth (*qv*) described one such occasion at Bradford, when the team made their entrance to a silence lasting perhaps five seconds, those present absorbing the fact that Laurel & Hardy really were there prior to giving them a thunderous ovation. Less overawed but equally affectionate were the children who, as ever, flocked to see them. In Rhyl, for example, twelve young competition-winners met the team backstage and received autographed books and pictures. A similar event is documented from the Chiswick Empire during the final tour, which opened in Dublin in early September, 1953. Their welcome here proved that, if anything, the passing years had enhanced the team's popularity. According to Harry Worth, besieging fans obliged the team to travel to the theatre by taxi. First UK date was the New Theatre, Northampton on 19 October, two days after appearing live on BBC TV. In Northampton they were filmed by Pathé News and recorded an item for radio. This time, Laurel & Hardy were performing *Birds of a Feather* (*qv*), another Laurel creation in which we see the aftermath of their job as whisky-tasters. There was a different sort of hiccup when Stan became unwell early in November, forcing the cancellation of their show at Finsbury Park (Babe appeared on-stage to introduce their deputies, Jimmy Jewell and Ben Warriss). Fortunately they were back in business later that month, playing Brixton, Newcastle and the Hippodrome, Birmingham, where they first met their future biographer, John McCabe (qv). Next was a fortnight in Hull followed by their special Christmas show at the Nottingham Empire, a four-week stay requiring more performances than usual, but allowing Stan to visit his sister, who ran a pub nearby. They were back on the road in mid-January. Their performance at Chiswick was reviewed by Kenneth Tynan in the *Daily Sketch* on the 29th. Tynan compared the experience to 'shaking hands with a legend' but considered their sketch 'feeble in the extreme'. He didn't laugh once but smiled throughout, appreciating 'the splendid relaxation, the economy of effort with which these two veterans work... anyone expecting to see a pair of pathetic oldsters straining for laughs will be disappointed... [they] are carrying on a tradition which stretches back to Andrew Aguecheek and Toby Belch. They deserve our respect'. The tour continued until May, curtailed at Plymouth by Babe's deteriorating health. The *Star* of 20 May 1954 ascribed his condition to 'a virus condition and complete exhaustion', but he was concealing the more serious news of a minor heart attack. Babe had completed the Plymouth show after an injection, administered by a doctor who monitored his condition from the wings. Babe's condition forbade any further visits, much as they would have enjoyed them. The team considered Britain to be the one remaining place 'where music-hall still has dignity' and benefited psychologically and financially from the visits. Though limited, their time overseas earned them countless friends and much Laurel & Hardy lore derives from these memorable tours.

(See also: Appendix 2; Alan, Ray; Boats, ships; Circuses; France; Grand Order of Water Rats, the; Golf; Guinness, Sir Alec; Interviews; Jefferson, Arthur; Letters; Marx Brothers, the; M-G-M; Murphy, Jimmy; Music-hall; Newsreels; Parrott, James; Publicity; Radio; Records; Reviews; Royalty; *Rum 'Uns From Rome, the*; Salaries; Shops; Television; Ties; Trains; Unfilmed projects; Vaudeville; Wartime; Waxworks; Wisdom, Norman)

STAMPS
For several years the Laurel & Hardy society, Sons of the Desert (qv), campaigned on both sides of the Atlantic for a postage stamp to honour the team. Other film stars had been similarly recognized, among them W. C. Fields in a US issue of 1980 and an array of UK talent (including Chaplin) in a series commemorating British Film Year in 1985. The first to feature them, on 6 February 1990, featured the face of Stan Laurel (visible only from the bridge of the nose down) in one of a package of British stamps featuring 'famous smiles'. They were intended for use in sending various types of greeting, and were available only in sets. The other designs featured Lewis Carroll's Cheshire Cat, the Man in the Moon, Mr Punch, Dennis the Menace (the version from UK comics), the Queen of Hearts, the Mona Lisa, a clown, a Teddy Bear and the Laughing Policeman, based on the famous music-hall song recorded by Charles Penrose. The availability of the Laurel stamp only as part of a package meant that Laurel & Hardy *aficionados* at this time found their correspondence easily distinguishable by the use of sometimes quite inappropriate greeting stamps. The Laurel stamp was issued in time for the comedian's centenary in June 1990. Many enterprising Sons commemorated the event by sending the stamp on custom-printed covers, some of them designed so that the stamp would

complete a head-and-shoulders portrait. When the series was reissued in March 1991 with a 'first class' logo replacing the original face value of 20p, the whole process was repeated by some for his 101st birthday (an absurdity Stan Laurel would have appreciated). The United States Postal Service finally responded during the summer of 1991, with Laurel & Hardy represented among a selection of comedians as caricatured by veteran artist Al Hirshfeld. Available in booklets of 20 stamps, the 'Comedians By Hirshfeld' set was launched outside the former Grauman's Chinese Theatre in Hollywood on 29 August 1991. Other designs in this series of 29-cent issues depict Jack Benny, Bergen & McCarthy, Fanny Brice and Abbott & Costello. A further series was issued in 1994. Hirshfeld has provided numerous movie-star caricatures in his long career. One of his better-known Laurel & Hardy portraits graced the cover of Richard J. Anobile's 1975 book *A Fine Mess* (qv). A surprising Laurel & Hardy stamp appeared from Fujeira, a sheikdom in the United Arab Emirates, representing the team in *Night Owls*. The Laurel & Hardy society, reporting this stamp in their *Intra-Tent Journal*, felt obliged to admit that this issue was from *real* Sons of the Desert!

(See also: Caricatures; Kilgore, Al)

STAN LAUREL PRODUCTIONS
Company established in the mid-1930s, receiving credit on *Our Relations* and *Way Out West* (both qv). Laurel's billing as producer is believed to have been a purely nominal independence, the rights to these films having very obviously remained with Roach, but the high standard of the two suggests that Laurel was at least allowed a completely free hand. The company produced a series of 'B' westerns starring Fred Scott. Trade announcements for the 1938-9 season detail six titles, crediting Jed Buell as producer. They were released by

Stan Laurel Productions reached its zenith with this series of Fred Scott westerns; Laurel also received producer credit on two of the team's Roach features
By courtesy of Robert G. Dickson

Spectrum, though copies now in British circulation seem to name a UK distributor without mention of Laurel. He is thought to have taken an active part in only three, *Songs and Bullets, Ranger's Roundup* and *Knight of the Plains*. Alice Ardell, with whom Stan had formed a long-term relationship, appears in the first; an ex-Karno colleague, Jimmy Aubrey (*qv*) is in the last; Rychard Cramer (*qv*) is present in all three. Later on, Stan, Babe and Ben Shipman (*qv*) formed Laurel &

Stand-ins: Charlie Phillips (left) and Ham Kinsey doubled for Laurel & Hardy in Swiss Miss

Hardy Feature Productions (*qv*).

(See also: Marriages; Salaries; Teaming; Westerns)

THE STAN JEFFERSON TRIO
See: Keystone Trio, the

STAND-INS
(Laurel & Hardy films *qv*)
'We aren't 30 any more', said Stan Laurel when explaining the team's less physical humour of latter days. Nor were they 30 during their peak years, which, combined with their value to the studio explains the necessity for stand-ins. Although Laurel & Hardy handled much of the action themselves (notably in *Liberty*) some of the more dangerous stunts required doubles. The usual deputies were Ham Kinsey for Stan Laurel and Cy Slocum for Oliver Hardy, although an on-set photo from *Swiss Miss* shows Charlie Phillips in the latter role. Ham Kinsey played occasional walk-ons in the Laurel & Hardy films: in *Chickens Come Home* he appears twice, first as one of Mr Hardy's aides ('Good morning, Mr Kinsey') and much later as a lift operator. Peter Cushing recalled the team's reshooting of long-shots originally employing doubles in *A Chump at Oxford*, the substitute team having tried too hard to be funny. Laurel & Hardy were themselves replaced by stand-ins when the studio refilmed the conclusion of *Block-Heads*.

(See also: Bicycles; Earthquakes; Freak Endings; Practical jokes)

STANTON, WILL (1885-1969)
British-born supporting actor, visible mostly in early Laurel & Hardys of 1927. He is most prominent as Baron Behr in *Sailors, Beware!* (1927), and appears among the convicts in *Pardon Us* (*qv*).

STEVENS, GEORGE (1904–75)
As a director, Stevens is noted for his Oscar-winning features *A Place in the Sun* (1951) and *Giant* (1956). Other features of note include *Gunga Din* (1939), *Woman of the Year* (1941), *Shane* (1953) and *The Diary of Anne Frank* (1959). He began as cameraman and sometime screenwriter at Roach Studios, photographing most of the Laurel & Hardy films before graduating to the director's chair in 1931 with Roach's *Boy Friends* series.

(See also: *Angora Love*; Butler, Frank; Deleted scenes; Guiol, Fred L.; *Hollywood Party*; Our Gang; Sutton, Grady; *Twice Two*)

STEVENS, JACK
See: Cameramen

STICK AROUND (1925)
A two-reeler pairing Oliver Hardy with tiny comedian Bobby Ray, *Stick Around* was directed by Ward Hayes and produced by Arrow, a small independent whose product was released on a State's rights basis. Producer credit on this series goes to Billy West (*qv*), former Chaplin imitator with whom Babe had worked during 1917-18. Other known entries include *Hop To It*. *Stick Around* was for several years confused with an alleged Lubin film called *The Paperhanger's Helper*, due mostly to a lapse in Babe's memory and the existence of a one-reel edition of *Stick Around* bearing a faked Lubin title. Although post-dating the formative Lubin period, *Stick Around* bears out Hardy's recollections of his work with Ray as having anticipated the on-screen relationship with Stan Laurel: as paperhangers, Hardy supervises his blank-faced assistant, who brings disaster upon them both. Quite early on, the two are left sitting in a pile of wallpaper, Ray looking vacuous and Hardy slapping him, as the scene fades. Ray draws their wagon, unassisted, up a steep hill; in true Laurel & Hardy fashion, it is the wrong one. Their job is to decorate a room in a sanitorium, where they arrive having unwittingly switched their wallpaper with some circus posters. Bobby makes

a mess while Babe makes time with a nurse. When she kisses Bobby, he collapses into a tub of whitewash, a reaction not unakin to Stan's fainting after a kiss in *The Fixer-Uppers* (*qv*). As Babe sleeps, Bobby proceeds to paper the room with circus posters. The proprietor tells them to leave but they insist on resigning; bowing graciously to the nurse, they back out of the room but forget they are not on the ground floor. They hit *terra firma* just before they are showered with circus posters. *Stick Around* is more significant as a prototype Laurel & Hardy comedy than for its gags; one of its clearest descendents is *The Finishing Touch* (*qv*). Although Ray was not in the Laurel class, the film was justly important to Babe, originating an embryonic form of his eventual screen character.

(See also: Characters; Lubin, Siegmund 'Pop'; Solo films)

THE STOLEN JOOLS
(Laurel & Hardy guest appearance) Distributed by Paramount and National Screen Service from April 1931. Two reels. Produced by Pat Casey for the NVA (National Variety Artists, a company union of the Albee theatre chain), to raise funds for their tuberculosis sanitarium in Saranac Lake, New York (now known as the Will Rogers Memorial Hospital for Respiratory Diseases). Production financed by Chesterfield cigarettes. Directed by William McGann. Released in Great Britain during 1932 as *The Slippery Pearls*.

With Norma Shearer, Wallace Beery, Edward G. Robinson, George E. Stone, Buster Keaton, Jack Hill, Allen Jenkins, J. Farrell MacDonald, Eddie Kane, Our Gang, Polly Moran, Stan Laurel and Oliver Hardy, Hedda Hopper, Joan Crawford, William Haines, Dorothy Lee, Edmund Lowe, Victor McLaglen, El Brendel, Charlie Murray, George Sidney, Winnie Lightner, Fifi D'Orsay, Warner Baxter,

Irene Dunne, Bert Wheeler and Robert Woolsey, Richard Dix, Claudia Dell, Lowell Sherman, Eugene Pallette, Stuart Erwin, Skeets Gallagher, Gary Cooper, Wynne Gibson, Buddy Rogers, Maurice Chevalier, Douglas Fairbanks Jr., Loretta Young, Richard Barthelmess, Charles Butterworth, Bebe Daniels, Ben Lyon, Barbara Stanwyck, Frank Fay, Jack Oakie, Fay Wray, Joe E. Brown, Gabby Hayes, 'Little Billy', Mitzi Green.

The annual screen stars' ball is followed by the news that Norma Shearer's jewels are missing; they have been stolen from the two criminals (Edward G. Robinson and George E. Stone) who took them in the first place. The news is reported to a police sergeant (Wallace Beery), a man more interested in parking offences than in murder. It is then relayed to a detective (Eddie Kane), who heads for Miss Shearer's residence with two of his best men - Stan and Ollie. They drive the detective to his destination, where their car collapses. When asked where they will be, Ollie replies 'Right here'; he turns to Stan, adding 'I told you not to make that last payment'. The investigation spreads throughout the film colony, allowing Victor McLaglen and Edmund Lowe (recreating their roles from *What Price Glory?* and *The Cock-Eyed World*) to trade idiocies with El Brendel; Wheeler and Woolsey to duplicate a routine from *Rio Rita* (they even say so); George Sidney and Charlie Murray to revive 'Cohen' and 'Kelly'; while individual stars obstruct the search (as when Charles Butterworth claims to be Louise Fazenda). The jewels are at last traced to Mitzi Green, who took the jewels to save them from Messrs. Robinson and Stone. She leaves us some invaluable advice: 'Never spank a child on an empty stomach'.

Until the end of the 1960s this charity short was among the most sought-after 'lost' Laurel & Hardy

films. It was first rediscovered in England, retitled *The Slippery Pearls*. The US title was verified later and other material has been located bearing the original credits. Once thought to have been from the Masquers Club series (with which it was grouped for domestic release), *The Stolen Jools* was an entirely separate item. Stars and their respective studios provided sequences free of charge; distribution was also *gratis*. Technical costs were borne as a public relations move by Chesterfield cigarettes and, in America at least, public donations were collected after each screening. While it seems absurd today that a cigarette manufacturer should help finance a hospital for respiratory diseases, it should be remarked that this film long predates any suggestion of the dangers of smoking.

(See also: Charities; Guest appearances; Keaton, Buster; Moran, Polly; Our Gang; Pallette, Eugene; Smoking)

STREAMLINERS
One of Roach's less successful endeavours was to conceive a featurette-length format as a compromise between the feature and short-subject markets. Known as 'Streamliners', examples include Laurel & Hardy's penultimate Roach film, *A Chump at Oxford* (*qv*). *Saps at Sea* (*qv*) is considered to be in this category, but at nearly an hour, it hardly qualifies. Confirmation of the above suspicion may be found by viewing the original trailers, which describe only the first as 'streamlined'. The original US edition of *Chump* runs for 42 minutes, although overseas and subsequent US releases have used the expanded version.

(See also: Feature films; Hal Roach Studios, the; Trailers)

STREETCARS
(Laurel & Hardy films *qv*) The streetcar, or 'tram' in Britain, belongs mostly to the past but is

Ollie and 'wife' brave the hotel lobby in **Sugar Daddies**

making a comeback. In Laurel & Hardy's time, they were a commonplace mode of transport, and are essential to the plot of a 1923 Laurel solo film, *A Man About Town* (*qv*). The mutilated Tin Lizzies in *Hog Wild* and *County Hospital* are victims of collisions with such vehicles, while Ollie, perched on a window-ledge in *Tit For Tat*, sarcastically tells Stan that he is 'waiting for a streetcar'. In *Lucky Dog* Stan is scooped by a streetcar's safety mechanism, having stepped out of the path of another; while in *Duck Soup* and its remake *Another Fine Mess*, the boys meet streetcars during a wild tandem ride. Elsewhere at Roach, other comedians built routines around streetcars, such as Harold Lloyd (*qv*) in *Off the Trolley* and Charley Chase (*qv*) in *Hasty Marriage*.

(See also: Buses; Cars)

STULL, WALTER
See: *Hungry Hearts*

STUNTMEN
See: Stand-ins

SUGAR DADDIES
(Laurel & Hardy film)
Released by M–G–M, 10 September 1927. Produced by Hal Roach. Directed by Fred L. Guiol. Camera: George Stevens. Two reels. Silent. With Stan Laurel, James Finlayson, Oliver Hardy, Edna Marian, Charlotte Mineau, Noah Young, Eugene Pallette.

Millionaire Cyrus Brittle (James Finlayson) lives up to his name when awakening after a hectic night. His butler (Oliver Hardy) has ice for the Master's throbbing head and the disquieting news that there is now a Mrs Brittle (Charlotte Mineau), who 'came over as First Mate on the *Mayflower*'. The unwelcome spouse awaits downstairs, accompanied by her daughter (Edna Marian) and homicidal brother (Noah Young). They plan to part Brittle from $50,000 in exchange for his liberty, but the millionaire hopes to avert disaster by calling his lawyer (Stan Laurel). Brittle greets the family, to be told immediately of their demands. The attorney arrives and, having removed the laundry from his briefcase, sets to work. Negotiations end as Brittle, his attorney and butler

flee from the brother and a loaded gun. The millionaire and his companions have taken refuge in a beachside hotel, where his wild parties continue to make headlines. Reading of Brittle's antics in a newspaper, the unwelcome family trace his whereabouts and arrive in the foyer. The attorney spots them first and races to his client's room, where they adopt a bizarre disguise. The brother reaches them just as the butler walks out with a 'wife' actually composed of the attorney perched on the millionaire's shoulders, the whole covered with a tent-like gown. They make their way from the hotel to an amusement park, followed by family and a suspicious policeman. Somehow they survive the various rides until caught in a crowd of people at the foot of a slide. The policeman remains outside and spots a lanky lady with a rotund, bowler-hatted gentleman. Thinking he has spotted his quarry, he lifts the skirts of a genuine woman, earning him a punch in the eye.

Their first M–G–M release, *Sugar Daddies* is little more than a reworking of *Love 'Em and Weep* (*qv*), simplifying its premise and expanding its best gag. Stan, in pince-nez and frock coat, forms a trio with James Finlayson (*qv*) and Oliver Hardy, who occupies a definite third place. Within a few months Stan and Babe would be an official team, although early publicity persisted in retaining Finlayson as an optional third member. Some of their interaction suggests better things: Stan knocks at the front door, fails to see Babe opening it and knocks again, catching him on the head. Otherwise it is the usual frantic mixture of the pre-teaming films, before comic film tempo was revolutionized by the new partnership.

(See also: Blackmail; Female impersonation; Funfairs; *Further Perils of Laurel & Hardy, the*; Marian, Edna; M–G–M; Pallette, Eugene; Teaming; Young, Noah)

SUICIDE (all films *qv*)
In *Come Clean* Laurel & Hardy rescue Mae Busch (*qv*) from a suicide attempt, and are given cause not to have bothered. During the similar *Chickens Come Home* Ollie threatens to do away with Mae Busch (again!) before turning the gun on himself and in the original version of this story, *Love 'Em and Weep*, James Finlayson (*qv*) puts a gun to his temple, but it jams. In *The Flying Deuces* a lovelorn Ollie chooses a watery grave until persuaded to join the Foreign Legion; in *Bonnie Scotland* they are ordered to shoot themselves, but Stan manages to miss; while the villain of *Nothing But Trouble* kills himself by accident. In his solo film *Half a Man* Stan escapes from an island full of girls by threatening to jump from a cliff; perhaps more plausible is the tragic tale of Sandy McLaurel, who is said (once more in *Bonnie Scotland*) to have committed suicide on seeing his baby son Stanley.

(See also: Black humour; Bruckman, Clyde; Murder)

SUPERSTITION
(Laurel & Hardy films *qv*)
Stan Laurel adopted that name because 'Stan Jefferson' has 13 letters; less well-known is that Oliver Hardy amended his billing after consulting a numerologist. Superstition abounds in theatre, understandable in a profession so dependent on good fortune. A Laurel solo film of 1922, *The Weak-End Party*, was built around fear of the number 13, while later examples include throwing salt over the left shoulder in *Pardon Us* and a scene in *Pick A Star* where Rosina Lawrence (*qv*) shows concern over a broken mirror. *The Live Ghost* and others come into this category, particularly when Noah Young (*qv*) is terrified by an apparition in *Do Detectives Think?* Ollie objects to being followed by a goat in *Angora Love* on the grounds that such creatures are 'bad luck'; while Ollie is clearly guarding against further misfortune in *Way Out West*

by crossing his fingers before being hauled into the air. The boys' fortune-telling scam in *The Bohemian Girl* plays on people's superstitions, while another opera, *Babes in Toyland*, lends flesh to a commonplace fantasy with its army of bogeymen.

(See also: Confidence tricks; Hereafter, the; Names; Solo films)

SUTHERLAND, A. EDWARD
(1895-1974)
Director, a former actor with experience at Sennett (*qv*). Sutherland's work with Eddie Cantor (*Palmy Days*) and W. C. Fields (*Mississippi*, *Poppy*) is well regarded, as is his 1940 film of *The Boys From Syracuse*. He produced *Zenobia* (*qv*) for Roach before being loaned to Boris Morros (*qv*) to direct Laurel & Hardy's *The Flying Deuces* (*qv*). An interview made shortly before Sutherland's death suggests disharmony between himself and Laurel at that time, not for any specific reason but more through what Sutherland described as 'chemistry'. On a different occasion, Sutherland told John McCabe (*qv*) that there was 'no overt disagreement, only two practitioners of comedy - Stan, myself - used to working in our different ways'. Sutherland, very much a 'hands on' director, found himself working with a similarly 'hands on' chief gag man (and *de facto* director) in Stan Laurel. 'If they wanted someone else who was used to being told how to direct the picture, they should have hired him', concluded Sutherland.

SUTTON, GRADY (b. 1908)
Comic actor specialising in ineffectual or rural types. Born in Tennessee, Sutton's early credits include Harold Lloyd's *The Freshman* (1925) and Leo McCarey's *The Sophomore* (1928). McCarey (*qv*) took the actor for a screen test at Roach, where he played 'Alabam' in the *Boy Friends* series under the direction of George Stevens (*qv*). He appears also in Stevens' RKO two-reel series *Blondes and Redheads*.

While at Roach, Sutton appeared with Laurel & Hardy in *Pack Up Your Troubles* (*qv*), as a nervous bridegroom. In a 1969 interview for *Film Fan Monthly* he recalled his friendship with Oliver Hardy, at whose home Sutton was a frequent guest. He is best remembered from W. C. Fields' features *Man On the Flying Trapeze*, *You Can't Cheat An Honest Man* and *The Bank Dick*, in the last as the splendidly-named Og Oggilby. Seen later in many feature films, commercials and TV shows.

(See also: Lloyd, Harold; Periodicals; *Twice Two*; Weddings)

SWEEPS
See: Businessmen and *Dirty Work*

SWISS CHEESE
See: *Swiss Miss* and Working titles

SWISS MISS
(Laurel & Hardy film)
Released by M-G-M, 20 May 1938. Produced by Hal Roach. Associate Producer: S. S. Van Keuren. Directed by John G. Blystone. Camera: Norbert Brodine, Art Lloyd. 72 minutes. With Stan Laurel and Oliver Hardy, Della Lind, Walter Woolf King, Eric Blore, Adia Kutznetzoff, Ludovico Tomarchio, Charles Judels, Anita Garvin.

Composer Victor Albert (Walter Woolf King) arrives at a Swiss hotel, hoping to gain inspiration for his new opera. The hotel's staff have been persuaded to wear traditional costume. Another reason for his retreat is to escape his wife, Anna (Della Lind), an opera star he believes would distract him from composing music about an ordinary, unsophisticated girl. Stan and Ollie are in Switzerland to sell mousetraps, acting on Stan's theory that Switzerland has the most cheese and, consequently, the most mice. They accept an offer to buy out their business but, when living it up at the Alpen Hotel, discover they have been paid in currency from a non-existent country. The pair are forced to work as kitchen hands to pay off the bill, with the complication of working an extra day for each plate they break; the tyrannical chef (Adia Kutznetzoff) ensures that plenty are broken. Anna, who has traced her husband to the hotel, is determined to prove she has the qualities to interest an ordinary man and is happy to encourage the romantic interest of both Ollie and the chef. To reinforce the point (and keep pestering Victor) she takes a job as chambermaid. Unaware that she is married, Ollie falls for Anna. He and Stan nearly take a different fall when transporting the composer's piano across a rickety rope bridge, a manoeuvre complicated by the appearance of a gorilla. At Stan's suggestion, Ollie invites Anna to join him at the Alpenfest, a local carnival. Serenading her, they are soaked by a jug of water from Ollie's rival, the chef. At the Alpenfest, Anna makes a convincing gypsy singer and she is

reunited with Victor. Stan and Ollie escape the chef and, learning of Anna's marriage, leave the hotel – pursued by the gorilla they had met earlier.

Swiss Miss followed two 'Stan Laurel Productions' (*qv*), neither of which were burdened with superfluous plotting. On this occasion the team's feature-film structure reverts to that of *Bonnie Scotland* (*qv*) in that too much time is devoted to the romantic sub-plot. There is at least an attempt to weave Laurel & Hardy into this story but tedium still results. Studio control over this enterprise is demonstrated by the huge associate producer credit for Roach's cousin, Sidney S. Van Keuren, and a famous anecdote: the bridge sequence is filled with shots of a drunken Stan crashing against the piano keys, which is rendered meaningless by Roach's order to delete a sequence in which the jealous chef, planning to murder the composer, plants a bomb to be set off by a

certain key. This scene is otherwise a highlight of the film, as is Ollie's serenade of Anna (Stan accompanying on sousaphone), Stan's fabrication of a 'snow storm' to obtain brandy from a St Bernard and an early scene with Laurel & Hardy demonstrating mousetraps. Most of the team's stock company are absent, though Anita Garvin (*qv*) returns after an absence of several years. Unrecognizable but nonetheless present is Charles Gemora, repeating his ape impersonation from *The Chimp* (*qv*).

(See also: Agee, James; Animals; Colour; Feature films; Judels, Charles; King, Walter Woolf; Kuznetzoff, Adia; Lind, Della; Songs; Teaming)

Ollie, Stan and a **Swiss Miss**, *Della Lind*

TASHLIN, FRANK (1913-72)
Director and screenwriter, initially for
cartoons. He reportedly contributed
gags to Laurel & Hardy's last three
shorts (all *qv*), *Tit For Tat*, *The Fixer-
Uppers* and *Thicker Than Water*. In his
Warner cartoon days, he was reported
as attending every Laurel & Hardy
and Chaplin film with a notebook, jot-
ting down the gags. A 1939 Looney
Tune, *Porky and Teabiscuit*, sees the
porcine hero duplicating the auction
scene of *One Good Turn* (*qv*). Tashlin
is credited with the celebrated joke in
A Night in Casablanca where Harpo
Marx, when asked if he is holding up
a building, turns out to be doing precisely that. As writer and director, he
worked on several films with Jerry
Lewis (*qv*); one of their collaborations,
The Bellboy (1960) commemorates the
Laurel connection.

(See also: Animation; Auctions; Marx
Brothers, the; Writers)

TATTOOS
Tattoos have been used for either
individual gags or as a plot element: a
famous example, from the Marx
Brothers' *Duck Soup*, shows a live dog
appearing from Harpo's tattoo of a
kennel. Laurel & Hardy avoided such
gags, though an early exception occurs
in the pre-teaming film *Why Girls
Love Sailors* (*qv*), when the ship
adorning Stan's chest is comple-
mented by a jug of water. This
absence from the repertoire may perhaps be explained by the genuine
tattoo, a leaf design, on Hardy's right
forearm. He acquired it as a youngster

and it is believed that his mother subsequently paid a visit to the tattooist,
bearing a horsewhip. The tattoo was
later kept well hidden but may be
glimpsed on occasion.

(See also: Hardy, Emily)

THE TAXI BOYS
A Roach series of 1932-3 that didn't
quite work, *The Taxi Boys* was a continuation of similar comedies made by
director Del Lord for Mack Sennett
(*qv*). The studio's press release for 30
May 1932 mentions *Thundering Taxis*
as the first to go into production,
quoting Lord as promising 'something
new in modernized slapstick which
will be the essence of the series'. Each
subject demonstrated instead a fondness for frenzy, 'impossible' gags
(such as stretched limbs) and finales
dependent on animated shots.
Thundering Taxis has Clyde Cook (*qv*)
as one of the cabbies; another early
title (sometimes quoted as the first),
What Price Taxi? pairs Cook with
Franklin Pangborn. The series was
recast with Billy Gilbert (*qv*), Charles
Rogers (*qv*) and Ben Blue, although
Rogers survived for only one short
(*Strange Innertube*) before Blue and
Gilbert settled down as leads. Blue
(1901-75), a former dancer, was an
accomplished club comic who was to
do reasonably well in films (notably
The Big Broadcast of 1938), but *The
Taxi Boys* presents him in remarkably
irritating form as a character unable to
stop twitching, twisting and mugging.
He and Gilbert were being groomed
as another Laurel & Hardy, but their

respective dolt and blusterer roles
were painted broadly. *Bring 'Em Back
a Wife* is a reworking of Laurel &
Hardy's *That's My Wife* (*qv*), while
the dialogue suggests a further influence when in *Wreckety Wrecks*, Gilbert
admonishes Blue with the remark 'see
what you got me into... you' (significantly, the funniest character in
Wreckety Wrecks is a drunk played by
Arthur Housman). *Hot Spot* typifies
some of the weak dialogue when Blue,
his cab being torn apart, tries a wise-
crack but can come up with nothing
better than 'What is this - a hobby?'
Call Her Sausage, one of several pun
titles based on features, jettisons the
whole Taxi format in favour of Billy
and Ben operating a general store.
Leonard Maltin (*qv*) has accurately
described the problem with the series
as 'everyone trying too hard'.

(See also: Costello, Lou; Housman,
Arthur; Impersonators; Parodies;
Reissues; Taxis; Weddings)

TAXIS (all films *qv*)
Stan and Ollie's encounters with taxi-
cabs are often memorable: a driver in
Their Purple Moment leaves the meter
running as the boys live it up; in
Liberty they try to change in the back
of a cab only to be surprised by
prospective passenger Jean Harlow
(*qv*). Another cab brings Miss Harlow
into *Double Whoopee*, shortly before
her dress is trapped in the door. The
same film pits the boys against a cab
driver who grows increasingly angry
when summoned unnecessarily. *Blotto*
concludes with an irate Mrs Laurel

checking the boys' escape by destroying their taxi with a shotgun. The cab driver is one of those who is fascinated by a jigsaw puzzle on Ollie's wedding day in *Me and My Pal*. Much of the plot in *Sons of the Desert* is outlined in a conversation between Laurel & Hardy during their cab ride home from a lodge meeting, and the team's last Fox film, *The Bullfighters*, demonstrates what seems to have been a shortage of cabs. British comedian Harry Worth (*qv*) recalled the team resorting to cabs as a means of escaping the crowds between hotel and theatre.

(See also: Shotguns; Stage appearances; *Taxi Boys, the*)

TAYLOR, SAM (1895-1958)
Veteran writer and director whose silent credits include screenwriting at Roach in the early 1920s and directing Harold Lloyd (*qv*) in *Hot Water* (1924) and *The Freshman* (1925). Taylor's name will forever be associated with a credit on the 1929 Pickford-Fairbanks talkie *The Taming of the Shrew*: 'By William Shakespeare, with additional dialogue by Sam Taylor'. He will *not* be remembered for directing Laurel & Hardy's *Nothing But Trouble* (*qv*), a task presumably given to Taylor in the belief that any 1920s refugee would suit the team's style.

(See also: M-G-M; St Clair, Malcolm; 20th Century-Fox)

TEACHERS
See: Education

TEAMING
(Laurel & Hardy films *qv*)
Laurel and Hardy had spent many years as solo comedians before circumstances finally dictated their teaming. Their joint appearance in *Lucky Dog* was mere coincidence: Joe Rock (*qv*) wanted Babe to support Stan, who was not then sufficiently confident to work with such a potential scene-stealer. The genesis of their

association really begins in 1925 at the Hal Roach lot where Laurel, fresh from starring roles at Rock, was training as a director under F. Richard Jones (*qv*) just as Hardy was settling at Roach. Their earliest connection at the studio is a one-reeler called *Yes, Yes, Nanette!* (*qv*), which was co-directed by Laurel and featured Hardy in the supporting cast. Laurel would direct his future partner into the next year, until Hardy withdrew from the cast of *Get 'Em Young*, a film with 'fading star' Harry Myers (who played the millionaire in Chaplin's *City Lights*). Hardy was badly scalded while cooking a leg of lamb, and Jones persuaded the reluctant

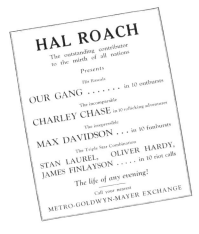

*Teaming: Neither Roach nor his new distributor, M-G-M, could decide if they were promoting a duo or a trio
By courtesy of Robert G. Dickson*

Laurel to take his place. Stan's return to acting was encouraged by a substantial raise in salary and it required a further raise to keep him before the cameras. Jones had noticed an additional zaniness in the Laurel persona and was anxious not to lose it; Stan in turn was placed in a difficult position, being officially barred from acting by his old contract with Rock. Both Laurel and Hardy were cast in *Forty-Five Minutes From Hollywood*, but in separate scenes; *Duck Soup*, by some monumental accident, presents them

almost in their later format; while *Slipping Wives, With Love and Hisses, Sailors Beware* and others keep them separate, the only noticeable progression being Hardy's increased prominence. *Do Detectives Think?* marks a return to their *Duck Soup* relationship, but this is jettisoned once more in *Flying Elephants* and *Sugar Daddies*. The last-named was the first to be released through M-G-M after Roach's break with Pathé. As the Laurel & Hardy films gained a following, the last Pathés were issued simultaneously, featuring them both, but billing Laurel solo. Audience confusion was matched only by that of the studio publicists, who alternated between promoting Laurel & Hardy and Laurel, Hardy and Finlayson. *The Second Hundred Years* was advertised as the first Laurel & Hardy film, but Roach and the comedians themselves considered the team official from *Putting Pants On Philip* and *The Battle of the Century*. *Philip* does not employ their standard characters, but there is no denying their teamwork; *Battle*, even in today's mangled edition, is one of their classics. An immediate difference in the Laurel & Hardy comedies is a deliberate decision to slow the pace. This decision was made by Leo McCarey (*qv*) and suited the team's slow-thinking characters. Short comedies had tended toward undue speed, which was sometimes exaggerated by under-cranking the camera (and emphasized all the more when projected at the later sound speed). Laurel & Hardy worked at a normal, realistic pace, which became especially fortunate when sound enforced it. Laurel & Hardy would continue to develop their characters, and by the early 1930s were artistically inseparable, but Stan's growing contractual difficulties with Roach threatened to end the partnership on several occasions. In 1935 such a split was announced, starting the first rumours of discord with Babe. This was not the case, and the comedians made a point of appearing together socially in order to dispel that impression. The British *Film Weekly* documents the sequence of events: in 1935 Stan told the magazine that the team would not split 'as long as we can pay our way... we're together until debt do us part'. More wrangling over money and artistic control begat further unfounded rumours of a split between the pair; in February 1938 *Film Weekly* published stills from the forthcoming *Swiss Miss*, claiming 'in spite of all the stories we've heard about disagreements between Laurel & Hardy, the twin comedians have proved that they've got over all that by beginning work on a new M-G-M comedy'. On 28 January 1939 the same magazine ran a full-page item on Stan after what seemed like a permanent split with Roach; Stan had been fired after taking a leave of absence from the studio. The magazine repeats a common misconception, that the team had previously been threatened by a studio disagreement over '[Laurel's] claim that he was worth more money than Hardy because of the extra work he did'. Stan was eventually re-hired, after Babe had appeared in Roach's *Zenobia* (*qv*) with Harry Langdon (*qv*). The *Film Weekly* piece, dwelling rather on Stan's recent marital catastrophes, noted Babe's 'new partner' and asked the question 'whither Laurel?' The team's reunion, with Laurel and Hardy able to sign concurrently as opposed to their hitherto staggered contracts, provided the answer but rumours of disharmony continued. Reviewers sometimes spoke condescendingly of their 'squabbling'. On July 15 1939, *Film Weekly* reported a reissue of *Bonnie Scotland* with a quote from Stan made 'just before the Laurel & Hardy partnership broke up', but five weeks later *Picturegoer* was able to report on their new project, *A Chump at Oxford*. In 1950 Babe was asked about he and Stan having been 'apart', but replied that 'they'd gotten us mixed up with other teams', adding that he and Stan were still friends after 23 years; 'I

think that's a record', said Babe. Rumour, however, is hard to crush and there was subsequently a story manufactured to satisfy it.

(See also: Apocrypha, Characters; Cook, Clyde; 'Fading stars'; *Four Clowns*; Finlayson, James; Hal Roach Studios; Marriages; Periodicals; Salaries; Short films; Solo films)

TELEGRAMS (all films *qv*)
As an adjunct to telephones (*qv*), telegrams serve an occasional purpose in the Laurel & Hardy films. Stan fabricates a telegram in *Blotto* as an excuse to leave the house. Ollie receives word of his wife's return in *Helpmates*, but is saved the job of reading it by an inquisitive telegraph boy. Perhaps worst of all is the telegram warning of financial disaster in *Me and My Pal* which is ignored until Ollie's fortune has been wiped out.

(See also: Letters)

TELEPHONES (all films *qv*)
Telephones provide gags involving dialogue (*qv*) as well as less obvious business. The absurd conversation of *Helpmates* is complicated when Stan inadvertently speaks into the rear end of a statue instead of the receiver. Another call is abandoned in *Saps at Sea* when Stan picks up a banana in lieu of the earpiece. Later in the film, Ollie hangs from an upstairs window with only the telephone lead keeping him from plummeting; less desperate but more claustrophobic is the scene in *Our Relations* where 'Alf' and 'Bert' share a telephone kiosk with Arthur Housman (*qv*). Ollie uses another booth to contact Stan in *Blotto*, but his plans for a night out with Stan are overheard by Mrs Laurel on an extension line. Stan in turn eavesdrops on Ollie's conversations in *Our Wife* and *Twice Two*, the latter complicated by an exchange of feedback through putting mouthpiece to earpiece, then by Stan blowing ink through the line.

Ollie is persuaded to postpone a seaside trip when friends call in *Be Big* and is too late when calling his broker in *Me and My Pal*. *Chickens Come Home* features several embarrassing calls to the Hardy residence; a police telephone has its cord severed in *The Midnight Patrol*; and a confused Stan answers the telephone when hearing a knock on the door in *Beau Hunks*. Later in the film, when the boys line up as Foreign Legion recruits, Stan gives his number as 'Hollywood 4368'. Stan's real-life telephone number, 'Oxford 0614', was used on-screen in *Blotto*; never reclusive about such matters, Stan kept his number listed in public directories until the end of his life.

(See also: Telegrams)

TELEVISION
(Laurel & Hardy films *qv*)
Although television has kept many people from the cinemas since the 1950s, it has served also to provide long-term audiences for numerous films and personalities. Laurel &

Television: As an aftermath of This is Your Life, *Hal Roach Sr. and Jr. dedicate their studio pool to Laurel & Hardy*

Hardy's popularity in the US had declined in the 1940s, but was rescued when their Roach films were released to television. A 1951 magazine article titled 'Popularity Rains on Laurel & Hardy' quotes Hardy to the effect that children who would say 'Get out of the way, Fat' had changed to a more civil 'You're Oliver Hardy, aren't you?', followed by a request for an autograph. Roach was then almost alone in supplying major film product to American TV, realizing where the future lay while his contemporaries regarded the new medium as an adversary (in a *Daily Express* interview of October 1953, Babe expresses a performer's anxiety at TV's ability to swallow up comic material).

Subsequent Roach product geared to television includes *The Gale Storm Show* and *Screen Directors' Playhouse*, one episode of which (*The Silent Partner*) stars Buster Keaton (*qv*). The Laurel & Hardy films have frequently suffered from inappropriate scheduling, with dedicated admirers sometimes having to set their alarm clocks for obscure hours in the morning. Both Laurel & Hardy became fairly avid viewers, although Laurel is known to have avoided seeing his own films because of drastic cutting. He admitted also to finding them too slow on the small screen, and would have been willing to edit TV versions if approached. When stations performed the task themselves (invariably for commercial rather than artistic reasons) the results could be disastrous. Especially notorious is the version of *Fra Diavolo* which was reduced to half its original 90 minutes. Even today, American television continues the process of mutilation, with the *Laurel & Hardy Show* package incorporating abridgments of certain subjects. British television has treated Laurel & Hardy with relative kindness, presenting both sound films and a number of the silents mostly intact. BBC screenings date back to at least 1947, a year when the team's popularity in the UK was reflected by a successful tour. The

BBC showings continued for some 35 years, deriving chiefly from Film Classics reissue prints and incorporating all but a few of the sound shorts and Roach features. Some, such as *Bonnie Scotland*, *The Bohemian Girl* and *Saps at Sea* went to commercial TV, which otherwise had to make do with several post-Roach appearances. A surprise deal took Laurel & Hardy to the ITV network early in the 1980s, producing examples of drastic cutting to rival American TV at its worst, such as the occasion when a large chunk of *Busy Bodies* was replaced by several feet of opaque leader. One positive aspect was that several ITV regions screened the silent films, hitherto ignored by British TV except in compilations (*qv*). A subsequent legal battle over film rights effectively blacked Laurel & Hardy from UK screens for a prolonged period; when the case was settled, the films reappeared on the BBC, with the addition of several features previously seen on ITV plus a few silent shorts. These copies of the silents superseded those of earlier years, deriving from new video masters prepared in Europe. The BBC has continued to use its own material for the talkies, but European-originated versions have appeared in such places as Eire and in UK video editions. Aside from a season in 1982, British TV has tended to slot Laurel & Hardy into children's schedules, although Channel Four once reached an opposite extreme with an after-midnight screening of *Fra Diavolo*. Widespread exposure has ensured the familiarity of the team's films, but less has been said of their work in television itself. Richard Finegan (in the Winter 1993 *Intra-Tent Journal*) has described a still-extant item from the *Erskine Johnson's Hollywood Reel* series, in which a solo Laurel is shown clowning at a children's swimming event at the Brentwood Bantam Club in California. Both Laurel & Hardy were interviewed by Leslie Mitchell for BBC TV's *Picture Page* in February 1952, and later took part in a

'comedy interview' written by Sid Colin and Talbot Rothwell for a 1953 BBC series, *Face the Music*, hosted by bandleader Henry Hall. Neither is believed to exist even in written form, a script for the latter containing a blank space in lieu of their contribution. Still in existence is Ralph Edwards' tribute to the team in his *This Is Your Life* series, broadcast live by NBC in December 1954. The team and lawyer Ben Shipman (*qv*) had arranged to meet British impresario Bernard Delfont at Hollywood's Knickerbocker Hotel, where they were surprised by the TV crew. Laurel is said to have resented both the programme's lack of preparation and the absence of any paid TV work (in 1952 he had told the *Daily Express* 'Television is the thing of the future, and we are considering it very seriously'), causing a delay which Edwards had to fill with ad-libs. In retrospect, Stan admitted some fondness for the tribute, but in the programme itself he maintains a level of polite taciturnity. Very few of the key names are present, though the team seem genuinely pleased to see Leo McCarey (*qv*), Vivian Blaine (*qv*) and Frank Fouce, a director from Stan's solo days. Some praise is also due the researchers for locating a childhood sweetheart of Babe's. Many years later this programme was adapted into a *Laurel & Hardy Show* segment incorporating additional interviews and clips, forming a more worthwhile tribute, but a direct legacy of the show was an offer from Roach Studios to star in a new series of colour TV films, provisionally titled *Laurel & Hardy's Fabulous Fables*. Producer was to be Hal Roach Jr., but the team's failing health led to the abandonment of the project. Their last TV work was a 1955 BBC programme about the Grand Order of Water Rats (*qv*) titled *This Is Music Hall*. Laurel & Hardy (who were unbilled in the BBC's listings magazine *Radio Times*) provide a filmed insert during which they reminisce about their friends in British variety. They conclude with thanks and a fond goodbye to their fans. Neither would have known this to be their farewell appearance but there could have been none more appropriate. The programme still exists in BBC archives but has not been revived for public viewing. After Laurel's death, American TV screened *A Salute to Stan Laurel*, hosted by Dick Van Dyke (*qv*). This rather notorious enterprise (described by one critic as 'unbelievably cheap and inept') allowed nothing for Hardy's contribution and little for that of Stan Laurel. Extracts were kept to a minimum as the mostly unrelated guests went through their paces. The presence of Buster Keaton (*qv*) provided some interest, as did a brief clip of Stan reacting to his Oscar, but Van Dyke was the only in-studio contributor to earn even scant praise. This programme also survives and, perhaps regrettably, *has* been made available for scrutiny.

(See also: Academy Awards; Anderson, G. M.; *Be Big*; *Berth Marks*; *Big Business*; *Blotto*; Colour; *Dancing Masters, The*; Documentaries; Hal Roach Studios, the; *Liberty*; *Men O'War*; *Midnight Patrol*; *Pack Up Your Troubles*; *Pardon Us*; Periodicals; Reissues; Roach, Hal E.; Stage appearances; *They Go Boom*; *Unaccustomed As We Are*; Unfilmed projects; Video releases; Wright, Basil)

TERRY, FRANK
See: Clifford, Nat

THAT'S MY WIFE
(Laurel & Hardy film)
Released by M-G-M, 23 March 1929. Produced by Hal Roach. Directed by Lloyd French. Two reels. Silent, with music and sound effects.
With Stan Laurel & Oliver Hardy, Vivien Oakland, Harry Bernard, William Courtwright, Jimmy Aubrey.

Permanent house guest Stan has brought Mrs Magnolia Hardy (Vivien Oakland) to the point of departure, despite Ollie's insistence that such a move would disbar the couple from Uncle Bernal's inheritance. Mrs Hardy has chosen to leave just before a surprise visit from Uncle himself, who promises to set up the Hardys in a fine new home - if they are happily married. Fortunately Uncle has never met the absent Magnolia, and Stan is called upon to impersonate her. The intricacies of balancing on high heels are matched by the task of maintaining an ersatz bosom (supplied by small barbells), but Stan convinces in the role. The imposture continues at dinner in the Pink Pup club, where Stan is pestered by an amorous drunk (Jimmy Aubrey) before a stolen necklace is dropped down the back of his dress. The drunk is disposed of by dumping a bowl of soup over his head, but the necklace is harder to dislodge, with Mr and 'Mrs' Hardy caught in several embarrassing positions, not least when suddenly on-stage in place of a floor show called 'The Pageant of Love'. Stan's disguise is revealed, leaving a disgruntled Uncle determined to leave his money to a cat's home. The returning drunk pours a bowl of soup over Ollie's head; as Stan grins, Ollie summons enough grace to follow his example.

Another of the late silents supplied with a music and effects track (part of it used as incidental music for Our Gang's *Bear Shooters*), *That's My Wife* echoes the plot of a 1926 Roach comedy with Oliver Hardy and Glenn Tryon (*qv*), *Along Came Auntie*. Vivien Oakland (*qv*) appears in both, although her role as Mrs Hardy has sometimes been miscredited to Dorothy Christy (*qv*) in filmographies. Just as *Liberty* (*qv*) is said to have been made in order to rescue a trouser-swapping gag deleted from a previous film, so *That's My Wife* is an excuse to rework the routine in a fashion even more risqué than the original. Stan's female disguise is by necessity more realistic than in many

Garrick and Lucille in "The Pageant of Love"; **That's My Wife**

instances; just convincing enough to attract a drunk, portrayed by Stan's flawlessly bleary Karno colleague Jimmy Aubrey (*qv*).

(See also: Courtwright, William; Female impersonation; *Further Perils of Laurel & Hardy, the*; *Laurel & Hardy's Laughing Twenties*; Risqué humour; Shoes; Sleeper, Martha; Women)

THAT'S THAT!
(Laurel & Hardy films *qv*)
A gag reel assembled by editor Bert Jordan (*qv*) for Stan's birthday in 1937, *That's That!* was unknown until Stan's personal copy was unearthed by his daughter in 1980. Screened at that year's British convention of the Sons of the Desert club (*qv*), the reel opens with full Roach/M-G-M titles followed by gag shots, outtakes and juxtapositions. Versions of *The Laurel-Hardy Murder Case* provide Ollie speaking Spanish before cutting to Stan's English reply of 'Gee, whizz'. The latter is a close-up unused in the release version; from the same film is a lengthy, alternate take of the boys' arrival at the Laurel mansion, suggesting a considerable amount of on-set revision. Between shots of skeletons and other momentary wonders (such as an alternate Finlayson dive downstairs in *Our Wife*) are two

glimpses of the Sheriff in *Way Out West*, first Tiny Sandford (*qv*) then his replacement in the role, Stanley Fields (*qv*). Stan's 16mm sound copy of *That's That!* was thought unique until a mute 35mm work print surfaced in private hands. At the time of writing it is unavailable for further examination although collectors hope it may some day reach home video.

(See also: Finlayson, James; Foreign versions; Home movies; Laurel, Lois; Out-takes; Scripts; Video releases)

THEIR FIRST MISTAKE
(Laurel & Hardy film)
Released by M-G-M, 5 November 1932. Produced by Hal Roach. Directed by George Marshall.
Two reels.
With Stan Laurel and Oliver Hardy, Mae Busch, Billy Gilbert, George Marshall.

Mrs Arabella Hardy (Mae Busch) is weary of the amount of time her husband spends with Mr Laurel. When Stan telephones, Ollie pretends it is his boss, 'Mr Jones', inviting him to a business meeting. Arabella is placated until Stan arrives from across the hall, explaining that it was him calling. The furious Mrs Hardy drives the boys into Stan's apartment, warning Ollie not to go out with Stan again. Stan believes that Ollie's household would benefit from the addition of a baby, in order to keep his wife occupied while the boys go out. Ollie decides to adopt a child, but on returning home is served papers to the effect that his wife is suing him for divorce and Stan for alienation of his affections. They are left to care for a screaming baby, complicated by complaints from the neighbours, Stan's plugging a standard lamp into a flashing hotel sign and the intricacies of feeding the child. Eventually some peace is restored until the sleeping Stan drinks from the baby's bottle; the teat comes loose, pouring milk over the bed.

Their First Mistake: the boys return to Ollie's home with a new resident

The somewhat abrupt finish mars *Their First Mistake*, but there is much to compensate. Stan's telephone call inviting Ollie to the Cement Workers' Bazaar ('They're going to give away a steam-shovel') is a priceless absurdity developed from similar business in *We Faw Down* (*qv*). When addressed as 'Mr Jones', Stan checks both the mirror and a letter in his pocket in order to verify his own identity. When Stan is prepared to abandon Ollie with a baby, there follows a risqué parody of Victorian melodrama, Ollie's 'ruined' pose reflecting in part Stan's kilted innocent in *Putting Pants On Philip* (*qv*). Today's prints tend to be from reissues, losing director credit for George Marshall (*qv*) plus the gag title, which reads, characteristically, 'Mr Hardy was married - Mr Laurel was also unhappy'.

(See also: Busch, Mae; Children; Gag titles; Gilbert, Billy; Melodrama; Reissues; Risqué humour; Scripts; Telephones)

THEIR PURPLE MOMENT
(Laurel & Hardy film)
Released by M-G-M, 19 May 1928. Produced by Hal Roach. Directed by James Parrott. Camera: George Stevens. Two reels. Silent.
With Stan Laurel and Oliver Hardy, Fay Holderness, Anita Garvin, Kay Deslys, Tiny Sandford, Jimmy Aubrey, Lyle Tayo, Leo Willis, Patsy O'Byrne.

Mr Pincher (Stan Laurel) and his wife (Fay Holderness) have a perfect financial arrangement: he earns it, she takes it. When Mr Pincher arrives home with his salary, Mrs Pincher notices a discrepancy of three dollars, an amount her husband claims was spent on a Chinese gramophone record. The three dollars actually reside under Mr Pincher's collar, and are later concealed in an ingenious hiding place, the inside pocket of a portrait hanging in the hallway. Mrs Pincher, seeing the manoeuvre, replaces her husband's accumulated money with the trading coupons she has been saving. 'Another husband', Mr Hardy, and his spouse (Lyle Tayo) visit the Pincher residence; quietly, the visiting husband tells Mr Pincher that 'she found my hide-out! She's a blood-hound!' Mr Pincher shows his friend the bulging wallet he has concealed inside the portrait. Believing them-selves financially equipped for doing the town, they leave the house on the pretext of visiting the bowling alley. Outside, they meet the town gossip (Patsy O'Byrne), who observes, cyni-cally, 'Fine day for mischief'. She is not far wrong, as when Mrs Pincher greets her at the door, the two hus-bands are already following a brace of young ladies. When spotted, the boys make a quick about-turn. Outside the Pink Pup café, they meet two girls (Anita Garvin and Kay Deslys) whose boyfriends have left them to pay the bill. The boys, offering to 'assume all responsibility', escort them back inside, and are seen once more by the gossip. The girls threaten dire revenge on the pair who let them down earlier: one carries a knife, the other a stiletto. Mr Pincher checks that his wallet is still in place, then goes on to make an impression with his trick of flicking a spoon into a glass. Ollie's attempt to follow suit sends the spoon down the back of a woman's dress. The floor show consists of a troupe of perform-ing midgets; deciding to treat them, Mr Pincher looks into the wallet and at last notices the absence of legal ten-der. His subsequent terror is compounded when the girls' taxi

... and the uninspired sequence that took its place

Their Purple Moment: *the planned ending, with Edgar Kennedy*

driver (Leo Willis) walks in, placing his still-running meter on the table; worse still, the driver is invited to dine at their table. Mr Pincher passes the wallet to Mr Hardy who, examining the contents, suggests a surreptitious exit. The subsequent arrival of the wives coincides with a request from the head waiter (Tiny Sandford) to settle the bill. When he discovers the truth, the boys are pursued to the kitchen. Cornered by head waiter and wives, Ollie decides to blame his friend for leading him to 'this den of vice'. Retribution follows with a pie aimed at Ollie, which instead hits Mrs Hardy. Ollie, responding in kind, acci-dentally sends a pie toward Mrs Pincher. Soon the entire kitchen is engaged in a free-for-all, culminating in the head waiter pushing a pie into Ollie's face.

The gag where Stan's money is concealed in the hinged door of a por-trait is among the most imaginative in the team's films. Indeed *Their Purple Moment* would be a clever film overall but for the degeneration into obvious slapstick for the finale. This is all the more incredible considering that stills

exist for a deleted ending in which Laurel & Hardy try to escape the café disguised as members of the midget troupe. Said to have been a decision made by the studio rather than the comedians themselves, the substitu-tion of a pie fight, without the satiric intent of *The Battle of the Century* (*qv*), relegates *Their Purple Moment* to a place among the team's lesser comedies.

(See also: Aubrey, Jimmy; Costumes; Deleted scenes; *Four Clowns*; Midgets; Night-clubs; Paintings; Slapstick; Taxis; *That's My Wife;* Women)

THEM THAR HILLS
(Laurel & Hardy film)
Released by M-G-M, 21 July 1934.
Produced by Hal Roach. Directed by
Charles Rogers. Camera: Art Lloyd.
Two reels.
With Stan Laurel and Oliver Hardy,
Mae Busch, Charlie Hall, Billy
Gilbert.

Dr Gilbert diagnoses Ollie's swollen

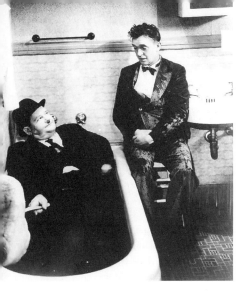

Them Thar Hills: *Ollie and his gouty foot get 'plenty of water'*

foot as gout and prescribes a trip to the mountains, where the patient should drink plenty of water. Stan suggests they rent a trailer. Helping Ollie downstairs, he provides him with his first dose of water, plunging them both straight into a bathful of the stuff. They duly arrive at a mountain retreat just after the locals have been forced to dump a load of moonshine into the well. Preparing baked beans and coffee (Stan: 'You sure know how to plan a meal') means drawing water from the well, but Stan notices how it 'tickles'. Ollie ascribes this to the way all mountain water tastes, adding 'it's good for your nerves'. Intricate kitchen details are accompanied by Ollie's gentle la-la version of 'The Old Spinning Wheel', punctuated by Stan's addition of 'pom-pom' until lightly struck on the head. Stan chops wood for the stove but amputates the toe of Ollie's shoe. A married couple (Mae Busch and Charlie Hall) arrive to borrow fuel for their car. By this time, the mountain water has soothed the boys' nerves to the point where they can barely stand. The visiting wife asks to stay while her husband fetches the car; she tries the laced water and has joined Stan and Ollie in a drunken version of their song by the time of her husband's return. The furious man

engages Stan and Ollie in an exchange of violence which gains momentum as a sink plunger is stuck to his head, his belt cut and a plate of beans dumped into his fallen trousers. He gains revenge by detaching the trailer from the boys' car, sending them crashing. They retaliate by emptying a tin of molasses over their victim, to which is added the contents of a pillow. This makeshift tar-and-feather treatment combines with the sink plunger to create the effect of a feathery unicorn. The mythical creature responds by pouring an oil lamp over the seat of Ollie's trousers, igniting the area with a match borrowed from Stan. The couple drive away leaving Ollie panicking. Stan recommends jumping in the well ('Thank you' says Ollie, pausing to shake his friend's hand), but the result is an explosion that sends Ollie heavenward before landing, head first, in a newly-created pit.

One of their funniest shorts, *Them Thar Hills* was such a hit that a sequel was made, *Tit For Tat* (*qv*). Mae Busch and Charlie Hall (both *qv*) work well together and Hall's finest moments are perhaps in these two films. The 'pom-pom' business has gained currency among *aficionados* worldwide; it has been known for jazz musicians to play 'The Old Spinning Wheel' for the sole purpose of adding such punctuation. Although never shown together theatrically, *Them Thar Hills* and *Tit For Tat* have been paired on British video and, very occasionally, the BBC.

(See also: Alcohol; Doctors; *Fra Diavolo*; Gilbert, Billy; Reciprocal destruction; Sequels; Shoes; Sickness; Television; Video releases)

THEY GO BOOM!
(Laurel & Hardy film)
Released by M-G-M, 21 September 1929. Produced by Hal Roach. Directed by James Parrott. Camera: Art Lloyd. Two reels.

With Stan Laurel and Oliver Hardy, Charlie Hall.

Ollie has 'the sniffles', something which has been aggravated variously by Stan's snoring, a rebellious roller blind and a framed motto over their bed ('Smile all the while') which refuses to stay put. In driving the nail back into the wall, Stan succeeds in puncturing a water pipe, causing Ollie some disquiet as its unidentified stream of water pours into the bed. Attempts at relieving Ollie's cold take the form of a mustard bath, chest plaster and 'painting his throat' with cotton wool dipped in cough mixture. The mustard turns solid around Ollie's feet, the chest plaster attaches itself to his rear and the cotton wool disappears down Ollie's gullet. In the ensuing squabble, Ollie is pushed on to the bed, flattening the inflatable mattress; his attempt to re-inflate it backfires, and it blows him up like a balloon. Once restored to his usual size, the scuffle resumes, bringing in the landlord (Charlie Hall) to complain about the noise. Stan has jumped into bed, leaving Ollie to take the blame. Ollie is threatened with eviction. The landlord gone, Ollie refills the mattress from a gas tap. The mattress now 'looks like a pudding', and the boys are unable to avoid rolling out of bed. The landlord reap-

They Go Boom!: *Stan has 'painted' Ollie's throat. Where's the cotton wool?*

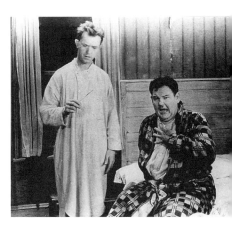

pears: he kicks Ollie, who pushes him into the tub of mustard. Exit the landlord, shouting threats. The boys return to bed and pretend to be asleep. The gas tap has been turned on and the mattress assumes giant proportions by the time the landlord has returned with the police. When Ollie sneezes, the mattress explodes; a further sneeze brings down the ceiling.

A claustrophobic but entertaining short, *They Go Boom!* is virtually unknown in the UK owing to its neglect by television. Several parts of the country saw a Canadian-originated print during the 1980s, but this had been deprived of its soundtrack. The full sound version appeared on video several years later. Considerably less adept in editing and sound recording than their other 1929 talkies, the film still contains a sequence (described under **Slapstick**) that could serve as a model of comedy structure. There are certain prints in which *They Go Boom!* belies its name, the climactic explosion consisting only of a muted thud and some isolated noises. Blackhawk Films (*qv*) had the film in release for some time before deciding to dub in a more convincing effect, which is included in today's copies.

(See also: Beds; Hall, Charlie; Landlords; Sickness; Sound; Stage appearances; Television; *Unaccustomed As We Are*; Video releases)

THICKER THAN WATER
(Laurel & Hardy film)
Released by M-G-M, 16 March 1935.
Produced by Hal Roach. Directed by James W. Horne. Camera: Art Lloyd. Two reels.
With Stan Laurel and Oliver Hardy, Daphne Pollard, James Finlayson, Charlie Hall, Harry Bowen, Grace Goodall, Bess Flowers, Gladys Gale.

Mr and Mrs Hardy are eating, accompanied by their lodger, Mr Laurel. Despite having consumed two pieces

Thicker Than Water: *Daphne insists that the dishes take precedence over baseball*

of pie, Stan, in true Oliver Twist fashion, asks for more. Mrs Hardy (Daphne Pollard) is more interested in receiving Stan's rent. 'I gave it to him' says Stan, indicating Ollie. The money is handed over. Stan and Ollie plan to leave for a ball game but Mrs Hardy insists her husband should remain to wash the dishes. If Ollie has to wash the dishes, Stan must be there to dry them; Mrs Hardy leaves them to the task. Stan pours a whole packet of soap powder into the bowl, creating a mass of suds. Once progress is established, Stan dries the dishes but puts them back into the bowl. When Ollie tells him to put them in a 'nice, dry place', Stan leaves them on a lighted gas ring, bringing disaster as Ollie picks them up. Ollie is soothing his singed digits when Mr Finlayson arrives to collect the Hardys' furniture payment. Mrs Hardy had given Ollie the money to pay in the previous day; it seems he gave it to Stan. From here it was returned to Ollie to pay Stan's room and board. This 'I gave it to him' principle escalates so that nobody knows what became of it (Stan: 'Well, if that was the money that you gave to him, to give to me to pay to him, it must've been the money that I gave him to give to you to pay my rent. Didn't I?'). Mrs Hardy pays Mr Finlayson and is tempted to throw Stan out; she can't, because the rent has been paid in advance. Ollie is disgusted: 'creditors hounding me at my

very fireside'. Stan suggests that the Hardys should withdraw their savings to pay off the furniture, thus avoiding any interest and, better still, 'you wouldn't have any hounds in your fireplace'. Mrs Hardy vetoes the suggestion but Ollie, asserting himself, draws out the money. On leaving the bank, Stan and Ollie pass an auction room whose sign declares them to be 'giving things away'. 'At last we get something for nothing', says Ollie. Inside there is fierce bidding for a grandfather clock; one of the bidders is a lady who has left her money at home. She asks Ollie to keep the bidding open until she returns. Ollie enters the fray, not realizing his chief opponent to be Stan. The clock finally goes to Ollie for $290, or precisely $10 less than the Hardys' savings. The lady has not reappeared, leaving Ollie with an unwanted clock. As the auction room's proprietor is Mr Finlayson, there is no arguing. Mrs Hardy visits the bank to arrange for nobody to draw any money but herself; she is told that Ollie has closed the account, and sets off in a fury. The boys negotiate their purchase through the streets, but Stan suggests they take a rest just in time for a lorry to shatter the clock. Mrs Hardy learns about the clock from Mr Finlayson, destroying Ollie's hope to 'keep everything in the dark'. Stan spills the beans completely and Ollie is knocked out with a frying pan. When Stan visits his friend in hospital, he is asked to donate blood for the patient. The reluctant Stan is dragged away, but worse is to come when a faulty valve takes too much blood; the operation is reversed despite the risk of mixing them up, and the nurse bids farewell to an Ollie who looks like Stan, and vice versa.

The team's last short comedy is marked by a degree of slowness but is remembered fondly as a prime specimen of absurd dialogue plus some excellent optical work. Several links (and the 'end' title) are achieved by physically pulling the next scene into view (one of these was adapted for the credits of *Laurel & Hardy's Laughing Twenties* [*qv*]). Inexplicably, the edition prepared for European video wipes into a replacement end title, something which may well have involved quite unnecessary expense. The British TV print and at least some other reissue copies betray a damaged master with some obvious, printed-in splices. *Thicker Than Water* has its origins in a brief sketch written by Stan which is reprinted by John McCabe (*qv*) in *The Comedy World of Stan Laurel*. Much of the film was reworked into *The Dancing Masters* (*qv*).

(See also: Auctions; Biographies; Courtliness; Dialogue; Doctors; Finlayson, James; Freak endings; Pollard, Daphne; Seawright, Roy; Titling; Video releases)

THIRTY YEARS OF FUN
(20th Century-Fox 1964)
For this compilation, Robert Youngson (*qv*), in sociological mood, combines silent comedy extracts with film of contemporary America. Little known in the UK since its initial release (at the time of writing it has yet to appear on British TV), *Thirty Years of Fun* incorporates what was then a recent Youngson discovery, *Lucky Dog* (*qv*). In his survey of Youngson's work for the Winter 1992 *Intra-Tent Journal*, Scott MacGillivray laments the domination of this film by Chaplin, Keaton, Langdon, Chase (all *qv*) and others, Laurel & Hardy being confined to the *Lucky Dog* clip plus a momentary glimpse of Babe with Max Davidson (*qv*).

(See also: Compilations; Periodicals; Teaming)

THIS IS YOUR LIFE
See: Television

THOMAS, DYLAN (1914-53)

LAWRENCE TIBBETT
'The ROGUE SONG'
with Catherine Dale Owen · Stan Laurel & Oliver Hardy
Directed by LIONEL BARRYMORE.
A Metro-Goldwyn-Mayer Picture.

*The boys support **Lawrence Tibbett** in his film debut*
BFI Stills, Posters and Designs

Welsh poet and playwright whose contribution to Laurel & Hardy history was made at a New York film society known as Cinema 16. Thomas listened uncomfortably to a theory about drama in film being horizontal and poetry vertical. When it came to his turn to speak, Thomas claimed not to understand. 'But', he said, 'I know there is such a thing as poetry in the film. I can't give you a scholarly definition, but I can give you an instance. I remember once a scene in which Laurel pushed Hardy down the stairs - ', at which point he broke into laughter. 'Ah', he continued, 'but I can't describe it. It would have to be seen. I say this only: that it was genuine poetry in every sense'. John McCabe (*qv*), who recounts this incident in *Mr Laurel and Mr Hardy*, records also Stan's reaction to the tale, starting with a solemn 'Yes?', followed by a pause and the remark 'The hell he says', punctuated by hearty laughter. Thomas, noted for the strategic deflation of pomp, might have joined in.

THOMAS, TONY
See: Interviews and Records

THREE COMIQUES, THE
See: Keystone Trio, the

TIBBETT, LAWRENCE
(1896-1960)

Baritone star of the Metropolitan Opera, first brought to the screen in *The Rogue Song* (*qv*). He also appears in *New Moon* (1930), *The Prodigal* (1931), *Cuban Love Song* (1932), *Metropolitan* (1936) and *Under Your Spell* (1937).

(See also: Academy Awards)

TIES (all films *qv*)
It is usual for Ollie to wear an ordinary tie and Stan to favour a bow. When this varies, as with Stan's conventional tie in *Their Purple Moment*, something seems amiss. It is remarkable that Stan's character is able to cope with the tying of a bow, the intricacies of which come into play during a meal in *Twice Two*. Ollie's tie-twiddling gesture is one of the team's most endearing trademarks, serving to convey embarrassment, coyness and a desire to ingratiate in a manner both childlike and genteel. It also emphasises the essentially grandiose Hardy persona through its concentration on the tie, a flowing garment which contrasts directly with the brief and rather useless variety favoured by his partner. Without it Ollie looks incomplete and is actually rather helpless: the indignities of *Big Business* leave

Ollie tieless in the face of an intimidating policeman; the open-necked 'Bert' of *Our Relations* must instead use the neckerchief worn by his friend 'Alf' (the twins are later differentiated by having their ties reversed); while there are those who find symbolism in *Oliver the Eighth* when Mae Busch (*qv*) snips off his tie below the knot. The gesture itself was born from an ad lib when Babe was caught off-guard by a bucket of water. Feeling obliged to react, he considered blowing his nose on his tie but, reconsidering this possibly tasteless idea, waved the tie in a twee fashion. He recalled this as occuring in *Why Girls Love Sailors*, but inspection of the film reveals Hardy in a polo neck. Such a gag takes place in *Sailors Beware*, although no tie-twiddle follows. It should be mentioned that in a different interview for the *South London Press* he claimed that he had originated the gesture when wiping pastry from his face in *The Battle of the Century*, though extant footage suggests no such action.

(See also: Characters; Costume)

TILBURY, ZEFFIE (1863-1950)
Veteran character actress brought into *The Bohemian Girl* (*qv*) during extensive retakes after the death of Thelma Todd (*qv*). Other films include *Werewolf of London*, *The Last Days of Pompeii* and *Tobacco Road*. She may also be glimpsed in *Block-Heads* (*qv*).

TIT FOR TAT
(Laurel & Hardy film)
Released by M-G-M, 5 January 1935. Produced by Hal Roach. Directed by Charles Rogers. Camera: Art Lloyd. Two reels.
With Stan Laurel and Oliver Hardy, Mae Busch, Charlie Hall, James C. Morton, Bobby Dunn.

Stan and Ollie's new electrical store is ready to open, having been delayed a day through Stan's 'nervous breakdown'. They decide to greet their

Stan finds a new toy from the wreckage of a watch: **Tit For Tat**

neighbours in the grocery, leaving the shop unattended (bearing a sign reading 'will be back soon') as a customer (Bobby Dunn) walks in. The boys recognize their neighbours as the couple they met during a mountain trip (in *Them Thar Hills*). Mrs Hall (Mae Busch) is quite happy to see them but her husband (Charlie Hall) bears a grudge. It is agreed that they should 'neither nod nor speak'. The boys return to business as their first customer exits with an unpaid-for item. Ollie climbs a ladder in order to put light bulbs in a display sign, but Stan operates a pavement lift that propels Ollie to the Halls' upstairs window ledge. Mrs Hall discovers their visitor and offers a cordial escort downstairs and through the shop. 'I've never been in a position like *that* before!' remarks Ollie, as Mr Hall fumes. He follows, challenging Ollie over a probable dalliance with his wife. I have *nothing* to say', replies Ollie; 'Neither have I' adds Stan, before Hall sits him in the bucket of light bulbs. Hall delivers a warning and exits. The customer leaves with more stolen items, pausing to say 'How do you do?' 'Who's that fella?' asks Stan, but more important business is at hand; Ollie's name has been 'dragged through the mud and mire'. Stan agrees that an apology is in order, claiming 'He who filters your good name, steals trash'. They depart for the grocery as their dubious patron returns for more goods. Hall's reaction to Ollie's complaint is a

smack on the head with a wooden spoon; Ollie's reaction to that is to ring the cash register, launching its drawer into Hall's chin. Ollie pauses to steal a marshmallow on the way out. Hall walks into the electrical store, promising a fight if one is required. He emphasizes his words by gesturing with a pair of curling tongs. Stan has plugged them in, burning Hall's fingers, but Ollie's laughter stops when the tongs are applied to his nose. Back to the grocery and another visit from the shoplifter. Ollie scoops up a spoonful of cottage cheese, sending it straight into Hall's face. 'Tit For Tat', says Ollie. Stan tips his hat obligingly. Exit the boys, taking a marshmallow each. Hall sabotages the marshmallows by sprinkling them with alum. He follows the boys to their shop, just as they blithely accept another liberation of their stock. Hall fills an electric mixer with a selection of watches, reducing them to fragments. Stan rescues a tiny component he can use as a spinning toy before he and Ollie start back for vengeance. The persistent thief returns with a wheelbarrow. Hall's cash register is opened and filled with honey; Ollie's hat is in turn put through a bacon slicer, excising its crown. The boys dump a tub of lard on Hall's head, patting it thoroughly so that its contents remain after the tub's removal. Exit once again, taking still more marshmallows. The alum takes effect, forcing the pursed-lipped pair to spray their mouths with a soda syphon. Hall is back, embarking on blind destruction before hitting upon the idea of swinging a ceiling light into its companion, starting a chain reaction culminating in the last crashing through the plate-glass window. '*Now* will you stop?' he asks, but it is too late for that: Mrs Hall looks on, aghast, as her husband is dumped into a crate of eggs, a second crate being emptied over his head. A policeman (James C. Morton) arrives as peacemaker. The misunderstanding is cleared up to an extent, though Hall kicks Stan in the pants when, following Ollie's example, he kisses Mrs Hall's hand. Stan and Ollie reach their shop just as the last item is being loaded into a truck. The cop, taking a marshmallow, orders the crowd to disperse as his speech disappears into alum-created oblivion.

As a sequel to *Them Thar Hills* (*qv*), *Tit For Tat* depends somewhat on the earlier film, especially when Mae Busch (*qv*) reprises their rendition of 'The Old Spinning Wheel' at the beginning. Both she and Charlie Hall (*qv*) are excellent as before, Mae Busch giving one of her rare sympathetic portrayals; Anita Garvin (*qv*) has said she had been intended for several roles played instead by Miss Busch and this rather out-of-character persona seems a prime candidate. *Tit For Tat* is the team's most prolonged exchange of violence since the silent *Big Business* (*qv*), to which there is a sly reference in their shop display. It suffers in comparison through being too obviously contrived, but there is no denying the range of gags or skill in execution. Further interest lies in the moment where Stan tips his hat in response to Ollie's remark of 'Tit For Tat': in England, this gets a laugh *before* Stan explains his mistake ('I thought you said 'Tip me hat''), because the expression means 'hat' in Cockney rhyming slang. Stan once admitted aiming certain gags at British audiences, though they were sufficiently qualified to make sense in America; here we have perhaps the most tangible example.

(See also: Academy Awards; Catchphrases; Dunn, Bobby; Eggs; Height, weight; 'In-jokes'; Morton, James C.; Policemen; Reciprocal destruction; Richard, Viola; Risqué humour; Sequels; Shops; Streetcars; Tashlin, Frank)

TIEMBLA Y TITUBEA
See: *Below Zero* and Foreign versions

TITLING (all films *qv*)
A film's titling makes an enormous difference to the total presentation and the Roach Studio took great care with its designs. Narrative and dialogue titles (in silents) would be the standard cloth-background type, sometimes replaced in new copies when only one or a few frames of each were retained in the negative (e.g. *Early to Bed* and *Should Married Men Go Home?*). Opening credits of the late 1920s-early 1930s favour elaborate Art-Deco designs, typical of the period and of M-G-M in particular. These are framed in a rectangular or, more commonly, elliptical border. Later Laurel & Hardy shorts often employed variations on a hatrack bearing twin bowlers, sometimes with Ollie's hat punctured by the hook or Stan's mysteriously hanging above it. Several employed animated or other moving titles, such as the greeting card opening of *The Fixer-Uppers*, windscreen wipers in *The Midnight Patrol* or the circular saw of *Busy Bodies*. Reissues (*qv*) have spoiled many of these, chiefly because of an apparent necessity to remove the M-G-M logo. Film Classics would omit the introductory lion trademark (though sometimes leaving its roar on the soundtrack), replacing the first card and, in several instances, the entire title sequence. The marble plaque design is an invention of Film Classics, as is the consciously 'period' style backed by a pleated effect. The company compounded its mutilation by mis-spellings and general carelessness, transforming Mae Busch (*qv*) into 'May Bush' (*Come Clean*) and rechristening Jacqueline Wells (*qv*) 'Jacoqueline' in *Any Old Port*. Plurals were taboo, *Men O'War* becoming *Man O'War* and *Chickens Come Home* being reduced to a solitary fowl. Irrespective of production date, every issue bore the same marble plaque, bearing in tiny print a 1933 copyright by M-G-M (each release having been passed by the 'National' Board of Review). Bad though these titles are,

collectors have even less time for the remade cards of Blackhawk Films (*qv*), whose white-on-black titling marred an otherwise excellent Laurel & Hardy range. Their excuse was again a legal obligation to omit the M-G-M logo, and the company even went so far as to amend their edition of *Two Tars* with reinstated Roach titles, but with their own logo obliterating the Metro lion. This excuse was somewhat belied not just by the M-G-M titling on a later issue of *The Battle of the Century* but through the replacement of titles not bearing that trademark in the first place. One of these is the curtain design of *Another Fine Mess*, which lifts prior to the entrance of twin girls (Beverly and Betty Mae Crane) who then offer spoken credits. This cute exploitation of early sound recurs in several Roach films of 1930, including some of those with Our Gang and Charley Chase (both *qv*). Blackhawk's version retains this spoken introduction. Fortunately the revived Blackhawk range seems to make a policy of using original titling where available. Most of the Laurel & Hardy features made at Roach have titling unique to each subject, designed to fit the subject matter (*Swiss Miss* has an appropriately Alpine look). The cartoons decorating *Block-Heads* have been attributed to Harry Langdon (*qv*).

(See also: Caricatures; *Chimp, the*; M-G-M; Seawright, Roy)

TODD, THELMA (1905/6-35)
(Laurel & Hardy films *qv*)
A former schoolteacher who after winning the title 'Miss Massachusetts' was enrolled in the Paramount Film School. She appears in films, sometimes under the pseudonym 'Alison Lloyd', from 1926. She was in Roach films from 1929, including the following Laurel & Hardy subjects: *Unaccustomed As We Are, Another Fine Mess, Chickens Come Home, Fra Diavolo* and *The Bohemian Girl*. Other Roach films include several with

Charley Chase (*qv*), *The Pip From Pittsburg*, *High C's* and its sequel *Rough Seas* being considered among the best of them. Another Roach series co-starred her with ZaSu Pitts, who was later replaced by Patsy Kelly (*qv*). One of the Pitts-Todd shorts, *On the Loose*, has a guest appearance by Laurel & Hardy. In 1933, Thelma Todd, Dennis King (*qv*) and James Finlayson (*qv*) travelled to England to promote *Fra Diavolo*. During the visit Miss Todd appeared with Stanley Lupino in a British film, *You Made Me Love You*. Other notable entries in the Todd filmography are the Marx Brothers' *Monkey Business* and *Horse Feathers*, the 1931 *Maltese Falcon*, Keaton's *Sneak Easily* and two Wheeler & Woolsey comedies *Hips, Hips, Hooray* and *Cockeyed Cavaliers*. After previews of *The Bohemian Girl*, Thelma Todd was found dead in her car, the victim of carbon monoxide poisoning. Though this was apparently a suicide, speculation has continued ever since about a possible murder. The actress was immensely popular among colleagues and greatly missed. The case has sometimes been examined in detail, as in the book *Hot Toddy*, which in turn is credited on a 1991 TV movie called *White Hot: the Mysterious Murder of Thelma Todd*. At the time of writing there are reports of another dramatization for cinema release. Her birthdate is usually quoted as 1905, but the death certificate reproduced in *Hot Toddy* claims 1906.

(See also: Guest appearances)

TOLER, SIDNEY (1874-1947)
Played the ship's Captain in *Our Relations* (*qv*); better known as 'Charlie Chan' in the long-running series produced (for a while) by Sol M. Wurtzel (*qv*) at Fox.

(See also: Moreland, Mantan)

TOPPER (1937)
Thorne Smith's novel *The Jovial Ghosts* provided the basis for this successful Roach feature, one of the studio's few full-length hits not to star Laurel & Hardy. Much of Marvin Hatley's score is shared with *Way Out West* (*qv*), including at least one theme written for but unused in the latter film. Constance Bennett and Cary Grant are the ghosts, with Roland Young as their flesh-and-blood friend Cosmo Topper. Billie Burke, who plays Topper's wife, appears also in Roach's *Zenobia* (*qv*). Two sequels followed, 1939's *Topper Returns* (minus Grant) and, two years later, *Topper Takes a Trip* (minus Grant and Bennett). Another Thorne Smith fantasy, *Turnabout*, was filmed by Roach in 1940 with Carole Landis, John Hubbard and Babe's old golfing opponent, Adolphe Menjou.

(See also: Golf; Hal Roach Studios, the; Hatley, Marvin; Hereafter, the; Kelly, Patsy; Music; *Of Mice and Men*; Patrick, Lee; Seawright, Roy)

A beautiful studio portrait of **Thelma Todd**

TORRENCE, DAVID (1864-1951)
Edinburgh-born character actor, originally a musician who sang baritone with the Savoy Opera Company. His native accent brought a singular authority to his role of Mr Miggs, the MacLaurel family lawyer, in *Bonnie Scotland* (*qv*). His brother, Ernest Torrence, is remembered by comedy fans for *Steamboat Bill, Jr.* (1928), starring Buster Keaton (*qv*).

TOURING
See: Stage appearances

TOWED IN A HOLE
(Laurel & Hardy film)
Released by M-G-M, 31 December 1932. Produced by Hal Roach. Directed by George Marshall. Camera: Art Lloyd. Two reels. With Stan Laurel and Oliver Hardy, Billy Gilbert.

Fish peddlers Stan and Ollie are driving through the streets, Ollie singing 'Fresh fish' with Stan supplying counterpoint on a flat-sounding horn. The day, bright in itself, seems all the sunnier because they are making money. Stan suggests they could make even more by catching their own fish, eliminating the middleman. Though unable to repeat the idea with lucidity, he conveys enough to Ollie for it to gain currency. Stan's notion to invest in fishpoles is superseded by Ollie's greater plan: they will buy a boat. Such a vessel is obtained from Joe's junk yard, not in pristine condition but eminently worth fixing up. To find any leaks, they fill the boat with water. Stan connects the hose and turns it on before passing it through the porthole; Ollie gets his first soaking. The boat is filled as Ollie paints the rudder; Stan turns it, pushing Ollie into the paint. Stan retreats slowly from Ollie before summoning sufficient courage to ask why Ollie has put 'that stuff' on his face. Ollie hurls a bucket at Stan, but it rebounds on an old bedstead, knocking its thrower into the water. The boys exchange soakings until Ollie decides they should not act like children; they continue to do exactly that but reason prevails. Ollie bravely steps forward on to a bar of soap, slipping straight back into the paint. Later, Ollie is

Towed in a Hole: *paint and petulance*

patching the hull while Stan scrubs the anchor and chain. The anchor slips through the hull, dragging Stan with it; both land on Ollie. Fade out. Fade up on Stan confined below decks, nursing a black eye. He has been doing chalk drawings, one of them a caricature of Ollie. He plays noughts and crosses, looking the other way when making a second move. Other amusement consists of his trick of blowing his finger to make his hat rise. Ollie is above, painting the mast; when Stan comes up to see him, he orders him to return below. When Stan closes the sliding hatch, Ollie overbalances into the paintbrush. Stan's head slides behind the lower part of the mast; Ollie is at the top while Stan tries to saw his way to freedom. The mast topples, pitching Ollie into a sizeable puddle. Fade out, fade in on the completed job. Stan has been tied behind a barrel; once freed, we see he has two black eyes. Ollie leads him to the car. The car cannot gain sufficient traction to tow the boat, so Ollie accepts Stan's suggestion to put up the sail. The boat gathers momentum, pushing the car along before Stan and Ollie can regain control. As boat and car lie wrecked, Stan rushes over and is delighted to find the horn still capable of sound. Ollie chases him away.

Towed in a Hole is one of the team's most popular films. The gags build perfectly, while much is said of their characters when Ollie admits to their being 'two grown-up men acting like a couple of children'. Ollie is therefore underqualified when he assumes the role of parent, leading Stanley to the car. This shift in their relationship provides ample illustration of Babe's definition of Ollie (see **Characters**). Director George Marshall (*qv*) later recalled a more elaborate finale planned for the film, with the boys riding an uncontrollable boat through the streets. This idea succumbed to then-current studio economies, themselves responsible for Marshall's

departure after *Towed in a Hole*'s completion.

(See also: Boats, ships; *Busy Bodies*; Cars; Dialogue; Fish; Slapstick)

TRAILERS (all films *qv*)
Trailers, in the 'coming attraction' sense, are quite usual practice for full-length productions. Such items have surfaced for a number of Laurel & Hardy features, among them *A Chump at Oxford* and *Saps at Sea*. Extant trailers for M-G-M's *Air Raid Wardens* and *Nothing But Trouble* tell us much of the studio's interpretation of them in addition to encapsulating the worst of 1940s slang. Slightly preferable is New Realm's British trailer for *The Flying Deuces*, in which a brace of coconuts turn around to reveal caricatures of Stan and Ollie. An original trailer for *Babes in Toyland* also exists in the UK. Even better would be the discovery of some reported trailers for the Laurel & Hardy shorts, a quite remarkable phenomenon for two-reel comedies.

(See also: Publicity; Streamliners)

TRAINS (Laurel & Hardy films *qv*)
Railway settings are sometimes necessary in the Laurel & Hardy films: *Berth Marks* and a parallel scene in *The Big Noise* are obvious candidates, as are the train journeys of *With Love and Hisses* and *A-Haunting We Will Go*. Trains are seen briefly in *A Chump at Oxford* and *Great Guns*, while plot twists in *Duck Soup* and *Be Big* depend on abortive train journeys. Footage also exists of some real-life train journeys made by the team. Perhaps their earliest train-related film still to exist is *Hustling For Health*, a Laurel solo film released in 1919.

(See also: Boats, ships; Buses; Newsreels; Rolin Film Co., the)

TRAMS
See: Streetcars

Trains: a hasty departure in Berth Marks

THE TREE IN A TEST TUBE
(Laurel & Hardy film)
Produced in 1943 by the US Department of Agriculture, Forest Service. Directed by Charles McDonald. Camera: A. H. C. Sintzenich. Edited by Boris Vermont. One reel. Made in 16mm Kodachrome colour.
With Stan Laurel and Oliver Hardy. Narrators: Pete Smith (Laurel & Hardy section); Lee Vickers (remaining portion).

One of the team's contributions to the war effort, *The Tree in a Test Tube* is reputed to have been shot during a lunch break at 20th Century-Fox (*qv*). The scenery is recognizably Fox's back lot, especially visible in Laurel & Hardy's *A Haunting We Will Go* and *The Dancing Masters* (both *qv*). The team's footage is silent, but timed to respond to the narration by Pete Smith, taking time out from his *Pete Smith Specialties* at M-G-M. Stan and Ollie are greeted by Smith with a cry of 'Hey, you mugs - I mean gentlemen', establishing early on that Smith plans to treat them as he would the buffooneries of Dave O'Brien in his own series. Asked if they are carrying any wood, the boys

are stuck until Smith points out the wood pulp used in a newspaper, plastic spectacle frames and pen. A billfold provides another example, similarly Mrs Laurel's stockings contained therein. There follow cigarette case and holder; 'Any more wood, my lads?' asks Smith, to which Ollie replies by rapping Stan's head. No actual wood there but Stan's hatband is imitation leather made from wood pulp. Stan replaces his hat, which springs into the air. Pipe, matchbook and penknife contain more wood products, as does the team's suitcase. Inside are slippers, bottles of witch hazel and cascara, imitation leather toilet case and contents, each of them deriving from wood. 'Let's take a look at some more of your junk - er, I mean your nice things', says Smith, and instead of miming where he should go the boys continue to display their luggage; this time a razor with plastic handle, items of stationery and a book, pyjamas and a pair of brightly-coloured underpants. Next are shirt, tie and socks, all of rayon.

Tree in a Test Tube: *Ollie and Stan greet an offscreen Pete Smith*

The boys have been stacking their possessions on the rear bumper of a car, which drives off as the boys give chase. 'Oh well,' comments Smith, 'they need exercise anyway. G'bye now!' The remaining footage concentrates on the importance of laboratory research into wood during wartime, closing with a superimposed shot of a tree inside a test tube. Aside from its value as a wartime curio, *The Tree in a Test Tube* attracts interest today as one of the team's few available colour films. Surviving prints vary in their colour rendition, many copies having acquired a reddish hue; even the faded examples provide a glimpse of Babe's golfing tan and Stan's red hair, although the latter is subdued through having been slicked down.

(See also: Colour; Colouring; M-G-M; *M-G-M's Big Parade of Comedy*; Wartime)

TRYON, GLENN (1899-1970)
Comedian and gagman with his own starring series at Roach in the late 1920s. One of these, *Forty-Five Minutes From Hollywood* (*qv*) is remembered today as the earliest Roach comedy with both Laurel and Hardy in the cast. Tryon was a breezy character but frankly too bland to carry this kind of farce; it is unsurprising to learn that his later work consisted of occasional screen roles mixed with behind-the-scenes contributions, such as gag writing for *Sons of the Desert* (*qv*). He is one of two associate producers credited on Olsen and Johnson's *Hellzapoppin'* (1941).

(See also: Teaming; *That's My Wife*; Writers)

TURNING POINT
See: Interviews and Radio

TURPIN, BEN (1874-1940)
Cross-eyed comedian who began his film career with Essanay, where he would in time work with a talented

Ben Turpin made his final screen appearance in Saps at Sea

newcomer, Charlie Chaplin (*qv*). He achieved considerable fame with Mack Sennett (*qv*), where his bizarre appearance contrasted neatly with comic exploits as daring explorer or man-about-town. Turpin moved to Weiss Brothers in the late 1920s, a downward move that coincided with the arrival of talkies. The wealthy comic went into retirement, making occasional guest appearances as in the 1932 W. C. Fields comedy *Million Dollar Legs*, a 1935 'revival' short called *Keystone Hotel* and another collection of veterans, *Hollywood Cavalcade* (1939). Two others were Laurel & Hardy's *Our Wife* and *Saps at Sea* (both *qv*), the latter being Turpin's final screen role.

(See also: Anderson, G. M.; *Golden Age of Comedy, the*; Hurlock, Madeline; Keaton, Buster; Oakland, Vivien; Pollard, Harry 'Snub'; *Two Tars*)

20TH CENTURY-FOX
(all films *qv*)
Formed in 1935 as a merger between the old Fox Film Corporation (for whom Babe had worked on occasion) and Twentieth-Century, a company owned by Joseph Schenck, former producer of pictures with Roscoe Arbuckle and Buster Keaton (both

qv). Production head was Darryl F. Zanuck, who delegated the studio's 'B' pictures to Sol M. Wurtzel (*qv*). It was to the latter unit that Laurel & Hardy were sent on joining the studio in 1941. On their departure from Roach, Stan and Babe had hoped to produce independently, but lack of capital forced a big studio deal. There was at least the promise of greater finance and facilities at a major company, but there was no room in such a studio for the creative methods possible at a small independent unit such as Roach. Stan in particular found himself handcuffed: signed only as an actor, he could not influence either direction or editing and was certainly not consulted on scripts. There is no reason to suggest the studio planned to wreck their careers but the resultant films virtually did so. 'Those Fox people', as Stan once called them, imposed their own ideas regarding content, make-up and even costume, while providing scripts designed for characters who could have been anyone but Stan and Ollie. Their idea of catering to the stars' needs consisted of the arbitrary revival of older routines regardless of context and the whole was placed in the hands of directors selected for their longevity rather than suitability. At Roach, the team had thrived under the direction of younger talents whose vitality combined with a receptiveness to Stan's ideas. Fox's directors were tired old

men, set in their ways. The absurdity of it all is highlighted by the simple fact that many Fox staffers could have saved themselves work (and made far better films) if they'd had the wit to turn it all over to Stan and just taken the money. Stan found these conditions unendurable and by the end had virtually given up. Babe, used to functioning only as actor, responded better but shared his partner's disgust with the result. Their genuine hurt is reflected by a story from their variety tours in Britain: a young comic elsewhere on the bill, Harry Worth (*qv*), attended a matinée revival of *The Dancing Masters* and was amazed to see Robert Mitchum (*qv*) in the cast. Returning to the theatre, he mentioned the film and was told of the unhappy conditions under which it was made. *The Dancing Masters* was fourth in the series; the others were *Great Guns*, *A-Haunting We Will Go*, *Jitterbugs*, *The Big Noise* and *The Bullfighters*. When Fox expressed a wish to continue with the team, they politely declined. Few of these films have earned praise from any quarter (the Medved brothers included *The Big Noise* in their book *The Fifty Worst Movies of All Time*), though *The Bullfighters* has its defenders and *Jitterbugs* benefits from an increased budget (having been used to introduce Vivian Blaine [*qv*]) and some amusing if uncharacteristic masquerades.

(See also: Banks, Monty; Characters; Costume; Crying; Hal Roach Studios, the; Home movies; Jordan, Bert; Laurel & Hardy Feature Productions; Make-up; M-G-M; Music; Salaries; Romance; Shipman, Ben; Stage appearances; St Clair, Malcolm; *Tree in a Test Tube, the*; Video releases; Werker, Alfred; Writers)

TWICE TWO
(Laurel & Hardy film)
Released by M-G-M, 25 February 1933. Produced by Hal Roach. Directed by James Parrott. Camera: Art Lloyd. Two reels.

With Stan Laurel and Oliver Hardy, Baldwin Cooke, Charlie Hall.

Oliver Hardy, Brain Specialist, and his 'Associate advisor', Mr Laurel, are about to celebrate the first anniversary of having married each other's sisters. They call their wives, offering to take them out for the evening, but are told to come home. Mrs Laurel (Oliver Hardy) and Mrs Hardy (Stan Laurel) are preparing a surprise; Stan accidentally blurts out this fact to Ollie. The girls arrange the dinner table rather as their husbands would, Ollie's sister

Twice Two: *the husbands ...*

being left with a cake on her head. The boys arrive home: Ollie's trousers, attached to a key chain, are ripped when the door is opened and the flowers he has brought are decapitated when the door is closed. Stan is dumped outside, knocks for re-admission but gains entrance instead through the kitchen door. Ollie goes to let him in, sees nobody and returns inside. Stan opens the door from the kitchen straight into Ollie's face; Ollie pushes the door back, hitting his wife. She breaks a plate over his head. Mrs Laurel is in the bedroom. She asks Stan for money, takes his bankroll and returns 15 cents for Stan to go out for strawberry ice cream. The others sit down to eat while Stan walks into a shop. As they haven't any strawberry

ice cream, he calls home. 'Get tutti-frutti', he is told. They have no tutti-frutti, either. Stan calls again. He should try chocolate; no luck there, and after a further call he asks for vanilla. The shop does not sell ice cream at all; Stan should try next door. He returns without ice cream ('I spent the fifteen cents calling you up'), joining the others for dinner. The uneasy meal descends into bickering, which Ollie halts with a desire to see the 'surprise'. Mrs Laurel is furious that Stan has betrayed the secret. The squabbling continues and the Hardys decide to eat out; they open the door to a deliveryman (Charlie Hall) carrying the 'surprise', a replacement cake. He asks Mrs Hardy to give the cake to Mrs Laurel; this she does, right over the head.

A variation of *Brats* (*qv*), *Twice Two* has none of its predecessor's pace or suitability. The team's characters are essentially masculine, if childlike, making them less than convincing as women (though it must be conceded that Babe makes a rather imposing female). The illusion is assisted by quick cutting, doubling and a small amount of matte work. Stan and Babe's female voices are dubbed by,

... phone their wives

respectively, Carol Tevis and May Wallace. The latter (who died five years later, aged 61) appears on screen, and is addressed by name in *County Hospital* (*qv*), and is present also in *Sailors, Beware!* and *Way Out West* (both *qv*); the former is visible doing her 'dizzy' portrayal in a contemporary series of RKO shorts directed by George Stevens (*qv*), *Blondes and Redheads*.

(See also: Characters; Dual roles; Dubbing; Female impersonation; Flowers; Seawright, Roy; Sutton, Grady; Telephones; Ties; Women)

TWO-REELERS
See: Short films

TWO TARS
(Laurel & Hardy film)
Released by M-G-M, 3 November 1928. Produced by Hal Roach. Directed by James Parrott. Camera: George Stevens. Two reels. Silent. With Stan Laurel and Oliver Hardy, Edgar Kennedy, Thelma Hill, Ruby Blaine, Charlie Hall, Charles Rogers, Sam Lufkin.

The USS *Oregon* has allowed its intrepid mariners ashore. Two of them, Stan and Ollie, are dangerous enough in their rented Model T before they meet the further distraction of two girls (Thelma Hill and Ruby Blaine), who are having problems with a gum machine. Ollie attempts to shake the contraption into submission, sending its spherical contents all over the pavement. The proprietor (Charlie Hall) appears just as Ollie tries to conceal the spilled gum in his shirt. The irate shopkeeper retrieves his stock, punctuating the manoeuvre with a blow to Ollie's stomach. The girls encourage Stan to intervene, but every swing he takes sends him spinning to the ground. The girls join the scuffle but the foursome soon beat a retreat. By late afternoon, Stan, Ollie and the girls are in party mood (having called the Admiral to say they might be late)

Two Tars: *Sam Lufkin, early in the battle*

when they run into a traffic jam. They drive past the line of cars, only to find a driver out of fuel blocking the first queue, and road-works blocking the new one they have just created. Obliged to back up, they collide with another car moving forward; an exchange of bumps damages the rear car's radiator. Ollie forces the other driver (Edgar Kennedy) back into the next car, breaking a headlight. The fight spreads down the line, reaching, among others, a car laden with camping equipment, a lorry driver, and so on. Stan and Ollie are the most active in the fray, pulling the front wheels from one car, and bending up the mudguards of another. A motorcycle policeman pulls up to survey the riot on the highway. The sight of a policeman sends the girls quietly away; the sound of a police whistle in turn silences the motorists, who blame the two sailors for starting the disturbance. The cop orders them to remain while the others move on, forming such a sorry parade of mutilated vehicles that the boys cannot keep straight faces. A heavy truck crushes the cop's motorcycle. Seeing their chance, Stan

and Ollie drive off, as the cop tries to hitch a lift from cars now unable to oblige. 'Everybody follow them sailors!' roars the policeman, and they do - into a railway tunnel. An oncoming train forces the pursuing cars to retreat, while Stan and Ollie emerge from the other side, their rented Tin Lizzie squashed sideways.

Two Tars usually ties with *Big Business* (qv) for first place among Laurel & Hardy silents; some consider it their greatest work. The civilized exchange of violence or, to use Laurel's term, 'reciprocal destruction' (qv) is a motif recurrent in their films but seldom executed with the skill, variety and careful construction demonstrated here. The precision with which the indignities escalate, gradually involving everyone nearby, is a model of comic film technique. The girls with whom Stan and Ollie spend their day, Thelma Hill and Ruby Blaine, appear with the team only on this one occasion. Ruby Blaine is believed to have been a lady wrestler who just happened to have been in the area; Thelma Hill (who died ten years later, aged only 31) is familiar from several 1920s comedies, among them Ben Turpin's *The*

Prodigal Bridegroom. Footage from this and *Two Tars* may be seen in the 1958 compilation *The Golden Age of Comedy* (qv). More from *Two Tars* surfaces in *Four Clowns* (qv), with each anthology employing better master material than most TV prints. Editions for British TV and video derive from the 16mm copies distributed by Blackhawk Films (qv), their vintage being determined by the sub-titling. Pre-1975 prints have replacements instead of the cloth-background originals, with one title (in the shopkeeper sequence) missing completely. The UK video release is from the later copy, but with new opening titles erroneously crediting Emmett Flynn (director of *Early to Bed*) instead of Parrott. A more recent American video edition has original titling throughout. It is known that *Two Tars* bore the title *Two Tough Tars* in previews and, at three reels, a similarly expanded length. It would be interesting to know which version so impressed an early audience that the evening's feature had to be postponed while *Two Tars* was re-run.

(See also: *Big Noise, the*; Boats, ships; Cars; Compilations; Deleted scenes; *Early to Bed*; Lufkin, Sam; *Men O'War*; Roberts, Thomas Benton; Sailors; Sound; Television; Titling; Turpin, Ben; Video releases; Youngson, Robert)

TWO TICKETS TO BROADWAY
See: Unfilmed projects

UNACCUSTOMED AS WE ARE

(Laurel & Hardy film)
Released by M-G-M, 4 May 1929.
Produced by Hal Roach. Directed by
Lewis R. Foster. Camera: George
Stevens, Len Powers, John McBurnie,
Jack Roach. Two reels.
With Stan Laurel & Oliver Hardy,
Mae Busch, Thelma Todd, Edgar
Kennedy.

Ollie has brought Stan home for dinner, promising a sumptuous menu.
Outside the Hardy residence they
meet neighbour Mrs Kennedy
(Thelma Todd), whose policeman
husband (Edgar Kennedy) has yet to
return home from work. Pleasantries
over, the boys enter Ollie's home for
Stan to meet that 'great scout', Mrs
Hardy (Mae Busch). Her reaction is
sufficiently hostile for Stan to ask if
they're in the right apartment. Mrs
Hardy decides to go back to her
mother rather than cook for another
of the 'bums' her husband brings
home, so leaving Ollie to prepare the
meal he has promised Stan. Ollie delegates the task of setting the table to
Stan, who makes enough of a mess for
Ollie to take over while Stan lights the
oven. Unable to find a match, Stan
returns to the living room, leaving the
gas taps still on. Ollie takes a lighted
match into the kitchen, and is
promptly blown back into the living
room. Mrs Kennedy, investigating the
commotion, volunteers to help but the
still-volatile cooker sets her dress on
fire. Draped in a sheet, she attempts
to return home but sees her husband
walking through the front door.

Fearing his reaction, she asks what to
do: Ollie, in command of the situation
as always, declares 'Why, we'll tell him
the truth!', only to retreat indoors at
the sight of his returning spouse. The
only option is to hide Mrs Kennedy in
a trunk, where she remains throughout Mrs Hardy's attempts at
reconciliation. Ollie, needing an
excuse to dispose of the trunk, rejects
his wife's pleas, claiming that Stan has
advised him to go to South America.
Mrs Hardy aims a selection of crockery at Stan, creating enough noise to
bring Officer Kennedy over. When
Mrs Hardy storms off into the bedroom, Kennedy learns that Stan and
Ollie have a woman in the trunk and,
being a man of the world, decides to
assist. Taking Mrs Hardy aside, he
promises to give the boys 'a good talking to' and tells them to take the trunk
to his apartment. Once there, he
advises Stan and Ollie to be as discreet
as he is with such illicit dalliances;
Mrs Kennedy, fuming, hears it all.
Kennedy sends the boys back to
Ollie's home and a peaceful meal,
while he prepares for a good time with
the 'cluck' in the trunk. The 'cluck'
provides a violent welcome and the
battered Kennedy reappears for
vengeance. In the hallway, Ollie takes
a severe beating, out of sight of his
wife and Stan. On his return, Stan is
summoned for the same treatment.
Once more in the hallway, Kennedy is
about to strike Stan when he is felled
by his vase-wielding wife. Stan calmly
returns to the Hardy home, picks up
his hat and leaves. The incredulous
Ollie inspects his unconscious

neighbour as Stan, pausing to say
goodnight, trips and vanishes downstairs, his descent suggested only by a
succession of crashes.

The familiar phrase 'Unaccustomed
as we are to public speaking' provided
an apt title for the team's entry into
talkies (superseding the intended
Their Last Word) and speak they do,
to surprising effect despite some
understandable nerves. Dialogue
ranges between the now somewhat
hackneyed and the genuinely amusing,
although the women in the cast seem
victims of a then-current fad for
increasing the pitch of female voices.
Even this early, there are some
delightful throw-away lines, as when
gallant Ollie unthinkingly offers to
help Mrs Kennedy change her dress.
Other uses of sound are as creative:
Mrs Hardy unconsciously starting to
nag in time to the gramophone record
Ollie is playing; various sound effects
suggesting off-screen calamity
(though some are ruined by inadequate volume); and Stan's whistling
'When Johnny Comes Marching
Home' after his apparent victory over
Kennedy. It is plain that Laurel &
Hardy had thought carefully about
ways to exploit the new medium,
rather than merely adding obvious
sound. Just as plainly, they had realized the continuing importance of
visuals, blending in sound as required
and avoiding the contemporary trap of
talking heads. For many years
Unaccustomed As We Are was in the
ironic position of being thought to
survive only in silent form, in versions

'*Good night, Mr Hardy!*'; a posed shot *from* **Unaccustomed As We Are**

either adapted from sound prints or as distributed in 1929 for theatres unequipped for the new technology. Fortunately, the late 1970s saw the discovery of a collection of early sound discs, among which was the complete soundtrack for this film; while somewhat worn, the quality was cleaned up sufficiently to permit new sound prints to be released. The restored version is particularly valuable today, not just as evidence of the comedians' immediate grasp of talkies but also as the prototype of their 1938 feature *Block-Heads* (*qv*). In 1983 one of Britain's ITV companies made the national press by announcing a screening of the team's first talking picture before going on to show the silent version; evidently they had not

examined the print before transmission. At least their copy had sub-titles; another early talkie, *They Go Boom* (*qv*), surfaced on the ITV network not merely silent but without any sub-titling.

(See also: Busch, Mae; Cameramen; Food; Kennedy, Edgar; Policemen; Records; Rediscoveries; Remakes; Shoes; Slapstick; Sound; Todd, Thelma; Video releases; Women)

UNFILMED PROJECTS
In addition to the team's prolific output, there were several projects that failed to materialize. One such is

Grand Mills Hotel, planned by Buster Keaton (*qv*) as a send-up of M-G-M's *Grand Hotel*. Keaton envisaged a plot in which Laurel & Hardy were, respectively, manufacturers of back and front collar studs, planning a merger. A highlight of the film was to be Oliver Hardy's seduction of Polly Moran (*qv*). At about the same time Roach visited Britain with the idea of making a Laurel & Hardy feature and an all-star assembly titled *The Roach Revue*; neither these nor a plan to film Karno's *Mumming Birds* (*qv*) (as *A Night in an English Music Hall*) materialized. When in 1935 contractual problems threatened to end Stan's association with Hal Roach, the studio announced Babe in *The Hardy Family*, co-starring Patsy Kelly (*qv*) and Our Gang's Spanky MacFarland. The rift was healed but a further dispute three years later brought details of Stan's first film with Sennett (*qv*), titled *Problem Child*. This tale of the normal-sized son of midgets was, mercifully, allowed to die on Laurel's return to Roach. Randy Skretvedt (*qv*) has detailed an abortive series of four-reelers scheduled for 1935, the first tentatively called *The Honesty Racket*. John McCabe (*qv*) has discovered an M-G-M campaign booklet (*Leo's Candid Camera Book*, distributed to exhibitors for the 1936-7 season) detailing the forthcoming *Our Relations* (*qv*) plus two further Laurel & Hardy feature projects. The last, untitled film presumably became *Way Out West* (*qv*), but the immediate successor to *Our Relations*, tentatively called *You'd Be Surprised*, was never made. The booklet summarizes its action thus:

Fancy these fascinatingly clumsy comics in top-hats, white ties and tails! They crash Society in this screaming feature production and they don't spare the rules. They bow low from the waist... and then collapse. They eat caviar, drive imported cars... but their pants are on backwards. It's a grand

lark of a yarn and the authors, **Richard Flourney and Charles Rogers, have given the boys brand new sparkling material to work with.**

Evidently it wasn't sparkling enough, and even allowing for publicists' terminology this does not sound appropriate material for the team. In 1937 Roach planned a co-production with none other than Mussolini, whose son had been placed in charge of Italy's film industry. *Rigoletto* may or may not have been planned for Laurel & Hardy but the project was abandoned after pressure from Roach's contemporaries. By 1947, Hollywood had virtually abandoned Laurel & Hardy, whose attentions were diverted instead to stage work in England. There were plans for a British production of *Robin Hood*, and a version of *Don Quixote*, the latter to be scripted by Will Hay (who proposed Babe's membership of the Water Rats) and directed by Val Guest; nothing was made though at the time of writing there are reports of a rediscovered script for *Robin Hood*. Earlier plans to film in Britain (with Laurel & Hardy 'regular' Art Lloyd [*qv*] behind the camera) had been interrupted by the outbreak of war; another abortive deal from this period involved a proposed series of Spanish-language subjects for distribution in South America. Howard Hughes' *Two Tickets to Broadway* (1951) offered them a way back into Hollywood as comic shopkeepers, but Stan's poor health after completing *Atoll K* meant that vaudeville team Smith and Dale were hired instead. There were other offers (one of them an Italian production of *Carmen*) but nothing happened until their appearance on *This Is Your Life* in 1954, when Hal Roach Jr. offered them a filmed series, to be aired in colour. *Laurel & Hardy's Fabulous Fables* (or *The Fables of Laurel & Hardy*) was abandoned when Stan, part-way through scripting, suffered a minor stroke. The first,

Babes in the Woods, had reached story-line stage, while three others, *Cinderella*, *Little Red Riding Hood* and *Jack and the Beanstalk* were being structured. Also planned were versions of *Dick Whittington*, *Beauty and the Beast*, *Hop 'O My Thumb*, *Aladdin*, *Puss-in-Boots*, *The Three Bears* and *The Three Wishes*. In *The Comedy World of Stan Laurel* John McCabe (*qv*) has described some of the gags in addition to samples of earlier, unused scripts. One of these describes Stan and Ollie's interest in a racehorse called 'Molly-O', a plot element jettisoned although much of the dialogue survives in *Thicker Than Water* (*qv*).

(See also: Deleted scenes; Foreign versions; Karno, Fred; Mexico; Pantomimes; Publicity; Rogers, Charles; Scripts; Stage appearances; Teaming; Television; Wartime; Waxworks)

UNITED ARTISTS
Originally formed in 1919 by Chaplin, Griffith, Mary Pickford and Douglas Fairbanks, United Artists became distributor for Hal Roach after his break with M-G-M (*qv*). Roach's last features with Laurel & Hardy, *A Chump at Oxford* and *Saps at Sea* (both *qv*), were distributed by UA, as was *Zenobia* (*qv*). *A Chump at Oxford* was produced during 1939 but not released until the following year, thus creating some confusion with its reference to UA's 20th anniversary over the closing titles.

(See also: Chaplin, Charlie; Hal Roach Studios, the)

UTOPIA
see: *Atoll K*

Vaudeville: Stan and Mae Laurel at the Los Angeles Pantages, 24–30 November, 1919. Coincidentally, one of Hal Roach's Snub Pollard comedies appears elsewhere on the bill
By courtesy of Robert G. Dickson

VAGRANCY
(Laurel & Hardy films *qv*)
The opening of *The Laurel-Hardy Murder Case* explains that Mr Laurel and Mr Hardy 'had been looking for work since 1921', illustrating the traditional motif of the comedian as outsider through the idea of vagrancy. Charlie Chaplin (*qv*) portrayed a nominal (if not always actual) tramp for a quarter of a century and many of the Laurel & Hardy films place them in the same category. Invariably such status brings trouble from the law, *Duck Soup*, *Another Fine Mess*, *Night Owls* and *Scram!* being obvious examples. An inheritance in *Early to Bed* elevates them from the city park to a mansion, but it is uncommon for their economic condition to vary within a single film. A tramp characterization permits its owner to wander into almost any given situation; Chaplin was certainly very aware of this and Laurel & Hardy are thus introduced into *Fra Diavolo* without undue explanation. It is clear that Stan and Ollie are experienced in the ways of the road: when in *One Good Turn* Ollie decides they should 'humiliate' themselves by begging for food, Stan's reply is 'What, again?' The more traditional nomads of *The Bohemian Girl* earn a living from picking pockets with considerable panache.

(See also: Businessmen; Confidence tricks; Costume; Gag titles; Judges; Policemen)

VANDERVEER, ELLINOR
(1886-1976) (all films *qv*)
An actress personifying *grandes dames*, Ellinor Vanderveer's dignity was punctured at every opportunity. In a 1928 'All-Star Comedy', *A Pair of Tights*, she sits on some ice cream cones left in the back of a car. Laurel & Hardy's *The Battle of the Century* and *The Hoose-Gow* permit her to be sullied along with lesser mortals, the latter giving her a hairdo caked with rice for two weeks afterwards. In *A Chump at Oxford* a society couple played by James Finlayson and Anita Garvin (both *qv*) are named 'Mr and Mrs Vanderveer', presumably either as a tribute or an in-house joke.

(See also: 'In-jokes'; Slapstick)

VAN DYKE, DICK (b. 1925)
Energetic comedian familiar from TV's *The Dick Van Dyke Show* of the early 1960s. His film career is erratic, ranging from excellent fantasies (*Mary Poppins*, *Chitty Chitty Bang Bang*), lesser family films (*Lt. Robin Crusoe USN*) and some very worthy social comedies (*Cold Turkey*, *Some Kind of a Nut*). Van Dyke knew Stan Laurel quite well in his later years, and would pay tribute to the man in both a funeral eulogy and in TV's *Salute to Stan Laurel*. Stan in turn had a considerable regard for Van Dyke, describing him as 'one of the very, very few comedians around who knows how to use his body for real comedy'. Stan disliked the idea of a film about his life but considered Van Dyke the best candidate for the role; he had in any case seen his Laurel impersonation on TV. In 1969 Dick Van Dyke starred in Carl Reiner's film *The Comic* (*qv*), playing a fictional silent-screen comedian believed by many to resemble Stan Laurel.

(See also: Impersonators; Television)

VAN KEUREN, S. S.
See: *Swiss Miss*

VAUDEVILLE
The American equivalent to music-hall (*qv*), vaudeville served not just an identical purpose but had a similar life span, being in obvious decline by the late 1920s. In *Berth Marks* (*qv*) Stan and Ollie describe themselves as a 'big-time vaudeville act', a status already anachronistic in 1929. Within the business, each vaudeville circuit was known as a 'time', owned by different concerns and possessing varying degrees of prestige, hence the expressions 'small' or 'big time' that have passed into the language. To the uninitiated, especially outside of the US, there is a tendency to bracket vaudeville with the term 'burlesque'; a grave error since vaudevillians would sooner play the smallest of small time than the burlesque houses, a world of unsubtle comics and girlie shows that earned vaudeville's lasting disdain. Later on burlesque was among the few outlets for aspiring comedians, but in vaudeville's heyday it was considered best avoided. Contemporary publicity for *Berth Marks* claims it to have been a conscious step back, particularly for Stan. Babe had his own

fling with vaudeville early on (he was more often in cabaret) but Stan's theatrical career was dominated by it, from the first visit with Fred Karno (qv) through the seemingly endless, umpteen-shows-a-day grind that finally terminated with regular picture work. In 1910 the Karno troupe arrived in Quebec, travelling to New York via Toronto to play on the Sullivan and Considine Circuit, 'big time' indeed. Their initial sketch, *The Wow-Wows*, needed work but sufficed during a three-month stint in New York. It made way for *A Night in an English Music Hall*, known in England as *Mumming Birds* (qv) for a twenty-week national tour. The Sullivan and Considine tour made sufficient impact for the troupe to be engaged for another 20 weeks, which commenced after a six-week New York run for the William Morris Agency. The company arrived back in England in June 1912 but returned four months later. Stan was particularly glad to return, having had some poor luck after returning home during the first tour. Repertoire and circuit were the same, though the conclusion was not. The star, Charlie Chaplin (qv) left for Keystone late in 1913 but a twelve-week engagement on the Nixon-Nirdlinger Circuit, commencing in Philadelphia, depended upon his presence. Alf Reeves, the company manager, informed the Circuit that Stan, as Chaplin's understudy, was equally as good, but a replacement from England was insisted upon. He arrived and the show flopped. Members of the troupe were offered the fare home but Stan was among those who decided to remain in America. Work was spasmodic, but included a day performing a shadow sketch called *The Evolution of Fashion*. Stan teamed with a married couple from the Karno company, Mr and Mrs Edgar Hurley, in a sketch that began life as *The Crazy Cracksman* (booked into Poli's 'family time' theatres) but developed into the 'big time' *Keystone Trio* (qv). This remained harmonious only for a while

and finished after Stan met Alice and Baldwin Cooke (qv) in 1915. Their act played the Fox, Proctor and Pantages Circuits until 1918, when Stan left to partner Mae Dahlberg, later called Mae Laurel (qv). Their act played mostly, but by no means exclusively, on the Orpheum and the Pantages time. John McCabe (qv) has recorded their itinerary for 1918-20, which took them from Kansas to Indiana, via Illinois and Michigan, between October and December 1918; from Illinois through the Midwest to Ontario by July 1919; back to Chicago, then more of Canada until reaching Montana in September; 12 days in Washington were followed by another 12 in British Columbia; then Washington again, moving on to Oregon, California, Utah, California again, Utah again, greeting 1920 in Colorado. From here they played Texas, New York, Ontario, more of New York, Massachusetts, New York again, Connecticut and Pennsylvania, opening on 11 September. Travel and the necessity to provide sometimes as many as four shows a day took its toll, and it is no surprise that Stan took whatever was available in films. There was at least work, and the act earned some excellent reviews (many of them collected by Jim Kerkhoff for *The Intra-Tent Journal* of summer 1987): their appearance at the Los Angeles Hippodrome in May 1918 (where Stan was offered his first film job) was described as creating 'the most uproar'; when playing the Majestic at Springfield, Illinois during November 1918, the *Illinois State Register* described their sketch, with Stan as a burglar impersonating a dentist (!), as 'something out of the ordinary... Laurels 'a-plenty' were certainly due these two clever actors... one of the best laugh producers seen at the Majestic this season'. In September 1919 Montana's *Helena Daily Independent* considered their skit to be 'the farce of the season'; the *Seattle Daily Times* called Stan's burglar song and vamp burlesque 'a knockout'; on

1 October, the *Seattle Post-Intelligence* hailed Stan Laurel as 'a travesty artist of the highest quality'; a few weeks later the *Tacoma Daily Ledger*, Washington, compared Stan to Chaplin, doubtless unaware of their former association; the *Los Angeles Times* of 25 November, 1919 spoke of an 'exceptionally clever sketch' with 'a plentitude of comedy'; while the *Oregon Journal* in September 1921 referred to a 'side-splitting laugh riot' from 'two delightfully entertaining artists'. By 1922, Stan's film career began to assume shape with a series for G. M Anderson (qv), but vaudeville remained a stand-by until the middle of the decade. Though it was not terribly remunerative, there were times when the rent had to be paid.

(See also: Circuses; Clifford, Nat; *Just Nuts*; Publicity; Rolin Film Co., the; Reeves, Alf; Reviews; *Rum 'Uns From Rome, the*; Stage appearances)

VELEZ, LUPE (1908-44)
Fiery Mexican actress whose early film work includes Laurel & Hardy's pre-teaming *Sailors, Beware!* (qv). After achieving stardom, she was reunited with the team in an egg-breaking routine for *Hollywood Party* (qv). In the 1940s she became associated chiefly with the *Mexican Spitfire* series. She took her own life after conceiving an illegitimate child.

(See also: Compilations; Eggs; Mexico; *M-G-M's Big Parade of Comedy*; Reciprocal destruction)

VIDA NOCTURNA, LA
See: *Blotto* and Foreign versions

VIDEO RELEASES
(Laurel & Hardy films qv)
The spread of domestic video has obliterated much of the former trade in 8mm cine film. Just as in home movie days, there is considerable interest in Laurel & Hardy material for home consumption and most of their films have been made available,

at least in Britain. In America, Blackhawk Films (*qv*) issued a number of Laurel & Hardy talkies on video before ceasing to trade. They offered collections of shorts plus features, with other Roach subjects added. Nostalgia Merchant released the films for a period, while later issues have been from Video Treasures and Cabin Fever. The former uses Film Classics reissues and some originals, with the added bonus of rarities; the latter range has computer-coloured subjects. In Britain, a number of early, obscure tape issues (some on the obsolete Philips 1700 system) were superseded by the series commenced by Virgin Vision (later renamed Vision Video) in 1986. Most seem to derive from the video masters issued for European TV and thus often have remade title cards. Among the first releases, *Way Out West* was minus the entire opening

sequence prior to Laurel & Hardy's arrival, but most black-and-white features are complete. There are some gems, such as talkie versions of *Unaccustomed As We Are*, *Berth Marks* and *They Go Boom*, all unused on British TV. There is also a comprehensive range of silents, the envy of American collectors until high-quality copies began to appear on the Nostalgia Archive label. Virgin/VVL have restored versions of *Early to Bed* and *Big Business*, making up somewhat for the copies of *Forty-Five Minutes From Hollywood* and *Slipping Wives* which are lacking subtitles. *Wrong Again* is presented with its 1929 disc track and *Do Detectives Think?* (on the same tape) is of outstanding picture quality. The company has also issued a number of the colour editions, starting with *Way Out West* (complete this time) and including the extra-length

versions of *Pardon Us* and *Laughing Gravy*. Some of the films have been coloured in abridged versions. A few solo films (*qv*) have been issued: *Zenobia* (*qv*) and a Laurel-only tape comprising *Save the Ship* (1923), *Eve's Love Letters* (*qv*), *White Wings* (1923) and *A Man About Town* (*qv*). Two solo tapes had appeared earlier from Palace Video, containing *Oranges and Lemons* (1923), *Pick and Shovel* (1923), *The Sleuth* (1925), *The Soilers* (*qv*), *Just Rambling Along* (see **Rolin**), *Near Dublin* (*qv*), *Kid Speed* (Semon/Hardy, 1924), *Stick Around* (*qv*) and *Smithy*. During 1992 the Semon/Hardy *Wizard of Oz* appeared from two different sources. VVL have also released compilations

Villains: Walter Long was always a tongue-in-cheek menace; this time it's from Any Old Port

and a documentary, *Laurel & Hardy: Archive Rarities*. M-G-M/UA have released much of the Laurel & Hardy material under their ownership, including *Bonnie Scotland*, *Air Raid Wardens*, *Nothing But Trouble* and the compilation *Laurel & Hardy's Laughing Twenties* (*qv*); another such anthology, *Days of Thrills and Laughter* (*qv*), has been released on tape at least once. The best M-G-M/UA-owned title, *Fra Diavolo*, has not been issued in the UK at the time of writing but has surfaced elsewhere; in America some have been released on the videodisc format. Fox Video have four titles in British release, *Great Guns*, *A-Haunting We Will Go*, *The Dancing Masters* and *The Bullfighters*; curiously, this selection avoids those with, respectively, the best and worst reputations, *Jitterbugs* and *The Big Noise*. *The Flying Deuces* and *Atoll K*, apparently in the public domain, have been issued by various labels in differing versions.

(See also: *Babes in Toyland*; *Below Zero*; *Blotto*; Colour; Compilations; Documentaries; Home movies; Lyn, Jacquie; M-G-M; Rediscoveries; Semon, Larry; Solo films; 20th Century-Fox; *Two Tars*)

VILLAINS
(all actors and Laurel & Hardy films *qv*)
Stereotypes are rare in the Laurel & Hardy world but, on occasion, full-blooded 'heavies' of the old school appear. Hardy himself had cornered this market before teaming with Laurel, particularly in his days with Billy West and Larry Semon and sometimes later, as in the Roach feature *No Man's Law*. Few actors could carry off an unshaven chin with such aplomb. In the embryonic months of the team, Hardy tended to continue as more or less a comic villain (as with his domineering sergeant in *With Love and Hisses*), but the role soon began to fall to others. Many early Laurel & Hardys benefit from the maniacal

tendencies of Noah Young, a Roach veteran from the 'teens whose best moments are perhaps as the psycho-pathic 'Tipton Slasher' in *Do Detectives Think?* Edgar Kennedy is really too helpless to qualify as a villain, while Tiny Sandford is a mostly gentle giant (as with his tolerant lawmen in *Big Business* and *The Hoose-Gow*). Genuine intimidation is provided by the bullet-headed Walter Long, whose menace, tempered by a slightly roguish manner, is given perhaps fullest rein in *Any Old Port*, *Going Bye-Bye!* and *Pardon Us*. Unredeemed by any roguishness (though he sometimes betrays a good comic sense), Rychard Cramer glowers his memorable way through four Laurel & Hardy comedies, most notably *Scram!* and *Saps at Sea*. Less bulky but altogether more sinister is Charles Middleton, who portrays an insidious orphanage official in *Pack Up Your Troubles*, a volatile artist in *The Fixer-Uppers* and the crazed commandant in Laurel & Hardy's two Foreign Legion tales, *Beau Hunks* and *The Flying Deuces*. Charlie Hall, diminutive stature notwithstanding, proves a splendidly mean landlord in *They Go Boom* and (especially) *Laughing Gravy*. James Finlayson, whose conniving ways permeate the Laurel & Hardy canon, parodies the standard villain most effectively in *One Good Turn* ('I have you in my clutches!'), while 'Mickey Finn' from *Way Out West* is Finlayson at his unrestrained best. The rather forgettable post-Roach films produce some appropriately ineffectual villains: an interesting exception is that of Robert Mitchum, who, at a time before achieving eminence, portrayed a convincingly seedy protection racketeer in *The Dancing Masters*. The prize for this category must go, however, to Henry Brandon, whose Silas Barnaby in *Babes in Toyland* must be one of the most unregenerate rascals in the history of filmic perfidy.

(See also: *Bullfighters, the*; Criminals;

Four Clowns; Landlords; Melodrama; Murder; Prison; Rediscoveries)

VIM COMEDIES
See: *Hungry Hearts* and Solo films

VITAGRAPH
One of the pioneering film companies and a member of the Motion Picture Patents Trust. Vitagraph established a reputation for both drama and comedy, elements skilfully blended in the films of Mr and Mrs Sidney Drew and, especially, John Bunny (1861-1915); his frequent co-star, Flora Finch, appears briefly in Laurel & Hardy's *Way Out West* (*qv*). More straightforward knockabout came later with Larry Semon (*qv*), whose entry into film had been as director for Jimmy Aubrey (*qv*). Stan Laurel appeared in at least three of Semon's Vitagraph comedies; Oliver Hardy supported both Semon and Aubrey at various times. Vitagraph was alone among Trust members to survive into the 1920s. The company was eventually acquired by Warner Brothers, who later reissued several Semon/Hardy comedies with added music and effects.

WAITE, MALCOLM
See: *Why Girls Love Sailors*

WAITING FOR GODOT
(Laurel & Hardy films *qv*)
Samuel Beckett's *avant-garde* play has as its principals two vagrants, Vladimir and Estragon, who have been compared to the Stan and Ollie characters. They are, of course, not exact parallels, but certainly the relationship between the two has some similarity, Vladimir slightly dominating his friend but in a spirit of comradely leadership. Beckett, whose regard for Laurel & Hardy is known, incorporates recognizable business with their hats, including a complex exchange of headgear between Vladimir, Estragon and a third participant, Lucky; there is even a malapropism worthy of Stan, when Estragon suggests they might 'strike the iron before it freezes'. In a 1971 edition of *Pratfall* Jordan Young examines the play in detail, comparing it to various scenes in the Laurel & Hardy films, for example Estragon's struggle to remove his boots (*Be Big*) and the tramps' contemplation of suicide (*The Flying Deuces*). *Waiting for Godot* has been said to differ from conventional situation-comedy in being 'change constantly promised, and never delivered' rather than 'change constantly threatened, but always avoided', in which respect it may be said to parallel the consistently thwarted ambitions of Laurel & Hardy. When Vladimir and Estragon consider the notion of parting, they decide instead that it is 'too late',

rather as Stan and Ollie's prolonged relationship has made the characters totally interdependent. One of Beckett's favoured interpreters, British comedian Max Wall (1908-90), played in *Waiting for Godot* for both stage revivals and on television, investing in it the qualities unique to a music-hall droll in the mould of Laurel, Chaplin (*qv*), Leno (*qv*), Grock and Little Tich. Stan Laurel maintained a regular correspondence with Max Wall.

(See also: Hats; Moreland, Mantan; Music-hall; Periodicals; Plays; Vagrancy)

WALKER, H. M. (1884-1937)
(Laurel & Hardy films *qv*)
Harley M. Walker, known as 'Beanie', turned from sportswriting to movies when he joined Roach in 1916. His combined role of editorial head and title-writer produced cards that have entered legend, both for silent films and as opening remarks for the earlier talkies (*Helpmates* opens with 'When the cat's away - the mice start looking up telephone numbers'). Though described as 'the Dean of the art' of title-writing (in a press release for *The Second Hundred Years*) Walker was less skilled at writing dialogue. Much of his work for Laurel & Hardy was so unwieldy and out of character that complete on-set revision was necessary. A hint of this occurs in titling for a few of the silents, as when in *Habeas Corpus* Stan is supposed to describe an eccentric professor as 'a trifle cuckoo', a phrase which suggests that Walker

has overdone the boys' gentility. He resigned from the Roach studio in 1932, probably in response to the economies imposed by a newly-appointed general manager, Henry Ginsberg. This unpopular man, dubbed 'the Expediter' by Stan Laurel, is said to have understood films only in terms of cost. The remaining five years of Walker's life were spent at Universal and Paramount. Evidently, Walker would stand for very little nonsense: Tay Garnett, a title-writer before his days as a director, recalled (in *Light Your Torches and Pull Up Your Tights*) applying for a job at Roach and being put on a one-day trial with Walker, whose comments on Garnett's work consisted of a growled 'yeah'. Garnett, who soon discovered Walker's 'yeahs' to be the equivalent to a round of applause, was told 'Come back tomorrow - on salary'.

(See also: Gag titles; *Half a Man*; Writers)

WALL, MAX
See: *Waiting for Godot*

WALLACE, MAY
See: *Twice Two*

WANDERING PAPAS
See: Cook, Clyde

WARDELL, NANCY
See: Home movies

WARTIME (all films *qv*)
America's entry into the Second

World War post-dates the release of *Great Guns* but such a move was widely anticipated at the time. By 1943, *Air Raid Wardens* had an entirely suitable subject, even if the US was spared the type of bombing that devastated Europe. Nazi saboteurs are the villains in this tale; other Axis types are blown to smithereens in *The Big Noise*. *Nothing But Trouble* gives us a little of the Home Front (its working title), dealing with the problems imposed by rationing and a shortage of manpower (a confidence trick in *Jitterbugs* offers 'gas pills' as a solution to fuel rationing). *The Tree in a Test Tube* is a short made by Laurel & Hardy to promote the work of the US Forestry Department. The team's other contributions to the war effort took the form of live appearances, sometimes on tour with the Hollywood Victory Caravan.

(See also: Aircraft; Army, the; Censorship; Confidence tricks; *Drivers' Licence Sketch, the*; Marx Brothers, the; M-G-M; Newsreels; Paintings; Stage appearances; 20th Century-Fox; Unfilmed projects; Working titles)

WAXWORKS

Lifelike effigies of Laurel & Hardy have appeared in several exhibitions, such as the short-lived presentation in the London Palladium cellars. More permanent (and notorious) is the Laurel & Hardy tableau in the Hollywood Wax Museum, purporting to represent a scene from *Perfect Day* (*qv*). The action is placed in a theatre lobby, where policeman Edgar Kennedy (*qv*) approaches the boys and their wrecked car. This bears no relation to the film itself, where no theatre is visible and Kennedy is dressed in civilian clothes. The exhibit has been refurbished in recent years but no attempt has been made to introduce some accuracy. In 1942 the Fox studio planned to star Laurel & Hardy in *Me and My Shadow*, in which the team operate a waxworks; the film was aborted at scripting stage. Five years later, the team visited Madame Tussaud's famous waxworks in London, where they posed for photographers while examining their reflections in distorting mirrors.

(See also: *Rum 'Uns From Rome, the*; 20th Century-Fox; Unfilmed projects)

WAY OUT WEST

(Laurel & Hardy film)
Released by M-G-M, 16 April 1937. Stan Laurel Productions for Hal Roach. Directed by James W. Horne. Camera: Art Lloyd, Walter Lundin. 65 minutes.
With Stan Laurel & Oliver Hardy, James Finlayson, Sharon Lynne, Rosina Lawrence, Stanley Fields, Vivien Oakland, Harry Bernard, James C. Morton, the Avalon Boys, Chill Wills.

Life in the western town of Brushwood Gulch centres around the saloon run by Mickey Finn (James Finlayson) and his wife, singer Lola Marcel (Sharon Lynne). Slaving in the kitchen is Mary Roberts (Rosina Lawrence), who has been in their charge since childhood. When two prospectors, Stan and Ollie, arrive with a deed to a gold mine left by Mary's late father, Finn, seeing an opportunity, passes Lola off as the heiress. By the time Stan and Ollie realize the deception, Mary has already been tricked into signing the deed over to the Finns. Attempts to retrieve it are not helped by the arrival of the town's Sheriff (Stanley Fields), who had ordered them out of town earlier that day. That night they break into the saloon, recover the deed and leave with Mary, with plans to settle 'way down south'.

Last of the team's two 'Stan Laurel Productions' (*qv*), *Way Out West* is one of their most popular films, a TV perennial and frequent rival to *Sons of the Desert* (*qv*) when evaluating their best feature-length films. The reasons

for this popularity are clear: most of their comedy's best elements are present, as is familiar foil James Finlayson (*qv*). The plot, as in the earlier feature, involves them completely and is enough to sustain the length without padding. Finlayson's melodramatic villainy finds a perfect setting, while Sharon Lynne (*qv*), whose background was in musicals, is ideal as his unscrupulous wife. Another bonus is the presence of three musical numbers involving the team, including a dance (much prized by impersonators) to 'At the Ball, That's All' and the song 'The Trail of the Lonesome Pine', which, when issued as a 45 rpm record late in 1975, reached number two in the charts. One of the highlights of the latter song is that Stan takes over the chorus, singing it first in a robust bass, thus annoying Ollie who, after asking the bartender for a large wooden mallet, proceeds to hit his pal firmly over the head. Stan's voice immediately changes from bass to high soprano, and he promptly falls down out of camera range. The bass voice was dubbed by Chill Wills, the soprano by Rosina Lawrence (*qv*), heroine of the film. As William K. Everson (*qv*) has noted, *Way Out West* differs from most comic westerns by actually parodying the genre rather than merely using a western setting. Mel Brooks' more recent *Blazing Saddles* attempts the same but is over-reliant on self-conscious dialogue references and suffers from a tendency to stray from the target.

Boarding a stagecoach in **Way Out West**

get. The success of *Way Out West* may owe something to Stan Laurel's early experience in parody (he was soon also to become a producer of westerns); similarly, Oliver Hardy's earlier work in silent westerns would have contributed. One might add that a sequence in which saloon-singer Lola uses a mirror to reflect the spotlight at various men in the audience (much imitated since), occurs in *The Show*, a 1922 film in which Hardy supports Larry Semon (*qv*). The parody element extends far enough to include a moment where Stanley rolls up a trouser leg to halt a stagecoach; a precise imitation of Claudette Colbert's hitchhiking methods in *It Happened One Night* (complete with close-up of braking wheel); it reflects the best Laurel parodies of the 1920s through being amusing in its own right. At least two accounts describe a sequence unique to British prints in which Laurel & Hardy are confused by a revolving signpost. Although stills exist suggesting such a scene, all available copies seem to derive from American material, usually the reissue by Film Classics or, less commonly, the original (distinguishable by the M-G-M logo on the main title card). The signpost sequence is detailed in the original shooting script, reprinted in the Winter 1991/2 edition of *Blotto* magazine from the collection of Ray Andrew. An interesting fragment in the gag reel *That's That!* (*qv*) juxtaposes shots of Stanley Fields with Tiny Sandford (both *qv*) in the role of Sheriff (Sandford was replaced during production). Coincidentally, the two had appeared together in the previous year's version of *Show Boat*. *Way Out West* became a flagship title when computer-colouring was applied to the Laurel & Hardy films. A simpler version of the process had been used with a few of the shorts, but *Way Out West* was the first to employ a genuinely convincing range, drawing favourable comment (technically if not artistically) when released to American TV and video in 1985. Six years later, it became the first computer-coloured Laurel & Hardy to be issued on British video, heralded by a large-screen presentation at BAFTA's London premises.

(See also: Britain; Colour; Dubbing; Melodrama; Music; Oakland, Vivien; Parodies; Records; Reissues; Songs; Titling; Villains; Westerns; 'White magic'; Working titles; Video releases)

WAYNE, JOHN
See: *Fighting Kentuckian, the*

WEDDINGS (all films *qv*)
Usually regarded as cause for celebration, weddings in the Laurel & Hardy films tend to be rather fraught. Ollie's big day in *Me and My Pal* is ruined by a present from his best man, Stan; Ollie's elopement with Babe London (*qv*) in *Our Wife* reaches a bizarre conclusion because of a cross-eyed judge; while Stan's wedding in a radio sketch is called off through indecision, first from Stan, then the bride and, finally, the Justice of the Peace. In *Pack Up Your Troubles* Stan and Ollie disrupt a society wedding by arriving with 'Eddie's baby'; bridegroom in this sequence is Grady Sutton (*qv*), while the bride, Muriel Evans, appeared more frequently with Charley Chase (*qv*). The wedding of Bo-Peep to the villainous Barnaby in *Babes in Toyland* is averted when the bride is revealed to be Stan; other unwelcome ceremonies are thwarted in *Any Old Port* and *Fra Diavolo*.

(See also: Marriages; Radio; Romance)

WEDDING NIGHT/PARTY, THE
See: Radio and Weddings

WE FAW DOWN
(Laurel & Hardy film)
Released by M-G-M, 29 December 1928. Produced by Hal Roach. Directed by Leo McCarey. Two reels. Silent, released with music and sound effects. Released in Britain as *We Slip Up*.

With Stan Laurel and Oliver Hardy, Vivien Oakland, Bess Flowers, Kay Deslys, Vera White, George Kotsonaros.

Stan and Ollie cannot escape their wives (Bess Flowers and Vivien Oakland) to go to a poker game with friends; when those same friends telephone to ask where they are, Ollie pretends it is the boss inviting Stan and himself to the Orpheum Theatre. The boys set out for the poker game but pause to assist two girls (Kay Deslys and Vera White) when one of them loses her hat. In retrieving it from under a car, the boys are drenched by a passing water-sprinkling wagon. They are invited to dry out at the girls' flat, where they are caught by a knife-wielding boyfriend (George Kotsonaros). This forces a quick retrieval of clothes and an exit via the window. Stan and Ollie are unaware that the Orpheum Theatre has just burned to the ground, and that their wives, *en route* to the scene, have spotted them making an undignified escape. At home, Ollie's great show of outrage at being doubted by his wife pales alongside his description of the acts they saw. Stan is horrified to see the front page of the evening paper: ORPHEUM THEATRE BURNS. Ollie claims they visited the Palace instead, an excuse so lame that Stan bursts out laughing. The proverbial last straw is reached when one of the girls appears with Ollie's waistcoat. The boys are chased from the house by their wives, who with a single shotgun blast send countless trouserless men leaping from every nearby apartment.

Typical of their matrimonial comedies, *We Faw Down* anticipates the plot of perhaps the best of them, the feature-length *Sons of the Desert* (*qv*). At least one source traces the plot of *We Faw Down* to a Keystone comedy of the teens, though according to a contemporary report by British journalist Margaret Chute (in *Royal Pictorial*

Magazine), the basic story was supplied by Babe, after listening to gossip from his laundress. Babe was self-effacing about his contribution to the gag content, but it is evident that he would supply worthwhile ideas on occasion (see **Remakes**). This silent comedy lacks the synchronized music and effects of its initial release, a fate it shares with *Habeas Corpus* (*qv*) although the other film's pacing is more affected by the loss. Of greater concern is the mutilation afflicting certain prints: older copies issued by Blackhawk Films (*qv*) lack the footage linking the boys' escape from the flat to their return home, a section that is replaced with a clumsy title card. This is the version currently available to UK video buyers; an earlier TV copy, originating in Canada, is complete, but with the irritating distraction of remade subtitles.

(See also: *Block-Heads*; Deslys, Kay; Flowers, Bess; *Golden Age of Comedy, the*; *Hats Off*; *Liberty*; Oakland, Vivien; Risqué humour; Shotguns; *Their First Mistake*; Women)

WEIGHT
See: Height, weight

WELLS, JACQUELINE (1917-?)
Leading lady of *Any Old Port* and *The Bohemian Girl* (both *qv*). The Colorado-born actress later changed her name to Julie Bishop, appearing in *Rhapsody in Blue* (1945), *Sands of Iwo Jima* (1949), and *The High and the Mighty* (1954), among others. She was also known as Jacqueline Brown.

(See also: Songs; Titling)

WERKER, ALFRED (1896-1975)
Veteran director from the silent era, whose key films of the period include *Little Lord Fauntleroy* (1921). By the late 1930s, he was with 20th Century-Fox (*qv*), for whom he directed the classic *Adventures of Sherlock Holmes* in 1939. His only Laurel & Hardy picture, *A-Haunting We Will Go* (*qv*) was

one of several instances of the studio automatically assigning to the pair a silent-film talent, irrespective of style.

WE SLIP UP

See: Alternate titles, *Golden Age of Comedy, the* and *We Faw Down*

WEST, BILLY (1893–1975)

When Charlie Chaplin (*qv*) reached the peak of his popularity in the mid-1910s, several comedians in his wake adopted his costume and style. One such was Stan Laurel, whose vaudeville routine was justified by his days as understudy to the original. This harmless tribute to a former colleague can not be compared to the bogus Chaplins who plied their trade in film, one of whom adopted the name 'Charles Aplin' and was sued by Chaplin. The most accomplished impostor was Billy West, a Russian-born comedian who had been brought to the US as a child. West (real name Roy Weissberg) had been dividing his time between the stage and cartooning until his imitation of Chaplin took him from vaudeville into films. West's films were actually very funny, but earned more money than respect:

according to John McCabe (*qv*), several trade journals would express their contempt by printing the name 'billy west' in lower case. It has been claimed, quite reasonably, that West did not so much imitate the Chaplin character as explore an alternative facet of it. Less accurate is a parallel defence to the effect that West did not borrow Chaplin's plots. Robert Youngson (*qv*) disproved this theory when he unearthed a West film, *The Villain* (1917), which was influenced directly by Chaplin's *Tillie's Punctured Romance*. Here, city slicker West deceives a rotund country girl. The 'girl' is played by Oliver Hardy, who was a regular foil in West's series for the King Bee company during 1917–18. Hardy would often portray a villain (in make-up reminiscent of Chaplin's 'heavy', Eric Campbell) or, as in *The Hobo* (1917), an amiable rival to whom the gallant West could ultimately surrender the girl. A highlight from this film sees Hardy devouring a lengthy string of sausages, a gag that may have served some practical purpose. Historian Kalton C. Lahue has recorded that Hardy's contract guaranteed a bonus of $2 for each pound

added to his weight, with a $250 bonus if he gained 50 pounds within six months. Also of note is *His Day Out* (1918), with Billy in charge of a barber's shop. Babe appears in top hat, cutaway coat and bushy moustache, the florid gestures of his later years being suggested somewhat in this cad of the old school. The film is known today mostly through extracts in *Four Clowns* and *The Further Perils of Laurel & Hardy* (both *qv*). Another West associate of the period was Charley Chase (*qv*) who, like Hardy, was to win his greatest fame at the Hal Roach studio. Both Hardy and Chase may be seen in West's *Playmates*, a 1918 comedy considered by William K. Everson (*qv*) to be the inspiration behind Laurel & Hardy's *Brats* (*qv*). The appropriate segment (revived in the TV series *Silents, Please*) is indeed a clear anticipation of the later short, with West and Hardy in children's costume, squabbling against an overscaled background. Hardy and Chase are known to have continued on the former King Bee lot after the company's closure; for his 1920s appearances West abandoned the Chaplin look for that of a man-about-town. He appeared in a series for an independent company, Arrow, in addition to producing their 'Mirthquake' comedies, starring Oliver Hardy and Bobby Ray (see **Stick Around**). West's obituary in *Boxoffice* refers to subsequent work as an assistant director at Columbia, where he and his wife Marian ran the 'Columbia Grill'. Billy West remained active in the film community almost until his death, maintaining his membership of the Directors' Guild of America up to the end.

(See also: Anderson, G. M.; *Days of*

Babe in support of Chaplin imitator **Billy West** *in* The Rogue *(1918). To the right is Mancunian comic Leo White, poached from the Chaplin company. Note West's left-handed violin playing, a precise match for Chaplin's*

Thrills and Laughter; Female imper-
sonation; Height, weight; *Keystone
Trio, the*; Lawrence, Rosina;
Melodrama; Sawmills; Seiter, William
A.; Solo films)

WESTERNS
Laurel & Hardy's only fully-fledged
excursion into this genre is their
famous spoof, *Way Out West* (*qv*),
though they appear as Mexican bandits
for a film-within-a-film sequence of
Pick A Star (*qv*). As solo talents they
contributed rather more: Babe is
known to have worked in some of Buck
Jones' westerns of the 1920s, and is in
Roach's *No Man's Law*. Stan's skills at
parody took him *West of Hot Dog*,
while his *The Soilers* (*qv*) is considered
a minor classic; another western, a late
solo Laurel released by Pathé in 1928,
is called *Should Tall Men Marry?* In
the 1930s, Stan produced a number of
B-westerns, contributing only in an
off-screen capacity.

(See also: *Four Clowns*; Parodies; Pathé
Exchange; Solo films; Stan Laurel
Productions)

WHEN COMEDY WAS KING
(20th Century-Fox 1960)
Second of the feature-length compilations by Robert Youngson (*qv*), *When*

*Babe in an unidentified western of the
'teens*

Comedy Was King covers a slightly
greater time-scale than its predecessor,
The Golden Age of Comedy (*qv*) in
extending a concentration on 1920s
films back to the Keystone comedies
of 1914-16. Laurel & Hardy are permitted less space (their reputation
having been restored by this time) but
Roach product is much in evidence,
notably through Chase's *Movie Night*,
Pollard's *It's A Gift* and the superb
'All-Star' comedy *A Pair of Tights* (*qv*).
Closing the show is most of Laurel &
Hardy's *Big Business* (*qv*), from the
usual American version but in superb
picture quality. Youngson took care to
obtain the best surviving material,
working from original negative where
possible. Music scoring in these early
Youngson anthologies takes the form
of a full orchestra with synchronized
sound effects: *Big Business* is greatly
enhanced here by a score that alter-
nates between the Laurel & Hardy
theme and 'The Campbells Are
Coming' as the action switches from
the boys to Scotsman James Finlayson
(*qv*). The style is very much of the
1950s, as is the narration: when
Charlie Chaplin (*qv*) is on screen, contemporary American attitudes have to

be salved by describing the early work
of this 'figure of controversy' as
'blameless'. Given the hostility shown
toward Chaplin in America less than a
decade before, Youngson's inclusion of
his footage can be considered a brave
move, even if this partial apology was
deemed necessary.

(See also: Chaplin, Charlie; Chase,
Charley; Compilations; Letters;
Music)

WHEN KNIGHTS WERE COLD
See: Anderson, G. M.

'WHITE MAGIC' (all films *qv*)
Stanley's occasional displays of super-
natural but trivial accomplishment
have been dubbed, appropriately,
'White magic' by John McCabe (*qv*).
The most celebrated examples are
linked, being the igniting of a thumb
as a cigarette lighter in *Way Out West*
and his smoking a clenched fist in lieu
of a pipe in *Block-Heads* (the imaginative impressionist might care to
combine the two). Stan smokes a clay
pipe in *Way Out West*, despite the
detachment of bowl from stem. Ollie,
of course, cannot imitate these feats,
bound as he is by the self-appointed
role of sensible, worldly bridge
between Stan and the rest of humanity. However, he can be caught
off-guard, first when trying to light
his own thumb behind Stan's back
and later, when such an attempt
brings success just when he is not
expecting it. *Block-Heads* has a running gag where Stan twice pulls down
the blind of the *shadow* cast by a window; on a subsequent attempt a
shadow hand beats him to it. At least
one critic has found fault with the
unworldly quality of these gags,
through being out of keeping with the
team's usual adherance to the credible.
One might counter this by considering the effectiveness of these
occasional fantasies within an otherwise realistic context (it is open to
debate whether the comparable antics
of, for example, Harpo Marx are any

more effective for the zanier context in which they are presented). Another objection is that Stan's inherent helplessness is undermined by such fantastic accomplishments, although it might be said in turn that his vulnerability is underlined by an ability to apply such skills only to unimportant tasks. Stanley is more strongly in the clown mould than Ollie, and clowns have by tradition been endowed with other-worldly qualities. Perhaps Stanley's permanent abstention from conscious thought enables his subconscious to produce these miracles. Advancing age saw such feats gradually supplanting the team's knockabout aspect: at sea in *Atoll K* Stan literally 'pours oil on troubled waters' in order to calm a storm.

(See also: Characters; *Great Guns*; Marx Brothers, the; Records; Standins; Titling)

WHISKY TASTERS, THE
See: *Birds of a Feather*

WHITE WINGS
See: Dentists and Video releases

WHY GIRLS LOVE SAILORS
(Laurel & Hardy film)
Released by Pathé Exchange, 17 July 1927. Produced by Hal Roach. Directed by Fred Guiol. Two reels. Silent.
With Stan Laurel, Viola Richard, Malcolm Waite, Oliver Hardy, Anita Garvin.

Winkle fisherman Willie Brisling (Stan Laurel) is happily engaged to Nelly (Viola Richard) until she is abducted and taken aboard ship by her former boyfriend, a visiting sea captain (Malcolm Waite). Following them, Willie finds a means of disguise in a theatrical trunk belonging to a female impersonator (!), in whose costume he lures each crew member to a knockout blow. Last in line is the Mate (Oliver Hardy), who is left, eyes closed, expecting a kiss while Willie

makes his way to the Captain's quarters. The Mate reopens his eyes to see a woman's leg clambering aboard; making a grab, he discovers its owner to be the Captain's wife (Anita Garvin), who has reappeared after being left at the last port. Having flattened the Mate, she enters her husband's cabin to discover him with the female-clad impostor. She is ready to shoot them both but Willie removes his wig and declares his impersonation to have been a test of the wife's love. Although off the hook, the Captain issues a muttered threat to Willie, who in retaliation produces

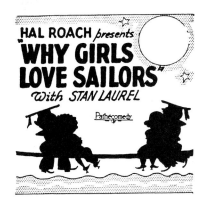

Why Girls Love Sailors: *as usual, the publicity has little to do with the film's content*
By courtesy of Robert G. Dickson

both Nelly and the information that three other girls had left earlier. As Willie and Nelly depart, a gunshot informs us of the Captain's demise; a further shot leaves the young couple in their underwear, and they scamper away.

Why Girls Love Sailors was for years the subject of considerable speculation. Long thought lost, nothing was known of the plot other than Laurel's vague recollection of a story similar to that above (but with Hardy as the Captain), complicated by the existence of the director's own notes detailing a quite different scenario. In this version, Laurel & Hardy are in

the US Navy and are united in their efforts to recover Stan's Chinese girlfriend (to be played by Anna May Wong) from a moneylender played by the Japanese actor, Sojin. Rumours of a 1971 screening at the Cinémathèque Française led to nothing until a 16mm print surfaced from a private collector in 1985. The available copy is in French (with subtitles decorated by often tasteless cartoons) and has music, sound effects and a slightly incongruous song added. Fortunately the text itself does not seem far from the original and is easy to translate. Its rediscovery confirmed not only the plot but its supporting cast: Malcolm Waite (1892–1949), best known from Chaplin's *The Gold Rush*, was not known to have appeared with Laurel & Hardy; the presence of Anita Garvin (*qv*) proved another surprise, all of her appearances with the team (of which this is one of the best) were thought documented. *Why Girls Love Sailors* is one of several instances where the status of a 'lost' film has been reduced by its rediscovery. Oliver Hardy credited the film as birthplace both of his camera-looks (*qv*) and 'tie-twiddle' (see **Ties**), and although the former claim was already in some doubt, the latter remained unassailable until an actual screening revealed Hardy wearing a polo neck, not a tie. His description suggests a confusion with another short of the same year, *Sailors Beware* (*qv*).

(See also: Boats, ships; Female impersonation; Foreign versions; In-jokes; Rediscoveries; Villains)

WILD POSES
(Laurel & Hardy guest appearance)
Released by M-G-M, 28 October 1933. Produced by Robert F. McGowan for Hal Roach. Directed by Robert F. McGowan. Camera: Francis Corby. Two reels.
With Our Gang (Spanky McFarland, Matthew 'Stymie' Beard, Tommy Bond, George [Darby] Billings, Jerry Tucker), Franklin Pangborn, Gay

Seabrook, Emerson Treacy, Stan Laurel and Oliver Hardy.

A door-to-door salesman is drumming up business for a photographer by describing the children of every household as being the most beautiful and photogenic he's ever seen; that statement extends even to a pair of babies who look remarkably like Stan and Ollie. The sales pitch is enough to persuade Spanky's parents (Gay Seabrook and Emerson Treacy), who take their son and his young friends to the studio of Otto Phocus (Franklin Pangborn). The photographer is a fragile sort ill-equipped to deal with such a difficult subject as Spanky, all the more so when the youngster hits Mr Phocus. He would be even more distressed to know that the Gang have ruined his film, paper and camera, replacing the lens with a bottle. He discovers the makeshift lens and replaces it, but is unaware that the bulb-release has been filled with water. Spanky is reluctant to be photographed until his father agrees to sit first; father is given a soaking. Spanky is still afraid of the camera but submits to a group portrait with his parents. This time, mother gets the water. 'One hour later' (according to a title), Phocus has a plan: Spanky should be asked to smile into one camera while Phocus snaps him with another. Spanky refuses to smile until his father disappears under the dummy camera, then laughs immoderately while Phocus takes his picture. All seems well until Phocus tries to develop the film, which comes out black. As his customers make for the door, Phocus pleads for 'one more bust'; Spanky returns to hit the photographer yet again.

Part of Roach's long-running Our Gang series (qv), *Wild Poses* is another of Laurel & Hardy's infrequent guest shots. Their sequence, lasting approximately ten seconds, shows them as babies squabbling over a milk bottle. The giant chair on which they are seated is believed to be a remnant of

the set for *Brats* (qv), while background music is the baroque version of their 'cuckoo' theme from *Fra Diavolo* (qv). The scene was incorporated into a 1981 compilation of Gang shorts called *Rascal Dazzle*, narrated by Jerry Lewis (qv).

(See also: Children; Guest appearances; Music)

WILLS, CHILL
See: Dubbing

WISDOM, NORMAN (b. 1915)
British comedian comparable to the greats of silent film and music-hall though taken for granted until recent years. Although familiar on TV, radio and the stage, he is associated chiefly with a thirteen-year run of features for the Rank Organisation, starting with *Trouble in Store* (1953). He was once tipped by Chaplin (qv) as a possible successor. His meetings with Laurel & Hardy are mentioned variously, as in a 1974 series of profiles in the long-defunct magazine *Reveille* and a biography by Richard Dacre, *Trouble in Store*. In 1947, Laurel & Hardy saw Wisdom at a Water Rats' charity show at the Victoria Palace, in which they also took part; they met him later on in Belgium, where Wisdom was appearing in the show *Piccadilly Nights*. Stan Laurel showed particular interest in the young comedian, offering both advice and to work (disguised) as Wisdom's feed; regrettably, management intervention prevented this intriguing partnership.

(See also: Grand Order of Water Rats, the; Music-hall; Stage appearances)

WITH LOVE AND HISSES
(Laurel & Hardy film)
Released by Pathé Exchange, 28 August 1927. Produced by Hal Roach. Directed by Fred Guiol. Two reels. Silent.
With Stan Laurel, Oliver Hardy, James Finlayson, Frank Brownlee, Anita Garvin, Eve Southern.

The army reserve, or 'Home Guards', are off for a weekend camp. Top Sergeant Banner (Hardy) is a ladies' man, whose interest in two attractive women earns him a reprimand from their escort, Captain Bustle (James Finlayson). On the train, Banner meets a further irritation, Cuthbert Hope (Laurel) a timid private. On a route march, the platoon stops to bathe in a nearby lake. Hope, who is left to guard their uniforms, deserts his post to join the others and fails to notice that Banner's discarded cigarette has reduced their clothing to ashes. The approach of the Colonel's

With Love and Hisses: *an unrecognizable Stan gets the boot in this contemporary newspaper advertisement; note that Babe does not as yet receive billing*
By courtesy of Robert G. Dickson

ladies compels the naked platoon to hide behind a convenient billboard, their heads replacing those in the poster. In attempting to sneak back to camp they knock over a hornets' nest, unleashing swarms of irate insects. For the finale, a title card tells us 'all's well that ends swell', a maxim illustrated by the men walking slowly away, posteriors expanded to giant proportions.

Surprisingly vulgar (but undeniably funny), *With Love and Hisses* relies heavily on things such as strong cheese or even stronger feet, the grimy atmosphere emphasized in surviving prints that look duped from 16mm. For an early pre-teaming film, Laurel and Hardy share a considerable amount of footage, albeit in roles requiring Hardy to be a bully and Laurel an effete but hyperactive simpleton. It has been suggested that Stan's effeminacy in this film was another experiment to find a suitable character, unlikely since these traits exist only to facilitate Stan's lampooning of his commanding officer, James Finlayson (*qv*).

(See also: Animals; Army, the; Garvin, Anita; Homosexuality; Insects; Mandy, Jerry; Names; Nudity; Pathé Exchange; Preservation; Risqué humour; Smoking; Teaming; Trains)

WOMEN (all films *qv*)

It is popularly believed that most Laurel & Hardy admirers are male, with the team's antics dismissed by women because they do not find them funny or resent the depiction of women in the films. How true this is remains open to conjecture, though the Sons of the Desert (*qv*) has a considerable female membership. There is just cause for complaint: most of the women in Laurel & Hardy's world are either shrewish wives, gossips, lunatics, gold-diggers or prostitutes. However, in fairness most of the male characters are no better, also serving the purpose of confronting the good-natured Stan and Ollie. Landlords (*qv*), best personified by Charlie Hall (*qv*), are the domestic rulers in one environment; wives, notably Mae Busch (*qv*), dominate another. When Ollie portrays a married man, Stan often remains a bachelor; *Blotto* is a rare exception, with Stan escaping his wife for a night's drinking with bachelor Ollie. *Blotto* works well despite Stan's greater suitability as a disruptive influence, as in *Their First Mistake*; when both have wives, as in *Sons of the Desert*, Ollie takes the lead in any rebellion. In some earlier comedies (such as *Perfect Day*), the boys are relatively assertive with their spouses,

but others (*Their Purple Moment*) suggest the domination to come. The childlike aspect of their characters leads naturally to the assumption of a somewhat parental role by their screen wives, usurping Ollie's leadership of Stan and subtly transforming their relationship into that of allies, a status otherwise reserved for their battles with such adversaries as James Finlayson (*qv*). It is important to note sympathetic female characters in the Laurel & Hardy repertoire: Mrs Hall in *Them Thar Hills* and *Tit For Tat*; the neighbouring ladies of *Unaccustomed As We Are* and its remake, *Block-Heads*; the heroines of *Babes in Toyland*, *The Bohemian Girl* and *Way Out West*; the not unjustly impatient Mrs Hardy of *Hog Wild*, to name a few.

(See also: Characters; Flowers; Hardy, Emily; Marriages; Risqué humour; Shotguns)

WOOD, 'WEE' GEORGIE, O.B.E. (1895-1979)

Diminutive British comedian acquainted with Stan Laurel from 1907 until Laurel's death. They first met in the Levy and Cardwell production of *Sleeping Beauty*, and again, years later as fellow members of the Water Rats maintaining a steady correspondence. Wood's later career included work as a columnist for *The Stage* and *Record Mirror*.

(See also: Grand Order of Water Rats, the; Music-hall; Pantomime)

WORKING TITLES

(Laurel & Hardy films *qv*)

Numerous films have borne production titles differing from those of the eventual release. Such changes tend to be aesthetic but several have been for commercial reasons, notably Laurel's 1923 *Robin Hood* parody, *When Knights Were Cold*, which jettisoned the name *Rob 'Em Good* when that title was used elsewhere (*Way Out West* usurped the name *Tonight's the Night* for similar

reasons). The improvised nature of the Laurel & Hardy films dictated the use of temporary labels, and *From Soup To Nuts* was previewed as *Let George Do It*. *Hog Wild* actually played as *Haywire* for a week in Los Angeles before being rechristened, while *The Chiselers* was redubbed *Be Big* only after being registered for copyright. *Be Big* is a title lifted directly from the film's dialogue; several working titles betray similar origins, such as *Just the Reverse* (*Wrong Again*), *Step On It* (*Perfect Day*), *The Sniffles* (*They Go Boom*) and *Calling Car Thirteen* (*The Midnight Patrol*). In the 1920s there was a trend for 'question' titles, seen in, among others, *Do Detectives Think?*, *Should Married Men Go Home?* and Laurel's *Should Tall Men Marry?* *Flying Elephants* nearly asked *Were Women Always Wild?* and *Do Cavemen Marry?* until someone decided to name it after a single gag shot. Working titles also provided an alternative for peculiarly American names, as when *You're Darn Tootin'* appeared in Britain as *The Music Blasters*. The retention of *Fraternally Yours* in lieu of *Sons of the Desert* may have been prompted by the comparative lack of national lodges in the UK, whose audiences also saw *Fra Diavolo* under its intended title instead of *The Devil's Brother*. The effort in finding a suitable pun for Laurel & Hardy's first talkie produced both *Their Last Word* and, more appropriately, *Unaccustomed As We Are*. *Pardon Us* began life as *The Rap*, and nearly reached theatres under a title used instead for a later film, *Their First Mistake*. Several changes may be considered minor, there being scant difference between *A Little Laughing Gas* and *Leave 'Em Laughing*, or *Swiss Cheese* and *Swiss Miss*; others, however, induce a sigh of relief, especially when learning how close *The Chimp* came to being called *Monkeydoodle*.

(See also: Alternate titles; *Bonnie Scotland*; *Jitterbugs*; *Two Tars*; Westerns; *Zenobia*)

WORTH, HARRY

Born Harry Illingworth, Harry Worth was among several British post-war talents who toured with Laurel & Hardy in variety. He came to know Babe Hardy particularly well, and it was through his guidance that Worth abandoned ventriloquism in favour of comic dithering: Worth had considered making such a move, but Babe's recommendation confirmed the decision. It was in this style that Worth became famous on stage and in his 1960s BBC TV sitcom *Here's Harry*. Later efforts for commercial TV received less widespread acclaim. He continued to work until the end, sometimes in pantomime and in a revival of his 1960s radio show, *Thirty Minutes Worth*. Died in 1989, aged 71.

(See also: Stage appearances; Taxis; 20th Century-Fox)

WOW-WOWS, THE

See: *Mumming Birds* and Vaudeville

WRIGHT, BASIL (1907-87)

(Laurel & Hardy films *qv*)
British film maker who pioneered documentary work, his best-known film being the 1936 GPO short *Night Mail*, co-directed by Harry Watt. In his parallel occupation as critic, Wright had special praise for Laurel & Hardy, comparing *Hog Wild* to the work of Eisenstein and regarding part of *Way Out West* ('a film I would choose to see on my deathbed') as a comic encapsulation of the *avant-garde* movement. In 1962, Wright was a faculty member at the University of California, Los Angeles; one of his students, a young Scot named Robert G. Dickson, had visited Stan Laurel on several occasions and arranged for them to meet. Wright's visit to the Laurel apartment, documented in his book *The Long View* (1974), brought the pleasant revelation that Stan remembered every last detail of his films and that he still found them funny, something evident also in the few recorded interviews. Wright noted

Basil Wright visits Stan in 1962. Note the portrait sent by Laurel & Hardy admirer John F. Kennedy
Photograph by kind permission of Robert G. Dickson

the comedian's dismay at the butchering of his films on American TV, Stan remarking plaintively 'It makes you weep'. Laurel autographed a copy of *Mr Laurel and Mr Hardy* to Wright, which he kept until his death.

(See also: Biographies; McCabe, John; Preservation; Reviews; Television)

WRITERS

The Roach comedies were created by a sizeable team, the most important members of which were perhaps the writers or, as they were more commonly called, gagmen. In the early days of Laurel & Hardy this team would be presided over by Stan Laurel and Leo McCarey (*qv*), Stan alone having final say after McCarey's departure from the studio. Membership of this group, as with most things at Roach, would be informal; several on-screen talents would contribute to the gags and vice versa, as when Carl Harbaugh (*qv*) took minor roles. Exclusively off-camera were those such as H. M. Walker, Frank Butler (both *qv*) and, briefly, Stan's former boss Fred Karno (*qv*). Those doubling as gagmen and actors included Eddie Dunn, Charles Rogers, Nat Clifford, Charlie Hall and Glenn Tryon (all *qv*). The features

required more extensive scripting and scenario work, recurring names here being Frank Butler, James Parrott (*qv*), Jack Jevne, Felix Adler, Charles Rogers and, later, Harry Langdon (*qv*). Stan had absolute say in what was chosen, a situation reversed after 1940. The initial Fox writer, Lou Breslow, (a former director of the Three Stooges), avoided any consultation with the comedian, as did his successor, W. Scott Darling (*qv*). Breslow presumably was given the assignment on the strength of having conceived the initial idea for Fox's *Hollywood Cavalcade* (1939), a self-conscious and largely inaccurate account of silent comedy's heyday; Darling was in turn a screenwriter left over from the 'teens. Better things were suggested by the presence of Jevne and Rogers on M-G-M's *Air Raid Wardens* (*qv*), but the production was marred by poor direction and a script to match. It has been speculated that the film's two other writers might have had more say, but one might similarly interpret this as illustration of Stan's contribution to his old writing team.

(See also: Keaton, Buster; M-G-M; Scripts; 20th Century-Fox)

WRONG AGAIN

(Laurel & Hardy film)
Released by M-G-M, 23 February 1929. Produced by Hal Roach. Directed by Leo McCarey. Two reels. Camera: George Stevens and Jack Roach. Silent, with music and sound effects.
With Stan Laurel and Oliver Hardy, Del Henderson, Josephine Crowell, Sam Lufkin.

Stable-hands Laurel & Hardy hear of the theft of 'Blue Boy' and, not realizing it to be a famous painting, assume the missing item to be a horse of that name which is in their care. Seeking a reward, they take him to the address of the painting's millionaire owner. On their arrival, the millionaire is in the bath, but throws down a key with a request to put 'Blue Boy' on the piano. Stan and Ollie assume the man to be eccentric. They lead the animal into the mansion, breaking a statue which Ollie reassembles with its midriff reversed. Getting a reluctant horse atop the piano proves difficult; keeping him there is as big a problem, particularly after the front piano leg breaks off. The piano is fixed (though not before Ollie's head is temporarily sandwiched between leg and piano!) in time for the return of the owner's mother. On his way downstairs, the millionaire asks Stan and Ollie to conceal their surprise behind a curtain. His mother has another surprise, the missing painting. When the millionaire explains *that* to be 'Blue Boy', Stan and Ollie laugh at their mistake before leading away the horse. Wielding a shotgun, the millionaire gives chase, knocking over the painting. It lands on Sullivan, the butler, whose face protrudes through that of the picture. The contrite millionaire is escorted home by a policeman, who complains that 'this man almost blew

my brains out'. When he turns to leave, we see smoking devastation in lieu of the seat of his trousers.

The final gag is reprised from one of their first appearances, *Slipping Wives* (*qv*), and would resurface later; otherwise *Wrong Again* is among the most original Laurel & Hardy comedies; its gags alternately bizarre, risqué and imaginative knockabout. The similarity to *Un Chien Andalou* (1928), in which Dali and Buñuel place donkeys on a piano, is probably coincidence although Leo McCarey (*qv*) might well have kept track of such avant-garde projects. The story developed from an afternoon spent by McCarey in a dentist's surgery, where he distracted himself from pain by devising a scenario around a copy of Gainsborough's *Blue Boy* hanging in the surgery. The best copies of *Wrong Again* (including that issued on UK video) incorporate a restored disc accompaniment from the original release. The skilled orchestral arrangement and appropriate sound effects transform the film into a minor masterpiece, reminding

modern audiences of the way silent films were presented at their zenith. Part of this soundtrack provides background music for the opening of *The Laurel-Hardy Murder Case* (*qv*).

(See also: *A-Haunting We Will Go*; Animals; *Big Noise, the*; *Chump at Oxford, a*; Henderson, Del; Insanity; *Laurel & Hardy's Laughing Twenties*; Music; Pianos; Risqué humour; Sound; Video releases)

WURTZEL, SOL M. (1890-1958) B-picture production executive at 20th Century-Fox (*qv*), responsible for most of the Laurel & Hardy films made at the studio. New York-born Wurtzel began with the old Fox company in 1914 as a stenographer and secretary, becoming secretary to William Fox and ultimately a producer, reaching the peak of his achievement with the *Charlie Chan* series.

(See also: Toler, Sidney)

Stan and Ollie have the wrong 'Blue Boy' in **Wrong Again**

X Y

X-CERTIFICATES
See: Censorship

YATES, HAL
Roach director, seldom associated with Laurel & Hardy though credited on *Sailors, Beware!* and *Hats Off* (both *qv*). Later directing work includes RKO shorts with Edgar Kennedy (*qv*), one of them a remake of *Hats Off*. Biographical details uncertain but in June 1956 *Variety* ran an obituary for a Minnesota-born Harold 'Hal' H. Yates, formerly of the vaudeville double-act Yates and Lawley; age at death reported as 61.

YES, YES, NANETTE! (1925)
The earliest known Laurel & Hardy link at Roach studios, *Yes, Yes, Nanette!* was directed by Stan Laurel with Keystone veteran Clarence Hennecke, an actor/director who died in 1969, aged 74. James Finlayson (*qv*) stars, with Oliver Hardy in support. At this time, Finlayson was being groomed as a star comedian, with Laurel training as director and Hardy (billed as 'Babe' in this film) establishing his position as a reliable character player. The plot concerns Finlayson arriving at the home of his new bride (Lyle Tayo) only to meet a hostile family: Finlayson's mother-in-law takes one look and retreats in tears; father accepts a cigar, only to crush it and stuff the remains into an oversized pipe; the bratty younger sister leaves chewing gum on the wall, to which Finlayson loses his toupée; eventually, the toupée adorns the fam-

ily dog. Worse still, the bride's former boyfriend, a 'refined steam fitter' played by Oliver Hardy, enters to make time with Mrs Finlayson. The battered bridegroom takes only so much before retaliating, sending the startled bully running and earning respect from his new family. The film is brimming with funny gags but has little substance, Finlayson being suited more to supporting roles and the studio itself more adept at logical silliness than spot gags. There is nonetheless a place for *Yes, Yes, Nanette!* in Laurel & Hardy history. Danish scholar Peter Mikkelsen has uncovered an interview recorded by Laurel & Hardy in Copenhagen, in the course of which their partnership is clearly regarded as having begun in the director-actor relationship established on this occasion.

(See also: Interviews; Sennett, Mack; Solo films; Teaming; Villains)

YOUNG, NOAH (1887-1958)
(Laurel & Hardy films *qv*)
Champion weightlifter used mostly as a villain. Despite his size, he was turned down by the US Navy through having too few teeth. Instead, he concentrated on menacing Harold Lloyd (*qv*) from the 'teens to the early 1930s, taking time out to do as much for Snub Pollard (*qv*), and Stan Laurel, both solo and with Hardy, as in *Do Detectives Think?*, *Sugar Daddies* and *The Battle of the Century*. Less prolific in talkies but present in two 1935 films, *The Fixer-Uppers* and *Bonnie*

Scotland. Other film work includes silent features such as Roach's *The Battling Orioles* (1924), various westerns and a prominent role in the 1928 *Sharp Shooters*.

(See also: Murder; Rolin Film Company, the; Villains)

YOUNGSON, ROBERT (1917-74)
Producer and compiler of anthologies, often credited with the rescue of much silent comedy. He began in short subjects, starting in newsreels before adapting old news film and other material into interest reels. *World of Kids* (1951) and *This Mechanical Age* (1954) won Academy Awards, while several others were nominated. There was also a feature, *Fifty Years Before Your Eyes* (1950). A progression into the compiling and condensing of entertainment films (as in *When the Talkies Were Young* and a feature-length revamp of the 1929 *Noah's Ark*) led to another full-length collection, *The Golden Age of Comedy* (*qv*). In 1969 Youngson told *Film Fan Monthly* that he had tried to create interest in the project for seven years before financing it himself with a partner. Its subsequent success did much to revive critical interest in Laurel & Hardy, whose work Youngson sought to promote. He would later attempt the same for Charley Chase and Snub Pollard (both *qv*). Subsequent Youngson features

Ollie would be better off training a seal or an elephant: **You're Darn Tootin'**

(all *qv*) are: *When Comedy Was King, Days of Thrills and Laughter, Thirty Years of Fun, M-G-M's Big Parade of Comedy, Laurel & Hardy's Laughing Twenties, The Further Perils of Laurel & Hardy* and *Four Clowns*.

(See also: Academy Awards; *Battle of the Century, the*; Compilations; *Lucky Dog*)

YOU'RE DARN TOOTIN'

(Laurel & Hardy film)
Released by M-G-M, 21 April 1928. Produced by Hal Roach. Directed by E. Livingston Kennedy (Edgar Kennedy). Camera: Floyd Jackman. Two reels. Silent. Released in Britain as *The Music Blasters*.
With Stan Laurel and Oliver Hardy, Otto Lederer, Agnes Steele, Sam Lufkin, Charlie Hall, Christian Frank, Rolfe Sedan.

Bandsmen Stan and Ollie disrupt a public performance and are dismissed. At their lodgings, they receive a note concerning back rent; eviction follows when the landlady discovers they are unemployed. The homeless musicians try their hand at busking, but meet an indifferent public. Ollie, growing impatient, breaks Stan's clarinet in half and throws it in the gutter; Stan responds by throwing Ollie's French horn into the road, where it is flattened by a passing lorry. An exchange of blows develops into a tearing of buttons, ripping of ties and kicking of shins. The shin-kicking involves passers-by, and after escalating to mass proportions switches to a trouser-tearing battle. Stan is next to last in losing his trousers: the very last is a policeman, from whom the boys flee, sharing the huge trousers they have stolen from a fat man.

Another of the Laurel & Hardy silents familiar from compilations (*qv*), *You're Darn Tootin'* contains what is in many respects the best of Laurel & Hardy's huge street battles. So good is this climactic sequence that other sections tend to be ignored: the opening bandstand segment is timed to a musical beat, Stan's sheet music going astray and Ollie's taking its place (despite being scored for a different instrument!) before his excruciating attempt to retrieve the missing pages from beneath the conductor's tapping foot. The scene cries out for synchronized music and effects, something it received when used in *The Further Perils of Laurel & Hardy* (*qv*). The more sedate boarding-house scene, contrasting neatly with the mayhem on either side, includes a gag wherein Stan loosens the salt and pepper shakers so that their entire contents plunge into Ollie's soup. This idea was reused in *The Hoose-Gow* (*qv*). Although released in Britain under its working title of *The Music Blasters*, modern UK copies of *You're Darn Tootin'* retain the American title. Reportedly, a US video release also includes the British main and censor titles.

(See also: Alternate titles; *Big Business*; Children; *Finishing Touch, the*; *Golden Age of Comedy, the*; Kennedy, Edgar; Lederer, Otto; Music; *Pair of Tights, a*; Sedan, Rolfe; Working titles)

Babe in costume for **Zenobia**

though Billie Burke, who worked for Roach in the *Topper* series (*qv*), is amusing as the doctor's wife. The film was produced for Roach by Edward Sutherland (*qv*), who directed Laurel & Hardy's *The Flying Deuces* (*qv*) soon after.

(See also: Animals; Parker, Jean; Solo films; Teaming)

ZOOS (all films *qv*)

The only full-scale zoo sequence in Laurel & Hardy is that in *Nothing But Trouble* where they attempt to part a lion from its meal. Billy Gilbert (*qv*) takes one look at *The Chimp* and declares his boarding house to be 'no zoo'. Stan and Ollie do not endear themselves to the Dean in *A Chump at Oxford* when suggesting his face to be more suited to a zoo or monkey-house; while a sizeable menagerie is on view at the finale of *Hollywood Party*.

(See also: Animals; Circuses)

ZENOBIA (1939)

Contractual problems kept Stan Laurel off the Roach payroll for much of 1939. In the interim, Oliver Hardy was paired with Harry Langdon (*qv*) in *Zenobia*, a feature released in Britain under its working title of *Elephants Never Forget*. Both titles refer specifically to the circus elephant around which the plot is centred. Set in a small southern town of the 1870s, *Zenobia* casts Babe as a physician more interested in treating needy patients without a fee than in pandering to wealthy hypochondriacs. His most unusual patient, the one with grey skin and a trunk, is brought to him by a travelling showman (Langdon). The grateful animal follows the kindly doctor everywhere, creating embarrassment and, soon, considerable hazard when the showman is inveigled into taking legal action. In court, the

doctor proves the elephant's interest in him to be unsolicited, while the real cause of the animal's discomfort is revealed when the physician delivers a *little* grey patient. Perhaps because of the circumstances under which it was made, *Zenobia* has a poor reputation among Laurel & Hardy admirers. Roach later made scathing comments as to its worth, but taken in isolation it remains a pleasing if unremarkable chance for Babe to display his skills at light comedy. The film received a fair amount of attention in the UK, the *Illustrated Sporting and Dramatic News* of 19 May 1939 referring to its forthcoming première (at the London Pavilion) 'in aid of the Invalid Kitchens of London. The Duchess of Gloucester has promised to attend'. Harry Langdon is not 'teamed' with Babe in the accepted sense and might have been given more comic business,

APPENDIX 1

The Laurel & Hardy Films

The following is a chronological guide of the films of Laurel & Hardy. Accounts of their solo credits undergo revision with such frequency that a truly definitive list remains very much in the future. A reasonable idea of their separate endeavours may be obtained from the **Solo films** entry and cross-references therefrom. Guest appearances are included but news-reels, radio, records, stage appearances (see also **Appendix 2**) and television are described only under the appropriate entries. (V) indicates at least one additional version in a foreign language. Titles are given in order of release.

c.1920: *Lucky Dog*

1926: *Forty-Five Minutes From Hollywood*

1927: *Duck Soup*
Slipping Wives
Love 'Em and Weep
Why Girls Love Sailors
With Love and Hisses
Sugar Daddies
Sailors, Beware!
The Second Hundred Years
Now I'll Tell One
Call of the Cuckoos
Hats Off
Do Detectives Think?
Putting Pants On Philip
The Battle of the Century

1928: *Leave 'Em Laughing*
Flying Elephants
The Finishing Touch
From Soup To Nuts
You're Darn Tootin'
Their Purple Moment
Should Married Men Go Home?
Early to Bed
Two Tars
Habeas Corpus
We Faw Down

1929: *Liberty*
Wrong Again
That's My Wife
Big Business
Unaccustomed As We Are
Double Whoopee
Berth Marks (V)
Men O'War
Perfect Day
They Go Boom
Bacon Grabbers
The Hoose-Gow
The Hollywood Revue of 1929
Angora Love

1930: *Night Owls* (V)
Blotto (V)
Brats (V)
Below Zero (V)
The Rogue Song
Hog Wild (V)
The Laurel-Hardy Murder Case (V)
Another Fine Mess

1931: *Be Big* (V)
Chickens Come Home (V)
The Stolen Jools
Laughing Gravy (V)
Our Wife
Pardon Us (V)
Come Clean
One Good Turn
Beau Hunks
On the Loose

1932: *Helpmates*
Any Old Port
The Music Box
The Chimp
County Hospital
Scram!
Pack Up Your Troubles
Towed in a Hole
Their First Mistake

1933: *Twice Two*
Me and My Pal
Fra Diavolo
The Midnight Patrol
Busy Bodies
Wild Poses
Dirty Work
Sons of the Desert

1934: *Oliver the Eighth*
Hollywood Party
Going Bye-Bye!
Them Thar Hills
Babes in Toyland
The Live Ghost

1935: *Tit For Tat*
The Fixer-Uppers
Thicker Than Water
Bonnie Scotland

1936: *The Bohemian Girl*
On the Wrong Trek
Our Relations

1937: *Way Out West*
Pick a Star

1938: *Swiss Miss*
Block-Heads

1939: *The Flying Deuces*

1940: *A Chump at Oxford*
Saps at Sea

1941: *Great Guns*

1942: *A-Haunting We Will Go*

1943: *The Tree in a Test Tube*
Air Raid Wardens
Jitterbugs
The Dancing Masters

1944: *The Big Noise*

1945: *Nothing But Trouble*
The Bullfighters

1951: *Atoll K*

APPENDIX 2

Variety tours of the UK, 1952-4

The following consists of tour dates from Laurel & Hardy's last two visits to the UK (see also **Stage appearances**). These were supplied by Hardy's widow, Lucille Hardy Price, to *The Laurel & Hardy Magazine* (then called *Helpmates News*), and are reprinted by kind courtesy of that magazine.

1952:

25 February-8 March
Embassy, Peterborough

10-15 March
Empire, Glasgow

17 March
Empire, Newcastle

24 March
Empire, Sunderlamd

31 March
Royal, Hanley

7 April
Empire, Leeds

14 April
Empire, Nottingham

21 April
Granada, Shrewsbury

28 April
Empire, Edinburgh

5 May
Hippodrome, Birmingham

12 May
Gaumont, Southampton

19 May
Empire, Liverpool

26 May-7 June
Olympia, Dublin

9-21 June
Grand Opera House, Belfast

30 June
Empire, Sheffield

7 July
Hippodrome, Brighton

14 July
Palace, Manchester

21 July
Queens, Rhyl

28 July
Alhambra, Bradford

4 August
Odeon, Southend-on-Sea

11 August
Hippodrome, Coventry

18 August
Garrick, Southport

25 August
Granada, Sutton

1 September
Hippodrome, Bristol

8 September
Theatre Royal, Portsmouth

15 September
Hippodrome, Dudley

22 September
Empire, Swansea

29 September
New Theatre, Cardiff

1953-4:

19 October
New Theatre, Northampton

26 October
Empire, Liverpool

2 November
Hippodrome, Manchester

9 November
Empire, Finsbury Park (cancelled due to Laurel's illness; Hardy introduced their deputies, Jewell & Warriss)

16 November
Empress, Brixton

23 November
Empire, Newcastle

30 November
Hippodrome, Birmingham

7 December
Palace, Hull

21 December-16 January
Empire, Nottingham

18 January
Theatre Royal, Portsmouth

25 January
Empire, Chiswick

1 February
Empire, Finsbury Park

8 February
Hippodrome, Brighton

15th February
Hippodrome, Norwich

22 February
Empire, Sunderland

1 March
Empire, Glasgow

8 March
Hippodrome, Wolverhampton

15 March
Empire, Sheffield

22 March
Empire, York

29 March
Palace, Grimsby

5 April
Empire, Leeds

12 April
Empire, Edinburgh

19 April
Her Majesty's, Carlisle

3 May
Alhambra, Bradford

10 May
Hippodrome, Aston

17 May
Palace, Plymouth (curtailed by
Hardy's illness)

APPENDIX 3

Bibliography

The information in this volume is
compiled from numerous sources,
often acknowledged within the text,
though much derives from personal
observation and conversation with
other enthusiasts. Original news cuttings are not always identifiable,
though a number are believed to be
from theatrical papers such as *Variety*
and *The Stage*. Cuttings from local or
national newspapers are identified in
the text where possible. Apologies to
any sources inadvertently neglected.
Readers are directed also to the entries
headed **Biographies** and
Periodicals. I owe particular grati-
tude to the works of John McCabe
and Randy Skretvedt.

Adamson, Joe, *Groucho, Harpo, Chico
and Sometimes Zeppo*, Coronet, 1974

Adeler, Edwin and West, Con,
Remember Fred Karno?, John Long
Ltd., 1939

Allen, H. Warner (ed.), *A Stag Party
with Men Only*, George Newnes Ltd.,
1955

Andrew, Ray, *On the Trail of Charlie
Hall*, published privately, 1988

Anobile, Richard J., *The Best of Laurel
& Hardy (aka A Fine Mess!)*, Michael
Joseph, 1975

Arliss, George, *On the Stage*, John
Murray, 1928

Barr, Charles, *Laurel & Hardy*,
University of California Press, 1968

Beck, Jerry and Friedwald, Will,
Looney Tunes and Merrie Melodies,
Henry Holt, 1989

Beckett, Samuel, *Waiting for Godot*,
Faber & Faber, 1959

Bentine, Michael, *The Long Banana
Skin*, Wolfe, 1975

Bergan, Ronald, *The Life and Times of
Laurel & Hardy*, Green Wood, 1992

Bermingham, Cedric Osmond (ed.),
Stars of the Screen, Herbert Joseph,
1933

Blesh, Rudi, *Keaton*, Secker &
Warburg, 1967

Bogdanovich, Peter, *Picture Shows:
Peter Bogdanovich on the Movies*,
George Allen & Unwin Ltd., 1975

Bullar, Guy, R. and Evans, Len (eds.),
The Performer Who's Who in Variety,
The Performer Ltd., 1950

Cahn, William, *Harold Lloyd's World
of Comedy*, George Allen & Unwin
Ltd., 1966

Capra, Frank, *The Name Above the
Title*, Macmillan, 1971

Chaplin, Charles, *My Autobiography*,
Bodley Head, 1964
   My Life in Pictures, Bodley Head,
1974

Chester, Charlie, *The World is Full of
Charlies*, New English Library, 1974

Conway, Michael and Ricci, Mark,
The Films of Jean Harlow, Citadel,
1965

Crowther, Bruce, *Laurel & Hardy:
Clown Princes of Comedy*, Columbus
Books, 1987

Cushing, Peter, *An Autobiography*,
Weidenfeld & Nicholson, 1987

Dacre, Richard, *Trouble in Store*, T. C.
Farries & Co, nd

Dardis, Tom, *Keaton: The Man who
Wouldn't Lie Down*, Andre Deutsch,
1979
   Harold Lloyd: The Man on the

Clock, Viking Penguin, 1984

Edmonds, Andy, *Hot Toddy*, Macdonald & Co., 1989

Elley, Derek (ed.), *Variety Movie Guide*, Hamlyn/Reed Consumer Books, 1982

Everson, William K., *The Films of Laurel & Hardy*, Citadel, 1967

Franklin, Joe, *Classics of the Silent Screen*, Citadel, 1959

Garnett, Tay with Dudley Balling, Freda, *Light Your Torches and Pull Up Your Tights*, Arlington House, 1973

Gehring, Wes D., *Laurel & Hardy: A Bio-Bibliography*, Greenwood Press, 1990

Guiles, Fred Lawrence, *Stan: The Life of Stan Laurel*, Michael Joseph, 1980

Hall, Henry, *Here's To The Next Time*, Odhams, 1955

Halliwell, Leslie, *The Filmgoer's Companion* , MacGibbon & Kee, first edition 1965; continuously updated

Hancock, Freddie and Nathan, David, *Hancock*, revised edition, Ariel/BBC, 1986

Huff, Theodore, *Charlie Chaplin*, Pyramid Books, 1964

Keaton, Buster with Samuels, Charles, *My Wonderful World of Slapstick*, George Allen & Unwin Ltd., 1967

King, Graham and Saxby, Ron, *The Wonderful World of Film Fun*, Clarke's New Press, 1985

Lahr, John, *Notes on a Cowardly Lion*, Bloomsbury, 1992

Lahue, Kalton, C., *World of Laughter:*

The Motion Picture Comedy Short, 1910-1930, University of Oklahoma Press, 1972
    with Sam Gill, *Clown Princes and Court Jesters*, A. S. Barnes & Co., 1970

Levin, Martin, *Hollywood and the Great Fan Magazines*, Harrison House, 1992

Lloyd, Harold, *An American Comedy*, Longmans, Green & Co., 1928

Lorentz, Pare, *Lorentz on Film*, Hopkinson and Blake, 1975

McCabe, John, *Mr Laurel and Mr Hardy*, Signet, 1966; Robson, 1976
    The Comedy World of Stan Laurel, Robson 1975 (revised) Moonstone 1990
    Babe: the Life of Oliver Hardy, Citadel, 1989
    with Kilgore, Al and Bann, Richard W., *Laurel & Hardy*, W. H. Allen, 1975

MacInnes, Colin, *Sweet Saturday Night*, Panther, 1969

Maltin, Leonard, *Of Mice and Magic: A History of American Animated Cartoons*, Plume, 1980
    Movie Comedy Teams, Signet, 1970
    The Great Movie Shorts, Bonanza, 1972
    The Great Movie Comedians, HarmonyBooks, 1982
    (ed.) *The Laurel & Hardy Book*, Curtis, 1973
    (ed.) *The Real Stars*, Curtis, 1973

Marx, Groucho, with Anobile, Richard J., *The Marx Brothers Scrapbook*, Michael Joseph, 1973
    with Arce, Hector, *The Groucho Phile*, W.H. Allen, 1978

Medved, Harry, with Dreyfuss, Randy, *The Fifty Worst Movies of all Time*, Angus & Robertson, 1978
    with Medved, Michael, *The Golden Turkey Awards*, Angus & Robertson, 1980

Motion Picture News, *1930 Blue Book*

Owen-Pawson, Jenny and Mouland, Bill, *Laurel Before Hardy*, Westmorland Gazette, Kendall, 1984

Ragan, David, *Who's Who in Hollywood* 1900-1976, Arlington House, 1976

Reilly, Adam, *Harold Lloyd, The King of Daredevil Comedy*, Andre Deutsch, 1978

Robinson, David, *The Great Funnies*, Studio Vista, 1969
    Chaplin: His Life and Art, McGraw Hill, 1985

Scagnetti, Jack, *The Laurel & Hardy Scrapbook*, Jonathan David Publishers, New York, 1982

Skretvedt, Randy, *Laurel & Hardy: The Magic Behind the Movies*, Moonstone, 1987

Slide, Anthony, *Early American Cinema*, Zwemer/Barnes, 1970

Stark, Graham, *Remembering Peter Sellers*, Robson, 1990

Taylor, Jack, *The Rogue Song Scrapbook*, Bijou Press, 1993

Truitt, Evelyn Mack, *Who Was Who On Screen*, R. R. Bowker, New York & London, 1984

Vonnegut, Kurt Jr., *Slapstick! Or Lonesome No More*, Panther, 1977

Walker, Alexander, *Peter Sellers: The Authorized Autobiography*, Wiedenfeld & Nicholson, 1981

Wilmut, Roger with Grafton, Jimmy, *The Goon Show Companion*, Robson, 1976

Winchester, Clarence (ed.), *The World Film Encyclopedia*, Amalgamated Press, 1932

Yallop, David A., *The Day the Laughter Stopped*, Hodder & Stoughton, 1976

Young, Jordan R., *Reel Characters*, Moonstone, 1987

The Picturegoer's Who's Who and Encyclopedia, Odhams, 1932

Bowler Dessert, Sons of the Desert, 1976 to date. (Scottish-based; news and historical data from a mainly UK viewpoint)

Classic Images (originally *8mm Collector* and, later, *Classic Film Collector*), 1962 to date. (Valuable source of news, general features on cinema, filmographies and obituaries. See especially the Laurel & Hardy edition [July 1982], the series 'Fighting for Reappraisal': 'The Laurel & Hardy Solo Films' by Rick de Croix, profiles of Siegmund Lubin [issues 78, 110], June Marlowe [issues 129, 130], The Taxi Boys [issue 119], Lucile Brown [issue 130] and Herbert Rawlinson [issue 107])

The Desert Song and *Shifting Sands*, Sons of the Desert, published 1985-7. (Useful for checking details of supporting players and solo films)

The Intra-Tent Journal, Sons of the Desert, 1974 to date. (Contact point for the society worldwide and a valuable source of material)

The Laurel & Hardy Magazine (formerly *Helpmates News*), ditto 1978 to date. (Published in England; UK viewpoint; news, views, reprints, critiques)

Pratfall, Sons of the Desert, 1969-1985. (Particularly valuable for interviews and archival reprints)

APPENDIX 4

The Sons of the Desert

Enquiries regarding *The Laurel and Hardy Magazine* should be addressed (enclosing sae) to:

63 Wollaston Close
Gillingham
Kent
ME8 95H

Subscription enquiries for *The Intra-Tent Journal* should be addressed (with sae) to:

Europe:

102 Hough Green Road
Widnes
Cheshire
WA8 9PF
England

USA/Canada

1602 Park Trail Drive
Westerville
OH 43081
USA